The Gallup Poll

PUBLIC OPINION 1935-1971

GEORGE H. GALLUP, Founder and Chairman of the
American Institute of Public Opinion (The Gallup Poll)
received a Ph. D. in Psychology from the University of
Iowa in 1928. From his undergraduate days he has had
three prime interests: survey research, public opinion,
and politics.

Dr. Gallup is the author of many articles on public
opinion and advertising research and he has published
the following books: *The Pulse of Democracy* (1940);
A Guide Book to Public Opinion Polls (1944); *The Gallup
Political Almanac* (1952); *Secrets of Long Life* (1960);
The Miracle Ahead (1964); and *The Sophisticated Poll
Watcher's Guide* (1970).

The Gallup Poll

PUBLIC OPINION 1935-1971

Dr. George H. Gallup,
Founder and Chairman,
American Institute of Public Opinion

VOLUME
ONE
1935-1948

RANDOM HOUSE  NEW YORK

Reference Series Editors:
William P. Hansen
Fred L. Israel
Assistant Editor:
June Rephan

Paul Perry's comments on pages xi–xxx are revised versions of articles that appeared in *Public Opinion Quarterly*, Vol. 24 (1960), pp. 531–42 and Vol. 26 (1962), pp. 272–79.

Library of Congress Cataloging in Publication Data

Gallup, George Horace, 1901–
The Gallup Poll, 1935–1971
1. Public opinion — U.S. I. Title.
HN90. P8G3   301. 15′ 43′ 32900973   77-39867
ISBN 0-394-47270-5

Preface

These volumes contain the findings of all Gallup Poll reports from the founding of the Gallup Poll in October 1935 through December 1971. The more than 7,000 reports present a view of changing American political and social thought since the New Deal.

From its founding, the American Institute of Public Opinion (The Gallup Poll) has functioned as a totally independent fact-finding organization whose sole purpose has been to determine public opinion. It is strictly impartial, has no political predilections, and espouses no public or private causes. The Poll's main source of income during its thirty-eight year existence has been subscriber newspapers, which have exclusive rights to publish the Gallup findings. Today, the Poll is carried by 153 newspapers with a daily readership of approximately thirty million people.

In addition to its regular polls, the Gallup organization has conducted hundreds of surveys of special groups such as college students, county chairmen of both major political parties, persons listed in *Who's Who in America*, etc. Surveys have also been conducted in many foreign countries through Gallup International, Ltd., an association which now consists of 30 Gallup affiliates conducting public opinion research in more than 50 nations.

Since the establishment of the Poll, approximately 20,000 questions have been asked of more than two million people. The decision as to what issues are to be surveyed rests with the various members of the Gallup Poll staff, although subscriber newspapers frequently provide suggestions.

Each report in these volumes contains all the statistical data as released to newspapers. Due to space limitations, the editorial and interpretative material accompanying the reports has been eliminated. Unless otherwise indicated, all data applies to a representative cross-section of the total United States adult, non-institutionalized population.

The date preceding each report indicates the newspaper release date. The headline following the date identifies the subject matter of the poll or polls that follow. The interviewing dates are in small type. To further identify and catalogue the polls, survey, index, and question numbers are provided. The questions appear exactly as they were asked.[1]

---

[1] Persons desiring tabular data other than that published in the Gallup reports should contact Mr. Philip K. Hastings, Roper Public Opinion Research Center, Williams College, Williamstown, Massachusetts 01267. The Roper Center has on file complete data card decks for all Gallup reports released since 1935.

All Gallup polls since 1950, excluding certain special surveys, have been based on a national probability sample of interviewing areas. Refinements in the sample design have been introduced at various points in time since then. However, over this period the design in its essentials has conformed to the current procedure, as follows:[2]

1. The United States is divided into seven size-of-community strata: cities of population 1,000,000 and over; 250,000 to 999,999; and 50,000 to 249,999; with the urbanized areas of all these cities forming a single stratum; cities of 2,500 to 49,999; rural villages; and farm or open country rural areas.
2. Within each of these strata, the population is further divided into seven regions: New England, Middle Atlantic, East Central, West Central, South, Mountain, and Pacific Coast.
3. Within each size-of-community and regional stratum the population is arrayed in geographic order and zoned into equal-sized groups of sampling units.
4. In each zone, pairs of localities are selected with probability of selection proportional to the size of each locality's population — producing two replicated samples of localities.
5. Within selected cities for which population data are reported by census tracts or enumeration districts, these sample subdivisions are drawn with probability of selection proportional to the size of the population.
6. For other cities, minor civil divisions, and rural areas in the sample for which population data are not reported by census tracts or enumeration districts, small, definable geographic areas are drawn, with the probability of selection proportional to size where available data permit; otherwise with equal probability.
7. Within each subdivision selected for which block statistics are available, a block or block cluster is drawn with probability of selection proportional to the number of dwelling units.
8. In cities and towns for which block statistics are not available, blocks are drawn at random, that is, with equal probability.
9. In subdivisions that are rural or open country in character, segments approximately equal in size of population are delineated and drawn with equal probability.
10. In each cluster of blocks and each segment so selected, a randomly selected starting point is designated on the interviewer's map of the area. Starting at this point, interviewers are required to follow a given direction in the selection of households, taking households in sequence, until their assigned number of interviews has been completed.
11. Within each occupied dwelling unit or household reached, the interviewer asks to speak to the youngest man 18 or older at home, or if no man is at home, the oldest woman 18 or older. This method of selection within the household has been developed empirically to produce an age distribution

[2]For a discussion of election survey procedures since 1950, see Paul Perry's comments, *supra*.

vi

by men and women separately which compares closely with the age distribution of the population. It increases the probability of selecting younger men, who are at home relatively infrequently, and the probability of reaching older women in the household who tend to be under-represented unless given a disproportionate chance of being drawn from among those at home. The method of selection among those at home within the household is not strictly random, but it is systematic and objective and eliminates interviewer judgment in the selection process.

12. Interviewing is conducted at times when adults are most likely to be at home, which means on weekends or if on weekdays, after 4:00 P.M. for women and after 6:00 P.M. for men.

13. Allowance for persons not at home is made by a "times-at-home" weighting procedure rather than by "call-backs." This procedure is a standard method for reducing the sample bias that would otherwise result from underrepresentation of persons who are difficult to find at home.

14. The pre-stratification by regions is routinely supplemented by fitting each obtained sample to the latest available Census Bureau estimates of the regional distribution of the population. Also minor adjustments of the sample are made by educational attainment (by men and women separately), based on the annual estimates of the Census Bureau derived from their Current Population Survey.

The sampling procedure described is designed to produce an approximation of the adult civilian population living in the United States, except for those persons in institutions such as prisons or hospitals.

Prior to 1950, the samples for all Gallup surveys, excluding special surveys, were a combination of what is known as a purposive design for the selection of cities, towns, and rural areas, and the quota method for the selection of individuals within such selected areas.

The first step in obtaining the sample was to draw a national sample of places (cities, towns, and rural areas). These were distributed by six regions and five or six city size, urban rural groups or strata in proportion to the distribution of the population of voting age by these regional-city size strata. The distribution of cases between the non-South and South, however, was on the basis of the vote in presidential elections.

Within each region the sample of such places was drawn separately for each of the larger states and for groups of smaller states. The places were selected to provide broad geographic distribution within states and at the same time in combination to be politically representative of the state or group of states in terms of three previous elections. Specifically they were selected so that in combination they matched the state vote for three previous elections within small tolerances. Great emphasis was placed on election data as a control in the era from 1935 to 1950.

Within the civil divisions in the sample, respondents were selected on the basis of age, sex and socio-economic quotas. Otherwise, interviewers were given considerable latitude within the sample areas, being permitted to draw their cases from households and from persons on the street anywhere in the community.

Many social scientists in the United States have warned of the dangers of attempting to predict human behavior. After the miscalculations of the poll takers in the 1948 presidential race, many in the field of market research added their voices to those who claimed that it was not feasible to predict what action people would take in given situations.

I have always held an opposite view. I believe that human behavior is predictable and, in fact, that we as researchers can make progress best by making predictions and learning from our mistakes when we make them. In fact, I believe that fear of being "wrong," with attendant penalties, has had a retarding effect upon all of the social sciences. It would be folly to argue that behavior can be predicted with perfect accuracy. It can't and never will be. But already' enough evidence has been accumulated in a number of different fields to prove that behavior can be predicted with a high degree of accuracy. The goal is to increase this accuracy.

Princeton
August 1, 1972

George H. Gallup

Contents

		VOLUME ONE
Preface	v	
Election Survey Procedures of the Gallup Poll by Paul Perry	xi	
Gallup Poll Election Survey Experience, 1950–1960 by Paul Perry	xxiii	
Election Survey Methods by Paul Perry	xxxi	
The Year 1935	1	
1936	9	
1937	45	
1938	83	
1939	133	
1940	199	
1941	257	
1942	315	
1943	363	
1944	425	
1945	481	
1946	553	
1947	617	
1948	697	

		The Year
VOLUME TWO	779	**1949**
	879	**1950**
	957	**1951**
	1033	**1952**
	1113	**1953**
	1199	**1954**
	1299	**1955**
	1389	**1956**
	1463	**1957**
	1533	**1958**
VOLUME THREE	1585	**1959**
	1649	**1960**
	1699	**1961**
	1749	**1962**
	1797	**1963**
	1857	**1964**
	1915	**1965**
	1981	**1966**
	2043	**1967**
	2099	**1968**
	2177	**1969**
	2231	**1970**
	2279	**1971**
	2341	**Gallup Election Accuracy Record**
	2343	**Index**

Election Survey Procedures
of the Gallup Poll

by Paul Perry, president The Gallup Organization

The development of sample surveys of the population has been accompanied by their highly publicized use as a means of determining the voting public's political preferences. The use of sample surveys for this purpose has provided a difficult test of the method, particularly in the United States, where a large part of the adult population fails to vote. Testimony to this effect appeared in Chapter I of *The Pre-Election Polls of 1948*, a Social Science Research Council publication issued in 1949. The statement was: "The committee and the staff would like to point out that pre-election polling and predictions constitute one of the more severe tests of polling or survey methodology. There are more steps in pre-election polling at which error can enter than there are in many other applications of survey technique."

Since a straightforward sample survey of the total adult population on opinion with respect to parties or candidates quantifies only one variable in the formula, this has provided the Gallup Poll with some difficult problems. What is specifically required, of course, is an estimation procedure that takes into account the major variables and conditions. Progress in the development of such an estimation procedure by the Gallup Poll has increased the reliability of its pre-election estimates of the division of the vote based on survey data. For this reason it probably has some intrinsic interest for many who are engaged in survey research, and the methods used may prove useful in other political research.

The methods of sampling the voting population used, relating voting participation to candidate preferences, dealing with the problem of the undecided, obtaining unbiased expressions of candidate preference, and measuring reactions to major events close to election day are of methodological concern to all engaged in political research.

In this discussion data reported concerning election surveys and samples are based on the United States excluding the South.[1] The South has been excluded because it presents special difficulties which introduce additional variables. For example, in congressional elections many districts in the South are uncontested. Another difficulty is presented by the fact that the South's share of the total vote fluctuates between elections to a much greater extent than is true for other major regions. The limited scope of this essay precludes going into the details of the methods of coping with these factors.

The data reported are based on Gallup Poll experience in the elections of 1950, 1952, 1954, 1956, and 1958. In 1950 certain of the basic elements in the estimation procedure here described were first adopted and

[1]States excluded: Alabama, Arkansas, Florida, Georgia, Kentucky, Louisiana, Mississippi, North Carolina, Oklahoma, South Carolina, Tennessee, Texas, and Virginia.

used. We believe it is noteworthy that as a result of using these methods, our pre-election estimates of how the popular vote divided in four elections (1950, 1954, 1956, and 1958) were the four most accurate estimates of the twelve which the Gallup Poll made in national elections up to that date. The first of the twelve estimates was made in the 1936 presidential election.

THE SAMPLE

The sample of areas used for the Gallup Poll election surveys is the same as the sample of areas used for the Gallup Poll surveys between election periods. These areas are drawn in accord with the principles of the theory of probability sampling. Between election periods the areas consist of block clusters and rural segments. In the two election surveys which provide the basis for the final pre-election estimate, the areas consist of election precincts, drawn in the same manner as the block clusters and rural segments. The change to election precincts in the period immediately preceding the election is made because of the greater control provided with regard to the political representativeness of the sample of areas. For surveys on most general issues the precinct as the basic areal sampling unit would have little or no advantage over block clusters and segments and might have some disadvantages.

The sample of areas is drawn in the following manner: A systematic sample of cities and minor civil divisions is drawn from regional-city size strata with probability of selection proportional to size. Within places so drawn, for election survey purposes a selection of smaller units for which election data are available is drawn in the same manner. In cities such smaller units are usually wards. Within these units precincts are selected. The selection of the precincts proceeds in this manner: Election results for the previous national election are obtained for each precinct in the ward. One precinct is then drawn with probability of selection proportional to the precinct's total vote. Within the precinct a systematic sample of households is selected, and one adult from each household is interviewed. The total number of adults in each household is obtained in the survey to provide for a size-of-household correction when necessary.

For each precinct so selected, the proportions in which the vote divided by parties in the previous one or two national elections is computed. In 1958, for example, the percentage voting for Eisenhower of the Eisenhower-Stevenson vote in 1956 was computed for each precinct drawn into the sample. Since the precincts were drawn with probability proportional to size, the mean Eisenhower percentage of the precincts in the sample served as a measure of the representativeness of the areas drawn. For example, if the mean Eisenhower percentage for such a sample was 58.5, the sample of precincts was 0.7 percentage points higher than the vote for Eisenhower in 1956, when, of the vote for Eisenhower and Stevenson, 57.8 per cent voted for Eisenhower. When such a bias is found to exist, a simple correction of the final estimate can be made, and the bias in the sample of precincts with respect to the previous election removed.

The vote in a previous election is perhaps the most efficient control one can use for an election survey (unless the span of time between elections is very great), either as a basis for stratification or as a part of the estimation procedure. However, difficulties are involved in using it as a basis for stratification in a national election, at least if precincts are the areal units. Precinct data are not available from a central source; a great deal of time and effort must be expended to obtain election results for even a modest number of precincts. The use of precinct data becomes quite laborious even with a double sampling procedure, in which a large sample of precincts is drawn first, strata are formed, and the final sample is drawn from the strata. Therefore, it appears to be more efficient to use the past voting data in forming the estimates after the sample is taken instead of using them in drawing the sample.

The correlation of the vote by precincts between elections is fairly high. For example, we have found the variance between precincts in terms of shift or change in the percentage of the vote for a candidate of a given party between two elections is only about two-thirds as large, typically, as the variance between them in terms of party or candidate preference in a single election.

In the 1950, 1952, and 1956 samples the deviation of the mean precinct party percentage for the previous election used as a control was small; in 1954 and 1958 it was of some consequence. The deviations of the means for each previous election are shown in Table 1.

TABLE 1

Deviations of the Means of the Samples of Precincts*
in Per Cent Republican of the Democratic-Republican Vote

Survey Year	Past Election Used	Deviations†	Number of Precincts
1950	1946	+0.7	50
1952	1948	+0.3	100
1954	1952	+2.8	105
1956	1952	−0.2	171
1958	1956	−2.2	156

*Outside the South.

†For example, the 1946 election results in precincts in the sample in 1950 had a mean per cent Republican vote 0.7 of a percentage point higher than was true in the United States outside the South. As a sample of precincts, they were this much in error in terms of the results of the previous election.

This step cannot be expected, of course, to improve matters in every instance. Some of the time it will make things worse. In view of the correlation between elections in the division of the vote, however, it can be expected to improve matters at least the majority of times.

The above illustrates one of the advantages of using precincts as the sampling unit as compared with other areal units such as census tracts or enumeration districts. While it is not possible to obtain for precincts census statistics such as those concerning demographic characteristics of the population, this disadvantage is more than offset in our opinion by the availability of election data. In fact, the availability of census data by small areal units is of limited value in any case, because it is useful only in the first few years following the decennial census.[2]

Within the precinct, unless it has an exceedingly large population, the sampling interval used in the selection of households requires the interviewer to cover the area entirely. That is to say, the sample does not, in most cases, consist of clusters of households. The interviewer is given a randomly selected starting point and takes every nth household throughout the precinct. In larger precincts, a sample of blocks or segments is selected and, within the blocks or segments drawn into the sample, a systematic sample of households is drawn as above. These are precincts where the sampling interval for coverage of all blocks in the precinct would be so large that it would create serious problems of maintaining an accurate count.

Within the household the individual who is interviewed is selected from among those who are at home, in the following manner: The interviewer asks first to speak to the youngest man of voting age who is at home; if no man is at home he asks to speak to the youngest woman who is at home. If no one is at home or the indicated person refuses, the interviewer is told to go to the next adjacent dwelling unit. In such a case the interviewer resumes the interval count from the original dwelling selected. The interviewer is given a male-female assignment. Thus if, following the procedure described above, the number of men assigned is obtained, in subsequent households the interviewer asks to speak only to the youngest woman at home. Interviewing hours are from 4 P.M. to 10 P.M. A record of refusals is kept, with information concerning the person's sex, estimated age, education, race, and whether the resident is in a high-, medium-, or low-rental area.

A point commonly made about the use of precincts as sampling units is that, since the boundaries of many of them are frequently changed, their usefulness is limited as a political control. This objection is based on a mistaken notion of how they are used. The vote in a previous election is the control, and therefore the boundaries of the precincts as they were at the time of that election are the ones used. It makes no difference whatsoever how frequently they are changed thereafter. It would be useful, of course, in analyzing the accuracy of the survey results if the boundaries were constant from election to election. We have found that, on the average, about 75 per cent of precincts remain the same over a four-year period, and we use these for error analysis.

---

[2]The use of precincts as the areal sampling unit in election surveys also has some practical advantages over use of other divisions such as census tracts or enumeration districts. For example, if interviewer failure causes loss of a sampling area too late for replacement, knowledge of the previous voting behavior of the area enables one to adjust statistically for any resultant political bias.

A discussion of the use of the precinct as the ultimate areal sampling unit in the design leads into a description of the method used to bring the measurement of voting intentions as close to the election as possible. The use of precincts on a large scale by the Gallup Poll began with the 1950 congressional election. Although a method of carrying out a late October survey and getting the results in time for pre-election publication had been worked out and used in 1940 and 1944 (unfortunately *not* in 1948), a less cumbersome method was sought. A combination of the telegraphic communication of survey results to the home office with the control provided by the use of precincts seemed to be particularly advantageous and was the method adopted. The two final election surveys are usually conducted in October. The first one usually takes place the first week in October; the second on Wednesday, Thursday, and Friday of the week prior to the election. The first survey questionnaires are returned by mail. However, the interviewers are also required to carry out all the steps involved in the final telegraphic survey, including tabulation of the results, recording and checking the tabulations on forms provided, and preparation of the telegram. We find that about 80 per cent of the interviewers do this quite precisely and accurately, about 15 per cent make small errors which cannot seriously affect the results, and the remainder make serious errors which have to be dealt with. In the latter case, the questionnaires are returned to the interviewers and they are requested to read their directions once again, do over the tabulation, and record the corrected data. Telephone consultations are then conducted with each of them to be sure their confusion has been eliminated. Those who make minor errors are also told about it, and once again great stress is laid on the necessity of accuracy. A simplified breakdown of the data has to be employed, of course, to minimize the possibility of errors. For example, interviewers are required only to divide their questionnaires into two easily classified groups — one group consisting of those who say they plan to vote, the second group comprising all others. They tabulate the voting preference only among those who say they plan to vote. Interviewers are also asked to tabulate and telegraph the educational attainment of all respondents in six categories, but not the *vote* by education categories. The latter step would increase the chance of transmission errors so much that it is not considered worth the risk.

As a variable closely associated with socio-economic status and income, the educational-attainment information is used to standardize the two surveys in this respect. Since the vote by education is not obtained, for the reason indicated above, any difference between the two samples by education is dealt with in this manner: The first survey is tabulated by the six education categories (college complete, college incomplete, high school complete, high school incomplete, grammar school seventh and eighth grades, grammar school sixth grade or less), and the vote or preference in each category. The data are then adjusted to fit the education distribution of the second sample, and the change in voting preference which results is applied to the results of the second survey. This sample control of the second survey is designed primarily to protect against the consequences of interviewer failure to do a careful coverage of the precinct the second time around. Since this control has been employed, the effect of the adjustment has been in no case more than one- or two-tenths of a percentage point.

TURNOUT

Another important step in the procedure for estimating election results is projecting the proportion of the population old enough to vote who will vote, or what might be called the turnout ratio. Our estimate of this ratio is derived from the results of several questions which are related to voting participation. Some combinations used, for example, are based on these two questions: "How much thought have you given to the coming November elections — quite a lot, or only a little?" and, "Do you, yourself, plan to vote in the election this November, or not?" If the answer is "yes," the respondent is asked, "How certain are you that you will vote — absolutely certain, fairly certain, or not certain?" For previous elections a record has been kept of the relationship between the proportion who answer such questions in a category indicating a likelihood of voting and the actual turnout ratio in the election. From these relationships a sufficiently accurate estimate of the turnout ratio can be made for estimating preference in that part of the sample representative of those who will vote. For example, the method projected a turnout percentage of 61 in 1956 as compared with the actual turnout ratio of 60; in 1958 it projected a turnout of 45 as compared with the actual turnout of 44. In 1950, 1952, and 1954, the turnout ratio was projected from available registration data.

The variable of voting participation is an important one in United States elections, and a technique for taking it into account is required. Surveys during the past three decades have shown that, during this period, in the aggregate those persons who favor the Democratic Party or candidate in national elections are less likely to vote than those who favor the Republican Party or candidate. Even if this were not true, however, so long as only a part of the electorate votes, steps have to be taken to provide a sample of

TABLE 2

**Per Cent of United States Population Old Enough
to Vote Who Voted in 1950, 1952, 1954, 1956, 1958**

Election	Type of Election	Per Cent Who Voted
1950	Congressional	41.9
1952	Presidential	62.5
1954	Congressional	42.4
1956	Presidential	60.4
1958	Congressional	43.9

that particular part of the population, because it may well differ from the total population old enough to vote. The turnout ratio is particularly low in national nonpresidential elections. The ratios for five elections are shown in Table 2. To make allowance for this factor we use questions such as these:

> How much thought have you given to the coming November elections — quite a lot, or only a little?
> Have you ever voted in this precinct or district?
> Where do people who live in this neighborhood go to vote?
> Are you now registered so that you can vote in the election this November?
> Do you plan to register so that you can vote in the November election?
> How often would you say you vote — always, nearly always, part of the time, or seldom?
> Do you, yourself, plan to vote in the election this November?
> How certain are you that you will vote — absolutely certain, fairly certain, or not certain?
> In the election in November, 1956 — when Eisenhower ran against Stevenson — did things come up which kept you from voting, or did you happen to vote?

Post-election studies indicate that the answers to these questions are related to voting participation, and indicate the extent to which they are related. A scoring system based on such studies is applied to the answers of respondents to each question. The scoring system is such that the greater their likelihood of voting, the higher their score. Respondents are then ranked on the basis of their scores.

Before using the turnout scale scores, all persons are excluded who say they are not registered and do not plan to register, or who say they do not plan to vote. Thus a person who is not registered and does not plan to register or who says he or she does not plan to vote is not included in the final sample of persons upon which the election estimate is based. These people are excluded because our studies and the studies of others have indicated that a negligible percentage of them vote, something on the order of between 1 and 5 per cent. Using the remaining sample of respondents, each class — on the basis of turnout scale scores — is tabulated on party or candidate preference (depending upon whether it is a national presidential or congressional election); the division of preference is then computed for the first scale position (those most likely to vote); the first and second scale positions combined; the first, second, and third scale positions combined; and so on. With this classification and accumulation, and the turnout ratio previously computed, that portion of the total sample with the greatest likelihood of voting (on the basis of these criteria) is selected, and the preference computed for that group. Usually this requires interpolation between classes.

THE UNDECIDED

For accurate estimation of the probable division of the vote, it is essential to minimize the proportion of replies which are in the category of undecided. For analytical purposes it is, of course, quite useful to use methods for maximizing the undecided, and this can be done quite easily. The opposite objective of reducing the undecided can be quite difficult, however, and, of course, when it is truly a case of being completely undecided, impossible. Two basic approaches we have adopted are (1) to use a question which makes the decision as easy as possible and (2) to ask the undecided person if he can say in which direction he is leaning in his preference. The question combination used in the 1960 Gallup Poll survey was:

> a. If the Presidential election were being held TODAY, which candidates would you vote for — Nixon and Lodge or Kennedy and Johnson? IF UNDECIDED OR REFUSED ASK:
> b. As of today, do you lean more to Nixon and Lodge or more to Kennedy and Johnson?

Before the "a" question is asked, the respondent is handed a card on which are printed the names of the two major parties and the respective candidates underneath their party designation.

The question has been framed to ask for the respondent's choice if the election were to be held "today" because it provokes less indecision than do questions which ask how a respondent expects to vote in November. Currently the use of the "leaning" question reduces the proportion of undecided by half. Sometimes the effect of a further reduction of the undecided can be obtained by the use of a secret ballot; this will be touched upon later.

COMPARING SURVEY RESULTS AND ELECTION RESULTS

Three sets of party- or candidate-preference survey results have been computed for each of the past five national elections, and the error computed for each. The three sets are (1) the total sample, with a shift adjustment based on the precinct vote in a previous election; (2) those in the sample who are registered or who plan to register and plan to vote, with shift adjustment; (3) the accumulated-classes method described above, with shift adjustment. The results are shown in Tables 3, 4, and 5, and provide a summation based on the final survey data illustrating how each step in the estimation procedure affected the results. As stated earlier, this summation is based on the vote excluding the South.

It should be emphasized that in actual practice we are unable to make complete use of the data obtained in the final pre-election survey. Insufficient time elapses between the last day of interviewing and the deadline for the release of the results to subscribing newspapers to receive the completed questionnaires through the mail, process them, and do a full analysis. In practice, in the case of the final survey, we have a simple basis for sorting out likely voters for the interviewers to use in their tabulations. The procedures described are used in processing the survey in early October; to the division of the vote obtained is applied any change observed between this survey and the final one. In comparing the two surveys, of course, the simplified basis used by interviewers in separating likely voters from non-

xviii

TABLE 3

Comparison of Election Results and
Survey Results in the Total Sample*:
Per Cent Republican of the Democratic-Republican Vote

Election	(N)	Survey Results	Election Results	Deviation
1950	(2,452)	48.0	52.7	−4.7
1952	(4,814)	53.2	56.8	−3.6
1954	(4,784)	45.6	50.5	−4.9
1956	(6,173)	61.8	59.0	+2.8
1958	(4,625)	42.6	46.1	−3.5
Mean†				3.9
Range†				2.8–4.9

*Corrected for bias in terms of a previous election.
†Disregarding signs.

TABLE 4

Comparison of Election Results and Survey Results
Among Those Registered, Plan to Register, and Plan to Vote*:
Per Cent Republican of the Democratic-Republican Vote

Election	(N)	Survey Results	Election Results	Deviation
1950	(1,999)	49.2	52.7	−3.5
1952	(4,229)	54.2	56.8	−2.6
1954	(3,733)	47.3	50.5	−3.2
1956	(5.438)	61.6	59.0	+2.6
1958	(3,662)	43.8	46.1	−2.3
Mean†				2.8
Range†				2.3–3.5

*Corrected for bias in terms of a previous election.
†Disregarding signs.

TABLE 5

Comparison of Election Results and Survey Results Among
Those Whose Turnout Score Placed Them in That Part of the
Sample Corresponding to the Expected Turnout Proportion:
Per Cent Republican of the Democratic-Republican Vote

Election	(N)	Survey Results	Election Results	Deviation
1950	(1,235)	52.4	52.7	−0.3
1952	(3,240)	55.3	56.8	−1.5
1954	(2,410)	50.0	50.5	−0.5
1956	(4,150)	62.1	59.0	+3.1
1958	(2,465)	45.9	46.1	−0.2
Mean*				1.1
Range*				0.2–3.1

*Disregarding signs.

voters for their telegraphic report is used for both. In the description here, however, the final survey materials as analyzed after the election have been used, because an accurate appraisal of the results of the methods can best be made with survey data obtained as close as possible to the election. The final survey interviewing period in the five elections covered in this description has centered five days before election day.

USE OF A SECRET BALLOT

Obtaining unbiased expressions of candidate preference is, of course, a matter of continuing great concern in election surveys. The traditional and obvious method of dealing with the problem is to use a secret ballot. Doing so in a completely satisfactory way in the typical survey situation presents difficulties, although the Gallup Poll has used a secret ballot at one time or another in election surveys from 1936 onward. Early in 1956 a method was worked out to incorporate a secret ballot procedure, making use of an approach developed by Sidney Goldish in the election surveys of the Minnesota Poll. In this approach, the interview is conducted in the usual manner (i.e. as an "open" interview) for all questionnaire items except the voting preference question. This enables the interviewer to establish rapport with the respondent in the manner customary in an "open" interview. After asking a series of introductory questions, the respondent is handed a card showing the parties and candidates and asked to check his choice privately, fold the card, and drop it in a ballot box carried by the interviewer. The remainder of the interview is carried out in the usual manner.

The secret ballot was employed in two Gallup Poll national surveys conducted in early October and mid-October of 1956 and in mid-September and mid-October of 1958. In these surveys an interpenetrating sample was used, with every second respondent interviewed using the secret questionnaire. A comparison of the two sets of data in 1956 showed a 60 per cent lower undecided in the secret survey and a relatively greater vote for the Democratic ticket of Stevenson and Kefauver than was true in the nonsecret

TABLE 6

Comparison of Election Results and Final Survey Results:
Per Cent Republican of the Democratic-Republican Vote

Election	Survey Results	Election Results	Deviation
1950	52.4	52.7	−0.3
1952	55.3	56.8	−1.5
1954	50.0	50.5	−0.5
1956	60.6	59.0	+1.6
1958	46.3	46.1	+0.2
Mean*			0.8
Range*			0.2–1.5

*Disregarding signs.

xx

survey. In 1958 the secret survey produced 30 per cent less undecided than the nonsecret survey and a relatively lower Democratic vote. An application of the secret-nonsecret differentials in 1956 lowered the Eisenhower-Nixon percentage of the vote one and a half percentage points in the non-South; in 1958 it produced a change of less than a percentage point.

Table 6 recapitulates the final estimates that were obtained using the final survey data in the non-South and utilizing all steps in the estimating procedure, including the secret ballot in 1956 and 1958. Actually, in 1956 and 1958 the difference between the secret and nonsecret was statistically significant only in the case of the per cent undecided. Nonetheless, the differential was applied to the party vote for the final estimate in both years and improved matters in 1956.

Gallup Poll Election Survey Experience, 1950-1960

by Paul Perry, president The Gallup Organization

This is a review of Gallup Poll election survey experience and methods incorporating the experience of the 1960 election. In view of the question often raised as to the accuracy of election survey data, an attempt is made to evaluate in terms of theoretical sampling error the deviations from election results of Gallup Poll data. That is to say, are the deviations greater than, less than, or about what sampling theory would lead one to expect?

This analysis is ex post facto of necessity because the final election survey ordinarily is completed three days before the election and reported from the field by telegram or telephone. The questionnaires of the final survey are not available for a complete application of the method until after the election. The final published pre-election release is based on reports from interviewers who have made a simple count of presidential preference among those of their respondents who say they are planning to vote. These reports are combined and related in an appropriate manner to a comparable survey in early October that has been processed with the full estimation procedure. The results of the complete method applied to the final survey are important, however, as an indication of its usefulness.

Although the analysis here reported is "after the fact," the record of published Gallup Poll pre-election estimates corresponds so closely as to provide substantiation for what might otherwise be regarded as a "record" of post election "judgment." For example, the final Gallup Poll release on Monday, November 6, 1960, the day before the last election, reported the survey vote for President to be divided as follows: Kennedy, 48 per cent; Nixon, 47 per cent; undecided, 5 per cent. Excluding the undecided, the report indicated that the division of the survey vote was Kennedy, 51; Nixon, 49.[1] The division of the popular vote for the two major candidates in the election was 50.1 per cent for Kennedy, 49.9 per cent for Nixon.

The Gallup Poll's election survey procedures may be briefly summarized as follows:

1. Sampling areas that comprise a probability sample of election precincts, making it possible to use as supplementary data the vote by precincts in a previous election to reduce the sampling variance.
2. Provision for a final survey to be taken during the week before election day and reported from the field by telegraph or telephone. This final survey is part of a system of two surveys in which the first is processed using the entire estimating method and the difference between the two surveys is applied to the estimate based on the first survey.

---

[1]The percentage division computed to a tenth of a per cent was Kennedy, 50.7 per cent; Nixon, 49.3 per cent. For publication, percentages were rounded to the nearest whole percentage.

3. A method for projecting the turnout ratio based on the joint results of questions on intention to vote and interest in the election.
4. A method for ranking respondents on likelihood of voting using a simple scale based on questions related to voting participation, as determined by post-election studies.
5. A method involving the use of the turnout ratio to derive the division of the vote based on those most likely to vote. Respondents are accumulated on the basis of the turnout scale scores until that share of the sample corresponding to the turnout ratio is reached, and then candidate or party preference is computed among these respondents.
6. Techniques to minimize undecided. These include wording the voting preference question in terms of voting preference "today" rather than in the future; using a forced-choice question which asks undecideds and refusals in which 'political direction they "lean"; and using a "secret ballot."

A major change in the procedure in 1960 was the manner in which the secret ballot was used. The secret ballot procedure requires the respondent to check his voting preference privately and drop the ballot into a slotted box. Two national surveys conducted late in the 1956 and 1958 campaigns used a split sample in which half of all respondents were asked for their voting preference openly and half used the secret ballot. The two methods of obtaining voting preference were alternated by respondent. The purpose was to determine the difference obtained using the ballot box method and apply this difference to the final survey, which was designed to use the open preference question. The secret ballot, or ballot box, method was expected to produce a more valid response than the open preference question, but, because of added duties for the interviewers in the final surveys, it was thought desirable not to give them the further burden of the ballot box procedure. Therefore, the open preference question was used, and the secret-nonsecret differentials were applied as a correction to the final survey results. In 1960, however, interviewers were given considerable practice in the use of the ballot box method before the final surveys, and we decided

TABLE 1

Deviations of the Means of the Samples of Precincts* in Per Cent Republican of the Democratic-Republican Vote

Survey Year	Past Election Used	Deviation†	Number of Precincts
1950	1946	+0.7	50
1952	1948	+0.3	100
1954	1952	+2.8	105
1956	1952	−0.2	171
1958	1956	−2.2	156
1960	1956	−0.7	198

*Outside the South.

†For example, the 1946 election results in precincts in the sample in 1950 had a mean per cent Republican vote 0.7 of a percentage point higher than was true in the United States outside the South. As a sample of precincts, they were this much in error in terms of the results of the previous election.

TABLE 2

Comparison of Election Results and Survey Results, Per Cent Republican of the Democratic-Republican Vote

Election	(N)	Non-South Survey Results	Voting Preference Method	Non-South Election Results	Deviation
In total sample:*					
1950	(2,452)	48.0	Open	52.7	−4.7
1952	(4,814)	53.2	Open	56.8	−3.6
1954	(4,784)	45.6	Open	50.5	−4.9
1956	(6,173)	61.8	Open	59.0	+2.8
1958	(4,625)	42.6	Open	46.1	−3.5
1960	(6,082)	49.8	Secret	50.1	−0.3
Mean†					3.3
Range†					0.3–4.9
Among those registered, plan to register, plan to vote:*					
1950	(1,999)	49.2	Open	52.7	−3.5
1952	(4,229)	54.2	Open	56.8	−2.6
1954	(3,733)	47.3	Open	50.5	−3.2
1956	(5,438)	61.6	Open	59.0	+2.6
1958	(3,662)	43.8	Open	46.1	−2.3
1960	(5,291)	49.6	Secret	50.1	−0.5
Mean†					2.5
Range†					0.5–3.5
Among those whose turnout score placed them in part of sample corresponding to expected turnout proportion:* Open preference question result:					
1950	(1,235)	52.4	Open	52.7	−0.3
1952	(3,240)	55.3	Open	56.8	−1.5
1954	(2,410)	50.0	Open	50.5	−0.5
1956	(4,150)	62.1	Open	59.0	+3.1
1958	(2,465)	45.9	Open	46.1	−0.2
1960	(4,360)	50.2	Secret	50.1	+0.1
Mean†					1.0
Range†					0.1–3.1
Converting 1956 and 1958 to secret ballot base:					
1950	(1,235)	52.4	Open	52.7	−0.3
1952	(3,240)	55.3	Open	56.8	−1.5
1954	(2,410)	50.0	Open	50.5	−0.5
1956	(4,150)	60.6	Secret	59.0	+1.6
1958	(2,465)	46.3	Secret	46.1	+0.2
1960	(4,360)	50.2	Secret	50.1	+0.1
Mean†					0.7
Range†					0.1–1.6

*Corrected for bias in terms of a previous election.
†Disregarding signs.

that all the interviewers would have had sufficient experience with it for us to use only the ballot box procedure in the final surveys without serious concern.

As in my first essay, the material here is for the United States excluding thirteen Southern states.[2] The relatively wide difference between presidential and congressional years in the turnout ratio in the South has made it desirable to exclude this variable in our analysis.

The data in Tables 1 and 2 are comparable to the data in tables appearing in the earlier article, with the addition of the appropriate 1960 data. Table 1 brings up to date the data concerning the representativeness of the precincts which were the primary sampling units for the final survey and the number of such units in each sample. Table 2 provides a comparison of election results and survey results in the total sample; among those registered, planning to register, and planning to vote; among those whose turnout score placed them in that part of the sample corresponding to the expected turnout proportion, using the open preference question result for all elections except 1960 (in 1960 only secret ballot data were available); and among those whose turnout score placed them in that part of the sample corresponding to the expected turnout proportion, but converting 1956 and 1958 results to the secret ballot base.

With the experience of six elections using essentially the same methods, it is useful to look at the reduction in deviations that occurs as the sample is defined to conform more and more closely to the universe of those who vote, and at these deviations in relation to the standard error for simple random samples of the sizes used (see Table 3).

The samples were drawn from among all persons old enough to vote who were living in private households. When the voting preference of all such persons is used (that is, without excluding any respondent on the basis of likelihood of not voting), the mean deviation for the six elections disregarding signs is 3.3 percentage points. The bias (the mean deviation taking signs into account) is −2.4 per cent Republican or +2.4 per cent Democratic.

When a first approach is made to restrict the universe sampled to one approximating the voting population, the sample is restricted to those who were registered or said they planned to register and also said they planned to vote. With this sample the mean deviation is 2.5 percentage points. The bias is −1.6 per cent Republican, or +1.6 per cent Democratic. This approach to an approximation of the voting population has reduced the mean deviation from 3.3 to 2.5 percentage points and the bias from 2.4 to 1.6 percentage points.

A more restrictive definition of the sample is used for the final estimate. This involves a turnout scale derived from a series of questions related to voting participation and a cutting point corresponding to the proportion of the adult population expected to vote. Those whose scale scores put them

[2]Alabama, Arkansas, Florida, Georgia, Kentucky, Louisiana, Mississippi, North Carolina, Oklahoma, South Carolina, Tennessee, Texas, and Virginia.

TABLE 3

A Comparison of the Standard Error of Per Cent Democratic (or Republican) with the Survey Deviation

Year	Actual Non-South Division of the Vote in the Election Per Cent Democratic	Per Cent Republican	(N)	Standard Error (σ)	Deviation between Survey Result and Election (d)	$\dfrac{d}{\sigma}$
All respondents:						
1950	47.3	52.7	(2,452)	1.0	−4.7	4.7
1952	43.2	56.8	(4,814)	0.7	−3.6	5.1
1954	49.5	50.5	(4,784)	0.7	−4.9	7.0
1956	41.0	59.0	(6,173)	0.6	+2.8	4.7
1958	53.9	46.1	(4,625)	0.7	−3.5	5.0
1960	49.9	50.1	(6,082)	0.6	−0.3	0.5
Mean					3.3*	4.5
Bias					−2.4†	
Those registered, plan to register, plan to vote						
1950	47.3	52.7	(1,999)	1.1	−3.5	3.2
1952	43.2	56.8	(4,229)	0.8	−2.6	3.2
1954	49.5	50.5	(3,733)	0.8	−3.2	4.0
1956	41.0	59.0	(5,438)	0.7	+2.6	3.7
1958	53.9	46.1	(3,662)	0.8	−2.3	2.9
1960	49.9	50.1	(5,291)	0.7	−0.5	0.7
Mean					2.5*	3.0
Bias					−1.6†	
Those whose turnout score placed them in part of sample corresponding to expected turnout proportion:						
1950	47.3	52.7	(1,235)	1.4	−0.3	0.2
1952	43.2	56.8	(3,240)	0.9	−1.5	1.7
1954	49.5	50.5	(2,410)	1.0	−0.5	0.5
1956	41.0	59.0	(4,150)	0.8	+3.1	3.9
1958	53.9	46.1	(2,465)	1.0	−0.2	0.2
1960	49.9	50.1	(4,360)	0.8	+0.1	0.1
Mean					1.0*	1.1
Bias					+0.1†	

*Mean deviation disregarding signs.
†Mean deviation taking signs into account.

above the cutting point constitute the sample of voters for the final estimate. With this sample the mean deviation is 1.0 percentage points. The bias is +0.1 per cent Republican or −0.1 Democratic. Again a further approach to an approximation of the voting population has reduced the mean deviation materially. The reduction in the mean deviation as compared with a sample of all persons of voting age is from 3.3 to 1.0 percentage points and the reduction in the bias is from 2.4 to 0.1 percentage points.

In the 1956, 1958, and 1960 elections, one further step taken to refine the measurement of voting intention, which had nothing to do with the sample, was the use of a secret ballot as described above. Since its purpose was to obtain a more valid measurement of voting intention, however, a "best estimate" would include it. With this final step the mean deviation for the six elections was 0.7 and the bias was +0.1 Republican or −0.1 Democratic.

At this final stage one can say that we have moved closer to the true universe of voters and increased the validity of responses. The mean deviation of the final estimates is very close to the theoretical mean error for random samples of the sizes used. The ratios of the standard error to the actual deviation in each election are shown in Table 4.

The deviations averaged 0.8 of the sampling standard errors. In a large number of random samples from a population, theory would lead us to expect the mean deviation of the estimates to be about 0.8 of the standard deviation or standard error. Also, theory would lead us to expect that the ratio between the deviations of the estimates from the true population value and the standard error would be the equivalent of 1.0 or less in a little more than two-thirds of the samples. Actually, 4 out of 6 of the ratios were in that category. Theory would also lead us to expect that in repeated samplings the ratio of the deviations to the standard error would have a value of 2.0 or less in about 95 out of 100 samples. All six of the examples shown had a d/σ of 2.0 or less.

TABLE 4

**A Comparison of the Standard Error of Per Cent
Democratic (or Republican) with the Deviation
of the Final Estimate**

Election	Standard Error (σ)	Deviation (d)	$\dfrac{d}{\sigma}$
1950	1.4	0.3	0.2
1952	0.9	1.5	1.7
1954	1.0	0.5	0.5
1956*	0.8	1.6	2.0
1958*	1.0	0.2	0.2
1960†	0.8	0.1	0.1
Mean	1.0	0.7	0.8

*Includes adjustment for the final data to a secret ballot base.
†All data obtained by secret ballot procedure.

We know that there were several sources of possible error: (1) the method used for approximating the voting population is subject to error, and as a result the final estimate is based upon a sample that includes some nonvoters and excludes some voters; (2) some respondents who said they would vote for one party or candidate undoubtedly finally voted for the other; (3) a small percentage remained undecided; and (4) several days elapsed between the survey and the election. Nevertheless, experience with the estimation procedure used by the Gallup Poll in the last six national elections closely approximated theoretical expectations, assuming a simple random sample drawn from the population of those who voted. In other words, if in these elections we had been able to draw random samples of the ballots actually cast in the election booth on election day, used samples of the size employed in these six election surveys, and computed the distribution of the vote in the six elections, we could expect to have done little if any better on the average than we did using survey data.

A point worthy of note is that in 1960 and 1956, as contrasted with the other four elections, use of the turnout scale made little difference, and one could have done about as well using the total sample with no exclusions as using the sample excluding those least likely to vote. *In this particular respect* 1956 and 1960 were elections in which it was easier to have a small error than in the other four elections. This fact points up the danger of evaluating an election survey method on the basis of one or two elections.

A summary of the data for the six non-South elections appears in Table 5. It will be seen that as the universe sampled was defined to conform more and more closely to the voting population and steps were taken to increase the validity of the voting preference response in 1956, 1958, and 1960, the mean deviation was markedly reduced and approached a level which conforms closely to the theoretical expectation for samples of the sizes used drawn as random samples.

TABLE 5

The Effect of the Progressive Elimination of Likely Nonvoters and Use of the Secret Ballot

	Mean Deviation between Survey Result and Election in Six Elections	*Mean of Ratios between Survey Deviation and Standard Error*
Total sample of all respondents*	3.3	4.5
Those who were registered, planned to register, and planned to vote*	2.5	3.0
Those whose turnout score placed them in that part of the sample corresponding to the expected turnout proportion*	1.0	1.1
Those whose turnout score placed them in that part of the sample corresponding to the expected turnout proportion †	0.7	0.8

*"Open" preference question in 1950, 1952, 1954, 1956, 1958; "secret" preference question in 1960.

†"Open" preference question in 1950, 1952, 1954; "secret" preference question in 1956, 1958, and 1960.

Of course, each election is a unique event, and the sources of error can be many and varied. An international crisis on the eve of an election, for example, conceivably could cause a shift of opinion sufficient to change enough votes to invalidate the results of all prior surveys. The experience here recorded, however, is some evidence bearing upon the accuracy of personal interview attitude surveys when the important variables in a given situation can be controlled and measured.

Election Survey Methods

by Paul Perry, president The Gallup Organization

In a presidential election year election survey results are prominent in the news. In 1964, activity began earlier than usual in connection with the presidential primary elections, and much was said and written about the results in the various news media. As is usually the case the publication of election survey results which in some instances differed from the division of the vote in these elections provoked considerable controversy. The conclusion of many commentators in such cases is that sample surveys have thereby demonstrated their lack of validity and reliability. Published survey results which agree well with election results are often either accepted as evidence of the survey practitioner's good luck or as cause for alarm. Also the automatic assumption of much commentary is that election survey results are "predictions" of what will happen on election day more or less regardless of how far in advance of the election they are taken. This and other oversimplification that frequently is a part of the reporting and interpretation of election surveys leads to adverse judgments regarding the usefulness of the survey method in general. Certain characteristics of election surveys and their methodology need to be kept in mind, and a clear idea of what they are and what they are not is required if they are to be properly interpreted and evaluated. On a different level political surveys provide data which are used by political scientists and others with an academic or professional interest, and it is important to users to have some evidence of their validity and reliability. In particular, polling agencies would seem to have a responsibility to inform political scientists what methods are being employed and provide data concerning their adequacy. With these two general objectives in mind, this paper is an extension of my first two papers describing Gallup Poll election survey procedures and experiences.

Pre-election survey results are more correctly to be regarded as measurements than forecasts or predictions. The problems of reliability and of validity are sufficiently difficult to make the matter of prediction something to be dealt with only after these have been solved with satisfactory approximations. If a good job of measurement can be done and the problem of doing this properly close to an election can be solved, an instrument is available for ascertaining the division of voter preference in a sequence of surveys up to the election. One might then hazard a prediction of the outcome by extrapolating the trend, if any, observable in the sequence of measurements. However, this final projection is necessary if one is to call it a prediction. Suppose the final survey is done some time prior to an election, say a month or two in advance. Any projection or prediction at that time would properly have to be made with an accompanying statement of assumptions. Relatively large swings in voter preference in short periods of time have been observed in survey results, changes large enough to have small likelihood of being chance fluctuations. Therefore, a prediction of the election outcome based solely on a survey as much as a month before an election is in the realm of prophecy rather than prediction in the scientific meaning of that word. An example was the case of the 1964 New Hampshire presidential primary. Polls in New Hampshire picked up a marked change in candidate standings in the last week.

This is not to say that a large margin of one man or party over another is weak evidence as to which one will win if such a result is obtained, say, a month before an election. However, it is not conclusive evidence as is sometimes inferred by post election accuracy claims for estimates that far in advance. Six months in advance or even three months in advance, even a large lead might be weak evidence. This would be especially true if the minority candidate is not well known and can be expected to be better known as he campaigns. He may make surprising headway in three months or even one month.

Long range political estimates based on survey data can be made, of course. This is a different process from that used in forming the typical election survey estimate. The typical survey estimate is designed to be a measurement of voting preference at a point in time in the same way that the Bureau of Labor Statistics' measures of unemployment are taken as an estimate of what a census would show at a point in time. Predictions of the amount of unemployment six months from now require something else in addition. As an example of what might be dignified as a long range political forecast, in 1958 on a visit to Canada someone there asked me to guess who would be the likely candidates in 1960 and who would win the election. On the basis of the results of Gallup Poll surveys on the political temper of the country and, of course, the results of surveys concerning the two possible candidates, the observation was made that Nixon and Kennedy would probably be the candidates and that if this happened, Kennedy would be almost sure to win. This could be categorized as sheer guessing if the estimate had been made without any prior knowledge. However, on the basis of available information the writer could have buttressed his opinion with supporting facts, made a few assumptions, and called it a prediction. If it proved correct, it would be perhaps interesting, but its correctness would be little evidence of the reliability or validity of the method used. If the background information were quantified, however, and put together in a systematic manner, the framework of a prediction system would be there with large gaps for unknown parameters and variables. Although these unknowns could not be evaluated that far in advance, a range of outcomes could be projected on the basis of various assumptions. The possible value of these in providing usable information could be very great, particularly for parties, candidates, or political scientists. This would be true even if the predictions had a wide range of possible error. However, their value would not be measured by the error. At that distance in time a right political prediction is likely to depend on so many things beyond the predictor's control that it becomes happenstance. One usually has a reasonable chance of being right in choosing between two candidates at even a relatively remote point in time. In other words, such a successful prediction is mildly interesting but nothing more because of the considerable element of chance involved. Unfortunately, some survey estimates several months in advance of elections are cited for their accuracy or inaccuracy with a similar lack of attention to the large element of chance involved because of possible changes over time. Analogously election surveys based on small samples which happen to be accurate are sometimes cited as evidence of the adequacy of small samples. Without reference to the theoretical confidence limits based on sample size and without reference to the broader error limits if the other sources of error are taken into account, such examples prove nothing.

To turn to the Gallup Poll estimates in national elections, each is an estimate of the division of voter preference at a particular time, or time period. With respect to the final pre-election estimate, interviewing for this survey usually ends four days prior to the elections. The time span centers five days prior to the election, that is on Thursday of the week preceding the election on Tuesday. Therefore, any net shift in voter preference between that time and election day will produce a deviation between the election result and a completely accurate final estimate. Ideally we would do the final survey on the Monday before election day. This is not feasible for us at the moment on a national basis and probably would serve little practical purpose if it could be done properly. Therefore, in attempting to refine our measurement procedures we have to make the assumption that little shift in voting intention occurs during this period.

SAMPLE SIZE

The sources of error in any measure of voter intention are greater than is generally recognized. Those who did such an excellent analysis of election polls for the Social Science Research Council after the 1948 election made this abundantly clear in their report.[1] Take the size of the sample used in a survey estimate, for example, an element which has such a direct bearing upon the sampling error. Sample size can be controlled at will, presuming the availability of a large enough sum of money. Practically speaking, however, distinct budgetary limitations control sample size. With the sample sizes usually available for election estimates, the sampling tolerances are large enough to make the sampling error a serious matter in close elections. Consider an election such as 1960 when Kennedy received 50.1 per cent and Nixon 49.9 per cent of the popular vote cast, excluding minor party candidates. In such an election a huge sample is required to estimate with a high degree of confidence which candidate has a majority of the popular vote assuming all the other sources of error are under control.

[1]Frederick Mosteller, Herbert Hyman, Philip J. McCarthy, Eli S. Marks, David B. Truman, *The Pre-Election Polls of 1948*, Social Science Research Council, Bulletin 60, 1949.

Given the Gallup Poll final 1960 pre-election estimate of 50.7 per cent Kennedy, 49.3 per cent Nixon, a sample of 14,000 binomial cases would be required to say with 95 per cent confidence that Kennedy had at least 50.0 plus per cent of the vote at the time of the survey. This, of course, would be assuming that one had in hand a simple random sample of an accurately defined universe of those going to the polls. An even larger sample would be required using the typical cluster sample.

In most elections the popular vote is not that close. If the population of voters divided 53 per cent for one candidate and 47 for another, then some 1,500 to 1,700 cases using a typical cluster sample would enable us to say with close to 95 per cent confidence that the leading candidate had at least 50.0+ per cent of the vote at the time of the survey, *if* we are sure we have an unbiased sample of those going to vote, *and* there is no refusal or undecided response. In any case, an evaluation of election survey procedures depends upon the size of the deviation from the election result in a number of elections. Also the relevant criterion is the size of the deviation rather than whether the results of the survey showed a majority preference for the actual winner.

MEASURING VOTER PREFERENCE

The major problems in measuring the division of candidate or party preference in the electorate seem to be the following: (1) Obtaining a valid expression of voting intention; (2) appraising the likely voting preference of the undecided or refusals; (3) defining a sample of those old enough to vote who are representative of those who will vote.

The Gallup Poll relies on the straightforward question "If the election for President were being held today, would you vote for the Democratic candidate (name of candidate) or the Republican candidate (name of candidate)?" The question asks for the vote "today" rather than at the time of election. Many persons cannot honestly say how they will vote a week, a month, or several months hence but can say how they might vote today. Asking about voting preference in the future usually produces a relatively large undecided unless asked close to an election. Since there is some reason to be concerned about the truthfulness of a response on political matters, we have in recent elections depended entirely upon a procedure in which respondents are asked to check their preference privately on a paper ballot. They are then asked to drop the ballot in a box carried by the interviewer. The reduction in the number of undecided or refusal responses this produces leads us to believe it increases the validity of the results we get. More elaborate and more indirect questioning techniques, of course, can be and have been used. With their use problems of interpretation can become quite difficult in the absence of considerable experimental data. For this reason a simple choice question at the moment seems preferable to us. It has the decided virtue of being a close simulation of the actual choice a voter makes in an election.

To further reduce the number of undecideds and refusals a supplemental forced choice question has long been used. This question asks respondents who cannot or will not make a choice to indicate in which direction they are leaning. This reduces the undecided[2] obtained in response to the initial question by as much as 50 per cent. Our judgment is that a forced choice can be used safely in this instance, and it appears to be borne out by the results.

We have used other techniques for analyzing the undecided. For example, one can determine how the undecideds and refusals on candidate preference answer questions concerning issues, personalities, and parties and compare their answers with how the decideds answer such questions. Take such a question as "Which party can do the best job of keeping the country prosperous in the next four years — the Democratic or Republican Party?" Usually on such a question the vote of undecideds in party or candidate preference falls somewhere between the vote of supporters of the Democratic candidate and the vote of supporters of the Republican candidate. A comparison of these three results provides an indication of the predispositions of the undecideds. A measure of this predisposition can be obtained by determining what weighted combination of Democrats and Republicans will reproduce the undecided responses on the question. With a little algebra one can say that the undecideds look like a combination of x per cent supporters of the Democratic candidate and y per cent supporters of the Republican candidate. After this has been done on a series of questions, the problem remains of how much weight to give the various items included in the analysis. One particular item may be more influential than several other items combined.

In the 1952 election, for example, such an analysis indicated the undecided to be at least 2 to 1 Democratic in terms of most domestic issues, in terms of past vote, in terms of party affiliation, and in terms of demographic characteristics. On the other hand it indicated a Republican or Eisenhower majority among them in their appraisal of the relative ability of the two candidates to keep the country out of war. In light of the election results the war and peace issue was presumably as influential as all other items combined. By making such an assumption one would have anticipated an approximately even division of the undecideds. Before the election this was not an easy assumption to make without considerably more data than were available. Therefore, in the final estimate in allocating undecided reliance was placed upon the analysis described which in sum indicated that the undecided and refusals were at least two to one Democratic in their predispositions. Use of the forced choice question which indicated an evenly divided preference among the undecided would have produced a significantly more accurate estimate. Relying on respondent testimony as

[2]For simplicity of presentation the "no choice" respondents will be referred to as "undecided" although they consist of a combination of "undecided" and "refusal." Actually it is nearly impossible to distinguish between them. Some who say "undecided" are covert refusals and some who refuse are really undecided.

in the forced choice question does have the great advantage of eliminating judgmental factors which are subject to a number of interpretations.

A particularly risky item to use directly in judging the pre-disposition of the undecided is a question concerning the vote in previous elections. It is risky for these reasons: (1) A response bias occurs in the direction of the winning candidates. That is to say, among those who claim to have voted, a larger percentage claim to have voted for the winning candidate than was actually the case. (2) A response bias occurs in the direction of having voted. A larger percentage claim to have voted than actually did vote. (3) A large shift such as occurred between 1948 and 1952 tends to negate the past vote as an indicator of present vote. It is unrealistic to assume no shift or a counter shift in the undecided voting group in the presence of a large shift among others. (4) Usually a sizable proportion of the undecided did not vote in a previous election.

A residual undecided on voting preference, of course, always remains. In the last two presidential elections for example — 1956 and 1960 — it was 3 per cent in both cases in Gallup Poll surveys a few days before the election. Post election validation studies of voting participation, determining which respondents voted by a check of registration records, suggest that anywhere from a third to two-thirds of these residual undecided did vote in the last seven national elections. Ideally these should be taken into account in the final estimate. However, they can not be without some kind of indirect method of measuring their predispositions. Also about seven or eight per cent of all those contacted refuse to be interviewed at all.

In discussing the size of the undecided vote realistically, it is necessary to define the universe, specify the question, and specify any procedures

TABLE 1

Per Cent Undecided in Final Pre-Election Surveys
Outside the South

Election	Type of Election	Total Sample of Voting Age Before "Leaning" Question	Total Sample of Voting Age After "Leaning" Question	Likely Voters* After "Leaning" Question	Likely Voters* Using "Secret" Ballot
1950	Congressional	18.8	10.5	5.3	
1952	Presidential	13.4	6.7	5.6	
1954	Congressional	16.6	8.2	5.9	
1956	Presidential	14.5	8.5	7.5	3.0
1958	Congressional	16.6	8.1	4.7	3.4
1960	Presidential	12.9	7.5	5.1	3.0
1962	Congressional	14.8	7.8	5.6	3.3
Mean		15.4	8.2	5.7	
Range		12.9–18.8	6.7–10.5	4.7–7.5	

*"Likely voters" were those in the sample with voting participation scale ratings placing them in that part of the sample regarded as most likely to vote.

used to probe for opinions. For example, it makes a difference whether one is talking about a total sample of voting age or a sample of those likely to vote. In the last two presidential elections, in the final Gallup Poll surveys outside the South, among all those of voting age the mean per cent undecided was 13.7. After using the "leaning" question probe, the mean per cent residual undecided was 8.0. Next, reducing the universe to those most likely to vote and using the "leaning" probe, the mean per cent undecided was 6.3. Finally using a ballot box and a paper ballot, the mean undecided was 3.0. This is a 78 per cent reduction from the per cent undecided that was obtained without the ballot box, without a probe, and without eliminating the most likely non voters. Table 1 gives Gallup Poll data on undecided for the seven national elections, 1950–1962.

TURNOUT

The other major problem is determining which respondents in the sample comprise a group representative of those who will vote. Our practice has been to sample the adult civilian population and then try to classify respondents in terms of their likelihood of voting. A sizeable minority of those old enough to vote do not, and most importantly the nonvoters differ from voters in their politics. It is essential to do something about this in developing a realistic estimate of the vote division. The percentage of the civilian population old enough to vote who do not has averaged about 38 per cent in the last five presidential elections and over 50 per cent in the last five congressional elections in non-presidential years.

Currently a turnout scale based on a series of eight questions is used by the Gallup Poll to make the classification of likelihood of voting. One question asks about voting in previous elections; one about registration; one about plans to vote in the coming election; one about interest in the election; one about usual voting habits; a knowledge question about location of the polling place; a question about previous voting in the local precinct; and one about interest in politics in general. These are used for a national general election; for a primary election additional questions would be required.

A score for each respondent is computed by giving a weight of 1 or 0 to each response category for each of the eight questions. This scoring is based on a Guttman scale analysis. In 1962 an additional scoring was used based on post election studies of voting participation in which the proportion in each response category who voted was ascertained. For example, if among respondents in earlier elections who said they were absolutely certain to vote, an average of 80 per cent voted, this was used to score such respondents in the 1962 samples. Each question response category provided such a score. A mean of such scores was computed for each respondent, and respondents were ranked on the basis of their scores. This latter scoring provided for a more detailed scaling than the previous scoring procedure — some 20 total scale positions as contrasted with 9 positions using the 1 or 0 scores.

After scoring and classification, the candidate preference question is tabulated by the weighted score categories. The most likely voter category is placed at the top of the array and the least likely voter category at the bottom. The groups are accumulated until a proportion of the sample is obtained corresponding to the expected turnout proportion. If, for example, it is estimated that 60 per cent of those old enough to vote will go to the polls, sample cases are accumulated until the 60 per cent of the sample most likely to vote is obtained. This is taken as the sample of voters. In 1962 both scales produced the same division of the vote at the position of the expected turnout proportion.[3]

The range between the most likely voter group and the least likely voter group in party preference was striking. In the top 11 per cent likelihood group the preference division was 56 per cent Republican, 40 per cent Democratic, 3 per cent "other", and 1 per cent undecided. In the lowest 22 per cent likelihood group the preference division was reversed with 30 per cent Republican, 52 per cent Democratic, 2 per cent "other", and 16 per cent undecided. The vote in six turnout groups is shown in Table 2.

TABLE 2

**Party Preference by Likelihood of Voting
in the 1962 Congressional Elections**

Voting Participation Scale Groups Ranging from Highest to Lowest Scores in Voting Likelihood Classified by Share of Sample		Responses to Voting Preference Question			
	(N)	Republican	Democratic	Other	Undecided and Refuse
%					
11 Most likely to vote	(492)	55.6	40.5	2.6	1.3
15	(659)	46.2	47.9	2.4	3.5
13	(585)	43.6	49.7	3.8	2.9
17	(805)	38.6	52.7	4.2	4.5
22	(1028)	35.4	52.5	3.1	9.0
22 Least likely to vote	(988)	30.1	51.6	2.2	16.1
100					

A relationship between likelihood of voting and candidate preference has been observed in primary elections also where voting participation may be as low as 10 per cent of the adult population. The difficulty presented in such a situation is clear. Unless the original sample drawn is quite large as survey samples go, one ends up with a sample too small to provide a satisfactory degree of statistical reliability. The inefficiency of sample surveys for elections with low rates of participation is thus very great if one is interested primarily in estimating the relative positions of the candidates. Even to

[3]In a sample of the precincts a post election study in 1962 indicated that among those sampled prior to the election, 77 per cent of the likely voter group actually voted and 25 per cent of the unlikely voter group voted.

analyze accurately the influential issues is difficult if one wishes to do it in relation to likely voters.

A practical difficulty of dealing with the turnout problem is that it requires taking a sample at least 50 per cent larger than the one used for estimating the division of the vote. Conceivably one could begin the interview with the series of questions related to voting participation and end the interview at some point in the series. This offers two obvious difficulties: (1) Since all the questions bear upon the classification of voting likelihood, it is not feasible to make the classification with less than all of them; (2) one does not then have a sample from a population with known parameters. It is always useful to be able to validate or balance the sample in certain respects. Therefore, the total sample must be drawn to include many who are excluded from the final estimate.

Post election studies by the Gallup Poll to determine how well the voter group classification approximates the actual voter group in terms of candidate or party preference have been made. These studies have been carried out in connection with national elections, both presidential and congressional. In each such study a subsample of precincts used for the final election surveys was drawn, and an investigation of voter lists made to see which respondents had voted. For nine elections the pre-election voting preference

TABLE 3

**Comparison of Pre-Election Preference of Those
in the Sample Who Voted and Those Regarded as
Likely Voters Using the Scale and Cutoff Technique**

	Pre-Election Preference in Per Cent Democratic of the Democratic-Republican Vote				
Election	*Those who Voted*	*(N)*	*Likely Voters Using the Scale & Cutoff Technique*	*(N)*	*Deviation of Likely Voters From Actual Voters*
1952 Presidential	42.1	(385)	41.2	(385)	−0.9
1954 Congressional	48.4	(339)	48.1	(339)	−0.3
1956 Presidential	31.4	(497)	31.2	(497)	−0.2
1958 Congressional	54.1	(438)	55.1	(438)	+1.0
1960 Presidential	47.1	(348)	46.5	(348)	−0.6
1962 Congressional	47.6	(290)	47.4	(290)	−0.2
1964 Presidential	61.0	(228)	64.0	(228)	+3.0
1966 Congressional	52.8	(333)	54.8	(333)	+2.0
1968 Presidential	38.9	(280)	39.6	(280)	+0.7
Mean*					1.0
Mean†					+0.5
Range					0.2–3.0

*Disregarding signs
†Taking signs into account

of these actual voters has been compared with the preferences of those deemed most likely to vote. The average deviation between likely voters and actual voters was 1.0 percentage points, with a range of 0.2 to 3.0. The data for the individual elections are shown in Table 3.

By way of contrast the average deviation between the pre-election preference of voters and nonvoters was 8.6 percentage points (Table 4).

TABLE 4

Comparison of Pre-Election Preference of Those in the Sample Who Voted and Those in the Sample Who Did Not Vote

| Election | *Pre-Election Preference in Per Cent Democratic of the Democratic-Republican Vote* | | | | |
	Those who Voted	*(N)*	*Those Who Did Not Vote*	*(N)*	*Deviation of Non Voters from Voters*
1952 Presidential	42.1	(385)	43.2	(81)	+ 1.1
1954 Congressional	48.4	(339)	56.2	(121)	+ 7.8
1956 Presidential	31.4	(497)	42.0	(250)	+10.6
1958 Congressional	54.1	(438)	59.0	(139)	+ 4.9
1960 Presidential	47.1	(348)	53.9	(91)	+ 6.8
1962 Congressional	47.6	(290)	63.9	(130)	+16.3
1964 Presidential	61.0	(228)	73.4	(79)	+12.4
1966 Congressional	52.8	(333)	62.3	(146)	+ 9.5
1968 Presidential	38.9	(280)	46.6	(196)	+ 7.7
Mean					+ 8.6
Range					1.1–16.3

The average deviation between the total sample and actual voters was 2.4 with a range of 0.2 to 5.0 (Table 5).

It should be noted that when using a total sample of all those of voting age, the average deviation was about three times as large as the average deviation using likely voters. Furthermore, the average net deviation or bias was +0.5 Democratic among likely voters and +2.4 percentage points Democratic in the total sample.

Without a turnout correction, that is, using the total sample without exclusions for likely nonvoters, the net deviation or bias was 2.2 percentage points Democratic in the presidential and 2.8 percentage points Democratic in the congressional. In other words, as expected, the difference between voter and nonvoter groups is a more serious problem in the off-year congressional elections. Nevertheless, the method of correcting for this factor so far is at least as successful in such elections as it is in presidential elections.

A part of the problem, of course, is to determine the proportion of the population of voting age who can be expected to vote — that is, to project turnout. We have found that it is possible to project the turnout ratio with

TABLE 5

Comparison of Pre-Election Preference of Those in the Sample Who Voted and the Preference of Voters and Nonvoters Combined

| Election | Pre-Election Preference in Per Cent Democratic of the Democratic-Republican Vote | | | | Deviation of Total Sample from Voters |
	Those who Voted	(N)	Total Sample: Voters & Nonvoters Combined	(N)	
1952 Presidential	42.1	(385)	42.3	(466)	+0.2
1954 Congressional	48.4	(339)	50.4	(460)	+2.0
1956 Presidential	31.4	(497)	34.9	(747)	+3.5
1958 Congressional	54.1	(438)	55.3	(577)	+1.2
1960 Presidential	47.1	(348)	48.5	(439)	+1.4
1962 Congressional	47.6	(290)	52.6	(420)	+5.0
1964 Presidential	61.0	(228)	64.2	(307)	+3.2
1966 Congressional	52.8	(333)	55.7	(479)	+2.9
1968 Presidential	38.9	(280)	41.4	(476)	+2.5
Mean					+2.4
Range					0.2–5.0

considerable accuracy from survey data. Our method of doing so has been quite accurate on the limited number of occasions we have used it. The comparison made here is based on the non-South. These projections were made in each instance on the basis of an early October survey. In 1962 we projected 55.2 per cent would vote; 54.5 per cent did vote. In 1960 the projection was 73.8 per cent, the actual 71.7. In 1958 the projection was 52.7, the actual 53.7; in 1956 the projection was 67.8, the actual 67.3. The average error was 1.1 percentage points and the maximum 2.1. Projections before 1956 were made using such supplementary information as registrations. The necessity of basing them on something better became apparent, and survey data were then developed for the purpose.

The method, briefly, is to relate the proportion who answer a question on interest and a question on voting intention to the proportion who voted in previous elections using various combinations of answers. Separate projections are made for each of these combinations (about 10 combinations are used) and a mean of the projections is the one used. This has been consistently more accurate than any one of the combinations.

SAMPLE DESIGN

The only particular feature about the sample design in Gallup Poll election surveys is the use of precincts as the primary sampling units which was first adopted on a large scale in 1950. This makes possible the use of the vote in a previous election or elections as supplementary information with which to form the estimates. The estimates can be formed by either the ratio method or the regression method, both of which provide an estimate with a lower sampling variance. The procedure is a simple one and is analogous to the use of stratification for the reduction of sampling variance. For example, using the ratio method: For each precinct to be sampled in year 1964, the per cent of the vote for Kennedy in 1960 was computed. The precincts had been drawn with probability of selection proportional to size so that they could be given equal weight. The mean Kennedy percentage in 1960 in the sample of precincts was then an unbiased estimate of the Kennedy per cent in the total vote for Kennedy and of Nixon. Let us suppose that it turned out to be 52.0 per cent Kennedy in 1960 in the sample of precincts as compared with the 50.1 per cent Kennedy polled of the total 1960 major party vote. Thus the sample of precincts as drawn in such a case has a positive bias in per cent Kennedy. A ratio adjustment would then be applied to the current candidate preference — that is, the current preference for the Democratic candidate will be reduced by the fraction 50.1/52.0 to remove the slight bias in the sample of precincts. This takes advantage of any significant correlation by precincts between the actual party division in the previous election and the survey party preference. Two things to bear in mind about such an adjustment: (1) Its advantages will only show up over a period of time — that is, in a number of estimates, and (2) other sources of error are potentially more serious.

In the ten national elections of 1950 through 1968 the ratio adjustment has in fact only slightly reduced the mean deviation of the results of the final surveys using the complete estimation procedure.

One final additional note on sampling error. The idea that samples of human populations are somehow less subject to random sampling error or are more amenable to the control of random sampling error than samples of other kinds of populations is not uncommon. Drawing samples of precincts is a good way to discover, if one has any doubts, the inexorability of sampling error with human populations. For example, in the ten elections from 1950 through 1968 we have drawn probability samples of precincts with the number of precincts drawn ranging from 50 in 1950 to 266 in 1960 (outside the South). The deviations of the mean percentage Democratic (or Republican) of the actual vote in the preceding election in each of the ten samples of precincts from the corresponding percentage of the national major party vote in that election conform closely to theoretical expectations. An estimated standard error for each sample was computed using a precinct standard deviation of 18 percentage points, a figure obtained from the combined samples of precincts. The ratios of the standard error to the actual deviation in each election average 0.7, which is about the same as the ratio of the mean deviation to the standard deviation for a normal distribution (Table 6).

These computations illustrate the built-in error one can start with even using as many as 150 or 200 sampling areas. In other words, a perfect sampling, or complete census of voters, if such were possible, in a relatively large number of sampling areas would still fail to account for the error accompanying a given sample of areas. The above experience illustrates

TABLE 6

Deviation of the Means of Samples of Precincts* in
Per Cent Democratic of the Democratic-Republican Vote

Survey Year	Number of Precincts	Previous Election Used	Mean % Democratic in Previous Election in Sample of Precincts†	Democratic % in Previous Election in All Precincts	Deviation of Sample Precincts From Universe of Precincts (d)	Standard Error‡ (σ)	$\dfrac{d}{\sigma}$
1950	50	1946	43.8	43.1	+0.7	2.6	0.3
1952	100	1948	52.4#	52.1#	+0.3	1.8	0.2
1954	105	1952	46.0	43.2	+2.8	1.8	1.6
1956	171	1952	43.0	43.2	−0.2	1.4	0.2
1958	156	1956	38.8	41.0	−2.2	1.4	1.5
1960	198	1956	41.3	41.0	−0.7	1.3	0.6
1962	155	1960	48.4	49.9	−1.5	1.5	1.0
1964	195	1960	48.8	49.9	−1.1	1.3	0.8
1966	243	1964	64.6	63.7	+0.9	1.2	0.8
1968	260	1964	63.7	63.7	0.0	1.1	0.0
Mean¶						1.0	0.7
Range						0.0–2.8	

*Outside the South.

†Drawn with probability of selection proportional to size and computing the mean giving each precinct equal weight.

‡Based on an estimated precinct standard deviation of 18 percentage points.

#Truman vote plus Wallace vote.

¶Disregarding sign.

that built-in sampling errors of two or three percentage points are not unusual in survey samples.

The final estimate of voter preference by the Gallup Poll is based on a system of two surveys, one taken in early October and a final survey in late October or early November. The first survey results are processed using the complete estimating procedure. The second survey is tabulated by the interviewers and telegraphed or telephoned to the central office. Both surveys are done in the same precincts. A simplified breakdown of the data by likely voters and nonvoters is employed to minimize tabulating and transmission errors by the interviewers. They tabulate the voting preference only among those who say they plan to vote. The trend if any in the "plan to vote" group is then applied to the results of the first survey obtained using the complete estimating procedure. The two surveys are standardized by educational attainment and other characteristics regarded as important to control. For example, in 1960 they were equated by religion as well as by education.

In arriving at an estimate based on the early October survey the sample is balanced by a number of other characteristics as well. The sample is balanced jointly by region, education, and sex; also by city size, and by age. A further weighting is by number of adults in the household, and finally the results by region are weighted on the basis of the regional distribution of the vote in recent elections. This distribution is nearly the same as the distribution of the population of voting age except for the South which usually includes from 15 to 20 per cent of the vote in presidential elections. It constitutes about 27 per cent of the population of voting age.

Election survey problems and methods have been presented here on the basis of Gallup Poll experience. No doubt much can be added by the experience of others. It would be highly worthwhile to have more of it published. Elections offer something of a challenge to those in survey research because they are not simple to deal with successfully. If taken full advantage of, however, they can be a useful proving ground for survey methods. Easy generalities about why surveys are accurate or inaccurate in relation to elections without careful analysis do a disservice to all concerned. On the other hand if approached with the respect they deserve as a test of method, much of usefulness to all those interested in the measurement and analysis of public opinion can be learned.

The Gallup Poll
PUBLIC OPINION 1935-1971

1935

OCTOBER 20

RELIEF AND RECOVERY

Interviewing Date 9/10–15/35
Survey #1   Question #1

Do you think expenditures by the Government for relief and recovery are too little, too great, or just about right?

Too little.......................... 9%
Too great.......................... 60
About right........................ 31

By Region
New England

Too little.......................... 6%
Too great.......................... 75
About right........................ 19

East Central

Too little.......................... 9%
Too great.......................... 62
About right........................ 19

Middle Atlantic

Too little.......................... 13%
Too great.......................... 61
About right........................ 26

South

Too little.......................... 5%
Too great.......................... 60
About right........................ 35

West Central

Too little.......................... 7%
Too great.......................... 58
About right........................ 35

Mountain

Too little.......................... 11%
Too great.......................... 44
About right........................ 45

Pacific

Too little.......................... 9%
Too great.......................... 58
About right........................ 33

By Political Affiliation
Republicans

Too little.......................... 4%
Too great.......................... 89
About right........................ 7

Democrats

Too little.......................... 11%
Too great.......................... 36
About right........................ 53

The American Institute of Public Opinion, a nonpartisan fact-finding organization which will report the trend of public opinion on one major issue each week, has collected this information by means of personal interviews and mail questionnaires from thousands of voters located in every state in the union. Persons in all walks of life have been polled in order to obtain an accurate cross section.

The results of these polls are being published for the first time today in leading newspapers—representing every shade of political preference.

OCTOBER 27
PRESIDENT ROOSEVELT'S
VOTER APPEAL

Interviewing Date 9/10–15/35
Survey #1   Question #2

Did you vote for Franklin Roosevelt in 1932? Would you vote for him today?

By Region

	1932	1935	Points of Change
New England....	51%	38%	−13%
Middle Atlantic..	53	46	−7
East Central.....	55	51	−4
West Central.....	63	56	−7
South..........	76	70	−6
Mountain........	60	65	+5
Pacific Coast.....	61	56	−5

NOVEMBER 3
SUPREME COURT

Interviewing Date 9/10–15/35
Survey #1   Question #3

As a general principle, would you favor limiting the power of the Supreme Court to declare acts of Congress unconstitutional?

Yes............................... 31%
No................................ 53
No opinion........................ 16

By Region
New England

Yes............................... 25%
No................................ 63
No opinion........................ 12

Middle Atlantic

Yes............................... 32%
No................................ 56
No opinion........................ 12

East Central

Yes............................... 27%
No................................ 50
No opinion........................ 23

West Central

Yes............................... 32%
No................................ 49
No opinion........................ 19

South

Yes............................... 35%
No................................ 52
No opinion........................ 13

Mountain

Yes............................... 35%
No................................ 41
No opinion........................ 24

Pacific

Yes............................... 33%
No................................ 51
No opinion........................ 16

By Political Affiliation
Democrats

Yes............................... 55%
No................................ 45

Republicans

Yes............................... 14%
No................................ 86

New Democrats*

Yes............................... 55%
No................................ 45

New Republicans*

Yes............................... 13%
No................................ 87

*Persons who have changed parties since the 1932 election.

NOVEMBER 11
ALCOHOLIC BEVERAGES

Interviewing Date 10/8–13/35
Survey #4   Question #2

In your locality is the situation in respect to the use of alcoholic beverages better, about the same, or worse than it was during the last few years of prohibition?

Better	36%
Worse	33
About the same	31

By Political Affiliation
Democrats

Better	47%
Worse	20
About the same	33

Republicans

Better	24%
Worse	50
About the same	26

NOVEMBER 17
NEUTRALITY

Interviewing Date 9/18–23/35
Survey #2   Question #4

In order to declare war, should Congress be required to obtain the approval of the people by means of a national vote?

Yes	75%
No	25

By Region

	Yes	No
New England	75%	25%
Middle Atlantic	75	25
East Central	75	25
West Central	77	23
South	70	30
Mountain	79	21
Pacific	77	23

Interviewing Date 10/8–13/35
Survey #3   Question #3a

If one foreign nation insists upon attacking another, should the United States join with other nations to compel it to stop?

Should join	29%
Should not	71

By Region

	Should	Should Not
New England	33%	67%
Middle Atlantic	30	70
East Central	29	71
West Central	30	70
South	27	73
Mountain	23	77
Pacific Coast	25	75

Views of Special Groups

	Should	Should Not
Persons on relief	23%	77%
Persons too young to vote in 1932	30	70

NOVEMBER 24
PRESIDENT ROOSEVELT'S VOTER APPEAL

Interviewing Date 11/9–14/35
Survey #9   Question #6b

Would you vote for President Roosevelt today?

Yes	53%
No	47

Definitely Republican States

New Hampshire	Pennsylvania
Vermont	Connecticut
Maine	Massachusetts
Rhode Island	New Jersey

Borderline Republican States

Delaware	Maryland
West Virginia	Indiana
Ohio	

Definitely Democratic States

Wisconsin	Nevada
Oregon	Oklahoma
New Mexico	Iowa
Colorado	Florida
North Dakota	Virginia
Kansas	Arizona
Wyoming	North Carolina
Kentucky	Utah
Washington	Arkansas
Missouri	Alabama
Idaho	Texas
Nebraska	Louisiana
California	Georgia
Montana	South Carolina
Tennessee	Mississippi

Borderline Democratic States

New York	Illinois
Michigan	Minnesota
South Dakota	

DECEMBER 1
REPUBLICAN PRESIDENTIAL CANDIDATES

Interviewing Date 10/14–19/35
Survey #5   Question #3

Republican voters were asked: Whom would you like to see the Republican party nominate for President in 1936?

Governor Alf Landon	33%
Senator William E. Borah	26
Herbert Hoover	12
Theodore Roosevelt Jr.	12
Frank Knox	8
Ogden Mills	5
Senator Arthur Vandenberg	3
Senator Lester Dickinson	1

By Region

	1st Choice	2nd Choice
New England	Borah	Landon-Roosevelt tied
Middle Atlantic	Landon	Borah
East Central	Landon	Borah
West Central	Landon	Borah
South	Landon	Borah
Mountain	Borah	Landon
Pacific Coast	Borah	Landon

DECEMBER 8
VETERANS BONUS

Interviewing Date 11/4–9/35
Survey #8   Question #1

Should the Federal Government pay the veterans their bonus now?

Yes	55%
No	45

The slight edge in favor of immediate payment is brought about largely by the vote of persons now receiving relief money, who vote for cash payment of the bonus by an overwhelming majority of 4–1. If this group were not included, public opinion on the bonus question would divide 50–50.

By Political Affiliation

	Yes	No
Democrats	59%	41%
Republicans	49	51

By Region

	Yes	No
New England	50%	50%
Middle Atlantic	56	44
East Central	56	44
West Central	53	47
South	57	43
Mountain	57	43
Pacific Coast	52	48

DECEMBER 15
MOST IMPORTANT PROBLEM

Interviewing Date 11/4–9/35
Survey #8   Question #3

What do you regard as the most vital issue before the American people today?

The following are listed in order of frequency of mention:

Employment
Economy in government
Neutrality
Reduction of taxes
Preservation of the Constitution
Ending the Depression
Less government control of business
Repudiation of the New Deal
Townsend Plan
Labor problems
Farm conditions
Pensions
Repudiation of President Roosevelt
Redistribution of wealth
Liquor control
Religion and morality
Maintenance of the New Deal
Political honesty
Social security
Reelection of President Roosevelt
Increased national defense
Payment of the soldiers' bonus

By Political Affiliation
Democrats

Employment
Neutrality
Economy
Ending Depression
Reduced taxes
Labor problems
Better farm conditions
Pensions
Support of New Deal
Townsend Plan
Support of Roosevelt
Redistribution of wealth

Social security
Religion
Increased national defense
Revised Constitution
Soldiers' bonus
Political honesty
Less control of business
Liquor control

Republicans

Economy
Employment
Preserving Constitution
Reduced taxes
Neutrality
Defeat of Roosevelt
Defeat of New Deal
Less control of business
Ending Depression
Liquor control
Townsend Plan
Labor problems
Religion
Better farm conditions
Political honesty
Pensions
Redistribution of wealth
Social security
Increased national defense
Soldiers' bonus

Third-Party Voters

Employment
Economy
Reduced taxes
Townsend Plan
Defeat of New Deal
Neutrality
Redistribution of wealth
Labor problems
Less control of business
Ending Depression
Political honesty
Soldiers' bonus
Increased national defense
Pensions
Social security

Religion
Liquor control
Better farm conditions
Preserving Constitution
Defeat of Roosevelt

DECEMBER 22
PRESIDENT ROOSEVELT'S
VOTER APPEAL

Interviewing Date 12/9–14/35
Survey #13   Question #1

Would you vote for President Roosevelt today?

Definitely Republican States

	Yes
Maine	39%
Rhode Island	41
Vermont	41
Pennsylvania	43
Connecticut	44
New Hampshire	46

Borderline Republican States

Ohio	47%
Massachusetts	47
Maryland	48
Illinois	48
West Virginia	48
New Jersey	48
Delaware	49
Indiana	49

On the Line State

New York	50%

Borderline Democratic States

Minnesota	52%
Michigan	52
Colorado	52
Kansas	53
Oregon	53
Wyoming	53

Definitely Democratic States

New Mexico	54%
Idaho	54
Wisconsin	54
Nebraska	54
Iowa	55
Kentucky	56
Missouri	56
South Dakota	56
Washington	56
North Dakota	57
Montana	58
Nevada	58
California	59
Utah	59
Oklahoma	61
Arizona	65
Tennessee	65
Virginia	66
Florida	68
North Carolina	70
Arkansas	71
Alabama	74
Texas	79
Georgia	81
Louisiana	84
South Carolina	85
Mississippi	88

DECEMBER 29
MILITARY APPROPRIATIONS

Interviewing Date 12/1–6/35
Survey #12   Question #3

Do you think that army (navy, air force) appropriations should be greater, smaller, or about the same as they are now?

	Greater	Smaller	About the Same
Army appropriations	48%	11%	41%
Navy appropriations	54	11	35
Air Force appropriations	74	7	19

Army Appropriations
By Region

	Greater	Smaller	About the Same
New England....	53%	8%	39%
Middle Atlantic..	55	11	34
East Central.....	44	11	45
West Central.....	30	18	52
South..........	49	11	40
Mountain........	45	11	44
Pacific..........	50	11	39

By Political Affiliation

	Greater	Smaller	About the Same
Democrats.......	51%	9%	40%
Republicans.....	44	14	42

Navy Appropriations
By Region

	Greater	Smaller	About the Same
New England....	60%	8%	32%
Middle Atlantic	63	10	27
East Central.....	51	11	38
West Central.....	30	20	50
South..........	57	10	33
Mountain.......	43	10	47
Pacific..........	59	9	32

By Political Affiliation

	Greater	Smaller	About the Same
Democrats.......	59%	8%	33%
Republicans......	52	13	35

Air Force Appropriations
By Region

	Greater	Smaller	About the Same
New England....	79%	5%	16%
Middle Atlantic..	80	6	14
East Central.....	71	7	22
West Central.....	62	11	27
South..........	73	7	20
Mountain.......	73	7	20
Pacific..........	83	4	13

By Political Affiliation

	Greater	Smaller	About the Same
Democrats.......	75%	5%	20%
Republicans......	72	9	19

1936

	Yes	No
New England	87%	13%
Middle Atlantic	89	11
East Central	88	12
West Central	90	10
South	88	12
Mountain	94	6
Pacific	92	8

By Political Affiliation

Democrats	94.5%	5.5%
Republicans	80	20

JANUARY 5
AGRICULTURAL ADJUSTMENT ACT

Interviewing Date 12/9–14/35
Survey #13 — Question #2

Do you favor or oppose the Agricultural Adjustment Act?

Favor	41%
Oppose	59

By Political Affiliation

	Favor	Oppose
Democrats	70%	30%
Republicans	8	92

By Region

New England	22%	78%
Middle Atlantic	30	70
East Central	34	66
West Central	44	56
South	57	43
Mountain	40	60
Pacific	29	71

JANUARY 12
OLD AGE PENSIONS

Interviewing Date 12/16–21/35
Survey #14 — Question #1

Are you in favor of Government old age pensions for needy persons?

Yes	89%
No	11

Interviewing Date 12/16–21/35
Survey #14 — Question #1a

Asked of those who replied in the affirmative: How much should be paid monthly to each single person?

National average	$40 mo.

By Region

New England	$50 mo.
Middle Atlantic	50 mo.
East Central	40 mo.
West Central	30 mo.
South	30 mo.
Mountain	50 mo.
Pacific	60 mo.

Interviewing Date 12/16–21/35
Survey #14 — Question #1b

Asked of those who replied in the affirmative: How much should be paid monthly to a husband and wife?

National average	$60 mo.

By Region

New England	$75 mo.
Middle Atlantic	80 mo.
East Central	65 mo.
West Central	60 mo.
South	50 mo.
Mountain	90 mo.
Pacific	100 mo.

Interviewing Date 12/16–21/35
Survey #14   Question #1c

Asked of those who replied in the affirmative: What age should a person be to qualify for an old age pension?

National average.................. 60 yrs.

Interviewing Date 12/16–21/35
Survey #14   Question #1d

Do you favor the Townsend Plan — that is paying $200 a month to each aged husband and wife?

Yes............................. 3.8%
No.............................. 96.2

By Region

	Yes	No
New England.........	2.9%	97.1%
Middle Atlantic.......	2.2	97.8
East Central..........	3.0	97.0
West Central..........	4.3	95.7
South................	1.2	98.8
Mountain.............	12.0	88.0
Pacific................	16.0	84.0

By Political Affiliation

	Yes	No
Democrats.............	3.3%	96.7%
Republicans...........	3.8	96.2

JANUARY 19
PRESIDENTIAL TRIAL HEAT

Interviewing Date 1/6–11/36
Survey #14   Question #5

For which candidate would you vote today — Franklin Roosevelt or the Republican candidate?

Roosevelt......................... 53%
Republican....................... 47

Persons Listed in *Who's Who in America*
Only

Roosevelt......................... 31%
Republican....................... 69

Reliefers Only

Roosevelt......................... 77%
Republican....................... 23

Definitely Republican

		For Roosevelt
Maine............................		36%
Vermont..........................		37
New Hampshire...................		43
Rhode Island.....................		45
Pennsylvania.....................		45
Connecticut......................		46
New Jersey.......................		46

Borderline Republican

Ohio.............................	48%
Massachusetts.....................	48
Illinois...........................	48
West Virginia.....................	49
Maryland.........................	49
Delaware.........................	49
Indiana..........................	49

On the Line

Michigan.........................	50
Colorado.........................	50
New York........................	50

Borderline Democratic

Minnesota........................	51%
Kansas...........................	52
Wyoming.........................	52
Wisconsin........................	52
South Dakota.....................	53

Definitely Democratic

Nebraska.........................	54%
Oregon...........................	55
Idaho............................	55
Washington.......................	56
North Dakota.....................	56
Iowa.............................	56
Kentucky.........................	57
Missouri.........................	57
California........................	58
New Mexico......................	59

Oklahoma........................ 60
Nevada.......................... 61
Montana......................... 61
Utah............................ 61
Arizona......................... 62
Florida......................... 66
Virginia........................ 67
Tennessee....................... 67
North Carolina.................. 70
Arkansas........................ 74
Alabama......................... 76
Texas........................... 79
Louisiana....................... 80
Georgia......................... 83
South Carolina.................. 87
Mississippi..................... 89

JANUARY 26
AUTOMOBILE SAFETY

Interviewing Date 12/30/35–1/5/36
Survey #15   Question #1a

*As a means of reducing the number and
severity of automobile accidents, would you
favor or oppose uniform traffic laws and
regulations for all states?*

Favor........................... 95%
Oppose.......................... 5

By Region

	Favor	Oppose
New England...............	94%	6%
Middle Atlantic............	95	5
East Central...............	94	6
West Central...............	94	6
South.....................	95	5
Mountain..................	98	2
Pacific....................	93	7

Interviewing Date 12/30/35–1/5/36
Survey #15   Question #1b

*Would you favor or oppose strict drivers'
tests including regular physical and mental
examinations?*

Favor........................... 86%
Oppose.......................... 14

By Region

	Favor	Oppose
New England...............	87%	13%
Middle Atlantic............	86	14
East Central...............	84	16
West Central...............	85	15
South.....................	89	11
Mountain..................	83	17
Pacific....................	86	14

Interviewing Date 12/30/35–1/5/36
Survey #15   Question #1c

*Would you favor or oppose stricter penalties
for violators of traffic laws?*

Favor........................... 82%
Oppose.......................... 18

By Region

	Favor	Oppose
New England...............	78%	22%
Middle Atlantic............	73	27
East Central...............	80	20
West Central...............	82	18
South.....................	89	11
Mountain..................	86	14
Pacific....................	83	17

Interviewing Date 12/30/35–1/5/36
Survey #15   Question #1d

*Would you favor or oppose compulsory
automobile liability insurance in every
state?*

Favor........................... 73%
Oppose.......................... 27

By Region

	Favor	Oppose
New England...............	73%	27%
Middle Atlantic............	73	27
East Central...............	79	21
West Central...............	68	32
South.....................	73	27
Mountain..................	64	36
Pacific....................	76	24

Interviewing Date 12 /30 /35–1 /5 /36
Survey #15   Question #1e

Would you favor or oppose special marking of cars whose drivers have been at fault in accidents?

Favor............................ 70%
Oppose........................... 30

By Region

	Favor	Oppose
New England...............	61%	39%
Middle Atlantic.............	61	39
East Central................	65	35
West Central...............	72	28
South.....................	78	22
Mountain..................	73	27
Pacific....................	67	33

Interviewing Date 12 /30 /35–1 /5 /36
Survey #15   Question #1f

Would you favor or oppose installation of "governors" to prevent speeds greater than 50 miles an hour?

Favor............................ 68%
Oppose........................... 32

By Region

	Favor	Oppose
New England...............	69%	31%
Middle Atlantic.............	66	34
East Central...............	61	39
West Central...............	71	29
South.....................	72	28
Mountain..................	66	34
Pacific....................	58	42

FEBRUARY 2
THE BUDGET

Interviewing Date 12 /30 /35–1 /5 /36
Survey #15   Question #3

Do you think it necessary at this time to balance the budget and start reducing the national debt?

Yes.............................. 70%
No.............................. 30

By Region

	Yes	No
New England................	75%	25%
Middle Atlantic..............	70	30
East Central.................	72	28
West Central.................	71	29
South.......................	67	33
Mountain....................	70	30
Pacific......................	66	34

By Political Affiliation

	Yes	No
Democrats...................	55%	45%
Republicans..................	89	11

Interviewing Date 12 /30 /35–1 /5 /36
Survey #15   Question #3a

Asked of those who voted in the affirmative: Should this be done by governmental economies, higher taxes, or both?

Governmental economies............. 80%
Higher taxes....................... 2
Both.............................. 18

FEBRUARY 9
GOVERNMENT REGULATION

Interviewing Date 1 /13–18 /36
Survey #16   Question #1

Would you favor an amendment to the Constitution transferring to the Federal Government the power to regulate agriculture and industry?

Yes.............................. 43%
No.............................. 57

By Region

	Yes	No
New England................	28%	72%
Middle Atlantic..............	39	61
East Central.................	39	61
West Central.................	41	59

South	55	45
Mountain	40	60
Pacific Coast	47	53

FEBRUARY 16
PRESIDENTIAL TRIAL HEAT

Interviewing Date 1/27–2/1/36
Survey #19   Question #6

For which candidate would you vote today — Franklin Roosevelt, the Republican candidate, the Socialist candidate, or a third party candidate?

Roosevelt	50.3%
Republican	43.
Third party	4.6
Socialist	2.1

Reliefers Only

Roosevelt	71.2%
Republican	21.8
Third party	4.0
Socialist	3.0

Minor Party Vote by Region

	Socialist	Third Party
New England	2.3%	4.2%
Middle Atlantic	2.7	4.3
East Central	1.8	4.6
West Central	1.9	5.1
South	.9	3.6
Mountain	1.5	5.5
Pacific	2.7	6.5

FEBRUARY 23
REPUBLICAN PRESIDENTIAL CANDIDATES

Interviewing Date 1/13–18/36
Survey #16   Question #2

Asked of Republicans: If you favor a Republican for President, which candidate would you like to support?

Landon	43%
Borah	28
Hoover	17
Knox	7
Vandenberg	4
Dickinson	1

By Region
New England

Landon	39%
Borah	28
Hoover	20
Knox	10
Vandenberg	2
Dickinson	1

Middle Atlantic

Landon	43%
Borah	26
Hoover	21
Knox	6
Vandenberg	3
Dickinson	1

East Central

Landon	39%
Borah	23
Hoover	15
Vandenberg	13
Knox	8
Dickinson	2

West Central

Landon	54%
Borah	26
Hoover	11
Knox	5
Vandenberg	2
Dickinson	2

South

Landon	40%
Borah	33
Hoover	16
Knox	7
Vandenberg	2
Dickinson	2

Mountain

Borah	43%
Landon	35
Hoover	14
Knox	5
Vandenberg	2
Dickinson	1

Pacific

Landon	44%
Borah	31
Hoover	20
Knox	2
Vandenberg	2
Dickinson	1

Republicans Who Voted for Roosevelt in 1932

Landon	41%
Borah	39
Hoover	7
Knox	7
Vandenberg	4
Dickinson	2

Reliefers Only

Borah	34%
Landon	32
Hoover	20
Knox	8
Vandenberg	3
Dickinson	3

MARCH 1
POLITICAL PHILOSOPHY

Interviewing Date 1/20–25/36
Survey #18   Question #3

Which theory of government do you favor — concentration of power in the Federal Government, or concentration of power in the state governments?

Federal Government	56%
State governments	44

By Political Affiliation

	Federal Govt.	State Govts.
Democrats	72%	28%
Republicans	35	65

By Special Groups

Reliefers	71%	29%
Leading citizens	25	75
Women	58	42

By Region

New England	47%	53%
Middle Atlantic	54	46
East Central	58	42
West Central	56	44
South	58	42
Mountain	66	34
Pacific	57	43

MARCH 8
WAR MUNITIONS

Interviewing Date 1/20–25/36
Survey #18   Question #4

Should the manufacture and sale of war munitions for private profit be prohibited?

Yes	82%
No	18

By Region

	Yes	No
New England	78%	22%
Middle Atlantic	81	19
East Central	82	18
West Central	83	17
South	82	18
Mountain	82	18
Pacific	88	12

By Political Affiliation

	Yes	No
Socialists	91%	9%
Democrats	85	15
Republicans	79	21

MARCH 15
PRESIDENTIAL TRIAL HEAT

Interviewing Date 2/24–3/1/36
Survey #23   Question #5

*For which candidate would you vote today
— Franklin Roosevelt, the Republican
candidate, the Socialist candidate, or a
third party candidate?*

Roosevelt........................ 51.1%
Republican....................... 43.4
Third party...................... 3.7
Socialist........................ 1.8

By Electoral Vote

Democratic (33 states)................ 343
Republican (11 states)................ 128
On the line (4 states)................ 60

The states that are listed as definitely Republican are: Maine, Vermont, New Hampshire, Delaware, Rhode Island, Massachusetts, and Pennsylvania. Borderline Republican states are: Connecticut, New Jersey, Ohio, and Colorado. The on the line states are: Michigan, Illinois, Kansas, and Wyoming.

MARCH 22
CURRENCY INFLATION

Interviewing Date 1/27–2/2/36
Survey #19   Question #3

Are you in favor of currency inflation?

Yes.............................. 27%
No............................... 73

By Region

	Yes	No
New England................	18%	82%
Middle Atlantic............	23	77
East Central...............	28	72
West Central...............	28	72
South......................	35	65
Mountain...................	30	70
Pacific....................	17	83

By Political Affiliation

Republicans.................	10%	90%
Democrats...................	40	60
Third party supporters......	41	59
Socialists..................	32	68

MARCH 29
CIVIL SERVICE REFORM

Interviewing Date 2/17–22/36
Survey #22   Question #2

*Should Government positions, except those
that have to do with important matters of
policy, be given to persons who help put
their political party in office, or persons who
receive the highest marks in Civil Service
examinations?*

Help political party................. 12%
Receive highest marks................ 88

By Political Affiliation

	Political Party	Highest Marks
Democrats..............	15%	85%
Republicans............	9	91

Interviewing Date 2/24–31/36
Survey #23   Question #3

*Should all postmasters hereafter be selected
by Civil Service examinations?*

Yes.............................. 86%
No............................... 14

By Political Affiliation

	Yes	No
Democrats..................	85%	15%
Republicans................	87	13

APRIL 5
REPUBLICAN PRESIDENTIAL CANDIDATES

Interviewing Date 2/24–3/1/36
Survey #23   Question #4

*Asked of Republicans: Which candidate
do you support for the Republican nomination for President?*

Landon.......................... 56%
Borah........................... 20
Hoover.......................... 14
Knox............................ 5
Vandenberg...................... 4
Dickinson....................... 1

By Region
New England

Landon.......................... 55%
Hoover.......................... 20
Borah........................... 16
Knox............................ 6
Vandenberg...................... 2
Dickinson....................... 1

Middle Atlantic

Landon.......................... 57%
Borah........................... 18
Hoover.......................... 17
Knox............................ 4
Vandenberg...................... 3
Dickinson....................... 1

East Central

Landon.......................... 53%
Borah........................... 16
Hoover.......................... 13
Vandenberg...................... 11
Knox............................ 6
Dickinson....................... 1

West Central

Landon.......................... 63%
Borah........................... 22
Hoover.......................... 9
Knox............................ 3
Vandenberg...................... 2
Dickinson....................... 1

South

Landon.......................... 53%
Borah........................... 24
Hoover.......................... 13

Knox............................ 6
Vandenberg...................... 2
Dickinson....................... 2

Mountain

Landon.......................... 46%
Borah........................... 38
Hoover.......................... 9
Knox............................ 3
Vandenberg...................... 3
Dickinson....................... 1

Pacific

Landon.......................... 60%
Borah........................... 17
Hoover.......................... 15
Knox............................ 4
Vandenberg...................... 3
Dickinson....................... 1

By City
New York

Landon.......................... 54%
Hoover.......................... 20
Borah........................... 19
Knox............................ 4
Vandenberg...................... 2
Dickinson....................... 1

Philadelphia

Landon.......................... 43%
Hoover.......................... 22
Borah........................... 20
Knox............................ 8
Vandenberg...................... 5
Dickinson....................... 2

Boston

Landon.......................... 71%
Hoover.......................... 12
Borah........................... 9
Knox............................ 6
Vandenberg...................... 1
Dickinson....................... 1

Women Only

Landon........................... 56%
Hoover........................... 18
Borah............................ 17
Knox............................. 4
Vandenberg....................... 4
Dickinson........................ 1

Farmers Only

Landon........................... 59%
Borah............................ 22
Hoover........................... 9
Knox............................. 4
Vandenberg....................... 4
Dickinson........................ 2

Reliefers Only

Landon........................... 45%
Borah............................ 29
Hoover........................... 15
Knox............................. 6
Dickinson........................ 3
Vandenberg....................... 2

Republicans Listed in
Who's Who in America

Landon........................... 60%
Hoover........................... 20
Borah............................ 7
Knox............................. 7
Vandenberg....................... 5
Dickinson........................ 1

APRIL 8
PRESIDENTIAL TRIAL HEAT

Interviewing Date 2/24–3/1/36
Survey #23   Question #1

Asked of New Jersey voters: If the presidential election were held today, for which candidate would you vote?

Roosevelt........................ 50%
Republican candidate............. 50

Based on major party vote.

APRIL 9
PRESIDENTIAL TRIAL HEAT

Interviewing Date 2/24–3/1/36
Survey #23   Question #1a

Asked of Kansas voters: If the presidential election were held today, for which candidate would you vote?

Roosevelt........................ 49%
Republican candidate............. 51

Based on major party vote.

APRIL 10
PRESIDENTIAL TRIAL HEAT

Interviewing Date 2/24–3/1/36
Survey #23   Question #1b

If the presidential election were held today, for which candidate would you vote?

Michigan Only

Roosevelt........................ 52%
Republican candidate............. 48

Detroit Only

Roosevelt........................ 58%
Republican candidate............. 42

Based on major party vote.

APRIL 11
PRESIDENTIAL TRIAL HEAT

Interviewing Date 2/24–3/1/36
Survey #23   Question #1c

Asked of Illinois voters: If the presidential election were held today, for which candidate would you vote?

Roosevelt........................ 49%
Republican candidate............. 51

Based on major party vote.

APRIL 12
PRESIDENTIAL TRIAL HEAT

Interviewing Date 2/24–3/1/36
Survey #23   Question #1d

Asked of New York State voters: If the presidential election were held today, for which candidate would you vote?

Roosevelt......................... 54.5%
Republican candidate.............. 45.5

Based on major party vote.

APRIL 19
HOURS AND WAGES

Interviewing Date 2/24–3/1/36
Survey #23   Question #3

One plan for reducing unemployment is to shorten the hours of labor in business and industry. Do you favor this plan?

Yes................................ 76%
No................................. 24

By Political Affiliation

	Yes	No
Democrats.............	86%	14%
Republicans..........	61	39
Socialists...........	88	12
Third party supporters	78	22

By Special Groups

	Yes	No
Farmers....................	63%	37%
Women.....................	80	20
Young people (21–24 years)	80	20
Reliefers..................	86	14

Interviewing Date 2/24–3/1/36
Survey #23   Question #2

If hours are reduced should the weekly wages of employees be lowered or remain the same?

Lowered.......................... 16%
Remain the same.................. 84

By Political Affiliation

	Lowered	Remain the same
Democrats..........	10%	90%
Republicans........	26	74
Socialists.........	6	94
Third party voters	10	90

By Special Groups

	Lowered	Remain the same
Farmers...................	34%	66%
Women....................	13	87
Young people (21–24 years)	11	89
Reliefers.................	6	94

APRIL 22
CAMPAIGN ISSUES

Special Survey

Asked of Republicans: What in your opinion will be the most important issue in the forthcoming presidential campaign?

The following are listed according to frequency of mention:

Government extravagance
Regulation of business
Disregard of the Constitution
Dictatorial government

Asked of Democrats: What in your opinion will be the most important issue in the forthcoming presidential campaign?

One issue leads all others. Roosevelt helped the common man.

APRIL 24
RELIEF

Special Survey

In your opinion does politics play a part in handling of relief in your locality?

West Virginia Only

Yes................................ 77%
No................................ 13
No opinion........................ 10

Pennsylvania Only

Yes................................ 67%
No................................ 18
No opinion........................ 15

APRIL 26
RELIEF

Interviewing Date 3/23–28/36
Survey #27   Question #4

In your opinion, does politics play a part in the handling of relief in your locality?

Yes................................ 65%
No................................ 18
No opinion........................ 17

By Political Affiliation
Democrats

Yes................................ 55%
No................................ 25
No opinion........................ 20

Republicans

Yes................................ 80%
No................................ 8
No opinion........................ 12

Socialists

Yes................................ 77%
No................................ 9
No opinion........................ 14

By Special Groups
Reliefers

Yes................................ 49%
No................................ 25
No opinion........................ 26

Farmers

Yes................................ 70%
No................................ 19
No opinion........................ 11

Women

Yes................................ 58%
No................................ 17
No opinion........................ 25

Young People (21–24 Years)

Yes................................ 60%
No................................ 14
No opinion........................ 26

Interviewing Date 3/23–28/36
Survey #27   Question #3

Should the responsibility of caring for all persons on relief be returned now to state and local governments?

Yes................................ 55%
No................................ 45

By Political Affiliation

	Yes	No
Democrats....................	44%	56%
Republicans..................	72	28
Socialists....................	38	62

By Special Groups

	Yes	No
Reliefers.....................	41%	59%
Farmers.....................	60	40
Women.....................	56	44
Young people (21–24 years).....	47	53

APRIL 27
PRESIDENTIAL TRIAL HEAT

Interviewing Date 2/24–3/1/36
Survey #23   Question #1e

Asked of Maine voters: If the presidential election were held today, for which candidate would you vote?

Roosevelt.......................... 33%
Republican candidate.............. 67

Based on major party vote.

APRIL 29
REPUBLICAN PRESIDENTIAL CANDIDATES

Special Survey

> Asked of Michigan Republicans: If you favor a Republican for President, which candidate would you like to support?

Vandenberg........................ 49%
Landon........................... 25
Borah............................ 11
Hoover........................... 11
Knox............................. 3
Dickinson........................ 1

MAY 1
REPUBLICAN PRESIDENTIAL CANDIDATES

Special Survey

> Asked of Republicans: If you favor a Republican for President, which candidate would you like to support?

New York City Only

Landon........................... 56%
Hoover........................... 18
Borah............................ 15
Knox............................. 5
Vandenberg....................... 5
Dickinson........................ 1

Philadelphia Only

Landon........................... 49%
Hoover........................... 20
Borah............................ 20
Knox............................. 5
Vandenberg....................... 5
Dickinson........................ 1

Boston Only

Landon........................... 64%
Hoover........................... 20
Knox............................. 8
Borah............................ 4
Vandenberg....................... 2
Dickinson........................ 2

MAY 2
REPUBLICAN PRESIDENTIAL CANDIDATES

Special Survey

> Asked of Idaho Republicans: If you favor a Republican for President, which candidate would you like to support?

Borah............................ 58%
Landon........................... 34
Hoover........................... 6
Others........................... 2

MAY 3
REPUBLICAN PRESIDENTIAL CANDIDATES

Interviewing Date 3/30–4/4/36
Survey #28   Question #1

> Asked of Republicans: Which candidate do you support for the Republican nomination for President?

Landon........................... 56%
Borah............................ 19
Hoover........................... 14
Knox............................. 5
Vandenberg....................... 5
Dickinson........................ 1

By Region
New England

Landon........................... 57%
Hoover........................... 21

Borah.......................... 11
Knox........................... 8
Vandenberg..................... 2
Dickinson...................... 1

Middle Atlantic

Landon......................... 58%
Borah.......................... 17
Hoover......................... 17
Knox........................... 4
Vandenberg..................... 3
Dickinson...................... 1

East Central

Landon......................... 50%
Borah.......................... 16
Hoover......................... 13
Vandenberg..................... 12
Knox........................... 8
Dickinson...................... 1

West Central

Landon......................... 62%
Borah.......................... 23
Hoover......................... 9
Knox........................... 3
Vandenberg..................... 2
Dickinson...................... 1

South

Landon......................... 55%
Borah.......................... 25
Hoover......................... 12
Knox........................... 5
Vandenberg..................... 2
Dickinson...................... 1

Mountain

Landon......................... 49%
Borah.......................... 36
Hoover......................... 10
Knox........................... 2
Vandenberg..................... 2
Dickinson...................... 1

Pacific

Landon......................... 57%
Borah.......................... 22
Hoover......................... 16
Knox........................... 3
Vandenberg..................... 1
Dickinson...................... 1

Midwest Farmers Only

Landon......................... 59%
Borah.......................... 21
Vandenberg..................... 8
Hoover......................... 6
Knox........................... 4
Dickinson...................... 2

Women Only

Landon......................... 56%
Hoover......................... 18
Borah.......................... 15
Knox........................... 5
Vandenberg..................... 5
Dickinson...................... 1

Reliefers Only

Landon......................... 46%
Borah.......................... 31
Hoover......................... 15
Knox........................... 4
Vandenberg..................... 3
Dickinson...................... 1

MAY 7
PRESIDENTIAL TRIAL HEAT

Special Survey

Asked of Iowa voters: If the presidential election were held today, for which candidate would you vote?

Roosevelt...................... 52%
Republican candidate........... 48

Based on major party vote.

MAY 8
PRESIDENTIAL TRIAL HEAT

Special Survey

> *Asked of Ohio voters: If the presidential election were held today, for which candidate would you vote?*

Roosevelt........................ 50%
Republican candidate............... 50

Based on major party vote.

MAY 9
PRESIDENTIAL TRIAL HEAT

Special Survey

> *Asked of college students: If the presidential election were held today, for which candidate would you vote?*

Roosevelt........................ 54%
Republican candidate............... 46

Based on major party vote.

MAY 10
PRESIDENTIAL TRIAL HEAT

Interviewing Date 3/30–4/4/36
Survey #28   Question #1a

> *If the presidential election were today, for which candidate would you vote?*

By City

	Roosevelt	Republican Candidate
Philadelphia..........	48%	52%
Chicago.............	54	46
Boston..............	56	44
Pittsburgh..........	57	43
Cleveland...........	59	41
St. Louis...........	59	41
Baltimore...........	60	40
Detroit.............	60	40
Los Angeles.........	63	37
New York...........	69	31

Small Towns Only (Under 2,500)

Roosevelt......................... 49%
Republican candidate............... 51

Based on major party vote.

MAY 13
EDUCATION

Interviewing Date 3/30–4/4/36
Survey #28   Question #3

> *Asked in Virginia: Should schools teach the facts about all forms of government, including communism, fascism, and socialism?*

Yes.............................. 54%
No............................... 46

MAY 15
EDUCATION

Interviewing Date 3/30–4/4/36
Survey #28   Question #3a

> *Should schools teach the facts about all forms of government, including communism, facism, and socialism?*

By City

	Yes	No
Baltimore...................	53%	47%
Boston.....................	56	44
New York..................	58	42
Philadelphia................	59	41

MAY 17
EDUCATION

Interviewing Date 3/30–4/4/36
Survey #28   Question #3

> *Should schools teach the facts about communism, fascism, and socialism?*

Yes.............................. 62%
No............................... 38

By Region

	Yes	No
New England	64%	36%
Middle Atlantic	60	40
East Central	60	40
West Central	63	37
South	64	36
Mountain	68	32
Pacific	61	39

By Political Affiliation

Democrats	62%	38%
Republicans	59	41
Socialists	85	15
Third party supporters	73	27

By Special Groups

College students	95%	5%
Young people (21–24 years)	78	22
College teachers	88	12
Teachers	87	13
Women	63	37
Reliefers	55	45
Farmers	60	40

By Community Size

Big cities (100,000 and over)	58%	42%
Small towns (under 2,500)	63	37

Interviewing Date 4/6–11/36
Survey #29   Question #3

Should college teachers be free to express their views on all subjects, including government and religion?

Yes.................................. 59%
No................................... 41

By Region

	Yes	No
New England	65%	35%
Middle Atlantic	57	43
East Central	55	45
West Central	57	43
South	64	36
Mountain	62	38
Pacific	51	49

MAY 20
CHILD LABOR

Special Survey

Asked in New York State: Do you favor or oppose an amendment to the Constitution giving Congress the power to limit, regulate, and prohibit the labor of persons under 18?

Favor............................... 63%
Oppose............................. 37

MAY 21
CHILD LABOR

Special Survey

Asked of farmers: Do you favor or oppose an amendment to the Constitution giving Congress the power to limit, regulate, and prohibit the labor of persons under 18?

Favor............................... 46%
Oppose............................. 54

MAY 24
CHILD LABOR

Interviewing Date 4/6–11/36
Survey #29   Question #1

Do you favor an amendment to the Constitution giving Congress the power to limit, regulate, and prohibit the labor of persons under 18?

Yes.................................. 61%
No................................... 39

By Political Affiliation

	Yes	No
Democrats	72%	28%
Republicans	46	54
Socialists	81	19

By Special Groups

	Yes	No
Farmers	46%	54%
Women	61	39
Reliefers	67	33
Young people (21–24 years)	72	28

By Community Size

Small towns (under 2,500)	57%	43%
Big cities (100,000 and over)	66	34

MAY 29
REPUBLICAN PRESIDENTIAL CANDIDATES

Special Survey

Asked of persons who voted for Roosevelt in 1932 but who would vote for a Republican today: Which candidate would you like to have the Republican convention nominate for President?

Landon	53%
Borah	27
Knox	8
Hoover	6
Vandenberg	5
Dickinson	1

MAY 31
REPUBLICAN PRESIDENTIAL CANDIDATES

Interviewing Date 4/6–11/36
Survey #29   Question #10

Asked of Republicans: If you favor a Republican today, which candidate would you like to support?

Landon	55%
Borah	18
Hoover	14
Knox	6
Vandenberg	6
Dickinson	1

By Region

	Landon	Borah	All Others
New England	59%	14%	27%
Middle Atlantic	58	15	27
East Central	47	18	35
West Central	61	21	18
South	57	21	22
Mountain	46	32	22
Pacific	53	21	26

By Special Groups

	Landon	Borah	All Others
Women	57%	13%	30%
Farmers	57	22	21
Reliefers	43	30	27
Young people (21–24 years)	55	20	25

JUNE 5
PRESIDENTIAL TRIAL HEAT

Special Survey

Asked in Kansas: Which candidate do you prefer for President?

Landon	53%
Roosevelt	47

Based on major party vote.

JUNE 6
PRESIDENTIAL TRIAL HEAT

Special Survey

Asked in Iowa: Which candidate do you prefer for President?

Roosevelt	51%
Landon	49

Based on major party vote.

JUNE 7
PRESIDENTIAL TRIAL HEAT

Interviewing Date 5/18–23/36
Survey #35   Question #8

*For which candidate would you vote —
Franklin Roosevelt, the Republican candidate, the Socialist candidate, or a third
party candidate?*

Roosevelt........................ 53.5%
Republican....................... 42.2
Third party...................... 2.5
Socialist........................ 1.8

By Income

| | Favoring Roosevelt | |
	Upper Two-thirds	All Classes
New England...........	30.0%	46.0%
Middle Atlantic.........	38.0	52.0
East Central...........	46.0	51.9
West Central...........	45.1	54.1
South.................	75.2	72.5
Mountain..............	57.6	59.2
Pacific................	52.7	51.5

JUNE 10
PRESIDENTIAL TENURE

Special Survey

*Asked in Cleveland: Are you in favor of
changing the length of the presidential term
from four to six years?*

Yes.............................. 23%
No............................... 77

JUNE 11
PRESIDENTIAL TENURE

Special Survey

*Asked in Mississippi: Are you in favor of
relaxing the rule against a third term for
the President?*

Yes.............................. 57%
No............................... 43

JUNE 12
PRESIDENTIAL TENURE

Special Survey

*Asked in Ohio: Are you in favor of relaxing
the rule against a third term for the President?*

Yes.............................. 36%
No............................... 64

JUNE 14
PRESIDENTIAL TENURE

Interviewing Date 5/18–23/36
Survey #35   Question #3

*Would you favor changing the term of
office of the President of the United States
to one six-year term with no reelection?*

Yes.............................. 26%
No............................... 74

By Region

	Yes	No
New England................	23%	77%
Middle Atlantic..............	28	72
East Central.................	27	73
West Central.................	24	76
South.......................	26	74
Mountain....................	28	72
Pacific......................	27	73

By Political Affiliation

Democrats...................	26%	74%
Republicans..................	27	73
Socialists....................	26	74
Others......................	29	71

Interviewing Date 5/18–23/36
Survey #35   Question #3a

*Should a President be eligible for a third
term?*

Yes............................. 43%
No.............................. 57

By Region

	Yes	No
New England................	44%	56%
Middle Atlantic..............	42	58
East Central.................	39	61
West Central................	42	58
South.......................	45	55
Mountain....................	44	56
Pacific......................	44	56

By Political Affiliation

Democrats...................	56%	44%
Republicans..................	22	78
Socialists....................	39	61
Others......................	29	71

JUNE 20
POLITICAL PARTIES

Interviewing Date 5/11–16/36
Survey #34   Question #3a

Asked of Middle Atlantic voters: If there were only two political parties in the country — Conservative and Liberal — which would you join?

Conservative....................... 60%
Liberal............................ 40

Maryland Only

Conservative....................... 76%
Liberal............................ 24

JUNE 24
ROOSEVELT ADMINISTRATION

Interviewing Date 5/18–23/36
Survey #35   Question #1

Asked of young voters (21–24 years): Are the acts of the present Administration helping or hindering recovery?

Helping.......................... 67%
Hindering........................ 33

JUNE 24
POLITICAL PARTIES

Interviewing Date 5/11–16/36
Survey #34   Question #3

If there were only two political parties in this country — Conservative and Liberal — which would you join?

Conservative....................... 53%
Liberal............................ 47

By Region

	Conservative	Liberal
New England..........	56%	44%
Middle Atlantic........	60	40
East Central..........	50	50
West Central..........	56	44
South................	49	51
Mountain.............	44	56
Pacific...............	48	52

By Special Groups

Women...............	48%	52%
Reliefers..............	31	69
Young people (21–24 years)..............	34	66
Farmers..............	51	49

By Community Size

Small towns (under 2,500)	52%	48%
10 biggest cities........	45	55

Interviewing Date 5/11–16/36
Survey #34   Question #4

Do you think the time has come to give up our present political parties and have two new ones — one for conservatives and one for liberals?

Yes............................. 30%
No.............................. 70

By Region

	Yes	No
New England................	34%	66%
Middle Atlantic..............	32	68
East Central.................	29	71
West Central.................	33	67
South.......................	25	75
Mountain....................	34	66
Pacific......................	36	64

By Political Affiliation

	Yes	No
Republicans..................	27%	73%
Democrats...................	28	72

By Special Groups

	Yes	No
Women.....................	27%	73%
Farmers.....................	29	71
Reliefers....................	30	70
Young people (21–24 years).....	34	66
College students..............	43	57

JUNE 26
ROOSEVELT ADMINISTRATION

Special Survey

Asked of Kansas voters: Are the acts of the present Administration helping or hindering recovery?

Helping...........................	49%
Hindering........................	51

JUNE 28
THE NEW DEAL

Interviewing Date 5/18–23/36
Survey #35   Question #1

Are the acts of the present Administration helping or hindering recovery?

Helping...........................	55%
Hindering........................	45

By Political Affiliation

	Helping	Hindering
Democrats..............	93%	7%
Republicans.............	10	90
Socialists...............	48	52
Others.................	24	76

JULY 1
CIVILIAN CONSERVATION CORPS

Interviewing Date 5/11–16/36
Survey #34   Question #1

Are you in favor of continuing the Civilian Conservation Corps camps?

Philadelphia Only

Yes...............................	74%
No................................	26

Boston Only

Yes...............................	82%
No................................	18

New York City Only

Yes...............................	73%
No................................	27

JULY 5
CIVILIAN CONSERVATION CORPS

Interviewing Date 5/11–16/36
Survey #34   Question #1

Are you in favor of continuing the C.C.C. camps?

Yes...............................	82%
No................................	18

By Political Affiliation

	Yes	No
Democrats....................	92%	8%
Socialists....................	79	21
Republicans..................	67	33
Third party supporters........	67	33

By Region

	Yes	No
New England	85%	15%
Middle Atlantic	82	18
East Central	80	20
West Central	80	20
South	83	17
Mountain	83	17
Pacific	87	13

Interviewing Date 5/11–16/36
Survey #34   Question #2

Should military training be included in the C.C.C. program?

Yes	77%
No	23

By Region

	Yes	No
New England	78%	22%
Middle Atlantic	74	26
East Central	75	25
West Central	69	31
South	83	17
Mountain	75	25
Pacific	73	27

By Political Affiliation

Democrats	80%	20%
Republicans	74	26
Third party supporters	59	41
Socialists	43	57

By Special Groups

Women	74%	26%
Farmers	77	23
Reliefers	78	22
Young people (21–24 years)	68	32
College students	59	41

JULY 12
PRESIDENTIAL TRIAL HEAT

Interviewing Date 6/22–27/36
Survey #40   Question #1

If the presidential election were today, for which candidate would you vote?

Roosevelt	51.8%
Landon	48.2

By Region

	Roosevelt	Landon
New England	41.3%	58.7%
Middle Atlantic	47.6	52.4
East Central	48.7	51.3
West Central	48.9	51.1
South	68.2	31.8
Mountain	53.6	46.4
Pacific	59.0	41.0

Based on major party vote.

JULY 15
MINIMUM WAGES

Special Survey

Do you favor an amendment to the Constitution to regulate minimum wages?

New York State Only

Yes	72%
No	28

New York City Only

Yes	82%
No	18

Boston Only

Yes	91%
No	9

Los Angeles Only

Yes	78%
No	22

Chicago Only

Yes	73%
No	27

JULY 19
MINIMUM WAGES

Interviewing Date 6/22–27/36
Survey #40   Question #3

Do you favor an amendment to the Constitution to regulate minimum wages?

Yes............................. 70%
No.............................. 30

By Political Affiliation

	Yes	No
Democrats.............	84%	16%
Republicans............	51	49
Socialists.............	84	16
Third party supporters..	78	22

By Special Groups

Young people (21–24 years).....	74%	26%
Reliefers....................	84	16
Farmers.....................	59	41
City residents (2,500 and over)...	74	26

By Region

New England.................	67%	33%
Middle Atlantic..............	70	30
East Central................	69	31
West Central................	66	34
South.......................	69	31
Mountain....................	70	30
Pacific.....................	74	26

Interviewing Date 6/22–27/36
Survey #40   Question #4

Asked of those in favor of the amendment: Should the power be given to Congress or to the individual states?

Congress........................ 56%
States.......................... 44

By Political Affiliation

	Congress	States
Democrats.............	65%	35%
Republicans............	40	60
Socialists.............	70	30
Third party supporters..	70	30

By Special Groups

Young people (21–24 years)..	54%	46%
Reliefers....................	60	40
Farmers.....................	51	49
City residents (2,500 and over)	57	43

By Region

New England.............	52%	48%
Middle Atlantic...........	52	48
East Central..............	56	44
West Central..............	58	42
South....................	62	38
Mountain.................	56	44
Pacific..................	57	43

JULY 26
COUGHLIN AND TOWNSEND ENDORSEMENTS

Interviewing Date 6/29–7/3/36
Survey #36   Question #1

Would Father Coughlin's endorsement of a candidate make any difference in your voting for the candidate, against the candidate, or would it make no difference in your vote?

Would vote for candidate............ 7%
Would vote against candidate......... 20
No difference...................... 73

By Political Affiliation

	For	Against	No Diff.
Democrats...........	7%	17%	76%
Republicans..........	3	25	72
Socialists.............	15	23	62
Third party supporters..	59	7	34

By Region

	For	Against	No Diff.
New England.........	12%	20%	68%
Middle Atlantic.......	9	21	70
East Central..........	8	12	80
West Central..........	9	21	70
South...............	5	20	75
Mountain............	5	14	81
Pacific...............	8	20	72

Interviewing Date 6/22–27/36
Survey #39   Question #4

Would Dr. Townsend's endorsement of a candidate make any difference in your voting for the candidate, against the candidate, or would it make no difference in your vote?

Would vote for candidate............ 10%
Would vote against candidate........ 22
No difference...................... 68

By Political Affiliation

	For	Against	No Diff.
Democrats...........	9%	19%	72%
Republicans..........	7	27	66
Socialists............	14	18	68
Third party supporters..	46	8	46

By Region

	For	Against	No Diff.
New England........	8%	24%	68%
Middle Atlantic.......	8	23	69
East Central.........	7	24	69
West Central.........	11	23	66
South...............	10	19	71
Mountain............	15	16	69
Pacific..............	18	20	62

JULY 29
ROOSEVELT ADMINISTRATION

Special Survey

Do you believe the acts and policies of the Roosevelt Administration may lead to a dictatorship?

New England Small Towns (Under 2,500)

Yes................................ 73%
No................................. 27

New England Cities (2,500 and Over)

Yes................................ 54%
No................................. 46

Middle Atlantic Small Towns (Under 2,500)

Yes................................ 59%
No................................. 41

Middle Atlantic Cities (2,500 and Over)

Yes................................ 43%
No................................. 57

JULY 30
ROOSEVELT ADMINISTRATION

Special Survey

Asked of young people (21–24 years): Do you believe the acts and policies of the Roosevelt Administration may lead to a dictatorship?

Yes................................ 27%
No................................. 73

AUGUST 2
ROOSEVELT ADMINISTRATION

Interviewing Date 6/22–27/36
Survey #40   Question #2

Do you believe the acts and policies of the Roosevelt Administration may lead to a dictatorship?

Yes................................ 45%
No................................. 55

By Region

	Yes	No
New England................	58%	42%
Middle Atlantic..............	47	53
East Central.................	46	54
West Central.................	47	53
South.......................	31	69
Mountain....................	42	58
Pacific......................	37	63

By Political Affiliation

	Yes	No
Democrats...................	9%	91%
Republicans..................	83	17
Third party supporters........	53	47
Socialists....................	30	70

By Special Groups

Reliefers	23%	77%
Women	44	56
Young people (21–24 years)	27	73
Farmers	46	54

By Community Size

Ten largest cities	35%	65%
Small towns (under 2,500)	52	48

AUGUST 9
PRESIDENTIAL TRIAL HEAT

Interviewing Date 7/20–25/36
Survey #43   Question #3

Which candidate do you prefer for President?

Roosevelt	49.3%
Landon	44.8
Lemke	3.4
Thomas	1.5
Others	1.0

Illinois Only

Landon	47.6%
Roosevelt	46.7
Lemke	3.8
Thomas	1.0
Others	.9

AUGUST 14
CIO

Special Survey

Asked in Pennsylvania: Do you favor or oppose John L. Lewis and his Committee for Industrial Organization's efforts to organize the steel industry?

Favor	47%
Oppose	53

AUGUST 16
UNIONS

Interviewing Date 7/20–25/36
Survey #43   Question #1

Are you in favor of labor unions?

Yes	76%
No	24

By Region

	Yes	No
New England	72%	28%
Middle Atlantic	76	24
East Central	76	24
West Central	74	26
South	74	26
Mountain	83	17
Pacific	78	22

By Political Affiliation

Democrats	83%	17%
Republicans	65	35
Socialists	91	9
Union party	85	15
Others	79	21

Interviewing Date 7/20–25/36
Survey #43   Question #1a

Asked of those who responded in the affirmative: Do you favor separate unions for each craft in an industry (like carpenters, masons, machinists, etc.), or one single union for all workers in an industry (the industrial union)?

Craft	59%
Industrial	41

By Region

	Craft	Industrial
New England	61%	39%
Middle Atlantic	57	43
East Central	56	44
West Central	57	43

	Craft	Industrial
South	63%	37%
Mountain	57	43
Pacific	52	48

By Political Affiliation

	Craft	Industrial
Democrats	53%	47%
Republicans	70	30
Socialists	34	66
Union party	41	59
Others	30	70

Labor Union Members Only

Craft	52%
Industrial	48

AUGUST 16
PRESIDENTIAL TRIAL HEAT

Interviewing Date 7/20–25/36
Survey #43   Question #2

If the presidential election were held today, for which candidate would you vote?

By Special Groups
Labor

Roosevelt	64.7%
Landon	24.3
Lemke	7.4
Thomas	3.1
Others	.5

Farmers

Roosevelt	51.3%
Landon	42.9
Lemke	3.4
Thomas	1.1
Others	1.3

Midwest Farmers

Roosevelt	46.1
Landon	45.7
Lemke	5.9
Thomas	1.2
Others	1.1

Women

Roosevelt	51.5%
Landon	44.0
Lemke	2.3
Thomas	1.0
Others	1.2

Young People

Roosevelt	58.1%
Landon	37.3
Thomas	2.2
Lemke	1.6
Others	.8

Reliefers

Roosevelt	75.9%
Landon	16.5
Thomas	4.8
Lemke	4.2
Others	1.6

AUGUST 23
PRESIDENTIAL TRIAL HEAT

Interviewing Date 8/10–15/36
Survey #46   Question #1

Whom do you prefer for President?

Roosevelt	49.2%
Landon	44.5
Lemke	4.6
Thomas	1.3
Others	.4

By Income

	Roosevelt	Landon
Upper third	41%	59%
Lower third	70	30
Reliefers	82	18

Based on major party vote.

Polls Conducted by Mail

	Roosevelt	Landon
Telephone lists	41%	59%
Automobile registration	44	56

Based on major party vote.

States for Landon
Safely Republican

Vermont
Maine
Massachusetts
Kansas
New Hampshire
Connecticut
Wyoming
Nebraska

Borderline Republican

New Jersey
Rhode Island
Delaware
Illinois
Indiana
Iowa
Pennsylvania
South Dakota
Minnesota
New York
Ohio

States for Roosevelt
Safely Democratic

Mississippi
South Carolina
Alabama
Texas
Georgia
Arkansas
Louisiana
North Carolina
Florida
Virginia
Nevada
North Dakota
Tennessee
Utah
Kentucky
California
New Mexico
Oklahoma
Arizona
Montana

Missouri
Maryland
Washington

Borderline Democratic

Oregon
Wisconsin
Idaho
Colorado
Michigan
West Virginia

AUGUST 27
PRESIDENTIAL TRIAL HEAT

Special Survey

Asked in Kansas: Will you vote for Franklin Roosevelt or Governor Landon?

Roosevelt.......................... 42%
Landon............................ 58

AUGUST 30
PRESIDENTIAL TRIAL HEAT

Interviewing Date 8/17–22/36
Survey #47–B   Question #1

Whom do you prefer for President?

Roosevelt........................ 49.2%
Landon........................... 44.5
Lemke............................ 4.6
Thomas........................... 1.3
Others........................... .4

According to today's results, Roosevelt would carry 29 states and 274 electoral votes to 19 states for Landon with 257 electoral votes.

By Special Groups
Farmers

Roosevelt........................ 51.3%
Landon........................... 42.3
Lemke............................ 5.0
Thomas........................... 1.0
Others........................... .4

Women

Roosevelt	52.1%
Landon	42.8
Lemke	3.4
Thomas	1.0
Others	.7

Young People

Roosevelt	56.9%
Landon	38.8
Lemke	2.0
Thomas	1.8
Others	.5

Reliefers

Roosevelt	76.1%
Landon	16.3
Lemke	5.3
Thomas	1.7
Others	.6

SEPTEMBER 3
PRESIDENTIAL TRIAL HEAT

Special Survey

Asked in the Midwest: Will you vote for Franklin Roosevelt or Governor Landon?

Roosevelt	47%
Landon	53

SEPTEMBER 4
PRESIDENTIAL TRIAL HEAT

Special Survey

Asked in Maryland: Whom do you prefer for President?

Roosevelt	52.7%
Landon	44.4
Lemke	2.1
Thomas	.7
Others	.1

SEPTEMBER 6
PRESIDENTIAL TRIAL HEAT

Interviewing Date 8/24–29/36
Survey #48   Question #1

Whom do you prefer for President?

Roosevelt	49.3%
Landon	44.3
Lemke	5.0
Thomas	1.1
Others	.3

States Safely Republican

Maine
Vermont
Kansas
Connecticut
Massachusetts
New Hampshire
South Dakota

States Borderline Republican

Iowa
Wyoming
Illinois
Indiana
Pennsylvania
Rhode Island
Delaware
New York
New Jersey
Nebraska
Michigan
Minnesota
Colorado

SEPTEMBER 10
PRESIDENTIAL TRIAL HEAT

Special Survey

Asked in Maine: Which candidate do you prefer for President?

Landon............................ 63.0%
Roosevelt......................... 31.1
Lemke............................. 4.8
Thomas............................ 1.0
Others............................ .1

Asked in the South: Whom do you prefer for President?

Roosevelt......................... 67.9%
Landon............................ 29.9
Lemke............................. 1.4
Thomas............................ .5
Others............................ .3

SEPTEMBER 13
PRESIDENTIAL TRIAL HEAT

Special Survey

Asked of reliefers: Whom do you prefer for President?

Roosevelt......................... 75.1%
Landon............................ 17.5
Lemke............................. 5.3
Thomas............................ 1.6
Others............................ .5

SEPTEMBER 27
PRESIDENTIAL TRIAL HEAT

Interviewing Date 9/7–12/36
Survey #50   Question #1

Which candidate do you prefer for President?

Roosevelt......................... 49.5%
Landon............................ 44.6
Lemke............................. 4.7
Thomas............................ 1.1
Others............................ .1

By Age

	Lemke	Thomas
21–24 Years	2.7%	1.3%
25–34 Years	3.8	1.0
35–44 Years	4.3	1.1
45–54 Years	5.3	1.0
55 Years and over	6.6	.8

SEPTEMBER 27
WAR REFERENDUM

Interviewing Date 8/17–22/36
Survey #47   Question #4

In order to declare war, should Congress be required to obtain the approval of the people by means of a national vote?

Yes............................... 71%
No................................ 29

By Region

	Yes	No
New England	71%	29%
Middle Atlantic	74	26
East Central	72	28
West Central	71	29
South	64	36
Mountain	66	34
Pacific	71	29

By Special Groups

	Yes	No
Women	81%	19%
Young people (21–24 years)	70	30
Farmers	71	29
Small-town residents (under 2,500)	66	34
City residents (2,500 and over)	72	28

By Political Affiliation

	Yes	No
Democrats	70%	30%
Republicans	68	32
Socialists	85	15
Union party	86	14

OCTOBER 1
PRESIDENTIAL TRIAL HEAT

Special Survey

Asked of Pennsylvania voters: Whom do you prefer for President?

Landon...........................	49.4%
Roosevelt.........................	45.4
Lemke............................	3.7
Thomas...........................	1.4
Others............................	.1

OCTOBER 4
PRESIDENTIAL TRIAL HEAT

Interviewing Date 9/21–26/36
Survey #52   Question #6

Which candidate do you prefer for President?

Roosevelt.........................	50.3%
Landon...........................	44.2
Lemke............................	4.3
Thomas...........................	1.0
Others............................	.2

By Region

	Roosevelt	Landon	Others
New England....	40.0%	51.1%	8.9%
Middle Atlantic..	47.0	47.9	5.1
East Central.....	47.4	46.8	5.8
West Central.....	46.8	45.5	7.7
South..........	68.3	30.0	1.7
Mountain........	52.8	41.9	5.3
Pacific..........	54.7	39.4	5.9

OCTOBER 11
PRESIDENTIAL TRIAL HEAT

Interviewing Date 8/24–29/36
Survey #48   Question #5

Asked of persons who identified themselves as church members: Which candidate do you prefer for President?

By Religion

	Roosevelt	Landon
Roman Catholic.........	78%	22%
Jewish.................	82	18
Baptist................	54	46
Methodist.............	43	57
Lutheran..............	46	54
Presbyterian...........	37	63
Episcopalian...........	37	63
Congregationalist........	22	78
Reformed Dutch........	28	72

Based on major party vote.

OCTOBER 11
THE NEGRO VOTE

Interviewing Date 8/24–29/36
Survey #48   Question #1

Asked of Negroes: Which candidate do you prefer for President?

Sixty-nine per cent said that they preferred Roosevelt. Roosevelt is especially popular among Negroes in New York State, where he receives 80%.

OCTOBER 12
PRESIDENTIAL TRIAL HEAT

Special Survey

Asked of Ohio voters: Which candidate do you prefer for President?

Roosevelt.........................	47.7%
Landon...........................	45.7
Lemke............................	5.6
Thomas...........................	.8
Others............................	.2

OCTOBER 18
PRESIDENTIAL TRIAL HEAT

Interviewing Date 10/3–8/36
Survey #54   Question #1

Which candidate do you prefer for President?

Roosevelt........................ 51.4%
Landon.......................... 43.8
Lemke........................... 3.6
Thomas......................... 1.0
Others.......................... .2

Roosevelt........................ 50.6%
Landon.......................... 46.3
Lemke........................... 2.8
Others.......................... .3

By City

For Roosevelt

Baltimore........................ 63%
Boston.......................... 58
Chicago......................... 53
Cleveland....................... 71
Detroit......................... 56
Los Angeles..................... 59
New York........................ 69
Philadelphia.................... 56
Pittsburgh...................... 61
St. Louis....................... 55

OCTOBER 20
PRESIDENTIAL TRIAL HEAT

Special Survey

Which candidate do you prefer for President?

Los Angeles County Only

Roosevelt........................ 59%
Landon.......................... 41

San Francisco Only

Roosevelt........................ 59%
Landon.......................... 41

Based on major party vote.

OCTOBER 24
PRESIDENTIAL TRIAL HEAT

Special Survey

Asked in Indiana: Which candidate do you prefer for President?

OCTOBER 25
PRESIDENTIAL TRIAL HEAT

Interviewing Date 10/12–17/36
Survey #55   Question #1

Which candidate do you prefer for President?

Roosevelt........................ 51.4%
Landon.......................... 43.8
Lemke........................... 3.6
Thomas......................... 1.0
Others.......................... .2

By Special Groups
Farmers

Roosevelt........................ 52.6%
Landon.......................... 42.1
Lemke........................... 4.5
Thomas......................... .6
Others.......................... .2

Women

Roosevelt........................ 51.4%
Landon.......................... 44.8
Lemke........................... 2.9
Thomas......................... .6
Others.......................... .3

Young People (21–24 Years)

Roosevelt........................ 57.4%
Landon.......................... 38.4
Lemke........................... 2.3
Thomas......................... 1.5
Others.......................... .4

Reliefers

Roosevelt........................ 78.8%
Landon.......................... 14.0
Lemke........................... 5.6
Thomas......................... 1.3
Others.......................... .3

OCTOBER 30
PRESIDENTIAL TRIAL HEAT

Special Survey

Which candidate do you prefer for President?

New York State Only

Roosevelt............................ 52%
Landon............................. 48

New York City Only

Roosevelt............................ 69%
Landon............................. 31

Based on major party vote.

NOVEMBER 1
PRESIDENTIAL TRIAL HEAT —
FINAL POLL

Interviewing Date 10/23–28/36
Survey #55–B   Question #1

Which candidate do you prefer for President?

Roosevelt........................ 53.8%
Landon........................... 42.8
Lemke............................ 2.2
Thomas........................... .9
Others............................ .3

States for Landon

	Electoral Vote
Maine...............................	5
Vermont............................	3
New Hampshire......................	4
	12

States for Roosevelt

Mississippi........................	9
South Carolina:....................	8
Georgia...........................	12

Alabama...........................	11
Louisiana..........................	10
Texas.............................	23
Arkansas...........................	9
North Carolina.....................	13
Tennessee..........................	11
Florida............................	7
Virginia...........................	11
Nevada............................	3
Utah..............................	4
North Dakota.......................	4
Oklahoma..........................	11
Montana...........................	4
Oregon............................	5
Washington.........................	8
Idaho.............................	4
Kentucky...........................	11
Maryland...........................	8
New Mexico........................	3
California..........................	22
Arizona............................	3
Missouri...........................	15
Wisconsin..........................	12
Colorado...........................	6
Minnesota..........................	11
New York..........................	47
Delaware...........................	3
Nebraska...........................	7
	315

Doubtful States

South Dakota.......................	4
Massachusetts......................	17
Kansas............................	9
Connecticut........................	8
Rhode Island.......................	4
Illinois............................	29
Iowa..............................	11
Michigan...........................	19
New Jersey.........................	16
Pennsylvania.......................	36
West Virginia.......................	8
Wyoming...........................	3
Indiana............................	14
Ohio..............................	26
	204

NOVEMBER 2
COMPARISON OF POLLS

The American Institute of Public Opinion forecasts the reelection of President Roosevelt in tomorrow's voting, while the *Literary Digest* shows a victory for Governor Landon in the battle of the preelection polls.

The *Digest*, after sending out more than 10,000,000 ballots, finds Governor Landon polling 57% of the major party vote and leading in 32 states with 370 electoral votes.

The Institute of Public Opinion, operating on a sampling method which calls for a representative cross section of voters, predicts Roosevelt's reelection with approximately 56% of the major party vote, and shows him leading in 40 states, of which 31 with 315 electoral votes are called "sure," and the others too close for positive prediction.

Literary Digest Final Poll

Landon	57%
Roosevelt	43
States for Landon	32
States for Roosevelt	16

A.I.P.O. (Gallup) Final Poll

Roosevelt	55.7%
Landon	44.3
States for Roosevelt	40
States for Landon	6
On the line	2

NOVEMBER 8
DISARMAMENT CONFERENCE

Special Survey

Would you favor a new international conference to limit and reduce armaments?

Yes	57%
No	43

By Political Affiliation

	Yes	No
Democrats	57%	43%
Republicans	57	43
Socialists	71	29

Asked of those who favor a new conference: Should the United States call such a conference?

Yes	72%
No	28

By Political Affiliation

	Yes	No
Democrats	75%	25%
Republicans	68	32
Socialists	81	19

NOVEMBER 15
WOMEN AND WORK

Interviewing Date 8/3–8/36
Survey #45   Question #1a

Should a married woman earn money if she has a husband capable of supporting her?

Yes	18%
No	82

By Region

	Yes	No
New England	10%	90%
Middle Atlantic	11	89
East Central	10	90
West Central	9	91
South	13	87
Mountain	10	90
Pacific	10	90

NOVEMBER 15
RELIGION

Interviewing Date 8/10–15/36
Survey #46–B   Question #4

A noted clergyman says the churches can build their influence in America by omitting sermons and lectures from Sunday worship for a period of one or two years. Do you agree with him?

Agree............................. 17%
Disagree.......................... 83

By Religion

	Agree	Disagree
Reformed Church.........	6%	94%
Methodists................	9	91
Baptists..................	11	89
Presbyterians..............	14	86
Lutherans................	14	86
Roman Catholics..........	14	86
Congregationalists.........	18	82
Jews.....................	22	78
Episcopalians.............	23	77
Other denominations........	15	85

By Region

New England..............	13%	87%
Middle Atlantic...........	19	81
East Central..............	16	84
West Central..............	19	81
South....................	13	87
Mountain.................	25	75
Pacific...................	20	80

NOVEMBER 15
NRA

Interviewing Date 9/21–26/36
Survey #52   Question #1

Should the NRA, in legal form, be revived?

Yes............................... 44%
No................................ 56

NOVEMBER 22
KING EDWARD

Interviewing Date 11/6–11/36
Survey #56   Question #9

Would you like to have King Edward marry Mrs. Simpson?

Yes............................... 61%
No................................ 39

By Special Groups

	Yes	No
Women.....................	60%	40%
City residents (2,500 and over)...	61	39
Small town residents (under 2,500)................	68	32
Farmers......................	57	43
Young persons................	65	45

NOVEMBER 22
OLD AGE INSURANCE

Interviewing Date 11/6–11/36
Survey #56   Question #5

Do you favor the compulsory old age insurance plan, starting in January, which requires employers and workers to make equal contributions to workers' pensions?

Yes............................... 68%
No................................ 32

By Political Affiliation

	Yes	No
Democrats...................	82%	18%
Republicans..................	50	50
Lemke supporters.............	73	27
Socialists....................	79	21

NOVEMBER 22
POST OFFICE

Interviewing Date 7/13–18/36
Survey #42   Question #4

Should the entire Post Office Department, including the Postmaster General, be put under Civil Service?

Yes............................... 86%
No................................ 14

By Political Affiliation

	Yes	No
Democrats	84%	16%
Republicans	88	12
Lemke supporters	87	13
Socialists	88	12

By Special Groups

	Yes	No
Farmers	82%	18%
Small town residents (under 2,500)	84	16
City residents (2,500 and over)	88	12
Women	87	13
Young people (21–24 years)	90	10
Reliefers	89	11

NOVEMBER 29
BIRTH CONTROL

Interviewing Date 5/18–23/36
Survey #35   Question #2

Should the distribution of information on birth control be made legal?

Yes	70%
No	30

By Special Groups

	Yes	No
Reliefers	58%	42%
Farmers	61	39
Women	71	29
Small town residents (under 2,500)	72	28
City residents (2,500 and over)	71	29
Young people (21–24 years)	81	19
College students	94	6

NOVEMBER 29
ROOSEVELT ADMINISTRATION

Interviewing Date 11/6–11/36
Survey #56   Question #3

Should President Roosevelt's second Administration be more liberal, more conservative, or about the same as his first?

More liberal	15%
More conservative	50
About the same	35

By Political Affiliation
Democrats

More liberal	19%
More conservative	50
About the same	31

Republicans

More liberal	4%
More conservative	88
About the same	8

Socialists

More liberal	53%
More conservative	40
About the same	7

Lemke Voters

More liberal	50%
More conservative	30
About the same	20

NOVEMBER 29
NRA

Interviewing Date 9/14–19/36
Survey #51   Question #2

Should the NRA be revived?

Yes	51%
No	49

By Region

	Yes	No
New England	58%	42%
Middle Atlantic	65	35
East Central	45	55
West Central	45	55
South	50	50
Mountain	42	58
Pacific	51	49

By Political Affiliation

	Yes	No
Democrats	69%	31%
Republicans	18	82
Socialists	64	36
Lemke supporters	65	35

DECEMBER 4
PRESIDENT ROOSEVELT

Interviewing Date 11/6–11/36
Survey #56   Question #8

Should President Roosevelt be a candidate for a third term in 1940?

Yes	31%
No	69

By Region

	Yes	No
New England	32%	68%
Middle Atlantic	35	65
East Central	25	75
West Central	29	71
South	32	68
Mountain	32	68
Pacific	29	71

By Special Groups

	Yes	No
Farmers	25%	75%
Small town residents (under 2,500)	20	80
City residents (2,500 and over)	33	67
Young people (21–24 years)	32	68
Women	33	67
Reliefers	60	40

DECEMBER 4
DIVORCE LAWS

Interviewing Date 4/13–18/36
Survey #30   Question #3

Should divorce be easier to obtain in your state?

Yes	23%
No	77

By Special Groups

	Yes	No
Farmers	16%	84%
Small town residents (under 2,500)	16	84
Women	19	81
Young people (21–24 years)	22	78
City dwellers (2,500 and over)	23	77
College students	25	75
Reliefers	31	69

New York State Only

Yes	51%
No	49

Wisconsin Only

Yes	9%
No	91

Maine Only

Yes	4%
No	96

DECEMBER 6
REGIONAL LEAGUE OF NATIONS

Interviewing Date 4/13–18/36
Survey #30   Question #5

Should the countries of North and South America form their own League of Nations?

Yes	56%
No	44

By Sex

	Yes	No
Men	59%	41%
Women	53	47

By Political Affiliation

	Yes	No
Democrats	60%	40%
Republicans	51	49
Socialists	53	47
Others	56	44

DECEMBER 13
FAMILY SIZE

Interviewing Date 11/15–20/36
Survey #57   Question #5

What do you think is the ideal family size?

One child...................	2%
Two children................	32
Three children..............	32
Four children...............	22
Five children...............	7
Six children................	3
More than six children......	2

Reliefers Only

One child...................	1%
Two children................	24
Three children..............	29
Four children...............	25
Five children...............	12
Six children................	6
More than six children......	3

DECEMBER 13
SUPREME COURT

Interviewing Date 11/15–20/36
Survey #57   Question #3

As a general principle would you favor limiting the power of the Supreme Court to declare acts of Congress unconstitutional?

Favor......................	41%
Oppose.....................	59

By Region

	Yes	No
New England.............	33%	67%
Middle Atlantic..........	41	59
East Central.............	38	62
West Central.............	35	65
South...................	46	54
Mountain................	44	56
Pacific.................	50	50

Interviewing Date 11/15–20/36
Survey #57   Question #3a

Should the Supreme Court be more liberal in reviewing New Deal measures?

Yes.......................	59%
No........................	41

By Political Affiliation

	Yes	No
Democrats................	80%	20%
Republicans..............	22	78
Socialists...............	67	33
Lemke supporters.........	52	48

DECEMBER 13
LOANS TO FARM TENANTS

Interviewing Date 9/28–10/2/36
Survey #53   Question #2

Would you favor Government loans, on a long time and easy basis, to enable farm tenants to buy the farms they now rent?

Yes.......................	83%
No........................	17

DECEMBER 20
BUSINESS OUTLOOK

Interviewing Date 11/6–11/36
Survey #56   Question #6

Do you think there will be another serious depression?

Yes.......................	67%
No........................	33

DECEMBER 20
PROHIBITION

Interviewing Date 12/2–5/36
Survey #59   Question #1

If the question of national prohibition should come up again, would you vote to make the country dry?

Yes.................................. 33%
No................................... 67

Interviewing Date 11/15–20/36
Survey #57   Question #1

Do you think liquor regulations in your state are too strict, too lax, or about right?

Too strict........................... 11%
Too lax............................. 39
About right......................... 50

DECEMBER 20
VENEREAL DISEASE

Interviewing Date 11/6–11/36
Survey #56   Question #10

Would you be in favor of a Government bureau that would distribute information concerning venereal diseases?

Yes.................................. 88%
No................................... 12

1937

CAPITAL PUNISHMENT

Interviewing Date 12/1–6/36
Survey #59   Question #3

Do you believe in the death penalty for murder?

Yes................................. 61%
No.................................. 39

Asked of those who answered in the affirmative: Are you in favor of the death penalty for persons under 21?

Yes................................. 46%
No.................................. 54

By Region

	Yes	No
New England	31%	69%
Middle Atlantic	50	50
East Central	48	52
West Central	50	50
South	46	54
Mountain	41	59
Pacific	46	54

JANUARY 3
RELIEF EXPENDITURES

Interviewing Date 12/9–14/36
Survey #60   Question #1

Do you approve of the Government's reduction in relief expenditures?

Yes................................. 60%
No.................................. 40

By Region

	Yes	No
New England	54%	46%
Middle Atlantic	55	45
East Central	69	31
West Central	56	44
South	65	35
Mountain	59	41
Pacific	53	47

Interviewing Date 12/9–14/36
Survey #60   Question #2

Do you believe reductions should be made in your own community?

Yes................................. 53%
No.................................. 47

By Region

	Yes	No
New England	44%	56%
Middle Atlantic	51	49
East Central	64	36
West Central	47	53
South	54	46
Mountain	56	44
Pacific	46	54

JANUARY 10
ROOSEVELT ADMINISTRATION

Interviewing Date 11/6–11/36
Survey #56   Question #3

Should President Roosevelt's second Administration be more liberal, more conservative, or about the same as his first?

More liberal....................... 15%
More conservative.................. 50
About the same..................... 35

JANUARY 10
REPUBLICAN PARTY

Interviewing Date 12/2–7/36
Survey #59   Question #2a

Do you think the Republican party is dead?

Yes............................... 27%
No................................ 73

By Political Affiliation

	Yes	No
Democrats	39%	61%
Republicans	8	92

Interviewing Date 12/2–7/36
Survey #59   Question #2b

Do you think the Republican party will win in 1940?

Yes............................... 31%
No................................ 69

By Political Affiliation

	Yes	No
Democrats	15%	85%
Republicans	65	35

JANUARY 10
REPUBLICAN PRESIDENTIAL CANDIDATES

Interviewing Date 12/9–14/36
Survey #60   Question #9

Republicans were asked: Who do you think will make the best Republican candidate for President in 1940?

The following are listed in order of frequency of mention:

Senator Vandenberg
Governor Landon
Senator Borah
Herbert Hoover
Colonel Knox
Henry Cabot Lodge

Theodore Roosevelt, Jr.
John Hamilton
Ogden Mills
Charles Taft

JANUARY 17
FUTURE WARS

Interviewing Date 12/16–21/36
Survey #61   Question #1

If there is another general European war, do you believe the United States can stay out of it?

Yes............................... 62%
No................................ 38

JANUARY 17
EUTHANASIA

Interviewing Date 11/15–20/36
Survey #57   Question #8

Do you favor mercy deaths under government supervision for hopeless invalids?

Yes............................... 46%
No................................ 54

By Region

	Yes	No
New England	43%	57%
Middle Atlantic	54	46
East Central	40	60
West Central	32	68
South	38	62
Mountain	63	37
Pacific	64	36

Women Only

Yes............................... 48%
No................................ 52

Young Persons (21–24 Years) Only

Yes............................... 54%
No................................ 46

JANUARY 17
INFLATION

Interviewing Date 11/22–27/36
Survey #58   Question #8

Do you think we will have inflation?

Yes............................... 46%
No................................ 54

By Region

	Yes	No
New England.................	47%	53%
Middle Atlantic..............	43	57
East Central.................	50	50
West Central.................	45	55
South.......................	38	62
Mountain....................	57	43
Pacific......................	63	37

JANUARY 24
MOST IMPORTANT PROBLEM

Interviewing Date 12/30/36–1/5/37
Survey #62   Question #3

What do you regard as the most vital issue before the American people today?

The following are listed in order of frequency of mention:

Unemployment
Neutrality
Social security
Labor and capital
Recovery
Government spending
Standard of living
Relief
Taxes

JANUARY 24
UNEMPLOYMENT

Interviewing Date 12/30/36–1/5/37
Survey #62   Question #6

Should the Federal Government appropriate money to make a national census of the unemployed?

Yes............................... 51%
No................................ 49

By Region

	Yes	No
New England.................	64%	36%
Middle Atlantic..............	57	43
East Central.................	43	57
West Central.................	48	52
South.......................	55	45
Mountain....................	41	59
Pacific......................	48	52

JANUARY 24
THE BUDGET

Interviewing Date 11/15–20/36
Survey #57   Question #4

In your opinion, whose responsibility for balancing the budget is greater, the President's or that of Congress?

President......................... 38%
Congress......................... 62

JANUARY 31
TRIAL JURIES

Interviewing Date 12/30/36–1/5/37
Survey #62   Question #5

Should trial juries, in cases not involving murder, be permitted to return a verdict by three-fourths majority instead of by unanimous vote as at present?

Yes............................... 57%
No................................ 43

By Region

	Yes	No
New England.................	54%	46%
Middle Atlantic..............	53	47
East Central.................	51	49
West Central.................	68	32
South.......................	58	42
Mountain....................	61	39
Pacific......................	56	44

Lawyers Only

Yes............................... 42%
No................................ 58

JANUARY 31
UNIVERSAL FINGERPRINTING

Interviewing Date 1/7–12/37
Survey #63   Question #1

Do you think everyone in the United States should be fingerprinted?

Yes............................... 68%
No................................ 32

By Region

	Yes	No
New England	70	30
Middle Atlantic	68	32
East Central	66	34
West Central	67	33
South	72	28
Mountain	71	29
Pacific	66	34

JANUARY 31
ANTI-LYNCHING LAWS

Interviewing Date 1/7–12/37
Survey #63   Question #5

Should Congress enact a law that would make lynching a federal crime?

Yes............................... 70%
No................................ 30

By Region

	Yes	No
New England	75%	30%
Middle Atlantic	72	28
East Central	77	23
West Central	70	30
South	65	35
Mountain	65	35
Pacific	59	41

By Special Groups

	Yes	No
Women	75%	25%
Young persons (21–24 Years)	77	23
Reliefers	72	28
Farmers	69	31

FEBRUARY 7
GENERAL MOTORS STRIKE

Interviewing Date 2/3–6/37
Survey #64   Question #7

In the current General Motors strike, are your sympathies with the John L. Lewis group of striking employees or with the employers?

Lewis group....................... 44%
Employers......................... 56

Interviewing Date 1/13–18/37
Survey #64   Question #7a

Is General Motors right in refusing to negotiate with the sit-down strikers until they leave the General Motors plants?

Yes............................... 66%
No................................ 34

Interviewing Date 1/13–18/37
Survey #64   Question #7b

Do you believe that John L. Lewis represents a majority of General Motors workers?

Yes............................... 38%
No................................ 62

FEBRUARY 7
FARM-LABOR PARTY

Interviewing Date 12/16–21/36
Survey #61   Question #6

Would you join a new farmer-labor party if one is organized?

Yes................................ 18%
No................................. 82

By Region

	Yes	No
New England.................	18%	82%
Middle Atlantic..............	18	82
East Central.................	17	83
West Central.................	20	80
South.......................	21	79
Mountain....................	15	85
Pacific......................	17	83

FEBRUARY 7
LABOR UNIONS

Interviewing Date 1/13–18/37
Survey #64   Question #2

Which do you favor: one single union for all workers in an industry, or separate unions for each craft in industry?

Industrial unions.................. 37%
Craft unions...................... 63

By Region

	Industrial Unions	Craft Unions
New England...........	40%	60%
Middle Atlantic..........	38	62
East Central............	31	69
West Central............	36	64
South..................	41	59
Mountain...............	40	60
Pacific.................	41	59

By Special Groups

Women................	37%	63%
Young people (21–24 years)	35	65
Reliefers...............	43	57
Farmers...............	35	65
Urban dwellers (2,500 and over)................	38	62

By Political Affiliation

Democrats..............	40%	60%
Republicans.............	29	71

FEBRUARY 9
SUPREME COURT

Special Survey

Do you favor President Roosevelt's plan to increase the size of the Supreme Court to make it more liberal?

New York City Only

Yes................................ 70%
No................................. 30

Upstate New York Only

Yes................................ 46%
No................................. 54

FEBRUARY 14
SPANISH CIVIL WAR

Interviewing Date 1/13–18/37
Survey #64   Question #8

In the present Civil War in Spain are your sympathies with the Loyalists who are now defending Madrid or with the Rebels, or are they with neither side?

Loyalists......................... 22%
Rebels........................... 12
Neutral, no opinion................. 66

By Region
New England

Loyalists......................... 32%
Rebels........................... 16
Neither.......................... 52

Middle Atlantic

Loyalists......................... 32%
Rebels........................... 19
Neither.......................... 49

East Central

Loyalists......................... 28%
Rebels........................... 14
Neither.......................... 58

West Central

Loyalists......................... 23%
Rebels............................ 20
Neither........................... 57

South

Loyalists......................... 29%
Rebels............................ 18
Neither........................... 53

Mountain

Loyalists......................... 30%
Rebels............................ 9
Neither........................... 61

Pacific

Loyalists......................... 35%
Rebels............................ 10
Neither........................... 55

The above tables record the views of only those who had an opinion.

FEBRUARY 14
WAR DEBTS

Interviewing Date 12/2–7/36
Survey #59   Question #4

Should the war debts be cancelled and forgotten, should they be reduced to a point where at least something might be collected, or should the United States continue to try to collect them in full?

Should be cancelled................. 9%
Should be reduced.................. 37
Should be collected................ 54

FEBRUARY 21
CHILD LABOR

Interviewing Date 2/3–8/37
Survey #67   Question #6

Do you favor an amendment to the Constitution giving Congress the power to limit, regulate, and prohibit the labor of persons under eighteen?

Yes.............................. 76%
No.............................. 24

FEBRUARY 21
WOMEN JURORS

Interviewing Date 2/3–8/37
Survey #67   Question #2

Are you in favor of permitting women to serve as jurors in your state?

Yes.............................. 69%
No.............................. 31

By Special Groups

	Yes	No
Women.....................	78%	22%
Young people (21–24 years).....	76	24
Farmers.....................	65	35
Reliefers....................	57	43

FEBRUARY 28
SUPREME COURT

Interviewing Date 2/17–22/37
Survey #70   Question #1

Are you in favor of President Roosevelt's proposal to reorganize the Supreme Court?

Yes.............................. 47%
No.............................. 53

By Region

	Yes	No
New England.................	40%	60%
Middle Atlantic..............	49	51
East Central.................	44	56
West Central.................	45	55
South.......................	53	47
Mountain....................	46	54
Pacific......................	57	43

Special Survey

Asked of lawyers: What three members of the present Supreme Court do you regard as the most able?

The following are listed according to frequency of mention:

Charles Evans Hughes
Louis Brandeis
Benjamin Cardozo

Special Survey

Asked of lawyers: Do you think that Supreme Court justices should quit when they reach 70?

Yes.................................. 29%
No.................................. 71

Special Survey

Asked of lawyers: Do you favor or oppose President Roosevelt's Court plan?

Favor................................ 23%
Oppose.............................. 77

MARCH 7
PRESIDENT ROOSEVELT'S VOTER APPEAL

Interviewing Date 2/24–3/1/37
Survey #71   Question #13

Would you vote for Franklin Roosevelt today?

Yes................................ 65.2%
No................................ 34.8

By Region

	Yes	No
New England	59%	41%
Middle Atlantic	65	35
East Central	60	40
West Central	61	39
South	79	21
Mountain	68	32
Pacific	70	30

MARCH 7
SUPREME COURT

Interviewing Date 2/24–3/1/37
Survey #71   Question #2

What action should Congress take on the Roosevelt plan to reorganize the Supreme Court — pass it, modify it, or defeat it?

Pass................................ 38%
Modify............................. 23
Defeat............................. 39

By Region
New England

Pass................................ 32%
Modify............................. 21
Defeat............................. 47

Middle Atlantic

Pass................................ 38%
Modify............................. 23
Defeat............................. 39

East Central

Pass................................ 34%
Modify............................. 23
Defeat............................. 43

West Central

Pass................................ 27%
Modify............................. 25
Defeat............................. 48

South

Pass................................ 48%
Modify............................. 27
Defeat............................. 25

Mountain

Pass................................ 37%
Modify............................. 20
Defeat............................. 43

Pacific

Pass................................ 35%
Modify............................. 28
Defeat............................. 37

By Political Affiliation
Democrats

Pass................................ 56%
Modify............................. 27
Defeat............................. 17

Republicans

Pass................................ 4%
Modify............................. 14
Defeat............................. 82

MARCH 14
NRA

Interviewing Date 2/17–22/37
Survey #70   Question #2

Do you think Congress and the President should seek to enact a second NRA?

Yes................................ 53%
No................................. 47

By Region

	Yes	No
New England.......	49%	51%
Middle Atlantic...	57	43
East Central......	53	47
West Central......	44	56
South.............	51	49
Mountain..........	46	54
Pacific...........	55	45

By Special Groups

	Yes	No
Farmers.......................	37%	63%
Small town residents (under 2,500)...............	44	56
Urban dwellers (2,500 and over)..	56	44
Young people (21–24 years).....	56	44
Reliefers.....................	76	24

By Political Affiliation

	Yes	No
Democrats.........	72%	28%
Republicans.......	20	80
Others............	56	44

MARCH 21
SIT-DOWN STRIKES

Interviewing Date 3/3–8/37
Survey #72   Question #7

Do you think this state should pass legislation making sit-down strikes illegal?

Yes................................ 67%
No................................. 33

By Region

	Yes	No
New England.......	67%	33%
Middle Atlantic...	70	30
East Central......	65	35
West Central......	65	35
South.............	73	27
Mountain..........	57	43
Pacific...........	65	35

By Special Groups

	Yes	No
Farmers.......................	73%	27%
Small town residents (under 2,500)...............	71	29
Women........................	71	29
City dwellers (2,500 and over)....	65	35
Young people (21–24 years).....	62	38
Reliefers.....................	47	53

By Political Affiliation

	Yes	No
Democrats.........	62%	38%
Republicans.......	80	20

By Several Strike Area States

	Yes	No
Michigan..........	64%	36%
Wisconsin.........	63	37
Illinois..........	70	30
Indiana...........	69	31
Ohio..............	59	41

Pennsylvania	71	29
New York	71	29
New Jersey	62	38
California	64	36

MARCH 21
PROTESTANT CHURCHES

Interviewing Date 2/24–3/1/37
Survey #71   Question #7

It has been suggested that all Protestant Churches in the United States combine into one Church. Do you think it would be a good thing?

Yes	44%
No	56

By Sects

	Yes	No
Northern Baptist	47%	53%
Southern Baptist	25	75
Methodist	43	57
Lutheran	33	67
Presbyterian	48	52
Episcopal	40	60
Congregational	65	35
Reformed	52	48
Others	59	41

By Region

	Yes	No
New England	61%	39%
Middle Atlantic	46	54
East Central	39	61
West Central	51	49
South	36	64
Mountain	42	58
Pacific	40	60

MARCH 25
SUPREME COURT

Interviewing Date 3/3–8/37
Survey #72   Question #2

Are you in favor of President Roosevelt's proposal to reorganize the Supreme Court?

Yes	47%
No	53

By Region

	Yes	No
New England	40%	60%
Middle Atlantic	49	51
East Central	44	56
West Central	45	55
South	53	47
Mountain	46	54
Pacific	57	43

By Political Affiliation

Democrats	70%	30%
Republicans	8	92

By Special Groups

Farmers	42%	58%
City voters	48	52
Reliefers	73	27
Lawyers	23	77

MARCH 28
CONGRESSIONAL AUTHORITY

Interviewing Date 3/3–8/37
Survey #72   Question #3

Would you favor an amendment to the Constitution giving Congress greater power to regulate industry and agriculture?

Yes	58%
No	42

By Region

	Yes	No
New England	57%	43%
Middle Atlantic	60	40
East Central	57	43
West Central	48	52
South	69	31
Mountain	54	46
Pacific	57	43

By Political Affiliation

	Yes	No
Democrats	75%	25%
Republicans	27	73
Others	62	38

MARCH 28
SUPREME COURT

Interviewing Date 3/17–22/37
Survey #74   Question #1

Are you in favor of President Roosevelt's proposal to reorganize the Supreme Court?

Yes	48%
No	52

By Region

	Yes	No
New England	44%	56%
Middle Atlantic	47	53
East Central	43	57
West Central	46	54
South	54	46
Mountain	50	50
Pacific	59	41

By Political Affiliation

	Yes	No
Democrats	73%	27%
Republicans	5	95

APRIL 4
WORLD WAR I

Interviewing Date 1/20–25/37
Survey #65   Question #1

Do you think it was a mistake for the United States to enter World War I?

Yes	70%
No	30

By Region

	Yes	No
New England	67%	33%
Middle Atlantic	71	29
East Central	74	26
West Central	68	32
South	61	39
Mountain	72	28
Pacific	70	30

APRIL 4
MOST LIKED COUNTRY

Interviewing Date 1/13–18/37
Survey #64   Question #8

Which European country do you like best?

England	55%
France	11
Germany	8
Finland	4
Ireland	4
Italy	3
Switzerland	3
Belgium	2
Norway	2
Sweden	2
Denmark	1
Greece	1
Holland	1
Russia	1
Others	2

APRIL 11
DEMOCRATIC PRESIDENTIAL CANDIDATES

Interviewing Date 3/12–17/37
Survey #73   Question #8

Asked of Democrats: If President Roosevelt is not a candidate in 1940, who do you think will make the best Democratic candidate?

The following are listed in order of frequency of mention:

James Farley
George Earle
Frank Murphy
Paul McNutt
John Garner
Herbert Lehman
Henry Wallace
John L. Lewis

APRIL 11
SUPREME COURT

Interviewing Date 4/1–6/37
Survey #76   Question #1

Are you in favor of President Roosevelt's proposal to reorganize the Supreme Court?

Yes............................... 49%
No................................ 51

By Region

	Yes	No
New England.................	45%	55%
Middle Atlantic..............	49	51
East Central.................	44	56
West Central.................	47	53
South.......................	48	52
Mountain....................	48	52
Pacific......................	58	42

By Special Groups

Reliefers.....................	74%	26%
Union members..............	66	34
Young persons (21–24 years)....	50	50
Women.....................	49	51
Farmers....................	45	55
Small town residents (under 2,500)...............	44	56
Urban dwellers (2,500 and over)..	50	50

By Political Affiliation

Democrats...................	74%	26%
Republicans.................	6	94

APRIL 18
SIT-DOWN STRIKES

Interviewing Date 4/1–6/37
Survey #76   Question #2

Do you think that state and local authorities should use force in removing sit-down strikers?

Yes............................... 65%
No................................ 35

By Region

	Yes	No
New England.................	65%	35%
Middle Atlantic..............	62	38
East Central.................	65	35
West Central.................	64	36
South.......................	71	29
Mountain....................	57	43
Pacific......................	64	36

By Special Groups

Urban dwellers (2,500 and over)..	62%	38%
Small town residents (under 2,500)...............	73	27
Farmers....................	74	26
Women.....................	67	33
Young people (21–24 years).....	64	36
Reliefers....................	65	35

APRIL 18
RELIEF EXPENDITURES

Interviewing Date 4/1–6/37
Survey #76   Question #3

Do you believe that the Federal Government should further reduce relief expenditures at this time?

Yes............................... 56%
No................................ 44

By Region

	Yes	No
New England.................	51%	49%
Middle Atlantic..............	45	55
East Central.................	54	46
West Central.................	50	50
South.......................	48	52
Mountain....................	49	51
Pacific......................	40	60

APRIL 19
FAVORITE SPORT

Interviewing Date 3/24–29/37
Survey #75   Question #6

What is your favorite sport to watch?

By Sex
Men
Baseball........................... 44%
Football........................... 28
Basketball........................ 7
Boxing............................ 5
Horse racing...................... 4
Others............................ 12

Women
Baseball........................... 27%
Football........................... 23
Basketball........................ 15
Tennis............................ 9
Horse racing...................... 8
Others............................ 18

By Age
17–20 Years
Baseball........................... 23%
Football........................... 44
Others............................ 33

21–24 Years
Baseball........................... 33%
Football........................... 39
Others............................ 28

25–34 Years
Baseball........................... 36%
Football........................... 35
Others............................ 29

35–44 Years
Baseball........................... 49%
Football........................... 24
Others............................ 27

45–54 Years
Baseball........................... 53%
Football........................... 24
Others............................ 23

55 Years and Over
Baseball........................... 58%
Football........................... 14
Others............................ 28

APRIL 25
SUPREME COURT JUSTICES

Interviewing Date 4/7–12/37
Survey #77   Question #1

Would you favor an amendment requiring Supreme Court justices to retire at some age between 70 and 75?

Yes................................ 64%
No................................ 36

By Region

	Yes	No
New England	52%	48%
Middle Atlantic	65	35
East Central	59	41
West Central	66	34
South	71	29
Mountain	58	42
Pacific	71	29

By Political Affiliation

Democrats	80%	20%
Republicans	35	65

APRIL 25
INFLATION

Interviewing Date 3/17–22/37
Survey #74   Question #8

Do you think we will have inflation?

Yes................................ 53%
No................................ 47

By Region

	Yes	No
New England	54%	46%
Middle Atlantic	53	47
East Central	50	50
West Central	53	47
South	53	47
Mountain	59	41
Pacific	55	45

By Political Affiliation

Democrats...................	46%	54%
Republicans.................	68	32
Others.....................	48	52

By Special Groups

Women.....................	51%	49%
Urban dwellers (2,500 and over)..	53	47
Farmers....................	53	47
Small town residents (under 2,500)................	47	53
Reliefers...................	40	60
Young people (21–24 years).....	48	52

MAY 2
SUPREME COURT

Interviewing Date 4/21–26/37
Survey #79   Question #1a

Should Congress pass the President's Supreme Court plan?

Yes...............................	47%
No................................	53

By Region

	Yes	No
New England................	41%	59%
Middle Atlantic..............	49	51
East Central.................	41	59
West Central.................	46	54
South.......................	53	47
Mountain....................	52	48
Pacific......................	56	44

Interviewing Date 4/21–26/37
Survey #79   Question #1b

Do you think the President will win his fight to enlarge the Court?

Yes...............................	61%
No................................	39

By Region

	Yes	No
New England................	56%	44%
Middle Atlantic..............	63	37

East Central.................	60	40
West Central.................	54	46
South.......................	67	33
Mountain....................	56	44
Pacific......................	65	35

By Political Affiliation

Democrats...................	75%	25%
Republicans.................	38	62

MAY 9
INCOME TAXES

Interviewing Date 4/7–12/37
Survey #77   Question #5

About how much do you think a married man earning $3,000 a year should pay in the form of income taxes? What about a man earning $5,000? A man earning $10,000? A man earning $100,000?

	Tax favored
$3,000.........................	$30
$5,000.........................	$100
$10,000........................	$500
$100,000.......................	$10,000

Interviewing Date 4/7–12/37
Survey #77   Question #6

Should state and federal employees be exempt from income taxes?

Yes...............................	12%
No................................	88

By Region

	Yes	No
New England................	10%	90%
Middle Atlantic..............	11	89
East Central.................	13	87
West Central.................	21	79
South.......................	9	91
Mountain....................	12	88
Pacific......................	8	92

MAY 9
VENEREAL DISEASE

Interviewing Date 1/7–12/37
Survey #63   Question #6

Should Congress appropriate $25 million to help control venereal disease?

Yes................................ 92%
No................................ 8

By Region

	Yes	No
New England................	89%	11%
Middle Atlantic..............	94	6
East Central.................	93	7
West Central.................	89	11
South.......................	93	7
Mountain....................	89	11
Pacific......................	94	6

MAY 16
LABOR UNIONS

Interviewing Date 4/14–19/37
Survey #78   Question #5

Do you think labor unions should be regulated by the Government?

Yes................................ 69%
No................................ 31

By Region

	Yes	No
New England................	64%	36%
Middle Atlantic..............	68	32
East Central.................	69	31
West Central.................	69	31
South.......................	77	23
Mountain....................	68	32
Pacific......................	69	31

By Special Groups

Farmers.....................	75%	25%
City dwellers (2,500 and over)....	66	34
Women.....................	69	31
Young persons (21–24 years)....	71	29
Reliefers....................	65	35

By Political Affiliation

Democrats...................	72%	28%
Republicans..................	67	33

MAY 16
UNEMPLOYMENT

Interviewing Date 4/21–26/37
Survey #79   Question #3

Do you think that the unemployment problem can be solved?

Yes................................ 65%
No................................ 35

By Region

	Yes	No
New England................	63%	37%
Middle Atlantic..............	67	33
East Central.................	69	31
West Central.................	62	38
South.......................	58	42
Mountain....................	67	33
Pacific......................	74	26

By Special Groups

Farmers.....................	58%	42%
City dwellers (2,500 and over)....	66	34
Women.....................	65	35
Young persons (21–24 years)....	63	37
Reliefers....................	72	28

By Political Affiliation

Democrats...................	67%	33%
Republicans..................	64	36

MAY 23
SUPREME COURT

Interviewing Date 5/5–10/37
Survey #81   Question #3

Should Congress pass President Roosevelt's Supreme Court plan?

Yes................................ 46%
No................................ 54

Interviewing Date 5/5–10/37
Survey #81   Question #3a

Would you favor a compromise on the President's Court plan which would permit him to appoint two new judges instead of six?

Yes.............................. 38%
No.............................. 62

By Political Affiliation

	Yes	No
Democrats	47%	53%
Republicans	21	79

Special Survey

Asked of lawyers: Whom would you like to see appointed to the Supreme Court?

The following are listed according to frequency of mention:

Felix Frankfurter
John W. Davis
Newton Baker
Robert Wagner
Roscoe Pound
Learned Hand
Joseph Robinson
Wharton Pepper

MAY 23
STERILIZATION

Interviewing Date 1/13–18/37
Survey #64   Question #6

Do you favor sterilization of habitual criminals and the hopelessly insane?

Yes.............................. 84%
No.............................. 16

By Region

	Yes	No
New England	75%	25%
Middle Atlantic	80	20
East Central	88	12
West Central	83	17
South	84	16

Mountain	92	8
Pacific	92	8

MAY 29
PARTY AFFILIATION

Interviewing Date 3/3–8/37
Survey #72   Question #8

Do you regard yourself as a Republican, a Democrat, a Socialist, or an Independent in politics?

Democrat......................... 50%
Republican....................... 33
Independent...................... 15
Socialist......................... 2

By Region
New England

Democrat......................... 34%
Republican....................... 39
Independent...................... 21
Socialist......................... 6

Middle Atlantic

Democrat......................... 46%
Republican....................... 33
Independent...................... 20
Socialist......................... 1

East Central

Democrat......................... 46%
Republican....................... 37
Independent...................... 16
Socialist......................... 1

West Central

Democrat......................... 44%
Republican....................... 40
Independent...................... 14
Socialist......................... 2

South

Democrat......................... 73%
Republican....................... 19
Independent...................... 7
Socialist......................... 1

Mountain

Democrat........................... 50%
Republican......................... 32
Independent........................ 16
Socialist............................ 2

Pacific

Democrat........................... 49%
Republican......................... 33
Independent........................ 16
Socialist............................ 2

The following are listed in order of frequency of mention:

Arthur Vandenberg
Alf Landon
William Borah
Herbert Hoover
Frank Knox
Theodore Roosevelt, Jr.
Henry Cabot Lodge
Ogden Mills
John Hamilton
Charles Taft

MAY 30
REPUBLICAN PARTY

Interviewing Date 5/12–17/37
Survey #82   Question #8

Should the Republican party change its leadership? Should the Republican party change its name? Should a new party be formed of anti-New Deal Democrats and Republicans?

Views of Republicans

	Yes	No
GOP should change leadership	59%	41%
GOP should change name	12	88
New party should be formed	14	86

Views of Democrats

	Yes	No
GOP should change leadership	72%	28%
GOP should change name	22	78
New party should be formed	31	69

MAY 30
REPUBLICAN PRESIDENTIAL CANDIDATES

Interviewing Date 4/21–26/37
Survey #79   Question #8

Republicans were asked: Who do you think will make the best Republican candidate in 1940?

JUNE 6
MINIMUM WAGES AND MAXIMUM WORK HOURS

Interviewing Date 5/19–24/37
Survey #83   Question #4

Do you think the Federal Government ought to set the lowest wage that employees should receive in each business and industry?

Yes............................... 61%
No................................ 39

By Region

	Yes	No
New England	60%	40%
Middle Atlantic	60	40
East Central	61	39
West Central	61	39
South	56	44
Mountain	69	31
Pacific	63	37

Interviewing Date 5/19–24/37
Survey #83   Question #3

Should Congress set a limit on the hours employees should work in each business and industry?

Yes............................... 58%
No................................ 42

By Region

	Yes	No
New England	50%	50%
Middle Atlantic	60	40
East Central	56	44
West Central	51	49
South	62	38
Mountain	65	35
Pacific	59	41

JUNE 13
RELIEF

Interviewing Date 4/14–19/37
Survey #78   Question #3

Should the Government do away with the WPA and give only cash, or direct, relief?

Yes. 21%
No. 79

By Region

	Yes	No
New England	25%	75%
Middle Atlantic	22	78
East Central	20	80
West Central	18	82
South	21	79
Mountain	19	81
Pacific	20	80

Interviewing Date 5/10–15/37
Survey #81   Question #1

Should state and local governments pay a greater share of the costs of relief?

Yes. 62%
No. 38

By Region

	Yes	No
New England	69%	31%
Middle Atlantic	63	37
East Central	65	35
West Central	59	41

South	63	37
Mountain	55	45
Pacific	51	49

JUNE 17
DISARMAMENT

Interviewing Date 6/3–8/37
Survey #85   Question #5a

Would you favor a world disarmament conference?

Yes. 66%
No. 34

By Region

	Yes	No
New England	67%	33%
Middle Atlantic	67	33
East Central	63	37
West Central	63	37
South	65	35
Mountain	66	34
Pacific	70	30

By Political Affiliation

	Yes	No
Democrats	70%	30%
Republicans	56	44

Interviewing Date 6/3–8/37
Survey #85   Question #5b

Do you think the time is ripe to bring the leading nations of the world together for this purpose?

Yes. 56%
No. 44

By Region

	Yes	No
New England	55%	45%
Middle Atlantic	59	41
East Central	51	49
West Central	61	39
South	57	43
Mountain	54	46
Pacific	46	54

By Political Affiliation

	Yes	No
Democrats	61%	39%
Republicans	47	53

Interviewing Date 6/3–8/37
Survey #85   Question #5c

Should President Roosevelt call such a conference?

Yes	41%
No	59

By Region

	Yes	No
New England	43%	57%
Middle Atlantic	45	55
East Central	38	62
West Central	41	59
South	43	57
Mountain	36	64
Pacific	36	64

By Political Affiliation

	Yes	No
Democrats	47%	53%
Republicans	32	68

Interviewing Date 6/3–8/37
Survey #85   Question #5d

If other nations agree to reduce their spending for armaments, should America agree to reduce its expenditures to the same extent?

Yes	79%
No	21

By Region

	Yes	No
New England	80%	20%
Middle Atlantic	78	22
East Central	78	22
West Central	84	16
South	82	18
Mountain	74	26
Pacific	75	25

By Political Affiliation

	Yes	No
Democrats	81%	19%
Republicans	73	27

Interviewing Date 6/3–8/37
Survey #85   Question #5e

Do you believe any nation or nations is responsible for the present armaments race?

Yes	77%
No	23

Asked of those who answered in the affirmative: Which nation?

Germany	38%
Italy	32
Japan	10
Soviet Union	9
Great Britain	3
France	3
Spain	2
"All"	2
United States	1

JUNE 20
PRESIDENT ROOSEVELT'S VOTER APPEAL

Interviewing Date 5/5–10/37
Survey #81   Question #7

If the election were being held today would you vote for President Roosevelt?

Yes	60.2%
No	39.8

JULY 4
LABOR

Interviewing Date 6/16–21/37
Survey #87   Question #3

Which labor leader do you prefer: Green of the A.F. of L. or Lewis of the C.I.O.?

Green............................. 67%
Lewis............................. 33

By Income

	Green	Lewis
Lower one-third..............	53%	47%
Upper two-thirds.............	74	26

Interviewing Date 6/9–14/37
Survey #86   Question #4

Which type of labor union do you favor: the A.F. of L. craft type, or the C.I.O. industrial type?

A.F. of L.......................... 64%
C.I.O............................. 36

Union members favor the A.F. of L.-type union by a margin of 57% to 43%.

Interviewing Date 6/16–21/37
Survey #87   Question #5

Has your attitude toward labor unions changed any during the last six months?

Yes............................... 50%
No................................ 50

Interviewing Date 6/16–21/37
Survey #87   Question #1

Those who said yes were asked: Are you more in favor or less in favor of labor unions?

More in favor...................... 29%
Less in favor...................... 71

Interviewing Date 6/16–21/37
Survey #87   Question #2

Should the militia be called out whenever strike trouble threatens?

Yes............................... 57%
No................................ 43

Interviewing Date 6/16–21/37
Survey #87   Question #4

Should the Post Office Department deliver food and other packages to workers in factories where strikes have been called?

Yes............................... 58%
No................................ 42

JULY 11
MINIMUM NEEDS FOR FAMILY OF FOUR

Interviewing Date 6/9–14/37
Survey #86   Question #9

What is the smallest weekly amount a family of four must have to live decently?

Median average................. $30 wk.

By Special Groups
(*Median Average*)

Professional people.............. $35 wk.
Merchants, businessmen.......... $35 wk.
Skilled workers.................. $35 wk.
Lower one-third income group..... $23 wk.
City dwellers (2,500 and over)...... $35 wk.
Small town residents (under 2,500)... $25 wk.
Farmers........................ $25 wk.

By Region
(*Median Average*)

New England.................... $30 wk.
Middle Atlantic................. $35 wk.
East Central.................... $30 wk.
West Central.................... $25 wk.
South (excluding Negroes)........ $25 wk.
Mountain....................... $30 wk.
Pacific......................... $35 wk.

The survey found that among Negroes living in the South the median average was $12 per week.

JULY 11
MINIMUM NEEDS FOR HEALTH AND COMFORT

Interviewing Date 2/10–15/37
Survey #68   Question #1

How much income a year do you think the average family of four needs for health and comfort?

Median average................. $38 wk.

By Special Groups
(*Median Average*)

Professional people.............. $40 wk.
Merchants, businessmen.......... $39 wk.
Skilled laborers................. $39 wk.
Lower one-third income group..... $28 wk.
City dwellers (2,500 and over)....... $39 wk.
Small town residents (under 2,500)... $29 wk.
Farmers........................ $28 wk.

By Region
(*Median Average*)

New England................... $39 wk.
Middle Atlantic................. $39 wk.
East Central.................... $38 wk.
West Central.................... $33 wk.
South (excluding Negroes)........ $33 wk.
Mountain...................... $38 wk.
Pacific......................... $39 wk.

JULY 18
CIVIL SERVICE EMPLOYEES

Interviewing Date 6/30–7/4/37
Survey #89   Question #4

Would you like to see the C.I.O. organize civil service employees throughout the country?

Yes.............................. 19%
No.............................. 81

By Region

	Yes	No
New England................	17%	83%
Middle Atlantic..............	21	79
East Central.................	16	84
West Central.................	18	82
South.......................	24	76
Mountain....................	19	81
Pacific......................	22	78

By Political Affiliation

Republicans...................	7%	93%
Democrats...................	26	74
Others......................	22	78

JULY 25
DEMOCRATIC PARTY

Interviewing Date 6/23–28/37
Survey #88   Question #11

Democrats were asked: If President Roosevelt is not a candidate for reelection in 1940, would you prefer a conservative type of candidate or a "New Dealer"?

New Dealer........................ 67%
Conservative...................... 33

By Region

	New Dealer	Conservative
New England.........	70%	30%
Middle Atlantic.......	72	28
East Central..........	64	36
West Central..........	58	42
South...............	68	32
Mountain.............	64	36
Pacific...............	67	33

JULY 25
PRESIDENT ROOSEVELT'S VOTER APPEAL

Interviewing Date 7/7–12/37
Survey #90   Question #2

Democrats were asked: Do you favor or oppose a third term for President Roosevelt?

Favor............................ 37%
Oppose........................... 63

By Region

	Favor	Oppose
New England	57%	43%
Middle Atlantic	65	35
East Central	56	44
West Central	54	46
South	55	45
Mountain	51	49
Pacific	54	46

JULY 25
TRAVEL

Interviewing Date 7/7–12/37
Survey #90   Question #1

If someone paid your expenses would you like to go by airplane to Europe and back?

Yes............................... 38%
No................................ 62

By Age

	Yes	No
18–20 Years	69%	31%
21–24 Years	50	50
25–34 Years	46	54
35–44 Years	35	65
45–54 Years	30	70
55 Years and over	18	82

Interviewing Date 7/7–12/37
Survey #90   Question #1a

If someone paid your expenses would you like to go by boat to Europe and back?

Yes............................... 84%
No................................ 16

By Age

	Yes	No
18–20 Years	92%	8%
21–24 Years	89	11
25–34 Years	91	9
35–44 Years	82	18
45–54 Years	84	16
55 Years and over	64	36

AUGUST 1
WORLD WAR

Interviewing Date 7/25–30/37
Survey #91   Question #1

Do you think there will be another world war?

Yes............................... 73%
No................................ 27

Asked of those saying there will be another war: Do you think it will come in the next year?

Yes............................... 16%
No................................ 84

Asked of those saying there will be another war: What nation or nations do you think will be responsible for starting it?

Germany........................... 30%
Italy.............................. 27
Japan............................. 19
Russia............................ 11
Spain............................. 5
China............................. 3
Great Britain..................... 2
Others............................ 3

Do you think America will stay out?

Yes............................... 56%
No................................ 44

Interviewing Date 6/23–28/37
Survey #88   Question #5

Do you consider any nation or nations chiefly guilty of causing the World War?

Yes............................... 45%
No................................ 30
No opinion........................ 25

Asked of those answering in the affirmative: If so, which nation?

Germany 77%
France 5
Great Britain 5
Austria 4
Russia 3
Others 6

Do you think the peace treaty after the war was too easy or too severe on Germany?

Too easy 41
Too severe 30
About right 29

AUGUST 8
VENEREAL DISEASE

Interviewing Date 7/28–8/2/37
Survey #93   Question #6

In strict confidence and at no expense to you, would you like to be given, by your own physician, a blood test for syphilis?

Yes 87%
No 13

By Region

	Yes	No
New England	83%	17%
Middle Atlantic	88	12
East Central	88	12
West Central	84	16
South	90	10
Mountain	89	11
Pacific	82	18

By Special Groups

	Yes	No
Farmers	88%	12%
Urban dwellers (2,500 and over)	86	14
Young persons (21–24 years)	90	10

By Sex

	Yes	No
Men	89%	11%
Women	85	15

AUGUST 8
LABOR UNIONS

Interviewing Date 7/14–19/37
Survey #91   Question #2

Should government employees join labor unions?

Yes 26%
No 74

AUGUST 8
CONGRESS

Interviewing Date 7/21–26/37
Survey #92   Question #2

Should Congress adjourn and go home, or should it stay in Washington to consider New Deal legislation on wages and hours, housing, farm tenancy, and the Supreme Court?

Adjourn 37%
Stay 63

By Political Affiliation

	Adjourn	Stay
Democrats	23%	77%
Republicans	63	37

AUGUST 15
VIGILANTE CITIZEN COMMITTEES

Interviewing Date 7/21–26/37
Survey #92   Question #4

Do you approve of citizen groups, called vigilantes, which have sprung up recently in strike areas?

Yes 24%
No 76

By Region

	Yes	No
New England	22%	78%
Middle Atlantic	22	78

East Central	22	78
West Central	28	72
South	31	69
Mountain	19	81
Pacific	34	66

AUGUST 15
WORK WEEK

Interviewing Date 5/26–31/37
Survey #84   Question #6

How many hours are you supposed to put in on your job in a regular week, excluding overtime?

Less than 40 hours	14%
40–45 hours	37
46–50 hours	24
51–55 hours	5
56–60 hours	10
61 hours and over	10

The median average is 47 hours. By region the highest median average is in the South — 50 hours — and the lowest is in New England, where the average work week is 45 hours. The survey also found that the average work week for women is 44 hours; for those in the professions, 44 hours; for business executives and merchants, 54 hours.

AUGUST 15
A WOMAN PRESIDENT

Interviewing Date 1/27–2/1/37
Survey #66   Question #8

Would you vote for a woman for President, if she qualified in every other respect?

Yes	34%
No	66

By Sex

	Yes	No
Men	27%	73%
Women	41	59

AUGUST 22
LABOR UNIONS

Interviewing Date 6/23–28/37
Survey #88   Question #7

Are you in favor of labor unions?

Yes	76%
No	24

Farmers Only

Yes	67%
No	33

AUGUST 22
FARMER-LABOR PARTY

Interviewing Date 7/28–8/2/37
Survey #93   Question #3

If a Farmer-Labor party is organized before the next presidential election, do you think you would join it?

Yes	21%
No	79

By Political Affiliation

	Yes	No
Democrats	24%	76%
Republicans	12	88
Others	23	77

Farmers Only

Yes	28%
No	72

AUGUST 22
AGRICULTURAL ADJUSTMENT ADMINISTRATION

Interviewing Date 2/17–22/37
Survey #70   Question #3

Would you like to see the AAA revived?

Yes	41%
No	59

By Region

	Yes	No
New England	26%	74%
Middle Atlantic	39	61
East Central	35	65
West Central	45	55
South	57	43
Mountain	41	59
Pacific	40	60

Farmers Only

Yes	53%
No	47

AUGUST 29
DEMOCRATIC PRESIDENTIAL CANDIDATES

Interviewing Date 8/11–16/37
Survey #95   Question #9

Asked of Democrats: If President Roosevelt is not a candidate in 1940, who do you think would make the best Democratic candidate?

The following are listed in order of frequency of mention:

James Farley
John Garner
George Earle
Alben Barkley
Frank Murphy
Herbert Lehman
John L. Lewis
Paul McNutt
Henry Wallace

AUGUST 29
PRESIDENTIAL TENURE

Interviewing Date 8/11–16/37
Survey #95   Question #2

Would you favor a constitutional amendment prohibiting any President to run for a third term?

Yes	49%
No	51

By Political Affiliation

	Yes	No
Democrats	38%	62%
Republicans	67	33

SEPTEMBER 5
PRESIDENT ROOSEVELT'S VOTER APPEAL

Interviewing Date 8/4–9/37
Survey #94   Question #10

Are you for or against President Roosevelt?

For	60.4%
Against	39.6

By Region

	For	Against
New England	55%	45%
Middle Atlantic	60	40
East Central	54	46
West Central	61	39
South	72	28
Mountain	62	38
Pacific	65	35

SEPTEMBER 5
CHINA

Interviewing Date 8/11–16/37
Survey #95   Question #7

Should we withdraw all troops in China to keep from getting involved in the fighting, or should the troops remain there to protect American citizens?

Withdraw	54%
Remain	46

By Region

	Withdraw	Remain
New England...........	46%	54%
Middle Atlantic.........	50	50
East Central............	50	50
West Central............	60	40
South..................	62	38
Mountain..............	52	48
Pacific.................	60	40

By Political Affiliation
Democrats

Too friendly.......................	29%
Not friendly enough................	15
About right.......................	56

Republicans

Too friendly.......................	80%
Not friendly enough................	8
About right.......................	12

SEPTEMBER 12
SUPREME COURT

Interviewing Date 8/25–30/37
Survey #97   Question #2

Would you like to have President Roosevelt continue his fight to enlarge the Supreme Court?

Yes.............................	32%
No..............................	68

By Region

	Yes	No
New England................	28%	72%
Middle Atlantic..............	37	63
East Central.................	29	71
West Central.................	28	72
South......................	35	65
Mountain...................	29	71
Pacific......................	30	70

SEPTEMBER 12
NEW DEAL AND LABOR

Interviewing Date 8/4–9/37
Survey #94   Question #7

Do you think that the New Deal has been too friendly toward labor, not friendly enough, or just about right?

Too friendly.......................	45%
Not friendly enough................	13
About right.......................	42

SEPTEMBER 12
SINO-JAPANESE WAR

Interviewing Date 8/4–9/37
Survey #94   Question #5

In the present fight between Japan and China with which side are your sympathies?

China............................	43%
Japan............................	2
Neither...........................	55

SEPTEMBER 19
REPUBLICAN PARTY

Interviewing Date 8/18–23/37
Survey #96   Question #9

Republicans were asked: Do you think the Republican party should hold a national convention next spring to strengthen the party for the congressional campaign of next year?

Yes.............................	88%
No..............................	12

Interviewing Date 8/18–23/37
Survey #96   Question #10

Republicans were also asked: In your opinion, who should guide the policies of the Republican party between now and 1940 — Hoover, Landon, or someone else?

Landon.......................... 31%
Hoover.......................... 22
Others.......................... 46

SEPTEMBER 19
AID TO CHINA AND JAPAN

Interviewing Date 9/9–14/37
Survey #98   Question #7

Should American banks lend money to Japan and China during the present war?

Yes............................... 5%
No................................ 95

SEPTEMBER 26
SUPREME COURT

Interviewing Date 9/18–23/37
Survey #99   Question #9

Would you like to have President Roosevelt continue his fight to enlarge the Supreme Court?

Throughout the United States, less than one voter in three answered in the affirmative. In the Midwest the yes vote was 28%; in the Mountain states it was 29%; in the Pacific states it was 30%.

SEPTEMBER 26
PRESIDENT ROOSEVELT AND THE CONGRESSIONAL ELECTIONS

Interviewing Date 9/9–14/37
Survey #98   Question #3

Democrats were asked: Do you think the Administration should try to defeat the reelection of Democratic congressmen who opposed the Supreme Court plan?

Yes............................... 27%
No................................ 73

By Region

	Yes	No
New England................	27%	73%
Middle Atlantic..............	33	67
East Central................	34	66
West Central................	26	74
South......................	19	81
Mountain...................	25	75
Pacific.....................	26	74

OCTOBER 3
HUGO BLACK

Interviewing Date 9/18–23/37
Survey #99   Question #2

If a man has been a member of the Ku Klux Klan, should this bar him from serving as a Supreme Court judge?

Yes............................... 57%
No................................ 43

Interviewing Date 9/18–23/37
Survey #99   Question #3

Should Justice Black resign from the Supreme Court if it is proved that he has been a member of the Ku Klux Klan?

Yes............................... 59%
No................................ 41

By Region

	Yes	No
New England................	66%	34%
Middle Atlantic..............	66	34
East Central................	61	39
West Central................	62	38
South......................	35	65
Mountain...................	57	43
Pacific.....................	67	33

By Political Affiliation

Democrats...................	55%	45%
Republicans.................	65	35

Negroes Only

Yes.................................. 82%
No................................. 18

Interviewing Date 9/18–23/37
Survey #99   Question #1

When President Roosevelt appointed Senator Black to the Supreme Court, did you approve of the nomination?

Yes.................................. 56%
No................................. 44

OCTOBER 3
LABOR UNIONS

Interviewing Date 9/9–14/37
Survey #98   Question #2

Would you like to see the C.I.O. and A.F. of L. labor unions settle their differences and work as one labor organization?

Yes.................................. 79%
No................................. 21

Union Members Only

Yes.................................. 75%
No................................. 25

OCTOBER 10
NEUTRALITY

Interviewing Date 9/9–14/37
Survey #98   Question #5

Which plan for keeping out of war do you have more faith in — having Congress pass stricter neutrality laws, or leaving the job up to the President?

Stricter laws........................ 69%
President's discretion................ 31

By Region

	Stricter Laws	President's Discretion
New England	72%	28%
Middle Atlantic	68	32

East Central	75	25
West Central	67	33
South	63	37
Mountain	71	29
Pacific	72	28

By Political Affiliation

| Democrats | 60% | 40% |
| Republicans | 87 | 13 |

OCTOBER 10
WAR REFERENDUM

Interviewing Date 9/9–14/37
Survey #98   Question #1

In order to declare war, should Congress be required to obtain the approval of the people by means of a national vote?

Yes.................................. 73%
No................................. 27

By Region

	Yes	No
New England	72%	28%
Middle Atlantic	72	28
East Central	74	26
West Central	75	25
South	75	25
Mountain	73	27
Pacific	67	33

By Sex

	Yes	No
Men	69%	31%
Women	79	21

OCTOBER 18
NATIONAL BUDGET

Interviewing Date 8/18–23/37
Survey #96   Question #4

Do you think President Roosevelt can balance the budget next year?

Yes............................ 16%
No............................. 84

By Political Affiliation

	Yes	No
Democrats...................	24%	76%
Republicans..................	6	94

OCTOBER 18
STOCK MARKET

Interviewing Date 9/18–23/37
Survey #99   Question #4a

Do you think that Government regulation of stock exchanges has helped investors?

Yes............................ 69%
No............................. 31

By Political Affiliation

	Yes	No
Democrats...................	83%	17%
Republicans..................	47	53

Investors Only

Yes............................ 62%
No............................. 38

Interviewing Date 9/18–23/37
Survey #99   Question #4b

Do you think stock prices will go higher or lower in the next six months?

Higher......................... 68%
Lower.......................... 32

By Political Affiliation

	Higher	Lower
Democrats................	78%	22%
Republicans..............	61	39

Investors Only

Higher......................... 70%
Lower.......................... 30

OCTOBER 23
BASEBALL

Special Survey

Do you follow big league baseball?

Yes............................ 40%
No............................. 60

Those who responded in the affirmative were asked: In your opinion, who was the most valuable player in the big leagues this year?

Joe DiMaggio.................... 29%
Lou Gehrig...................... 17
Carl Hubbell.................... 16
Joe Medwick.................... 8
Lefty Gomez.................... 7
Charley Gehringer.............. 6
Gabby Hartnett................. 5
Others......................... 12

OCTOBER 24
SINO-JAPANESE WAR

Interviewing Date 10/6–11/37
Survey #100   Question #7

In the present fight between China and Japan, are your sympathies with Japan, China, or neither side?

Japan.......................... 1%
China.......................... 59
Neither side................... 40

By Region

	China	Japan	Neither
New England..........	62%	1%	37%
Middle Atlantic.......	64	1	35
East Central..........	52	1	45
West Central..........	54	1	45
South................	57	1	42
Mountain.............	63	2	35
Pacific...............	73	2	25

By Political Affiliation

Democrats............	59%	1%	40%
Republicans.........	64	1	35
Third party voters.....	56	1	43

Asked of those who said their sympathies were with China: Is your sympathy for China great enough to keep you from buying goods made in Japan?

Yes...............................	37%
No...............................	63

By Region

	Yes	No
New England................	44%	56%
Middle Atlantic..............	47	53
East Central.................	30	70
West Central.................	28	72
South.......................	30	70
Mountain....................	39	61
Pacific......................	50	50

By Political Affiliation

	Yes	No
Democrats...................	40%	60%
Republicans.................	39	61
Third party supporters........	32	68

OCTOBER 24
HUGO BLACK

Interviewing Date 10/6–11/37
Survey #100   Question #6a

Should Justice Hugo Black resign from the Supreme Court?

Yes...............................	44%
No...............................	56

By Region

	Yes	No
New England................	58%	42%
Middle Atlantic..............	56	44
East Central.................	42	58
West Central.................	39	61
South.......................	27	73

Mountain....................	32	68
Pacific......................	46	54

By Political Affiliation

Democrats...................	36%	64%
Republicans.................	61	39

Negroes Only

Yes...............................	68%
No...............................	32

Interviewing Date 10/6–11/37
Survey #100   Question #6b

Asked of those replying in the affirmative: If Justice Black does not resign, should Congress remove him?

Yes...............................	31%
No...............................	69

By Political Affiliation

	Yes	No
Democrats...................	25%	75%
Republicans.................	45	55

OCTOBER 31
LIVING STANDARDS

Interviewing Date 10/6–11/37
Survey #100   Question #1

In your opinion is the cost of living higher, lower, or about the same compared to a year ago?

Higher...........................	86%
Lower...........................	1
About the same...................	13

By Region

	Higher	Lower	Same
New England.........	92%	1%	7%
Middle Atlantic.......	85	2	13
East Central..........	88	1	11
West Central..........	82	1	17

	Higher	Lower	Same
South	79%	1%	20%
Mountain	89	1	10
Pacific	91	1	8

Interviewing Date 10/6–11/37
Survey #100   Question #2

Compared with a year ago is your family income now higher, lower, or about the same?

Higher	35%
Lower	15
About the same	50

By Region

	Higher	Lower	Same
New England	26%	23%	51%
Middle Atlantic	30	16	54
East Central	44	11	45
West Central	36	12	52
South	34	14	52
Mountain	41	18	41
Pacific	32	16	52

Interviewing Date 10/6–11/37
Survey #100   Question #3

Considering your income and your cost of living, do you feel you are better off today than a year ago?

Yes	38%
No	62

By Region

	Yes	No
New England	25%	75%
Middle Atlantic	33	67
East Central	40	60
West Central	48	52
South	40	60
Mountain	40	60
Pacific	37	63

By Political Affiliation

	Yes	No
Democrats	39%	61%
Republicans	28	72

OCTOBER 31
PRESIDENTIAL POWER

Interviewing Date 7/28–8/2/37
Survey #93   Question #2a

Do you think the President of the United States should have more power or less power than he has now?

More	18%
Less	35
About the same	47

By Political Affiliation
Democrats

More	27%
Less	15
About the same	58

Republicans

More	3%
Less	71
About the same	26

OCTOBER 31
PAROLE SYSTEMS

Interviewing Date 2/17–22/37
Survey #69   Question #7a

Do you believe the parole system helps to restore prisoners to a useful place in society?

Yes	46%
No	54

Interviewing Date 2/17–22/37
Survey #69   Question #7b

Should parole boards be more strict, less strict, or about the same as they are now in granting paroles?

More strict	82%
Less strict	3
About the same	15

NOVEMBER 7
BUSINESS OUTLOOK

Interviewing Date 10/20–25/37
Survey #101   Question #5

Do you expect general business conditions to be better or worse in the next six months?

Better............................ 64%
Worse............................ 36

By Region

	Better	Worse
New England	67%	33%
Middle Atlantic	60	40
East Central	60	40
West Central	70	30
South	67	33
Mountain	65	35
Pacific	78	22

By Political Affiliation

Democrats	69%	31%
Republicans	51	49

NOVEMBER 7
STOCK MARKET

Interviewing Date 10/20–25/37
Survey #101   Question #3

Do you think that the fall of stock market prices means that a new depression is coming?

Yes.............................. 26%
No.............................. 74

By Region

	Yes	No
New England	22%	78%
Middle Atlantic	32	68
East Central	25	75
West Central	20	80
South	30	70
Mountain	25	75
Pacific	22	78

By Political Affiliation

Democrats	24%	76%
Republicans	32	68

By Income

Above average	21%	79%
Average	22	78
Below average	27	73
Poor	30	70
On relief	40	60

NOVEMBER 14
ANTI-LYNCHING LEGISLATION

Interviewing Date 10/30–11/4/37
Survey #102   Question #3

Should Congress pass a law that would make lynching a federal crime?

Yes.............................. 72%
No.............................. 28

By Region

	Yes	No
New England	75%	25%
Middle Atlantic	79	21
East Central	77	23
West Central	78	22
South	57	43
Mountain	75	25
Pacific	65	35

NOVEMBER 14
GERMANY

Interviewing Date 10/30–11/4/37
Survey #102   Question #2

Should the colonies taken from Germany after the war be given back to her?

Yes.............................. 24%
No.............................. 76

	Yes	No
New England	26%	74%
Middle Atlantic	26	74
East Central	23	77
West Central	26	74
South	22	78
Mountain	22	78
Pacific	24	76

This same question was asked of Britons in a special survey conducted by the Gallup affiliate in Great Britain with the same results.

NOVEMBER 14
CHILDBIRTH AID

Interviewing Date 8/11–16/37
Survey #95   Question #5

Should the Federal Government help state and local governments in providing medical care for mothers at childbirth?

Yes.............................. 81%
No.............................. 19

NOVEMBER 21
PRESIDENT ROOSEVELT'S VOTER APPEAL

Interviewing Date 10/30–11/4/37
Survey #102   Question #8

Are you for or against President Roosevelt?

For............................. 62.8%
Against......................... 37.2

By Region

	For	Against
New England	57%	43%
Middle Atlantic	61	39
East Central	58	42
West Central	64	36
South	76	24
Mountain	61	39
Pacific	68	32

NOVEMBER 21
DUKE AND DUCHESS OF WINDSOR

Interviewing Date 10/30–11/4/37
Survey #101   Question #7

Would you like to have the Duke and Duchess of Windsor live in this country?

Yes.............................. 61%
No.............................. 39

By Region

	Yes	No
New England	51%	49%
Middle Atlantic	62	38
East Central	65	35
West Central	60	40
South	59	41
Mountain	68	32
Pacific	61	39

NOVEMBER 28
BUSINESS TAXES AND PROFIT SHARING

Interviewing Date 10/30–11/4/37
Survey #102   Question #7

It has been suggested that the Federal Government reduce taxes on companies that distribute profits to their workers. Do you favor this plan?

Yes.............................. 65%
No.............................. 35

By Region

	Yes	No
New England	69%	31%
Middle Atlantic	74	26
East Central	73	27
West Central	54	46
South	58	42
Mountain	51	49
Pacific	54	46

By Occupation

Professional	62%	38%
Businessmen	67	33
Farmers	48	52
Skilled workers	71	29
Unskilled workers	71	29
Unemployed	74	26

NOVEMBER 28
LABOR-MANAGEMENT RELATIONS

Interviewing Date 11/14–19/37
Survey #103   Question #2

Do you think corporations would have less labor trouble if workers had the right to elect a representative on the board of directors?

Yes	67%
No	33

NOVEMBER 28
PARTY STRENGTH

Interviewing Date 10/30–11/4/37
Survey #102   Question #4

What candidate for Congress from your district do you think you will vote for in the next congressional election — the Democratic candidate, the Republican candidate, or another party's candidate?

The minor parties have been excluded from the results.

Democratic candidate	56%
Republican candidate	44

By Region

	Democrat	Republican
New England	47%	53%
Middle Atlantic	52	48
East Central	49	51
West Central	54	46
South	82	18
Rocky Mountain	66	34
Pacific	62	38

DECEMBER 5
REPUBLICAN PARTY

Interviewing Date 11/14–19/37
Survey #103   Question #8a

Asked of Republicans: Are you satisfied with the present leadership of the Republican party?

Yes	39%
No	61

Interviewing Date 11/14–19/37
Survey #103   Question #8b

Asked of Republicans: Which do you think the Republicans need more — new leaders or a new program?

New leaders	61%
New program	39

Interviewing Date 11/14–19/37
Survey #103   Question #8c

Asked of Republicans: If you were running the Republican party, on what main issue would you appeal for votes?

The issues are listed in order of frequency of mention:

Economy in government spending
Restoration of business prosperity
Reduction of taxes
Honest governmental policies
Protection of Constitution and Courts
A policy favorable to labor

Interviewing Date 11/14–19/37
Survey #103   Question #8d

Asked of Republicans: Do you think the time has come to abandon the Republican party and form a new party of anti-New Deal Democrats and Republicans?

Yes	23%
No	77

Interviewing Date 11/14–19/37
Survey #103   Question #8e

Asked of Republicans: Whom would you like to see as the Republican candidate in 1940?

The following are listed in order of frequency of mention:

Vandenberg
Landon
La Guardia
Hoover
Borah
Dewey

Interviewing Date 11/14–19/37
Survey #103   Question #8f

Should the Republican party be more liberal, or more conservative, than in 1936?

More liberal........................ 47%
More conservative.................. 12
About the same.................... 41

Interviewing Date 11/14–19/37
Survey #103   Question #1b

Asked of those answering in the affirmative: Do you think the Roosevelt Administration is to blame for this decline entirely, partly, or not at all?

Entirely.......................... 19%
Partly............................ 39
Not at all........................ 42

By Region

	Entirely	Partly	Not at all
New England.........	16%	41%	43%
Middle Atlantic.......	18	41	41
East Central..........	20	39	41
West Central..........	18	45	37
South................	19	35	46
Mountain.............	23	32	45
Pacific...............	14	40	46

By Political Affiliation

	Entirely	Partly	Not at all
Democrats...........	6%	31%	63%
Republicans..........	40	49	11

DECEMBER 12
BUSINESS CONDITIONS

Interviewing Date 11/14–19/37
Survey #103   Question #1a

Have you noticed any decline in business in this community during the last two months?

Yes............................... 63%
No................................ 37

By Region

	Yes	No
New England..................	69%	31%
Middle Atlantic...............	60	40
East Central..................	70	30
West Central..................	61	39
South........................	63	37
Mountain.....................	61	39
Pacific.......................	59	41

DECEMBER 12
MERCHANT MARINE

Interviewing Date 11/14–19/37
Survey #103   Question #6a

Should the Government appropriate money to build a new United States merchant fleet?

Yes............................... 52%
No................................ 48

By Region

	Yes	No
New England..................	62%	38%
Middle Atlantic...............	62	38
East Central..................	50	50
West Central..................	41	59
South........................	45	55
Mountain.....................	40	60
Pacific.......................	50	50

By Political Affiliation

Democrats	58%	42%
Republicans	41	59

DECEMBER 12
UNEMPLOYMENT

Interviewing Date 11/21–26/37
Survey #104   Question #3c

Do you think all the unemployed should register weekly at some such place as the post office so that the Government can know each week how many are out of work?

Yes	62%
No	38

Employed Persons Only

Yes	62%
No	38

Unemployed Persons Only

Yes	64%
No	36

By Age

	Yes	No
18–24 Years	73%	27%
25–34 Years	64	36
35–44 Years	58	42
45–54 Years	60	40
55 Years and over	65	35

DECEMBER 19
AGRICULTURE

Interviewing Date 12/1–6/37
Survey #105   Question #6d

Farmers were asked: Secretary Wallace has a schedule of what he considers fair prices for farm products. What do you consider a fair price for the following?

	Median average
Wheat, per bushel	$1.00
Corn, per bushel	.75
Cotton, per pound	.14
Hogs, per hundredweight	8.25
Tobacco, per pound	.24

Interviewing Date 12/1–6/37
Survey #105   Question #9

Farmers were asked: Do you think Henry Wallace has done a good job as Secretary of Agriculture?

Yes	69%
No	31

By Type of Farmer

	Yes	No
Tobacco farmers	89%	11%
Cotton farmers	80	20
Wheat farmers	71	29
Corn farmers	68	32
Other farmers	63	37

Interviewing Date 12/1–6/37
Survey #105   Question #12b

Tenant farmers were asked: Would you be interested in buying a farm if the Government loaned you the money at 3% interest and gave you 40 years to repay the loan?

Yes	74%
No	26

Interviewing Date 12/1–6/37
Survey #105   Question #4

Farmers were asked: If a farmer goes over his quota, should he merely lose the Government loan or payment, or should he be penalized by a tax?

By Region

	Lose loans	Pay tax
New England	54%	46%
Middle Atlantic	54	46

	Lose loans	Pay tax
East Central.........	56%	44 %
West Central.........	45	55
South...............	41	59
Mountain.............	65	35
Pacific..............	50	50

Interviewing Date 12/1–6/37
Survey #105   Question #3

Farmers were asked: If two-thirds of the farmers producing any one crop agree to have marketing quotas set by the Department of Agriculture, should the other one-third be compelled to stay within these quotas?

By Region

	Yes	No
New England...........	81%	19%
Middle Atlantic........	69	31
East Central...........	51	49
West Central...........	48	52
South.................	75	25
Mountain..............	63	37
Pacific...............	50	50

By Type of Farmer

Cotton farmer.........	78%	22%
Corn farmer..........	52	48
Wheat farmer.........	52	48
Hog farmer...........	52	48
Tobacco farmer........	83	17
Others...............	64	36

DECEMBER 26
MOST INTERESTING EVENTS

Interviewing Date 12/1–6/37
Survey #105   Question #10

Which events interested you most in 1937?

Ohio floods..............	28.3%
Sino-Japanese war........	27.8
Supreme Court fight.......	27.5

Windsor marriage.........	25
Amelia Earhart lost.......	21
Present business slump.....	20
Texas school explosion.....	18
Justice Black and the Klan..	16
General Motors strike......	16
Supreme Court decisions on New Deal	13

By Sex
Men

Supreme Court fight.......	33%
Sino-Japanese war........	32
Ohio floods.............	25
Present business slump.....	24
General Motors strike......	20
Justice Black and the Klan..	19
Supreme Court decisions on New Deal..	18
Texas school explosion.....	14
Windsor marriage.........	12
Spanish Civil war........	12

Women

Windsor marriage.........	39%
Ohio floods.............	32
Amelia Earhart lost.......	31
Sino-Japanese war........	24
Texas school explosion.....	23
Supreme Court fight.......	22
Present business slump.....	16
Coronation of George VI....	15
Justice Black and the Klan..	14
General Motors strike......	11

DECEMBER 26
GOVERNMENT SPENDING

Interviewing Date 12/1–6/37
Survey #105   Question #8

Do you think the Government should start spending again to help get business out of its present slump?

Yes...................	38%
No....................	62

By Region

	Yes	No
New England	39%	61%
Middle Atlantic	46	54
East Central	36	64
West Central	30	70
South	41	59
Mountain	30	70
Pacific	34	66

By Income

	Yes	No
Above average	19%	81%
Average	30	70
Below average	47	53
Poor	47	53
On Relief	69	31

1938

Interviewing Date 11/21–26/37
Survey #104   Question #3

Is it your understanding that you will get a job because you sent in an unemployment census card?

Yes............................... 20%
No................................ 80

JANUARY 5
PRESIDENT ROOSEVELT'S VOTER APPEAL

Interviewing Date 12/15–20/37
Survey #106   Question #12

Are you for or against Franklin Roosevelt today?

For.............................. 62.1%
Against.......................... 37.9

By Region

	For	Against
New England................	55%	45%
Middle Atlantic..............	60	40
East Central.................	57	43
West Central................	61	39
South.......................	75	25
Mountain....................	64	36
Pacific......................	70	30

A majority of voters polled in the upper one-third income group are against President Roosevelt. The survey also found that 72% of wage earners and 62% of white-collar workers support the President.

JANUARY 2
BUSINESS OUTLOOK

Interviewing Date 12/15–20/37
Survey #106   Question #8

Do you expect general business conditions will be better or worse during the next six months?

Better............................ 58%
Worse............................ 42

By Region

	Better	Worse
New England..............	69%	31%
Middle Atlantic............	62	38
East Central...............	66	34
West Central..............	55	45
South.....................	48	52
Mountain..................	31	69
Pacific....................	50	50

JANUARY 2
UNEMPLOYMENT CENSUS

Interviewing Date 11/21–26/37
Survey #104   Question #3b

Asked of unemployed persons: Did you send in an unemployment census card last week?

	Yes	No
Totally unemployed............	74%	26%
Partly unemployed.............	43	57

JANUARY 7
PRESIDENT ROOSEVELT

Interviewing Date 12/1–6/37
Survey #105   Question #4

Do you favor a third term for President Roosevelt?

Yes............................... 33%
No................................ 67

By Income

	Yes	No
Upper	17%	83%
Middle	32	68
Lower	44	56

JANUARY 9
RELIEF

Interviewing Date 12/15–20/37
Survey #106   Question #3a

Do you think relief should be given as work relief or as direct cash relief?

Work relief	90%
Direct cash	10

By Political Affiliation

	Work Relief	Direct Relief
Republicans	88%	12%
Democrats	90	10
Other parties	91	9

By Region

New England	93%	7%
Middle Atlantic	88	12
East Central	91	9
West Central	90	10
South	89	11
Mountain	94	6
Pacific	81	19

Interviewing Date 12/15–20/37
Survey #106   Question #3

Do you think it is the Government's responsibility to pay the living expenses of needy people who are out of work?

Yes	69%
No	31

By Political Affiliation

	Yes	No
Republicans	57%	43%
Democrats	76	24

JANUARY 9
WAGES AND HOURS

Interviewing Date 10/30–11/4/37
Survey #102   Question #5

Do you favor or oppose a federal law providing for minimum wages and maximum hours?

Favor	69%
Oppose	31

By Region

	Favor	Oppose
New England	72%	28%
Middle Atlantic	75	25
East Central	72	28
West Central	64	36
South	63	37
Mountain	67	33
Pacific	55	45

JANUARY 12
ARMED FORCES

Interviewing Date 12/30/37–1/4/38
Survey #107   Question #14

Should the United States build a larger navy?

Yes	74%
No	26

Interviewing Date 12/30/37–1/4/38
Survey #107   Question #14a

Should the United States build a bigger army?

Yes	69%
No	31

Interviewing Date 12/30/37–1/4/38
Survey #107   Question #14b

Should the United States build a bigger air force?

Yes	80%
No	20

JANUARY 14
NEWSPAPERS

Interviewing Date 12/30–1/4/38
Survey #107   Question #4

Are the newspapers you read fair or unfair to the Roosevelt Administration?

Fair............................. 73%
Unfair.......................... 27

By Political Affiliation

	Yes	No
Democrats....................	65%	35%
Republicans..................	85	15

Among Democrats, belief in the political fairness of the press is highest in the South, where the papers are virtually all Democratic, and in the East. The vote of confidence among Democrats is somewhat lower in the Middle West and on the Pacific Coast. But even in these sections, one-half of the Roosevelt supporters interviewed say the papers they read are fair to the New Deal.

JANUARY 16
CAPITAL PUNISHMENT

Interviewing Date 12/1–6/37
Survey #105   Question #1a

Do you favor or oppose capital punishment for murder?

Favor............................ 65%
Oppose.......................... 35

By Sex

	Favor	Oppose
Men......................	69%	31%
Women....................	57	43

Interviewing Date 12/1–6/37
Survey #105   Question #1b

Do you favor or oppose capital punishment for women convicted of murder?

Favor............................ 58%
Oppose.......................... 42

JANUARY 16
SINO-JAPANESE WAR

Interviewing Date 12/30/37–1/4/38
Survey #107   Question #12

Which policy should the Government follow with regard to American citizens in China — warn them to leave and withdraw our soldiers, or continue to maintain our present armed forces in China for their protection?

Withdraw........................ 70%
Stay............................. 30

By Region

	Withdraw	Stay
New England............	64%	36%
Middle Atlantic..........	65	35
East Central............	71	29
West Central............	77	23
South..................	74	26
Mountain...............	66	34
Pacific.................	65	35

JANUARY 19
FORD LABOR DISPUTE

Interviewing Date 12/28/37–1/4/38
Survey #107   Question #1

In the present dispute between Henry Ford and the Automobile Workers Union are your sympathies with Ford or with the union?

With Ford........................ 66%
With union....................... 34

Automobile Owners Only

With Ford........................ 73%
With union....................... 27

Non-Automobile Owners Only

With Ford........................ 54%
With union....................... 46

JANUARY 21
ANTI-LYNCHING LAW

Interviewing Date 10/30–11/4/37
Survey #102   Question #3a

Congress is now considering a lynching bill which would give the Federal Government power to fine and imprison those police officers who are negligent in protecting a prisoner from a lynch mob. Do you approve or disapprove of this bill?

Approve............................ 53%
Disapprove........................ 47

JANUARY 23
SOCIAL SECURITY

Interviewing Date 12/30/37–1/4/38
Survey #107   Question #9

Do you think the Social Security law should be changed to make the employer pay the whole amount of the security tax?

Yes................................ 15%
No................................. 85

By Political Affiliation

	Yes	No
Republicans..................	9%	91%
Democrats...................	17	83

By Region

	Yes	No
New England.................	15%	85%
Middle Atlantic...............	18	82
East Central.................	14	86
West Central.................	20	80
South.......................	10	90
Mountain....................	12	88
Pacific......................	12	88

Interviewing Date 12/30/37–1/4/38
Survey #107   Question #8

Do you approve of the present Social Security tax on wages?

Yes................................ 73%
No................................. 27

By Region

	Yes	No
New England.................	74%	26%
Middle Atlantic...............	79	21
East Central.................	69	31
West Central.................	65	35
South.......................	74	26
Mountain....................	74	26
West........................	76	24

By Political Affiliation

	Yes	No
Republicans..................	55%	45%
Democrats...................	83	17

Interviewing Date 12/30/37–1/4/38
Survey #107   Question #10

The present Social Security law does not cover household help, sailors, farm workers, and employees in small shops. Do you think the law should be extended to include these workers?

Yes................................ 74%
No................................. 26

By Region

	Yes	No
New England.................	74%	26%
Middle Atlantic...............	80	20
East Central.................	75	25
West Central.................	72	28
South.......................	65	35
Mountain....................	78	22
Pacific......................	76	24

JANUARY 26
SYPHILIS

Interviewing Date 1/13–18/38
Survey #108   Question #8

Women were asked: Would you favor a law requiring doctors to give every expectant mother a blood test for syphilis?

Yes.............................. 88%
No............................... 12

By Age

	Yes	No
18–24 Years..................	93%	7%
25–34 Years..................	91	9
35–44 Years..................	89	11
45–54 Years..................	89	11
55 Years and over............	84	16

By Income

	Yes	No
Above average...............	95%	5%
Average.....................	88	12
Below average...............	95	5
Poor........................	90	10
Reliefers...................	81	19

JANUARY 28
PRESIDENTS

Interviewing Date 1/13–18/38
Survey #108   Question #2

Fifty years from now who do you think will be regarded as the greater President, Theodore Roosevelt or Franklin Roosevelt?

Franklin Roosevelt.................. 58%
Theodore Roosevelt................. 42

JANUARY 28
ANGLO-AMERICAN TRADE

Special Survey

Asked in Great Britain by Gallup affiliate: Are you in favor of a trade agreement between the United States and England?

Yes.............................. 96%
No............................... 4

JANUARY 30
TOM MOONEY

Interviewing Date 12/30/37–1/4/38
Survey #107   Question #3b

Do you think Tom Mooney was guilty?

Yes.............................. 47%
No............................... 53

By Region

	Yes	No
New England.................	51%	49%
Middle Atlantic..............	31	69
East Central.................	54	46
West Central.................	52	48
South.......................	69	31
Mountain....................	48	52
Pacific......................	52	48

California Only

Yes.............................. 52%
No............................... 48

Interviewing Date 12/30/37–1/4/38
Survey #107   Question #3c

Should Tom Mooney be pardoned and released from prison?

Yes.............................. 64%
No............................... 36

By Region

	Yes	No
New England.................	66%	34%
Middle Atlantic..............	77	23
East Central.................	58	42
West Central.................	57	43
South.......................	52	48
Mountain....................	65	35
Pacific......................	55	45

California Only

Yes.............................. 55%
No............................... 45

JANUARY 30
UNEMPLOYMENT

Interviewing Date 8/4–9/37
Survey #94   Question #2

Are you in favor of the Richmond Plan, which makes it possible for the unemployed to make goods for self-use?

	Yes	No
Yes	85%	
No	15	

	Yes	No
Better	78%	
Worse	22	

By Region

	Yes	No
New England	80%	20%
Middle Atlantic	81	19
East Central	86	14
West Central	88	12
South	88	12
Mountain	87	13
Pacific	86	14

By Region

	Better	Worse
New England	77%	23%
Middle Atlantic	79	21
East Central	81	19
West Central	76	24
South	75	25
Mountain	82	18
Pacific	77	23

FEBRUARY 2
PRESIDENT ROOSEVELT'S VOTER APPEAL

Special Survey

Small businessmen were asked: For which presidential candidate did you vote in 1936?

Landon	58%
Roosevelt	42

The vote for minor party candidates has been eliminated.

Small businessmen also were asked: Are you for or against President Roosevelt today?

Outside South Only

For	39%
Against	61

South Only

For	72%
Against	28

FEBRUARY 4
BUSINESS OUTLOOK

Interviewing Date 1/20–25/38
Survey #109–A   Question #8

Do you think business will be better or worse six months from now?

FEBRUARY 6
DEMOCRATIC PRESIDENTIAL CANDIDATES

Interviewing Date 1/20–25/38
Survey #109–A   Question #11

Democrats were asked: If President Roosevelt is not a candidate for reelection in 1940, would you prefer a conservative type of candidate or a "New Dealer"?

New Dealer	63%
Conservative type	37

By Region

	New Dealer	Conservative type
New England	69%	31%
Middle Atlantic	59	41
East Central	65	35
West Central	57	43
South	55	45
Mountain	69	31
Pacific	69	31

By Community Size

Farms	55%	45%
Small towns	66	34
Urban areas	64	36

Interviewing Date 1/13–18/38
Survey #108   Question #7b

Those who voted for Franklin Roosevelt in 1936 were asked: If President Roosevelt does not run in 1940 whom would you favor as the Democratic candidate for President?

The following are listed in order of frequency of mention:

Farley
Garner
Earle
Hull
La Guardia
Barkley
Murphy
La Follette
Lehman
Wallace
McNutt
Byrd

FEBRUARY 9
GOVERNMENT SPENDING

Interviewing Date 1/20–25/38
Survey #109–A   Question #10

Do you think Government spending should be increased to help get business out of its present slump?

Yes............................... 37%
No................................ 63

FEBRUARY 11
CENSORSHIP

Interviewing Date 1/27–2/2/38
Survey #110   Question #3

Radio owners were asked: Do you think Government censorship of the radio would do harm or good?

Harm............................. 59%
Good............................. 41

Interviewing Date 1/27–2/2/38
Survey #110   Question #2

Radio owners also were asked: During the past year have you heard any broadcast that has offended you by its vulgarity?

Yes............................... 15%
No................................ 85

FEBRUARY 13
PRESIDENT ROOSEVELT'S VOTER APPEAL

Interviewing Date 1/27–2/1/38
Survey #110   Question #11a

Are you for or against Franklin Roosevelt today?

For.............................. 61.2%
Against.......................... 38.8

By Region

	For	Against
New England...............	54%	46%
Middle Atlantic.............	58	42
East Central................	57	43
West Central................	60	40
South.......................	76	24
Mountain....................	63	37
Pacific.....................	67	33

FEBRUARY 13
REPUBLICAN PARTY

Special Survey

Asked of Republicans: Do you favor a new party composed of anti-New Deal Democrats and Republicans?

Yes............................... 31%
No................................ 69

Asked of Republicans: Do you favor or oppose changing the name of the Republican party?

Favor............................ 10%
Oppose........................... 90

FEBRUARY 16
HOURS AND WAGES

Interviewing Date 1/27–2/2/38
Survey #110   Question 4a

In your opinion, what is the lowest hourly wage that workers should receive in this community?

Median average in non-farm areas for a
  44-hour work week................ 40¢
Median average in farm areas......... 30¢

Interviewing Date 1/27–2/2/38
Survey #110   Question #4b

What is the largest number of hours per week workers should work in this community?

Median average................. 44 hours

Interviewing Date 1/27–2/2/38
Survey #110   Question #4c

Would you favor a federal law requiring employers to maintain the wage and hour standards you have suggested?

Yes............................... 67%
No................................ 33

FEBRUARY 18
SINO-JAPANESE WAR

Interviewing Date 2/5–10/38
Survey #111–B   Question #6

Do you think the United States should allow shipment of arms or ammunition from this country to China?

Yes............................... 36%
No................................ 64

Interviewing Date 10/6–11/37
Survey #100   Question #7

In the present war between China and Japan are your sympathies with China, Japan, or neither side?

China............................. 59%
Japan............................. 1
Neither side...................... 40

FEBRUARY 20
PROHIBITION

Interviewing Date 12/15–20/37
Survey #106   Question #10

If the question of national prohibition should come up again, would you vote to make the country dry?

Yes............................... 34%
No................................ 66

By Region

	Yes	No
New England	26%	74%
Middle Atlantic	24	76
East Central	36	64
West Central	41	59
South	47	53
Mountain	42	58
Pacific	24	76

By Political Affiliation

	Yes	No
Republicans	43%	57%
Democrats	29	71

By Community Size

	Yes	No
Farms	48%	52%
Small towns	45	55
Cities	28	72

FEBRUARY 23
PHILIPPINE INDEPENDENCE

Interviewing Date 2/5–10/38
Survey #111–A   Question #7

Are you in favor of granting immediate independence to the Filipinos?

Yes............................... 24%
No................................ 76

	Yes	No
Republicans	21%	79%
Democrats	25	75

By Sex

	Yes	No
Men	22%	78%
Women	26	74

By Region

	Yes	No
New England	22%	78%
Middle Atlantic	29	71
East Central	24	76
West Central	21	79
South	20	80
Mountain	21	79
Pacific	18	82

FEBRUARY 24
LEAGUE OF NATIONS

Special Survey

Asked of Britons: Should Great Britain remain a member of the League of Nations?

Yes	60%
No	12
Qualified	13
No opinion	15

FEBRUARY 25
RAILROADS

Interviewing Date 12/15–20/37
Survey #106   Question #7

Do you believe the Government should buy, own, and operate the railroads?

Yes	30%
No	70

Interviewing Date 1/27–2/2/38
Survey #110   Question #7b

Do you think the railroads would be run more efficiently if the Government owned and operated them?

Yes	36%
No	64

FEBRUARY 27
VETERAN PENSIONS

Interviewing Date 2/5–10/38
Survey #111–A   Question #1a

When a World War veteran dies from causes not connected with the war, should his widow and children be given a government pension?

Yes	44%
No	56

By Region

	Yes	No
New England	45%	55%
Middle Atlantic	45	55
East Central	49	51
West Central	46	54
South	38	62
Mountain	45	55
Pacific	39	61

Interviewing Date 2/5–10/38
Survey #111–A   Question #1b

Would you be willing to see taxes increased in order to pay these pensions?

Yes	32%
No	68

By Region

	Yes	No
New England	32%	67%
Middle Atlantic	32	68
East Central	32	68
West Central	31	69
South	29	71
Mountain	35	65
Pacific	25	75

FEBRUARY 27
SPANISH CIVIL WAR

Interviewing Date 2/5–10/38
Survey #111–A   Question #4b

Which side do you sympathize with in the Spanish civil war?

Loyalists........................... 75%
Insurgents......................... 25

Fifty-two per cent expressed no opinion.

MARCH 4
DISARMAMENT

Interviewing Date 2/16–21/38
Survey #112–A   Question #6

If other nations signed a disarmament treaty with the United States, would you favor giving up our plans to build a larger navy?

Yes................................ 52%
No................................ 48

MARCH 6
REPUBLICAN PRESIDENTIAL CANDIDATES

Interviewing Date 2/5–10/38
Survey #111–A   Question #11

Republicans were asked: Whom would you like to see as the Republican candidate for President in 1940?

Senator Arthur Vandenberg received 36% of the votes, three times as many as the next candidate, Senator William Borah. Fifteen other candidates were named. Among them: Henry Cabot Lodge, Hamilton Fish, Glenn Frank, Henry Stimson, Theodore Roosevelt, Jr., Charles Taft, Charles Evans Hughes, Frank Gannett, and Harold Hoffman.

MARCH 6
PARTY STRENGTH

Interviewing Date 2/16–21/38
Survey #112–A   Question #8

If a congressional election were held in this district today, do you think you would vote for the Democratic candidate or for the Republican candidate?

By Region

	Democratic	Republican
New England.........	45%	55%
Middle Atlantic........	47	53
East Central..........	48	52
West Central..........	51	49
South................	77	23
Mountain.............	57	43
Pacific...............	62	38

MARCH 9
CRIME AND PUNISHMENT

Interviewing Date 8/4–9/37
Survey #94   Question #1

Are you in favor of restoring the whipping post as a means of punishing certain types of criminals?

Yes................................ 39%
No................................ 61

By Sex

	Yes	No
Men......................	43%	57%
Women...................	35	65

Interviewing Date 8/4–9/37
Survey #94   Question #1a

Those who responded in the affirmative were asked: What types of criminals?

Sex offenders were mentioned by the largest number of voters, with wife-beaters and habitual drunkards listed next. Thieves, petty criminals, juvenile offenders, and "repeaters" who fail to be cured of crime by ordinary prison sentences were also named.

MARCH 11
BRITISH FOREIGN POLICY

Special Survey

Asked in Great Britain by Gallup affiliate: Do you favor Mr. Chamberlain's proposed foreign policy?

Favor........................... 24%
Oppose.......................... 56
No opinion...................... 20

Do you believe Mr. Eden was right in resigning?

Yes............................. 73%
No.............................. 13
No opinion...................... 14

Do you agree with Mr. Eden's reasons for resigning?

Yes............................. 68%
No.............................. 11
No opinion...................... 21

MARCH 12
INCOME TAX

Interviewing Date 1/20–25/38
Survey #109–A   Question #3b

Do you think a single man earning less than $1,000 a year should be required to pay a federal income tax?

Yes............................. 13%
No.............................. 87

By Region

	Yes	No
New England...............	9%	91%
Middle Atlantic..............	15	85
East Central.................	9	91
West Central.................	13	87
South.......................	17	83
Mountain....................	8	92
Pacific......................	15	85

Interviewing Date 1/20–25/38
Survey #109–A   Question #3a

Do you think that a married man earning less than $2,500 a year should be required to pay a federal income tax?

Yes............................. 20%
No.............................. 80

By Region

	Yes	No
New England.................	20%	80%
Middle Atlantic..............	23	77
East Central.................	16	84
West Central.................	21	79
South.......................	20	80
Mountain....................	11	89
Pacific......................	21	79

MARCH 13
THE NAVY

Interviewing Date 2/16–21/38
Survey #112–A   Question #1

Do you think a larger navy, as now proposed by President Roosevelt, will be more likely to get us into war or keep us out of war?

Keep us out of war................ 73%
Get us into war................... 27

MARCH 16
TRADE POLICY

Interviewing Date 2/16–21/38
Survey #112-B   Question #7

Do you approve of Secretary Hull's policy in seeking a reciprocal trade agreement with Great Britain?

Yes............................. 73%
No.............................. 27

Interviewing Date 2/16–21/38
Survey #112-A   Question #7b

If Great Britain reduces tariffs on American goods should we reduce tariffs on British goods?

Yes................................. 73%	Yes................................. 39%
No................................. 27	No................................. 61

MARCH 18
WAR DEBTS

Interviewing Date 2/28–3/4/38
Survey #113   Question #2

What is your opinion regarding the war debts owed this country? Should we continue to try to collect in full, or should they be reduced to a point where at least something might be collected, or should they be cancelled and forgotten?

Collect in full...................... 47%
Reduce............................ 42
Cancel............................ 11

MARCH 20
FREIGHT TRUCKS

Special Survey

Would you favor laws to restrict and reduce the use of the highways by large freight trucks?

Automobile Owners Only

Yes................................. 66%
No................................. 34

Non-Automobile Owners Only

Yes................................. 63%
No................................. 37

MARCH 23
OLYMPIC GAMES

Interviewing Date 2/28–3/4/38
Survey #113   Question #5

Do you think the United States should refuse to take part in the 1940 Olympic games if they are held in Japan?

MARCH 25
PROFITS TAX

Interviewing Date 3/10–15/38
Survey #114–A   Question #10a

Have you followed the arguments for and against the federal undistributed profits tax?

Yes................................. 30%
No................................. 70

Interviewing Date 3/10–15/38
Survey #114–A   Question #10b

Those who responded in the affirmative were asked: Should the federal undistributed profits tax be repealed, reduced, or left unchanged?

Repealed.......................... 40%
Reduced........................... 29
Unchanged........................ 31

MARCH 27
DIRIGIBLES

Interviewing Date 3/10–15/38
Survey #114–B   Question #1

Do you think the United States Navy should build any more dirigibles?

Yes................................. 41%
No................................. 59

MARCH 27
PRESIDENT ROOSEVELT'S
VOTER APPEAL

Interviewing Date 3/10–15/38
Survey #114–B   Question #13a

Are you for or against Franklin Roosevelt today?

For............................ 58.5%
Against......................... 41.5

By Region

	For	Against
New England................	48%	52%
Middle Atlantic..............	57	43
East Central.................	56	44
West Central................	57	43
South.......................	72	28
Mountain....................	58	42
Pacific......................	63	37

MARCH 30
AUTOMOBILE TRAVEL

Interviewing Date 2/28–3/4/38
Survey #113   Question #6b

Automobile owners were asked: About how many miles did you go in your car last year?

Median average................ 9,000 miles

Interviewing Date 2/28–3/4/38
Survey #113   Question #6c

What was the longest car trip that you made last year?

Median average................ 500 miles

Interviewing Date 2/28–3/4/38
Survey #113   Question #6d

If you had been able to make that long trip on a special high-speed highway, such as the Federal Government has been urged to build, would you have paid one cent a mile for use of that highway?

Yes............................. 27%
No.............................. 73

Interviewing Date 2/28–3/4/38
Survey #113   Question #6e

Would you have paid one-half cent a mile for use of that highway?

Yes............................. 39%
No.............................. 61

MARCH 30
CORPORATE SALARIES

Interviewing Date 3/17–22/38
Survey #115–A   Question #7

Do you think salaries over $15,000 a year that are paid by corporations should be made public by the Federal Government?

Yes............................. 49%
No.............................. 51

By Income

	Yes	No
Upper.......................	33%	67%
Middle......................	48	52
Lower.......................	61	39

APRIL 1
GOVERNMENT SPENDING

Interviewing Date 3/17–22/38
Survey #115–B   Question #3

Do you think Government spending should be increased to help get business out of its present slump?

Yes............................. 37%
No.............................. 63

By Political Affiliation

	Yes	No
Democrats...................	46%	54%
Republicans.................	18	82

APRIL 3
DEMOCRATIC PRESIDENTIAL CANDIDATES

Interviewing Date 3/17–22/38
Survey #115–B   Question #5

Democrats were asked: If President Roosevelt does not run in 1940, whom would you favor as the Democratic candidate for President?

The following are listed in order of frequency of mention:

Hull
Garner
Farley
Earle
Jackson
Barkley
Wallace
Lehman
Murphy
Wheeler

APRIL 3
PRESIDENT ROOSEVELT

Interviewing Date 3/17–22/38
Survey #115–B   Question #4

Would you favor a third term for President Roosevelt?

Yes................................. 30%
No.................................. 70

APRIL 6
GERMANY

Interviewing Date 3/17–22/38
Survey #115–B   Question #1

Do you think the United States will have to fight Germany again in your lifetime?

Yes................................. 46%
No.................................. 54

APRIL 8
PRESIDENTIAL POWER

Interviewing Date 3/10–15/38
Survey #114–B   Question #9

Do you think the President of the United States should have more power or less power than he now has?

More................................. 17%
Less................................. 42
Same................................ 41

By Political Affiliation
Republicans

More................................. 3%
Less................................. 75
Same................................ 22

Democrats

More................................. 25%
Less................................. 25
Same................................ 50

By Income
Upper

More................................. 8%
Less................................. 62
Same................................ 30

Middle

More................................. 14%
Less................................. 43
Same................................ 43

Lower

More................................. 27%
Less................................. 30
Same................................ 43

APRIL 10
HITCHHIKERS

Interviewing Date 2/16–21/38
Survey #112–B   Question #4b

Have you ever given rides to hitchhikers?

Yes................................. 43%
No.................................. 57

Interviewing Date 2/16–21/38
Survey #112–B   Question #4c

Do you think strict laws should be enforced against hitchhikers?

Yes.............................. 54%
No............................... 46

APRIL 13
RICHARD WHITNEY

Interviewing Date 3/25–30/38
Survey #116–A   Question #3a

Have you heard about the Wall Street case of Richard Whitney?

Yes.............................. 63%
No............................... 37

Interviewing Date 3/25–30/38
Survey #116–A   Question #3b

Those who answered in the affirmative were asked: Do you think it calls for further regulation of Wall Street?

Yes.............................. 74%
No............................... 26

APRIL 15
BOMBING OF CIVILIANS

Interviewing Date 4/2–7/38
Survey #117–A   Question #5a

Do you think all nations should agree not to bomb civilians in cities during wartime?

Yes.............................. 91%
No............................... 9

By Sex

	Yes	No
Men	89%	11%
Women	94	6

Interviewing Date 4/2–7/38
Survey #117–A   Question #5b

Should the United States call a conference of all nations to make such an agreement?

Yes.............................. 61%
No............................... 39

By Sex

	Yes	No
Men	58%	42%
Women	65	35

APRIL 17
CIVILIAN CONSERVATION CORPS

Interviewing Date 3/25–30/38
Survey #116–A   Question #1a

Do you think the Civilian Conservation Corps should be made permanent?

Yes.............................. 78%
No............................... 22

By Political Affiliation

	Yes	No
Republicans	62%	38%
Democrats	85	15

Interviewing Date 3/25–30/38
Survey #116–A   Question #1b

Should military training be part of the duties of those who join the Civilian Conservation Corps?

Yes.............................. 75%
No............................... 25

APRIL 17
THE 1938 RECESSION

Interviewing Date 4/2–7/38
Survey #117–B   Question #9

Businessmen were asked: In your opinion, which will do more to get us out of the current recession — increased Government spending for relief and public works or helping business by reducing taxes?

Helping business.................. 79%
Increased spending................ 21

APRIL 20
TAX ON BONDS

Interviewing Date 3/25–30/38
Survey #116–B   Question #2

Should people who have federal, state, and municipal securities be required to pay taxes on the income from these securities?

Yes............................... 74%
No............................... 26

By Income

	Yes	No
Upper.	65%	35%
Middle.	74	26
Lower.	80	20

APRIL 22
CHILDBIRTH PICTURES

Interviewing Date 4/15–20/38
Survey #119–A   Question #8a

Did you see the pictures of "The Birth of a Baby" in Life *magazine?*

In the first ten days after copies of the magazine were put on sale, it is estimated that 17,000,000 adults saw the childbirth pictures.

Interviewing Date 4/15–20/38
Survey #119–A   Question #8b

Those who responded in the affirmative were asked: In your opinion do these pictures violate the law against publication of material which is obscene, filthy, or indecent?

Yes............................... 24%
No............................... 76

Interviewing Date 4/15–20/38
Survey #119–A   Question #8c

Those who responded in the negative also were asked: Do you approve of this method of teaching the public about childbirth and care of mothers?

Approve........................... 61%
Disapprove........................ 39

APRIL 24
RELIEF

Interviewing Date 3/25–30/38
Survey #116–A   Question #5a

Do you think people on relief in your community are getting as much as they should?

Yes............................... 71%
No............................... 29

By Region

	Yes	No
New England.....	64%	36%
Middle Atlantic.	68	32
East Central....	70	30
West Central....	80	20
South...........	68	32
Mountain........	74	26
Pacific.........	73	27

Interviewing Date 3/25–30/38
Survey #116–A   Question #5b

Do you think the United States will have to continue relief appropriations permanently?

Yes............................... 67%
No............................... 33

By Political Affiliation

	Yes	No
Republicans.	63%	37%
Democrats.	69	31

Reliefers Only

Yes............................... 75%
No............................... 25

APRIL 27
THE 1938 RECESSION

Interviewing Date 4/2–7/38
Survey #117–A   Question #6

If you were in President Roosevelt's place, what would you do to fight the current recession?

The following three suggestions are listed in order of frequency of mention:

Remove restrictions on business initiative, such as high taxes

Reduce government spending and try to balance budget

Increase government spending

Interviewing Date 4/8–13/38
Survey #118   Question #1a

Would you call the present state of business a recession or a depression?

Recession............................ 42%
Depression.......................... 58

By Political Affiliation

	Recession	Depression
Republicans..........	28%	72%
Democrats..........	50	50

APRIL 29
POLITICAL PARTIES

Interviewing Date 4/8–13/38
Survey #118   Question #2a

Do you think the time has come to give up our two present political parties and have two new ones, one for liberals and the other for conservatives?

Yes................................ 30%
No................................. 70

By Political Affiliation

	Yes	No
Republicans..................	26%	74%
Democrats..................	31	69

Interviewing Date 4/8–13/38
Survey #118   Question #2b

If there were only two political parties, one for liberals and one for conservatives, which party do you think you would like to join?

By Political Affiliation

	Conservative	Liberal
Republicans............	85%	15%
Democrats.............	36	64

MAY 1
PRESIDENT ROOSEVELT'S VOTER APPEAL

Interviewing Date 4/21–26/38
Survey #120–A   Question #11a

Are you for or against Franklin Roosevelt today?

For................................ 55%
Against............................ 45

By Region

	For	Against
New England................	49%	51%
Middle Atlantic..............	53	47
East Central.................	51	49
West Central.................	54	46
South.......................	66	34
Mountain....................	58	42
Pacific......................	59	41

MAY 1
PISTOL REGISTRATION

Interviewing Date 4/1–6/38
Survey #117–A   Question #1

Do you think all owners of pistols and revolvers should be required to register with the Government?

Yes................................ 84%
No................................. 16

By Region

	Yes	No
New England	90%	10%
Middle Atlantic	82	18
East Central	86	14
West Central	83	17
South	83	17
Mountain	84	16
Pacific	85	15

MAY 4
STANDARD OF LIVING

Interviewing Date 4/8–13/38
Survey #118   Question #8

Are you better off today than you were a year ago?

Yes	36%
No	64

By Political Affiliation

	Yes	No
Democrats	40%	60%
Republicans	20	80

By Region

	Yes	No
New England	26%	74%
Middle Atlantic	32	68
East Central	33	67
West Central	38	62
South	46	54
Mountain	45	55
Pacific	36	64

Persons Who Have Turned Against Roosevelt Since 1936 Only

Yes	23%
No	77

Roosevelt Supporters Only

Yes	47%
No	53

MAY 6
GOVERNMENT SPENDING

Interviewing Date 4/21–26/38
Survey #120–A   Question #2b

Do you think Government spending should be increased to help get business out of its present slump?

Yes	42%
No	58

Persons Who Heard Roosevelt's Fireside Chat Only

Yes	49%
No	51

Persons Who Did Not Hear Roosevelt's Fireside Chat Only

Yes	40%
No	60

MAY 8
PARTY STRENGTH

Interviewing Date 4/29–5/4/38
Survey #121–B   Question #11

If the congressional elections were being held today, would you vote for the Republican or for the Democratic candidate?

By Region

	Republican	Democratic
New England	60%	40%
Middle Atlantic	59.5	40.5
East Central	54	46
West Central	58	42
South	23	77
Mountain	39	61
Pacific	43	57

MAY 8
FATHER CHARLES COUGHLIN

Interviewing Date 4/8–13/38
Survey #118   Question #3b

Do you listen to Father Coughlin's radio broadcasts?

From time to time..   6,250,000 radio families
Regularly........   2,250,000 radio families
No.............   <u>15,750,000 radio families</u>
                 24,250,000   total   radio
                                  families

Approximately 77% of American families are radio owners.

Interviewing Date 4/8–13/38
Survey #118   Question #3d

Those who said that they do listen to Father Coughlin's broadcasts were asked: Do you approve or disapprove of what Father Coughlin says?

Approve........................... 83%
Disapprove........................ 17

MAY 8
WAGNER LABOR ACT

Interviewing Date 4/15–20/38
Survey #119–B   Question #9b

Do you think the Wagner Labor Act should be revised, repealed, or left unchanged?

Revised........................... 43%
Repealed.......................... 19
Left unchanged.................... 38

By Political Affiliation
Democrats

Revised........................... 39%
Repealed.......................... 11
Unchanged......................... 50

Republicans

Revised........................... 49
Repealed.......................... 32
Unchanged......................... 19

By Region
New England

Revised........................... 35%
Repealed.......................... 19
Unchanged......................... 46

Middle Atlantic

Revised........................... 45%
Repealed.......................... 13
Unchanged......................... 42

East Central

Revised........................... 48%
Repealed.......................... 33
Unchanged......................... 19

West Central

Revised........................... 39%
Repealed.......................... 25
Unchanged......................... 36

South

Revised........................... 38%
Repealed.......................... 22
Unchanged......................... 40

Mountain

Revised........................... 37%
Repealed.......................... 21
Unchanged......................... 42

Pacific

Revised........................... 48%
Repealed.......................... 26
Unchanged......................... 26

MAY 11
WAGES AND HOURS

Interviewing Date 4/21–26/38
Survey #120–B   Question #8

Should Congress pass a bill regulating wages and hours before ending this session?

Yes............................... 59%
No................................ 41

By Region

	Yes	No
New England.................	74%	26%
Middle Atlantic	62	38

	Yes	No
East Central	58%	42%
West Central	50	50
South	56	44
Mountain	61	39
Pacific	59	41

MAY 13
RELIEF AND POLITICS

Interviewing Date 4/29–5/3/38
Survey #121–B   Question #2

Would you favor a law making it a crime for a relief official to attempt to influence the vote of persons on relief?

Yes.............................. 86%
No.............................. 14

Reliefers Only

Yes.............................. 82%
No.............................. 18

Interviewing Date 3/25–30/38
Survey #116–B   Question #6

How large a part does politics play in giving relief in your community, none, a little, or quite a bit?

None............................ 16%
A little......................... 31
Quite a bit...................... 53

By Political Affiliation
Republicans

None............................ 13%
A little......................... 27
Quite a bit...................... 60

Democrats

None............................ 20%
A little......................... 34
Quite a bit...................... 46

Reliefers Only

None............................ 23%
A little......................... 30
Quite a bit...................... 47

MAY 15
REPUBLICAN PRESIDENTIAL CANDIDATE

Interviewing Date 4/2–7/38
Survey #117–A   Question #8

Republicans were asked: Do you think the Republican party would be wise to nominate a conservative Democrat for President in 1940?

Yes.............................. 28%
No.............................. 72

MAY 15
VENEREAL DISEASE

Interviewing Date 4/29–5/4/38
Survey #121–A   Question #7a

Do you think Congress should appropriate money to aid states in fighting venereal disease?

Yes.............................. 86%
No.............................. 14

Interviewing Date 4/29–5/4/38
Survey #121–A   Question #7b

Those who responded in the affirmative were asked: Would you be willing to pay higher taxes for this purpose?

Yes.............................. 69%
No.............................. 31

21–29 Years Only

Yes.............................. 90%
No.............................. 10

MAY 15
KENTUCKY SENATORIAL PRIMARY

Special Survey

Democrats in Kentucky were asked: Whom do you plan to vote for in the upcoming primary, Alben Barkley or A. B. Chandler?

Barkley......................... 65%
Chandler........................ 35

The undecided and those who do not intend to vote have been eliminated.

MAY 15
WAGES AND HOURS BILL

Special Survey

Southerners were asked: Should Congress pass a bill regulating wages and hours before the end of this session?

Yes.............................. 59%
No............................... 41

MAY 18
LOTTERIES

Interviewing Date 4/15–20/38
Survey #119–A   Question #1a

Would you favor lotteries in your state to help pay the cost of government?

Favor............................ 49%
Oppose........................... 51

By Region

	Favor	Oppose
New England..............	59%	41%
Middle Atlantic...........	58	42
East Central..............	45	55
West Central..............	39	61
South....................	37	63
Mountain.................	43	57
Pacific...................	58	42

By Sex

Men.....................	60%	40%
Women...................	40	60

By Income

Upper....................	45%	55%
Middle...................	45	55
Lower....................	55	45

Interviewing Date 4/15–20/38
Survey #119–A   Question #1b

Do you think government lotteries would produce an unwholesome gambling spirit in this country?

Yes.............................. 51%
No............................... 49

MAY 20
ELECTION OF 1936

Interviewing Date 5/14–19/38
Survey #122–A   Question #10a

For which candidate did you vote in the 1936 presidential election?

By Special Groups

	For Roosevelt	For Landon
Reliefers...............	80%	20%
Recipients of home or land loans................	73	27
Recipients of crop control payments............	68	32
Recipients of soldiers' bonus.................	62	38
Persons who received no money from the government................	57	43

Only those who said that they voted for either Roosevelt or Landon have been included.

MAY 22
REPUBLICAN PRESIDENTIAL CANDIDATES

Interviewing Date 4/29–5/3/38
Survey #121–A   Question #10

Republicans were asked: Whom would you like to see as the Republican candidate for President in 1940?

The following are listed in order of frequency of mention:

Vandenberg
Dewey
Lodge
Hoover
Landon
Borah
Knox

Fifty per cent of those interviewed expressed no opinion.

MAY 25
FEDERAL LICENSING OF CORPORATIONS

Interviewing Date 4/29–5/4/38
Survey #121–B   Question #9a

Do you think all companies doing business in more than one state should be required to obtain a license from the Federal Government?

Yes................................ 57%
No................................ 43

Approximately one voter in four was undecided.

Farmers Only

Yes................................ 64%
No................................ 36

MAY 27
NATIONAL PROGRESSIVE PARTY

Interviewing Date 5/14–19/38
Survey #122–A   Question #6a

Have you heard of the new National Progressive party led by the La Follette brothers?

Yes................................ 60%
No................................ 40

Interviewing Date 5/14–19/38
Survey #122–A   Question #6b

Those who responded in the affirmative were asked: Do you think you would like to join it?

Yes................................ 9%
No................................ 91

By Political Affiliation

	Yes	No
Republicans.	6%	94%
Democrats.	12	88

MAY 29
SUPREME COURT

Interviewing Date 4/15–20/38
Survey #119–A   Question #6

Do you think Supreme Court justices should be required to retire after reaching a certain age?

Yes................................ 70%
No................................ 30

By Region

	Yes	No
New England.	68%	32%
Middle Atlantic.	69	31
East Central.	66	34
West Central.	72	28
South.	74	26
Mountain.	74	26
Pacific.	71	29

Interviewing Date 4/15–20/38
Survey #119–A   Question #6a

Those who responded in the affirmative were asked: At what age should they be required to retire?

Median average................. 70 years

Interviewing Date 4/15–20/38
Survey #119–A   Question #7

Would you favor an amendment to the Constitution to fix the number of justices at nine?

Yes............................... 61%
No................................ 39

By Political Affiliation

	Yes	No
Republicans....................	64%	36%
Democrats....................	60	40

MAY 29
LEGALIZED BETTING

Interviewing Date 4/21–26/38
Survey #120–A   Question #1

Do you think betting on horses should be made legal in your state?

Yes............................... 61%
No................................ 39

By Region

	Yes	No
New England..................	65%	35%
Middle Atlantic...............	70	30
East Central..................	55	45
West Central..................	59	41
South........................	52	48
Mountain.....................	60	40
Pacific.......................	66	34

Businessmen Only

Yes............................... 64%
No................................ 36

JUNE 1
MINIMUM WAGE LAW

Interviewing Date 5/14–19/38
Survey #122–A   Question #5a

If Congress passes a minimum wage law do you think the minimum wage per hour should be the same all over the country, or should it be different for different sections?

Same.............................. 38%
Different.......................... 62

Interviewing Date 5/14–19/38
Survey #122–A   Question #5b

If the minimum hourly wage is set higher in this part of the country than in other sections, do you think it will hurt business here?

Yes............................... 37%
No................................ 63

JUNE 3
CHURCH LOTTERIES

Interviewing Date 5/6–11/38
Survey #121   Question #2a

Do you approve of churches raising money by lotteries and games of chance?

Yes............................... 31%
No................................ 69

By Religion

	Yes	No
Catholics.....................	58%	42%
Protestants...................	21	79
Others.......................	23	77

Non-Church Members Only

Yes............................... 35%
No................................ 65

JUNE 5
PRESIDENT ROOSEVELT'S
VOTER APPEAL

Interviewing Date 5/22–27/38
Survey #123   Question #14a

Are you for or against Franklin Roosevelt today?

For............................... 54.4%
Against........................... 45.6

By Region

	For	Against
New England	47%	53%
Middle Atlantic	53	47
East Central	49	51
West Central	54	46
South	68	32
Mountain	63	37
Pacific	60	40

Young Voters (21–24 Years) Only

For	60%
Against	40

Reliefers Only

For	80%
Against	20

Interviewing Date 5/22–27/38
Survey #123   Question #8

Do you think President Roosevelt is more popular or less popular today than he was when he was reelected in 1936?

More popular	15%
Less popular	62
About the same	23

JUNE 8
PRESIDENT ROOSEVELT'S VOTER APPEAL

Interviewing Date 5/29–6/4/38
Survey #124–B   Question #11c

How would you rate Franklin Roosevelt's performance as President?

Favorable	54%
Unfavorable	46

By Income

	Favorable	Unfavorable
Upper	31%	69%
Middle	48	52
Lower	61	39
Reliefers	80	20

JUNE 10
PRESIDENT ROOSEVELT

Interviewing Date 5/22–27/38
Survey #123   Question #8

Do you favor a third term for President Roosevelt?

Yes	30%
No	70

By Political Affiliation

	Yes	No
Republicans	3%	97%
Democrats	46	54

JUNE 12
MEDICAL CARE

Interviewing Date 5/22–27/38
Survey #123   Question #10c

Have you ever put off going to a doctor because of the cost?

Yes	48%
No	52

By Region

	Yes	No
New England	35%	65%
Middle Atlantic	45	55
East Central	35	65
West Central	44	56
South	48	52
West	45	55

Interviewing Date 5/14–19/38
Survey #122–A   Question #1a

Do you think the Government should be responsible for providing medical care for people who are unable to pay for it?

Yes	81%
No	19

By Region

	Yes	No
New England	77%	23%
Middle Atlantic	84	16
East Central	79	21
West Central	79	21
South	83	17
West	83	17

Interviewing Date 5/22–27/38
Survey #123   Question #2a

If you were assured of complete medical and hospital care for yourself in case of accident or illness (excluding dentistry), would you be willing to pay something for this service?

Yes........................... 53%
No............................ 13
No opinion.................... 34

Interviewing Date 5/22–27/38
Survey #123   Question #1b

Those who answered in the affirmative were asked: Would you be willing to pay higher taxes for this purpose?

Yes........................... 59%
No............................ 41

JUNE 15
MEDICAL CARE

Special Survey

Medical doctors were asked: Do you approve of the principle of voluntary medical insurance where an individual insures himself for medical and hospital care by making regular payments to a health fund?

Yes........................... 73%
No............................ 27

Do you think the movement for voluntary health insurance will grow in this country during the next III years?

Yes........................... 82%
No............................ 18

If voluntary health insurance is widely adopted, do you think it will increase or decrease the income of the medical profession?

Increase...................... 51%
Decrease...................... 49

Do you think the standards of medical practice are raised when physicians practice in groups, as in clinics?

Yes........................... 53%
No............................ 47

Do you believe many persons in your community go without adequate medical care because they are unable to pay doctor's fees?

Yes........................... 37%
No............................ 63

JUNE 17
GOVERNMENT SPENDING

Interviewing Date 5/22–27/38
Survey #123   Question #11

Do you think Government spending should be increased to help get business out of its present slump?

Yes........................... 38%
No............................ 62

By Income

	Yes	No
Upper	23%	77%
Middle	32	68
Lower	57	43

WORKS PROGRESS ADMINISTRATION

Interviewing Date 5/29–6/4/38
Survey #124–B   Question #1a

Do you think the Roosevelt administration is using the W.P.A. to elect New Deal candidates to Congress?

Yes............................... 54%
No............................... 46

By Region

	Yes	No
New England................	56%	44%
Middle Atlantic..............	57	43
East Central.................	57	43
West Central.................	54	46
South.......................	48	52
West.......................	46	54

Interviewing Date 5/29–6/4/38
Survey #124-B   Question #1b

Do you, or would you, approve of such use of the W.P.A.?

Yes............................... 9%
No............................... 91

By Region

	Yes	No
New England................	8%	92%
Middle Atlantic..............	11	89
East Central................	7	93
West Central................	8	92
South.......................	10	90
West.......................	9	91

JUNE 19
HUMAN INTEREST POLL

Interviewing Date 5/14–19/38
Survey #122–A   Question #3

In Chicago recently a family had to decide between letting its newborn baby die and letting it have an operation that would leave the baby blind for life. Which course would you have chosen?

Operate........................... 63%
Let baby die...................... 37

By Religion

	Operate	Let Baby Die
Catholic................	73%	27%
Protestants..............	63	37
Non-church members.....	58	42

JUNE 24
RANSOM TO A KIDNAPPER

Interviewing Date 6/11–16/38
Survey #125–A   Question #1

Do you think it should be against the law for a family to pay ransom to a kidnapper?

Yes............................... 67%
No............................... 33

JUNE 26
THE 1938 RECESSION

Interviewing Date 5/29–6/4/38
Survey #124-B   Question #8

What is your explanation of the cause of the present recession?

Business, natural economic trends, bad distribution of wealth, lingering effects of the World War................ 70%
Roosevelt and New Deal policies....... 30

By Income
Upper

Business........................... 10%
Roosevelt and New Deal............. 42
Other causes....................... 48

Middle

Business........................... 11%
Roosevelt and New Deal............. 31
Other causes....................... 58

Lower

Business	16%
Roosevelt and New Deal	21
Other causes	63

By Income

Upper	10%	90%
Middle	22	78
Lower	48	52

JUNE 26
RELIGION

Interviewing Date 5/22–27/38
Survey #123   Question #12

Protestants were asked: Do you think it would be a good thing for all Protestant churches in the United States to combine into one church?

Yes	47%
No	53

By Religious Denomination

	Yes	No
Northern Baptists	46%	54%
Southern Baptists	14	86
Methodists	50	50
Lutherans	40	60
Presbyterians	50	50
Episcopalians	44	56
Congregationalists	60	40
Others	47	53

JUNE 29
ROOSEVELT ADMINISTRATION

Interviewing Date 6/11–16/38
Survey #125–A   Question #4

During the next two years would you like to see the Roosevelt Administration be more liberal or more conservative?

More liberal	28%
More conservative	72

By Political Affiliation

	More Liberal	More Conservative
Democrats	41%	59%
Republicans	7	93

JULY 1
DEMOCRATIC PRIMARIES

Interviewing Date 6/11–16/38
Survey #125–B   Question #5

Democrats were asked: Do you think the Roosevelt Administration should try to defeat in the primary elections Democratic senators who opposed the President's plan to enlarge the Supreme Court?

Yes	31%
No	69

JULY 3
THE CABINET

Interviewing Date 5/29–6/4/38
Survey #124–B   Question #4

Do you think the following cabinet members have done a good or a poor job in office?

	Good	Poor	No Opin.
Hull	53%	8%	39%
Swanson	44	8	48
Morgenthau	44	13	43
Farley	39	26	35
Woodring	37	8	55
Ickes	37	22	41
Wallace	37	23	40
Cummings	36	13	51
Perkins	31	37	32
Roper	26	12	62

Democrats Only

	Good	Poor	No Opin.
Hull	58%	5%	37%
Swanson	50	5	45

	Good	Poor	No Opin.
Morgenthau	52%	8%	40%
Farley	53	14	33
Woodring	43	5	52
Ickes	47	14	39
Wallace	49	15	36
Cummings	44	7	49
Perkins	40	30	30
Roper	32	9	59

JULY 3
POLITICAL PARTIES

Interviewing Date 4/8–13/38
Survey #118   Question #2b

Democrats were asked: If there were only two political parties in this country — one for liberals and one for conservatives — which would you join?

Liberal............................ 72%
Conservative....................... 28

JULY 8
KENTUCKY SENATORIAL PRIMARY

Special Survey

Kentucky Democrats were asked: Do you favor Alben Barkley or A.B. Chandler for United States senator?

Barkley............................ 64%
Chandler........................... 36

JULY 8
PRESIDENT ROOSEVELT'S VOTER APPEAL

Special Survey

Ohio voters were asked: Are you for or against President Roosevelt today?

For................................ 51%
Against............................ 49

JULY 9
PRESIDENT ROOSEVELT'S VOTER APPEAL

Special Survey

Asked in Oklahoma: Are you for or against Franklin Roosevelt today?

For................................ 60%
Against............................ 40

JULY 10
RELIEF

Special Survey

Those on relief were asked: Do you think relief assistance would be harder or easier to obtain if we had a Republican President?

Harder............................. 89%
Easier............................. 11

Forty per cent were undecided.

JULY 12
PRESIDENT ROOSEVELT'S VOTER APPEAL

Special Survey

Colorado voters were asked: Do you favor or oppose President Roosevelt?

Favor.............................. 58%
Oppose............................. 42

JULY 14
PRESIDENT ROOSEVELT'S VOTER APPEAL

Special Survey

California voters were asked: Do you favor or oppose President Roosevelt?

Favor.............................. 63%
Oppose............................. 37

JULY 17
AUTOMOBILE INSURANCE

Interviewing Date 4/21–26/38
Survey #120–A   Question #5c

*Should every automobile owner be required
by law to carry accident insurance?*

Yes.................................. 84%
No................................... 16

Automobile Owners Only

Yes.................................. 81%
No................................... 19

Non-Automobile Owners Only

Yes.................................. 89%
No................................... 11

JULY 17
PARTY STRENGTH

Interviewing Date 7/4–9/38
Survey #127   Question #11

*If you were voting for a congressman today,
would you be most likely to vote for a
Republican, Democrat, or the candidate of
another party?*

By Region

	For Democrat
New England	45%
Middle Atlantic	48
East Central	48
West Central	52
South	77
West	59

JULY 20
PRESIDENT ROOSEVELT'S
VOTER APPEAL

Interviewing Date 7/4–9/38
Survey #127   Question #13c

*If Franklin Roosevelt were running for
President today, would you vote for or
against him?*

By Region

	For	Against
New England	48%	52%
Middle Atlantic	54	46
East Central	51	49
West Central	57	43
South	67	33
West	64	36

By Income

Upper	33%	67%
Middle	53	47
Lower	73	27
Reliefers	84	16

JULY 22
PRESIDENT ROOSEVELT

Interviewing Date 7/4–11/38
Survey #127   Question #5a

*Do you think President Roosevelt will run
for a third term?*

Yes.................................. 36%
No................................... 64

JULY 24
DISARMAMENT CONFERENCE

Interviewing Date 6/11–16/38
Survey #125–B   Question #8a

*Would you favor a world disarmament
conference?*

Yes.................................. 68%
No................................... 32

Interviewing Date 6/11–16/38
Survey #125–B   Question #8b

*Do you think the time is ripe to bring
together the leading nations of the world
for this purpose?*

Yes.................................. 48%
No................................... 52

Interviewing Date 6/11–16/38
Survey #125–B   Question #8c

Should President Roosevelt call such a conference?

Yes............................... 37%
No................................ 63

JULY 24
KENTUCKY SENATORIAL PRIMARY

Special Survey

Democrats in Kentucky were asked: Whom do you plan to vote for in the upcoming primary, Alben Barkley or A. B. Chandler?

Barkley........................... 61%
Chandler.......................... 39

The undecided and those who do not intend to vote have been eliminated.

JULY 27
EUROPEAN WAR

Interviewing Date 5/29–6/4/38
Survey #124–B   Question #2b

If England and France have a war with Germany and Italy, which side would you support?

England and France................ 65%
Germany and Italy................. 3
Neither side...................... 32

JULY 29
INCOME TAX

Special Survey

Do you think married men earning less than $2,500 a year should be required to pay a federal income tax?

Yes............................... 20%
No................................ 80

Do you think a single person earning less than $1,000 a year should be required to pay a federal income tax?

Yes............................... 13%
No................................ 87

Should people who own federal, state, and municipal securities be required to pay taxes on the income from these securities?

Yes............................... 74%
No................................ 26

Would you favor an amendment to the Constitution requiring employees of state and local governments to pay federal income taxes?

Yes............................... 82%
No................................ 18

JULY 31
DEMOCRATIC PRESIDENTIAL CANDIDATES

Special Survey

Democrats were asked: If Franklin Roosevelt were not a candidate, whom would you like to see the Democrats nominate for President in 1940?

Garner............................ 23%
Farley............................ 16
Hull.............................. 12
McNutt............................ 5
Earle............................. 5
Joseph Kennedy.................... 4
Wallace........................... 3
Lehman............................ 3
Murphy............................ 2
Barkley........................... 2
Others, no opinion................ 25

JULY 31
RELIEF

Special Survey

> Those on relief were asked: If you had a job and then lost it, do you think it would be hard to get relief assistance again?

Yes............................... 61%
No................................ 39

South Only

Yes............................... 46%
No................................ 54

AUGUST 3
PRESIDENT ROOSEVELT'S VOTER APPEAL

Interviewing Date 7/15–20/38
Survey #128   Question #10c

> What is your attitude toward President Roosevelt?

	Favor	Oppose
Home or property owners....	48%	52%
Non-property owners........	65	35
Investors..................	35	65
Non-investors..............	62	38

AUGUST 5
KENTUCKY SENATORIAL PRIMARY

Special Survey

> Kentucky Democrats were asked: Do you favor Alben Barkley or A.B. Chandler for United States senator?

Barkley............................ 59%
Chandler........................... 41

AUGUST 7
PRESIDENT ROOSEVELT'S POLICIES

Interviewing Date 7/15–20/38
Survey #128   Question #1a

> If you had been a member of Congress during the past two years, would you have supported every bill recommended by President Roosevelt?

Yes............................... 23%
No................................ 77

By Region

	Yes	No
New England.................	18%	82%
Middle Atlantic..............	28	72
East Central.................	21	79
West Central.................	18	82
South.......................	29	71
West........................	20	80

Roosevelt Voters in 1936 Only

Yes............................... 38%
No................................ 62

By Region

	Yes	No
New England.................	35%	65%
Middle Atlantic..............	46	54
East Central.................	36	64
West Central.................	34	66
South.......................	35	65
West........................	32	68

AUGUST 7
PRESIDENT ROOSEVELT'S VOTER APPEAL

Interviewing Date 7/15–20/38
Survey #128   Question #10c

> C.I.O. and A.F. of L. members were asked: Are you for or against President Roosevelt today?

C.I.O. Members

For............................... 79%
Against........................... 21

A.F.L. Members

For............................... 70%
Against........................... 30

AUGUST 10
PRESIDENT ROOSEVELT'S
VOTER APPEAL

Special Survey

Are you for or against Franklin Roosevelt today?

Florida Only

For............................... 67%
Against......................... .. 33

Georgia Only

For............................... 72%
Against........................... 28

AUGUST 12
NATIONAL LABOR
RELATIONS BOARD

Interviewing Date 7/29–8/4/38
Survey #129   Question #7a

Have you an opinion on the National Labor Relations Board?

Yes............................... 34%
No............................... 66

Interviewing Date 7/29–8/4/38
Survey #129   Question #7b

Asked of those who responded in the affirmative: In your opinion, have its decisions been fair to employers?

Yes............................... 41%
No............................... 59

Interviewing Date 7/29–8/4/38
Survey #129   Question #7c

Asked of those who replied in the affirmative to the first question: Regarding the C.I.O. and the A.F. of L., do you think the Board's decisions have been partial to one union more than the other?

Has been partial.................... 68%
Has not been partial................ 32

Interviewing Date 7/29–8/4/38
Survey #129   Question #7d

Asked of those who replied that the Board has been partial: Partial to which union?

Partial to A.F. of L................. 8%
Partial to C.I.O.................... 92

AUGUST 14
PRESIDENT ROOSEVELT'S
VOTER APPEAL

Interviewing Date 7/29–8/4/38
Survey #129   Question #10c

Are you for or against Franklin Roosevelt today?

For............................... 56%
Against........................... 44

By Region

	For	Against
New England................	48%	52%
Middle Atlantic..............	53	47
East Central.................	52	48
West Central.................	56	44
South......................	67	33
West.......................	65	35

By Income

Upper......................	30%	70%
Middle.....................	53	47
Lower......................	74	26

AUGUST 14
RELIEFERS

Interviewing Date 7/15–20/38
Survey #128   Question #10a

Asked of persons receiving federal unemployment relief: If you were given a chance to go on a farm where you could have a house and make enough to pay living expenses, would you take it?

Yes............................... 52%
No............................... 48

AUGUST 16
WALTER GEORGE

Special Survey

Georgia voters were asked: Do you think President Roosevelt should have made the Barnesville speech criticizing Senator George?

Yes............................... 25%
No............................... 75

AUGUST 17
FRANKLIN ROOSEVELT

Interviewing Date 7/29–8/4/38
Survey #129   Question #2a

Would you like to see Franklin Roosevelt run for a third term?

Yes............................... 31%
No............................... 69

Interviewing Date 7/29–8/4/38
Survey #129   Question #2b

If Franklin Roosevelt did run for a third term, would you vote for him?

Yes............................... 40%
No............................... 60

AUGUST 21
FREIGHT TRUCKS

Interviewing Date 7/29–8/4/38
Survey #129   Question #1

Do you think that freight trucks should be kept off highways during certain hours on Sundays and holidays?

Yes............................... 73%
No............................... 27

AUGUST 21
PRESIDENT ROOSEVELT'S
VOTER APPEAL

Special Survey

Voters in Erie County, Ohio, were asked: As of today, do you support or oppose Franklin Roosevelt?

Support......................... 54.5%
Oppose.......................... 45.5

Voters in Erie County also were asked: Are you in favor of a third term for President Roosevelt?

Favor............................. 34%
Oppose.......................... 66

AUGUST 24
ECONOMIC SECURITY

Interviewing Date 7/29–8/4/38
Survey #129   Question #4

If you (or your husband) lost your (or his) job and could not find other work, about how long could you hold out before you had to apply for relief?

One month or less.................. 31%
Two to six months.................. 20
Longer, would never ask for relief..... 49

AUGUST 26
WAGNER LABOR ACT

Special Survey

A sampling of people listed in Who's Who in America *were asked: Do you think the Wagner Labor Act should be revised, repealed, or left unchanged?*

Revised............................ 65%
Repealed........................... 25
Left unchanged..................... 10

Do you think the Act is fair or unfair to employees?

Fair............................... 52%
Unfair............................. 48

Do you think the Act is fair or unfair to employers?

Fair............................... 20%
Unfair............................. 80

AUGUST 28
ROOSEVELT ADMINISTRATION

Interviewing Date 7/29–8/4/38
Survey #129   Question #3

During the next two years, would you like to see the Roosevelt Administration continue along its present lines or become more conservative?

More conservative.................. 66%
Continue along present lines....... 34

By Political Affiliation

	Rep.	Dem.
More conservative............	98%	35%
Continue along present lines....	2	65

AUGUST 28
WORKS PROGRESS ADMINISTRATION

Special Survey

W.P.A. workers were asked: Do you like your W.P.A. job?

Like............................... 72%
Dislike............................ 28

W.P.A. workers also were asked: Do you find the work you are doing in the W.P.A. harder or easier than in your former job?

Harder............................. 41%
Easier............................. 59

AUGUST 30
MARYLAND SENATORIAL PRIMARY

Special Survey

Democrats in Maryland were asked: Whom do you plan to vote for in the forthcoming senatorial primary, Millard Tydings or David Lewis?

Tydings............................ 58%
Lewis.............................. 42

Twenty-five per cent expressed no opinion.

SEPTEMBER 4
JAMES ROOSEVELT

Interviewing Date 8/18–23/38
Survey #131   Question #7a

Have you followed the discussion about James Roosevelt and his insurance business?

Yes................................ 40%
No................................. 60

By Political Affiliation

	Yes	No
Republicans...................	42%	58%
Democrats.....................	38	62

Interviewing Date 8/18–23/38
Survey #131   Question #7b

Those who responded in the affirmative were asked: Do you think James Roosevelt has made improper use of his relation to the President to get insurance business?

By Political Affiliation

	Yes	*No*
Republicans	72%	28%
Democrats	30	70

SEPTEMBER 4
GEORGIA SENATORIAL PRIMARY

Special Survey

Georgia Democrats were asked: Whom do you favor for United States senator in the forthcoming primary, Walter George, Lawrence Camp, or Eugene Talmadge?

George	52%
Camp	28
Talmadge	20

SEPTEMBER 7
LABOR ENDORSEMENTS

Interviewing Date 5/29–6/4/38
Survey #124–A   Question #7

If the A.F. of L. endorses a candidate for Congress from this state, would it influence you to vote for or against the candidate?

For	12%
Against	55
No difference	33

Interviewing Date 5/29–6/14/38
Survey #124–A   Question #7a

If the A.F. of L. endorses a candidate for Congress from this state, would it influence you to vote for or against the candidate?

For	22%
Against	25
No difference	53

SEPTEMBER 9
GEORGIA SENATORIAL PRIMARY

Special Survey

Georgia Democrats were asked: Whom do you favor for United States senator in the forthcoming primary, Walter George, Lawrence Camp, or Eugene Talmadge?

George	52%
Camp	24
Talmadge	24

SEPTEMBER 11
THE ROOSEVELT "PURGE"

Interviewing Date 8/18–23/38
Survey #131   Question #14

Democrats were asked: Do you approve or disapprove of President Roosevelt's campaign to defeat Democrats who oppose his views?

Approve	39%
Disapprove	61

By Region

	Approve	*Disapprove*
New England	33%	67%
Middle Atlantic	45	55
East Central	40	60
West Central	38	62
South	34	66
West	39	61

SEPTEMBER 11
MARYLAND SENATORIAL PRIMARY

Special Survey

Democrats in Maryland were asked: Whom do you plan to vote for in the forthcoming senatorial primary, Millard Tydings or David Lewis?

Tydings............................ 57%
Lewis.............................. 43

SEPTEMBER 13
GEORGIA SENATORIAL PRIMARY — FINAL POLL

Special Survey

Georgia Democrats were asked: Whom do you favor for United States senator in the forthcoming primary?

Walter George...................... 46%
Eugene Talmadge.................... 28
Lawrence Camp..................... 25
William McRae..................... 1

By Income
Upper

George............................. 71%
Talmadge........................... 11
Camp.............................. 17
McRae............................. 1

Middle

George............................. 54%
Talmadge........................... 23
Camp.............................. 22
McRae............................. 1

Lower

George............................. 34%
Talmadge........................... 36
Camp.............................. 29
McRae............................. 1

By Community Size
10,000 and Over

George............................. 59%
Talmadge........................... 12
Camp.............................. 28
McRae............................. 1

2,500–10,000

George............................. 64%
Talmadge........................... 12
Camp.............................. 23
McRae............................. 1

Rural

George............................. 54%
Talmadge........................... 21
Camp.............................. 25
McRae............................. *

*Less than 1%.

Farms

George............................. 36%
Talmadge........................... 43
Camp.............................. 20
McRae............................. 1

Under Georgia primary law, candidates are nominated by county unit votes rather than by popular vote. Each county has from two to six votes in the nominating convention. There are 410 unit votes in all, and whoever receives a majority — 206 votes — wins.

A study of Senator George's strength by counties indicates that his vote in the convention will be about twice as large as the combined votes of his two principal opponents.

SEPTEMBER 16
GOVERNMENT PENSIONS

Interviewing Date 8/12–17/38
Survey #130–A   Question #2

Asked of those who favor Government pensions: Should Government pensions be paid to all old people or only to those in need?

All old people...................... 21%
Those in need...................... 79

SEPTEMBER 18
PRESIDENT ROOSEVELT'S VOTER APPEAL

Interviewing Date 8/18–23/38
Survey #131   Question #13a

Are you for or against Franklin Roosevelt?

For................................ 55.2%
Against............................ 44.8

By Region

	For	Against
New England	47%	53%
Middle Atlantic	53	47
East Central	51	49
West Central	55	45
South	67	33
West	64	36

SEPTEMBER 18
PRESIDENTIAL TENURE

Interviewing Date 8/18–23/38
Survey #131   Question #15

Would you favor a constitutional amendment prohibiting any President of the United States from serving a third term?

Yes	48%
No	52

By Political Affiliation

	Yes	No
Democrats	37%	63%
Republicans	72	28

SEPTEMBER 21
POLITICAL PARTIES

Special Survey

A cross section of persons listed in Who's Who in America *were asked: Do you think the time has come to give up our two present political parties and have two new ones, one for conservatives and the other for liberals?*

Yes	52%
No	48

SEPTEMBER 23
SUPREME COURT

Special Survey

Lawyers were asked: Whom would you like to see President Roosevelt nominate to the Supreme Court?

Felix Frankfurter	27%
Learned Hand	5
John W. Davis	5
Walter George	4
Samuel Bratton	3
J. C. Hutcheson	3
Samuel Sibley	2
Ferdinand Pecora	2
Robert Wagner	2
Cordell Hull	2
John J. Parker	2
Others	43

SEPTEMBER 25
BRITISH TRADE AGREEMENT

Special Survey

A cross-section of persons listed in Who's Who in America *were asked: Do you approve of Secretary Hull's policy in seeking a reciprocal trade agreement with Great Britain?*

Yes	86%
No	14

SEPTEMBER 25
PARTY STRENGTH

Interviewing Date 8/18–23/38
Survey #131   Question #12

If you were voting for congressman today, would you be more likely to vote for the Republican candidate or the Democratic candidate?

By Region

	Democratic	Republican
New England	42%	58%
Middle Atlantic	48	52
East Central	48	52
West Central	50	50
South	79	21
West	59	41

SEPTEMBER 28
RAILROADS

Interviewing Date 8/18–23/38
Survey #131   Question #9a

In view of the present financial troubles of the railroads, should the railroad workers accept a pay cut?

Yes............................... 52%
No............................... 48

SEPTEMBER 30
EUROPEAN WAR

Interviewing Date 9/15–20/38
Survey #132   Question #4b

If England and France go to war against Germany, which side do you think will win?

England and France................. 86%
Germany.......................... 14

OCTOBER 2
EUROPEAN WAR

Interviewing Date 9/15–20/38
Survey #132   Question #4

If England and France go to war against Germany do you think the United States can stay out?

Yes............................... 57%
No............................... 43

By Region

	Yes	No
New England.................	46%	54%
Middle Atlantic...............	61	39
East Central..................	60	40
West Central..................	57	43
South........................	60	40
West.........................	51	49

OCTOBER 2
POWER TO DECLARE WAR

Interviewing Date 9/15–20/38
Survey #132   Question #3

In order to declare war, except when our country is invaded, should Congress be required to obtain the approval of the people by means of a national vote?

Yes............................... 68%
No............................... 32

OCTOBER 5
NEWS REPORTING

Interviewing Date 9/15–20/38
Survey #132   Question #6f

Do you think news columns in this newspaper treat the Roosevelt Administration fairly or unfairly?

Fair............................... 82%
Unfair........................... 18

By Region

	Fair	Un-fair
New England.................	87%	13%
Middle Atlantic...............	83	17
East Central..................	77	23
West Central..................	84	16
South........................	88	12
West.........................	73	27

OCTOBER 7
WILLIAM GREEN AND JOHN L. LEWIS

Interviewing Date 9/25–30/38
Survey #133   Question #10

Which labor leader do you like better, William Green of the A.F.L. or John L. Lewis of the C.I.O.?

Green............................ 78%
Lewis............................ 22

By Income

	Green	Lewis
Upper	88%	12%
Middle	82	18
Lower	66	34

OCTOBER 9
RELIEFERS

Interviewing Date 9/15–20/38
Survey #132   Question #7a

It has been suggested that reliefers should not be allowed to vote. Do you agree with this suggestion?

Agree	19%
Disagree	81

By Region

	Agree	Disagree
New England	20%	80%
Middle Atlantic	21	79
East Central	18	82
West Central	20	80
South	23	77
West	15	85

By Political Affiliation

Republican	32%	68%
Democratic	12	88
Others	19	81

OCTOBER 9
PRESIDENT ROOSEVELT'S VOTER APPEAL

Interviewing Date 10/3–8/38
Survey #134   Question #11b

Farmers were asked: Are you for or against President Roosevelt today?

For	54%
Against	46

Southern Farmers Only

For	72%
Against	28

OCTOBER 14
THE MUNICH AGREEMENT

Interviewing Date 10/3–8/38
Survey #134   Question #4

Do you believe that England and France did the best thing in giving in to Germany instead of going to war?

Yes	59%
No	41

Interviewing Date 10/3–8/38
Survey #134   Question #3

Do you think that Germany's demand for the annexation of the Sudeten German areas in Czechoslovakia was justified?

Yes	23%
No	77

Interviewing Date 10/3–8/38
Survey #134   Question #5

Do you think that this settlement (agreed to by England, France, and Germany) will result in peace for a number of years or in a greater possibility of war?

Peace	40%
War	60

Interviewing Date 10/3–8/38
Survey #134   Question #6

Do you think the colonies taken from Germany after the World War by England, France, and Japan should be given back?

Yes	22%
No	78

OCTOBER 16
ARMED FORCES

Interviewing Date 9/25–30/38
Survey #133   Question #2a

Should the United States build a larger navy?

Yes.............................. 71%
No.............................. 29

By Region

	Yes	No
New England.................	71%	29%
Middle Atlantic..............	77	23
East Central.................	68	32
West Central.................	58	42
South........................	75	25
West.........................	72	28

Interviewing Date 9/25–30/38
Survey #133   Question #2b

Should the United States build a larger army?

Yes.............................. 65%
No.............................. 35

By Region

	Yes	No
New England.................	67%	33%
Middle Atlantic..............	70	30
East Central.................	63	37
West Central.................	56	44
South........................	71	29
West.........................	66	34

OCTOBER 16
PRESIDENT ROOSEVELT'S VOTER APPEAL

Interviewing Date 10/10–15/38
Survey #135   Question #5c

In general, do you approve or disapprove of Franklin Roosevelt as President today?

Approve......................... 59.6%
Disapprove...................... 40.4

By Region

	Approve	Disapprove
New England.........	50%	50%
Middle Atlantic........	57	43
East Central..........	56	44
West Central..........	59	41
South................	69	31
West.................	70	30

OCTOBER 19
NEVILLE CHAMBERLAIN

Special Survey

Asked in Great Britain: Do you approve or disapprove of Mr. Chamberlain as Prime Minister?

Approve.......................... 57%
Disapprove....................... 43

OCTOBER 19
REPUBLICAN PARTY

Interviewing Date 10/10–15/38
Survey #135   Question #6

Asked of Republicans: Would you like to see the Republican party be more liberal or more conservative than it was in the presidential campaign of 1936?

More liberal....................... 56%
More conservative................. 15
About the same................... 29

The highest vote for change comes from Republicans in the cities, 60% of whom would like to see the party become more liberal. Small towns also vote "more liberal," by a majority of 55%.

Republican farmers, on the other hand, are much less in favor of liberalizing the party. A slight majority, 53%, think it should be either more conservative or about the same as in 1936, while 47% vote "more liberal."

OCTOBER 23
PARTY STRENGTH

Interviewing Date 9/25–30/38
Survey #133   Question #11

If you were voting for congressman today, would you be more likely to vote for the Republican candidate or the Democratic candidate?

Democratic........................ 53%
Republican........................ 47

By Region

	Democratic	Republican
New England........	42%	58%
Middle Atlantic......	51	49
East Central.........	50	50
West Central.........	45	55
South..............	79	21
West...............	59	41

OCTOBER 23
GERMANY

Interviewing Date 10/10–15/38
Survey #135   Question #4

Do you think the United States will have to fight Germany again in your lifetime?

Yes............................... 48%
No................................ 52

OCTOBER 24
NEW YORK POLITICS

Special Survey

Asked in New York State: For whom do you plan to vote for governor — Herbert Lehman or Thomas Dewey?

Lehman........................... 50%
Dewey............................ 50

Nine per cent expressed no opinion.

Upstate Only

Lehman........................... 42%
Dewey............................ 58

New York City Only

Lehman........................... 57%
Dewey............................ 43

By Age

	Lehman	Dewey
21–29 Years..............	49%	51%
30–49 Years..............	50	50
50 Years and over.........	50	50

By Sex

Men....................	51%	49%
Women..................	49	51

By Income

Upper....................	43%	57%
Middle...................	46	54
Lower....................	57	43

Persons on relief are included in the lower income group. Taken separately, they favor Lehman to Dewey 65% to 35%.

By Community Size

Farms....................	27%	73%
Small towns...............	42	58
Medium-sized cities.........	39	61
Larger cities (excluding N.Y.C.).......	50	50

OCTOBER 26
PARTY STRENGTH

Interviewing Date 10/19–24/38
Survey #136   Question #12

New voters were asked: If you were voting for congressman today, would you be most likely to vote for the Republican candidate or the Democratic candidate?

Democratic........................ 55%
Republican........................ 45

OCTOBER 28
FORMER GERMAN COLONIES

Special Survey

Asked in Great Britain by Gallup affiliate: Are you in favor of giving back any former German colonies?

Favor............................. 15%
Oppose............................ 85

Those who said that they opposed this also were asked: Would you rather fight than hand them back?

Yes............................... 81%
No................................ 19

OCTOBER 30
CONGRESSIONAL ELECTIONS

Interviewing Date 10/19–24/38
Survey #136   Question #12
Which party do you intend to support in the upcoming congressional elections?

Democratic........................ 53%
Republican........................ 47

By Income

	Democratic	Republican
Upper.............	35%	65%
Middle............	50	50
Lower.............	66	34

OCTOBER 30
RELIEF

Interviewing Date 10/10–15/38
Survey #135   Question #16
Do you favor the proposal that California pay its citizens who are not employed $30 every Thursday in script money?

Favor............................. 32%
Oppose............................ 68

By Income

	Favor	Oppose
Upper....................	9%	91%
Middle..................	26	74
Lower...................	54	46

By Age

21–29 Years...............	33%	67%
30–49 Years...............	32	68
50 Years and over..........	34	66

By Region

New England..............	35%	65%
Middle Atlantic............	36	64
East Central..............	35	65
West Central..............	28	72
South....................	27	73
West....................	28	72

California Only

Favor............................. 33%
Oppose............................ 67

NOVEMBER 3
NEW YORK POLITICS

Special Survey

Asked in New York State: For whom do you plan to vote for governor — Herbert Lehman or Thomas Dewey?

Lehman........................... 50.5%
Dewey............................ 49.5

Upstate Only

Lehman........................... 37%
Dewey............................ 63

New York City Only

Lehman........................... 65%
Dewey............................ 35

By Income

	Lehman	Dewey
Upper...................	38%	62%
Middle..................	48	52
Lower...................	61	39

By Age

21–29 Years	55%	45%
30–49 Years	53	47
50 Years and over	44	56

NOVEMBER 6
CONGRESSIONAL ELECTIONS — FINAL POLL

Special Survey
Interviewing Date 10/28–11/1/38

Which party do you intend to support in the upcoming congressional elections?

Democratic	54%
Republican	46

By Region

	Democratic	Republican
New England	39%	61%
Middle Atlantic	51	49
East Central	49	51
West Central	49	51
South	80	20
West	61	39

NOVEMBER 7
NEW YORK POLITICS — FINAL POLL

Special Survey

Asked in New York State: For whom do you plan to vote for governor — Herbert Lehman or Thomas Dewey?

Lehman	50.2%
Dewey	49.8

NOVEMBER 11
ADOLF HITLER

Interviewing Date 10/19–24/38
Survey #136   Question #1

Chancellor Hitler says that he has no more territorial ambitions in Europe. Do you believe him?

Yes	8%
No	92

NOVEMBER 13
WAGNER LABOR ACT

Interviewing Date 10/10–15/38
Survey #135   Question #8b

Do you think the Wagner Labor Act should be repealed, revised, or left unchanged?

Repealed	18%
Revised	52
Unchanged	30

By Political Affiliation
Democrats

Repealed	14%
Revised	50
Unchanged	36

Republicans

Repealed	30%
Revised	58
Unchanged	12

By Region
New England

Repealed	19%
Revised	53
Unchanged	28

Middle Atlantic

Repealed	17%
Revised	52
Unchanged	31

East Central

Repealed	22%
Revised	56
Unchanged	22

West Central

Repealed	18%
Revised	52
Unchanged	30

South

Repealed	19%
Revised	61
Unchanged	20

West

Repealed	23%
Revised	53
Unchanged	24

Great Britain	48%
France	12
Switzerland	6
Sweden	5
Finland	5
Germany	4
Ireland	4
Italy	3
Russia	2
Netherlands	2
Others	9

NOVEMBER 16
PRESIDENT ROOSEVELT'S VOTER APPEAL

Interviewing Date 11/7–12/38
Survey #137   Question #7b

In general, do you approve or disapprove of Franklin Roosevelt as President?

Approve	54%
Disapprove	46

NOVEMBER 18
POLITICAL PARTIES

Interviewing Date 9/15–20/38
Survey #132   Question #8b

Do you think we should give up the Republican and Democratic parties and have two new parties, one for liberals and the other for conservatives?

Yes	30%
No	70

NOVEMBER 20
BEST LIKED COUNTRY

Interviewing Date 10/3–8/38
Survey #134   Question #7

Which European country do you like best?

NOVEMBER 23
ELECTION OF 1940

Interviewing Date 11/7–12/38
Survey #137   Question #2

Which political party do you think will win the presidential election in 1940?

Republicans	50%
Democrats	50

NOVEMBER 25
RELIEF AND RECOVERY

Interviewing Date 10/19–24/38
Survey #136   Question #8

In deciding where and how to spend federal money for relief and recovery, who should have the greater say, Congress or the President?

Congress	78%
President	22

By Political Affiliation

	Congress	President
Republicans	90%	10%
Democrats	68	32

NOVEMBER 27
PERSONAL EXPERIENCES

Interviewing Date 7/15–20/38
Survey #128   Question #7a

During the past year, have you done any of the following things?

	Yes
Bought a ticket in a church raffle.......	29%
Bought a number on a punch board.....	26
Played a slot machine...............	23
Played cards for money..............	21
Bet on an election..................	19
Bought a sweepstakes ticket..........	13
Bet on a horse race.................	10
Played the numbers game............	9
None of these.....................	47

NOVEMBER 27
REPUBLICAN PRESIDENTIAL CANDIDATES

Interviewing Date 11/7–12/38
Survey #137   Question #8

Republicans were asked: Whom would you like to see as the Republican candidate for President in 1940?

Dewey..........................	33%
Vandenberg......................	18
Taft............................	18
Landon.........................	6
Hoover.........................	6
Lodge..........................	5
Others.........................	14

DECEMBER 2
DEMOCRATIC PRESIDENTIAL CANDIDATES

Interviewing Date 11/24–29/38
Survey #139   Question #10

Asked of Democrats: If Franklin Roosevelt does not run, whom would you like to see nominated by the Democratic party for President in 1940?

The following are listed according to frequency of mention:

Garner
Hull
Farley
Bennett Clark
Lehman

McNutt
Barkley
Murphy
Hopkins
Joseph Kennedy

DECEMBER 4
TOM MOONEY

Interviewing Date 11/16–21/38
Survey #138   Question #3a

Are you familiar with the Tom Mooney case?

Yes..............................	85%
No..............................	15

Interviewing Date 11/16–21/38
Survey #138   Question #3b

Asked of those who replied in the affirmative: Would you like to see the new governor of California free Tom Mooney?

Yes..............................	66%
No..............................	34

By Political Affiliation

	Yes	No
Democrats...................	74%	26%
Republicans..................	49	51

Throughout the country persons in the upper and middle income groups are most familiar with the Mooney issue but the greatest sentiment for freeing him comes from those in the lower income group and from labor union members.

DECEMBER 4
PRESIDENT ROOSEVELT'S VOTER APPEAL

Interviewing Date 11/16–21/38
Survey #138   Question #6c

In general, do you approve or disapprove of Franklin Roosevelt as President today?

Approve.........................55.5%
Disapprove......................44.5

By Region

	Approve	Disapprove
New England..........	47%	53%
Middle Atlantic........	57	43
East Central..........	52	48
West Central..........	51	49
South................	64	36
West.................	62	38

By Income

Upper................	34%	66%
Middle...............	51	49
Lower		
(including reliefers)...	71	29
Reliefers (separately)....	84	16

DECEMBER 7
CORDELL HULL

Interviewing Date 11/24–29/38
Survey #139   Question #7

Do you think Cordell Hull has done a good job or a poor job as Secretary of State?

Good job...........................85%
Poor job...........................15

DECEMBER 9
NAZI PERSECUTIONS

Interviewing Date 11/24–29/38
Survey #139   Question #1a

Do you approve or disapprove of the Nazi treatment of Jews in Germany?

Approve............................6%
Disapprove.........................94

Interviewing Date 11/24–29/38
Survey #139   Question #1b

Do you approve or disapprove of the Nazi treatment of Catholics in Germany?

Approve............................3%
Disapprove.........................97

DECEMBER 11
THE DIES COMMITTEE

Interviewing Date 11/16–21/38
Survey #138   Question #5a

Have you heard about the Dies Committee for investigating un-American activities?

Yes...............................60%
No................................40

Interviewing Date 11/16–21/38
Survey #138   Question #5b

Those who responded in the affirmative were asked: Do you think its findings have been important enough to justify continuing the investigation?

Yes...............................74%
No................................26

By Region

	Yes	No
New England.................	72%	28%
Middle Atlantic...............	69	31
East Central.................	80	20
West Central.................	78	22
South.......................	80	20
West........................	70	30

By Political Affiliation

Democrats...................	68%	32%
Republicans..................	83	17
Third party supporters........	71	29

By Income

Upper.......................	77%	23%
Middle......................	73	27
Lower.......................	74	26

DECEMBER 11
WAR BETWEEN GERMANY AND RUSSIA

Interviewing Date 11/16–21/38
Survey #138   Question #4

If there were a war between Germany and Russia, which side would you rather see win?

Russia........................... 83%
Germany......................... 17

DECEMBER 14
PRESIDENT ROOSEVELT

Interviewing Date 11/7–12/38
Survey #137   Question #1a

Do you favor or oppose a third term for President Roosevelt?

Favor........................... 30%
Oppose.......................... 70

By Political Affiliation

	Favor	Oppose
Republicans..........	3%	97%
Democrats..........	49	51

DECEMBER 16
UNIVERSAL MILITARY TRAINING

Interviewing Date 12/4–9/38
Survey #140–B   Question #1a

Should every able-bodied American boy 20 years old be required to go into the army or navy for one year?

Yes............................. 37%
No.............................. 63

Interviewing Date 12/4–9/38
Survey #140–B   Question 1b

Do you think military training should be part of the duties of the boys in the Civilian Conservation Corps camps?

Yes............................. 75%
No.............................. 25

DECEMBER 17
RADIOS

Interviewing Date 10/10–15/38
Survey #135   Question #12a

Does your family own a radio?

Yes............................. 77%
No.............................. 23

By Region

	Yes	No
New England..................	92%	8%
Middle Atlantic...............	88	12
East Central.................	86	14
West Central.................	79	21
South......................	52	48
Mountain....................	80	20
Pacific......................	88	12

DECEMBER 18
PROHIBITION

Interviewing Date 10/10–15/38
Survey #135   Question #1a

If the question of national prohibition should come up again, would you vote for it?

Yes............................. 36%
No.............................. 64

Dry States Only

Yes............................. 56%
No.............................. 44

Interviewing Date 10/10–15/38
Survey #135   Question #1b

Do you think drunkenness is increasing or decreasing in this community?

Increasing........................ 40%
Decreasing........................ 24
About the same.................... 36

Interviewing Date 10/10–15/38
Survey #135   Question #1c

Do you think liquor regulations in your state are too strict, not strict enough, or about right?

Too strict......................... 4%
Not strict enough.................. 53
About right....................... 43

By Region
New England

Too strict................................ 5%
Not strict enough.................. 49
About right....................... 46

Middle Atlantic

Too strict........................ 6%
Not strict enough.................. 41
About right....................... 53

East Central

Too strict........................ 4%
Not strict enough.................. 53
About right....................... 43

West Central

Too strict........................ 3%
Not strict enough.................. 65
About right....................... 32

South

Too strict........................ 4%
Not strict enough.................. 65
About right....................... 31

West

Too strict........................ 4%
Not strict enough.................. 52
About right....................... 44

Interviewing Date 10/10–15/38
Survey #135   Question #1d

Do you think young people would be better off if we had national prohibition again?

Yes............................... 43%
No................................ 57

Dry States Only

Yes............................... 63%
No................................ 37

DECEMBER 18
BOYCOTT OF GERMAN GOODS

Interviewing Date 11/24–29/38
Survey #139   Question #5

Would you join a movement in this country to stop buying German-made goods?

Yes............................... 61%
No................................ 39

By Religion

	Yes	No
Protestants....................	61%	39%
Catholics.....................	64	36
Jews.........................	96	4
Others.......................	50	50

DECEMBER 21
NEVILLE CHAMBERLAIN

Special Survey

Britons were asked by Gallup affiliates abroad: Do you approve or disapprove of Neville Chamberlain as Prime Minister?

Approve........................... 55%
Disapprove....................... 45

DECEMBER 23
HARRY HOPKINS

Interviewing Date 11/24–29/38
Survey #139   Question #8a

Do you think Harry Hopkins has done a good job or a poor job as director of the W.P.A.?

Good job.......................... 47%
Poor job.......................... 53

One voter in every four had no opinion.

By Political Affiliation

	Good job	Poor job
Republicans............	22%	78%
Democrats............	60	40

Interviewing Date 11/24–29/38
Survey #139   Question #8b

Hopkins has been mentioned for the post of Secretary of Commerce. Would you approve or disapprove of his appointment?

Approve........................... 34%
Disapprove........................ 66

Forty per cent of those polled said that they had no opinion.

By Political Affiliation

	Approve	Disapprove
Republicans...........	14%	86%
Democrats............	45	55

DECEMBER 25
WORKING WOMEN

Interviewing Date 10/19–24/38
Survey # 13–B   Question #6

Do you approve of a married woman earning money in business or industry if she has a husband capable of supporting her?

Approve........................... 22%
Disapprove........................ 78

By Sex

	Approve	Disapprove
Men.................	19%	81%
Women.............	25	75

Younger men and women are the least critical of married women working.

DECEMBER 25
MOST INTERESTING NEWS STORY

Interviewing Date 11/24–29/38
Survey #13a   Question #11

Which news story of 1938 do you consider the most interesting?

Czech crisis.........................	23%
Nazi persecutions....................	12
Republican gains....................	10
Corrigan's flight....................	7
Wage and hour bill.................	6
New England hurricane.............	5
Business slump.....................	5
World Series.......................	5
Struggle between Japan and China.....	4
C.I.O. and A.F.L. troubles...........	4
Others.............................	19

By Sex
Men

Czech crisis.........................	22%
Nazi persecutions....................	11
Republican gains....................	11
Wage and hour bill.................	7
Corrigan's flight....................	6
Business slump.....................	6
World series.......................	6
C.I.O. and A.F.L. troubles...........	4
New England hurricane.............	4
Struggle between Japan and China.....	4
Others.............................	19

Women

Czech crisis.........................	24%
Nazi persecutions....................	14
Republican gains....................	9
Corrigan's flight....................	7
New England hurricane.............	7
Wage and hour bill.................	5
Struggle between Japan and China.....	5
Business slump.....................	4
California unemployment plan........	4
Roosevelt "purge"..................	3
Others.............................	18

DECEMBER 28
ARMED FORCES

Interviewing Date 11/24–29/38
Survey #139   Question #6a

Should the United States build a larger navy?

Yes............................... 86%
No................................ 14

Interviewing Date 11/24–29/38
Survey #139   Question #6b

Should the United States enlarge the army?

Yes............................... 82%
No................................ 18

Interviewing Date 11/24–29/38
Survey #139   Question #6c

Should the United States enlarge the air force?

Yes............................... 90%
No................................ 10

DECEMBER 30
SPANISH CIVIL WAR

Interviewing Date 12/18–23/38
Survey #141   Question #5a

Which side do you sympathize with in the Spanish Civil War?

Loyalists........................... 76%
Franco............................. 24

By Religion

	Loyalists	*Franco*
Catholics..................	42%	58%
Protestants................	83	17

Thirty-three per cent declared that they sympathized with neither side.

1939

JANUARY 1
NEW YEAR RESOLUTIONS

Interviewing Date 12/18–23/38
Survey #141   Question #3a

Are you planning to make any New Year resolutions?

Yes................................ 28%
No................................ 72

Interviewing Date 12/18–23/38
Survey #141   Question #3b

Asked of those who responded in the affirmative: What New Year resolutions do you plan to make?

The following are listed in order of frequency of mention:

Save more money
Improve my character
Better myself in business
Stop smoking
Be more religious; go to church oftener

JANUARY 2
WAGE AND HOURS LAW

Interviewing Date 12/4–9/38
Survey #140–A   Question #7

Are you in favor of the new wage and hours law?

Yes................................ 71%
No............................... 29

By Region
	Yes	No
New England..................	79%	21%
Middle Atlantic...............	77	23
East Central..................	66	34
West Central..................	75	25
South.........................	59	41
West..........................	73	27

By Political Affiliation
	Yes	No
Democrats....................	80%	20%
Republicans..................	51	49

Interviewing Date 12/4–9/38
Survey #140–A   Question #6c

Asked of employees: Do you think your employer pays you a fair wage?

Yes................................ 79%
No................................ 21

By Occupation
	Yes	No
Skilled.......................	80%	20%
Unskilled.....................	75	25
White collar..................	84	16
Professional..................	77	23

Interviewing Date 12/4–9/38
Survey #140–A   Question #6e

Asked of employees: Do you think your employer requires you to work too many hours a week?

Yes................................ 13%
No................................ 87

JANUARY 3
GERMANY AND RUSSIA

Special Survey
Interviewing Date 11/16–21/38 (U.S. only)
Survey #138–K   Question #4

If there were a war between Germany and Russia which side would you rather see win?

Russia............................ 83%
Germany.......................... 17

Great Britain Only

Russia............................ 85%
Germany.......................... 15

Approximately one-third of the American and British voters would not express an opinion.

JANUARY 4
DUKE AND DUCHESS OF WINDSOR

Special Survey

> *Asked in Great Britain: Would you like the Duke and Duchess of Windsor to make their home in England?*

Yes.............................. 79%
No............................... 21

Twenty per cent expressed no opinion.

JANUARY 6
GOVERNMENT SPENDING

Interviewing Date 12/25–30/38
Survey #142   Question #4

> *Do you think the Federal Government is spending too much, too little, or about the right amount of money at this time?*

Too much......................... 61%
Too little........................ 10
About right....................... 29

By Political Affiliation
Democrats

Too much......................... 46%
Too little........................ 13
About right....................... 41

Republicans

Too much......................... 89%
Too little........................ 3
About right....................... 8

JANUARY 8
FATHER CHARLES COUGHLIN

Interviewing Date 12/18–23/38
Survey #141   Question #1a

> *Have you listened to any of Father Coughlin's radio talks in the last month?*

Projecting the results of this survey, approximately 15,000,000 persons listened to one or more of the Sunday broadcasts of Father Coughlin during December 1938. Approximately 3,500,000 would classify themselves as regular listeners.

Interviewing Date 12/18–23/38
Survey #141   Question #1b

> *Asked of a cross section of those who listened to Father Coughlin: In general, do you approve or disapprove of what he says?*

	Approve	Disapprove
Regular listeners.......	67%	33%
Occasional listeners.....	51	49

Interviewing Date 12/18–23/38
Survey #141   Question #1c

> *Asked of those who do not listen to Father Coughlin's radio talks: In general, do you approve or disapprove of what he says?*

Approve.......................... 30%
Disapprove....................... 70

Seventy-five per cent expressed no opinion.

JANUARY 9
PRESIDENT ROOSEVELT'S
VOTER APPEAL

Interviewing Date 12/25–30/38
Survey #142   Question #11c

> *In general, do you approve or disapprove of Franklin Roosevelt as President?*

Approve.......................... 58%
Disapprove....................... 42

By Region

	Approve	Disapprove
New England	51%	49%
Middle Atlantic	57	43
East Central	55	45
West Central	56	44
South	68	32
West	64	36

By Community Size

Farms	53%	47%
Small towns	56	44
Cities of 500,000 and over	66	34

JANUARY 15
ELEANOR ROOSEVELT

Interviewing Date 12/25–30/38
Survey #142   Question #1

Do you approve of the way Mrs. Roosevelt has conducted herself as "First Lady"?

Yes............................... 67%
No............................... 33

By Region

	Yes	No
New England	66%	34%
Middle Atlantic	72	28
East Central	64	36
West Central	66	34
South	67	33
West	66	34

By Sex

Men	62%	38%
Women	73	27

By Political Affiliation

Democrats	81%	19%
Republicans	43	57

Interviewing Date 12/25–30/38
Survey #142   Question #3

Mrs. Roosevelt has taken a position on the Board of Directors in her son's insurance company. Do you approve or disapprove of this?

Approve........................... 44%
Disapprove........................ 56

JANUARY 15
MOST INTERESTING BOOK

Interviewing Date 10/19–24/38
Survey #136   Question #9

What is the most interesting book you have ever read?

The following are listed in order of frequency of mention:

The Bible
Gone With the Wind
Anthony Adverse
The Citadel
How To Win Friends and Influence People
The Good Earth
Ben Hur
Northwest Passage
Little Women
A Tale of Two Cities
Les Miserables
Magnificent Obsession

By Age

	Naming Bible
21–29 Years	6%
30–49 Years	17
50 Years and over	37

JANUARY 16
WORLD'S FAIR

Interviewing Date 12/25–30/38
Survey #142   Question #2a

Do you plan to visit the World's Fair during 1939?

By Region

	Projected Figures of Those Planning To Attend
New England	3,400,000
Middle Atlantic	14,600,000
East Central	5,700,000
West Central	2,600,000
South	5,600,000
West	1,100,000
Total	33,000,000

JANUARY 18
UNEMPLOYMENT RELIEF

Interviewing Date 12/25–30/38
Survey #142   Question #7a

Would you favor having a national committee made up of members of both major political parties to handle unemployment relief?

Yes............................... 73%
No................................ 27

By Political Affiliation

	Yes	No
Democrats	72%	28%
Republicans	74	26

JANUARY 20
DEFENSE PROGRAMS

Interviewing Date 1/9–14/39
Survey #143–A   Question #1a

As part of the national defense program the Government is planning to train young men in schools and colleges to fly airplanes. Do you favor this plan?

Yes............................... 87%
No................................ 13

By Age

	Yes	No
Under 30 Years	91%	9%
Over 30 Years	85	15

Interviewing Date 1/9–14/39
Survey #143–A   Question #1b

Asked of those between the ages of 19 and 30: Would you like to receive such training?

Yes............................... 74%
No................................ 26

JANUARY 23
RELIEF AND POLITICS

Interviewing Date 1/9–14/39
Survey #143–A   Question #8a

Would you favor a law prohibiting any person on relief from contributing money to a political campaign?

Yes............................... 78%
No................................ 22

Interviewing Date 1/9–14/39
Survey #143–A   Question #8b

Would you favor a law prohibiting any relief official from contributing money to a political campaign?

Yes............................... 70%
No................................ 30

Interviewing Date 1/9–14/39
Survey #143–A   Question #9

Should employees of the Federal Government be prohibited from contributing money to political campaigns?

Yes............................... 62%
No................................ 38

Interviewing Date 12/25–30/38
Survey #142   Question #8

Do you think officials in charge of relief should be under civil service?

Yes............................... 75%
No................................ 25

JANUARY 25
PRESIDENTIAL TENURE

Interviewing Date 12/18–23/38
Survey #141   Question #4

*Would you favor changing the term of office
of the President of the United States to one
six year term with no reelection?*

Yes.............................. 24%
No.............................. 76

JANUARY 27
FINGERPRINTING

Interviewing Date 1/12–17/39
Survey #144–A   Question #5

*Do you think all persons living in this
country who are not citizens should be
fingerprinted and registered with the
Federal Government?*

Yes.............................. 84%
No.............................. 16

Interviewing Date 1/12–17/39
Survey #144–B   Question #5

*Do you think everybody in this country
should be fingerprinted by the Federal
Government?*

Yes.............................. 71%
No.............................. 29

JANUARY 29
FELIX FRANKFURTER

Interviewing Date 1/12–17/39
Survey #144–B   Question #7

*Do you think Felix Frankfurter will make a
good United States Supreme Court justice?*

Yes.............................. 82%
No.............................. 18

By Political Affiliation

	Yes	No
Republicans.	72%	28%
Democrats.	90	10

By Region

	Yes	No
New England.	90%	10%
Middle Atlantic.	87	13
East Central.	80	20
West Central.	77	23
South.	77	23
West.	78	22

JANUARY 30
EUROPEAN WAR

Interviewing Date 1/12–17/39
Survey #144–A   Question #3a

*Do you believe there will be a war between
any of the big European countries this year?*

Yes.............................. 44%
No.............................. 56

Interviewing Date 1/12–17/39
Survey #144–A   Question #3b

*If there is such a war, which country do you
think will be responsible for starting it?*

Germany alone..................... 62%
Italy alone....................... 12
Germany and Italy................. 20
Others............................ 6

Interviewing Date 1/12–17/39
Survey #144–A   Question #3c

*If there is such a war, do you think the
United States will be drawn in?*

Yes.............................. 57%
No.............................. 43

By Region

	Yes	No
New England	57%	43%
Middle Atlantic	56	44
East Central	55	45
West Central	55	45
South	61	39
West	57	43

JANUARY 31
BRITISH VIEWS ON FRANKLIN ROOSEVELT

Special Survey

Asked in Great Britain: Do you think the world would or would not benefit if President Roosevelt were elected for a third term?

Would benefit	91%
Would not benefit	9

FEBRUARY 1
AID TO SPANISH LOYALISTS

Interviewing Date 1/9–14/39
Survey #143–A   Question #2a

Should Congress change the Neutrality Act to permit the shipment of arms to the Loyalists in Spain?

Yes	21%
No	79

Seventeen per cent expressed no opinion.

FEBRUARY 3
GERMAN COLONIES

Interviewing Date 1/22–27/39
Survey #145–A   Question #7

Should the colonies taken from Germany after the World War be given back to her?

Yes	17%
No	83

FEBRUARY 6
PRESIDENT ROOSEVELT

Interviewing Date 1/12–17/39
Survey #144–A   Question #10a

Do you favor a third term for President Roosevelt?

Yes	31%
No	69

By Political Affiliation

	Yes	No
Democrats	47%	53%
Republicans	2	98

Interviewing Date 1/12–17/39
Survey #144–A   Question #10b

Would you like to see the Senate go on record against a third term for President Roosevelt?

Yes	49%
No	51

FEBRUARY 8
INCOME TAXES

Interviewing Date 1/22–27/39
Survey #145–A   Question #3

Do you think people who work for the state and local governments should pay federal income taxes on their salaries?

Yes	87%
No	13

Interviewing Date 1/22–27/39
Survey #145–A   Question #4

Should people who own United States government bonds or state or municipal bonds have to pay federal income taxes on their incomes from these securities?

Yes............................... 75%
No............................... 25

By Income

	Yes	No
Upper......................	69%	31%
Middle.....................	73	27
Lower......................	81	19

FEBRUARY 12
DEMOCRATIC PRESIDENTIAL CANDIDATES

Interviewing Date 11/16–21/38
Survey #138   Question #7a

Asked of Democrats: If President Roosevelt is not a candidate for re-election in 1940, would you prefer a conservative type of candidate or a New Dealer?

Conservative........................ 41%
New Dealer......................... 59

Interviewing Date 1/22–27/39
Survey #145–A   Question #15

Asked of Democrats: If Franklin Roosevelt is not a candidate for President in 1940, would you prefer a conservative type of candidate like John Garner, Bennett Clark, or Harry Byrd, or a New Dealer like Harry Hopkins, Henry Wallace, or Alben Barkley?

Conservative........................ 52%
New Dealer......................... 48

By Region

	Conservative	New Dealer
New England..........	58%	42%
Middle Atlantic........	47	53
East Central..........	53	47
West Central..........	57	43
South.................	54	46
West.................	42	58

FEBRUARY 13
GOVERNMENT CONSTRUCTION

Interviewing Date 1/27–2/1/39
Survey #146–B   Question #5a

Have you heard of the proposal to build a ship canal across Florida?

Yes............................... 50%
No............................... 50

Interviewing Date 1/27–2/1/39
Survey #146–B   Question #5b

Asked of those who replied in the affirmative: Should the Federal Government spend $150,000,000 for this project?

Yes............................... 25%
No............................... 75

By Political Affiliation

	Yes	No
Democrats...................	34%	66%
Republicans.................	13	87

Interviewing Date 1/27–2/1/39
Survey #146–A   Question #5a

Have you heard of the Passamaquoddy power project in Maine?

Yes............................... 50%
No............................... 50

Interviewing Date 1/27–2/1/39
Survey #146–A   Question #5b

Asked of those who replied in the affirmative: Should the Federal Government spend $36,000,000 for this project?

Yes............................... 27%
No............................... 73

By Political Affiliation

	Yes	No
Democrats...................	43%	57%
Republicans.................	7	93

FEBRUARY 15
ECONOMIC RECOVERY

Interviewing Date 1/27–2/1/39
Survey #146–A   Question #6

Do you think that, to create new jobs and reduce unemployment, it would be better to follow the ideas of big businessmen or the ideas of the Roosevelt Administration?

Follow businessmen................. 55%
Follow Administration.............. 45

By Political Affiliation

	Businessmen	Administration
Democrats.........	36%	64%
Republicans........	96	4

FEBRUARY 17
REPUBLICAN PRESIDENTIAL CANDIDATES

Interviewing Date 2/4–9/39
Survey #147–A   Question #14

Asked of Republicans: Whom would you like to see as the Republican candidate for President in 1940?

Dewey........................... 27%
Vandenberg...................... 21
Taft............................. 16
Landon.......................... 7
Borah........................... 4
Hoover.......................... 4
La Guardia...................... 4
Others.......................... 17

Forty-eight per cent expressed no opinion.

FEBRUARY 19
PRESIDENT ROOSEVELT'S VOTER APPEAL

Interviewing Date 1/9–14/39
Survey #143   Question #12c

In general, do you approve or disapprove of Franklin Roosevelt as President?

Approve........................... 58%
Disapprove....................... 42

By Region

	Approve	Disapprove
New England.........	53%	47%
Middle Atlantic.......	58	42
East Central..........	54	46
West Central..........	54	46
South................	68	32
West.................	63	37

By Income

Upper................	37%	63%
Middle...............	53	47
Lower................	75	25

FEBRUARY 20
GONE WITH THE WIND

Interviewing Date 1/27–2/1/39
Survey #146–A   Question #10a

Have you read the Book Gone With the Wind?

Nearly three years after its first publication, the Institute estimates that a total of 14,000,000 persons have read all or a part of the book. The great majority have read library or rental-library copies. More than twice as many women as men have read the book.

Interviewing Date 1/27–2/1/39
Survey #146–A   Question #10b

Asked of those who have read the book: Whom do you think was the most interesting character?

The overwhelming majority considered Scarlet O'Hara the most interesting character with Rhett Butler the next most interesting.

Interviewing Date 1/27–2/1/39
Survey #146–A   Question #10c

When Gone With the Wind *comes out as a movie, what are the chances of your seeing it?*

The Institute finds at this time that approximately 56,500,000 persons or 65% of the total movie-going population intends to see the film.

Interviewing Date 1/27–2/1/39
Survey #146–A   Question #10d

Asked of those who intend to see the film: Would you rather see the film come out in color or in black and white?

Color............................... 57%
Black and white..................... 21
No difference....................... 22

Interviewing Date 1/27–2/1/39
Survey #146–A   Question #10e

Asked of those who read the book: Which actress was your choice for Scarlett O'Hara?

The following are listed according to frequency of mention:

Bette Davis
Katherine Hepburn
Norma Shearer
Miriam Hopkins

Of those who intend to see the film, 29% did not know of the selection of Vivien Leigh to play the part of Scarlett O'Hara. Of the others, 35% said they were satisfied with Miss Leigh, 16% were dissatisfied, and 20% had no opinion.

FEBRUARY 22
EUROPEAN WAR

Interviewing Date 2/4–9/39
Survey #147–A   Question #3a

If Germany and Italy go to war against England and France, do you think we should do everything possible to help England and France win, except go to war ourselves?

Yes............................... 69%
No............................... 31

Six per cent expressed no opinion.

By Political Affiliation

	Yes	No
Democrats...................	71%	29%
Republicans..................	69	31
Third party supporters........	65	35

By Income

Upper.......................	73%	27%
Middle......................	70	30
Lower.......................	66	34

Interviewing Date 2/4–9/39
Survey #147–A   Question #4a

If Germany and Italy defeated England and France in a war, do you think Germany and Italy would then start a war against the United States?

Yes............................... 62%
No............................... 38

Sixteen per cent expressed no opinion.

FEBRUARY 24
PRESIDENTIAL TRIAL HEAT

Interviewing Date 1/22–27/39
Survey #145–A   Question #2

If Harry Hopkins runs for President in 1940 on the Democratic ticket against Thomas Dewey on the Republican ticket, which candidate would you prefer?

Dewey........................... 61%
Hopkins.......................... 39

Twenty-two per cent expressed no opinion.

By Political Affiliation

	Dewey	Hopkins
Democrats..............	39%	61%
Republicans..............	96	4
Third party supporters....	59	41

By Income

	Dewey	Hopkins
Upper	80%	20%
Middle	66	34
Lower (including reliefers)	47	53
Reliefers only	40	60

MARCH 20
DAUGHTERS OF THE AMERICAN REVOLUTION

Interviewing Date 3/4–9/39
Survey #150–A   Question #1

The Daughters of the American Revolution would not allow a well-known Negro singer to give a concert in one of their halls. As a protest against this, Mrs. Roosevelt resigned from the organization. Do you approve of her action?

Yes................................ 67%
No................................ 33

Fifteen per cent expressed no opinion.

By Political Affiliation

	Yes	No
Democrats	68%	32%
Republicans	63	37

By Region

	Yes	No
New England	79%	21%
Middle Atlantic	75	25
East Central	71	29
West Central	65	35
South	43	57
West	80	20

FEBRUARY 26
PENSIONS

Interviewing Date 1/12–17/39
Survey #144–A   Question #1a

Do you believe in Government old-age pensions?

Yes................................ 94%
No................................ 6

Interviewing Date 1/12–17/39
Survey #144–A   Question #1c

Asked of those who replied in the affirmative: About how much pension per month should be paid to a single person?

Median average.................... $40

Interviewing Date 1/12–17/39
Survey #144–A   Question #1d

Asked of those who replied in the affirmative: About how much pension per month should be paid to a married couple?

Median average.................... $60

FEBRUARY 27
AIRPLANE TRAVEL

Interviewing Date 2/4–9/39
Survey #147–A   Question #1b

If someone paid your way and you could go, would you be willing to fly across the Atlantic Ocean in one of the new commercial airplanes?

Yes................................ 41%
No................................ 59

By Sex

	Yes	No
Men	47%	53%
Women	36	64

By Age

	Yes	No
21–29 Years	61%	39%
30–49 Years	40	60
50 Years and over	25	75

Of those who have flown, 64% would be willing to fly to Europe. Of those who have never flown, 32% are willing.

MARCH 1
FEDERAL LICENSING

Interviewing Date 1/27–2/1/39
Survey #146–B   Question #4

Do you think all companies doing business in more than one state should be required to get a license from the Federal Government?

Yes............................. 57%
No.............................. 43

By Income

	Yes	No
Upper.....................	38%	62%
Middle....................	55	45
Lower.....................	69	31

Interviewing Date 2/4–9/39
Survey #147–B   Question #6

Do you think every labor union should be required to take out a license (permit) from the Federal Government?

Yes............................. 75%
No.............................. 25

By Income

	Yes	No
Upper.....................	76%	24%
Middle....................	73	27
Lower.....................	72	28

MARCH 3
SIT-DOWN STRIKES

Interviewing Date 2/4–9/39
Survey #147–A   Question #7

Do you think sit-down strikes should be made illegal in your state?

Yes............................. 75%
No.............................. 25

By Region

	Yes	No
New England.....................	68%	32%
Middle Atlantic...............	76	24
East Central...................	80	20
West Central..................	79	21
South.........................	74	26
West..........................	67	33

MARCH 5
NATIONAL ANTHEM

Interviewing Date 2/4–9/39
Survey #147–B   Question #10a

Can you tell me the name of the official national anthem (song) of the United States?

Correct............................ 68%
Incorrect.......................... 32

Thirteen per cent of those interviewed said they knew all the words to "The Star-Spangled Banner."

Interviewing Date 2/4–9/39
Survey #147–A   Question #10a

It has been suggested that the national anthem be played at the end of every performance and when radio stations sign off at night. Do you favor or oppose this idea?

Favor............................. 48%
Oppose............................ 52

MARCH 6
DIES COMMITTEE

Interviewing Date 2/18–23/39
Survey #148–A   Question #9a

Have you heard or read about the Dies Committee — The special House Committee on Un-American Activities?

Yes............................... 67%
No................................ 33

Interviewing Date 2 /18–23 /39
Survey #148–A   Question #9b

Asked of those who responded in the affirmative: What do you consider the most important area of investigation for the Dies Committee?

War propaganda.................... 42%
Nazi activities in U.S............... 32
Communist activities in U.S.......... 26

Thirty per cent expressed no opinion.

Interviewing Date 2 /18–23 /39
Survey 148–A   Question #9c

Have you heard or read about the La Follette Senate Committee on Civil Liberties?

Yes............................... 24%
No................................ 76

MARCH 8
WAR REFERENDUM

Interviewing Date 2 /18–23 /39
Survey #148–A   Question #8

Should the Constitution be changed to require Congress to obtain the approval of the people in a national vote before the United States could take part in a war overseas?

Yes............................... 58%
No................................ 42

By Political Affiliation

	Yes	No
Democrats	57%	43%
Republicans	54	46

By Income

	Yes	No
Upper	45%	55%
Middle	54	46
Lower	67	33

MARCH 10
WAGNER LABOR ACT

Interviewing Date 1 /27–2 /1 /39
Survey #146–A   Question #2b

Do you think the Wagner Labor Act should be revised, repealed, or left unchanged?

Revised........................... 48%
Repealed.......................... 18
Left unchanged.................... 34

By Income
Upper

Revised........................... 58%
Repealed.......................... 25
Left unchanged.................... 17

Middle

Revised........................... 51%
Repealed.......................... 18
Left unchanged.................... 31

Lower

Revised........................... 34%
Repealed.......................... 13
Left unchanged.................... 53

By Political Affiliation
Democrats

Revised........................... 45%
Repealed.......................... 12
Left unchanged.................... 43

Republicans

Revised........................... 56%
Repealed.......................... 29
Left unchanged.................... 15

MARCH 12
INCOME TAX

Interviewing Date 2 /18–23 /39
Survey #148–A   Question #10a

Do you think a single man earning $15 to $20 a week should be required to pay a federal income tax?

Yes.............................. 12%
No............................... 88

Interviewing Date 2/18–23/39
Survey #148–A   Question #10b

Do you think a married man earning $40 to $50 a week should be required to pay a federal income tax?

Yes.............................. 36%
No............................... 64

MARCH 13
EUROPEAN WAR

Interviewing Date 2/19–24/39
Survey #148–B   Question #8a

In case a war breaks out, should we sell Britain and France food supplies?

Yes.............................. 76%
No............................... 24

Interviewing Date 2/19–24/39
Survey #148–B   Question #8b

Should we sell them airplanes and other war materials?

Yes.............................. 52%
No............................... 48

By Political Affiliation

	Yes	No
Democrats	53%	47%
Republicans	54	46
Others	46	54

Interviewing Date 2/19–24/39
Survey #148–B   Question #8c

Should we send our army and navy abroad to help England and France?

Yes.............................. 17%
No............................... 83

Approximately 6% expressed no opinion to the above questions. Less than 1% said their sympathies would be with Germany and Italy in case of another war.

MARCH 15
DISARMAMENT CONFERENCE

Interviewing Date 2/18–23/39
Survey #148–A   Question #5a

Would you favor a conference of the leading nations to reduce the size of all armies and navies at this time?

Yes.............................. 43%
No............................... 57

Interviewing Date 2/18–23/39
Survey #148–A   Question #5b

Asked of those who replied in the affirmative: Should President Roosevelt call this disarmament conference?

Yes.............................. 28%
No............................... 72

MARCH 17
ROOSEVELT ADMINISTRATION
AND BUSINESS

Interviewing Date 3/4–9/39
Survey #150–B   Question #4

Do you think that the general attitude of the Roosevelt Administration toward business is too friendly or not friendly enough?

Too friendly...................... 9%
Not friendly enough............... 52
About right....................... 39

Interviewing Date 3/4–9/39
Survey #150–B   Question #5

Do you think the attitude of the Roosevelt Administration toward business is delaying business recovery?

Yes, a lot......................... 41%
Yes, a little...................... 26
No............................... 33

MARCH 20
RELIGION

Interviewing Date 2/24–3/1/39
Survey #149–A   Question #6f

Did your parents go to church more often or less often than you do?

More often........................ 50%
Less often........................ 18
About the same.................... 32

Interviewing Date 2/24–3/1/39
Survey #149–A   Question #6e

Do you think interest in religion in this community has increased or decreased during the last few years?

By Community Size
Farms

Increased......................... 27%
Decreased......................... 40
About the same.................... 33

Small Towns

Increased......................... 29%
Decreased......................... 46
About the same.................... 25

Cities

Increased......................... 42%
Decreased......................... 32
About the same.................... 26

By Age
21–29 Years

Increased......................... 37%
Decreased......................... 34
About the same.................... 29

30–49 Years

Increased......................... 38%
Decreased......................... 36
About the same.................... 26

50 Years and Over

Increased......................... 32%
Decreased......................... 40
About the same.................... 28

Interviewing Date 2/24–3/1/39
Survey #149–A   Question #6d

What can churches do to increase the interest of the public in religion?

The following are listed according to frequency of mention:

Select ministers who are more intelligent.
Arrange more social activities around the churches.
Become more modern and liberal.
Eliminate hypocrisy.
Stop emphasizing money and contributions.
Let church people be more friendly.

A majority thought there was nothing the churches could do or expressed no opinion.

MARCH 22
REPUBLICAN PRESIDENTIAL CANDIDATES

Interviewing Date 3/4–9/39
Survey #150–A   Question #10a

Asked of Republicans: Whom would you like to see as the Republican candidate for President in 1940?

Dewey............................ 50%
Vandenberg....................... 15
Taft.............................. 13
Hoover............................ 5
Landon............................ 4
Lodge............................. 2
Borah............................. 2
Others............................ 9

Fifty-four per cent expressed no opinion.

MARCH 24
PRESIDENT ROOSEVELT'S
VOTER APPEAL

Interviewing Date 3/10–15/39
Survey #151   Question #9d

In general, do you approve or disapprove of Franklin Roosevelt as President?

Approve......................... 58.2%
Disapprove...................... 41.8

By Income

	Approve	Disapprove
Upper..............	35%	65%
Middle..............	54	46
Lower (including reliefers)....	74	26
Reliefers only.........	83	17

MARCH 26
DEMOCRATIC PRESIDENTIAL
CANDIDATES

Interviewing Date 3/10–15/39
Survey #151–A   Question #3

Asked of Democrats: If President Roosevelt is not a candidate in 1940, whom would you like to see as the Democratic candidate for President?

Garner........................... 42%
Farley........................... 10
Hull............................. 10
Hopkins.......................... 8
McNutt........................... 5
Lehman........................... 3
Clark............................ 2
Barkley.......................... 2
Kennedy.......................... 2
Murphy........................... 2
Others........................... 14

MARCH 27
THE DRAFT

Interviewing Date 3/10–15/39
Survey #151–B   Question #6

Should the Constitution be amended to require a national vote before the country could draft men to fight overseas?

Yes.............................. 61%
No............................... 39

MARCH 29
PARTY STRENGTH

Interviewing Date 3/10–15/39
Survey #151–A   Question #2

Which party would you like to see win the presidential election in 1940?

Republican....................... 51%
Democratic....................... 49

Interviewing Date 3/10–15/39
Survey #151–A   Question #10

Suppose these are the candidates for President and Vice President in 1940, for which combination would you rather vote: Democratic ticket — John Garner for President and James Farley for Vice President; Republican ticket — Thomas Dewey for President and Robert Taft for Vice President?

Dewey-Taft....................... 52%
Garner-Farley.................... 48

Sixteen per cent expressed no opinion.

MARCH 31
NEVILLE CHAMBERLAIN

Special Survey

Asked in Great Britain by the Gallup affiliate. Are you satisfied with Mr. Neville Chamberlain as Prime Minister?

Yes.............................. 58%
No............................... 42

APRIL 2
SOCIAL AND INCOME CLASS

Interviewing Date 3/4–9/39
Survey #150–A   Question #2a

*To what social class in this country do you
feel you belong — lower, middle, or upper?*

Lower............................. 6%
Middle............................ 88
Upper............................. 6

Interviewing Date 3/4–9/39
Survey #150–A   Question #2b

*To what income class in this country do you
feel you belong — lower, middle, or upper?*

Lower............................. 31%
Lower middle...................... 21
Middle............................ 41
Upper middle...................... 6
Upper............................. 1

APRIL 3
PERSONAL SECURITY

Interviewing Date 3/4–9/39
Survey #150–A   Question #3d

*Asked of employers, business owners, and
employees: If you lost your present job (or
business) and could not find other work,
how long do you think you could hold out
before you would have to apply for relief?*

Three years and over................ 35%
Six months to three years........... 13
One to six months................... 16
One month or less................... 19
On relief now....................... 17

Interviewing Date 3/4–9/39
Survey #150–A   Question #3e

*Will you tell me in your own words what
your attitude is today toward President
Roosevelt?*

By Personal Security Level

	Favor	Oppose
Three years and over........	44%	56%
Six months to three years.....	56	44
One to six months..........	58	42
One month or less..........	61	39
On relief now..............	81	19

Interviewing Date 3/4–9/39
Survey #150–A   Question #3f

*Asked of farmers: If you lost your farm
(or farm job), how long do you think you
could hold out before you would have to
apply for relief?*

Three years and over................ 42%
Six months to three years........... 16
One to six months................... 15
One month or less................... 27

APRIL 7
AUTOMOBILE ACCIDENTS

Interviewing Date 3/6–11/39
Survey #150–B   Question #1

*To reduce automobile accidents, would you
favor any of the following measures?*

	All Voters	Car-Owners Only (Favoring)
Compulsory brake and headlight inspection................	90%	88%
Strict drivers' tests with physical and mental examinations.....	87	86
Revoke licenses of drunken drivers.................	95	95
Strict laws against jay-walking..	89	90
Speed governors.............	67	61
Compulsory auto liability insurance.....................	76	72

APRIL 9
EUROPEAN WAR

Interviewing Date 3/23–28/39
Survey #152–A   Question #5a

*In case a war breaks out, should we sell
Britain and France food supplies?*

Yes............................ 82%
No............................. 18

Interviewing Date 3/23–28/39
Survey #152–A   Question #5b

*Should we sell them airplanes and other war
materials?*

Yes............................ 66%
No............................. 34

By Political Affiliation

	Yes	No
Democrats.......................	70%	30%
Republicans....................	65	35

Interviewing Date 3/23–28/39
Survey #152–A   Question #5c

*Should we send our army and navy abroad
to help England and France?*

Yes............................ 16%
No............................. 84

Approximately 5% expressed no opinion to
the above questions. Of all sections of the
country, the South shows the greatest inclination for sending troops — 24%.

APRIL 10
SWING MUSIC

Interviewing Date 3/23–28/39
Survey #152–A   Question #11a

Do you like swing music?

Yes............................ 56%
No............................. 44

By Age

	Yes	No
21–29 Years.................	74%	26%
30–49 Years.................	56	44
50 Years and over............	35	65

APRIL 12
GERMANY

Interviewing Date 3/23–28/39
Survey #152–A   Question #4

*Would you join a movement in this country
to stop buying German-made goods?*

Yes............................ 65%
No............................. 35

Interviewing Date 3/23–28/39
Survey #152–B   Question #4

*Our Government is showing its disapproval
of Germany's policies by putting a special
tax on German-made goods brought into
the United States. Are you in favor of this
special tax?*

Yes............................ 78%
No............................. 22

APRIL 14
NEUTRALITY

Interviewing Date 4/2–7/39
Survey #153–A   Question #1

*Our present Neutrality Law prevents this
country from selling war materials to any
countries fighting in a declared war. Do you
think the law should be changed so that we
could sell war materials to England and
France in case of war?*

Yes............................ 57%
No............................. 43

APRIL 16
CANCER

Interviewing Date 4/2–7/39
Survey #153–A   Question #4b

Do you think cancer is contagious?

Yes................................ 20%
No................................. 59
Don't know........................ 21

Interviewing Date 4/2–7/39
Survey #153–B   Question #4a

Do you think cancer is curable?

Yes................................ 64%
No................................. 36

Interviewing Date 4/2–7/39
Survey #153–A   Question #4a

Which of these diseases would you hate most to have?

Cancer............................. 76%
Tuberculosis....................... 13
Heart trouble...................... 9
Pneumonia......................... 2

APRIL 17
EUROPEAN WAR

Interviewing Date 3/23–28/39
Survey #152–A   Question #1a

Do you believe there will be a war between any of the big European countries this year?

Yes................................ 51%
No................................. 49

Interviewing Date 3/23–28/39
Survey #152–A   Question #1b

If there is such a war, do you think the United States will be drawn into it?

Yes................................ 58%
No................................. 42

APRIL 19
PRESIDENTIAL TRIAL HEAT

Interviewing Date 4/2–7/39
Survey #153–B   Question #3

If Vice President Garner runs for President in 1940 on the Democratic ticket and Senator Arthur Vandenberg runs against him on the Republican ticket, which one do you think you would prefer?

Garner............................. 57%
Vandenberg........................ 43

Twenty-five per cent expressed no opinion.

By Region

	Garner	Vandenberg
New England.........	57%	43%
Middle Atlantic.......	54	46
East Central..........	50	50
West Central..........	51	49
South................	78	22
West.................	61	39

APRIL 21
FEDERAL SPENDING

Interviewing Date 4/2–7/39
Survey #153–A   Question #2a

Do you think federal spending should be reduced by 10% on expenditures for the army and navy?

Yes................................ 19%
No................................. 81

Interviewing Date 4/2–7/39
Survey #153–A   Question #2b

Do you think farm benefits should be reduced by 10%?

Yes................................ 38%
No................................. 62

Interviewing Date 4/2–7/39
Survey #153–A   Question #2c

Do you think relief spending should be cut by 10%?

Yes.................................. 57%
No.................................. 43

Interviewing Date 4/2–7/39
Survey #153–B   Question #2a

Do you think public works spending should be cut by 10%?

Yes.................................. 53%
No.................................. 47

Interviewing Date 4/2–7/39
Survey #153–B   Question #2b

Do you think ordinary operating expenses should be reduced by 10%?

Yes.................................. 69%
No.................................. 31

Interviewing Date 4/2–7/39
Survey #153–B   Question #2c

Do you think old-age pensions should be reduced by 10%?

Yes.................................. 14%
No.................................. 86

APRIL 23
INTERNATIONAL PEACE CONFERENCE

Interviewing Date 3/23–28/39
Survey #152–A   Question #3a

Would you like to see the heads of the leading nations of the world meet in a new peace conference to settle the claims of Germany and Italy?

Yes.................................. 73%
No.................................. 27

By Region

	Yes	No
New England...............	76%	24%
Middle Atlantic..............	69	31
East Central.................	74	26
West Central.................	76	24
South......................	77	23
West......................	69	31

By Political Affiliation

	Yes	No
Democrats...................	74%	26%
Republicans..................	68	32
Others.....................	75	25

APRIL 24
EUTHANASIA

Interviewing Date 1/22–27/39
Survey #145–B   Question #12

Do you favor mercy deaths under Government supervision for hopeless invalids?

Yes.................................. 46%
No.................................. 54

By Sex

	Yes	No
Men........................	49%	51%
Women.....................	42	58

By Age

	Yes	No
21–29 Years.................	52%	48%
30–49 Years.................	44	56
50 Years and over.............	41	59

APRIL 26
RELIEFERS

Interviewing Date 4/8–13/39
Survey #154–A   Question #4a

Do you think there are any persons on relief in your community who could get jobs in private industry if they tried?

Yes................................ 69%

No................................ 31

Interviewing Date 4/8–13/39
Survey #154–A   Question #4b

> Asked of those who replied in the affirmative: What proportion of those on relief in your community could obtain jobs in private industry if they tried?

Median average.................... 25%

APRIL 28
PRESIDENT ROOSEVELT

Interviewing Date 4/21–26/39
Survey #155–A   Question #2a

> Do you approve or disapprove of President Roosevelt's action in sending his message to Hitler and Mussolini, suggesting a conference to settle Europe's war problems?

Approve.......................... 60%
Disapprove....................... 40

By Political Affiliation

	Approve	Disapprove
Democrats.............	69%	31%
Republicans...........	47	53

APRIL 30
BRITISH ARMED FORCES

Special Survey

> Asked in Great Britain by the Gallup affiliate: It has been decided to enlarge the British Army to 33 field divisions. Are you in favor of obtaining the necessary recruits on a planned and compulsory basis, or by leaving it to individuals to enroll voluntarily?

Favor compulsory system............ 42%
Favor voluntary system............. 58

By Political Affiliation

	Compulsory	Voluntary
Government supporters........	51%	49%
Opposition voters....	33	67

APRIL 30
TELEVISION

Special Survey

> At present, are you interested in purchasing a home television set?

Yes................................ 13%
No................................ 87

MAY 1
PARTY STRENGTH

Interviewing Date 4/8–13/39
Survey #154–A   Question #1

> Which party do you think will win the presidential election in 1940?

Democratic....................... 48%
Republican....................... 52

By Political Affiliation

	Democratic	Republican
Democrats............	67%	33%
Republicans...........	17	83
Third party voters.......	54	46

By Region

New England.........	47%	53%
Middle Atlantic........	43	57
East Central..........	42	58
West Central..........	43	57
South................	68	32
West.................	60	40

MAY 3
EUROPEAN WAR

Interviewing Date 3/23–28/39
Survey #152–A   Question #5a

> If war breaks out in Europe, are you in favor of sending American troops abroad?

By Region

	Yes	No
New England	18%	82%
Middle Atlantic	16	84
East Central	12	88
West Central	13	87
South	24	76
West	17	83

By Income

Upper	18%	82%
Middle	14	86
Lower	19	81

MAY 5
PRESIDENTIAL TRIAL HEAT

Special Survey

If President Roosevelt runs for a third term in 1940 on the Democratic ticket against Thomas E. Dewey on the Republican ticket, which one do you think you would prefer?

Roosevelt	45%
Dewey	55

Twelve per cent expressed no opinion.

Roosevelt Voters in 1936 Only

Roosevelt	67%
Dewey	33

Landon Voters in 1936 Only

Roosevelt	4%
Dewey	96

MAY 7
PRESIDENT ROOSEVELT'S VOTER APPEAL

Interviewing Date 4/21–26/39
Survey #155   Question #15e

In general, do you approve or disapprove of Franklin Roosevelt as President?

Approve	56.1%
Disapprove	43.9

By Region

	Approve	Disapprove
New England	48%	52%
Middle Atlantic	53	47
East Central	54	46
West Central	56	44
South	67	33
West	63	37

MAY 10
REPUBLICAN PRESIDENTIAL CANDIDATES

Interviewing Date 4/8–13/39
Survey #154–A   Question #2

Asked of Republicans: Whom do you prefer from this list (on card) for the Republican presidential nomination in 1940?

Dewey	54%
Taft	15
Vandenberg	13
Hoover	4
Borah	3
Landon	3
Bricker	1
Lodge	1
La Guardia	1
Barton	1
Others	4

Forty-one per cent expressed no opinion.

MAY 12
FARM POLICIES

Interviewing Date 4/21–26/39
Survey #155–A   Question #11a

Do you think the Roosevelt Administration has done a good job or a poor job in handling the farm problem?

Good job......................... 48%
Poor job......................... 52

Twenty-five per cent expressed no opinion.

Southern and Midwestern Farmers Only

Good job......................... 53%
Poor job......................... 47

Interviewing Date 4/21–26/39
Survey #155–A   Question #11b

Do you think Henry Wallace has done a good job as Secretary of Agriculture?

Yes............................... 58%
No................................ 42

Southern and Midwestern Farmers Only

Yes............................... 55%
No................................ 45

MAY 14
MOST IMPORTANT PROBLEM

Interviewing Date 4/21–26/39
Survey #155–A   Question #1

What do you regard as the most important problem before the American people today?

Keeping out of war.................. 37%
Solving unemployment............... 36
Recovery for business................ 8
Adequate relief..................... 4
Balancing the budget................ 3
Farm aid........................... 2
Adjustment of labor problems........ 2
Reduction of taxes.................. 1
Others............................. 7

MAY 15
EUROPEAN WAR

Interviewing Date 4/21–26/39
Survey #155–B   Question #5b

In case Germany and Italy go to war against England and France should we lend money to England and France to buy airplanes and other war materials from the United States?

Lend money....................... 31%
Do not lend money................. 69

Five per cent expressed no opinion.

By Region

	Lend	Do Not Lend
New England.......	18%	82%
Middle Atlantic......	34	66
East Central........	30	70
West Central........	21	79
South.............	45	55
West..............	33	67

MAY 17
WORLD'S FAIR

Special Survey

Asked of those who visited the World's Fair: Which exhibit did you like the best?

The following are listed according to frequency of mention:

General Motors
Theme Center
A. T. & T. Exhibit
Ford Motor Co. Exhibit
Soviet Building
British Building
Railroad Exhibit

MAY 19
EUROPEAN WAR

Interviewing Date 5/4–9/39
Survey #156–A   Question #2a

Do you believe there will be a war between any of the big European countries this year?

Yes............................... 32%
No................................ 68

By Sex

	Yes	No
Men	29%	71%
Women	36	64

MAY 21
DEMOCRATIC PRESIDENTIAL CANDIDATES

Interviewing Date 4/21–26/39
Survey #155–A   Question #12

Asked of Democrats: If Franklin Roosevelt is not a candidate, whom from this list (on card) would you like to see nominated by the Democratic party in 1940?

Garner	50%
Hull	13
Farley	9
Hopkins	3
McNutt	3
Murphy	3
Clark	2
Wallace	2
Barkley	2
Lehman	2
Others	11

MAY 22
ROYALTY

Interviewing Date 5/4–9/39
Survey #156–A   Question #5a

When Americans are presented to the King and Queen of England on their visit to this country, do you think American women should curtsy or shake hands?

Curtsy	22%
Shake hands	78

Interviewing Date 5/4–9/39
Survey #156–A   Question #5b

Do you think American men should bow or shake hands?

Bow	21%
Shake hands	79

MAY 24
PRESIDENTIAL TRIAL HEAT

Interviewing Date 4/21–26/39
Survey #155–A   Question #14

If Cordell Hull runs for President in 1940 on the Democratic ticket and Thomas Dewey runs against him on the Republican ticket, which one do you think you would prefer?

Dewey	52%
Hull	48

Eighteen per cent expressed no opinion.

Interviewing Date 5/4–9/39
Survey #156–A   Question #9

If Cordell Hull runs for President in 1940 on the Democratic ticket and Robert Taft runs against him on the Republican ticket, which one do you think you would prefer?

Hull	50%
Taft	50

Fifteen per cent expressed no opinion.

MAY 26
RELIEF

Interviewing Date 5/4–9/39
Survey #156–A   Question #6

Which way do you think relief should be given — in the form of work relief (such as W.P.A. jobs) or as direct cash relief?

Work relief	89%
Cash relief	11

MAY 28

ROOSEVELT ADMINISTRATION AND BUSINESS

Interviewing Date 5/12–17/39
Survey #157–A Question #7a

Do you think that the general attitude of the Roosevelt Administration toward business is too friendly or not friendly enough?

Not friendly enough................ 54%
Too friendly....................... 11
About right........................ 35

Interviewing Date 5/12–17/39
Survey #157–B Question #7a

Do you think the general attitude of business toward the Roosevelt Administration is too friendly or not friendly enough?

Not friendly enough................ 65%
Too friendly....................... 11
About right........................ 24

Interviewing Date 5/12–17/39
Survey #157–B Question #7a

Do you think the attitude of the Roosevelt Administration toward business is delaying business recovery?

Yes............................... 63%
No................................ 37

Interviewing Date 5/12–17/39
Survey #157–A Question #7b

Do you think the attitude of business toward the Roosevelt Administration is delaying business recovery?

Yes............................... 69%
No................................ 31

Approximately 16% had no opinion to the above questions.

MAY 29

LEARNING TO FLY AN AIRPLANE

Interviewing Date 5/12–17/39
Survey #157–A Question #1a

If it did not cost you anything, would you like to learn how to fly an airplane?

Yes............................... 42%
No................................ 58

By Sex

	Yes	No
Men.......................	50%	50%
Women.....................	34	66

By Age

18–29 Years.................	62%	38%
30–49 Years.................	39	61
50 Years and over............	23	77

Thirty-four per cent of those interviewed have been up in an airplane and 66% of this group are in favor of learning to fly.

MAY 31

PRESIDENTIAL TRIAL HEAT

Interviewing Date 3/23–28/39
Survey #152–B Question #8

If President Roosevelt runs for a third term in 1940 on the Democratic ticket against Senator Robert Taft on the Republican ticket, which one would you prefer?

Roosevelt......................... 50%
Taft.............................. 50

Sixteen per cent expressed no opinion.

Roosevelt Voters in 1936

Roosevelt......................... 75%
Taft.............................. 25

Landon Voters in 1936

Roosevelt......................... 6%
Taft.............................. 94

JUNE 2

PRESIDENT ROOSEVELT'S
VOTER APPEAL

Interviewing Date 5/20–25/39
Survey #158–A   Question #12c

In general, do you approve or disapprove of Franklin Roosevelt as President?

By Income

	Approve	Disapprove
Upper..................	38%	62%
Middle...............	54	46
Lower................	74	26
Reliefers..............	82	18

JUNE 4

WAR DEBTS

Interviewing Date 5/12–17/39
Survey #157–A   Question #2

If England and France pay something on the war debts they now owe us, should the United States lend them more money?

Yes............................... 21%
No................................ 79

Nine per cent expressed no opinion.

JUNE 5

ROOSEVELT ADMINISTRATION

Interviewing Date 5/12–17/39
Survey #157–A   Question #6a

What do you think is the greatest accomplishment of the Roosevelt Administration during the six years it has been in office?

Relief and the W.P.A................. 28%
Banking reforms.................... 21
Civilian Conservation Corps.......... 11
Social Security..................... 7
Farm program..................... 5
Labor policies...................... 4
Repeal of prohibition............... 3
Foreign policy...................... 3
Public works construction........... 2
N.R.A............................ 1
Others............................ 15

By Political Affiliation
Democrats

Relief and the W.P.A................. 35%
Banking reforms.................... 19
Civilian Conservation Corps.......... 8
Farm program..................... 8
Social Security..................... 6
Others............................ 24

Republicans

Banking reforms.................... 34%
Civilian Conservation Corps.......... 13
Relief and the W.P.A................. 12
Social Security..................... 10
Foreign policy...................... 4
Others............................ 27

Interviewing Date 5/12–17/39
Survey #157–A   Question #6b

What do you think is the worst thing the Roosevelt Administration has done in the past six years?

Relief and the W.P.A................. 23%
Spending policy.................... 16
Farm program..................... 12
Foreign Policy..................... 6
Labor policy....................... 6
Interference with business............ 5
Supreme Court plan................. 5
N.R.A............................ 4
Repeal of prohibition............... 3
Raising taxes...................... 2
Others............................ 18

By Political Affiliation
Democrats

Relief and the W.P.A.	20%
Farm program	16
Spending policy	12
Labor policy	7
Supreme Court plan	7
Others	38

Republicans

Spending policy	24%
Relief and the W.P.A.	22
Interference with business	9
Labor policy	8
Farm program	7
Others	30

JUNE 7
BUSINESS PROSPERITY

Interviewing Date 5/20–25/39
Survey #158–A   Question #11

Do you think business would be more prosperous or less prosperous if we had a Republican President in the White House?

More prosperous	50%
Less prosperous	26
No difference	24

By Political Affiliation
Democrats

More prosperous	29%
Less prosperous	42
No difference	29

Republicans

More prosperous	85%
Less prosperous	3
No difference	12

By Income
Upper

More prosperous	62%
Less prosperous	20%
No difference	18

Middle

More prosperous	54%
Less prosperous	22
No difference	24

Lower

More prosperous	40%
Less prosperous	34
No difference	26

Reliefers

More prosperous	37%
Less prosperous	38
No difference	25

JUNE 9
PRESIDENTIAL TRIAL HEAT

Interviewing Date 5/4–9/39
Survey #156–B   Question #9

If Vice President Garner runs for President in 1940 on the Democratic ticket and Senator Robert Taft runs against him on the Republican ticket, which one do you think you would prefer?

Garner	54%
Taft	46

Twenty-four per cent expressed no opinion.

JUNE 11
UNIONS

Interviewing Date 5/20–25/39
Survey #158–B   Question #6

Are you in favor of labor unions?

Yes	70%
No	30

Interviewing Date 5/28–6/3/39
Survey #159–A   Question #3

Would you favor a law requiring employers and unions to submit their differences to a federal labor board before a strike could be called?

Yes............................. 86%
No.............................. 14

Interviewing Date 5/20–25/39
Survey #158–B   Question #7

Are you in favor of the so-called closed shop — that is, hiring only persons who are already members of the union?

Yes............................. 27%
No.............................. 73

Interviewing Date 5/20–25/39
Survey #158–A   Question #7

Are you in favor of the so-called union shop — that is, requiring every worker to join the union?

Yes............................. 29%
No.............................. 71

Interviewing Date 5/20–25/39
Survey #158–A   Question #8

Which labor leader do you like the best — William Green of the A.F. of L. or John L. Lewis of the C.I.O.?

Green........................... 80%
Lewis........................... 20

Approximately 12% had no opinion on the above questions.

JUNE 12
VOTING AGE

Interviewing Date 5/20–25/39
Survey #158–A   Question #1

Do you favor reducing the age at which American citizens can vote from 21 to 18?

Yes............................. 17%
No.............................. 83

By Age

	Yes	No
21–30 Years.	17%	83%
30–49 Years.	17	83
50 Years and over.	18	82

JUNE 14
DEMOCRATIC PRESIDENTIAL CANDIDATES

Interviewing Date 5/20–25/39
Survey #158–A   Question #9

Asked of Democrats: In case Franklin Roosevelt is not a candidate for a third term, whom would you like to see the Democratic party nominate for President in 1940?

Garner........................... 47%
Farley........................... 16
Hull............................. 12
Hopkins.......................... 5
McNutt........................... 3
Wallace.......................... 3
Murphy........................... 3
Clark............................ 2
Barkley.......................... 1
Kennedy.......................... 1
Others........................... 7

Fifty-one per cent expressed no opinion.

JUNE 16
JAPAN

Interviewing Date 5/20–25/39
Survey #158–A   Question #4

In the present fight between Japan and China, with which side do you sympathize?

Japan............................ 2%
China............................ 74
Neither.......................... 24

Interviewing Date 5/20–25/39
Survey #158–B   Question #3

Would you join a movement in this country to stop buying goods made in Japan?

Yes............................... 66%
No............................... 34

Interviewing Date 5/20–25/39
Survey #158–A   Question #5

Do you think the United States should forbid shipment of arms or ammunition from this country to Japan?

Yes............................... 72%
No............................... 28

Interviewing Date 5/20–25/39
Survey #158–B   Question #5

Do you think the United States should forbid shipment of arms or ammunition from this country to China?

Yes............................... 40%
No............................... 60

JUNE 18
PRESIDENT ROOSEVELT

Interviewing Date 5/28–6/3/39
Survey #159–A   Question #6a

Do you think President Roosevelt will run for a third term in 1940?

By Income

	Yes	No
Upper	46%	54%
Middle	46	54
Lower	54	46
Reliefers	60	40

Interviewing Date 5/28–6/3/39
Survey #159–A   Question #6b

Do you think he will be elected if he runs?

Yes............................... 45%
No............................... 55

By Political Affiliation

	Yes	No
Democrats	61%	39%
Republicans	16	84

Interviewing Date 5/28–6/3/39
Survey #159–A   Question #6c

If he runs for a third term in 1940, would you vote for him no matter what Republican runs against him?

Yes............................... 39%
No............................... 61

By Income

	Yes	No
Upper	19%	81%
Middle	34	66
Lower	55	45
Reliefers	66	34

JUNE 19
EUROPEAN WAR

Interviewing Date 5/28–6/3/39
Survey #159–A   Question #4

If England, France, and Russia were involved in a war with Germany and Italy, which side do you think would win?

England, France, Russia............. 83%
Germany and Italy.................. 17

JUNE 21
INCOME TAX

Interviewing Date 5/12–17/39
Survey #157–A   Question #11a

Do you pay any income tax?

Yes............................... 75%
No............................... 25

By Income

	Yes	No
Upper	93%	7%
Middle	81	19
Lower	60	40

JUNE 23
PRESIDENTIAL TRIAL HEAT

Interviewing Date 6/9–14/39
Survey #160–A   Question #8

If President Roosevelt runs for a third term on the Democratic ticket against Thomas Dewey on the Republican ticket, which one would you prefer?

Roosevelt	48%
Dewey	52

Thirteen per cent expressed no opinion.

Roosevelt Voters in 1936

Roosevelt	74%
Dewey	26

Landon Voters in 1936

Roosevelt	2%
Dewey	98

JUNE 25
VIEWS OF RELIEFERS

Special Survey

Asked of reliefers: What do you blame for the present unemployment in this country?

Increasing use of machinery	23%
Short-sighted policies of business	13
Capital not being invested	10
New Deal interfering with business	8
Lack of adjustment since World War	4
Lack of money in circulation	4
Conflict between business and labor	4
People not willing to borrow	3

Overproduction back in 1920's	3
Business frightened by what happened in 1929	2
Republican party policies	2
Increasing employment of women	2
Others	22

Do you think jobs in private industry are harder to get now than ten years ago?

Yes	94%
No	6

Do you think you or your husband will find a job in private industry within the next two years?

Yes	53%
No	47

How long has it been since you or your husband has had a steady job other than W.P.A.?

Median average	2 yrs. 10 mos.

Do you think you would be better off or worse off if there were a Republican administration in the White House?

Better off	24%
Worse off	44
No difference	32

JUNE 27
JOE LOUIS VS. TONY GALENTO

Interviewing Date 5/12–17/39
Survey #157   Question #4a

Which man would you like to see win the fight — Joe Louis or Tony Galento?

Louis	53%
Galento	47

Thirty-four per cent expressed no opinion.

Interviewing Date 5/12–17/39
Survey #157   Question #4b

Asked of those who expressed an opinion on the first question: Which man do you think will win the fight?

Louis............................. 95%
Galento........................... 5

JUNE 28
TUBERCULOSIS

Interviewing Date 5/28–6/3/39
Survey #159–A   Question #5a

What do you think is the cause of tuberculosis?

Germs............................. 18%
Run-down condition................ 17
Malnutrition...................... 13
Poor living conditions............ 12
Bad heredity...................... 11
Exposure to weather............... 11
Bad food.......................... 8
Colds............................. 6
Others............................ 4

Interviewing Date 5/28–6/3/39
Survey #159–A   Question #5b

Do you think tuberculosis is contagious?

Yes............................... 76%
No................................ 24

Interviewing Date 5/28–6/3/39
Survey #159–A   Question #5c

Do you think tuberculosis is inherited at birth?

Yes............................... 52%
No................................ 48

Interviewing Date 5/28–6/3/39
Survey #159–A   Question #5d

Do you think tuberculosis is curable?

Yes............................... 86%
No................................ 14

Interviewing Date 5/28–6/3/39
Survey #159–A   Question #5e

What do you think is the best way to cure tuberculosis?

Rest.............................. 43%
Proper diet....................... 36
Fresh air......................... 26
Climate........................... 25
Sanitarium treatment.............. 13
                                 —————
                                 143%

(Note: table adds to more than 100% because some people gave more than one answer.)

JUNE 30
THE JUDICIARY

Interviewing Date 6/9–14/39
Survey #160–A   Question #3a

In general, do you think judges in the federal courts of this country are honest?

Yes............................... 86%
No................................ 14

Interviewing Date 6/9–14/39
Survey #160–B   Question #3a

In general, do you think judges in the state courts are honest?

Yes............................... 76%
No................................ 24

Interviewing Date 6/9–14/39
Survey #160–A   Question #3b

In general, do you think judges in the municipal or local courts are honest?

Yes............................... 72%
No................................ 28

By Region

	Yes	No
New England	80%	20%
Middle Atlantic	67	33
East Central	67	33
West Central	75	25
South	77	23
West	76	24

JULY 2
POLITICS

Special Survey

Asked in New York State: Which party would you like to see win the presidential election in 1940?

Republican	53%
Democratic	47

Asked in New York State: If President Roosevelt runs for a third term in 1940, do you think you will vote for him?

Yes, will	42%
No, will not	58

Asked in New York State: If President Roosevelt runs for a third term on the Democratic ticket against Thomas Dewey on the Republican ticket, which one would you prefer?

Roosevelt	43%
Dewey	57

Asked of New York State Democrats: If President Roosevelt is not a candidate in 1940, whom would you like to see the Democratic convention nominate for President?

Garner	51%
Farley	12
Hull	11
Hopkins	4

Lehman	4
Kennedy	3
Others	15

JULY 3
SUMMER FASHIONS

Interviewing Date 6/9–14/39
Survey #160–A   Question #2a

Do you think it is indecent for women to wear shorts for street wear?

Yes	63%
No	37

By Sex

	Yes	No
Men	57%	43%
Women	70	30

Most conservative were Southerners, who voted 79% against women wearing shorts for street wear, while Western voters were 53% against it.

Interviewing Date 6/9–14/39
Survey #160–A   Question #2b

Do you think it is indecent for men to wear topless bathing suits for swimming?

Yes	33%
No	67

JULY 5
REPUBLICAN PARTY

Interviewing Date 6/18–23/39
Survey #161–AR   Question #4

Asked of Republicans: Do you think the Republican party should be more liberal or more conservative than it was in the 1936 presidential campaign?

More liberal	55%
More conservative	17
About the same	28

Interviewing Date 6/18–23/39
Survey #161–BR   Question #4

Asked of Republicans: Do you think the Republican party has a better chance or a worse chance of winning in 1940 if it nominates a liberal candidate and adopts a liberal platform?

Better chance...................... 77%
Worse chance...................... 14
Makes no difference................. 9

JULY 7

REPUBLICAN PRESIDENTIAL CANDIDATES

Interviewing Date 6/18–23/39
Survey #161–AR   Question #5a

Asked of Republicans: Whom from this list (on card) would you like to see the Republican convention nominate for President in 1940?

Dewey.......................... 47%
Vandenberg...................... 19
Taft............................ 13
Hoover.......................... 6
Landon.......................... 4
Borah........................... 3
La Guardia...................... 2
Lodge........................... 1
Bricker......................... 1
Others.......................... 4

JULY 9

POLITICAL LABELS

Interviewing Date 6/18–23/39
Survey #161–AR   Question #3b

How do you classify each of the following (on card) political leaders — as a conservative, a liberal, or a radical?

	Conservative	Liberal	Radical
Harry Hopkins.....	4%	55%	41%
President Roosevelt.	1	62	37
Fiorello La Guardia.	8	64	28

James Farley.......	13	63	24
Thomas Dewey.....	45	47	8
Cordell Hull.......	51	46	3
John Garner.......	64	32	4
Arthur Vandenberg.	67	29	4
Robert Taft........	86	13	1
Herbert Hoover....	92	5	3

No opinion: Hopkins, 27%; Roosevelt, 2%; La Guardia, 15%; Farley, 12%; Dewey, 22%; Hull, 22%; Garner, 13%; Vandenberg, 45%; Taft, 37%; Hoover, 8%.

Interviewing Date 6/18–23/39
Survey #161–AR   Question #3a

In politics do you consider yourself a radical, a liberal, or a conservative?

Radical............................ 2%
Liberal............................ 46
Conservative....................... 52

By Political Affiliation
Democrats

Radical............................ 2%
Liberal............................ 56
Conservative....................... 42

Republicans

Radical............................ 1%
Liberal............................ 26
Conservative....................... 73

Third Party Voters

Radical............................ 5%
Liberal............................ 51
Conservative....................... 44

JULY 10

PRESIDENTIAL VISIT TO ENGLAND

Interviewing Date 6/18–23/39
Survey #161–AR   Question #1a

It has been suggested that President and Mrs. Roosevelt go to England to pay a return visit to the King and Queen. Do you favor this idea?

Yes................................ 51%
No................................. 49

Twelve per cent expressed no opinion.

By Region

	Yes	No
New England................	47%	53%
Middle Atlantic..............	54	46
East Central.................	47	53
West Central................	48	52
South.......................	62	38
West........................	46	54

JULY 12
DEMOCRATIC PRESIDENTIAL CANDIDATES

Special Survey

Asked of Iowa Democrats: If Franklin Roosevelt is not a candidate for a third term, would you prefer Henry Wallace or Harry Hopkins as the Democratic candidate for President?

Wallace........................... 54%
Hopkins........................... 46

Twenty-five per cent expressed no opinion.

By Region

	Wallace	Hopkins
Farms..................	66%	34%
Small towns (under 2,500)..	55	45
Urban areas (2,500 and over)........	42	58

JULY 14
POLITICS

Special Survey

Asked in Pennsylvania: Which party would you like to see win the presidential election in 1940?

Republican........................ 54%
Democratic........................ 46

Five per cent of all Republicans would like to see a Democrat win while 25% of all Democrats would like to see a Republican win.

Asked in Pennsylvania: If Franklin Roosevelt runs for a third term in 1940, do you think you will vote for him?

Yes................................ 46%
No................................. 54

Asked in Pennsylvania: If Franklin Roosevelt runs for a third term on the Democratic ticket against Thomas Dewey on the Republican ticket, which one would you like to see win?

Dewey............................. 55%
Roosevelt.......................... 45

Asked of Pennsylvania Democrats: If Franklin Roosevelt is not a candidate in 1940, whom would you like to see the Democratic party nominate for President?

Garner............................ 60%
Farley............................. 12
Hull............................... 9
Murphy............................ 4
Others............................ 15

Asked of Pennsylvania Republicans: Whom would you like to see nominated by the Republican party for President in 1940?

Dewey............................. 53%
Taft............................... 16
Vandenberg........................ 14
James.............................. 5
Hoover............................ 4
Landon............................ 3
Borah............................. 2
Others............................ 3

JULY 17
AUTOMOBILE DRIVERS

Interviewing Date 6/18–23/39
Survey #161–AR   Question #2a

Would you rather ride in a car driven by a man or a woman?

Man............................. 60%
Woman........................... 8
No difference.................... 32

By Sex
Men

Man............................. 72%
Woman........................... 4
No difference.................... 24

Women

Man............................. 48%
Woman........................... 12
No difference.................... 40

Interviewing Date 6/18–23/39
Survey #161–AR   Question #2b

What is a safe speed for driving on a normal stretch of good straight road outside of town and without crossroads?

Median average................. 50 mph

Interviewing Date 6/18–23/39
Survey #161–AR   Question #2e

Have you ever had an accident while you were driving?

By Sex

	Yes	No
Men	44%	56%
Women	32	68

Interviewing Date 6/18–23/39
Survey #161–AR   Question #2f

What is the fastest speed that you have ever driven an automobile?

Men............................. 75 mph
Women........................... 65 mph

JULY 17
POLITICS

Special Survey

Asked in California: Which party would you like to see win the presidential election in 1940?

Democratic....................... 60%
Republican....................... 40

Asked of California Democrats: In case Franklin Roosevelt is not a candidate for a third term, whom would you like to see the Democratic party nominate for President in 1940?

Garner........................... 51%
Farley........................... 14
Hull............................. 12
Hopkins.......................... 8
McNutt........................... 3
Others........................... 12

Fifty-two per cent expressed no opinion.

Asked in California: If President Roosevelt runs for a third term in 1940, will you vote for him?

Yes.............................. 36%
No............................... 64

JULY 19
PRESIDENT ROOSEVELT'S VOTER APPEAL

Interviewing Date 7/10–15/39
Survey #163   Question #1c

In general, do you approve or disapprove of Franklin Roosevelt as President?

Approve.......................... 57.7%
Disapprove........................ 42.3

By Region

	Approve	Disapprove
New England.........	51%	49%
Middle Atlantic........	57	43
East Central..........	55	45
West Central..........	57	43
South................	65	35
West.................	63	37

JULY 21

FAVORITE COUNTRY AND FAVORITE LEADER

Special Survey
Interviewing Date 7/1–6/39 (U.S. only)
Survey #162   Question #1

What country do you like best?

England.......................... 43%
France............................ 11
Finland.......................... 4
Switzerland....................... 4
Sweden........................... 4
Ireland........................... 3
Germany.......................... 3
Italy............................. 2
Norway........................... 2
Russia............................ 1
Others............................ 7
No opinion........................ 16

Great Britain Only

United States..................... 33%
France............................ 22
Russia............................ 12
Scandinavia....................... 3
Germany........................... 3
Switzerland....................... 2
Holland........................... 1
Belgium........................... 1
Others............................ 4
No opinion........................ 19

France Only

United States..................... 26%
England........................... 23
Switzerland....................... 15
Belgium........................... 9
Russia............................ 7
Italy............................. 4.5
Sweden............................ 2.5
Spain............................. 1.5
Others............................ 7
No opinion........................ 5.5

Special Survey
Interviewing Date 7/1–6/39 (U.S. only)
Survey #162   Question #2

What country do you like least?

Germany.......................... 58%
Italy............................. 12
Russia............................ 8
Others............................ 22

Great Britain Only

Germany.......................... 54%
Japan............................ 11
Italy............................. 9
Others............................ 26

France Only

Germany.......................... 70%
Italy............................. 9
Russia............................ 5
Others............................ 16

Special Survey
Interviewing Date 7/1–6/39 (U.S. only)
Survey #162   Question #3

Who is your favorite foreign statesman?

Chamberlain...................... 27%
Eden.............................. 13
Daladier.......................... 4
Mussolini......................... 3
Hitler............................ 2
Others............................ 11
No opinion........................ 40

France Only

Roosevelt.......................... 58%
Chamberlain....................... 22
Stalin............................. 4.5
Eden.............................. 3.5
Salazar (Portugal)................. 1.5
Others............................ 7
No opinion........................ 3.5

Special Survey
Interviewing Date 7/1–6/39 (U.S. only)
Survey #162   Question #4

Which foreign statesman do you least like?

Both American and French voters named Hitler, Mussolini, and Stalin, in that order.

JULY 23
PRESIDENTIAL TRIAL HEAT

Special Survey

Asked of Ohio Republicans: If it came to a choice between Senator Robert Taft and Governor John Bricker for Republican candidate for President in 1940, which would you favor?

Taft............................... 62%
Bricker............................ 38

Sixteen per cent expressed no opinion.

By Income

	Taft	Bricker
Upper......................	70%	30%
Middle.....................	62	38
Lower......................	50	50

By Community Size

Farms......................	59%	41%
Small towns.................	59	41
Cities.....................	63	37

JULY 23
CHINA

Interviewing Date 7/1–6/39
Survey #162–A   Question #7

How far do you think the United States Government should go to protect American interests in China — fight Japan — protest to Japan through the State Department — stop all shipments of war materials from this country to Japan — do nothing? (on card)

Fight............................. 6%
Protest........................... 18
Stop shipments.................... 51
Do nothing........................ 25

By Region
New England

Fight............................. 7%
Protest........................... 44
Stop shipments.................... 15
Do nothing........................ 34

Middle Atlantic

Fight............................. 4%
Stop shipments.................... 49
Protest........................... 20
Do nothing........................ 27

East Central

Fight............................. 5%
Stop shipments.................... 50
Protest........................... 17
Do nothing........................ 28

West Central

Fight............................. 7%
Stop shipments.................... 46
Protest........................... 18
Do nothing........................ 29

South

Fight............................. 11%
Stop shipments.................... 50
Protest........................... 18
Do nothing........................ 21

West

Fight	9%
Stop shipments	61
Protest	15
Do nothing	15

Special Survey

Asked in Great Britain: How far should Britain go at the present time to defend her interests in China?

Fight Japan if necessary	22%
Forbid all trade between Britain and Japan	37
Supply credits and munitions to China	17
Withdraw our ambassador as a protest	9
Do nothing	15

JULY 26
WORKS PROGRESS ADMINISTRATION

Interviewing Date 7/10–15/39
Survey #163–A   Question #5

The head of the W.P.A. says W.P.A. workers who go on strike will be dropped from the W.P.A. after five days on strike. Do you approve or disapprove of this action?

Approve	74%
Disapprove	26

Nine per cent expressed no opinion.

W.P.A. Workers Only

Approve	49%
Disapprove	51

By Income

	Approve	Disapprove
Upper	88%	12%
Middle	78	22
Lower	62	38

JULY 28
ALCOHOLIC BEVERAGES

Interviewing Date 6/9–14/39
Survey #160–A   Question #5a

Do you ever drink any alcoholic beverages (such as wine, beer, cocktails, high balls)?

Yes	58%
No	42

By Sex

	Yes	No
Men	70%	30%
Women	45	55

By Community Size

	Yes	No
Cities	63%	37%
Small towns	50	50
Farms	43	57

By Age

	Yes	No
21–29 Years	67%	33%
30–49 Years	62	38
50 Years and over	42	58

Interviewing Date 6/9–14/39
Survey #160–A   Question #5b

Asked of those who replied in the negative: Do you disapprove of other people drinking?

Yes	45%
No	55

By Sex

	Yes	No
Men	37%	63%
Women	49	51

By Community Size

	Yes	No
Cities	35%	65%
Small towns	55	45
Farms	60	40

By Age

	Yes	No
21–29 Years	30%	70%
30–49 Years	42	58
50 Years and over	56	44

Asked in Michigan: If the question of national prohibition should come up again, would you vote to make the country dry?

Yes............................... 31%
No................................ 69

JULY 30
PRESIDENT ROOSEVELT

Interviewing Date 7/19–24/39
Survey #164–A   Question #12a

If President Roosevelt runs for a third term in 1940, will you vote for him or will you vote against him, no matter who the Republican candidate happens to be?

For him........................... 38%
Against him....................... 40
Don't know or depends on candidate.... 22

Roosevelt Voters in 1936

For him........................... 57%
Against him....................... 19
Don't know or depends on candidate.... 24

Landon Voters in 1936

For him........................... 4%
Against him....................... 83
Don't know or depends on candidate.... 13

"Don't Know" or "Depends on Candidate"
By Income

	For Roosevelt
Upper	3%
Middle	12
Lower	7
	22%

By Age

21–29 Years	7%
30–49 Years	10
50 Years and over	5
	22%

Interviewing Date 7/19–24/39
Survey #164–A   Question #12b

Asked of those who responded "don't know" or "depends on candidate": Whom would you like to see elected President in 1940?

Dewey............................ 26%
Garner........................... 25
Vandenberg....................... 9
Hull............................. 8
McNutt........................... 5
Farley........................... 3
Others........................... 24

JULY 31
PRESIDENTIAL TENURE

Interviewing Date 7/10–15/39
Survey #163–A   Question #10b

As far as you know, has any President of the United States ever served a third term?

Yes.............................. 3%
No............................... 85
Don't know....................... 12

By Income
Upper

Yes.............................. 2%
No............................... 88
Don't know....................... 10

Middle

Yes.............................. 4%
No............................... 82
Don't know....................... 14

Lower

Yes.............................. 5%
No............................... 67
Don't know....................... 28

Interviewing Date 7/10–15/39
Survey #163–A   Question #10c

As far as you know, does the Constitution of the United States say that a President cannot serve a third term?

Yes	4%
No	78
Don't know	18

By Income
Upper

Yes	2%
No	91
Don't know	7

Middle

Yes	3%
No	88
Don't know	9

Lower

Yes	4%
No	78
Don't know	18

AUGUST 2
POLITICS

Special Survey

Asked in Illinois: Which party would you like to see win the Presidential election in 1940?

Republican	54%
Democratic	46

Asked in Illinois: If President Roosevelt runs for a third term in 1940, do you think you will vote for him?

Yes	39%
No	61

Asked of Illinois Republicans: Whom would you like to see the Republican party nominate for President in 1940?

Dewey	41%
Vandenberg	32
Taft	14
Landon	5
Borah	2
Others	6

Asked of Illinois Democrats: In case Franklin Roosevelt does not run for a third term, whom would you like to see the Democrats nominate for President in 1940?

Garner	49%
Farley	17
McNutt	8
Hull	7
Hopkins	5
Others	14

AUGUST 4
DEMOCRATIC PRESIDENTIAL CANDIDATES

Interviewing Date 7/28–8/2/39
Survey #165–A   Question #5b

Asked of Democrats: If Franklin Roosevelt is not a candidate for a third term, whom would you like to see the Democratic party nominate for President in 1940?

Garner	46%
McNutt	13
Hull	12
Farley	12
Hopkins	3
Murphy	3
Barkley	1
Clark	1
Wallace	1
Others	8

AUGUST 6
WORKS PROGRESS ADMINISTRATION

Interviewing Date 7/19–24/39
Survey #164–A   Question #2

Have you heard or read about the new relief law that requires all W.P.A. workers to work an average of 30 hours a week (130 hours a month)?

Yes	80%
No	20

Asked of those who replied in the affirmative: What do you think of this law?

W.P.A. Workers Only

Approve strongly	28%
Approve mildly	25
Disapprove strongly	31
Disapprove mildly	16

All Other Voters

Approve strongly	46%
Approve mildly	25
Disapprove strongly	16
Disapprove mildly	13

Do you think W.P.A. workers should be paid more or less than workers in private industry?

Less than workers in private industry	73%
About the same as in private industry	26
More than workers in private industry	1

AUGUST 7
POLITICS

Special Survey

Asked in Ohio: Which party would you like to see win the presidential election in 1940?

Republican	52%
Democratic	48

Asked in Ohio: If President Roosevelt runs for a third term in 1940, will you vote for him?

Yes	35%
No	65

Asked of Ohio Republicans: Whom would you like to see nominated by the Republican party for President in 1940?

Taft	33%
Dewey	29

Vandenberg	19
Bricker	12
Hoover	3
Landon	1
Others	3

Asked of Ohio Democrats: In case Franklin Roosevelt is not a candidate for a third term, whom would you like to see the Democratic party nominate for President in 1940?

Garner	57%
Farley	12
McNutt	9
Hull	8
Donahey	4
Lehman	2
Hopkins	2
Others	6

AUGUST 9
POLITICS

Special Survey

Asked in Michigan: Which party would you like to see win the presidential election in 1940?

Republican	54%
Democratic	46

Asked of Michigan Republicans: Whom would you like to see nominated by the Republican party for President in 1940?

Vandenberg	62%
Dewey	29
Taft	5
Landon	2
Hoover	1
Others	1

Asked of Michigan Democrats: In case Franklin Roosevelt is not a candidate for a third term, whom would you like to see the Democratic party nominate for President in 1940?

Garner	49%
Murphy	25
Farley	10
Hull	7
McNutt	2
Wheeler	2
Others	5

Asked in Michigan: If President Roosevelt runs for a third term in 1940, will you vote for him?

Yes	34%
No	66

Asked of Wisconsin Democrats: In case Franklin Roosevelt is not a candidate for a third term whom would you like to see the Democratic party nominate for President in 1940?

Garner	67%
Farley	8
Wallace	6
McNutt	4
Murphy	4
Others	11

Asked in Wisconsin: If President Roosevelt runs for a third term in 1940, will you vote for him?

Yes	34%
No	66

AUGUST 11
RELIEF

Interviewing Date 7/28–8/2/39
Survey #165–A   Question #2

Pennsylvania has a law requiring all able-bodied people on relief (including W.P.A.) to accept any job offered by a local government, no matter what kind of job it is. If they refuse to take the job, their relief is cut off. Do you favor this law?

Yes	81%
No	19

Reliefers Only

Yes	64%
No	36

Pennsylvania Only

Yes	84%
No	16

AUGUST 13
REPUBLICAN PRESIDENTIAL CANDIDATES

Interviewing Date 7/28–8/2/39
Survey #165–A   Question #5a

Asked of Republicans: Whom would you like to see the Republican party nominate for President in 1940?

Dewey	45%
Vandenberg	25
Taft	14
Hoover	6
Landon	3
Borah	2
Bricker	2
Others	3

Forty-one per cent expressed no opinion.

By Income
Upper

Dewey	39%
Vandenberg	31
Taft	14
Others	16

Middle

Dewey	46%
Vandenberg	23
Taft	13
Others	18

Lower

Dewey	47%
Vandenberg	24
Taft	16
Others	13

By Age
21–29 Years

Dewey	56%
Vandenberg	19
Taft	13
Others	12

30–49 Years

Dewey	47%
Vandenberg	24
Taft	12
Others	17

50 Years and Over

Dewey	38%
Vandenberg	28
Taft	16
Others	18

By Region
Urban

Dewey	44%
Vandenberg	29
Taft	12
Others	15

Small Towns

Dewey	52%
Vandenberg	17
Taft	15
Others	16

Farms

Dewey	40%
Vandenberg	22
Taft	18
Others	20

AUGUST 14
POLITICS

Special Survey

Asked in Massachusetts: Which party would you like to see win the presidential election in 1940?

Republican	55%
Democratic	45

Asked in Massachusetts: If President Roosevelt runs for a third term in 1940, will you vote for him?

Yes	36%
No	64

Asked of Massachusetts Republicans: Whom would you like to see the Republican party nominate for President in 1940?

Dewey	45%
Lodge	14
Vandenberg	14
Taft	12
Hoover	8
Landon	2
Bridges	2
Others	3

Asked of Massachusetts Democrats: If Franklin Roosevelt does not run for a third term, whom would you like to see the Democratic party nominate for President in 1940?

Garner	55%
McNutt	12
Smith	5
Farley	5
Hull	4
Murphy	4
Kennedy	3
Hopkins	3
Others	9

AUGUST 16
POLITICS

Special Survey

Asked in Wisconsin: Which party would you like to see win the presidential election in 1940?

Republican........................ 52%
Democratic........................ 48

Asked of Wisconsin Republicans: Whom would you like to see nominated by the Republican party for President in 1940?

Dewey............................ 37%
Vandenberg........................ 24
Taft.............................. 16
Hoover............................ 5
La Guardia........................ 4
Others............................ 14

AUGUST 17
POLITICS

Special Survey

Asked of Democrats between the ages of 20–29 years: Do you favor a third term for President Roosevelt?

Yes.............................. 52%
No............................... 48

Asked of Democrats 20–29: If President Roosevelt runs for a third term in 1940, will you vote for him?

Yes.............................. 62%
No............................... 38

Asked of Democrats 20–29: If Franklin Roosevelt is not a candidate for a third term, whom would you like to see the Democratic party nominate for President in 1940?

Garner........................... 41%
McNutt........................... 16
Hull............................. 15
Farley........................... 11
Hopkins.......................... 4
Murphy........................... 2
Others........................... 11

AUGUST 20
EUROPEAN WAR

Interviewing Date 7/28–8/2/39
Survey #165–B   Question #3

If England and France have a war with Germany and Italy, do you think the United States will be drawn in?

Yes.............................. 76%
No............................... 24

Twenty-five per cent expressed no opinion.

By Region

	Yes	No
New England	69%	31%
Middle Atlantic	74	26
East Central	78	22
West Central	78	22
South	75	25
West	75	25

By Political Affiliation

Democrats	76%	24%
Republicans	78	22
Others	71	29

AUGUST 21
WORLD'S FAIR

Special Survey

Asked of those who visited the World's Fair: Did you like or dislike the Fair?

Liked very much................... 83%
Liked moderately.................. 14
Disliked.......................... 3

Asked of those who visited the World's Fair: Do you want to return?

Yes............................. 84%
No.............................. 16

Asked of those who have not visited the World's Fair: Why have you not visited it?

Can't afford to go................. 63%
Can't get away.................... 16
Not interested.................... 9
Saw Chicago Fair — all fairs alike...... 3
Other reasons.................... 9

AUGUST 23
PRESIDENT ROOSEVELT'S VOTER APPEAL

Interviewing Date 8/10–15/39
Survey #166–A   Question #14c

In general, do you approve or disapprove of Franklin Roosevelt as President?

Favor........................... 56.6%
Oppose.......................... 43.4

By Region

	Favor	Oppose
New England...............	51%	49%
Middle Atlantic.............	54	46
East Central...............	51	49
West Central...............	55	45
South.....................	70	30
West.....................	64	36

Reliefers Only

Favor........................... 82%
Oppose.......................... 18

AUGUST 25
THANKSGIVING DAY

Interviewing Date 8/19–24/39
Survey #167–A   Question #1

Do you approve or disapprove of President Roosevelt's plan to change Thanksgiving Day to one week earlier?

Approve......................... 38%
Disapprove...................... 62

Twenty per cent expressed no opinion.

By Political Affiliation

	Approve	Disapprove
Democrats............	52%	48%
Republicans...........	21	79

AUGUST 27
CONGRESS

Interviewing Date 8/10–15/39
Survey.#166–A   Question #3

In general, do you think the present Congress has done a good job or a poor job?

Good job......................... 57%
Poor job......................... 43

Twenty-four per cent expressed no opinion.

By Political Affiliation

	Good	Poor
Democrats..................	52%	48%
Republicans.................	36	64

By Income

Upper.....................	60%	40%
Middle....................	61	39
Lower.....................	45	55

By Region

New England...............	62%	38%
Middle Atlantic.............	57	43
East Central...............	56	44
West Central...............	59	41
South.....................	55	45
West.....................	56	44

Interviewing Date 8/10–15/39
Survey #166–A   Question #5a

Do you think Congress was right in defeating President Roosevelt's three-billion-dollar lending bill?

Yes............................... 68%
No................................ 32

By Political Affiliation

	Yes	No
Democrats...................	51%	49%
Republicans..................	93	7

AUGUST 28
BUSINESS OUTLOOK

Interviewing Date 8/10–15/39
Survey #166–A   Question #2

Do you personally expect business conditions throughout the country to be more prosperous or less prosperous during the next six months than they are now?

More prosperous.................... 64%
Less prosperous.................... 36

Thirty-two per cent expressed no opinion.

By Region

	More	Less
New England.................	80%	20%
Middle Atlantic..............	66	34
East Central.................	61	39
West Central.................	55	45
South.......................	72	28
West........................	63	37

AUGUST 30
JAPAN

Interviewing Date 8/10–15/39
Survey #166–A   Question #4a

Do you approve or disapprove of the Government's action in cancelling the American-Japanese treaty?

Approve........................... 81%
Disapprove........................ 19

Interviewing Date 8/10–15/39
Survey #166–A   Question #4b

At the end of six months, when the treaty expires, should the United States sell Japan any more war materials?

Yes............................... 18%
No................................ 82

Approximately 12% expressed no opinion.

SEPTEMBER 1
DANZIG AND POLISH CORRIDOR

Interviewing Date 8/19–24/39
Survey #167–A   Question #3b

Do you think Hitler's claims to Danzig are justified?

Yes............................... 13%
No................................ 87

Interviewing Date 8/19–24/39
Survey #167–B   Question #5b

Do you think Hitler's claims to the Polish Corridor are justified?

Yes............................... 14%
No................................ 86

Twenty-four per cent expressed no opinion.

Interviewing Date 8/19–24/39
Survey #167–A   Question #3a

Would you like to see England, France, and Poland agree to Germany's demands regarding Danzig?

Yes............................... 12%
No................................ 88

By Region

	Yes	No
New England................	15%	85%
Middle Atlantic..............	13	87
East Central.................	17	83
West Central.................	5	95
South.......................	11	89
West........................	6	94

Interviewing Date 8/19–24/39
Survey #167–A   Question #5a

If war breaks out in Europe, do you think President Roosevelt should call a special session of Congress?

Yes...............................	71%
No................................	29

Fifteen per cent expressed no opinion.

SEPTEMBER 3
NEUTRALITY

Interviewing Date 8/19–24/39
Survey #167–A   Question #5b

Should Congress change the present Neutrality Law so that the United States could sell war materials to England and France?

Yes...............................	50%
No................................	50

Sixteen per cent expressed no opinion.

By Political Affiliation

	Yes	No
Democrats...................	56%	44%
Republicans..................	47	53

By Region

	Yes	No
New England................	49%	51%
Middle Atlantic..............	52	48
East Central.................	45	55
West Central.................	49	51
South.......................	60	40
West........................	51	49

By Sex

	Yes	No
Men.........................	53%	47%
Women......................	47	53

By age groups, persons 21–29 years old were the least in favor of changing the Neutrality Law.

SEPTEMBER 4
NATIONAL HOLIDAYS

Interviewing Date 8/19–24/39
Survey #167–A   Question #2

Would you approve or disapprove a plan to have all holidays like the Fourth of July celebrated on Mondays so as to make a longer weekend?

Approve...........................	51%
Disapprove.......................	49

By Region

	Approve	Disapprove
New England.........	58%	42%
Middle Atlantic.......	57	43
East Central..........	51	49
West Central..........	35	65
South................	41	59
West.................	46	54

SEPTEMBER 6
INTERNATIONAL POLICE FORCE

Interviewing Date 8/19–24/39
Survey #167–A   Question #4a

Do you think the time will come when there will be a strong international army or police force for maintaining world peace?

Yes...............................	30%
No................................	70

Interviewing Date 8/19–24/39
Survey #167–A   Question #4b

Asked of those who responded in the affirmative: How soon do you think this will be possible?

25 years or less...................... 60%
More than 25 years.................. 40

Interviewing Date 8/19–24/39
Survey #167–A   Question #4c

Would you like to see the United States join in a movement to establish an international police force to maintain world peace?

Yes................................. 53%
No.................................. 47

Fourteen per cent expressed no opinion.

By Political Affiliation

	Yes	No
Democrats....................	55%	45%
Republicans..................	46	54

SEPTEMBER 8
EUROPEAN WAR

Interviewing Date 9/1–6/39
Survey #168–SA   Question #7

Which country or countries do you consider responsible for causing the present war?

Germany........................ 82%
England and France............... 3
Versailles Treaty.................... 3
Poland........................... 1
All others......................... 5
No opinion........................ 6

SEPTEMBER 10
THE DRAFT

Interviewing Date 9/1–6/39
Survey #168–SA   Question #9

Should the Constitution be changed to require a national vote before Congress could draft men for war overseas?

Yes................................. 51%
No................................. 49

Eight per cent expressed no opinion.

By Sex

	Yes	No
Men........................	44%	56%
Women.....................	58	42

By Region

	Yes	No
New England.................	51%	49%
Middle Atlantic...............	50	50
East Central..................	57	43
West Central..................	56	44
South........................	37	63
West........................	47	53

By Political Affiliation

	Yes	No
Democrats....................	47%	53%
Republicans..................	52	48

SEPTEMBER 11
JULIUS HEIL

Special Survey

Asked in Wisconsin: In general do you approve or disapprove of Julius Heil as Governor?

Approve........................... 42%
Disapprove........................ 58

SEPTEMBER 13
DEMOCRATIC PRESIDENTIAL CANDIDATES

Interviewing Date 8/19–24/39
Survey #167–A   Question #9b

Asked of Democrats: If Franklin Roosevelt is not a candidate, whom would you like to see nominated by the Democratic party for President in 1940?

Garner.......................... 45%
McNutt......................... 21
Farley.......................... 10
Hull............................ 10
Murphy......................... 2
Clark........................... 1
Hopkins........................ 1
Barkley........................ 1
Others......................... 9

SEPTEMBER 15
NEUTRALITY

Interviewing Date 9/1–6/39
Survey #168–SA   Question #5

Should the United States allow its citizens to travel on ships of countries which are now at war?

Yes............................. 18%
No.............................. 82

Four per cent expressed no opinion.

By Region

	Yes	No
New England...............	16%	84%
Middle Atlantic..............	19	81
East Central.................	14	86
West Central................	18	82
South......................	16	84
West.......................	22	78

By Political Affiliation

Democrats...................	17%	83%
Republicans.................	19	81

Interviewing Date 9/1–6/39
Survey #168–SA   Question #6

Should the United States allow American ships to carry goods anywhere, or should our ships be kept out of war zones?

Anywhere....................... 16%
Keep out of war zones.............. 84

Six per cent expressed no opinion.

By Region

	Any- where	Keep out of War zones
New England............	17%	83%
Middle Atlantic..........	17	83
East Central.............	16	84
West Central........	16	84
South..................	19	81
West...................	17	83

By Political Affiliation

Democrats..............	15%	85%
Republicans.............	17	83

SEPTEMBER 18
MINNESOTA POLITICS

Special Survey

Asked in Minnesota: In general, do you approve or disapprove of Harold Stassen as Governor?

Approve.......................... 81%
Disapprove....................... 19

Asked in Minnesota: What party would you like to see win the presidential election in 1940?

Republican....................... 50%
Democratic....................... 50

SEPTEMBER 18
EUROPEAN WAR

Interviewing Date 8/30–9/5/39
Survey #167–S   Question #2a

Should we send our army and navy abroad to fight Germany?

Yes............................. 16%
No.............................. 84

Six per cent expressed no opinion.

By Income

	Yes	No
Upper	12%	88%
Middle	15	85
Lower (including reliefers)	20	80
Reliefers only	21	79

By Sex

	Yes	No
Men	19%	81%
Women	12	88

By Political Affiliation

	Yes	No
Democrats	18%	82%
Republicans	13	87

Interviewing Date 8/30–9/5/39
Survey #167–S   Question #3

If it looks within the next few months as if England and France might be defeated, should the United States declare war on Germany and send our troops abroad?

Yes................................ 44%
No................................ 56

Ten per cent expressed no opinion.

By Political Affiliation

	Yes	No
Democrats	46%	54%
Republicans	42	58

Interviewing Date 9/1–6/39
Survey #168–SA   Question #1b

Which side do you think will win the war?

Allies............................. 82%
Germany........................... 7
Qualified, no opinion.............. 11

Interviewing Date 8/30–9/5/39
Survey #168–SA   Question #1a

About how long do you think the present war will last?

One year or less................... 49%
More than one year................. 51

SEPTEMBER 22
PRESIDENT ROOSEVELT'S VOTER APPEAL

Interviewing Date 9/13–18/39
Survey #169–B   Question #14c

In general, do you approve or disapprove of Franklin Roosevelt as President?

Approve............................ 61%
Disapprove......................... 39

By Region

	Approve	Disapprove
New England	53%	47%
Middle Atlantic	58	42
East Central	59	41
West Central	60	40
South	72	28
West	65	35

Interviewing Date 9/13–18/39
Survey #169–B   Question #14d

How strongly do you feel about this?

Approve strongly................... 33%
Approve mildly..................... 28
                                    —
                                    61%

Disapprove strongly................ 24%
Disapprove mildly.................. 15
                                    —
                                    39%

SEPTEMBER 24
NEUTRALITY

Interviewing Date 9/13–18/39
Survey #169–A   Question #1

Do you think the Neutrality Law should be changed so that England and France could buy war supplies here?

Yes................................ 57%
No................................ 43

Nine per cent expressed no opinion.

By Political Affiliation

	Yes	No
Democrats	62%	38%
Republicans	54	46

Interviewing Date 9/13–18/39
Survey #169–A　　　　　　　　Question #2a

If the Neutrality Act is changed should England and France be required to pay cash for goods or should we give them credit if they cannot pay?

Cash	90%
Credit	10

Three per cent expressed no opinion.

Interviewing Date 9/13–18/39
Survey #169–A　　　　　　　　Question #2b

Should England and France be required to carry the goods away in their own ships?

Yes	94%
No	6

Four per cent expressed no opinion.

SEPTEMBER 25
SOUTHERN POLITICS

Special Survey

Asked in the South: Do you think the South would be better off if there were two political parties in the South of about equal strength, instead of only one strong party as at present?

Yes	57%
No	43

By Political Affiliation

	Yes	No
Democrats	45%	55%
Republicans	99	1

SEPTEMBER 27
FOREIGN NEWS REPORTS

Interviewing Date 9/13–18/39
Survey #169–A　　　　　　　　Question #7

The British say that the trans-Atlantic liner Athenia *was sunk by a German submarine. The Germans say they did not sink it. Do you believe the Germans sank the* Athenia?

Germans sank it	60%
Germans did not	40

Interviewing Date 9/13–18/39
Survey #169–A　　　　　　　　Question #8b

Do you have confidence in the news from Germany at the present time?

Yes, complete confidence	1%
Yes, some confidence	33
No confidence	66

Interviewing Date 9/13–18/39
Survey #169–A　　　　　　　　Question #8a

Do you have confidence in the news from England and France at the present time?

Yes, complete confidence	8%
Yes, some confidence	62
No confidence	30

Approximately 5% expressed no opinion on these questions.

SEPTEMBER 29
WAR WITH GERMANY

Interviewing Date 9/13–18/39
Survey #169–A　　　　　　　　Question #4

If Germany should defeat England, France, and Poland in the present war, do you think Germany would start a war against the United States sooner or later?

Yes.............................. 63%
No............................... 37

Seven per cent expressed no opinion.

OCTOBER 1
PRESIDENT ROOSEVELT

Interviewing Date 9/21–26/39
Survey #170–A   Question #9a

If President Roosevelt runs for a third term, will you vote for him?

Yes.............................. 43%
No............................... 57

By Political Affiliation

	Yes	No
Democrats....................	66%	34%
Republicans..................	3	97

Interviewing Date 9/21–26/39
Survey #170–A   Question #10

If the war is still going on next year, and if President Roosevelt runs for a third term, would you vote for him?

Yes.............................. 52%
No............................... 48

By Political Affiliation

	Yes	No
Democrats....................	76%	24%
Republicans..................	10	90

OCTOBER 2
MILITARY TRAINING

Interviewing Date 9/13–18/39
Survey #169–A   Question #9a

Should the Civilian Conservation Corps camps be permitted to give military training to the young men who request it?

Yes.............................. 90%
No............................... 10

Four per cent expressed no opinion.

OCTOBER 4
NEUTRALITY

Interviewing Date 9/21–26/39
Survey #170–A   Question #3a

Do you think Congress should change the Neutrality Law so that England and France could buy war supplies here?

Yes.............................. 62%
No............................... 38

Strongly in favor................... 41%
Mildly in favor.................... 21
Strongly opposed................... 25
Mildly opposed.................... 13

Eleven per cent expressed no opinion.

By Region

	Yes	No
New England...............	56%	44%
Middle Atlantic..............	65	35
East Central..................	57	43
West Central.................	55	45
South......................	77	23
West.......................	65	35

By Sex

	Yes	No
Men......................	64%	36%
Women....................	58	42

By Income

	Yes	No
Upper.......................	59%	41%
Middle......................	64	36
Lower......................	62	38

By Age

	Yes	No
21–29 Years................	56%	44%
30–49 Years................	64	36
50 Years and over............	63	37

OCTOBER 6
WAR WITH GERMANY

Interviewing Date 9/24–29/39
Survey #171–A   Question #6a

What should be the policy in the present European war? Should we declare war and send our army and navy abroad to fight Germany?

Yes............................... 5%
No................................ 95

By Nationality

Persons whose fathers were born in:

	Yes	No
United States.................	5%	95%
Russia.......................	3	97
Italy.........................	4	96
Germany.....................	3	97
Ireland......................	4	96
Canada......................	7	93
Austria......................	7	93
England......................	8	92
Poland.......................	11	89
Others.......................	4	96

OCTOBER 8
DEFENSE OF WESTERN HEMISPHERE

Interviewing Date 9/24–29/39
Survey #171–A   Question #2

If Canada is actually invaded by any European power, do you think the United States should use its army and navy to aid Canada?

Yes............................... 73%
No................................ 27

Seven per cent expressed no opinion.

Interviewing Date 9/24–29/39
Survey #171–A   Question #3

If Cuba or any other country within 1,500 miles of the Panama Canal is actually in-vaded by any European power, do you think the United States should fight to keep the European country out?

Yes............................... 72%
No................................ 28

Eleven per cent expressed no opinion.

Interviewing Date 9/24–29/39
Survey #171–A   Question #4

If Brazil, Chile, or any other South American country is actually invaded by any European power, do you think the United States should fight to keep that European country out?

Yes............................... 53%
No................................ 47

Thirteen per cent expressed no opinion.

OCTOBER 9
UNIVERSAL MILITARY TRAINING

Interviewing Date 9/21–26/39
Survey #170–A   Question #1a

Do you think every able-bodied young man 20 years old should be made to serve in the army or the navy for one year?

Yes............................... 39%
No................................ 61

Five per cent expressed no opinion.

OCTOBER 11
NEUTRALITY

Interviewing Date 10/5–10/39
Survey #172–A   Question #1a

Do you think Congress should change the Neutrality Law so that England and France or any other nations can buy war supplies here?

Yes................................ 60%

No................................. 40

Among those voters who want to see the arms embargo lifted, the chief reason is economic — that such a step might help American business and reduce unemployment. The second reason is one of sympathy for England and France. Those voters who think the Neutrality Act should remain unchanged and the arms embargo kept in force argue principally that to lift the embargo would lead the United States into war.

OCTOBER 13
REPUBLICAN PRESIDENTIAL CANDIDATES

Interviewing Date 10/5–10/39
Survey #172–A   Question #8a

Asked of Republicans: Whom would you like to see nominated by the Republican party for President in 1940?

Dewey............................ 39%

Vandenberg....................... 27

Taft............................. 17

Hoover............................ 5

Landon............................ 4

Borah............................. 3

Lindbergh......................... 1

Bricker........................... 1

Others............................ 3

Fourteen per cent expressed no opinion.

OCTOBER 16
NEUTRALITY

Interviewing Date 9/13–18/39
Survey #169–A   Question #1b, 2a

In what country was your father born? Do you think Congress should change the Neutrality Law so that England, France, or any other nation can buy war supplies here?

By Nationality

Persons whose fathers were born in:

	Yes	No
United States...............	60%	40%
Great Britain.................	68	32
Russia.......................	67	33
Ireland......................	61	39
Canada.......................	60	40
Italy........................	55	35
Germany.....................	45	55
Others.......................	58	42

OCTOBER 16
PARTY STRENGTH

Interviewing Date 9/24–29/39
Survey #171–A   Question #10b

Which party do you think will win the presidential election in 1940?

Democratic........................ 65%

Republican........................ 35

Twenty-seven per cent expressed no opinion.

By Region

	Democratic	Republican
New England........	59%	41%
Middle Atlantic......	63	37
East Central........	61	39
West Central........	58	42
South..............	81	19
West...............	73	27

Interviewing Date 9/24–29/39
Survey #171–A   Question #10a

Which party would you like to see win the presidential election in 1940?

Democratic........................ 57%

Republican........................ 43

Twenty-four per cent expressed no opinion.

OCTOBER 18
EUROPEAN WAR

Interviewing Date 10/5–10/39
Survey #173–A   Question #4a

Hitler says that the Polish question is settled and England and France have no reason to continue the war with Germany. Do you agree?

Yes............................... 14%
No................................ 86

Thirteen per cent expressed no opinion.

OCTOBER 20
EUROPEAN WAR

Interviewing Date 10/5–10/39
Survey #172   Question #5

If it appears that Germany is defeating England and France, should the United States declare war on Germany and send our army and navy to Europe to fight?

Yes............................... 29%
No................................ 71

OCTOBER 23
EUROPEAN WAR

Interviewing Date 10/5–10/39
Survey #172–A   Question #3

Which side do you want to see win the war?

Allies............................. 84%
Germany.......................... 2
No opinion, neutral................ 14

Interviewing Date 10/5–10/39
Survey #172–A   Question #5

What should be the policy of the United States in the present European war — Should we declare war on Germany and

send our army and navy abroad to fight or should we not send our armed forces overseas?

Should fight....................... 5%
Should not fight................... 95

Interviewing Date 10/5–10/39
Survey #172–A   Question #4a

Do you think the United States should do everything possible to help England and France win the war, except go to war ourselves?

Yes............................... 62%
No................................ 38

Interviewing Date 10/5–10/39
Survey #172–B   Question #1

Do you think Congress should make changes in the Neutrality Law so that England and France or any other nation can buy war supplies, including arms and airplanes, in the United States?

Yes............................... 60%
No................................ 40

By Region

	Yes	No
New England	56%	44%
Middle Atlantic	59	41
East Central	57	43
West Central	60	40
South	75	25
West	68	42

Interviewing Date 10/5–10/39
Survey #172–A   Question #4b

Do you think the United States should do everything possible to help England and France win the war, even at the risk of getting into the war ourselves?

Yes............................... 34%
No................................ 66

OCTOBER 25
EUROPEAN WAR

Interviewing Date 10/12–17/39
Survey #173–A   Question #1

Do you think the United States will go into the war in Europe, or do you think we will stay out of the war?

Will go in......................... 46%
Will stay out...................... 54

Thirteen per cent expressed no opinion.

By Region

	Will Go In	*Will Stay Out*
New England............	50%	50%
Middle Atlantic..........	41	59
East Central.............	45	55
West Central.............	49	51
South...................	50	50
West....................	51	49

OCTOBER 26
PRESIDENT ROOSEVELT'S VOTER APPEAL

Interviewing Date 10/5–10/39
Survey #172–A   Question #9c

In general, do you approve or disapprove of Franklin Roosevelt as President?

Approve........................... 64.9%
Disapprove........................ 35.1

By Region

	Approve	*Disapprove*
New England..........	59%	41%
Middle Atlantic........	65	35
East Central..........	61	39
West Central..........	63	37
South................	76	24
West.................	67	33

By Income

Upper...............	46%	54%
Middle...............	62	38
Lower................	78	22

OCTOBER 29
NEUTRALITY

Special Survey

Do you think Congress should make changes in the Neutrality Law so that England and France or any other nation can buy war materials, including arms and airplanes, in the United States?

Yes............................... 58%
No................................ 42

OCTOBER 30
INTERNATIONAL CONFERENCE

Interviewing Date 10/12–17/39
Survey #173–A   Question #5a

Would you favor a conference of the leading nations of the world to try to end the present war and settle Europe's problems?

Yes............................... 69%
No................................ 31

Interviewing Date 10/12–17/39
Survey #173–A   Question #5b

If such a conference is called, should the United States take part in it?

Yes............................... 50%
No................................ 50

By Political Affiliation

	Yes	*No*
Democrats...................	52%	48%
Republicans.................	45	55
Others......................	54	46

NOVEMBER 1
DIES COMMITTEE

Interviewing Date 10/20–25/39
Survey #174–A   Question #13

Do you think Congress should provide money to continue the Dies Committee for another year?

Yes.............................. 53%
No.............................. 14
No opinion........................ 33

By Political Affiliation
Democrats

Yes.............................. 52%
No.............................. 16
No opinion........................ 32

Republicans

Yes.............................. 63%
No.............................. 11
No opinion........................ 26

NOVEMBER 3
NEUTRALITY

Interviewing Date 10/26–31/39
Survey #175–A   Question #1a

Do you think Congress should make changes in the Neutrality Law so that England and France, or any other nations, can buy war materials, including arms and airplanes, in the United States?

Yes.............................. 56%
No.............................. 44

Interviewing Date 10/26–31/39
Survey #175–B   Question #1a

Do you think Congress should repeal the existing arms embargo in the Neutrality Law so that nations at war can buy airplanes, arms, and munitions in the United States?

Yes.............................. 56%
No.............................. 44

Special Survey

Asked of persons listed in Who's Who in America: *Do you think Congress should make changes in the Neutrality Law so that England and France, or any other nations can buy war materials, including arms and airplanes, in the United States?*

Yes.............................. 78%
No.............................. 22

NOVEMBER 5
PRESIDENT ROOSEVELT

Interviewing Date 10/20–25/39
Survey #174–A   Question #9a

Do you think President Roosevelt will run for a third term?

Yes.............................. 57%
No.............................. 43

By Political Affiliation

	Yes	No
Democrats..................	72%	28%
Republicans.................	31	69

Interviewing Date 10/20–25/39
Survey #176–A   Question #9b

Do you think President Roosevelt will be elected if he runs?

Yes.............................. 56%
No.............................. 44

NOVEMBER 6
DEMOCRATIC PRESIDENTIAL CANDIDATES

Interviewing Date 10/26–31/39
Survey #175–A   Question #8a

Asked of Democrats: Whom would you like to see elected President in 1940?

Roosevelt........................ 83%
Garner........................... 8
McNutt.......................... 3
Hull.............................. 3
Farley............................ 1
Others........................... 2

Taft.............................. 18
Hoover........................... 5
Landon........................... 3
Borah............................ 3
Lindbergh........................ 1
Lodge............................ 1
Others........................... 4

Interviewing Date 10/26–31/39
Survey #175–A   Question #8b

Asked of Democrats: If President Roosevelt is not a candidate, whom would you like to see elected?

Garner........................... 45%
McNutt.......................... 18
Hull.............................. 13
Farley............................ 8
Murphy.......................... 3
Smith............................ 2
Barkley.......................... 1
Ickes............................. 1
Clark............................. 1
Others........................... 8

Interviewing Date 10/26–31/39
Survey #175–A   Question #8b

Asked of Republicans: If it came to a choice among Robert Taft, Thomas Dewey, and Arthur Vandenberg for President, which one would you prefer?

Dewey............................ 44%
Vandenberg....................... 31
Taft.............................. 25

NOVEMBER 8
WORLD WAR I

Interviewing Date 10/20–25/39
Survey #174–A   Question #3a

Do you think it was a mistake for the United States to enter the World War?

Yes.............................. 68%
No............................... 32

NOVEMBER 10
REPUBLICAN PRESIDENTIAL CANDIDATES

Interviewing Date 10/26–31/39
Survey #175–A   Question #8a

Asked of Republicans: Whom would you like to see elected President in 1940?

Dewey............................ 39%
Vandenberg....................... 26

NOVEMBER 12
ARMED FORCES

Interviewing Date 9/24–29/39
Survey #171–A   Question #1a

Do you think the United States should increase the size of the army?

Yes.............................. 86%
No............................... 14

Interviewing Date 9/24–29/39
Survey #171–A   Question #2a

Asked of those who replied in the affirmative: Would you be willing to pay more money in taxes to support a larger army?

Yes.............................. 64%
No............................... 36

Interviewing Date 9/24–29/39
Survey #171–A   Question #1b

Do you think the United States should increase the size of the navy?

Yes.............................. 88%
No............................... 12

Asked of those who replied in the affirmative: Would you be willing to pay more money in taxes to support a larger navy?

Yes............................... 67%
No................................ 33

Do you think the United States should increase the size of the air force?

Yes............................... 91%
No................................ 9

Asked of those who replied in the affirmative: Would you be willing to pay more money in taxes to support a larger air force?

Yes............................... 70%
No................................ 30

NOVEMBER 13
WAR DEBT

Would you be willing to have the United States trade the war debts which Great Britain owes us for some islands in the West Indies near the Panama Canal?

Yes............................... 66%
No................................ 34

NOVEMBER 15
ADOLF HITLER

Do you think the people of Germany are in favor of Hitler?

Yes............................... 34%
No................................ 66

By Income

	Yes	No
Upper	43%	57%
Middle	34	66
Lower	30	70

NOVEMBER 16
PENNSYLVANIA POLITICS

Special Survey

Asked in Pennsylvania: Do you approve or disapprove of Arthur James as governor?

Approve........................... 55%
Disapprove........................ 45

By Community Size

	Approve	Disapporve
Rural	65%	35%
Small towns	55	45

Asked in Pennsylvania: What party would you like to see win the presidential election in 1940?

Republican........................ 52%
Democratic........................ 48

NOVEMBER 19
PARTY STRENGTH

Which party would you like to see win the presidential election in 1940?

Democratic........................ 54%
Republican........................ 46

Twenty per cent expressed no opinion.

By Region

	Democratic	Republican
New England........	44%	56%
Middle Atlantic......	51	49
East Central........	50	50
West Central........	51	49
South..............	77	23
West...............	59	41

NOVEMBER 19
POLITICS

Special Survey

Asked of a cross section of Democrats listed in Who's Who in America: *Whom would you like to see elected President in 1940?*

Roosevelt...........................	60%
Hull...............................	15
Garner............................	12
Murphy...........................	3
Wallace...........................	2
Others............................	8

Asked of a cross section of Democrats listed in Who's Who in America: *If Franklin Roosevelt is not a candidate, whom would you like to see elected President in 1940?*

Hull...............................	38%
Garner............................	21
Wallace...........................	6
Murphy...........................	5
McNutt............................	5
William Douglas....................	4
Others............................	21

Asked of a cross section of Republicans listed in Who's Who in America: *Whom would you like to see elected President in 1940?*

Vandenberg........................	26%
Taft...............................	24
Hoover............................	20
Dewey............................	19
Borah.............................	2
Others............................	9

NOVEMBER 22
PRESIDENT ROOSEVELT'S VOTER APPEAL

Interviewing Date 10/26–31/39
Survey #175–A   Question #9c

In general, do you approve or disapprove of Franklin Roosevelt as President?

Approve..........................	62.7%
Disapprove.......................	37.3

By Income

	Approve	Disapprove
Upper.................	43%	57%
Middle...............	60	40
Lower...............	76	24

NOVEMBER 24
RELIEFERS

Special Survey

The Government has tried out a food stamp plan which lets people on relief buy certain surplus farm products below their regular selling price. The Government makes up the difference to the merchant. Do you approve or disapprove of this plan?

Approve..........................	70%
Disapprove.......................	30

Twelve per cent expressed no opinion.

By Political Affiliation

	Approve	Disapprove
Democrats.............	80%	20%
Republicans...........	60	40

Would you approve of extending the food stamp plan to families earning less than $20 a week as well as to persons on relief?

Yes............................... 57%
No................................ 43

NOVEMBER 26
GOVERNMENT PENSIONS

Interviewing Date 11/10–15/39
Survey #176–A   Question #2a

Do you believe in Government old-age pensions?

Yes............................... 90%
No................................ 10

Interviewing Date 11/10–15/39
Survey #176–A   Question #2b

Asked of those who replied in the affirmative: Do you think pensions should be given to old people who are in need, or to all old people?

Needy only........................ 77%
All old people.................... 23

NOVEMBER 26
PRESIDENT ROOSEVELT

Special Survey

Asked of persons listed in Who's Who in America: Do you think President Roosevelt will run for a third term in 1940?

Will run.......................... 54%
Will not run...................... 46

Asked of persons listed in Who's Who in America: Do you think President Roosevelt will be elected if he does run?

Will be elected................... 45%
Will not be elected............... 55

NOVEMBER 29
THE COMMUNIST PARTY

Interviewing Date 11/10–15/39
Survey #176–A   Question #6

Which of these statements (on card) best describes your opinion about the Communist party in the United States?

The Communist party in this country takes orders directly from Russia..... 25%
The policies of the Communist party in the United States are decided on by Communists in this country in consultation with Russia................. 27
The policies of the American Communist party are decided entirely by Communists in the United States........ 9
Know nothing about the Communist party........................... 39

DECEMBER 1
BUSINESS PROSPERITY

Interviewing Date 11/10–15/39
Survey #176–B   Question #14

Do you think business would be more prosperous or less prosperous, if we had a Republican President in the White House?

By Political Affiliation
Democrats

More prosperous................... 10%
Less prosperous................... 50
No difference..................... 40

Republicans

More prosperous................... 79%
Less prosperous................... 2
No difference..................... 19

DECEMBER 3
WORLD WAR I

Interviewing Date 10/20–25/39
Survey #174–A   Question #3b

Why do you think we entered the last war?

America was the victim of propaganda
and selfish interests................ 34%
America had a just cause............ 26
America entered for its safety........ 18
Other reasons..................... 8
No opinion....................... 14

21–29 Years.............	57%	43%
30–49 Years.............	52	48
50 Years and over........	48	52

By Income

Upper..................	33%	67%
Middle.................	49	51
Lower..................	66	34
Reliefers...............	73	27

DECEMBER 4
MOST IMPORTANT PROBLEM

Interviewing Date 11/10–15/39
Survey #176–A   Question #1

What do you think is the most important problem before the American people today?

Keeping out of war................. 47%
Solving unemployment.............. 24
Recovery for business.............. 6
Adjustment of labor problems........ 3
Threats to democratic institutions...... 3
Adequate relief.................... 3
Balancing the budget............... 2
Farm aid......................... 1
Old-age pensions.................. 1
Spiritual needs.................... 1
Others........................... 9

DECEMBER 6
PRESIDENTIAL TRIAL HEAT

Interviewing Date 12/1–5/39
Survey #178–A   Question #5

If Thomas Dewey runs for President on the Republican ticket against Franklin Roosevelt running for a third term on the Democratic ticket, which would you prefer?

Roosevelt......................... 54%
Dewey........................... 46

By Political Affiliation

	Roosevelt	Dewey
Democrats..............	88%	12%
Republicans.............	8	92

DECEMBER 8
WAR WITH GERMANY

Interviewing Date 10/26–31/39
Survey #175–B   Question #2

Should the United States declare war on Germany and send her army and navy abroad to fight?

Yes.............................. 4%
No.............................. 96

DECEMBER 9
EUROPEAN WAR

Interviewing Date 11/17–22/39
Survey #177–B   Question #9

If England and France defeat Germany, should the peace treaty be more severe on Germany or less severe than the treaty at the end of the last war?

More severe....................... 58%
Less severe....................... 36
About the same.................... 6

Seventeen per cent expressed no opinion.

DECEMBER 10
LABOR UNIONS

Interviewing Date 11/17–22/39
Survey #177–A   Question #5a

Are you in favor of labor unions?

Yes................................ 74%
No................................ 26

Interviewing Date 11/17–22/39
Survey #177–A   Question #5b

Do you think labor unions should be regulated to a greater extent by the Federal Government?

Yes................................ 79%
No................................ 21

By Region

	Yes	No
Urban centers	78%	22%
Small towns	77	23
Farms	84	16

Interviewing Date 11/17–22/39
Survey #177–B   Question #8a

Do you think it would be a good thing for business if the A.F.L. and the C.I.O. got together?

Yes................................ 93%
No................................ 7

Union Members Only

Yes................................ 94%
No................................ 6

Interviewing Date 11/17–22/39
Survey #177–B   Question #8b

Do you think it would be a good thing for labor if the A.F.L. and the C.I.O. got together?

Yes................................ 95%
No................................ 5

Union Members Only

Yes................................ 93%
No................................ 7

DECEMBER 13
PARTY BEST ABLE TO MAINTAIN PEACE

Interviewing Date 12/2–7/39
Survey #178–A   Question #7

Which political party do you think is more likely to keep us out of war — the Republican or the Democratic?

Republican........................ 21%
Democratic........................ 27
No difference..................... 52

By Political Affiliation
Republicans

Republican........................ 42%
Democratic........................ 3
No difference..................... 55

Democrats

Republican........................ 5%
Democratic........................ 48
No difference..................... 47

DECEMBER 13
BRITISH CONDUCT OF THE WAR

Special Survey

Asked in Great Britain by the Gallup affiliate: Are you satisfied or dissatisfied with the Government's conduct of the war?

Satisfied.......................... 61%
Dissatisfied....................... 18
War should be stopped, no opinion..... 21

By Political Affiliation

	Government Voters	Opposition Voters
Satisfied	74%	46%
Dissatisfied	10	31
War should be stopped, no opinion	16	23

DECEMBER 15
DIES COMMITTEE

Interviewing Date 12/2–7/39
Survey #178–A   Question #4a

Do you think Congress should provide money to continue the Dies Committee another year?

Should............................ 75%
Should not........................ 25

Interviewing Date 12/2–7/39
Survey #178–A   Question #4b

What is your opinion regarding the Dies Committee?

Congress should appoint some other
committee to do the work.......... 12%
Congress should provide money so the
Dies Committee can continue for another year....................... 75
The investigations should be discon-
tinued........................... 13

DECEMBER 17
FREIGHT TRUCKS

Special Survey

Do you think freight trucks should be kept off highways during certain hours on Sundays and holidays?

Yes............................... 67%
No................................ 33

	By Age	Yes	No
21–29 Years.................		66%	34%
30–49 Years.................		65	35
50 Years and over..........		72	28

DECEMBER 18
LOUISIANA POLITICS

Special Survey

Asked of Louisiana voters: Do you think elections in Louisiana in recent years have been honestly conducted?

Yes............................... 25%
No................................ 60
No opinion........................ 15

Do you think that if the present state administration is returned to office next year it will clean house in the state government?

Yes............................... 30%
No................................ 51
No opinion........................ 19

Do you think that the state courts are honest?

Yes............................... 27%
No................................ 45
No opinion........................ 28

During this Louisiana survey, 20% indicated that they were afraid to talk for fear of political reprisals or for other reasons, even though voters were given every assurance as to the confidential nature of the interview.

DECEMBER 20
HUEY LONG

Special Survey

Asked in Louisiana: Taking everything into consideration, do you think that Huey P. Long was a bad or a good influence in Louisiana?

Good influence.................... 60%
Bad influence..................... 24
Both good and bad................. 16

Nine per cent expressed no opinion.

DECEMBER 22
LOUISIANA POLITICS

Special Survey

Asked in Louisiana: For which candidate do you intend to vote for Governor next month?

Earl Long.......................... 34%
Sam Jones......................... 34
Jimmy Noe........................ 20
James Morrison.................... 10
Vincent Moseley................... 2

DECEMBER 24
TAXES FOR DEFENSE

Interviewing Date 12/2–7/39
Survey #178–A   Question #2

If Congress decides to increase the army and navy, should this increase be paid for by extra taxes next year or by borrowing more money?

Extra taxes......................... 58%
More borrowing.................... 42

Twenty-five per cent expressed no opinion. The number of persons undecided was considerably higher (31%) in the lower income group than among higher income voters (19%).

By Political Affiliation

	Taxes	Borrowing
Democrats..............	55%	45%
Republicans.............	61	39

By Income

Upper...................	66%	34%
Middle.................	60	40
Lower (including reliefers).	48	52
Reliefers only............	44	56

DECEMBER 24
GERMAN MUSIC AND LANGUAGE

Special Survey

Do you think orchestras and bands in this country should stop playing German music?

Yes............................... 9%
No............................... 91

Six per cent expressed no opinion.

By Age

	Yes	No
21–29 Years.................	4%	96%
30–49 Years.................	8	92
50 Years and over............	13	87

Do you think American colleges and high schools should stop teaching the German language?

Yes............................... 12%
No............................... 88

Six per cent expressed no opinion.

By Age

	Yes	No
21–29 Years.................	6%	94%
30–49 Years.................	11	89
50 Years and over............	18	82

DECEMBER 27
PRESIDENT ROOSEVELT'S VOTER APPEAL

Interviewing Date 12/2–7/39
Survey #178–A   Question #14c

In general, do you approve or disapprove today of Franklin Roosevelt as President?

Approve........................... 63.5%
Disapprove........................ 36.5

By Income

	Approve	Disapprove
Upper.................	42%	58%
Middle..............	61	39
Lower................	76	24

DECEMBER 29
NEVILLE CHAMBERLAIN

Special Survey

Asked in Great Britain: In general do you approve or disapprove of Mr. Chamberlain as Prime Minister?

Approve........................... 71%
Disapprove........................ 29

Asked in Great Britain: Are you satisfied or dissatisfied with the Government's conduct of the war?

Satisfied........................... 61%
Dissatisfied........................ 18
"Just stop the war"................. 11
No opinion......................... 10

DECEMBER 31
MOST INTERESTING NEWS EVENTS

Interviewing Date 12/2–7/39
Survey #178   Question #10

Which two of these news events of 1939 interested you most? (on card)

The following are listed according to frequency of mention:

England and France declare war on Germany.
Special session of Congress lifts arms embargo.
Attempt on Hitler's life in Munich bombing.
Scuttling of the *Graf Spee*.
German "blitzkrieg" in Poland.
Visit of the King and Queen of England.
Russia's invasion of Finland.
Germany seizes Bohemia and Moravia.
Roosevelt's Thanksgiving proclamation.
Russo-German treaty of friendship.

By Sex
Men
England and France declare war on Germany.
Special session of Congress lifts arms embargo.

Attempt on Hitler's life in Munich bombing.
German "blitzkrieg" in Poland.
Russia's invasion of Finland.
Scuttling of the *Graf Spee*.
Germany seizes Bohemia and Moravia.
Russo-German treaty of friendship.
Dies Committee hearings.
Yankees win fourth straight World's Series.

Women
England and France declare war on Germany.
Special session of Congress lifts arms embargo.
Scuttling of the *Graf Spee*.
Visit of the King and Queen of England.
Attempt on Hitler's life in Munich bombing.
German "blitzkrieg" in Poland.
Russia's invasion of Finland.
Roosevelt's Thanksgiving proclamation.
Germany seizes Bohemia and Moravia.
Sinking of submarines *Squalus* and *Phoenix*.

DECEMBER 31
RUSSO-FINNISH WAR

Interviewing Date 12/14–19/39
Survey #179   Question #4a

In the present crisis, are your sympathies with Finland or Russia?

Finland............................ 88%
Russia............................. 1
Neutral, no opinion................ 11

1940

JANUARY 3
DEMOCRATIC PRESIDENTIAL CANDIDATES

Interviewing Date 12/24–29/39
Survey #180–A   Question #11a

Asked of Democrats: Whom would you like to see nominated by the Democratic party for President in 1940?

Roosevelt......................... 78%
Garner............................ 13
McNutt............................ 4
Hull.............................. 2
Murphy............................ 1
Farley............................ 1
Others............................ 1

Twenty-five per cent expressed no opinion.

Interviewing Date 12/24–29/39
Survey #180–A   Question #11b

Asked of Democrats: If Franklin Roosevelt is not a candidate, whom would you like to see nominated?

Garner............................ 58%
McNutt............................ 17
Hull.............................. 8
Farley............................ 5
Others............................ 12

Fifty-two per cent expressed no opinion.

JANUARY 5
DIES COMMITTEE

Interviewing Date 12/24–29/39
Survey #180–A   Question #3a

Have you heard or read about the Dies Committee?

Yes............................... 74%
No................................ 26

Interviewing Date 12/24–29/39
Survey #180–A   Question #3b

Asked of those who responded in the affirmative: Which of the following do you consider more important for the Dies Committee to investigate — Communist activities in this country, or Nazi activities in this country?

Communist activities.............. 70%
Nazi activities................... 30

Twenty-five per cent expressed no opinion.

JANUARY 7
REPUBLICAN PRESIDENTIAL CANDIDATES

Interviewing Date 11/17–22/39
Survey #177–A   Question #9c

Asked of Republicans: Whom would you like to see the Republican party nominate for President this year?

Dewey............................. 60%
Vandenberg........................ 16
Taft.............................. 11
Hoover............................ 5
James............................. 1
Lodge............................. 1
Bricker........................... 1
Borah............................. 1
Landon............................ 1
Others............................ 3

Thirty-seven per cent expressed no opinion.

By Age

	Naming Dewey
21–29 Years	72%
30–49 Years	61
50 Years and over	53

JANUARY 8
NEW YEAR RESOLUTIONS

Interviewing Date 12 /24–29 /39
Survey #180–A   Question #4a

Are you going to make any New Year resolutions?

Yes.. 17%
No... 83

Interviewing Date 12 /24–29 /39
Survey #180–A   Question #4b

Asked of those who replied in the affirmative: What New Year resolutions do you plan to make?

The following are listed according to frequency of mention:

Better myself in my business or job
Save more money
Stop smoking
Stop drinking
Improve my character

JANUARY 10
WORKS PROJECTS ADMINISTRATION

Interviewing Date 12 /24–29 /39
Survey #180–A   Question #7a

Should people on W.P.A. be allowed to form W.P.A. unions?

Yes.. 21%
No... 79

Ten per cent expressed no opinion.

Interviewing Date 12 /24–29 /39
Survey #180–A   Question #7b

Do you think people on W.P.A. should have the right to strike?

Yes.. 15%
No... 85

Ten per cent expressed no opinion.

JANUARY 12
PRESIDENT ROOSEVELT

Interviewing Date 12 /24–29 /39
Survey #180–A   Question #13c

In general, do you approve or disapprove today of Franklin Roosevelt as President?

Approve.................................... 63.5%
Disapprove................................. 36.5

Interviewing Date 12 /15–20 /39
Survey #179–A   Question #11

If President Roosevelt runs for a third term will you vote for him?

Yes.. 46%
No... 54

By Political Affiliation

	Yes	No
Democrats	79%	21%
Republicans	7	93

JANUARY 12
VIEWS OF LEADING
AMERICAN WRITERS

Special Survey

Asked of American writers by the Gallup Poll in collaboration with *The Saturday Review of Literature.*

Do you think the United States will go into war in Europe or do you think we will stay out of the war?

Go in............................ 31%
Stay out......................... 69

Twenty-four per cent expressed no opinion.

Do you think the United States should declare war on Germany and send our army and navy abroad to fight?

Yes.............................. 6%
No............................... 94

Ten per cent expressed no opinion.

What party would you like to see win the presidential election in 1940?

Democratic....................... 70%
Republican....................... 30

Twenty-two per cent expressed no opinion.

In general do you approve or disapprove of Franklin Roosevelt as President?

Approve.......................... 69%
Disapprove....................... 31

Seven per cent expressed no opinion.

If President Roosevelt runs for a third term will you vote for him?

Yes.............................. 53%
No............................... 47

Thirteen per cent expressed no opinion.

Do you think Congress should provide money to continue the Dies Committee another year?

Yes.............................. 43%
No............................... 57

Five per cent expressed no opinion.

Do you think the Wagner Labor Act should be revised, repealed, or left unchanged?

Revised.......................... 57%
Repealed......................... 9
Left unchanged................... 34

Sixteen per cent expressed no opinion.

Which country or countries do you consider responsible for the present war?

Germany.......................... 54%
England and France............... 3
Both sides....................... 19
All countries.................... 8
Versailles Treaty................ 5
Others........................... 8
No opinion....................... 3

About how long do you think the war in Europe will last?

Less than one year............... 10%
One year......................... 13
Two years........................ 31
Three years...................... 12
Four years....................... 6
Five years or more............... 28

Fifty-one per cent expressed no opinion.

Which side do you think will win?

England and France............... 59%
Germany.......................... 1
An agreement will be reached..... 14
Russia........................... 5
Qualified answers................ 4
No opinion....................... 17

Whom would you like to see elected President in 1940?

By Political Affiliation
Democrats

Roosevelt........................ 74%
Hull............................. 8
Byrd............................. 5
Murphy........................... 5
Douglas.......................... 2

Lehman	2
Wheeler	1
Eleanor Roosevelt	1
Wallace	1
McNutt	1

Twenty-seven per cent expressed no opinion.

Republicans

Dewey	50%
Vandenberg	20
Hoover	14
Taft	10
J.P. Morgan	3
Stone	3

Thirty-two per cent expressed no opinion.

Third Parties

Thomas	40%
La Guardia	20
Others	40

Forty-eight per cent expressed no opinion.

For which presidential candidate did you vote in 1936?

Roosevelt	66%
Landon	25
Lemke	1
Thomas	6
Browder	2

Fourteen per cent did not vote.

JANUARY 14
PARTY AFFILIATION

Interviewing Date 12/24–29/39
Survey #180–A   Question #2

In politics do you consider yourself a Democrat, Independent, Socialist, or Republican?

Democrat	42%
Republican	38

Independent	19
Socialist, other	1

Four per cent expressed no opinion.

By Region
New England

Democrat	27%
Republican	43
Independent	28
Socialist, other	2

Middle Atlantic

Democrat	39%
Republican	41
Independent	19
Socialist, other	1

East Central

Democrat	38%
Republican	42
Independent	20
Socialist, other	*

West Central

Democrat	38%
Republican	42
Independent	19
Socialist, other	1

South

Democrat	70%
Republican	20
Independent	10
Socialist, other	*

West

Democrat	45%
Republican	34
Independent	20
Socialist, other	1

*Less than 1%.

By Occupation
Professional

Democrat.......................... 29%
Republican........................ 44
Independent....................... 25
Socialist, other.................. 2

Businessmen

Democrat.......................... 29%
Republican........................ 48
Independent....................... 22
Socialist, other.................. 1

Skilled

Democrat.......................... 44%
Republican........................ 36
Independent....................... 19
Socialist, other.................. 1

Semiskilled

Democrat.......................... 47%
Republican........................ 33
Independent....................... 18
Socialist, other.................. 2

White Collar

Democrat.......................... 40%
Republican........................ 36
Independent....................... 22
Socialist, other.................. 2

Farmers

Democrat.......................... 49%
Republican........................ 38
Independent....................... 12
Socialist, other.................. 1

Farmers Outside South Only

Democrat.......................... 40%
Republican........................ 45
Independent....................... 14
Socialist, other.................. 1

JANUARY 17
WAGNER LABOR ACT

Interviewing Date 12/15–20/39
Survey #179–A   Question #5a

Do you think the Wagner Labor Act should be revised, repealed, or left unchanged?

Revised........................... 53%
Repealed.......................... 18
Left unchanged.................... 29

Fifty-eight per cent expressed no opinion.

By Political Affiliation
Democrats

Revised........................... 50%
Repealed.......................... 10
Left unchanged.................... 40

Republicans

Revised........................... 58%
Repealed.......................... 27
Left unchanged.................... 15

JANUARY 19
PARTY STRENGTH

Interviewing Date 12/24–29/39
Survey #180–A   Question #12

Which party would you like to see win the presidential election this year?

Democratic........................ 54%
Republican........................ 46

Fifteen per cent expressed no opinion.

JANUARY 21
PROHIBITION

Interviewing Date 12/15–20/39
Survey #179–A   Question #1

If the question of national prohibition should come up again, would you vote to make the country dry?

Yes................................ 34%
No................................ 66

Five per cent expressed no opinion.

By Region

	Yes	No
New England.................	27%	73%
Middle Atlantic..............	23	77
East Central.................	37	63
West Central.................	41	59
South.......................	50	50
West........................	32	68

Interviewing Date 12/15–20/39
Survey #179–A   Question #1c

Do you think liquor regulations in your community are too strict, not strict enough, or about right?

Too strict.......................... 7%
Not strict enough.................. 51
About right....................... 42

Nine per cent expressed no opinion.

Interviewing Date 12/15–20/39
Survey #179–A   Question #1b

Do you think drunkenness is increasing or decreasing in your community?

Increasing......................... 39%
Decreasing........................ 24
About the same.................... 37

Eight per cent expressed no opinion.

Interviewing Date 12/16–21/39
Survey #179–B   Question #1d

Do you think young people would be better off if we had national prohibition again?

Yes................................ 42%
No................................ 58

Seven per cent expressed no opinion.

JANUARY 22
PARTY STRENGTH

Interviewing Date 12/24–29/39
Survey #180–A   Question #12

Which party would you like to see win the presidential election this year?

Middle Atlantic States Only

Democratic........................ 52%
Republican........................ 48

East Central States Only

Democratic........................ 48%
Republican........................ 52

Sixteen per cent expressed no opinion.

JANUARY 24
BIRTH CONTROL

Interviewing Date 1/13–18/40
Survey #181–T   Question #8

Would you approve or disapprove of having government health clinics furnish birth control information to married people who want it?

Approve........................... 77%
Disapprove........................ 23

Eleven per cent expressed no opinion.

JANUARY 26
LENGTH OF WAR

Special Survey

Asked in Great Britain: For how long do you think the war will continue?

One year or less.................... 30%
One to two years................... 25
Three years or more................ 30
No opinion........................ 15

JANUARY 26
PRESIDENT ROOSEVELT'S POPULARITY

Interviewing Date 1/13–18/40
Survey #181–K   Question #11c

In general, do you approve or disapprove today of Franklin Roosevelt as President?

Approve........................ 63.5%
Disapprove..................... 36.5

JANUARY 28
WORLD PEACE

Interviewing Date 1/12–17/40
Survey #181–K   Question #2a

Have you given any thought to what should be done to maintain world peace after the present European war is over?

Yes............................. 34%
No.............................. 66

Interviewing Date 1/12–17/40
Survey #181–K   Question #2b

Asked of those who replied in the affirmative: In your opinion, what should be done?

The following are listed according to frequency of mention:

Some sort of international organization in which the member nations would surrender a few of their claims to national sovereignty.

Some kind of political, economic or moral reform within nations themselves or among all nations.

Complete disarmament.

A new attempt to create a World Court.

JANUARY 29
THE DRAFT

Interviewing Date 1/12–17/40
Survey #181–K   Question #3

Should the Constitution be changed to require a national vote before Congress could draft men for service overseas?

Yes............................. 60%
No.............................. 40

Five per cent expressed no opinion.

By Region

	Yes	No
New England.................	60%	40%
Middle Atlantic...............	60	40
East Central..................	62	38
West Central..................	63	37
South........................	50	50
West.........................	59	41

JANUARY 31
GREAT BRITAIN

Special Survey

Asked in Great Britain: If you had the choice between Mr. Chamberlain and Mr. Churchill, which would you have as Prime Minister?

Chamberlain...................... 52%
Churchill......................... 30
No opinion....................... 18

Are you in favor of the blackout being made less strict?

Yes............................. 75%
No.............................. 23
No opinion....................... 2

Asked of those who responded in the affirmative: Would you still be in favor of making the blackout less strict if it increased the risk of an air attack?

Yes............................. 37%
No.............................. 50
No opinion....................... 13

Are you satisfied or dissatisfied with the Government's conduct of the war?

Satisfied............................ 61%
Dissatisfied......................... 18
Stop the war........................ 11
No opinion......................... 10

For how long do you think the war will continue?

One year or less..................... 30%
One to two years.................... 25
Three years or more................ 30
No opinion......................... 15

Would you like to see the Royal Air Force bomb enemy military objectives, even if it means that the Germans would bomb England in return?

Yes................................ 52%
No................................. 41
No opinion......................... 7

Do you think the Government's decision to compel parents to pay something for the upkeep of evacuated children is fair or unfair?

Fair............................... 76%
Unfair............................. 18
No opinion......................... 6

Should the evacuation of children be compulsory?

Yes................................ 43%
No................................. 46
No opinion......................... 11

Do you think the Government's food rationing scheme is necessary or unnecessary?

Necessary.......................... 60%
Unnecessary........................ 28
No opinion......................... 12

FEBRUARY 2
POLITICS

Interviewing Date 12/15–20/39
Survey #179–A   Question #11

Asked of labor union members: If President Roosevelt runs for a third term, will you vote for him?

Yes................................ 59%
No................................. 41

Ten per cent expressed no opinion.

Interviewing Date 1/22–27/40
Survey #182–T   Question #8

Asked of labor union members: Which party would you like to see win the presidential election this year?

Democratic......................... 66%
Republican......................... 34

Eighteen per cent expressed no opinion.

FEBRUARY 4
RECIPROCAL TRADE

Interviewing Date 1/21–26/40
Survey #182–K   Question #3a

What is your understanding of the term "reciprocal trade?"

Approximately 10% had an understanding of the term.

Interviewing Date 1/12–17/40
Survey #181–K   Question #4a

Asked of those who had an understanding of the term: What is your personal opinion about Secretary Hull's reciprocal trade treaties?

Approve............................ 71%
Disapprove......................... 29

Interviewing Date 1/21–26/40
Survey #182–K   Question #3b

Asked of those who had an understanding of the term: Do you think Congress should give Secretary Hull the power to make more such treaties?

Yes............................... 57%
No................................ 43

Approximately 50% had no opinion.

FEBRUARY 5
POLITICS

Interviewing Date 12/22–27/39
Survey #182–T   Question #8

Asked of Negro voters: Which party would you like to see win the presidential election in November?

Democratic........................ 66%
Republican........................ 34

Interviewing Date 12/22–27/39
Survey #182–T   Question #9

Asked of Negro voters: In general, do you approve or disapprove of Franklin Roosevelt as President?

Approve........................... 82%
Disapprove........................ 18

FEBRUARY 7
FINLAND

Interviewing Date 1/21–26/40
Survey #182–K   Question #2a

Some members of Congress favor our Government lending Finland money to buy farm products and other nonmilitary supplies in this country. Others say this might get us into war. Do you think the Government should lend money to Finland?

Yes............................... 58%
No................................ 42

Nine per cent expressed no opinion.

Interviewing Date 1/21–26/40
Survey #182–K   Question #2b

Asked of those who responded in the affirmative: Would you favor the United States lending money to Finland for airplanes, arms, and other war materials?

Yes............................... 39%
No................................ 61

FEBRUARY 9
BRITISH AID TO FINLAND

Special Survey

Asked in Great Britain: Do you approve or disapprove of Britain sending arms to help Finland?

Approve........................... 74%
Disapprove........................ 18
No opinion........................ 8

Would you approve or disapprove of sending British troops to help Finland?

Approve........................... 33%
Disapprove........................ 50
No opinion........................ 17

FEBRUARY 11
REPUBLICAN PARTY

Interviewing Date 1/21–26/40
Survey #182–K   Question #10a

Asked of Republicans: Would you like to see the Republican party be more liberal or more conservative than it was in the 1936 presidential campaign?

More liberal...................... 59%
More conservative................. 17
About the same.................... 24

Interviewing Date 1/21–26/40
Survey #182–K   Question #10b

Asked of Republicans: Do you think the Republican party has a better chance or a worse chance of winning this year's election if it nominates a liberal candidate and adopts a liberal program?

Better chance...................... 77%
Worse chance...................... 10
No difference...................... 13

FEBRUARY 12
REPUBLICAN PRESIDENTIAL CANDIDATES

Interviewing Date 2/1–6/40
Survey #183–K   Question #9a

Asked of Republicans: Whom would you like to see the Republican party nominate for President this year?

Dewey............................ 56%
Vandenberg....................... 17
Taft.............................. 17
Hoover........................... 3
Others........................... 7

Thirty-six per cent expressed no opinion.

FEBRUARY 14
JAPAN

Interviewing Date 1/22–27/40
Survey #182–T   Question #4

Do you think our Government should forbid the sale of arms, airplanes, gasoline, and other war materials to Japan?

Yes.............................. 75%
No.............................. 25

Six per cent expressed no opinion.

FEBRUARY 16
NEUTRALITY

Interviewing Date 2/2–7/40
Survey #183–K   Question #1a

Do you think the United States will go into the war in Europe, or do you think we will stay out of the war?

Go into war...................... 32%
Stay out......................... 68

Interviewing Date 2/2–7/40
Survey #183–K   Question #1b

Asked of those who responded that we will stay out: Why do you think the United States will stay out of the European war?

The following are the three chief reasons:

The people are overwhelmingly against war and would not stand for American participation.

The United States learned its lesson in the last war.

The nation would have everything to lose and nothing to gain.

FEBRUARY 18
DEMOCRATIC PRESIDENTIAL CANDIDATES

Interviewing Date 2/8–13/40
Survey #184–K   Question #10a

Asked of Democrats: Whom would you like to see nominated by the Democratic party for President this year?

Roosevelt........................ 78%
Garner.......................... 10
Hull............................ 6
McNutt.......................... 2
Wheeler......................... 1
Farley.......................... 1
Others.......................... 2

Twenty per cent expressed no opinion.

Interviewing Date 2 /8–13 /40
Survey #184–K   Question #10b

Asked of Democrats: If Franklin Roosevelt is not a candidate, whom would you like to see nominated?

Garner......................... 40%
Hull........................... 25
McNutt......................... 11
Farley......................... 8
Wheeler........................ 4
La Guardia..................... 3
Jackson........................ 1
Murphy......................... 1
Others......................... 7

Fifty per cent expressed no opinion.

By Income

Upper

Hull........................... 34%
Garner......................... 30
McNutt......................... 12
Wheeler........................ 8
Farley......................... 5
La Guardia..................... 2
Jackson........................ 1
Others......................... 8

Middle

Garner......................... 37%
Hull........................... 29
McNutt......................... 11
Farley......................... 7
Wheeler........................ 4
La Guardia..................... 3
Jackson........................ 1
Others......................... 8

Lower

Garner......................... 48%
Hull........................... 17
McNutt......................... 10
Farley......................... 10
Wheeler........................ 4
La Guardia..................... 3
Jackson........................ 2
Others......................... 6

FEBRUARY 19
ANTI-LYNCHING LAW

Interviewing Date 1 /12–17 /40
Survey #181–K   Question #6

Under the proposed federal law against lynching, the Federal Government would (1) fine and imprison local police officers who fail to protect a prisoner from a lynch mob, and (2) make a county in which a lynching occurs pay a fine up to $10,000 to the victim or his family. Do you approve or disapprove of this law?

Approve........................ 55%
Disapprove..................... 45

Nine per cent expressed no opinion

South Only

Approve........................ 45%
Disapprove..................... 55

Negroes Only

Approve........................ 89%
Disapprove..................... 11

FEBRUARY 19
PRESIDENT ROOSEVELT

Interviewing Date 2 /2–7 /40
Survey #183–K   Question #9a

Do you think President Roosevelt will run for a third term?

Yes............................ 52%
No............................. 48

Eighteen per cent expressed no opinion.

By Political Affiliation

	Yes	No
Democrats..................	57%	43%
Republicans................	47	53

Interviewing Date 2/2–7/40
Survey #183–K   Question #9b

Do you think President Roosevelt will be reelected if he runs for a third term?

Yes................................. 60%
No.................................. 40

Ten per cent expressed no opinion.

By Political Affiliation

	Yes	No
Democrats....................	80%	20%
Republicans..................	33	67

FEBRUARY 19
FEDERAL BUDGET

Interviewing Date 2/2–7/40
Survey #183–K   Question #8a

President Roosevelt proposes an increase of 28% (about one-fourth) in spending for national defense. Do you approve or disapprove of this increase?

Approve............................ 79%
Disapprove......................... 21

Ten per cent expressed no opinion.

By Political Affiliation

	Approve	Disapprove
Democrats.............	85%	15%
Republicans...........	72	28

By Income

Upper.................	75%	25%
Middle...............	78	22
Lower................	83	17

Interviewing Date 2/2–7/40
Survey #183–K   Question #8b

The President proposes a 28% (about one-fourth) reduction in Federal Government spending for relief. Do you approve or disapprove of this cut?

Approve............................ 59%
Disapprove......................... 41

Ten per cent expressed no opinion.

By Political Affiliation

	Approve	Disapprove
Democrats.............	49%	51%
Republicans...........	73	27

By Income

Upper.................	79%	21%
Middle...............	67	33
Lower................	38	62

Interviewing Date 2/2–7/40
Survey #183–K   Question #8c

The President proposes a 21% (about one-fifth) reduction in Federal Government spending for public works. Do you approve or disapprove of this cut?

Approve............................ 62%
Disapprove......................... 38

Nine per cent expressed no opinion.

By Political Affiliation

	Approve	Disapprove
Democrats.............	52%	48%
Republicans...........	74	26

By Income

Upper.................	69%	31%
Middle...............	52	48
Lower................	45	55

Interviewing Date 2/2–7/40
Survey #183–K   Question #8d

The President proposes a 30% (about one-third) reduction in payments by the Government to help farmers. Do you approve or disapprove of this cut?

Approve.......................... 52%
Disapprove....................... 48

Fourteen per cent expressed no opinion.

By Political Affiliation

	Approve	Disapprove
Democrats.............	45%	55%
Republicans............	63	37

By Income

Upper................	69%	31%
Middle...............	52	48
Lower...............	45	55

FEBRUARY 21
EUROPEAN WAR

Interviewing Date 2/2–7/40
Survey #183–K   Question #6

If it appears that Germany is defeating England and France, should the United States declare war on Germany and send our army and navy to Europe to fight?

Yes.............................. 23%
No.............................. 77

Seven per cent expressed no opinion.

FEBRUARY 23
THE BUDGET

Interviewing Date 2/2–7/40
Survey #183–K   Question #3b

Which political party do you think is more likely to balance the Federal Government's budget in the next four years — the Republican or the Democratic?

Republican....................... 42%
Democratic....................... 23
Neither.......................... 35

Sixteen per cent expressed no opinion.

By Political Affiliation
Democrats

Republican....................... 15%
Democratic....................... 41
Neither.......................... 44

Republicans

Republican....................... 75%
Democratic....................... 4
Neither.......................... 21

FEBRUARY 28
POLITICAL CONTRIBUTIONS

Interviewing Date 2/2–7/40
Survey #183–K   Question #7

Do you think it is all right for people to solicit money for political campaigns from Government employees, or do you think this should be prevented by law?

All right to solicit.................. 23%
Soliciting should be prevented........ 77

Twelve per cent expressed no opinion.

MARCH 1
PRESIDENT ROOSEVELT'S POPULARITY

Interviewing Date 2/8–13/40
Survey #184–K   Question 12d

In general, do you approve or disapprove of Franklin Roosevelt as President?

Approve.......................... 64%
Disapprove....................... 36

MARCH 3
PARTY STRENGTH

Interviewing Date 2/8–13/40
Survey #184–K   Question #11

Which party would you like to see win the presidential election this year?

Democratic......................... 55%
Republican......................... 45

Sixteen per cent expressed no opinion.

By Income

	Democratic	Republican
Upper..............	36%	64%
Middle.............	51	49
Lower..............	69	31

By Region

New England.......	45%	55%
Middle Atlantic......	53	47
East Central........	49	51
West Central........	51	49
South..............	75	25
West...............	59	41

MARCH 4
EUROPEAN WAR

Interviewing Date 2/8–13/40
Survey #184–K   Question #3

If it looked as though England and France would lose the war unless we loaned them money to buy war supplies here, would you favor or oppose lending them money?

Favor............................. 55%
Oppose............................ 45

MARCH 6
GOVERNMENT SPENDING

Interviewing Date 2/2–7/40
Survey #183–K   Question #3a

Suppose there were two candidates for United States Senator in your state. One candidate promises to vote to reduce all Federal Government spending. The other promises to vote to spend more Federal Government money in your state. Other things being equal, which candidate would you vote for?

Candidate for reduced spending........ 64%
Candidate for more spending.......... 36

Thirteen per cent expressed no opinion.

By Income

	Candidate for	
	Reduced Spending	More Spending
Upper..................	81%	19%
Middle.................	69	31
Lower..................	49	51

MARCH 10
PEACE IN EUROPE

Interviewing Date 2/22–27/40
Survey #185–K   Question #6a

If Hitler offers to make peace this spring, do you think England and France should meet with the Germans and try to end the war?

Yes............................... 75%
No................................ 25

Interviewing Date 2/22–27/40
Survey #185–K   Question #5a

Do you think now is the right time for the leading nations of the world to have a conference to try to settle Europe's problems and end the war between Germany and England and France?

Yes............................... 58%
No................................ 42

Interviewing Date 2/22–27/40
Survey #185–K   Question #5b

If such a conference is held, should the United States take part in it?

Yes............................... 55%
No................................ 45

Interviewing Date 2/22–27/40
Survey #185–K Question #6b

If peace could be reached by letting Germany keep Czecho-Slovakia, would you favor this?

Yes............................ 38%
No............................. 62

Interviewing Date 2/22–27/40
Survey #185–T Question #6b

If peace could be reached by letting Germany keep Poland, would you favor this?

Yes............................ 30%
No............................. 70

Approximately 9% had no opinion on the above questions.

MARCH 11
FINLAND

Interviewing Date 2/8–13/40
Survey #184–K Question #4

Would you approve or disapprove of letting Finland raise money for her war against Russia by selling bonds to Americans?

Approve......................... 73%
Disapprove...................... 27

By Political Affiliation

	Approve	Disapprove
Democrats............	72%	28%
Republicans..........	75	25

MARCH 13
THIRD TERM

Interviewing Date 12/15–20/39
Survey #179–A Question #11

If President Roosevelt is a candidate for a third term, will you vote for him?

Yes............................ 47%
No............................. 53

MARCH 13
BRITISH AID FOR SWEDEN

Special Survey

Asked in Great Britain: If Sweden is attacked by Russia, would you approve or disapprove of Britain's sending arms and war materials to help her?

Approve......................... 51%
Disapprove...................... 31
No opinion...................... 18

Would you favor sending troops to help Sweden if Russia attacks her?

Yes............................ 33%
No............................. 47
No opinion...................... 20

MARCH 15
PARTY STRENGTH

Special Survey

Asked in New York State: Which party would you like to see win the presidential election this year?

Democratic...................... 53%
Republican...................... 47

New York City Only

Democratic...................... 69%
Republican...................... 31

MARCH 17
FARM POLICY

Special Survey

Asked of farmers: Do you think the present administration's program, as a whole, has helped or hurt the farmers?

Helped.......................... 66%
Hurt............................ 22
Neither......................... 12

Midwestern Farmers Only

Helped............................ 64%
Hurt.............................. 20
Neither........................... 16

Asked of farmers: Do you think Henry Wallace has done a good job or a poor job as Secretary of Agriculture?

Good job.......................... 73%
Poor job.......................... 27

Midwestern Farmers Only

Good job.......................... 68%
Poor job.......................... 32

Asked of Midwestern farmers: Would you prefer to see the Democrats or the Republicans win the presidential election this year?

Republicans....................... 54%
Democrats......................... 46

Asked of Midwestern farmers: If President Roosevelt runs for a third term this year, will you vote for him?

Yes............................... 37%
No................................ 63

MARCH 18
FARM POLICY

Special Survey

Asked of farmers: Considering costs of production, do you think the price for your chief cash crop is fair?

Yes............................... 36%
No................................ 64

By Crop

	Yes	No
Wheat	25%	75%
Corn	45	55
Cotton	11	89
Tobacco	32	68

MARCH 18
ELEANOR ROOSEVELT

Interviewing Date 2/22–27/40
Survey #185–K   Question #1

Do you approve or disapprove of the way Mrs. Roosevelt has conducted herself as First Lady?

Approve........................... 68%
Disapprove........................ 32

By Income

	Approve	Disapprove
Upper	56%	44%
Middle	68	32
Lower	75	25

MARCH 20
POLITICS

Special Survey

Asked in Pennsylvania: Which party would you like to see win the presidential election this year?

Democratic........................ 51%
Republican........................ 49

Asked in Pennsylvania: If President Roosevelt is a candidate for a third term, will you vote for him?

Yes............................... 49%
No................................ 51

MARCH 22
POLITICS

Special Survey

Asked in California: Which party would you like to see win the presidential election this year?

Democratic........................ 58%
Republican........................ 42

Asked in California: If President Roosevelt runs for a third term, will you vote for him?

Yes............................... 51%
No................................ 49

MARCH 24
REPUBLICAN PRESIDENTIAL CANDIDATES

Special Survey

Asked of Midwestern Republicans: If it came to a choice between Thomas Dewey and Arthur Vandenberg for the Republican presidential nomination, which one would you prefer?

Dewey............................ 45%
Vandenberg....................... 33
No opinion........................ 22

MARCH 25
PRESIDENT ROOSEVELT

Special Survey

Asked of lawyers listed in standard legal directories: If President Roosevelt runs for a third term, will you vote for him?

Yes............................... 29%
No................................ 71

MARCH 27
POLITICS

Special Survey

Asked in New Jersey: Which party would you like to see win the presidential election this year?

Republican....................... 53%
Democratic....................... 47

Asked in New Jersey: If President Roosevelt is a candidate for a third term, will you vote for him?

Yes............................... 46%
No................................ 54

MARCH 29
POLITICS

Special Survey

Asked in Massachusetts: Which party would you like to see win the presidential election this year?

Republican....................... 54%
Democratic....................... 46

Asked in Massachusetts: If President Roosevelt is a candidate for a third term, will you vote for him?

Yes............................... 45%
No................................ 55

MARCH 31
EUROPEAN WAR

Interviewing Date 3/8–13/40
Survey #186–K   Question #6a

Which side do you want to see win the present war — England and France or Germany?

England and France................. 84%
Germany.......................... 1
No opinion........................ 15

APRIL 1
POLITICS

Special Survey

Asked in Iowa: Which party would you like to see win the presidential election this year?

Republican...................... 54%
Democratic...................... 46

Asked in Iowa: If President Roosevelt is a candidate for a third term, will you vote for him?

Yes............................. 40%
No.............................. 60

Asked in Iowa: In general, do you approve or disapprove of Franklin Roosevelt as President?

Approve......................... 58%
Disapprove...................... 42

APRIL 3
POLITICS

Special Survey

Asked in Michigan: Which party would you like to see win the presidential election this year?

Republican...................... 54%
Democratic...................... 46

Fourteen per cent expressed no opinion.

If President Roosevelt is a candidate for a third term, will you vote for him?

Yes............................. 40%
No.............................. 60

Nine per cent expressed no opinion.

APRIL 5
POLITICS

Special Survey

Which party would you like to see win the presidential election this year?

Texas Only

Democratic...................... 93%
Republican...................... 7

Oklahoma Only

Democratic...................... 68%
Republican...................... 32

If President Roosevelt is a candidate for a third term, will you vote for him?

Texas Only

Yes............................. 73%
No.............................. 27

Oklahoma Only

Yes............................. 49%
No.............................. 51

APRIL 7
CANCER

Interviewing Date 3/8–13/40
Survey #186–K   Question #3a

In your opinion, which of the following is the most serious public health problem — tuberculosis, syphilis, cancer, or infantile paralysis?

Syphilis........................ 46%
Cancer.......................... 29
Tuberculosis.................... 16
Infantile paralysis............. 9

Interviewing Date 3/8–13/40
Survey #186–K   Question #3b

Do you think cancer is contagious?

Yes............................. 15%
No.............................. 57
No opinion...................... 28

Interviewing Date 3/8–13/40
Survey #186–K   Question #3c

Do you think cancer is curable?

Yes.............................. 56%
No............................... 27
No opinion....................... 17

Interviewing Date 3/8–13/40
Survey #186–K   Question #3d
What do you think causes cancer?

The following are listed according to frequency of mention:

Bruises, injuries, constant irritation of body
    tissues and tumors
Hereditary tendencies
Poor diet
Moles and warts
Liquor
Smoking
Frequent childbearing
Constipation
Mental distress
Wrong functioning of glands
Neglected teeth

Interviewing Date 3/8–13/40
Survey #186–K   Question #3e
Do you happen to know any of the symptoms of cancer?

Yes.............................. 38%
No............................... 62

Interviewing Date 3/8–13/40
Survey #186–K   Question #3g
Do you think there is anything shameful in having cancer?

Yes.............................. 2%
No............................... 98

APRIL 8
POLITICS

Special Survey
Which party would you like to see win the presidential election this year?

Oregon Only

Democratic....................... 55%
Republican....................... 45

Washington Only

Democratic....................... 57%
Republican....................... 43

If President Roosevelt is a candidate for a third term, will you vote for him?

Oregon Only

Yes.............................. 47%
No............................... 53

Washington Only

Yes.............................. 50%
No............................... 50

APRIL 10
POLITICS

Special Survey
Which party would you like to see win the presidential election this year?

Maryland Only

Democratic....................... 62%
Republican....................... 38

West Virginia Only

Democratic....................... 57%
Republican....................... 43

Delaware Only

Democratic....................... 54%
Republican....................... 46

If President Roosevelt is a candidate for a third term, will you vote for him?

Maryland Only

Yes.............................. 52%
No............................... 48

West Virginia Only

Yes................................ 51%
No................................ 49

Delaware Only

Yes................................ 49%
No................................ 51

APRIL 12
POLITICS

Special Survey

Which party would you like to see win the presidential election this year?

Ohio Only

Republican........................ 51%
Democratic........................ 49

Indiana Only

Democratic........................ 52%
Republican........................ 48

If President Roosevelt is a candidate for a third term, will you vote for him?

Ohio Only

Yes................................ 42%
No................................ 58

Indiana Only

Yes................................ 42%
No................................ 58

APRIL 14
POLITICS

Special Survey

Which party would you like to see win the presidential election this year?

Virginia Only

Democratic........................ 72%
Republican........................ 28

Kentucky Only

Democratic........................ 60%
Republican........................ 40

If President Roosevelt is a candidate for a third term, will you vote for him?

Virginia Only

Yes................................ 59%
No................................ 41

Kentucky Only

Yes................................ 51%
No................................ 49

APRIL 15
PRESIDENTIAL TRIAL HEAT

Interviewing Date 3/27–4/1/40
Survey #188–K   Question #5b

If President Roosevelt runs for a third term on the Democratic ticket against Senator Vandenberg on the Republican ticket, which one would you prefer?

Roosevelt.......................... 53%
Vandenberg........................ 47

Twelve per cent expressed no opinion.

By Region

	Roosevelt	Vandenberg
New England.......	52%	48%
Middle Atlantic......	52	48
East Central........	46	54
West Central........	49	51
South..............	71	29
West...............	59	41

Interviewing Date 3/27–4/1/40
Survey #188–K   Question #5a

If Cordell Hull runs for President on the Democratic ticket against Senator Vandenberg on the Republican ticket, which one would you prefer?

Hull. 58%
Vandenberg. 42

Eleven per cent expressed no opinion.

By Region

	Hull	Vandenberg
New England.	59%	41%
Middle Atlantic.	59	41
East Central.	51	49
West Central.	49	51
South.	79	21
West.	58	42

APRIL 15
BRITISH POLITICS

Special Survey

Asked in Great Britain: If Mr. Chamberlain were to retire, whom would you like to see succeed him as Prime Minister?

Eden. 28%
Churchill. 25
Halifax. 7
Attlee. 6
Others. 23
No opinion. 11

APRIL 17
POLITICS

Special Survey

Asked in Kansas: Which party would you like to see win the presidential election this year?

Republican. 56%
Democratic. 44

Thirteen per cent expressed no opinion.

If President Roosevelt is a candidate for a third term, will you vote for him?

Yes. 37%
No. 63

APRIL 19
PARTY STRENGTH

Special Survey

Which party would you like to see win the presidential election this year?

Wisconsin Only

Republican. 55%
Democratic. 45

Illinois Only

Republican. 55%
Democratic. 45

Nebraska Only

Republican. 51%
Democratic. 49

APRIL 21
PARTY STRENGTH

Interviewing Date 4/11–16/40
Survey #190–T   Question #5

Which party would you like to see win the presidential election this year?

The Democrats are out in front as the campaign gets under way, the state-by-state tabulations show. If the election were today the indications are that the Democratic party would lead in 31 of the 48 states, capturing about 317 out of a total of 531 electoral votes. But the Democratic lead in several states is so slim — notably in New York and Minnesota — that a shift of only 1% would completely alter the picture and throw a majority of electoral votes to the GOP.

APRIL 24
PARTY BEST ABLE TO KEEP PEACE

Interviewing Date 4/5–10/40
Survey #189–K   Question #1a

Which political party do you think is more likely to keep us out of war — the Republican or the Democratic?

Democratic........................ 35%
Republican........................ 33
No difference..................... 32

Sixteen per cent expressed no opinion.

By Political Affiliation
Democrats

Democratic........................ 62%
Republican........................ 6
No difference..................... 32

Republicans

Democratic........................ 5%
Republican........................ 65
No difference..................... 30

APRIL 26
NEVILLE CHAMBERLAIN

Special Survey

> *Asked in Great Britain: In general, do you approve or disapprove of Mr. Chamberlain as Prime Minister?*

Approve........................... 61%
Disapprove........................ 39

Seven per cent expressed no opinion.

APRIL 28
EUROPEAN WAR

Interviewing Date 4/11–16/40
Survey #190–K   Question #1a

> *Do you think Germany was justified in marching into Denmark and Norway?*

Yes............................... 7%
No................................ 93

Seven per cent expressed no opinion.

Interviewing Date 3/28–4/3/40
Survey #188–T   Question #1b

> *Should we declare war on Germany and send our armed forces abroad to fight?*

Yes............................... 4%
No................................ 96

Interviewing Date 4/11–16/40
Survey #190–K   Question #1c

> *Should the United States loan money to Norway to buy war supplies in the United States?*

Yes............................... 43%
No................................ 57

APRIL 29
DAYLIGHT SAVING TIME

Interviewing Date 3/15–20/40
Survey #187–K   Question #3a

> *Are you in favor of daylight saving time?*

Yes............................... 60%
No................................ 40

Nineteen per cent expressed no opinion.

By Region

	Yes	No
New England	75%	25%
Middle Atlantic	75	25
East Central	64	36
West Central	45	55
South	44	56
West	54	49

MAY 1
CRITICISM OF JUDGES

Interviewing Date 4/11–16/40
Survey #190–K   Question #2

> *Which do you think is more important (A) that newspapers should be allowed to criticize the decisions of judges; or (B) that judges should be free from such criticism?*

Newspapers can criticize............. 75%
Judges should be free of criticism...... 25

Twelve per cent expressed no opinion.

Missouri Only

Newspapers can criticize............. 75%
Judges should be free of criticism...... 25

Seven per cent of those polled in Missouri expressed no opinion.

MAY 2
POLITICS

Special Survey

Asked in Minnesota: Which party would you like to see win the presidential election this year?

Democratic...................... 51%
Republican...................... 49

Asked in Minnesota: If President Roosevelt is a candidate for a third term, will you vote for him?

Yes............................. 42%
No.............................. 58

Asked in Minnesota: In general, do you approve or disapprove of Franklin Roosevelt as President?

Approve......................... 65%
Disapprove...................... 35

MAY 5
PRESIDENTIAL TRIAL HEAT

Interviewing Date 4/19–24/40
Survey #191–K   Question #8a

If President Roosevelt runs for a third term on the Democratic ticket against Senator Robert Taft on the Republican ticket, which one would you prefer?

Roosevelt....................... 58%
Taft............................ 42

Ten per cent expressed no opinion.

By Region

	Roosevelt	Taft
New England.............	56%	44%
Middle Atlantic...........	56	44
East Central.............	51	49
West Central.............	57	43
South...................	72	28
West....................	64	36

Roosevelt Supporters in 1936 Only

Roosevelt....................... 84%
Taft............................ 16

Landon Supporters in 1936 Only

Roosevelt....................... 8%
Taft............................ 92

Interviewing Date 4/19–24/40
Survey #191–K   Question #8b

If Cordell Hull runs on the Democratic ticket against Senator Robert Taft on the Republican ticket, which one would you prefer?

Hull............................ 63%
Taft............................ 37

Twenty-two per cent expressed no opinion.

By Region

	Hull	Taft
New England.............	61%	39%
Middle Atlantic.............	61	39
East Central..............	54	46
West Central..............	62	38
South.....................	81	19
West......................	66	34

Roosevelt Supporters in 1936 Only

Hull............................ 84%
Taft............................ 16

Landon Supporters in 1936 Only

Hull............................ 21%
Taft............................ 79

Interviewing Date 4/19–24/40
Survey #191–K   Question #8c

If John Garner runs on the Democratic ticket against Senator Robert Taft on the Republican ticket, which one would you prefer?

Garner.......................... 51%
Taft............................ 49

Eighteen per cent expressed no opinion.

Roosevelt Supporters in 1936 Only

Garner.......................... 74%
Taft............................ 26

Landon Supporters in 1936 Only

Garner.......................... 11%
Taft............................ 89

MAY 6
PARTY STRENGTH

Interviewing Date 4/19–24/40
Survey #191–K   Question #9

Which party would you like to see win the presidential election?

Democratic...................... 54%
Republican...................... 46

MAY 8
REPUBLICAN PRESIDENTIAL CANDIDATES

Interviewing Date 4/25–30/40
Survey #192–K   Question #1a

Asked of Republicans: Whom would you like to see the Republican party nominate for President this year?

Dewey........................... 67%
Vandenberg...................... 14
Taft............................ 12

Willkie......................... 3
Hoover.......................... 2
Others.......................... 2

Twenty-eight per cent expressed no opinion.

MAY 10
NEUTRALITY

Interviewing Date 4/19–24/40
Survey #191–K   Question #7

If you were voting for President, which type of candidate (on card) do you think you would be more likely to vote for: (A) A candidate who promises to keep us out of war and refuses to give any more help to England and France than we are now giving them, even if they are being defeated by Germany; or (B) A candidate who promises to keep us out of war, but who is willing to give England and France all the help they want, except sending our army and navy.

Refuses help.................... 34%
Aid except troops............... 66

Nine per cent expressed no opinion.

By Political Affiliation

	Refuses Help	Aid Except Troops
Democrats.......	32%	68%
Republicans.....	36	64

By Income

Upper..............	28%	72%
Middle.............	34	66
Lower..............	37	63

MAY 12
PRESIDENTIAL TRIAL HEAT

Interviewing Date 5/5–10/40
Survey #193–K   Question #7a

If President Roosevelt runs for a third term on the Democratic ticket against Thomas

Dewey on the Republican ticket, which one would you prefer?

Roosevelt........................... 52%
Dewey.............................. 48

Eight per cent expressed no opinion.

By Income

	Roosevelt	Dewey
Upper................	31%	69%
Middle...............	48	52
Lower (including reliefers)............	66	34
Reliefers.............	74	26

Roosevelt Voters in 1936

Roosevelt........................... 79%
Dewey.............................. 21

Landon Voters in 1936

Roosevelt........................... 5%
Dewey.............................. 95

By Region

	Roosevelt	Dewey
New England.........	46%	54%
Middle Atlantic.......	53	47
East Central..........	46	54
West Central..........	48	52
South................	71	29
West.................	55	45

Interviewing Date 5/5–10/40
Survey #193–K   Question #4c

If Cordell Hull runs for President on the Democratic ticket against Thomas Dewey on the Republican ticket, which one would you prefer?

Hull............................... 51%
Dewey.............................. 49

Fifteen per cent expressed no opinion.

By Income

	Hull	Dewey
Upper................	40%	60%
Middle...............	49	51
Lower (including reliefers)............	59	41
Reliefers.............	65	35

Roosevelt Voters in 1936

Hull.............................. 75%
Dewey.............................. 25

Landon Voters in 1936

Hull.............................. 12%
Dewey.............................. 88

By Region

	Hull	Dewey
New England.........	43%	57%
Middle Atlantic.......	49	51
East Central..........	46	54
West Central..........	49	51
South................	75	25
West.................	50	50

MAY 13
POLITICAL CONTRIBUTIONS

Interviewing Date 4/25–30/40
Survey #192–K   Question #5

Do you think it is all right to ask state and other local government employees for money for state political campaigns or do you think this should be prevented by law?

Practice all right.................... 21%
Should be prevented................ 79

Fifteen per cent expressed no opinion.

By Political Affiliation

	All Right	Should Be Prevented
Democrats..........	25%	75%
Republicans.........	17	83

MAY 15

DEMOCRATIC PRESIDENTIAL CANDIDATES

Interviewing Date 5/5–10/40
Survey #193–K   Question #3b

Asked of Democrats: If Franklin Roosevelt is not a candidate, whom would you like to see the Democratic party nominate for President?

Hull.............................. 47%
Garner............................ 21
Farley............................ 16
McNutt........................... 6
Wheeler.......................... 4
Jackson.......................... 1
La Guardia....................... 1
Others........................... 4

Forty-five per cent expressed no opinion.

MAY 17

REPUBLICAN PRESIDENTIAL CANDIDATES

Interviewing Date 5/5–10/40
Survey #193–K   Question #3a

Asked of Republicans: Whom would you like to see nominated by the Republican party for President this year?

Dewey............................ 62%
Taft.............................. 14
Vandenberg....................... 13
Willkie........................... 5
Hoover............................ 2
Others........................... 4

Twenty-six per cent expressed no opinion.

MAY 19

EUROPEAN WAR

Interviewing Date 5/5–10/40
Survey #193–K   Question #2a

The war between England and France and Germany has been going on for eight months. Which side do you think is ahead so far?

Germany.......................... 67%
England and France................ 8
Even............................. 13
No opinion....................... 12

Interviewing Date 5/5–10/40
Survey #193–K   Question #2b

Which side do you think will win the war?

Allies........................... 55%
Germany.......................... 17
No opinion....................... 28

Interviewing Date 5/5–10/40
Survey #193–K   Question #1a

Do you think the United States will go into the war in Europe?

Yes.............................. 51%
No............................... 49

MAY 20

PRESIDENTIAL TRIAL HEAT

Interviewing Date 5/5–10/40
Survey #193–K   Question #3a

If Thomas Dewey runs for President on the Republican ticket against James Farley on the Democratic Ticket, which one would you prefer?

Dewey............................ 58%
Farley........................... 42

Fifteen per cent expressed no opinion.

By Region

	Dewey	Farley
New England........	62%	38%
Middle Atlantic......	61	39
East Central.........	64	36
West Central.........	62	38
South..............	32	68
West...............	60	40

MAY 22
ARMED FORCES

Interviewing Date 5/16–21/40
Survey #194–K   Question #1a

Do you think the United States should increase the size of its armed forces?

Yes................................ 90%
No................................ 10

MAY 24
EUROPEAN WAR

Interviewing Date 5/16–21/40
Survey #194–K   Question #6

If England and France are unable to pay cash for airplanes they buy in this country, do you think we should sell them planes on credit supplied by our Government?

Yes................................ 51%
No................................ 49

Six per cent expressed no opinion.

MAY 26
ARMED FORCES

Interviewing Date 5/18–23/40
Survey #195–K   Question #2a

Congress has set aside two billion dollars for the army, navy, and air forces for the next 12 months. President Roosevelt has now asked Congress to increase this by another one billion dollars. Do you approve or disapprove of this increase?

Approve........................... 86%
Disapprove........................ 14

Five per cent expressed no opinion.

By Political Affiliation

	Approve	Disapprove
Democrats	93%	7%
Republicans	83	17

Interviewing Date 5/18–23/40
Survey #195–K   Question #2b

Would you be willing to pay a special tax to cover this increased expenditure?

Yes................................ 76%
No................................ 24

By Income

	Yes	No
Upper	80%	20%
Middle	76	24
Lower	74	26

MAY 27
FOREIGN AFFAIRS

Interviewing Date 4/19–24/40
Survey #191–K   Question #6a

Which possible presidential candidate (on card) do you think would handle this country's foreign affairs the best?

By Political Affiliation
Democrats

Roosevelt.......................... 62%
Hull............................... 24
Garner............................. 3
Hoover............................. 3
Others............................. 8

Republicans

Hoover............................. 22%
Dewey.............................. 21
Hull............................... 21
Vandenberg......................... 10
Roosevelt.......................... 10
Taft............................... 9
Others............................. 7

Approximately one person in seven was undecided or without an opinion.

MAY 29
EUROPEAN WAR

Interviewing Date 5/18–23/40
Survey #195–K   Question #5

Do you think the United States should declare war on Germany and send our army and navy abroad to fight?

Yes................................. 7%
No................................. 93

MAY 31
REPUBLICAN PRESIDENTIAL CANDIDATES

Interviewing Date 5/18–23/40
Survey #195–K   Question #12a

Asked of Republicans: Whom would you like to see elected President this year?

Dewey............................. 56%
Taft............................... 16
Vandenberg........................ 12
Willkie............................ 10
Hoover............................. 2
Others............................. 4

Thirty-two per cent expressed no opinion.

JUNE 2
NATIONAL DEFENSE

Interviewing Date 5/18–23/40
Survey #195–K   Question #2

Do you think our country's army, navy, and air forces are strong enough so that the United States is safe from attack by any foreign nation?

Yes................................. 15%
No................................. 85

Ten per cent expressed no opinion.

Interviewing Date 5/16–21/40
Survey #194–K   Question #1d

Should the United States require every able-bodied young man 20 years old to serve in the army, navy, or the air forces for one year?

Yes................................. 50%
No................................. 50

Seven per cent expressed no opinion.

By Age

	Yes	No
21–29 Years.................	44%	56%
30–49 Years.................	49	51
50 Years and over...........	55	45
21–29 Years (men only).......	41	59

Interviewing Date 5/18–23/40
Survey #195–K   Question #1

Do you think that the C.C.C. camps should give military training to every young man in the C.C.C.?

Yes................................. 85%
No................................. 15

Seven per cent expressed no opinion.

Interviewing Date 4/11–16/40
Survey #190–K   Question #1d

If Germany should defeat England and France in the present war, do you think Germany would start a war against the United States sooner or later?

Yes................................. 65%
No................................. 35

Ten per cent expressed no opinion.

By Region

	Yes	No
New England................	64%	36%
Middle Atlantic..............	64	36
East Central.................	61	39

West Central................ 61   39
South...................... 82   18
West....................... 62   38

JUNE 5
PRESIDENT ROOSEVELT

Interviewing Date 5/18–23/40
Survey #195–K   Question #16

If President Roosevelt runs for a third term, will you vote for him?

Yes............................... 57%
No................................ 43

By Political Affiliation

	Yes	No
Democrats...	91%	9%
Republicans.	8	92

By Income

	Yes	No
Upper..	37%	63%
Middle.	54	46
Lower..	70	30

Interviewing Date 5/18–23/40
Survey #195–K   Question #4

Do you think Roosevelt has done a good job or a poor job in dealing with the war crisis in Europe?

Good job....................... 79%
Fair job....................... 7
Poor job....................... 14

By Political Affiliation
Democrats

Good job....................... 91%
Fair job....................... 4
Poor job....................... 5

Republicans

Good job....................... 60%
Fair job....................... 12
Poor job....................... 28

JUNE 7
DEFENSE OF PANAMA CANAL

Interviewing Date 5/25–30/40
Survey #196–K   Question #9

If Germany defeats the Allies, should the United States fight if necessary to keep Germany out of the British, French, and Dutch possessions located in the area of the Panama Canal?

Yes............................... 84%
No................................ 16

Twelve per cent expressed no opinion.

By Region

	Yes	No
New England...	82%	18%
Middle Atlantic	82	18
East Central...	83	17
West Central...	84	16
South.........	90	10
West..........	90	10

JUNE 9
EUROPEAN WAR

Interviewing Date 5/25–30/40
Survey #196–K   Question #5a

Asked of men under age 45: If the United States is attacked, would you personally volunteer to fight?

Yes............................... 86%
No................................ 7
No opinion........................ 7

Interviewing Date 5/25–30/40
Survey #196–K   Question #5b

If Canada is invaded and the United States goes to her aid, would you personally volunteer to fight?

Yes............................... 63%
No................................ 24
No opinion........................ 13

JUNE 10
THE CENSUS

Interviewing Date 5/25–30/40
Survey #196–K   Question #10

Has a Government census taker called at your home and obtained the information for the Government about you?

Yes.............................. 91%
No............................... 6
Called but didn't get information...... 1
Don't know....................... 2

JUNE 10
ALIEN REGISTRATION

Interviewing Date 5/25–30/40
Survey #196–K   Question #4

Should all people who are not United States citizens be required to register with the Government?

Yes.............................. 95%
No............................... 5

Five per cent expressed no opinion.

By Region

	Yes	No
New England.................	93%	7%
Middle Atlantic..............	93	7
East Central.................	95	5
West Central.................	94	6
South.......................	98	2
West.......................	97	3

JUNE 12
REPUBLICAN PRESIDENTIAL CANDIDATES

Interviewing Date 5/25–30/40
Survey #196–K   Question #12a

Asked of Republicans: Whom would you like to see elected President this year?

Dewey........................... 52%
Willkie.......................... 17
Taft............................ 13
Vandenberg....................... 12
Hoover.......................... 2
Landon.......................... 1
Others.......................... 3

Twenty-one per cent expressed no opinion.

Interviewing Date 5/25–30/40
Survey #196–K   Question #13a

Asked of Republicans: If it came to a choice between Thomas Dewey, Wendell Willkie, Robert Taft, and Arthur Vandenberg for the Republican presidential nomination, which man would you prefer?

Dewey........................... 50%
Willkie.......................... 18
Taft............................ 16
Vandenberg....................... 16

Twenty-four per cent expressed no opinion.

JUNE 14
PURCHASE OF ALLIED TERRITORY

Interviewing Date 6/1–6/40
Survey #197–K   Question #5

If the Allies need more money for running the war, would you be in favor of the United States and other American republics buying the British, French, and Dutch possessions in the area of the Panama Canal?

Yes.............................. 81%
No............................... 19

Seventeen per cent expressed no opinion.

JUNE 16
PARTY STRENGTH

Interviewing Date 6/9–14/40
Survey #198–K   Question #11

Which party would you like to see win the presidential election this year?

Democratic........................ 58%
Republican........................ 42

Sixteen per cent expressed no opinion.

JUNE 17
REPUBLICAN CONVENTION

Interviewing Date 5/18–23/40
Survey #195–K   Question #6

Asked of Republicans: It has been suggested that the Republican party postpone their presidential convention from June to August, in order to wait and see what is going to happen in Europe. Do you approve or disapprove of this proposal?

Approve........................... 43%
Disapprove........................ 57

Twenty-five per cent expressed no opinion.

JUNE 19
CANADA

Interviewing Date 5/25–30/40
Survey #196–K   Question #8

If Canada is actually invaded by a European power, do you think the United States should use its army and navy to aid Canada?

Yes............................... 87%
No................................ 13

Six per cent expressed no opinion.

JUNE 21
REPUBLICAN PRESIDENTIAL CANDIDATES

Interviewing Date 6/9–14/40
Survey #198–K   Question #10a

Asked of Republicans: Whom would you like to see elected President this year?

Dewey............................. 47%
Willkie........................... 29
Taft.............................. 8

Vandenberg........................ 8
Hoover............................ 6
Others............................ 2

Thirty-four per cent expressed no opinion.

JUNE 24
UNIVERSAL MILITARY TRAINING

Interviewing Date 6/13–18/40
Survey #198–J   Question #1

Do you think every abled-bodied young man 20 years old should be made to serve in the armed forces for one year?

Yes............................... 64%
No................................ 36

Six per cent expressed no opinion.

By Region

	Yes	No
New England	68%	32%
Middle Atlantic	68	32
East Central	61	39
West Central	54	46
South	68	32
West	60	40

Families with Men 18–30 Years

Yes............................... 61%
No................................ 39

Families without Men 18–30 Years

Yes............................... 67%
No................................ 33

JUNE 26
ENGLISH AND FRENCH REFUGEES

Interviewing Date 6/13–18/40
Survey #198–J   Question #6a

Should the United States permit English and French women and children to come to this country to stay until the war is over?

Yes.............................. 58%
No............................... 42

Fourteen per cent expressed no opinion.

Interviewing Date 6/13–18/40
Survey #198–J   Question #6b

If English and French refugees are allowed to come to this country, would you be willing to take care of one or more of these children in your home until the war is over?

Yes.............................. 25%
No............................... 54
Undecided........................ 21

JUNE 28
PRESIDENT ROOSEVELT

Interviewing Date 6/1–6/40
Survey #197–K   Question #15

If President Roosevelt runs for a third term, would you vote for him?

Yes.............................. 57%
No............................... 43

Thirteen per cent expressed no opinion.

By Region

	Yes	No
New England...	57%	43%
Middle Atlantic	57	43
East Central...	52	48
West Central...	53	47
South..........	73	27
West...........	55	45

JUNE 30
AID TO ENGLAND AND FRANCE

Interviewing Date 6/13–18/40
Survey #198–J   Question #4

President Roosevelt has taken action making it possible for England and France to buy some airplanes that were being used by our army and navy. Do you approve or disapprove of this action?

Approve.......................... 80%
Disapprove....................... 20

Seven per cent expressed no opinion.

By Political Affiliation

	Approve	Disapprove
Democrats....	85%	15%
Republicans..	76	24

JULY 1
DEMOCRATIC PRESIDENTIAL CANDIDATES

Interviewing Date 6/9–14/40
Survey #198–K   Question #10a

Asked of Democrats: Whom would you like to see nominated by the Democratic party for President?

Roosevelt........................ 92%
Hull............................. 3
Garner........................... 2
Farley........................... 1
McNutt........................... 1
Others........................... 1

Seventeen per cent expressed no opinion.

Interviewing Date 6/9–14/40
Survey #198–K   Question #10b

Asked of Democrats: If Franklin Roosevelt is not a candidate, whom would you like to see the Democratic party nominate for president?

Hull............................. 47%
Garner........................... 23
Farley........................... 12
McNutt........................... 9
Wheeler.......................... 3
Jackson.......................... 1
La Guardia....................... 1
Others........................... 4

Forty-eight per cent expressed no opinion.

JULY 5
FRANK KNOX AND HENRY STIMSON

Interviewing Date 6/27–7/3/40
Survey #199–K   Question #11

President Roosevelt has named two Republicans, Frank Knox and Henry Stimson, to be Secretaries of Navy and War in his cabinet. Do you approve or disapprove of his action?

Approve............................ 71%
Disapprove........................ 29

Twenty-eight per cent expressed no opinion.

By Political Affiliation

	Approve	Disapprove
Democrats.............	85%	15%
Republicans...........	57	43

JULY 7
EUROPEAN WAR

Interviewing Date 6/27–7/2/40
Survey #199–K   Question #5

If the question of the United States going to war against Germany and Italy came up for a national vote within the next two weeks, would you vote to go into the war or to stay out of the war?

Go to war......................... 14%
Stay out........................... 86

Eight per cent expressed no opinion.

By Region

	Go to War	Stay Out
New England..........	14%	86%
Middle Atlantic........	14	86
East Central..........	10	90
West Central..........	11	89
South................	23	77
West.................	16	84

By Income

Upper.................	10%	90%
Middle...............	14	86
Lower................	16	84

Interviewing Date 6/27–7/2/40
Survey #199–K   Question #12

Which side do you think will win the war?

Allies............................. 32%
Axis.............................. 35
No opinion........................ 33

JULY 8
REPUBLICAN PRESIDENTIAL CANDIDATES

Special Survey conducted between June 25–27, 1940.

Asked of Republicans: Whom would you like to see elected President this year?

Willkie............................ 44%
Dewey............................ 29
Taft.............................. 13
Others, no opinion................. 14

JULY 10
UNIVERSAL MILITARY TRAINING

Interviewing Date 6/27–7/2/40
Survey #199–K   Question #1

Asked of men between ages 21–25: Do you think every able-bodied young man 20 years old should be made to serve in the army or the navy for one year?

Yes............................... 52%
No............................... 48

Interviewing Date 6/27–7/2/40
Survey #199–K   Question #6

Asked of men between ages 21–46: If the United States were attacked by some foreign country, which branch of the armed forces would you prefer to serve in?

Army.............................. 44%
Air force.......................... 29
Navy.............................. 24
Others............................ 3

Eleven per cent expressed no opinion.

By Age
21–30 Years

Army.............................. 34%
Air force.......................... 34
Navy.............................. 29
Others............................ 3

30–45 Years

Army.............................. 50%
Air force.......................... 26
Navy.............................. 22
Others............................ 2

JULY 12
PRESIDENTIAL TRIAL HEAT

Interviewing Date 7/5–10/40
Survey #200–K   Question #9

*If President Roosevelt runs for a third term
on the Democratic ticket against Wendell
Willkie on the Republican ticket how would
you vote?*

Roosevelt.......................... 53%
Willkie............................ 47

Ten per cent expressed no opinion.

JULY 12
NEVILLE CHAMBERLAIN

Special Survey

*Asked in Great Britain: Do you think
Neville Chamberlain should be dropped
from the Government?*

Yes............................... 77%
No................................ 23

JULY 14
PARTY PLATFORMS

Interviewing Date 7/5–10/40
Survey #200–K   Question #8a

Have you read or heard about the Republican party platform?

Yes............................... 26%
No................................ 74

By Political Affiliation

	Yes	No
Democrats...................	22%	78%
Republicans..................	31	69

Interviewing Date 7/5–10/40
Survey #200–K   Question #8c

*Do you think many voters pay attention to
political platforms today?*

Yes............................... 27%
No................................ 73

Interviewing Date 7/5–10/40
Survey #200–K   Question #8d

*Should the platform of a political party be
drawn up by the convention or by the man
nominated for President?*

Convention........................ 67%
President.......................... 33

JULY 15
NATIONAL DEFENSE

Interviewing Date 6/27–7/3/40
Survey #199–K   Question #2

*Which party do you think would do the
better job of strengthening our country's
national defenses — the Republican or the
Democratic?*

Republican........................ 38%
Democratic........................ 38
No difference..................... 24

Twelve per cent expressed no opinion.

By Political Affiliation

Democrats

Republican........................ 5%
Democratic........................ 71
No difference..................... 24

Republicans

Republican........................ 69%
Democratic........................ 8
No difference..................... 23

JULY 18
WORKS PROJECTS ADMINISTRATION

Special Survey

The head of the W.P.A. says W.P.A. workers who go on strike will be dropped from the W.P.A. after five days on strike. Do you approve or disapprove of this action?

Approve............................ 74%
Disapprove......................... 26

JULY 19
AID TO ENGLAND

Interviewing Date 7/5–10/40
Survey #200–K   Question #3d

Do you think we are giving enough help to England, or do you think more ways should be found to give England help, short of going to war?

Give more help..................... 53%
Enough help now.................... 41
Give less help..................... 6

Ten per cent expressed no opinion.

By Political Affiliation
Democrats

Give more help..................... 56%
Enough help now.................... 38
Give less help..................... 6

Republicans

Give more help..................... 50%
Enough help now.................... 44
Give less help..................... 6

JULY 20
PRESIDENTIAL TRIAL HEAT

Special Survey

Asked in New York State: If the presidential election were held today, would you vote for Franklin Roosevelt or Wendell Willkie?

Roosevelt.......................... 49%
Willkie............................ 51

Fourteen per cent expressed no opinion.

JULY 22
PANAMA CANAL

Interviewing Date 7/5–10/40
Survey #200–K   Question #7

If Germany defeats England, should the United States take immediate possession of the English, French, and Dutch territories in the area of the Panama Canal?

Yes................................ 87%
No................................. 13

Thirteen per cent expressed no opinion.

By Political Affiliation

	Yes	No
Democrats....................	89%	11%
Republicans..................	86	14

By Region

New England................	87%	13%
Middle Atlantic.............	87	13
East Central................	84	16
West Central................	87	13
South.......................	94	6
West........................	88	12

JULY 24
THIRD TERM

Interviewing Date 7/5–10/40
Survey #200–K Question #10

Would you favor an amendment to the Constitution to prevent any President of the United States from serving a third term?

Yes............................... 41%
No................................ 59

By Political Affiliation

	Yes	No
Democrats....................	14%	86%
Republicans..................	69	31

JULY 26
GOVERNMENT REGULATION OF BUSINESS AND UNIONS

Interviewing Date 5/5–10/40
Survey #193–K Question #6a

During the next four years do you think business should be regulated to a greater extent by the Federal Government?

Yes............................... 33%
No................................ 67

Seventeen per cent expressed no opinion.

Interviewing Date 5/5–10/40
Survey #193–K Question #6b

Do you think labor unions should be regulated to a greater extent by the Federal Government?

Yes............................... 75%
No................................ 25

Eighteen per cent expressed no opinion.

JULY 28
PRESIDENTIAL TRIAL HEAT

Special Survey

Asked in Pennsylvania: If the presidential election were held today, would you vote for Franklin Roosevelt or Wendell Willkie?

Roosevelt........................ 48%
Willkie........................... 52

Thirteen per cent expressed no opinion.

JULY 29
UNIVERSAL MILITARY TRAINING

Interviewing Date 7/21–26/40
Survey #203–K Question #1

Do you think every able-bodied young man 20 years old should be made to serve in the armed forces for one year?

Yes............................... 67%
No................................ 33

Seven per cent expressed no opinion

By Age

	Yes	No
15–20 Years..................	67%	33%
21–29 Years..................	62	38
30–49 Years..................	69	31
50 Years and over............	68	32

By Sex

	Yes	No
Men..........................	70%	30%
Women.......................	64	36

JULY 31
PRESIDENTIAL TRIAL HEAT

Special Survey

Asked in California: If the presidential election were held today, would you vote for Franklin Roosevelt or Wendell Willkie?

Roosevelt.......................... 54%
Willkie........................... 46

Fourteen per cent expressed no opinion.

AUGUST 2
PRESIDENTIAL TRIAL HEAT

Special Survey

Asked in Texas: If the presidential election were held today, would you vote for Franklin Roosevelt or Wendell Willkie?

Roosevelt.......................... 85%
Willkie........................... 15

Nine per cent expressed no opinion.

AUGUST 4
PARTY AFFILIATION

Interviewing Date 7/21–26/40
Survey #203–K   Question #4

In politics, do you consider yourself a Democrat, Republican, Socialist, or Independent?

Democrat.......................... 41%
Republican........................ 38
Socialist.......................... 1
Independent....................... 20

Four per cent expressed no opinion.

By Region

	Independent
New England...................	30%
Middle Atlantic................	21
East Central...................	23
West Central...................	21
South..........................	10
West...........................	21

AUGUST 5
PRESIDENTIAL TRIAL HEAT

Interviewing Date 7/21–26/40
Survey #203–T   Question #2

If the presidential election were held today, would you vote for the Republican candidate, Wendell Willkie, or the Democratic candidate, Franklin Roosevelt?

Roosevelt.......................... 51%
Willkie........................... 49

Thirteen per cent expressed no opinion.

AUGUST 7
PRESIDENTIAL TRIAL HEAT

Interviewing Date 7/21–26/40
Survey #203–T   Question #2

Asked of first voters: If the presidential election were held today, would you vote for Franklin Roosevelt or Wendell Willkie?

Roosevelt.......................... 54%
Willkie........................... 46

By Income

	Roosevelt	Willkie
Upper..............	50%	50%
Middle.............	50	50
Lower..............	63	37

AUGUST 9
MOTION PICTURES

Interviewing Date 7/13–18/40
Survey #201–K   Question #15

Would you rather go to a motion picture theater showing a single feature or to one showing a double feature?

Single feature..................... 57%
Double feature.................... 43

By Age

	Single	Double
6–12 Years	23%	77%
12–17 Years	42	58
18–24 Years	60	40
24 Years and over	68	32

By Income

Upper	75%	25%
Middle	63	37
Lower	47	53
Reliefers	42	58

AUGUST 11
UNIVERSAL MILITARY TRAINING

Interviewing Date 7/21–26/40
Survey #203–K   Question #1

Do you think every able-bodied young man 20 years old should be made to serve in the armed forces for one year?

Yes	66%
No	34

Eight per cent expressed no opinion.

By Sex

	Yes	No
Men	68%	32%
Women	63	37

By Political Affiliation

Democrats	73%	27%
Republicans	60	40

AUGUST 14
PRESIDENTIAL TRIAL HEAT

Interviewing Date 8/2–7/40
Survey #204–K   Question #12

Asked in cities over 500,000 in population: If the presidential election were held today, would you vote for Franklin Roosevelt or Wendell Willkie?

Roosevelt	57%
Willkie	43

By City

	Roosevelt	Willkie
New York	62%	38%
Chicago	51	49
Philadelphia	56	44

AUGUST 14
WINSTON CHURCHILL

Special Survey

Asked in Great Britain: In general, do you approve or disapprove of Mr. Churchill as Prime Minister?

Approve	88%
Disapprove	7
No opinion	5

AUGUST 16
NATIONAL GUARD

Interviewing Date 8/2–7/40
Survey #204–T   Question #4

Do you think the National Guard should be called for one year of training?

Yes	85%
No	15

Nine per cent expressed no opinion.

AUGUST 18
BRITISH REFUGEES

Interviewing Date 8/2–7/40
Survey #204–K   Question #9

It has been suggested that the United States send American passenger ships to England to bring English refugee women and children to the United States to stay until the war is over. Would you approve or disapprove of sending our ships if Germany and Italy agree not to attack them?

Approve.......................... 63%
Disapprove....................... 37

Eight per cent expressed no opinion.

By Region

	Approve	Disapprove
New England..........	64%	36%
Middle Atlantic........	64	36
East Central..........	59	41
West Central..........	64	36
South................	67	33
West.................	60	40

AUGUST 19
DEFENSE PRODUCTION

Interviewing Date 8/2–7/40
Survey #204–K   Question #8a

Are you satisfied with the present rate of production of airplanes, tanks, warships, and guns for our national defense program?

Yes.............................. 32%
No............................... 40
No opinion....................... 28

By Region
New England and Middle Atlantic

Yes.............................. 34%
No............................... 41
No opinion....................... 25

East Central

Yes.............................. 27%
No............................... 42
No opinion....................... 31

West Central

Yes.............................. 37%
No............................... 33
No opinion....................... 30

South

Yes.............................. 27%
No............................... 42
No opinion....................... 31

West

Yes.............................. 33%
No............................... 39
No opinion....................... 28

By Political Affiliation
Democrats

Yes.............................. 35%
No............................... 37
No opinion....................... 28

Republicans

Yes.............................. 29%
No............................... 42
No opinion....................... 29

Interviewing Date 8/2–7/40
Survey #204–K   Question #8b

Do you happen to know whether or not tank production has been substantially increased?

Believe it has.................... 19%
Believe it has not................ 6
Don't know....................... 75

AUGUST 19
AID TO ENGLAND

Interviewing Date 8/11–16/40
Survey #206–K   Question #2

General Pershing says the United States should sell to England 50 of our destroyer ships which were built during the last World War and are now being put back in service. Do you approve or disapprove of our Government selling these destroyers to England?

Approve........................... 62%
Disapprove....................... 38

Eight per cent expressed no opinion.

Interviewing Date 8/11–16/40
Survey #206–T   Question #2

England needs destroyer ships to replace those which have been damaged or sunk. The United States has some destroyers which were built during the last World War and are now being put back in active service. Do you think we should sell some of these ships to England?

Yes.............................. 61%
No.............................. 39

Nine per cent expressed no opinion.

Note: The question covering the issue was worded in two different ways, and each version was put to a separate but comparable cross section of voters. The two wordings brought almost exactly the same result.

AUGUST 21
PRESIDENTIAL TRIAL HEAT

Special Survey

Asked in Ohio: If the presidential election were held today, would you vote for Franklin Roosevelt or Wendell Willkie?

Roosevelt......................... 47%
Willkie........................... 53

AUGUST 23
PRESIDENTIAL TRIAL HEAT

Special Survey

Asked in New Jersey: If the presidential election were held today, would you vote for Franklin Roosevelt or Wendell Willkie?

Roosevelt........................... 49%
Willkie............................ 51

AUGUST 24
PRESIDENTIAL TRIAL HEAT

Special Survey

If the presidential election were held today, would you vote for Franklin Roosevelt or Wendell Willkie?

Roosevelt......................... 51%
Willkie........................... 49

Twelve per cent expressed no opinion.

AUGUST 28
PRESIDENTIAL TRIAL HEAT

Special Survey

If the presidential election were held today, would you vote for Franklin Roosevelt or Wendell Willkie?

By Income

	Roosevelt	Willkie
Upper..............	29%	71%
Middle.............	47	53
Lower..............	66	34
Reliefers............	75	25

AUGUST 30
THE DRAFT

Interviewing Date 8/11–16/40
Survey #206–K   Question #1a

Do you favor increasing the size of our army and navy now by drafting men between the ages of 21 and 31 to serve in the armed forces for one year?

Yes.............................. 71%
No.............................. 29

Five per cent expressed no opinion.

Montana Only

Yes.............................. 62%
No............................... 38

Eleven per cent of those polled in Montana expressed no opinion.

Interviewing Date 8/11–16/40
Survey #206–K   Question #1b

Asked of men between the ages of 16 and 20: If the draft law is passed, will you, personally, have any objection to spending a year in some branch of military service?

Yes.............................. 19%
No.............................. 81

AUGUST 31
PARTY STRENGTH

Special Survey

Asked in Maine: Which party would you like to see win the presidential election this year?

Republican....................... 64%
Democratic....................... 36

Twelve per cent expressed no opinion.

SEPTEMBER 2
EUROPEAN WAR

Interviewing Date 8/2–7/40
Survey #204–K   Question #7a

If there is starvation in France, Holland, and Belgium this winter, should the United States try to send food to those countries in our ships?

Yes.............................. 38%
No.............................. 62

Ten per cent expressed no opinion.

By Region

	Yes	No
New England..................	37%	63%
Middle Atlantic..............	37	63
East Central.................	41	59
West Central.................	38	62
South........................	37	63
West.........................	38	62

Farmers Only

Yes.............................. 35%
No.............................. 65

Interviewing Date 8/2–7/40
Survey #204–K   Question #7b

Asked of those who replied in the affirmative: Would you be willing to send food even if some might go to the Germans?

Yes.............................. 22%
No.............................. 78

SEPTEMBER 3
PRESIDENTIAL TRIAL HEAT

Interviewing Date 8/24–29/40
Survey #207–K   Question #9a

Whom do you favor for President — Franklin Roosevelt or Wendell Willkie?

Roosevelt........................ 51%
Willkie.......................... 49

Ten per cent expressed no opinion.

SEPTEMBER 4
EUROPEAN WAR

Interviewing Date 8/10–15/40
Survey #205–K   Question #6

If England is defeated between now and election time and it looks as though the United States might have to fight Germany, which candidate would you prefer for President — Willkie or Roosevelt?

Roosevelt.......................... 58%
Willkie........................... 42

Ten per cent expressed no opinion.

SEPTEMBER 5
EUROPEAN WAR

Interviewing Date 8/11–16/40
Survey #206–K   Question #2

England needs destroyer ships to replace those which have been damaged or sunk. The United States has some destroyers which were built during the last World War and are now being put back in active service. Do you think we should sell some of these ships to England?

Yes.............................. 60%
No............................... 40

Ten per cent expressed no opinion.

By Political Affiliation

	Yes	No
Democrats..................	63%	37%
Republicans.................	58	42

SEPTEMBER 6
PRESIDENTIAL CAMPAIGN

Interviewing Date 8/24–29/40
Survey #207–K   Question #1

Wendell Willkie proposed that he and President Roosevelt hold a series of debates, both speaking from the same platform. Do you think the President should accept the proposal?

Yes.............................. 49%
No............................... 51

Fourteen per cent expressed no opinion.

SEPTEMBER 8
THE CENSUS

Interviewing Date 5/16–21/40
Survey #194–K   Question #8

Has a Government census taker called at your home and obtained the information for the Government about you?

Yes.............................. 98%
No............................... 2

SEPTEMBER 8
PRESIDENTIAL TRIAL HEAT

Special Survey

Asked in Maine: If the presidential election were held today, would you vote for Franklin Roosevelt or Wendell Willkie?

Roosevelt.......................... 36%
Willkie........................... 64

SEPTEMBER 11
EUROPEAN WAR

Interviewing Date 9/5–10/40
Survey #209–K   Question #1

Which side do you think will win the war?

England........................... 43%
Germany........................... 17
No opinion........................ 40

Interviewing Date 8/24–29/40
Survey #207–K   Question #7

Recently the English claimed that they shot down 387 German planes in one week and lost only 94 of their own. Do you think this report is accurate?

Yes.............................. 19%
No............................... 58
No opinion........................ 23

Interviewing Date 8/24–29/40
Survey #207–T   Question #7

Recently the Germans claimed that they shot down 427 English planes in one week and lost only 99 of their own. Do you think this report is accurate?

Yes.............................. 3%
No............................... 86
No opinion........................ 11

SEPTEMBER 13
PRESIDENTIAL TRIAL HEAT

Interviewing Date 8/24–29/40
Survey #207–K   Question #9a

Asked of labor union members: If the presidential election were held today, would you vote for Franklin Roosevelt or Wendell Willkie?

Roosevelt......................... 64%
Willkie........................... 36

Twelve per cent expressed no opinion.

A.F.L. Members Only

Roosevelt......................... 62%
Willkie........................... 38

C.I.O. Members Only

Roosevelt......................... 75%
Willkie........................... 25

SEPTEMBER 15
EUROPEAN WAR

Interviewing Date 8/24–29/40
Survey #207–K   Question #3a

Mr. Bullitt, our Ambassador to France, says that if Great Britain is defeated the Germans will invade the United States. Do you think they will?

Yes.............................. 42%
No............................... 45
No opinion........................ 13

Interviewing Date 8/2–7/40
Survey #204–K   Question #6b

Without mentioning names, do you think there are any fifth columnists in this community?

Yes.............................. 48%
No............................... 26
No opinion........................ 26

SEPTEMBER 15
PRESIDENTIAL TRIAL HEAT

Special Survey

If the presidential election were held today, would you vote for Franklin Roosevelt or Wendell Willkie?

Missouri Only

Roosevelt......................... 53%
Willkie........................... 47

Ten per cent expressed no opinion.

Kentucky Only

Roosevelt......................... 55%
Willkie........................... 45

Nine per cent expressed no opinion.

West Virginia Only

Roosevelt......................... 55%
Willkie........................... 45

Thirteen per cent expressed no opinion.

Maryland Only

Roosevelt......................... 56%
Willkie........................... 44

Thirteen per cent expressed no opinion.

Delaware Only

Roosevelt......................... 55%
Willkie........................... 45

Twelve per cent expressed no opinion.

SEPTEMBER 20
PRESIDENTIAL TRIAL HEAT

Interviewing Date 9/5–10/40
Survey #209–K   Question #4

Whom do you favor for President — Franklin Roosevelt or Wendell Willkie?

Roosevelt	55%
Willkie	45

Eleven per cent expressed no opinion.

Roosevelt States

	Roosevelt	Willkie
South Carolina	98%	2%
Mississippi	95	5
Georgia	86	14
Louisiana	86	14
Alabama	85	15
Texas	83	17
Arkansas	80	20
Florida	75	25
North Carolina	72	28
Virginia	70	30
Tennessee	69	31
Arizona	69	31
Oklahoma	63	37
New Mexico	63	37
Nevada	62	38
Maryland	61	39
Montana	60	40
Delaware	60	40
California	58	42
Kentucky	58	42
West Virginia	57	43
Washington	57	43
Utah	57	43
Missouri	56	44
Connecticut	56	44
Rhode Island	56	44
Idaho	55	45
New Jersey	54	46
Michigan	54	46
Wyoming	54	46
Illinois	53	47
Ohio	53	47
Oregon	53	47
New York	52	48
Pennsylvania	52	48
Colorado	52	48
Minnesota	51	49
Wisconsin	51	49

Willkie States

	Willkie	Roosevelt
Maine	56%	44%
Vermont	56	44
South Dakota	55	45
Iowa	54	46
North Dakota	54	46
Kansas	53	47
Nebraska	53	47
Massachusetts	51	49
Indiana	51	49
New Hampshire	51	49

SEPTEMBER 21
DEFENSE PRODUCTION

Interviewing Date 9/5–10/40
Survey #208   Question #1a

Are you satisfied with the present rate of production of airplanes, tanks, warships, and guns for our national defense program?

Yes	40%
No	41
No opinion	19

By Political Affiliation
Democrats

Yes	46%
No	36
No opinion	18

Republicans

Yes	32%
No	48
No opinion	20

Asked of those who responded in the negative: Who do you think is responsible for defense delays?

Roosevelt	14%
Congress	11
Industry	3
Public apathy	2
Others	3
No opinion	8
	41%

SEPTEMBER 23
NEUTRALITY

Which of these two things do you think is the most important for the United States to try to do — to keep out of war ourselves or to help England win, even at the risk of getting into the war?

Keep out	48%
Help England	52

Five per cent expressed no opinion.

By Region

	Keep Out	Help England
New England	48%	52%
Middle Atlantic	48	52
East Central	52	48
West Central	57	43
South	30	70
West	46	54

SEPTEMBER 25
PRESIDENTIAL TRIAL HEAT

Special Survey

Asked of Independent voters: If the presidential election were held today, would you vote for Franklin Roosevelt or Wendell Willkie?

New York Only

Roosevelt	49%
Willkie	51

Twenty per cent expressed no opinion

Pennsylvania Only

Roosevelt	62%
Willkie	38

Nineteen per cent expressed no opinion.

Ohio Only

Roosevelt	52%
Willkie	48

Nineteen per cent expressed no opinion.

Illinois Only

Roosevelt	46%
Willkie	54

Nineteen per cent expressed no opinion.

Michigan Only

Roosevelt	53%
Willkie	47

Nineteen per cent expressed no opinion.

California Only

Roosevelt	52%
Willkie	48

Sixteen per cent expressed no opinion.

SEPTEMBER 27
PRESIDENTIAL TRIAL HEAT

Special Survey

If the presidential election were held today, would you vote for Franklin Roosevelt or Wendell Willkie?

By Community Size

	Roosevelt	Willkie
500,000 and over.....	61%	39%
2,500–500,000........	55	45
2,500 and under......	51	49
Farms..............	53	47
Midwestern farms only	46	54

By Age

	Roosevelt	Willkie
21–24 Years........	59%	41%
25–29 Years........	59	41
30–49 Years........	56	44
50 Years and over....	54	46

SEPTEMBER 28
ELECTION FORECAST

Interviewing Date 9/19–24/40
Survey #210–K   Question #8

Regardless of how you yourself plan to vote, who do you think will be elected President?

Roosevelt........................... 68%
Willkie............................. 32

Sixteen per cent expressed no opinion.

By Political Affiliation

	Roosevelt	Willkie
Democrats..........	96%	4%
Republicans.........	27	73

OCTOBER 1
PRESIDENTIAL TRIAL HEAT

Special Survey

Asked in Nebraska: If the presidential election were held today, would you vote for Franklin Roosevelt or Wendell Willkie?

Roosevelt........................... 43%
Willkie............................. 57

Eight per cent expressed no opinion.

OCTOBER 2
PRESIDENTIAL TRIAL HEAT

Special Survey

Asked in Massachusetts: If the presidential election were held today, would you vote for Franklin Roosevelt or Wendell Willkie?

Roosevelt........................... 52%
Willkie............................. 48

Six per cent expressed no opinion.

OCTOBER 4
PRESIDENTIAL TRIAL HEAT

Special Survey

If the presidential election were held today, would you vote for Franklin Roosevelt or Wendell Willkie?

California Only

Roosevelt........................... 57%
Willkie............................. 43

Nine per cent expressed no opinion.

Oregon Only

Roosevelt........................... 56%
Willkie............................. 44

Eleven per cent expressed no opinion.

Washington Only

Roosevelt........................... 58%
Willkie............................. 42

Ten per cent expressed no opinion.

OCTOBER 6
PRESIDENTIAL TRIAL HEAT

Interviewing Date 9/28–10/3/40
Survey #212–K   Question #2

Whom do you favor for President, Franklin Roosevelt or Wendell Willkie?

Roosevelt.......................... 56%
Willkie........................... 44

Nine per cent expressed no opinion. One per cent named a third party candidate.

OCTOBER 9
COMMUNIST PARTY

Interviewing Date 9/22–27/40
Survey #211-K   Question #2a

Should Communist party candidates be allowed the same amount of time on the radio as the Democratic and Republican candidates?

Yes............................... 29%
No................................ 71

Ten per cent expressed no opinion.

Interviewing Date 9/22–27/40
Survey #211-K   Question #2b

Do you think Communist party candidates should be allowed any time on the radio?

Yes............................... 37%
No................................ 63

Thirteen per cent expressed no opinion.

Interviewing Date 9/22–27/40
Survey #211–T   Question #2a

Should Communist party candidates be allowed the same amount of free time on the radio as the Democratic and Republican candidates?

Yes............................... 25%
No................................ 75

Eleven per cent expressed no opinion.

Interviewing Date 9/22–27/40
Survey #211–T   Question #2b

Do you think Communist party candidates should be allowed any free time on the radio?

Yes............................... 31%
No................................ 69

Fifteen per cent expressed no opinion.

OCTOBER 13
PRESIDENTIAL TRIAL HEAT

Special Survey

Asked of property owners: If the presidential election were held today, would you vote for Franklin Roosevelt or Wendell Willkie?

Roosevelt.......................... 47%
Willkie........................... 53

Ten per cent expressed no opinion.

OCTOBER 14
EUROPEAN WAR

Interviewing Date 9/28–10/5/40
Survey #212–K   Question #1

If you were asked to vote today on the question of the United States entering the war against Germany and Italy, how would you vote — to go into the war or to stay out of the war?

Go in............................. 17%
Stay out.......................... 83

Eight per cent expressed no opinion.

By Region

	Go In	Stay Out
New England.......	18%	82%
Middle Atlantic......	20	80
East Central........	12	88
West Central........	14	86
South..............	24	76
West..............	20	80

OCTOBER 15
PRESIDENTIAL TRIAL HEAT

Special Survey

If the presidential election were being held today, would you vote for Franklin Roosevelt or Wendell Willkie?

Illinois Only

Roosevelt........................... 48%
Willkie............................. 52

Eleven per cent expressed no opinion.

Ohio Only

Roosevelt........................... 52%
Willkie............................. 48

Ten per cent expressed no opinion.

Indiana Only

Roosevelt........................... 47%
Willkie............................. 53

Nine per cent expressed no opinion.

Michigan Only

Roosevelt........................... 48%
Willkie............................. 52

Nine per cent expressed no opinion.

OCTOBER 20
JAPAN

Interviewing Date 10/2–7/40
Survey #213–K   Question #5

Do you think our Government should forbid the sale of arms, airplanes, gasoline, and other war materials to Japan?

Yes............................... 90%
No............................... 10

Eight per cent expressed no opinion.

By Political Affiliation

	Yes	No
Democrats....................	90%	10%
Republicans..................	90	10

Interviewing Date 10/2–7/40
Survey #213–K   Question #6

President Roosevelt has forbidden the shipment of scrap iron from this country to Japan. Do you approve or disapprove?

Approve........................... 96%
Disapprove........................ 4

Eight per cent expressed no opinion.

By Political Affiliation

	Approve	Disapprove
Democrats.............	96%	4%
Republicans...........	95	5

OCTOBER 21
PRESIDENTIAL CANDIDATES

Interviewing Date 10/2–7/40
Survey #213–T   Question #4

Asked of Willkie supporters: Have you, at any time since President Roosevelt was renominated, planned to vote for him?

Yes............................... 8%
No............................... 92

Interviewing Date 10/2–7/40
Survey #213–T   Question #4a

Asked of those who replied in the affirmative: What was the main reason that changed your mind?

The following are listed in order of frequency of mention:

Anxiety over a third term
Roosevelt's policies will get us into war
Favorable impression of Willkie

Interviewing Date 10/2–7/40
Survey #213–T   Question #4b

Asked of Roosevelt supporters: Have you, at any time since Mr. Willkie was nominated, planned to vote for him?

Yes............................... 10%
No................................ 90

Interviewing Date 10/2–7/40
Survey #213–T   Question #4c

Asked of those who replied in the affirmative: What was the main reason that changed your mind?

The following are listed in order of frequency of mention:

Disappointment with Willkie's speeches and campaign

Roosevelt's experience is needed in current war crisis

OCTOBER 22
PRESIDENTIAL TRIAL HEAT

Interviewing Date 10/7–12/40
Survey #214–T   Question #3

If there were no war in Europe today, which presidential candidate would you vote for, Franklin Roosevelt or Wendell Willkie?

Roosevelt........................... 47%
Willkie............................. 53

Eight per cent expressed no opinion.

OCTOBER 25
PRESIDENTIAL TRIAL HEAT

Interviewing Date 10/11–16/40
Survey #215–K   Question #5

Asked in New York State: If the presidential election were held today, would you vote for Franklin Roosevelt or Wendell Willkie?

Roosevelt........................... 51%
Willkie............................. 49

Nine per cent expressed no opinion.

New York City Only

Roosevelt........................... 61%
Willkie............................. 39

Upstate Only

Roosevelt........................... 40%
Willkie............................. 60

OCTOBER 26
PRESIDENTIAL TRIAL HEAT

Interviewing Date 10/11–16/40
Survey #215–K   Question #5

If the presidential election were held today, would you vote for Franklin Roosevelt or Wendell Willkie?

Maine Only

Roosevelt........................... 46%
Willkie............................. 54

Six per cent expressed no opinion.

New Hampshire Only

Roosevelt........................... 49%
Willkie............................. 51

Eight per cent expressed no opinion.

Vermont Only

Roosevelt........................... 43%
Willkie............................. 57

Eight per cent expressed no opinion.

Massachusetts Only

Roosevelt........................... 51%
Willkie............................. 49

Seven per cent expressed no opinion.

Rhode Island Only

Roosevelt.......................... 55%
Willkie............................ 45

Eight per cent expressed no opinion.

Connecticut Only

Roosevelt.......................... 54%
Willkie............................ 46

Eleven per cent expressed no opinion.

OCTOBER 26
MINNESOTA POLITICS

Interviewing Date 10/11–16/40
Survey #215–K   Question #12

*Asked in Minnesota: For whom do you
plan to vote for Governor?*

Harold Stassen..................... 59%
Hjalmar Petersen................... 28
Ed Murphy......................... 13

Ten per cent expressed no opinion.

OCTOBER 27
PRESIDENTIAL TRIAL HEAT

Interviewing Date 10/11–16/40
Survey #215–K   Question #5

*If the presidential election were held today,
would you vote for Franklin Roosevelt or
Wendell Willkie?*

Roosevelt......................... 54.5%
Willkie........................... 45.5

Seven per cent expressed no opinion.

OCTOBER 30
PRESIDENTIAL TRIAL HEAT

Interviewing Date 10/11–16/40
Survey #215–K   Question #5

*If the presidential election were held today,
would you vote for Franklin Roosevelt or
Wendell Willkie?*

Ohio Only

Roosevelt.......................... 49%
Willkie............................ 51

Four per cent expressed no opinion.

Indiana Only

Roosevelt.......................... 47%
Willkie............................ 53

Four per cent expressed no opinion.

OCTOBER 31
EUROPEAN WAR

Special Survey

*Asked in Great Britain: From what you
have experienced or read or heard about
during the past few weeks do you think it
is possible or impossible for Germany to
win the war by air attack alone on this
country?*

Possible........................... 6%
Impossible......................... 80
Don't know........................ 14

OCTOBER 31
PRESIDENTIAL TRIAL HEAT

Interviewing Date 10/11–16/40
Survey #215–K   Question #2a

*If the presidential election were held today,
would you vote for Franklin Roosevelt or
Wendell Willkie?*

Missouri Only

Roosevelt.......................... 49%
Willkie............................ 51

Seven per cent expressed no opinion.

Kentucky Only

Roosevelt.......................... 54%
Willkie............................ 46

Seven per cent expressed no opinion.

Oklahoma Only

Roosevelt............................ 55%
Willkie............................. 45

Ten per cent expressed no opinion.

NOVEMBER 1
PRESIDENTIAL TRIAL HEAT

Interviewing Date 10/24–29/40
Survey #217   Question #2a

If the presidential election were held today, would you vote for Franklin Roosevelt or Wendell Willkie?

Wisconsin Only

Roosevelt........................... 48%
Willkie............................. 52

Michigan Only

Roosevelt........................... 48%
Willkie............................. 52

Minnesota Only

Roosevelt........................... 51%
Willkie............................. 49

Maryland Only

Roosevelt........................... 58%
Willkie............................. 42

NOVEMBER 4
PRESIDENTIAL TRIAL HEAT —
FINAL POLL

Interviewing Date 10/26–31/40
Survey #218–K   Question #2a

If the presidential election were held today, would you vote for Franklin Roosevelt or Wendell Willkie?

Roosevelt........................... 52%
Willkie............................. 48

By State
Roosevelt States

	Roosevelt
South Carolina.....................	97%
Mississippi........................	94
Georgia............................	87
Alabama............................	86
Louisiana..........................	86
Arkansas...........................	82
Texas..............................	79
North Carolina.....................	72
Florida............................	72
Virginia...........................	70
Tennessee..........................	64
Arizona............................	61
Maryland...........................	59
West Virginia......................	59
California.........................	58
Montana............................	57
Washington.........................	57
Nevada.............................	56
Oklahoma...........................	56
Delaware...........................	56
Utah...............................	55
Kentucky...........................	54
Oregon.............................	54
Rhode Island.......................	54
Wyoming............................	53
New Mexico.........................	53
Connecticut........................	53
New Jersey.........................	52
Massachusetts......................	51
Minnesota..........................	51

Willkie States

	Willkie
Nebraska...........................	59%
South Dakota.......................	59
Vermont............................	58
Maine..............................	57
Kansas.............................	57
Iowa...............................	55
Indiana............................	55
Colorado...........................	55
North Dakota.......................	54
Illinois...........................	52
Michigan...........................	52

	Willkie
Wisconsin	52%
Ohio	51
New York	51
Pennsylvania	51
Missouri	51
New Hampshire	51
Idaho	51

NOVEMBER 9
ELECTION ANALYSIS

The American Institute of Public Opinion's final preelection report showed Franklin Roosevelt with 52% of the total popular vote, or 2.5% less than he received in the election returns.

By Region

	Gallup Poll For Roosevelt	Error
New England	50.5%	−2.6%
Middle Atlantic	49.5	−2.9
East North Central	47.8	−3.1
West North Central	46.6	−2.2
South Atlantic	68.1	−0.4
East South Central	66.1	−4.0
West South Central	73.1	−1.1
Mountain	51.7	−4.2
Pacific	56.0	−2.0
Average Error		2.5%

NOVEMBER 10
NATIONAL DEFENSE

Interviewing Date 10/24–29/40
Survey #220   Question #4

Who do you think will do the better job of strengthening our national defense — Roosevelt or Willkie?

Roosevelt	61%
Willkie	39

Thirteen per cent expressed no opinion.

Interviewing Date 10/24–29/40
Survey #220   Question #5

If the United States should get into the war, which man would you prefer to have as President — Roosevelt or Willkie?

Roosevelt	60%
Willkie	40

Nine per cent expressed no opinion.

NOVEMBER 15
EUROPEAN WAR

Special Survey

Asked in Great Britain: In view of the indiscriminate bombing of this country, would you approve or disapprove if the R.A.F. adopted a similar policy of bombing the civilian population of Germany?

Approve	46%
Disapprove	46
No opinion	8

NOVEMBER 18
AID TO ENGLAND

Interviewing Date 10/11–16/40
Survey #215–K   Question #1a

If it appears that England will be defeated by Germany and Italy unless the United States supplies her with more food and war materials, would you be in favor of giving more help to England?

Yes	90%
No	10

Six per cent expressed no opinion.

By Region

	Yes	No
New England	92%	8%
Middle Atlantic	92	8
East Central	87	13
West Central	86	14
South	94	6
West	90	10

NOVEMBER 20
NEUTRALITY

Interviewing Date 10/7–12/40
Survey #219–K   Question #1

The Johnson Act prevents any country that has stopped paying interest on its debt of the last World War from borrowing money in the United States. Would you approve of changing this law so that England could borrow money from our Government?

Yes.................................. 54%
No.................................. 46

Twelve per cent expressed no opinion.

NOVEMBER 22
BUSINESS AND LABOR REGULATION

Interviewing Date 10/26–31/40
Survey #219–K   Question #4a

During the next four years do you think there should be more or less regulation of business by the Federal Government than at present?

More.............................. 27%
Less.............................. 51
Same.............................. 22

Twenty per cent expressed no opinion.

Interviewing Date 10/26–31/40
Survey #219–K   Question #4b

During the next four years do you think there should be more or less regulation of labor unions by the Federal Government than at present?

More.............................. 60%
Less.............................. 21
Same.............................. 19

Twenty-seven per cent expressed no opinion.

NOVEMBER 24
AID TO ENGLAND

Interviewing Date 10/11–16/40
Survey #215–K   Question #1d

Should the United States send more airplanes to England, even though this might delay our own national defense program?

Yes.................................. 60%
No.................................. 40

Ten per cent expressed no opinion.

By Region

	Yes	No
New England................	60%	40%
Middle Atlantic..............	60	40
East Central.................	54	46
West Central.................	56	44
South.......................	72	28
West.......................	64	36

NOVEMBER 25
PROHIBITION

Interviewing Date 11/5–10/40
Survey #223   Question #1

If the question of national prohibition should come up again, would you vote for prohibition?

Yes.................................. 32%
No.................................. 68

Seven per cent expressed no opinion.

By Region

	Yes	No
New England................	24%	76%
Middle Atlantic..............	23	77
East Central.................	35	65
West Central.................	36	64
South.......................	44	56
West.......................	44	56

By Community Size

100,000 and over.............. 21% 79%
10,000–100,000................ 29 71
Under 10,000................. 38 62
Farms....................... 46 54

NOVEMBER 27
EUROPEAN WAR

Interviewing Date 10/25–29/40
Survey #221   Question #1

Which side do you think will win the war?

England........................... 63%
Germany........................... 7
No opinion........................ 30

NOVEMBER 29
AID TO GREECE

Interviewing Date 11/21–26/40
Survey #224–T   Question #14

Do you think the United States should lend money to Greece for the purchase of arms, airplanes, and other war materials?

Yes............................... 60%
No................................ 40

Fifteen per cent expressed no opinion.

NOVEMBER 30
EUROPEAN WAR

Special Survey

Asked in Great Britain: From what you have experienced or read or heard about during the past few weeks, do you think it is possible or impossible for Germany to win the war by air attack alone on this country?

Possible.......................... 6%
Impossible........................ 80
No opinion........................ 14

DECEMBER 2
EUROPEAN WAR

Interviewing Date 10/26–31/40
Survey #219–K   Question #1

Do you think the United States will go into the war in Europe sometime before it is over, or do you think we will stay out of the war?

Go in............................. 59%
Stay out.......................... 41

Six per cent expressed no opinion.

DECEMBER 4
DIES COMMITTEE

Interviewing Date 11/21–26/40
Survey #224–K   Question #12b

Do you think the Dies Committee should be continued?

Yes............................... 65%
No................................ 7
No opinion, never heard of Committee. 28

DECEMBER 11
EUROPEAN WAR

Special Survey

Asked in Great Britain: If someone in your presence suggested that it would be a good idea to have a negotiated peace with Germany now, what would you do?

Agree that it would be a good idea..... 7%
Contradict him.................... 59
Report him to the authorities........ 13
Say nothing, no opinion............. 21

DECEMBER 8
NEUTRALITY

Interviewing Date 10/11–16/40
Survey #215–K   Question #1b

Should the Neutrality Law be changed so that American ships can carry war supplies to England?

Yes................................ 40%
No................................ 60

Fourteen per cent expressed no opinion.

By Political Affiliation

	Yes	No
Democrats...................	48%	52%
Republicans..................	33	67

The South is the only section where a majority of those with opinions favor relaxing the Neutrality Law. Fifty-three per cent of Southerners voted yes, as compared with 40% in the East, and 33% in the farm-belt states of the Mississippi Valley.

DECEMBER 13
PANAMA CANAL

Interviewing Date 12/1–6/40
Survey #225–K   Question #4

If England offers to pay its World War debt to the United States by giving us islands or land near the Panama Canal, would you approve our accepting this offer?

Yes................................ 88%
No................................ 12

Ten per cent expressed no opinion.

DECEMBER 15
EUROPEAN WAR

Special Survey

Asked in Great Britain: Do you think our enemy is the German people or only the Nazi Government?

People............................ 52%
Government...................... 48

Less than 1% expressed no opinion.

DECEMBER 16
WORLD WAR I

Interviewing Date 11/21–36/40
Survey #224–K   Question #6

Do you think it was a mistake for the United States to enter the last World War?

Yes................................ 39%
No................................ 42
No opinion....................... 19

By Political Affiliation
Democrats

Yes................................ 33%
No................................ 46
No opinion....................... 21

Republicans

Yes................................ 46%
No................................ 38
No opinion....................... 16

By Age
21–34 Years

Yes................................ 36%
No................................ 39
No opinion....................... 25

35–49 Years

Yes................................ 37%
No................................ 44
No opinion....................... 19

50 Years and Over

Yes................................ 44%
No................................ 42
No opinion....................... 14

DECEMBER 18
DRAFTING OF WOMEN

Interviewing Date 12/1–6/40
Survey #225–K   Question #2

Would you be in favor of starting now to draft American women between the ages 21 and 35 to train them for jobs in war time?

Yes................................ 48%
No................................. 52

Six per cent expressed no opinion.

By Sex

	Yes	No
Men	44%	56%
Women	52	48

By Income

	Yes	No
Upper	41%	59%
Middle	44	56
Lower	55	45

Women Ages 21–35 Only

Yes................................ 54%
No................................. 46

DECEMBER 20
JOHNSON ACT

Interviewing Date 12/4–9/40
Survey #225–T   Question #3

The Johnson Act prevents any country that has stopped paying interest on its debt of the last World War from borrowing money in the United States. Would you approve of changing this law so that England could borrow money from our Government?

Yes................................ 55%
No................................. 45

Nine per cent expressed no opinion.

By Region

	Yes	No
New England	57%	43%
Middle Atlantic	57	43
East Central	49	51
West Central	49	51
South	69	31
West	57	43

DECEMBER 21
CONSCIENTIOUS OBJECTORS

Interviewing Date 12/4–9/40
Survey #225–T   Question #1

A group of students studying for the ministry who are concientious objectors refused to register for the draft and were sentenced to a year in jail. Do you think this punishment was too severe or not severe enough?

About right........................ 55%
Too severe......................... 24
Not severe enough.................. 21

DECEMBER 22
EUROPEAN WAR

Special Survey

Asked in Great Britain: Do you think the Government should draw up and publish our war aims?

Yes................................ 42%
No................................. 35
No opinion......................... 23

DECEMBER 23
HEALTH

Interviewing Date 12/1–6/40
Survey #225–K   Question #10a

Would the health of your family be better if you had more money each week to spend on food?

Yes................................ 40%
No................................. 60

Interviewing Date 12/1–6/40
Survey #225–K   Question #10b

Asked of those who responded in the affirmative: If you had more money, what foods would you spend it on?

Meat............................... 37%
Vegetables......................... 31
Fruit.............................. 27

Dairy products...................... 21
"Good solid food"................... 16
Bread and Cereals.................. 7
Eggs.............................. 7
Sweets............................ 5
Others............................ 16
                                   ———
                                   167%

Note: table adds to more than 40% because most people mentioned more than one item.

Interviewing Date 11/21–26/40
Survey #224–K   Question #14b

Do you happen to take regular physical exercise now?

Yes............................... 24%
No................................ 76

Interviewing Date 12/1–6/40
Survey #225–K   Question #11a

It has been suggested that the Federal Government organize a national program to interest more people in taking regular exercise to improve the health of the country. Would you approve or disapprove of such a program?

Approve........................... 71%
Disapprove........................ 29

Interviewing Date 12/1–6/40
Survey #225–K   Question #11b

Would you be willing to take part in such a program?

Yes............................... 65%
No................................ 35

DECEMBER 26
PERSONAL SECURITY

Interviewing Date 12/1–6/40
Survey #225–K   Question #8a

If you lost your present job or business and couldn't find other work, how long do you think you could hold out before you would have to apply for relief?

One month or less.................. 25%
Two to six months.................. 19
Six months to three years.......... 13
Three years and over............... 29
Already on relief.................. 14

Interviewing Date 12/1–6/40
Survey #225–K   Question #8b

Asked of these groups: For which candidate did you vote for President — Franklin Roosevelt or Wendell Willkie?

	Roosevelt	Willkie
One month or less....	60%	40%
Two to six months....	58	42
Six months to three years........	49	51
Three years and over..	39	61
Already on relief.....	80	20

DECEMBER 27
GERMANY

Special Survey

Have you read or heard about the speech of a Nazi official published recently which said that the Germans plan to make slaves of the people in Europe and to control American industry and trade?

Yes............................... 33%
No................................ 67

Asked of those who replied in the affirmative: Do you believe that the Germans plan to do this?

Yes............................... 80%
No................................ 20

DECEMBER 29
THE DRAFT

Interviewing Date 12/18–23/40
Survey #226–K   Question #10b

Do you think the draft is being handled fairly?

Yes.............................. 92%
No.............................. 8

Eleven per cent expressed no opinion.

Interviewing Date 12/18–23/40
Survey #226–K   Question #10a
Do you think the draft is a good thing?

Yes.............................. 89%
No.............................. 11

Twelve per cent expressed no opinion.

Interviewing Date 12/18–23/40
Survey #226–K   Question #10c
Do you think the Army is taking good care of the men drafted so far?

Yes.............................. 91%
No.............................. 9

Twelve per cent expressed no opinion.

DECEMBER 30
EUROPEAN WAR

Interviewing Date 12/1–6/40
Survey #225–K   Question #5
If you were asked to vote on the question of the United States entering the war against Germany and Italy, how would you vote — to go into the war or to stay out of the war?

Go in.............................. 12%
Stay out.............................. 88

Three per cent expressed no opinion.

By Region

	Go In	Stay Out
New England........	13%	87%
Middle Atlantic......	13	87
East Central........	10	90
West Central........	9	91
South..............	17	83
West..............	14	86

Interviewing Date 12/18–23/40
Survey #226–K   Question #1
Which of these two things do you think is the more important for the United States to try to do — to keep out of war ourselves, or to help England win even at the risk of getting into the war?

Keep out.............................. 40%
Help England.............................. 60

Two per cent expressed no opinion.

By Region

	Keep Out	Help England
New England........	38%	62%
Middle Atlantic......	38	62
East Central........	46	54
West Central........	46	54
South..............	25	75
West..............	35	65

1941

JANUARY 3
EUROPEAN WAR

Interviewing Date 12/18–23/40
Survey #226–K   Question #3

Do you think our country's future safety depends on England winning this war?

Yes.................................. 68%
No.................................. 26
No opinion......................... 6

Interviewing Date 12/18–23/40
Survey #226–K   Question #5

If the United States stopped sending war materials to England, do you think England would lose the war?

Yes.................................. 85%
No.................................. 8
No opinion......................... 7

Interviewing Date 12/18–23/40
Survey #226–K   Question #4b

If Germany tries to invade England within the next year, do you think she will be successful in conquering England?

Yes.................................. 11%
No.................................. 74
No opinion......................... 15

JANUARY 4
WARPLANE PRODUCTION

Interviewing Date 12/18–23/40
Survey #226–K   Question #11a

Do you think America's warplane production is going ahead fast enough?

Yes.................................. 28%
No.................................. 58
No opinion......................... 14

Interviewing Date 12/18–23/40
Survey #226–K   Question #11b

Asked of those who responded in the negative: Whose fault do you think it is?

The following are listed according to frequency of mention:

Roosevelt Administration
Labor and union leaders
Industry and business leaders
Congress and politicians
Government red tape

Interviewing Date 12/18–23/40
Survey #226–K   Question #11c

About how many warplanes would you guess the United States is now producing a month?

Less than 800...................... 25%
800–1,000......................... 12
More than 1,000................... 13
No opinion......................... 50

The correct answer is approximately 700.

JANUARY 5
DEFENSE INDUSTRIES

Interviewing Date 12/18–23/40
Survey #226–K   Question #11c

In order to speed up defense production, should factories making war materials hire enough men to work 24 hours a day (three shifts)?

Yes................................ 89%
No................................. 7
Undecided.......................... 4

Interviewing Date 12/18–23/40
Survey #226–K   Question #13

If a factory refuses to make defense materials for the Government at a price considered reasonable by the Defense Commission, should the Government take over that factory?

Yes................................ 71%
No................................. 22
Undecided.......................... 7

Interviewing Date 12/2–7/40
Survey #225–K   Question #7a

Should employees of industries working on defense contracts have the right to protest if they believe they are underpaid?

Yes................................ 69%
No................................. 22
Undecided.......................... 9

Interviewing Date 12/2–7/40
Survey #225–K   Question #7b

Should they have the right to strike if their protests are not taken care of?

Yes................................ 27%
No................................. 61
Undecided.......................... 12

By Income
Upper

Yes................................ 17%
No................................. 76
Undecided.......................... 7

Middle

Yes................................ 27%
No................................. 64
Undecided.......................... 9

Lower

Yes................................ 30%
No................................. 51
Undecided.......................... 19

JANUARY 8
TAXES

Interviewing Date 12/18–23/40
Survey #226–K   Question #18

To pay the cost of defense, should every American family not on relief pay an income tax based on the family's earnings, no matter how little?

Yes................................ 51%
No................................. 41
No opinion......................... 8

By Income
Upper

Yes................................ 54%
No................................. 38
No opinion......................... 8

Middle

Yes................................ 54%
No................................. 38
No opinion......................... 8

Lower

Yes................................ 44%
No................................. 48
No opinion......................... 8

Interviewing Date 12/18–23/40
Survey #226–T   Question #18

In order to help pay the cost of defense, should the United States Government collect a national sales tax on everything that people buy?

Yes................................ 42%
No................................. 49
No opinion......................... 9

Which kind of tax would you prefer to raise money for defense — a national sales tax on everything you buy, or an income tax based upon the amount of income you receive, and collected from every family except those on relief?

Sales tax	30%
Income tax	54
Both	8
Other	3
No opinion	5

JANUARY 10
EUROPEAN WAR

Which of these two things do you think it is more important for the United States to try to do — to keep out of the war ourselves, or to help England win, even at the risk of getting into the war?

Keep out	40%
Help England	60

By Region

	Keep Out	Help England
New England	37%	63%
Middle Atlantic	37	63
East Central	45	55
West Central	45	55
South	24	76
West	34	66

If you were asked to vote on the question of the United States entering the war against Germany and Italy, how would you vote — to go into the war, or to stay out of the war?

Go in	12%
Stay out	88

By Region

	Go In	Stay Out
New England	13%	87%
Middle Atlantic	13	87
East Central	10	90
West Central	9	91
South	17	83
West	14	86

Do you think it was a mistake for the United States to enter the last World War?

Yes	39%
No	42
No opinion	19

By Region
New England and Middle Atlantic

Yes	37%
No	44
No opinion	19

East Central

Yes	43%
No	35
No opinion	22

West Central

Yes	45%
No	42
No opinion	13

South

Yes	24%
No	55
No opinion	21

West

Yes	42%
No	38
No opinion	20

JANUARY 12
STATEHOOD FOR HAWAII

Interviewing Date 12/18–23/40
Survey #226–T   Question #21

Do you favor admitting Hawaii into the Union as a state?

Yes.............................. 48%
No.............................. 23
No opinion....................... 29

JANUARY 13
IRELAND

Interviewing Date 1/2–7/41
Survey #227–K   Question #3

Would you like to see the Irish give up their neutrality and let the English use war bases along the Irish coast?

Yes.............................. 63%
No.............................. 16
No opinion....................... 21

Irish-Americans Only

Yes.............................. 40%
No.............................. 52
No opinion....................... 8

JANUARY 15
EUROPEAN WAR

Interviewing Date 12/18–23/40
Survey #226–K   Question #1

Which of these two things do you think is the more important for the United States to try to do — keep out of the war ourselves, or help England win, even at the risk of war?

Roosevelt Voters in 1940

Keep out......................... 38%
Help England..................... 62

Willkie Voters in 1940

Keep out......................... 40%
Help England..................... 60

Interviewing Date 12/18–23/40
Survey #226–K   Question #3

Do you think our country's future safety depends on England winning this war?

Roosevelt Voters in 1940

Yes.............................. 72%
No.............................. 22
No opinion....................... 6

Willkie Voters in 1940

Yes.............................. 65%
No.............................. 30
No opinion....................... 5

Interviewing Date 12/18–23/40
Survey #226–K   Question #4

If a factory refuses to make defense materials for the Government at a price considered reasonable by the Defense Commission, should the Government take over that factory?

Roosevelt Voters in 1940

Yes.............................. 79%
No.............................. 15
No opinion....................... 6

Willkie Voters in 1940

Yes.............................. 64%
No.............................. 31
No opinion....................... 5

JANUARY 17
AID TO ENGLAND

Interviewing Date 1/2–7/41
Survey #227–K   Question #2a

Since the English have lost many ships, they may not be able to come and get the war materials we make for them. If this proves to be the case, should American ships with American crews be used to carry war materials to England?

Yes.............................. 42%
No............................... 45
No opinion....................... 13

By Region
New England and Middle Atlantic

Yes.............................. 39%
No............................... 47
No opinion....................... 14

East Central

Yes.............................. 38%
No............................... 50
No opinion....................... 12

West Central

Yes.............................. 38%
No............................... 49
No opinion....................... 13

South

Yes.............................. 58%
No............................... 26
No opinion....................... 16

West

Yes.............................. 45%
No............................... 42
No opinion....................... 13

Interviewing Date 1/2–7/41
Survey #227–K   Question #2b

Asked of those who responded in the affirmative: If American ships and American crews are used to carry war materials to England, should these ships be guarded by our navy while crossing?

Yes.............................. 82%
No............................... 12
No opinion....................... 6

JANUARY 19
DEFENSE PRODUCTION

Interviewing Date 12/18–23/40
Survey #226–K   Question #15b

If it would help speed up the defense program, would you be willing to work more hours per week at the same rate of pay per hour as you are getting now?

Yes.............................. 68%
No............................... 27
No opinion....................... 5

JANUARY 20
DEFENSE WORK

Interviewing Date 1/2–7/41
Survey #227–K   Question #4b

Would you personally be willing to spend an hour each day training for home-guard, nursing, first-aid work, ambulance driving, or other defense work?

Yes.............................. 67%
No............................... 22
No opinion....................... 11

By Region
New England and Middle Atlantic

Yes.............................. 70%
No............................... 20
No opinion....................... 10

East Central

Yes.............................. 65%
No............................... 25
No opinion....................... 10

West Central

Yes.............................. 57%
No............................... 25
No opinion....................... 18

South

Yes	71%
No	18
No opinion	11

West

Yes	70%
No	20
No opinion	10

JANUARY 22
LEND-LEASE

Interviewing Date 1/11–16/41
Survey #228–K   Question #4

If the British are unable to pay cash for war materials bought in this country, should our Government lend or lease war materials to the British, to be paid back in the same materials and other goods after the war is over?

Approve	68%
Disapprove	26
Undecided	6

By Political Affiliation
Democrats

Approve	74%
Disapprove	20
No opinion	6

Republicans

Approve	62%
Disapprove	32
No opinion	6

JANUARY 27
PRESIDENT ROOSEVELT'S POPULARITY

Interviewing Date 1/11–16/41
Survey #228–K   Question #9c

In general, do you approve or disapprove of Franklin Roosevelt as President?

Approve	71%
Disapprove	29

Nine per cent expressed no opinion.

JANUARY 31
EUROPEAN WAR

Interviewing Date 1/11–16/41
Survey #228–K   Question #8

Which of these two things do you think England should do now — try to make the best possible peace now with Germany, or keep on fighting in the hope of defeating Germany?

Make peace now	15%
Keep on fighting	79
No opinion	6

FEBRUARY 2
NATIONAL DEFENSE TRAINING

Interviewing Date 1/2–7/41
Survey #227–K   Question #5a

Do you think that boys between the ages of 16 and 21, who are out of high school, should spend one year in a training camp learning things useful to our defense program?

Yes	79%
No	14
No opinion	7

Interviewing Date 1/2–7/41
Survey #227–K   Question #5b

Do you think that girls between the ages of 16 and 21, who are out of high school, should spend one year in a training camp learning things useful to our defense program?

Yes	56%
No	34
No opinion	10

FEBRUARY 3
EUROPEAN WAR

Interviewing Date 12/2–7/40
Survey #225–K   Question #5

If you were asked to vote on the question of the United States entering the war against Germany and Italy, how would you vote — to go into the war or to stay out of the war?

Go in.............................. 15%
Stay out........................... 85

Nine per cent expressed no opinion.

FEBRUARY 5
SENDING TROOPS OVERSEAS

Interviewing Date 12/18–23/40
Survey #226–K   Question #9

Should a vote of the people be required before Congress can send men to fight overseas?

Yes............................... 52%
No................................ 48

Five per cent expressed no opinion.

Men Ages 21–36 Only

Yes............................... 52%
No................................ 48

FEBRUARY 10
LEND-LEASE

Interviewing Date 1/24–29/41
Survey #229–K   Question #4b

Do you think Congress should pass the President's Lend-Lease Bill?

Yes............................... 54%
No................................ 22
Qualified......................... 15
No opinion........................ 9

By Political Affiliation
Democrats

Yes............................... 69%
No................................ 13
Qualified......................... 10
No opinion........................ 8

Republicans

Yes............................... 38%
No................................ 30
Qualified......................... 23
No opinion........................ 9

By Region
New England and Middle Atlantic

Yes............................... 54%
No................................ 21
Qualified......................... 16
No opinion........................ 9

East Central

Yes............................... 39%
No................................ 35
Qualified......................... 17
No opinion........................ 9

West Central

Yes............................... 53%
No................................ 22
Qualified......................... 15
No opinion........................ 10

South

Yes............................... 77%
No................................ 8
Qualified......................... 10
No opinion........................ 5

West

Yes............................... 55%
No................................ 20
Qualified......................... 16
No opinion........................ 9

FEBRUARY 16
BLACKOUTS

Interviewing Date 1/24–29/41
Survey #229–K   Question #6

New York City is planning to have a practice blackout next month. Do you think all towns and cities in your state should have practice blackouts every few months?

Yes............................ 42%
No............................. 45
No opinion..................... 13

By Region

	Yes
New England	50%
Middle Atlantic	50
East Central	34
West Central	31
South	39
West	46

FEBRUARY 17
NEUTRALITY

Special Survey

If American ships with American crews are used to carry war materials to Britain and some of them are sunk by the Germans on the way over, would you be in favor of going to war against Germany?

Yes............................ 27%
No............................. 61
No opinion..................... 12

FEBRUARY 19
LOTTERIES

Interviewing Date 1/11–16/41
Survey #228–K   Question #8

Would you favor lotteries in this country run by the Federal Government to help pay some of the cost of national defense?

Yes............................ 51%
No............................. 38
No opinion..................... 11

By Region
New England and Middle Atlantic

Yes............................ 60%
No............................. 30
No opinion..................... 10

East Central

Yes............................ 50%
No............................. 39
No opinion..................... 11

West Central

Yes............................ 39%
No............................. 46
No opinion..................... 15

South

Yes............................ 45%
No............................. 40
No opinion..................... 15

West

Yes............................ 47%
No............................. 43
No opinion..................... 10

Interviewing Date 1/11–16/41
Survey #228–K   Question #11

Would you favor lotteries in your state run by the state government to help pay the cost of old-age pensions?

Yes............................ 45%
No............................. 41
No opinion..................... 14

By Region
New England and Middle Atlantic

Yes............................ 59%
No............................. 31
No opinion..................... 10

East Central

Yes............................... 40%
No................................ 44
No opinion........................ 16

West Central

Yes............................... 36%
No................................ 51
No opinion........................ 13

South

Yes............................... 31%
No................................ 51
No opinion........................ 18

West

Yes............................... 43%
No................................ 43
No opinion........................ 14

FEBRUARY 21
SOUTH AMERICA

Special Survey

If Brazil, Argentina, Chile, or any other Central or South American country is actually attacked by any Euronean power, do you think the United States should fight to keep that European power out?

Yes............................... 86%
No................................ 14

Eight per cent expressed no opinion.

Which of the following statements best describes Central and South America? (on card)

Central and South America have very few natural resources such as good farm land, oil, coal, silver, gold, water-power, etc., and will probably always be poor, weak, and backward........ 8%

Central and South America have many natural resources and some time may become fairly wealthy and strong..... 33

Central and South America have many natural resources and probably will become very wealthy and powerful.... 48

Don't know........................ 11

Do you think Germany will try to get control of Central and South American countries?

Yes............................... 50%
Germany is already trying........... 38
No................................ 7
Don't know........................ 5

Do you think it is important for the United States to keep Germany from getting more influence or control over Central and South American countries than she now has?

Yes............................... 93%
No................................ 4
No opinion........................ 3

Do you think the United States should lend money to Central and South American countries to help them build up their industries, railroads, and defenses?

Yes............................... 58%
Qualified opinion.................. 12
No................................ 22
No opinion........................ 8

FEBRUARY 22
EUROPEAN WAR

Special Survey

Asked in Great Britain: What are your thoughts when you hear there has been a very heavy air-raid?

Wonder how bombed people are getting on..................... 28%

Intensify our bombing of
  German military targets............ 24
Bomb German civilians in retaliation.... 22
Get better protection for people
  in this country................... 16
Find some way to end war........... 10

*Asked in Great Britain: Are you sleeping
less than before the war?*

Yes............................... 44%
No................................ 52
Don't know........................ 4

FEBRUARY 24
JAPAN

Interviewing Date 2/16–21/41
Survey #230–T   Question #7a

*Do you think the United States should try
to keep Japan from seizing the Dutch East
Indies and Singapore?*

Yes............................... 56%
No................................ 24
No opinion........................ 20

Interviewing Date 2/16–21/41
Survey #230–T   Question #7b

*Do you think the United States should risk
war with Japan, if necessary, in order to
keep Japan from taking the Dutch East
Indies and Singapore?*

Yes............................... 39%
No................................ 46
No opinion........................ 15

FEBRUARY 26
THE MOVIES

Special Survey

*Are there any motion pictures here that you
especially liked? (Card listed pictures re-*
*leased between January 1 and November
30, 1940.)*

The following are listed in order of frequency
of mention:

Boom Town
Knute Rockne
Rebecca
Northwest Passage
Strike up the Band
The Fighting 69th

Frequent Theatergoers
(*Once a Week or More*)

Boom Town
Knute Rockne
Northwest Passage
Rebecca
Strike Up the Band
The Fighting 69th

Infrequent Theatergoers
(*Less than Once a Week*)

Rebecca
Boom Town
Northwest Passage
Knute Rockne
The Fighting 69th
All This and Heaven Too

By Sex
Men

Knute Rockne
Boom Town
Northwest Passage
The Fighting 69th
Sea Hawk
Strike Up the Band

Women

Rebecca
All This and Heaven Too
Boom Town
My Favorite Wife
Strike Up the Band
Waterloo Bridge

FEBRUARY 28
LEND-LEASE

Interviewing Date 2/16–21/41
Survey #230–K   Question #1b

Do you think Congress should pass the President's Lease-Lend Bill?

Yes.............................. 55%
No............................... 20
Qualified........................ 11
No opinion....................... 14

By Political Affiliation
Democrats

Yes.............................. 67%
No............................... 13
Qualified........................ 6
No opinion....................... 14

Republicans

Yes.............................. 41%
No............................... 28
Qualified........................ 18
No opinion....................... 13

MARCH 3
WENDELL WILLKIE

Interviewing Date 2/16–21/41
Survey #230–K   Question #10c

Do you think Wendell Willkie would have made a good President if he had been elected last November?

Yes.............................. 60%
No............................... 40

By Political Affiliation

	Yes	No
Democrats	39%	61%
Republicans	85	15

MARCH 5
POSTWAR PEACE

Interviewing Date 2/16–21/41
Survey #230–K   Question #6a

Have you given any thought to what should be done to maintain world peace after the present European war is over?

Yes.............................. 34%
No............................... 66

Interviewing Date 2/16–21/41
Survey #230–K   Question #6b

Asked of those who responded in the affirmative: In your opinion, what should be done?

The following are listed according to frequency of mention:

An international federation
Moral, social, and political reform based on toleration and Christian principles
Divide Germany among the victors

MARCH 8
EUROPEAN WAR

Special Survey

Asked in Great Britain: Do you think the United States should take part in the peace settlement after the war?

Should........................... 65%
Should not....................... 15
No opinion....................... 20

Asked in Great Britain: Was Erie right in refusing to allow Britain to use naval bases like Cobh, Berehaven, and Lough Swilly?

Yes.............................. 14%
No............................... 62
No opinion....................... 24

MARCH 10
LEND-LEASE

Interviewing Date 2/16–21/41
Survey #230–K   Question #1b

Do you think Congress should pass the Lend-Lease Bill?

Well-Informed Voters

Yes............................... 59%
No............................... 21
Qualified......................... 17
No opinion........................ 3

Fairly Well-Informed Voters

Yes............................... 58%
No............................... 22
Qualified......................... 14
No opinion........................ 6

Uninformed Voters

Yes............................... 53%
No............................... 23
Qualified......................... 6
No opinion........................ 18

Interviewing Date 2/16–21/41
Survey #230–K   Question #1c

If you were asked to vote today on the question of the United States entering the war against Germany and Italy, how would you vote — to go into the war or to stay out of the war?

Well-Informed Voters

Go in............................. 17%
Stay out.......................... 78
No opinion........................ 5

Fairly Well-Informed Voters

Go in............................. 13%
Stay out.......................... 81
No opinion........................ 6

Uninformed Voters

Go in............................. 12%
Stay out.......................... 78
No opinion........................ 10

The voters were classified well-informed if they correctly answered five of the following questions, fairly informed if they correctly answered two to five, uninformed if they answered less than two.

1) Can you tell me the name of the country where the armies of Greece and Italy are fighting?
Correct (Albania).................. 55%

2) Can you name four leaders of European countries and tell me wnat country each one heads?
Correct........................... 62%

3) Can you tell me the five countries that Germany has conquered since the war began?
Correct........................... 54%

4) Can you tell me what country controls Gibraltar?
Correct........................... 68%

5) About how many miles would you say it is from London to Berlin?
Correct (600 miles)............... 27%

6) How many years has Hitler been in power?
Correct (8 years)................. 47%

MARCH 14
JAPAN

Interviewing Date 2/16–21/41
Survey #230–T   Question #7a

Do you think the United States should risk war with Japan, if necessary, to keep Japan from taking the Dutch East Indies and Singapore?

Yes............................... 40%
No............................... 39
No opinion........................ 21

MARCH 16
PRESIDENT ROOSEVELT'S POPULARITY

Interviewing Date 2/16–21/41
Survey #230–K   Question #11c

In general, do you approve or disapprove of the way Franklin Roosevelt is handling his job as President today?

Approve........................... 72%
Disapprove....................... 28

Six per cent expressed no opinion.

MARCH 17
INCOME TAX

Interviewing Date 2/28–3/5/41
Survey #231–K   Question #5a

Suppose you were a member of the United States Congress and it was your job to set the amount of taxes people must pay in the coming year. Let's take a typical family of four — a husband, wife, and two children. How much do you think this family, with a total income of $3,000 a year — that is $60 a week — should pay in personal income taxes next year?

Average
If public set tax rate................. $60
(Approximate 1941 tax rate.......... $0)

Interviewing Date 2/28–3/5/41
Survey #231–K   Question #5b

How much do you think this family, with a total income of $5,000 a year — that is $100 a week — should pay in personal income taxes next year?

Average
If public set tax rate................. $200
(Approximate 1941 tax rate.......... $130)

Interviewing Date 2/28–3/5/41
Survey #231–K   Question #5c

How much do you think this family, with a total income of $10,000 a year — that is $200 a week — should pay in personal income taxes next year?

Average
If public set tax rate................ $600
(Approximate 1941 tax rate......... $720)

Interviewing Date 2/29–3/5/41
Survey #231–K   Question #5d

How much do you think this family, with a total income of $100,000 a year — that is $2,000 a week — should pay in personal income taxes next year?

Average
If public set tax rate............. $10,000
(Approximate 1941 tax rate....... $46,000)

MARCH 19
HEALTH

Interviewing Date 2/28–3/5/41
Survey #231–K   Question #4a

The army has been rejecting volunteers and draftees who have not been able to pass the physical examination because they have bad teeth. Do you think the army should accept these men for duty and fix their teeth before they begin training?

Yes............................... 80%
No................................ 13
No opinion........................ 7

Interviewing Date 2/28–3/5/41
Survey #231–K   Question #4b

Do you think men who have a venereal disease that can be cured should be accepted by the army and placed in special camps until they are cured before starting training?

Yes............................... 65%
No................................ 25
No opinion........................ 10

MARCH 21
EUROPEAN WAR

Interviewing Date 3/9–14/41
Survey #232–K   Question #8a

If you were asked to vote on the question of the United States entering the war against Germany and Italy, how would you vote — to go into the war, or to stay out of the war?

Go in............................. 17%
Stay out.......................... 83

The Southern states show the highest vote for war, 20%, and the West Central states the lowest, 14%.

MARCH 23
LEASING DESTROYERS TO ENGLAND

Interviewing Date 3/9–14/41
Survey #232–K   Question #2

Would you approve or disapprove of the United States leasing about 40 additional destroyers to England?

Approve........................... 52%
Disapprove........................ 26
No opinion........................ 22

Interviewing Date 3/9–14/41
Survey #232–T   Question #2

Would you approve or disapprove of the United States leasing about five destroyers a month to England?

Approve........................... 55%
Disapprove........................ 25
No opinion........................ 20

MARCH 24
DEFENSE PRODUCTION

Interviewing Date 3/9–14/41
Survey #232–K   Question #5a

Do you think America's production of arms, airplanes, and other war materials is going ahead fast enough?

Yes.............................. 30%
No.............................. 53
No opinion....................... 17

By Region
New England and Middle Atlantic

Yes.............................. 30%
No.............................. 50
No opinion....................... 20

East Central

Yes.............................. 30%
No.............................. 57
No opinion....................... 13

West Central

Yes.............................. 35%
No.............................. 47
No opinion....................... 18

South

Yes.............................. 21%
No.............................. 63
No opinion....................... 16

West

Yes.............................. 29%
No.............................. 53
No opinion....................... 18

Interviewing Date 3/9–14/41
Survey #232–K   Question #5b

Asked of those who replied in the negative: What do you think is the chief reason why production isn't going ahead faster?

Strikes........................... 52%
Politics and red tape.............. 11
Shortage of plants and materials....... 6
Lack of organization................ 5
Lack of public interest.............. 4
Shortage of skilled labor............. 3
Sabotage.......................... 3
Profit-seeking businessmen........... 2
Others............................ 2
No opinion........................ 12

MARCH 26
LABOR AND BUSINESS LEADERS

Interviewing Date 3/9–14/41
Survey #232–K   Question #7a

Do you think labor union leaders are helping the national defense production program as much as they should?

Yes.............................. 18%
No.............................. 68
No opinion........................ 14

Interviewing Date 3/9–14/41
Survey #232–K   Question #7b

Do you think business leaders are helping the national defense production program as much as they should?

Yes.............................. 51%
No.............................. 31
No opinion........................ 18

Interviewing Date 3/9–14/41
Survey #232–K   Question #7c

Which do you think is trying harder to help national defense production — labor union leaders or business leaders?

Labor leaders...................... 10%
Business leaders.................... 56
About the same.................... 16
No opinion........................ 18

MARCH 29
LABOR UNIONS

Interviewing Date 3/9–14/41
Survey #232–K   Question #10

Henry Ford says he will refuse to recognize labor unions in his plants. Do you agree or disagree with this viewpoint?

Agree............................. 58%
Disagree........................... 29
No opinion........................ 13

Interviewing Date 3/9–14/41
Survey #232–K   Question #11

Westbrook Pegler, the newspaper writer, claims that many labor union leaders are racketeers. Do you agree or disagree with him?

Agree............................. 72%
Disagree........................... 14
No opinion........................ 14

APRIL 2
POLL TAX

Interviewing Date 2/16–21/41
Survey #230–T   Question #2

Some Southern states require every voter to pay a poll tax amounting to $1 a year or more before they can vote. Do you think these poll taxes should be abolished?

Yes.............................. 63%
No.............................. 25
No opinion........................ 12

Southern States without Poll Tax*

Yes.............................. 51%
No.............................. 36
No opinion........................ 13

*The five Southern states without a poll tax are: Kentucky, North Carolina, Florida, Oklahoma, and Louisiana.

Southern States with Poll Tax — Persons Who Have Paid**

Yes.............................. 34%
No.............................. 59
No opinion........................ 7

Southern States with Poll Tax — Persons Who Have Not Paid**

Yes.............................. 35%
No.............................. 53
No opinion........................ 12

**The eight Southern states with a poll tax are: Alabama, Arkansas, Georgia, Mississippi, South Carolina, Tennessee, Texas, and Virginia.

APRIL 4
FEDERAL SALES TAX

Interviewing Date 3/9–14/41
Survey #232–K   Question #4

In order to help pay the cost of national defense, would you favor, or oppose, a federal sales tax of 2% on everything you buy (in addition to state and local sales taxes now in effect)?

Favor............................ 54%
Oppose........................... 46

Eight per cent expressed no opinion.

Lower Income Group Only

Favor............................ 48%
Oppose........................... 52

APRIL 6
WORLD WAR I

Interviewing Date 1/24–29/41
Survey #229–K   Question #3

Do you think it was a mistake for the United States to enter the last war?

Yes.............................. 39%
No............................... 43
No opinion....................... 18

APRIL 6
IDEAL FAMILY SIZE

Interviewing Date 3/21–26/41
Survey #233–K   Question #7a

What do you consider the ideal family size — a husband and wife and how many children?

One.............................. 1%
Two.............................. 31
Three............................ 27

Four............................. 27
Five............................. 6
Six or more...................... 8

By Age
21–34 Years

One.............................. 1%
Two.............................. 40
Three............................ 32
Four............................. 21
Five............................. 3
Six or more...................... 3

35–49 Years

One.............................. 1%
Two.............................. 31
Three............................ 27
Four............................. 29
Five............................. 6
Six or more...................... 6

50 Years and Over

One.............................. *%
Two.............................. 23
Three............................ 23
Four............................. 33
Five............................. 9
Six or more...................... 12

*Less than ½ of 1%.

Interviewing Date 3/21–26/41
Survey #233–K   Question #7b

What do you think is the main reason why couples do not have more children?

Not enough money................. 57%
More children interfere with parents' freedom.......................... 20
Uncertainty of the future........ 5
Parents' health.................. 2
Dislike of children.............. 1
Too many children already........ 1
Other............................ 3
No opinion....................... 11

APRIL 7
EUROPEAN WAR

Interviewing Date 3/9–14/41
Survey #232–K   Question #10

Which of these two things do you think is the more important for the United States to try to do — to keep out of war ourselves, or to help England win, even at the risk of getting into the war?

Keep out........................... 33%
Help England....................... 67

APRIL 9
WAGE AND PRICE CONTROLS

Interviewing Date 3/21–26/41
Survey #233–K   Question #3a

Would you like to see the Federal Government fix prices so that as long as the war in Europe lasts everything you buy will cost the same as it does now?

Yes............................... 68%
No................................ 32

Nine per cent expressed no opinion.

By Occupation

	Yes	No
Businessmen...................	53%	47%
Farmers.......................	61	39
White collar..................	68	32
Skilled, semiskilled, unskilled....	80	20

Interviewing Date 3/21–26/41
Survey #233–K   Question #3b

Would you like to see the Federal Government keep all salaries and wages at the present level so that nobody's wage could be cut and nobody could get an increase as long as they did the same kind of work, until the present war in Europe is over?

Yes............................... 52%
No................................ 48

Twelve per cent expressed no opinion.

By Occupation

	Yes	No
Businessmen...................	42%	58%
Farmers.......................	55	45
White collar..................	47	53
Skilled, semiskilled, unskilled....	57	43

APRIL 11
MOST IMPORTANT BRITISH PROBLEM

Special Survey

Asked in Great Britain: What do you consider the most important war problem the British Government must solve this winter?

Shipping losses and food supply........ 44%
Night bombing..................... 8
Preparation for an offensive.......... 7
Others............................ 41

APRIL 12
THE FLU

Interviewing Date 3/21–26/41
Survey #233–K   Question #8c

Have you had the flu or grippe since October?

Yes............................... 25%
No................................ 75

By Sex

	Yes	No
Men..........................	24%	76%
Women........................	27	73

By Income

	Yes	No
Under $1,000.................	27%	73%
$1,000–$2,500................	25	75
Over $2,500..................	23	77

By Community Size

Farms	27%	73%
Under 10,000	27	73
10,000–100,000	24	76
Over 100,000	21	79

By Region

New England	23%	77%
Middle Atlantic	23	77
East Central	22	78
West Central	26	74
South	29	71
West	26	74

Interviewing Date 3/21–26/41
Survey #233–K   Question #8d

Asked of those who replied in the affirmative: How many times have you had the flu since October?

Once	22%
More than once	3
	25%

APRIL 14
PERSONAL HEALTH

Interviewing Date 3/21–26/41
Survey #233–K   Question #8a

Have you had any colds this winter, that is since last October?

Yes	64%
No	36

By Sex

	Yes	No
Men	63%	37%
Women	65	35

By Income

Upper	61%	39%
Middle	63	37
Lower	67	33

By Community Size

Under 10,000	66%	34%
10,000–100,000	63	37
Over 100,000	61	39
Farms	65	35

By Region

New England	64%	36%
Middle Atlantic	64	36
East Central	63	37
West Central	64	36
South	72	28
West	58	42

Interviewing Date 3/21–26/41
Survey #233–K   Question #8b

Asked of those who replied in the affirmative: How many colds?

One cold	38%
Two colds	17
Three or more	9
	64%

Interviewing Date 3/21–26/41
Survey #233–K   Question #11b

Have you found that the things you eat have any effect on the general state of your health?

Yes	50%
No	50

APRIL 18
PRESIDENT ROOSEVELT'S POPULARITY

Interviewing Date 4/10–15/41
Survey #234–K   Question #24c

In general, do you approve or disapprove today of Franklin Roosevelt as President?

Approve	73%
Disapprove	27

Six per cent expressed no opinion.

APRIL 21
EUROPEAN WAR

Interviewing Date 3/21–26/41
Survey #233–K   Question #4

Do you think the United States should send part of our army to Europe to help the British?

Yes	17%
No	79
No opinion	4

Interviewing Date 3/21–26/41
Survey #233–K   Question #5b

Do you think the United States should send part of our air force with American pilots to Europe to help the British?

Yes	24%
No	69
No opinion	7

Interviewing Date 3/21–26/41
Survey #233–K   Question #5a

Do you think the United States should send part of our warships manned by American sailors to Europe to help the British?

Yes	27%
No	67
No opinion	6

APRIL 23
EUROPEAN WAR

Interviewing Date 4/10–15/41
Survey #234–K   Question #3

Should the United States navy be used to guard ships carrying war materials to Britain?

Yes	41%
No	50
No opinion	9

By Region
New England and Middle Atlantic

Yes	41%
No	49
No opinion	10

East Central

Yes	35%
No	56
No opinion	9

West Central

Yes	33%
No	58
No opinion	9

South

Yes	59%
No	30
No opinion	11

West

Yes	42%
No	52
No opinion	6

Interviewing Date 4/10–15/41
Survey #234–K   Question #7

If it appears certain that Britain will be defeated unless we use part of our navy to protect ships going to Britain, would you favor or oppose such convoys?

Favor	71%
Oppose	21
No opinion	8

APRIL 25
EUROPEAN WAR

Interviewing Date 4/10–15/41
Survey #234–K   Question #6a

Which side do you think will win the war — Germany and Italy, or England?

Germany and Italy................ 11%
England........................ 57
Stalemate...................... 8
No opinion..................... 24

Interviewing Date 4/10–15/41
Survey #234–K   Question #13

Do you think Britain should try to get to-gether with Germany to work out some sort of peace, or do you think Britain should go on fighting?

Make peace.................... 29%
Go on fighting................ 71

Nine per cent expressed no opinion.

APRIL 27
EUROPEAN WAR

Interviewing Date 4/10–15/41
Survey #234–K   Question #1a

Do you think the United States will go into the war in Europe sometime before it's over, or do you think we will stay out of the war?

Will go in 82%
Will stay out................. 18

APRIL 28
EUROPEAN WAR

Interviewing Date 4/10–15/41
Survey #234–K   Question #8a

If you were asked to vote today on the question of the United States entering the war against Germany and Italy, how would you vote — to go into the war, or to stay out of the war?

Go in......................... 19%
Stay out...................... 81

Interviewing Date 4/10–15/41
Survey #234–K   Question #8b

If it appeared certain that there was no other way to defeat Germany and Italy except for the United States to go to war against them, would you be in favor of the United States going to war?

Yes........................... 68%
No............................ 24
No opinion.................... 8

APRIL 30
LABOR STRIKES

Interviewing Date 4/10–15/41
Survey #234–K   Question #15

When workers in a factory working on de-fense contracts vote to go on strike, do you think they should be required by law to wait for 60 days before the strike can start?

Yes........................... 89%
No............................ 11

Eight per cent expressed no opinion.

Interviewing Date 4/10–15/41
Survey #234–K   Question #18

A bill has been proposed that would treat any worker who goes on strike in a defense industry as a traitor, to be punished by one year in prison. Would you like to see Congress pass such a law?

Yes........................... 37%
No............................ 63

Nine per cent expressed no opinion.

MAY 2
EUROPEAN WAR

Interviewing Date 4/10–15/41
Survey #234–K   Question #4

If the United States navy is used to guard merchant ships crossing the Atlantic, and some of our warships are sunk by German submarines, would you be in favor of going to war against Germany?

Yes................................ 40%
No................................ 50
No opinion......................... 10

Interviewing Date 4/10–15/41
Survey #234–T   Question #5

If the United States sends merchant ships to Britain with war materials, and some of them are sunk by German submarines, would you be in favor of going to war against Germany?

Yes................................ 34%
No................................ 58
No opinion......................... 8

MAY 3
EUROPEAN WAR

Interviewing Date 4/10–15/41
Survey #234–K   Question #12

Do you think Britain will call for help from the American army before the war is over?

Yes................................ 57%
No................................ 20
Is already......................... 14
No opinion......................... 9

MAY 5
LABOR STRIKES

Interviewing Date 4/10–15/41
Survey #234–K   Question #17a

Do you think communists in unions are responsible for the strikes in defense industries?

Yes................................ 78%
No................................ 8
No opinion......................... 14

Interviewing Date 4/10–15/41
Survey #234–K   Question #17b

If it were up to you to decide, what would you do about the Communist party in this country?

Repressive measures................ 64%
Put them in prison................. 5
Do nothing......................... 8
No opinion......................... 23

MAY 7
CONCENTRATION OF POWER

Interviewing Date 4/10–15/41
Survey #234–K   Question #20

Do you think there is too much power in the hands of the Government in Washington?

Yes................................ 32%
No................................ 56
No opinion......................... 12

Interviewing Date 4/10–15/41
Survey #234–K   Question #19

Do you think there is too much power in the hands of a few rich men and large corporations in the United States?

Yes................................ 59%
No................................ 27
No opinion......................... 14

Interviewing Date 4/10–15/41
Survey #234–K   Question #21

Do you think there is too much power in the hands of the leaders of labor unions in this country?

Yes................................ 75%
No................................ 13
No opinion......................... 12

By Income
Upper

Yes................................ 82%
No................................ 13
No opinion......................... 5

Middle

Yes.............................. 76%
No............................... 14
No opinion....................... 10

Lower

Yes.............................. 71%
No............................... 13
No opinion....................... 16

MAY 9
CHARLES LINDBERGH

Interviewing Date 4/27–5/1/41
Survey #235–K   Question #15a

Are you familiar with the views which Charles Lindbergh has expressed concerning American foreign policy?

Yes.............................. 58%
No............................... 42

Interviewing Date 4/27–5/1/41
Survey #235–K   Question #15b

Asked of those who responded in the affirmative: Do you agree or disagree with what Charles Lindbergh says?

Agree............................ 24%
Disagree......................... 63
No opinion....................... 13

MAY 10
CANADA

Interviewing Date 4/27–5/1/41
Survey #235–K   Question #14

If Canada is actually invaded by any European power, do you think the United States should use its army and navy to aid Canada?

Yes.............................. 90%
No............................... 5
No opinion....................... 5

MAY 12
THE DRAFT

Interviewing Date 4/27–5/1/41
Survey #235–K   Question #1

At present men between the ages of 18 and 21 are not drafted. Do you think the law should be changed so that men between the ages of 18 and 21 would be included in the draft, along with those from 21 to 35?

Yes.............................. 51%
No............................... 44
No opinion....................... 5

By Region
New England and Middle Atlantic

Yes.............................. 53%
No............................... 41
No opinion....................... 6

East Central

Yes.............................. 56%
No............................... 38
No opinion....................... 6

West Central

Yes.............................. 53%
No............................... 44
No opinion....................... 3

South

Yes.............................. 45%
No............................... 51
No opinion....................... 4

West

Yes.............................. 47%
No............................... 49
No opinion....................... 4

By Sex
Men

Yes.............................. 58%
No............................... 37
No opinion....................... 5

Women

Yes.............................. 43%
No............................... 52
No opinion....................... 5

MAY 14
SOUTH AMERICA

Special Survey

> *If Brazil, Argentina, Chile, or any other Central or South American country is actually attacked by any European power, do you think the United States should fight to keep that European power out?*

Yes.............................. 86%
No............................... 14

Six per cent expressed no opinion.

MAY 16
BOMBING OF GERMANY

Special Survey

> *Asked in Great Britain: Would you approve or disapprove if the R.A.F. adopted a policy of bombing the civilian population of Germany?*

Approve.......................... 53%
Disapprove....................... 38
Undecided........................ 9

MAY 16
EUROPEAN WAR

Interviewing Date 5/8–13/41
Survey #236–K   Question #7

> *If you were asked to vote today on the question of the United States entering the war against Germany and Italy, how would you vote — to go into the war or to stay out of the war?*

Go in............................ 21%
Stay out......................... 79

Five per cent expressed no opinion.

By State

	Go In	Stay Out
Wisconsin....................	14%	86%
Minnesota....................	15	85
Iowa........................	15	85
Indiana.....................	15	85
Ohio........................	15	85
Massachusetts...............	17	83
New Hampshire...............	17	83
Illinois....................	17	83
Michigan....................	18	82
Nebraska....................	18	82
South Dakota................	18	82
Connecticut.................	19	81
Kansas......................	20	80
North Dakota................	21	79
Maine.......................	21	79
Rhode Island................	22	78
Pennsylvania................	22	78
Washington..................	22	78
Vermont.....................	23	77
New Jersey..................	23	77
Missouri....................	23	77
South Carolina..............	23	77
California..................	23	77
New York....................	24	76
New Mexico..................	24	76
Nevada......................	24	76
Delaware....................	25	75
Oklahoma....................	25	75
Louisiana...................	26	74
Tennessee...................	26	74
Montana.....................	26	74
Utah........................	26	74
Maryland....................	27	73
West Virginia...............	27	73
Kentucky....................	27	73
Idaho.......................	27	73
Oregon......................	27	73
Georgia.....................	28	72
Arkansas....................	28	72

	Go In	Stay Out
Virginia	28%	72%
Mississippi	28	72
Colorado	28	72
North Carolina	29	71
Alabama	29	71
Texas	29	71
Wyoming	29	71
Arizona	33	67
Florida	35	65

MAY 21
EUROPEAN WAR

Interviewing Date 5/8–13/41
Survey #236–K   Question #5a

Should the United States navy be used to guard ships carrying war materials to Britain?

Yes.................................. 52%
No................................... 41
No opinion........................... 7

By Region
New England and Middle Atlantic

Yes.................................. 55%
No................................... 38
No opinion........................... 7

East Central

Yes.................................. 43%
No................................... 50
No opinion........................... 7

West Central

Yes.................................. 42%
No................................... 50
No opinion........................... 8

South

Yes.................................. 74%
No................................... 20
No opinion........................... 6

West

Yes.................................. 51%
No................................... 44
No opinion........................... 5

MAY 23
THE DRAFT

Interviewing Date 5/8–13/41
Survey #236–K   Question #10a

Do you think the draft has been handled fairly in your community?

Yes.................................. 93%
No................................... 7

Eleven per cent expressed no opinion.

Interviewing Date 5/8–13/41
Survey #236–K   Question #11

Do you think big league baseball players should be exempted from the draft until the present season is over?

Yes.................................. 16%
No................................... 84

Baseball Fans Only*

Yes.................................. 21%
No................................... 79

*Those stating they follow big-league baseball regularly.

MAY 24
PRESIDENT ROOSEVELT

Interviewing Date 5/8–13/41
Survey #236–K   Question #13

Do you think President Roosevelt has gone too far in his policies of helping Britain, or not far enough?

Too far............................. 21%
About right......................... 59
Not far enough...................... 20

Roosevelt Voters in 1940

Too far............................... 11%
About right........................ 66
Not far enough..................... 23

Willkie Voters in 1940

Too far............................... 34%
About right........................ 49
Not far enough..................... 17

MAY 26
TAXES

Interviewing Date 5/8–13/41
Survey #236–K   Question #14

It has been suggested that every family not on relief should pay an income tax which would amount to, say $10, for families with yearly incomes of a thousand dollars, and larger taxes for families with larger incomes. Would you favor such a tax?

Favor.............................. 58%
Oppose............................ 31
No opinion........................ 11

Interviewing Date 5/8–13/41
Survey #236–K   Question #4

In order to meet the increased cost of national defense, would you be willing to pay a tax of about two weeks' salary per year in addition to the taxes you have been paying?

Yes................................ 59%
No................................. 33
No opinion......................... 8

Interviewing Date 5/8–13/41
Survey #236–K   Question #3a

Have you heard or read about the new money-raising proposals now being discussed in Congress?

Yes................................ 66%
No................................. 34

Interviewing Date 5/8–13/41
Survey #236–K   Question #3b

Asked of those who replied in the affirmative: How should the Federal Government pay the increased cost of defense — chiefly by extra taxes or chiefly by borrowing more money?

Extra taxes........................ 70%
By borrowing...................... 18
No opinion........................ 12

MAY 28
EUROPEAN WAR

Interviewing Date 5/22–27/41
Survey #237–K   Question #2a

If you were asked to vote today on the question of the United States entering the war against Germany and Italy, how would you vote — to go into the war, or to stay out of the war?

Go in.............................. 20%
Stay out........................... 80

Families with Men Ages 16–24

Go in.............................. 22%
Stay out........................... 78

Interviewing Date 4/27–5/1/41
Survey #235–K   Question #9b

If it appeared certain that there was no other way of defeating Germany and Italy, except for the United States to go to war against them, would you be in favor of the United States going into the war?

Yes................................ 66%
No................................. 34

Families with Men Ages 16–24

Yes................................ 68%
No................................. 32

Interviewing Date 5/8–13/41
Survey #236–T   Question #1

Which of these two things do you think is more important for the United States to try to do — to keep out of war ourselves, or to help England even at the risk of getting into the war?

Keep out........................... 39%
Help England...................... 61

Families with Men Ages 16–24

Keep out........................... 38%
Help England...................... 62

Interviewing Date 4/27–5/1/41
Survey #235–K   Question #2

Do you think the United States will go into the war in Europe sometime before it is over, or do you think we will stay out of the war?

We are already in.................. 13%
We will go in...................... 64
We will stay out................... 14
No opinion......................... 9

Families with Men Ages 16–24

We are already in.................. 12%
We will go in...................... 65
We will stay out................... 14
No opinion......................... 9

Interviewing Date 5/22–27/41
Survey #237–K   Question #1a

Should the United States navy be used to guard ships carrying war materials to Britain?

Yes................................ 52%
No................................. 40
No opinion......................... 8

Families with Men Ages 16–24

Yes................................ 52%
No................................. 42
No opinion......................... 6

MAY 31
EUROPEAN WAR

Interviewing Date 5/8–13/41
Survey #236–K   Question #8

If Germany and Italy should defeat Britain in the present war, do you think Germany and Italy would start a war against the United States within the next 10 years?

Yes................................ 62%
No................................. 29
No opinion......................... 9

JUNE 2
EUROPEAN WAR

Interviewing Date 5/8–13/41
Survey #236–K   Question #6

Would you rather see Britain surrender to Germany than have the United States go into the war?

Yes................................ 26%
No................................. 62
No opinion......................... 12

JUNE 4
EUROPEAN WAR

Interviewing Date 5/22–27/41
Survey #237–K   Question #1a

Should the United States navy be used to guard ships carrying war materials to Britain?

Yes................................ 52%
No................................. 40
No opinion......................... 8

By State
New York

Yes................................ 50%
No................................. 44
No opinion......................... 6

Pennsylvania

Yes........................... 52%
No............................ 41
No opinion.................... 7

Illinois

Yes........................... 46%
No............................ 48
No opinion.................... 6

Ohio

Yes........................... 48%
No............................ 43
No opinion.................... 9

California

Yes........................... 50%
No............................ 44
No opinion.................... 6

JUNE 5
FIORELLO LA GUARDIA

Special Survey

Asked in New York City: If Fiorello La Guardia runs for reelection as mayor next fall, will you vote for or against him?

For........................... 59%
Against....................... 26
No opinion.................... 15

Roosevelt Voters in 1940

For........................... 71%
Against....................... 16
No opinion.................... 13

Willkie Voters in 1940

For........................... 43%
Against....................... 40
No opinion.................... 17

JUNE 7
WAR WORK FOR BRITISH WOMEN

Special Survey

Asked in Great Britain: Do you approve or disapprove of women being compelled to do war work?

Approve....................... 72%
Disapprove.................... 23
Undecided..................... 5

JUNE 9
LEAGUE OF NATIONS

Interviewing Date 5/22–27/41
Survey #237–K   Question #6

Would you like to see the United States join a league of nations after this war is over?

Yes........................... 51%
No............................ 49

Eleven per cent expressed no opinion.

By Region

	Yes	No
New England	52%	48%
Middle Atlantic	52	48
East Central	46	54
West Central	48	52
South	52	48
West	51	49

By Income

Upper	53%	47%
Middle	48	52
Lower	49	51

Roosevelt Voters in 1940

Yes........................... 53%
No............................ 47

Willkie Voters in 1940

Yes........................... 43%
No............................ 57

JUNE 11
LABOR STRIKES

Interviewing Date 5/22–27/41
Survey #237–K   Question #3

Should the Government forbid strikes in industries manufacturing materials for our national defense program, or should the workers in those industries continue to have the right to go on strike?

Forbid strikes...................... 76%
Allow strikes....................... 19
No opinion.......................... 5

JUNE 13
LABOR UNIONS

Interviewing Date 5/31–6/4/41
Survey #238–K   Question #11

Do you favor or oppose labor unions?

Favor.............................. 67%
Oppose............................. 33

Ten per cent expressed no opinion.

By Region

	Favor	*Oppose*
New England...............	74%	26%
Middle Atlantic.............	74	26
East Central................	70	30
West Central...............	55	45
South......................	51	49
West......................	72	28

JUNE 14
LABOR AND BUSINESS LEADERS

Interviewing Date 5/31–6/4/41
Survey #238–K   Question #13a

Do you think labor union leaders are helping the national defense production program as much as they should?

Yes............................... 12%
No................................ 78
No opinion........................ 10

Interviewing Date 5/31–6/4/41
Survey 238–K   Question #13b

Do you think business leaders are helping the national defense production program as much as they should?

Yes............................... 42%
No................................ 41
No opinion........................ 17

JUNE 15
EUROPEAN WAR

Interviewing Date 6/9–14/41
Survey #239–K   Question #2

Do you think the United States navy should be used to guard ships carrying materials to Britain?

Yes............................... 55%
No................................ 38
No opinion........................ 7

By Region
New England and Middle Atlantic

Yes............................... 55%
No................................ 38
No opinion........................ 7

East Central

Yes............................... 48%
No................................ 44
No opinion........................ 8

West Central

Yes............................... 49%
No................................ 45
No opinion........................ 6

South

Yes............................... 75%
No................................ 17
No opinion........................ 8

West

Yes............................. 53%
No.............................. 39
No opinion....................... 8

Interviewing Date 5/22–27/41
Survey #237–K   Question #4

As far as you are personally concerned, do you think President Roosevelt has gone too far in his policies of helping Britain or not far enough?

Too far.......................... 23%
About right...................... 55
Not far enough................... 22

JUNE 18
COMMUNIST PARTY

Interviewing Date 5/22–27/41
Survey #237–K   Question #8

Do you think membership in the Communist party in this country should be forbidden by law?

Yes............................. 71%
No.............................. 22
No opinion....................... 7

By Income
Upper

Yes............................. 70%
No.............................. 28
No opinion....................... 2

Middle

Yes............................. 71%
No.............................. 24
No opinion....................... 5

Lower

Yes............................. 72%
No.............................. 16
No opinion....................... 12

JUNE 20
SENDING SOLDIERS OVERSEAS

Interviewing Date 5/31–6/4/41
Survey #238–K   Question #9

Should a vote of the people be required before Congress can send men to fight overseas?

Yes............................. 56%
No.............................. 44

Six per cent expressed no opinion.

JUNE 25
DAYLIGHT SAVING TIME

Interviewing Date 6/9–14/41
Survey #239–K   Question #9a

To save electricity and to increase daylight working hours, it has been suggested that the entire country be put on daylight saving time until the end of September. Do you favor or oppose this suggestion?

Favor........................... 67%
Oppose.......................... 19
No opinion....................... 14

By Community Size
Under 10,000

Favor........................... 64%
Oppose.......................... 20
No opinion....................... 16

Over 10,000

Favor........................... 77%
Oppose.......................... 13
No opinion....................... 10

Farms

Favor........................... 45%
Oppose.......................... 34
No opinion....................... 21

Interviewing Date 6/9–14/41
Survey #239–K   Question #9b

Would you favor or oppose keeping the country on daylight saving time throughout the coming year?

Favor............................ 38%
Oppose........................... 41
No opinion....................... 21

JUNE 27
PRESIDENT ROOSEVELT'S POPULARITY

Interviewing Date 6/9–14/41
Survey #239–K   Question #11c

In general, do you approve or disapprove of the way Franklin Roosevelt is handling his job as President today?

Approve.......................... 76%
Disapprove....................... 24

Five per cent expressed no opinion.

JUNE 27
EUROPEAN WAR

Special Survey

Asked in Great Britain: In general, are you satisfied or dissatisfied with the Government's conduct of the war?

Satisfied........................ 58%
Dissatisfied..................... 30
Undecided........................ 12

JUNE 28
EUROPEAN WAR

Interviewing Date 6/9–14/41
Survey #239–K   Question #6

If peace could be obtained today on the basis of Germany holding the countries it has conquered so far, and with Britain

keeping the British Empire as it now stands, would you be in favor of such a peace?

Yes.............................. 29%
No.............................. 62
Undecided........................ 9

JUNE 29
EUROPEAN WAR

Interviewing Date 6/9–14/41
Survey #239–K   Question #4a

If you were asked to vote today on the question of the United States entering the war now against Germany and Italy, how would you vote — to go into the war now or to stay out of the war?

Go in............................ 24%
Stay out......................... 76

Nine per cent expressed no opinion.

JULY 2
EUROPEAN WAR

Special Survey

Asked in Great Britain: Would you approve or disapprove if the British Government were to discuss peace proposals with Germany now?

Approve.......................... 12%
Disapprove....................... 82
No opinion....................... 6

JULY 7
PERSONAL FINANCES

Interviewing Date 6/26–7/1/41
Survey #240–K   Question #9

Financially, are you better off or worse off than last year?

Better off......................... 30%
Worse off......................... 20
Same............................. 50

By Region
New England

Better off......................... 35%
Worse off......................... 20
Same............................. 45

Middle Atlantic

Better off......................... 30%
Worse off......................... 22
Same............................. 48

East Central

Better off......................... 33%
Worse off......................... 18
Same............................. 49

West Central

Better off......................... 30%
Worse off......................... 16
Same............................. 54

South

Better off......................... 27%
Worse off......................... 22
Same............................. 51

West

Better off......................... 28%
Worse off......................... 22
Same............................. 50

By Age
21–29 Years

Better off......................... 47%
Worse off......................... 15
Same............................. 38

30–49 Years

Better off......................... 31%
Worse off......................... 18
Same............................. 51

50 Years and Over

Better off......................... 17%
Worse off......................... 26
Same............................. 57

By Occupation
Professional

Better off......................... 34%
Worse off......................... 16
Same............................. 50

Business

Better off......................... 32%
Worse off......................... 19
Same............................. 49

Farmers

Better off......................... 26%
Worse off......................... 16
Same............................. 58

White Collar

Better off......................... 38%
Worse off......................... 17
Same............................. 45

Skilled

Better off......................... 34%
Worse off......................... 21
Same............................. 45

Semiskilled

Better off......................... 32%
Worse off......................... 23
Same............................. 45

Unskilled

Better off......................... 24%
Worse off......................... 24
Same............................. 52

Reliefers

Better off......................... 11%
Worse off......................... 33
Same............................. 56

JULY 9
EUROPEAN WAR

Interviewing Date 6/26–7/1/41
Survey #240–K   Question #2

Should the United States enter the war now?

Yes.................................. 21%
No.................................. 79

Interviewing Date 6/26–7/1/41
Survey #240–K   Question #1

Do you think the United States navy should be used to convoy ships carrying war materials to Britain?

Yes.................................. 56%
No.................................. 35
No opinion....................... 9

JULY 11
AID TO ENGLAND

Interviewing Date 6/26–7/1/41
Survey #240–K   Question #4a

Has the new war between Germany and Russia changed your attitude toward helping Britain?

Yes.................................. 12%
No.................................. 83
Undecided....................... 5

Interviewing Date 6/26–7/1/41
Survey #240–K   Question #4b

Asked of those who responded in the affirmative: Are you now more in favor or less in favor of aiding Britain?

More in favor.................... 8%
Less in favor.................... 4
                         12%

JULY 12
BRITISH POLITICS

Special Survey

Asked in Great Britain: If anything should happen to Mr. Churchill, whom do you think would be the best man to take his place as Prime Minister?

Eden............................. 37%
Bevin............................ 7
Beaverbrook.................... 7
Hore-Belisha.................... 4
Lloyd George................... 3
Halifax.......................... 2
Morrison......................... 2
Attlee........................... 1
Others, no opinion............. 37

JULY 14
EUROPEAN WAR

Interviewing Date 6/26–7/1/41
Survey #240–K   Question #6a

In the present war between Germany and Russia, which side would you like to see win?

Germany.......................... 4%
Russia........................... 72
No difference................... 17
No opinion....................... 7

By Income
Upper

Germany.......................... 5%
Russia........................... 72
No difference, no opinion....... 23

Middle

Germany.......................... 4%
Russia........................... 73
No difference, no opinion....... 23

Lower

Germany	3%
Russia	72
No difference, no opinion	25

By Religion
Catholics

Germany	6%
Russia	65
No difference, no opinion	29

Protestants

Germany	3%
Russia	74
No difference, no opinion	23

Interviewing Date 6/26–7/1/41
Survey #240–K   Question #6b

Which side do you think will win the war?

Germany	47%
Russia	22
Stalemate	8
No opinion	23

JULY 16
WORLD WAR I

Interviewing Date 6/26–7/1/41
Survey #240–K   Question #10a

Do you happen to have any idea how much money the United States spent in the first World War?

Yes	15%
No	85

The estimated cost of the war is approximately $33 billion. Five per cent were able to name a figure between $18 billion and $45 billion.

Interviewing Date 6/26–7/1/41
Survey #240–K   Question #10c

If we go into the war, would you say that it will cost our country more money or less money than the first World War?

More	87%
Less	1
About the same	5
No opinion	7

Interviewing Date 6/26–7/1/41
Survey #240–K   Question #10d

If we go into the war, would you say that we will have more soldiers and sailors killed, or fewer, than in the first World War?

More	45%
Fewer	31
About the same	9
No opinion	15

Interviewing Date 6/26–7/1/41
Survey #240–K   Question #10b

Do you happen to have any idea how many Americans were killed as a result of the first World War?

Yes	21%
No	79

Army and navy records list 50,510 killed. Six per cent named a figure between 40,000 and 60,000.

JULY 19
DAYLIGHT SAVING TIME

Interviewing Date 6/9–14/41
Survey #239–K   Question #9a

To save electricity and to increase daylight working hours, it has been suggested that the entire country be put on daylight saving time until the end of September. Do you favor or oppose the suggestion?

Favor	67%
Oppose	19
No opinion	14

By Region

New England and Middle Atlantic

Favor............................. 78%
Oppose........................... 13
No opinion........................ 9

East Central

Favor............................. 66%
Oppose........................... 21
No opinion........................ 13

West Central

Favor............................. 56%
Oppose........................... 25
No opinion........................ 19

South

Favor............................. 64%
Oppose........................... 16
No opinion........................ 20

West

Favor............................. 58%
Oppose........................... 27
No opinion........................ 15

Interviewing Date 6/9–14/41
Survey #239–K   Question #9b

Would you favor or oppose keeping the country on daylight saving time throughout the coming year?

Favor............................. 46%
Oppose........................... 54

Twenty per cent expressed no opinion.

JULY 20
EUROPEAN WAR

Interviewing Date 6/26–7/1/41
Survey #240–K   Question #2

If you were asked to vote today on the question of the United States entering the war now against Germany and Italy, how would you vote — to go into the war now or to stay out of the war?

Go in............................. 21%
Stay out.......................... 79

Persons Listed in *Who's Who in America*

Go in............................. 45%
Stay out.......................... 55

Interviewing Date 6/26–7/1/41
Survey #240–K   Question #1

Do you think the United States navy should be used to convoy ships carrying war materials to Britain?

Yes............................... 56%
No............................... 35
No opinion........................ 9

Persons Listed in *Who's Who in America*

Yes............................... 64%
No............................... 29
No opinion........................ 7

Interviewing Date 6/26–7/1/41
Survey #240–K   Question #3

So far as you are personally concerned, do you think President Roosevelt has gone too far in his policies of helping Britain or not far enough?

Too far........................... 23%
About right....................... 55
Not far enough.................... 22

Persons Listed in *Who's Who in America*

Too far........................... 16%
About right....................... 53
Not far enough.................... 31

JULY 23
BRITISH VIEWS ON WAR PRODUCTION

Special Survey

Asked in Great Britain: Do you think that we are producing in our factories the greatest possible amount of war material?

Yes............................... 21%
No................................ 54
No opinion........................ 25

Asked in Great Britain: Do you think America's production of arms, airplanes, and other war materials is going ahead fast enough?

Yes............................... 30%
No................................ 53
No opinion........................ 17

Asked in Great Britain: Do you think the United States will eventually come into the war?

Yes............................... 72%
No................................ 14
No opinion........................ 14

JULY 25
ICELAND

Interviewing Date 7/11–16/41
Survey #241–K   Question #8

Do you approve or disapprove of the Government's action in taking over the defense of Iceland?

Approve........................... 61%
Disapprove........................ 17
No opinion........................ 22

JULY 28
WENDELL WILLKIE

Interviewing Date 7/11–16/41
Survey #241–K   Question #12a

Has your opinion of Wendell Willkie changed since the election?

Yes............................... 39%
No................................ 61

Interviewing Date 7/11–16/41
Survey #241–K   Question #12b

Asked of those who responded in the affirmative: Do you like him better or not as well as then?

Like him better................... 20%
Like him less..................... 19
                                  ____
                                  39%

By Political Affiliation
Democrats

Like him better................... 30%
Like him less..................... 7
Haven't changed opinion........... 63

Republicans

Like him better................... 9%
Like him less..................... 38
Haven't changed opinion........... 53

AUGUST 2
POSTWAR LEAGUE OF NATIONS

Special Survey

Asked of a cross section of people listed in Who's Who in America: *Would you like to see the United States join a league of nations after the war is over?*

Yes............................... 61%
No................................ 23
No opinion........................ 16

AUGUST 6
THE DRAFT

Interviewing Date 7/24–29/41
Survey #242–K   Question #1

Do you think drafted men should be kept in active service for longer than one year, or should they be released at the end of one year?

Should be kept...................... 50%
Should be released.................. 45
No opinion......................... 5

By Region
New England and Middle Atlantic

Should be kept...................... 51%
Should be released.................. 44
No opinion......................... 5

East Central

Should be kept...................... 39%
Should be released.................. 56
No opinion......................... 5

West Central

Should be kept...................... 44%
Should be released.................. 52
No opinion......................... 4

South

Should be kept...................... 63%
Should be released.................. 32
No opinion......................... 5

West

Should be kept...................... 57%
Should be released.................. 36
No opinion......................... 7

Interviewing Date 7/24–29/41
Survey #242–K   Question #2

The army has asked Congress to change the law that says drafted men cannot be sent to fight outside the Western Hemisphere. Do you think Congress should give the army power to sent drafted men to points outside the Western Hemisphere?

Yes............................... 37%
No................................ 50
No opinion......................... 13

AUGUST 8
PENSIONS

Interviewing Date 7/11–16/41
Survey #241–K   Question #1c

What do you think is the smallest income per month that a single person over 60 needs for a decent living in your community?

Median average.................. $42 mo.

By Region

New England.................... $50 mo.
Middle Atlantic................. 50 mo.
East Central.................... 42 mo.
West Central................... 37 mo.
South......................... 32 mo.
West.......................... 48 mo.

Interviewing Date 7/11–16/41
Survey #241–K   Question #1d

What do you think is the smallest income per month that a married couple over 60 needs for a decent living in your community?

Median average.................. $73 mo.

By Region

New England.................... $78 mo.
Middle Atlantic................. 78 mo.
East Central.................... 74 mo.
West Central................... 59 mo.
South......................... 59 mo.
West.......................... 76 mo.

Interviewing Date 7/11–16/41
Survey #241–K   Question #1a

Are you in favor of Government old-age pensions?

Yes............................... 91%
No................................ 7
No opinion......................... 2

Asked at what age pensions should begin, most voters named 60 years of age.

AUGUST 9
PENSIONS

Interviewing Date 7/11–16/41
Survey #241–K   Question #2

Would you be willing to pay three cents out of every dollar of your income until you are 60 years old in order to get a pension from the Government of $50 a month after you are 60?

Yes............................... 76%
No............................... 18
No opinion....................... 6

AUGUST 11
INCOME TAX

Interviewing Date 7/24–29/41
Survey #242–K   Question #12a

In order to help pay for defense, the Government will be forced to increase income taxes. If you were the one to decide, how much income tax, if any, would you ask a typical family of four with an income of $1,000 to pay?

                                        Average
If public set tax rate................... $6
(Proposed federal tax rate............. $0)

Interviewing Date 7/24–29/41
Survey #242–K   Question #12b

In order to help pay for defense, the Government will be forced to increase income taxes. If you were the one to decide, how much income tax, if any, would you ask a typical family of four with an income of $3,000 to pay?

                                        Average
If public set tax rate................. $140
(Proposed federal tax rate........... $ 11)

Interviewing Date 7/24–29/41
Survey #242–K   Question #12c

In order to help pay for defense, the Government will be forced to increase income

taxes. If you were the one to decide, how much income tax, if any, would you ask a typical family of four with an income of $10,000 to pay?

                                        Average
If public set tax rate................ $1,123
(Proposed federal tax rate......... $ 998)

Interviewing Date 7/24–29/41
Survey #242–K   Question #12d

In order to help pay for defense, the Government will be forced to increase income taxes. If you were the one to decide, how much income tax, if any, would you ask a typical family of four with an income of $100,000 to pay?

                                        Average
If public set tax rate.............. $24,000
(Proposed federal tax rate........ $52,738)

AUGUST 13
THE AIR FORCE

Interviewing Date 7/24–29/41
Survey #242–K   Question #6

At present the air force is a part of both the army and navy and not a separate branch of our armed forces. Do you think the air force should be made a separate branch of the armed forces?

Yes............................... 42%
No............................... 33
No opinion....................... 25

AUGUST 16
EUROPEAN WAR

Interviewing Date 7/31–8/4/41
Survey #243–K   Question #7

In the war between Britain and Germany, do you think the Vichy Government is helping one side rather than the other?

Vichy is helping Germany............ 58%
Vichy is helping Britain.............. 4
Vichy is neutral..................... 13
No opinion........................ 25

Lack of plants and equipment......... 3
Lack of enthusiasm in plants......... 3
Graft............................. 2
Others............................ 10
No opinion........................ 3

AUGUST 18
EUROPEAN WAR

Interviewing Date 7/31–8/4/41
Survey #243–K   Question #4

If the United States does enter the war against Germany and Italy, do you think it will be necessary to send our army to Europe to fight?

Yes............................... 65%
No............................... 30
No opinion........................ 5

AUGUST 20
DEFENSE PRODUCTION

Interviewing Date 7/24–29/41
Survey #242–K   Question #7a

Do you think America's production of arms, airplanes, and other war materials is going ahead fast enough?

Yes............................... 39%
No............................... 43
No opinion........................ 18

Interviewing Date 7/24–29/41
Survey #242–K   Question #7b

Asked of those who responded in the negative: What do you think is the chief reason why production isn't going ahead faster?

Strikes and labor disputes............ 48%
Poor administration................. 18
Sabotage.......................... 6
Lack of materials................... 4
Sending too much material abroad..... 3

AUGUST 22
INSTALLMENT BUYING

Interviewing Date 8/7–12/41
Survey #244–K   Question #7a

As one way to help defense production, it has been suggested that the Government forbid installment buying until the war in Europe is over. Do you approve or disapprove of this suggestion?

Approve........................... 43%
Disapprove........................ 49
No opinion........................ 8

By Income
Upper

Approve........................... 48%
Disapprove........................ 48
No opinion........................ 4

Middle

Approve........................... 43%
Disapprove........................ 50
No opinion........................ 7

Lower

Approve........................... 41%
Disapprove........................ 49
No opinion........................ 10

Interviewing Date 8/7–12/41
Survey #244–K   Question #7b

Are you paying for anything on the installment plan?

Yes............................... 36%
No............................... 64

AUGUST 23
LEAGUE OF NATIONS

Interviewing Date 7/31–8/4/41
Survey #243–K   Question #5

Do you think the United States should have joined the League of Nations after the last war?

Yes............................. 37%
No.............................. 37
No opinion....................... 26

By Region
New England and Middle Atlantic

Yes............................. 39%
No.............................. 36
No opinion....................... 25

East Central

Yes............................. 35%
No.............................. 39
No opinion....................... 26

West Central

Yes............................. 27%
No.............................. 45
No opinion....................... 28

South

Yes............................. 39%
No.............................. 30
No opinion....................... 31

West

Yes............................. 42%
No.............................. 35
No opinion....................... 23

AUGUST 25
PRESIDENT ROOSEVELT'S POPULARITY

Interviewing Date 8/7–12/41
Survey #244–K   Question #11c

Do you approve or disapprove of the way Franklin Roosevelt is handling his job as President?

Approve.......................... 73%
Disapprove....................... 20
No opinion....................... 7

AUGUST 27
ADMISSION TO WEST POINT AND ANNAPOLIS

Interviewing Date 7/24–29/41
Survey #242–K   Question #8

Should young men who want to go to West Point or Annapolis be permitted to apply directly for entrance, or should they first be required to get an appointment from their Congressman, as at present?

Apply directly...................... 64%
Through Congressman............... 19
No opinion....................... 17

AUGUST 29
MILITARY SALARIES

Interviewing Date 8/7–12/41
Survey #244–K   Question #1

For the duration of the war, would you be in favor of the Government paying an extra $30 a month to everybody in the army and navy who has been in active service for more than one year, not including officers?

Yes............................. 70%
No.............................. 22
No opinion....................... 8

AUGUST 30
EUROPEAN WAR

Special Survey

Asked in Great Britain: What do you think we are fighting for?

Freedom, liberty, democracy......... 46%
To stop fascism, to stop aggression..... 14
"It's them or us".................... 8

A better world, for peace............ 7
We are fighting for our lives......... 5
Others........................... 13
No opinion....................... 7

SEPTEMBER 1
EUROPEAN WAR

Interviewing Date 7/24–29/41
Survey #242–T   Question #9

If Germany were to offer peace on the basis that she would keep only the territory won from Russia — and give up France, Scandinavia, and other conquered countries — would you favor such a peace?

Yes.............................. 34%
No.............................. 58
No opinion....................... 8

SEPTEMBER 3
EUROPEAN WAR

Interviewing Date 8/21–26/41
Survey #245–K   Question #5

Do you think the American navy should be used to convoy ships carrying war materials to England?

Yes.............................. 52%
No.............................. 39
No opinion....................... 9

SEPTEMBER 5
AID FOR FREE FRENCH

Interviewing Date 8/21–26/41
Survey #245–K   Question #8c

Do you think the United States should send war materials under the Lend-Lease program to the Free French forces of General de Gaulle?

Yes.............................. 74%
No.............................. 16
No opinion....................... 10

SEPTEMBER 6
DRAFTEE MORALE

Interviewing Date 8/21–26/41
Survey #245–K   Question #1a

From what you have heard or read, do you think the morale of drafted men in the army is good or poor?

Good............................ 39%
Fair............................. 22
Poor............................ 25
No opinion....................... 14

SEPTEMBER 7
JAPAN

Interviewing Date 8/21–26/41
Survey #245–K   Question #13

Should the United States take steps now to keep Japan from becoming more powerful, even if it means risking a war with Japan?

Yes.............................. 70%
No.............................. 18
No opinion....................... 12

By Region
New England and Middle Atlantic

Yes.............................. 72%
No.............................. 19
No opinion....................... 9

East Central

Yes.............................. 61%
No.............................. 24
No opinion....................... 15

West Central

Yes.............................. 64%
No.............................. 21
No opinion....................... 15

South

Yes.............................. 76%
No.............................. 11
No opinion....................... 13

West

Yes........................... 76%
No............................ 14
No opinion.................... 10

SEPTEMBER 10
EUROPEAN WAR

Interviewing Date 8/21–26/41
Survey #245–K   Question #2

*Which side do you think will win the war —
England or Germany?*

England....................... 69%
Germany....................... 6
Stalemate, no opinion......... 25

SEPTEMBER 12
WAGE AND PRICE CONTROL

Interviewing Date 8/26–9/2/41
Survey #246–K   Question #4c

*As one way to prevent prices from going up
rapidly, would you be willing to have the
Government keep your salary rate where it
now is, if the Government also keeps the
prices of the things you buy where they are
now?*

Yes........................... 62%
No............................ 32
No opinion.................... 6

By Income
Upper

Yes........................... 63%
No............................ 32
No opinion.................... 5

Middle

Yes........................... 65%
No............................ 30
No opinion.................... 5

Lower

Yes........................... 57%
No............................ 35
No opinion.................... 8

Interviewing Date 8/26–9/2/41
Survey #246–K   Question #4b

*Do you consider that you are now being
paid a fair salary?*

Yes........................... 64%
No............................ 33
No opinion.................... 3

SEPTEMBER 13
WAGE AND PRICE CONTROLS

Interviewing Date 8/7–12/41
Survey #244–K   Question #5c

*Asked of farmers: Considering costs of
production, do you think that the price you
are now getting for your chief cash crop or
product is a fair price?*

Yes........................... 52%
No............................ 34
No opinion.................... 14

Midwestern Farmers Only

Yes........................... 56%
No............................ 29
No opinion.................... 15

Interviewing Date 8/7–12/41
Survey #244–K   Question #5d

*Asked of farmers: Would you be willing to
have the Government keep prices where
they are now on the things you sell, provided the Government also fixes the prices
of the things you buy at the present level?*

Yes........................... 55%
No............................ 28
No opinion.................... 17

Midwestern Farmers Only

Yes................................. 54%
No................................. 28
No opinion......................... 18

SEPTEMBER 15
POSSIBLE PRESIDENTIAL CANDIDATES

Special Survey

Who do you think will be the next President of the United States?

The following are listed according to frequency of mention:

Willkie
Hull
Dewey
Wallace
La Guardia
Farley
Taft
Vandenberg
McNutt
Hoover

SEPTEMBER 17
EUROPEAN WAR

Special Survey

Asked in Great Britain: Do you think America will come fully into the war?

Yes................................. 57%
No................................. 23
No opinion......................... 20

Asked of those who responded in the affirmative: When do you think America will enter the war?

This year........................... 19%
Next summer....................... 25
By end of next year................ 13
                                                         —
                                                         57%

Are you satisfied or dissatisfied with the amount of help the United States is giving Britain?

Satisfied........................... 61%
Dissatisfied........................ 25
No opinion......................... 14

SEPTEMBER 20
EUROPEAN WAR

Special Survey

Asked in Great Britain: What do you think is the most important war problem the British Government must solve in the next few months?

The following are listed according to frequency of mention:

Invading the Continent
Increasing speed of war production
Maintaining food supply
Fighting the bombing
Help to Russia
Checking submarine attacks and shipping losses

SEPTEMBER 22
NEUTRALITY

Interviewing Date 8/21–26/41
Survey #245–K   Question #11b

If Lindbergh, Wheeler, Nye, and others start a "Keep-Out-of-War" party and enter candidates in the next congressional elections, would you vote for the candidate of this party?

Yes................................. 16%
No................................. 84

By Region

	Yes	No
New England...............	18%	82%
Middle Atlantic..............	18	82

East Central................. 19   81
West Central................. 17   83
South....................... 9   91
West....................... 13   87

SEPTEMBER 26
EUROPEAN WAR

Interviewing Date 9/19–24/41
Survey #248–K   Question #6

Do you approve or disapprove of having the United States shoot at German submarines or warships on sight?

Approve........................... 56%
Disapprove........................ 34
No opinion........................ 10

SEPTEMBER 28
PERSONAL SACRIFICES

Interviewing Date 9/11–16/41
Survey #247–K   Question #1a

Have you had to make any personal sacrifices or do without things as a result of the war?

Yes.............................. 26%
No.............................. 74

Twelve per cent expressed no opinion.

SEPTEMBER 29
REPUBLICAN PARTY

Interviewing Date 9/11–16/41
Survey #247–K   Question #11

Asked of Republicans: Should the Republican party support the Administration's foreign policy, or oppose it?

Support.......................... 60%
Oppose........................... 23
No opinion....................... 17

OCTOBER 1
NEUTRALITY

Interviewing Date 9/19–24/41
Survey #248–K   Question #7

Should the Neutrality Act be changed to permit American merchant ships with American crews to carry war materials to Britain?

Yes.............................. 46%
No.............................. 40
No opinion....................... 14

By Political Affiliation
Democrats

Yes.............................. 51%
No.............................. 33
No opinion....................... 16

Republicans

Yes.............................. 42%
No.............................. 48
No opinion....................... 10

OCTOBER 3
EUROPEAN WAR

Interviewing Date 9/19–24/41
Survey #248–K   Question #6

In general, do you approve or disapprove of having the United States navy shoot at German submarines or warships on sight?

Approve........................... 62%
Disapprove........................ 28
No opinion........................ 10

By Region
New England and Middle Atlantic

Approve........................... 61%
Disapprove........................ 29
No opinion........................ 10

East Central

Approve	56%
Disapprove	35
No opinion	9

West Central

Approve	56%
Disapprove	31
No opinion	13

South

Approve	78%
Disapprove	15
No opinion	7

West

Approve	64%
Disapprove	27
No opinion	9

By Political Affiliation
Democrats

Approve	68%
Disapprove	22
No opinion	10

Republicans

Approve	56%
Disapprove	36
No opinion	8

OCTOBER 4
GAMBLING

Interviewing Date 9/19–24/41
Survey #248–K   Question #12a

During the past year, have you done any of the following things: Bought a ticket in a church raffle or lottery?

Yes	24%
No	76

Bet on an election or some sports event?

Yes	21%
No	79

Played cards or dice for money?

Yes	24%
No	76

Bought a number on a punch board?

Yes	23%
No	77

Played a slot machine?

Yes	21%
No	79

Bet on a horse race?

Yes	9%
No	91

Played the numbers game?

Yes	8%
No	92

Interviewing Date 9/19–24/41
Survey #248–K   Question #12b

Asked of those who responded in the affirmative: On the whole, have you made or lost money on these games of chance?

Made money	14%
Lost money	86

OCTOBER 5
EUROPEAN WAR

Interviewing Date 9/19–24/41
Survey #248–K   Question #4a

Which of these two things do you think is the more important — that this country keep out of war or that Germany be defeated?

Keep out of war	30%
Germany be defeated	70

By Political Affiliation

	Keep Out	*Defeat Germany*
Democrats...........	23%	77%
Republicans...........	36	64

By Region

New England..........	30%	70%
Middle Atlantic.......	30	70
East Central..........	37	63
West Central..........	36	64
South...............	12	88
West...............	31	69

By Income

Upper...............	24%	76%
Middle...............	26	74
Lower...............	35	65

OCTOBER 8
PRESIDENT ROOSEVELT

Interviewing Date 9/19–24/41
Survey #248–K   Question #5

So far as you personally are concerned, do you think President Roosevelt has gone too far in his policies of helping Britain, or not far enough?

Too far...........................	27%
About right........................	57
Not far enough.....................	16

Ten per cent expressed no opinion.

By Region
New England and Middle Atlantic

Too far...........................	27%
About right........................	55
Not far enough.....................	18

East Central

Too far...........................	34%
About right........................	51
Not far enough.....................	15

West Central

Too far...........................	31%
About right........................	59
Not far enough.....................	10

South

Too far...........................	14%
About right........................	61
Not far enough.....................	25

West

Too far...........................	24%
About right........................	62
Not far enough.....................	14

OCTOBER 11
COMMON COLD

Interviewing Date 10/3–8/41
Survey #249   Question #6b

Do any of the people in your home, including yourself, have a cold at present?

Yes...............................	10%
No...............................	90

By Region

	Yes	No
New England................	8%	92%
Middle Atlantic...............	8	92
East Central.................	12	88
West Central.................	12	88
South.......................	8	92
West.......................	12	88

OCTOBER 17
PRESIDENT ROOSEVELT

Special Survey

Asked in New York City: In general do you approve or disapprove of President Roosevelt's foreign policy?

Approve............................ 67%
Disapprove........................ 33

This question was asked of those who are registered to vote in the forthcoming election for mayor. Less than 50% of the adult population of the city is registered.

OCTOBER 18
COURSES IN MILITARY TRAINING

Interviewing Date 10/3–8/41
Survey #249   Question #1

Do you think courses in military training should be given boys in high school in your community?

Yes.............................. 69%
No............................... 31

Four per cent expressed no opinion.

OCTOBER 19
NEUTRALITY

Interviewing Date 10/9–14/41
Survey #250–K   Question #4

Should the Neutrality Act be changed to permit American ships to be armed?

Yes.............................. 72%
No............................... 21
No opinion........................ 7

By Political Affiliation
Democrats

Yes.............................. 76%
No............................... 17
No opinion........................ 7

Republicans

Yes.............................. 66%
No............................... 27
No opinion........................ 7

Interviewing Date 10/9–14/41
Survey #250–K   Question #2

Should the Neutrality Act be changed to permit American merchant ships with American crews to carry war materials to England?

Yes.............................. 46%
No............................... 40
No opinion........................ 14

By Political Affiliation
Democrats

Yes.............................. 53%
No............................... 33
No opinion........................ 14

Republicans

Yes.............................. 40%
No............................... 48
No opinion........................ 12

OCTOBER 25
PRO-AND ANTI-WAR GROUPS

Interviewing Date 10/9–14/41
Survey #250–K   Question #4

What persons or groups do you think are most active in trying to keep us out of war?

The following are listed according to frequency of mention:

Charles Lindbergh, Burton Wheeler, and
   Gerald Nye
America First Committee
Roosevelt Administration
Nazi agents and fifth columnists
Church groups

Interviewing Date 10/9–14/41
Survey #250–K   Question #5

What persons or groups do you think are most active in trying to get us into war?

The following are listed according to frequency of mention:

Roosevelt Administration and the Democratic
party
Big business and profiteers
British organizations and agents
American groups with pro-British sympathies
Jews

OCTOBER 26
LABOR UNIONS

Interviewing Date 10/3–8/41
Survey #249   Question #7

Are you in favor of labor unions?

Yes............................... 67%
No................................ 33

Interviewing Date 10/9–14/41
Survey #250–K   Question #13

*Do you believe that many labor union
leaders are racketeers?*

Yes............................... 74%
No................................ 17
No opinion........................ 9

Interviewing Date 10/9–14/41
Survey #250–K   Question #12

*Do you believe that many labor union
leaders are communists?*

Yes............................... 61%
No................................ 25
No opinion........................ 14

OCTOBER 29
THE CLOSED SHOP

Interviewing Date 10/3–8/41
Survey #249   Question #11

*Are you in favor of the closed shop — that
is, requiring every worker in a company to
belong to a union before he can be hired?*

Yes............................... 13%
No................................ 77
No opinion........................ 10

OCTOBER 31
LABOR UNIONS

Interviewing Date 10/3–8/41
Survey #249   Question #9

*Do you think labor unions should be re-
quired to make yearly public reports of the
money they collect and spend?*

Yes............................... 87%
No................................ 6
No opinion........................ 7

Union Members Only

Yes............................... 81%
No................................ 14
No opinion........................ 5

Interviewing Date 10/3–8/41
Survey #249   Question #12

*Should companies having a closed or union
shop take union dues out of worker's pay
envelopes and turn the money over to the
unions, or should the unions collect the dues
themselves?*

Companies should collect............ 15%
Unions should collect............... 60
No opinion........................ 25

NOVEMBER 1
GOVERNMENT EMPLOYEES

Interviewing Date 10/9–14/41
Survey #250–K   Question #8

*Should Government employees be allowed
to join labor unions?*

Yes............................... 28%
No................................ 64
No opinion........................ 8

Interviewing Date 10/9–14/41
Survey #250–K   Question #9

*Should people who work for the Govern-
ment be allowed to go on strike?*

Yes............................... 17%
No............................... 79
No opinion........................ 4

NOVEMBER 2
EUROPEAN WAR

Interviewing Date 9/19–24/41
Survey #248–K   Question #5

So far as you personally are concerned, do you think President Roosevelt has gone too far or not far enough in his policy of aiding Britain?

Too far............................ 27%
About right........................ 57
Not far enough..................... 16

Union Members Only

Too far............................ 27%
About right........................ 55
Not far enough..................... 18

Interviewing Date 10/9–14/41
Survey #250–K   Question #3

Which of these two things do you think is the more important — that this country keep out of war, or that Germany be defeated?

Keep out of war.................... 32%
Defeat Germany..................... 68

Union Members Only

Keep out of war.................... 34%
Defeat Germany..................... 66

NOVEMBER 3
LABOR STRIKES

Interviewing Date 10/9–14/41
Survey #250–K   Question #10a

Should the Government forbid strikes in defense industries, or should the workers in those industries continue to have the right to go on strike?

Forbid strikes..................... 73%
Right to strike.................... 23
No opinion......................... 4

Union Members Only

Forbid strikes..................... 56%
Right to strike.................... 39
No opinion......................... 5

NOVEMBER 5
NEUTRALITY

Interviewing Date 10/24–29/41
Survey #251–K   Question #4

Should the Neutrality Act be changed to permit American merchant ships to be armed?

Yes............................... 81%
No............................... 14
No opinion........................ 5

Interviewing Date 10/24–29/41
Survey #251–K   Question #3

Should the Neutrality Act be changed to permit American merchant ships with American crews to carry war materials to Britain?

Yes............................... 61%
No............................... 31
No opinion........................ 8

NOVEMBER 7
THE ARMY

Interviewing Date 10/9–14/41
Survey #250–K   Question #6

The army has asked Congress to change the law that says drafted men cannot be sent to fight outside of North or South America or this country's possessions. Do you think Congress should give the army the right to send drafted soldiers to any part of the world?

Yes................................. 42%
No.................................. 53
No opinion.......................... 5

By Political Affiliation
Democrats

Yes................................. 48%
No.................................. 47
No opinion.......................... 5

Republicans

Yes................................. 38%
No.................................. 58
No opinion.......................... 4

By Sex
Men

Yes................................. 49%
No.................................. 48
No opinion.......................... 3

Women

Yes................................. 36%
No.................................. 58
No opinion.......................... 6

NOVEMBER 10
WAGE AND PRICE CONTROL

Interviewing Date 10/24–29/41
Survey #251–K   Question #10

A new law in Canada keeps prices from going higher than they are now and also keeps wage and salary rates from going higher. Would you approve or disapprove of such a law in the United States?

Approve............................ 67%
Disapprove......................... 24
No opinion......................... 9

Interviewing Date 9/11–16/41
Survey #247–K   Question #3c

As one way to prevent prices from going up rapidly, would you be willing to have the

Government keep your wage (salary) rate where it is now, if the Government also keeps the prices of the things you buy where they are now?

Yes................................. 66%
No.................................. 28
No opinion.......................... 6

Interviewing Date 9/11–16/41
Survey #247–K   Question #3b

Do you consider that you are now being paid a fair wage (salary)?

Yes................................. 64%
No.................................. 33
No opinion.......................... 3

Union Members Only

Yes................................. 65%
No.................................. 33
No opinion.......................... 2

NOVEMBER 12
BRITISH WAR EFFORT

Special Survey

Asked in Great Britain: Do you feel that Britain has taken or has not taken full advantage of the opportunities offered by the German attack on Russia?

Has................................. 29%
Has not............................. 49
Undecided.......................... 22

Asked in Great Britain: Are you satisfied or dissatisfied with the Government's conduct of the war?

Satisfied........................... 44%
Dissatisfied....................... 38
No opinion......................... 18

Asked in Great Britain: Do you approve or disapprove of Winston Churchill as Prime Minister?

Approve........................... 84%
Disapprove....................... 11
No opinion....................... 5

NOVEMBER 14
JAPAN

Interviewing Date 10/24–29/41
Survey #251–K   Question #9

Should the United States take steps now to prevent Japan from becoming more powerful, even if this means risking a war with Japan?

Yes.............................. 64%
No............................... 25
No opinion....................... 11

NOVEMBER 15
LABOR STRIKES

Interviewing Date 10/9–14/41
Survey #250–K   Question #11

Should all workers in defense industries who have been deferred from the draft because they are defense workers, be drafted if they go on strike?

Yes.............................. 76%
No............................... 20
No opinion....................... 4

NOVEMBER 17
LABOR UNIONS AND STRIKES

Interviewing Date 11/7–12/41
Survey #252–K   Question #4

Should the Government forbid strikes in defense industries, or should the workers in those industries continue to have the right to go on strike?

By Occupation
Businessmen
Forbid strikes..................... 78%
Allow strikes...................... 17
No opinion....................... 5

Professionals
Forbid strikes..................... 67%
Allow strikes...................... 27
No opinion....................... 6

Skilled Workers
Forbid strikes..................... 64%
Allow strikes...................... 29
No opinion....................... 7

Unskilled Workers
Forbid strikes..................... 63%
Allow strikes...................... 27
No opinion....................... 10

White Collar
Forbid strikes..................... 72%
Allow strikes...................... 22
No opinion....................... 6

Farmers
Forbid strikes..................... 78%
Allow strikes...................... 13
No opinion....................... 9

Interviewing Date 10/3–8/41
Survey #249   Question #7

Are you in favor of labor unions?

Yes.............................. 67%
No............................... 33

By Occupation

	Yes	No
Businessmen	66%	34%
Professionals	77	23
Skilled workers	75	25
Unskilled workers	71	29
White collar	69	31
Farmers	52	48

NOVEMBER 19
JOHN L. LEWIS

Interviewing Date 11/7–12/41
Survey #252–K   Question #6

What is your opinion of John L. Lewis?

Generally favorable comments......... 14%
Generally unfavorable comments...... 70
No opinion......................... 16

NOVEMBER 21
JOHN L. LEWIS

Interviewing Date 11/7–12/41
Survey #252–K   Question #7a

Have you heard or read about the strike in the captive coal mines which John L. Lewis called last month?

Yes.............................. 82%
No............................... 18

Interviewing Date 11/7–12/41
Survey #252–K   Question #7a

Asked of those who replied in the affirmative: Do you think John L. Lewis was justified in calling this strike?

Yes.............................. 8%
No............................... 60
No opinion....................... 14
                                  82%

Skilled and Unskilled Workers Only

Yes.............................. 10%
No............................... 52
No opinion....................... 16
Not familiar with strike......... 22

NOVEMBER 22
EUROPEAN WAR

Interviewing Date 11/7–12/41
Survey #252–K   Question #11

It has been suggested that Congress pass a resolution declaring that a state of war exists between the United States and Germany. Would you favor or oppose such a resolution at this time?

Favor............................. 26%
Oppose............................ 63
No opinion........................ 11

NOVEMBER 24
COMMON COLD

Interviewing Date 11/7–12/41
Survey #252–K   Question #8b

Do any of the people in your home, including yourself, have a cold at present?

Yes.............................. 14%
No............................... 86

By Region

	Yes	No
New England.................	12%	88%
Middle Atlantic..............	12	88
East Central.................	16	84
West Central.................	17	83
South.......................	14	86
West........................	13	87

By Income

	Yes	No
Upper.......................	14%	86%
Middle......................	14	86
Lower.......................	16	84

NOVEMBER 26
DEFENSE BONDS

Interviewing Date 10/24–29/41
Survey #251–K   Question #11a

Have you heard about Defense Savings Bonds and Stamps?

Yes.............................. 97%
No............................... 3

Interviewing Date 10/24–29/41
Survey #251–K   Question #11b

Asked of those who responded in the affirmative: Have you purchased or have you made plans to purchase any?

Already purchased................... 21%
Plan to purchase.................... 17
No plans to purchase............... 62

By Income

Upper

Already purchased................... 38%
Plan to purchase.................... 20
No plans to purchase............... 42

Middle

Already purchased................... 28%
Plan to purchase.................... 18
No plans to purchase............... 54

Lower

Already purchased................... 12%
Plan to purchase.................... 15
No plans to purchase............... 73

By Community Size

10,000 and Over

Already purchased................... 24%
Plan to purchase.................... 18
No plans to purchase............... 58

10,000 and Under

Already purchased................... 20%
Plan to purchase.................... 16
No plans to purchase............... 64

Farms

Already purchased................... 14%
Plan to purchase.................... 15
No plans to purchase............... 71

NOVEMBER 28
PRICE OUTLOOK

Interviewing Date 11/15–20/41
Survey #253–K   Question #4a

Do you think prices on most products you buy will be higher, lower, or about the same six months from now?

Higher........................... 83%
Lower............................ 1
Same............................ 10
Don't know...................... 6

Interviewing Date 11/15–20/41
Survey #253–K   Question #5

Have you laid in any goods or products in order to protect yourself against higher prices later on?

Yes.............................. 18%
No.............................. 82

NOVEMBER 30
CHURCH DISCUSSION OF WAR

Interviewing Date 11/15–20/41
Survey #253–K   Question #12a

Do you think preachers and priests should discuss from the pulpit the question of American participation in the war?

Yes.............................. 34%
No.............................. 55
No opinion...................... 11

By Religion
Catholics

Yes.............................. 31%
No.............................. 59
No opinion...................... 10

Protestants

Yes.............................. 37%
No.............................. 54
No opinion...................... 9

Church Members

Yes.............................. 36%
No............................... 55
No opinion....................... 9

Non-Church Members

Yes.............................. 25%
No............................... 58
No opinion....................... 17

Interviewing Date 11/15–20/41
Survey #253–K   Question #12b

Asked of those who replied in the affirmative: What course of action would you like to see them recommend?

Should advocate staying out of war..... 20%
Should advocate getting into war....... 12
Should deal with the kind of peace needed after war................. 11
Should advocate aid to Britain but no troops........................... 10
Should stress U.S. defenses.......... 9
Should say what they believe......... 5
No opinion....................... 33

DECEMBER 1
RELIGION

Interviewing Date 11/15–20/41
Survey #253–K   Question #11

Have you noticed an increase in interest in religion in your community since the war began?

Yes.............................. 31%
No............................... 57
No opinion....................... 12

By Community Size
100,000 and Over

Yes.............................. 37%
No............................... 52
No opinion....................... 11

100,000 and Under

Yes.............................. 27%
No............................... 60
No opinion....................... 13

Farms

Yes.............................. 22%
No............................... 66
No opinion....................... 12

Interviewing Date 11/15–20/41
Survey #253–K   Question #10

Do you think young people in this community are more interested or less interested in religion now than young people were ten years ago?

More............................. 18%
Less............................. 49
About the same................... 24
No opinion....................... 9

DECEMBER 2
EUROPEAN WAR

Special Survey

Asked in Great Britain: Do you feel that Britain has taken or has not taken full advantage of the opportunities offered by the German attack on Russia?

Has.............................. 35%
Has not.......................... 32
Undecided........................ 33

Asked in Great Britain: Would you approve or disapprove of the Government's compelling women to join the women's auxiliary forces?

Approve.......................... 55%
Disapprove....................... 35
No opinion....................... 10

Asked in Great Britain: Would you approve or disapprove of allowing women to become fighting members of the armed forces?

Approve............................ 26%
Disapprove........................ 66
No opinion........................ 8

DECEMBER 5
FOOD

Interviewing Date 11/15–20/41
Survey #253–K   Question #6a

Would the health of your family be better if you had more money to spend on food?

Yes............................... 39%
No................................ 61

Lower Income Only

Yes............................... 57%
No................................ 43

Interviewing Date 11/15–20/41
Survey #253–K   Question #6b

Those who responded in the affirmative were asked: If you had more money, what foods would you spend it on?

Meat.............................. 45%
Vegetables........................ 33
Dairy products.................... 33
Fruits............................ 30
Bread, cereals.................... 5
Sugar content foods............... 2
Miscellaneous..................... 22
No opinion........................ 8
                                 ――――
                                 178%

(Note: table adds to more than 100% because some persons named more than one item.)

DECEMBER 6
CANADIAN AND BRITISH AID TO RUSSIA

Special Survey

Asked in Canada: Do you approve of Britain and Canada sending arms and other war supplies to Russia?

Yes............................... 91%
No................................ 6
No opinion........................ 3

DECEMBER 7
VITAMINS

Interviewing Date 11/15–20/41
Survey #253–K   Question #1

Is there any one vitamin that you have heard about a lot in recent months?

Vitamin A......................... 7%
Vitamin B-1, B-2.................. 42
Vitamin C......................... 2
Vitamin D......................... 7
Other vitamins.................... 2
Have not heard.................... 46
                                 ――――
                                 106%

(Note: table adds to more than 100% because some persons named more than one vitamin.)

Interviewing Date 11/15–20/41
Survey #253–K   Question #9f

Are vitamins a passing fad?

Yes............................... 25%
No................................ 68
No opinion........................ 7

By Sex
Men

Yes............................... 29%
No................................ 64
No opinion........................ 7

Women

Yes............................... 21%
No................................ 73
No opinion........................ 6

Interviewing Date 11/15–20/41
Survey #253–K   Question #9a

Asked of housewives: Can you explain the difference between a vitamin and a calorie?

Correct........................... 16%
Incorrect......................... 84

DECEMBER 10
JAPAN

Interviewing Date 11/27–12/1/41
Survey #254–K Question #4

Do you think the United States will go to war against Japan sometime in the near future?

Yes............................... 52%
No................................ 27
No opinion........................ 21

DECEMBER 13
BOMBING OF CITIES

Special Survey

Do you think there is any chance that your city will be bombed?

West Coast

Yes............................... 49%
No................................ 40
No opinion........................ 11

East Coast

Yes............................... 45%
No................................ 44
No opinion........................ 11

Where would you go in case of an air raid?

Would stay indoors or get into large
   public building.................... 26%
Would go to a basement.............. 26
Would stay wherever they happened to
   be.............................. 15
Would go to street, park, field, or subway 12
Miscellaneous...................... 9
Would not know what to do......... 12

DECEMBER 15
WAGE AND PRICE CONTROLS

Interviewing Date 11/27–12/1/41
Survey #254–K Question #9

A new law in Canada keeps wages and salaries from going higher than they are now and also keeps all prices, including prices of farm products, from going higher. Would you approve or disapprove of such a law in the United States?

Approve........................... 63%
Disapprove........................ 28
No opinion........................ 9

By Region
New England and Middle Atlantic

Approve........................... 60%
Disapprove........................ 30
No opinion........................ 10

East Central

Approve........................... 61%
Disapprove........................ 29
No opinion........................ 10

West Central

Approve........................... 61%
Disapprove........................ 29
No opinion........................ 10

South

Approve........................... 66%
Disapprove........................ 25
No opinion........................ 9

West

Approve........................... 69%
Disapprove........................ 24
No opinion........................ 7

DECEMBER 17
EUROPEAN WAR

Interviewing Date 11/15–20/41
Survey #253–K Question #13

Which of these two things do you think is the more important — that this country keep out of war, or that Germany be defeated?

Keep out of war................... 32%
Defeat Germany.................... 68

DECEMBER 19
INCENDIARY BOMBS

Interviewing Date 12/12–17/41
Survey #255   Question #11d

How would you put out an incendiary bomb?

Would use sand, earth, or spray with
water............................ 38%
Would put bomb in pail of water, use
fire extinguisher, smother with blanket 18
Don't know........................ 44

DECEMBER 20
CANADIAN MANPOWER

Special Survey

Asked in Canada: Do you think the Government should have the power to decide which men are to be used in industry, which men are to be used in farming, and which in the armed forces?

Yes.............................. 72%
No............................... 20
No opinion........................ 8

DECEMBER 22
WAR INDUSTRIES

Interviewing Date 12/12–17/41
Survey #255   Question #1a

Do you think our country's production of arms, airplanes, and other war materials is going ahead fast enough?

Yes.............................. 45%
No............................... 45
No opinion....................... 10

Interviewing Date 12/12–17/41
Survey #255   Question #12g

Asked of war industry workers: Would you be willing to work eight hours more a week at your present job?

Yes.............................. 88%
No............................... 12

DECEMBER 23
THREAT TO AMERICA'S FUTURE

Interviewing Date 12/12–17/41
Survey #255   Question #6

Which country is the greater threat to America's future — Germany or Japan?

Germany.......................... 64%
Japan............................ 15
Equal threats.................... 15
No opinion....................... 6

DECEMBER 25
BRITISH POLITICS

Special Survey

Asked in Great Britain: If anything should happen to Mr. Churchill, who do you think would be the best man to take his place?

Eden............................. 38%
Beaverbrook...................... 11
Bevin............................ 7
Attlee........................... 3
Morrison......................... 2
Shinwell......................... 2
Lloyd George..................... 2
Others........................... 12
No opinion....................... 23

DECEMBER 29
ILLNESS

Interviewing Date 12/12–17/41
Survey #255   Question #12c

During the past four weeks, have you been absent from work at any time because of illness?

Yes................................ 8%
No................................ 92

The illness that affected the largest number of workers—approximately 50%—was the common cold. The results projected for the entire country indicate that 23 days out of every 1,000 man-days were lost because of illness.

DECEMBER 30
PHYSICAL EXERCISE

Interviewing Date 11/27–12/1/41
Survey #254–K   Question #12a

Apart from your job do you do anything for physical exercise?

Yes................................ 42%
No................................ 58

1942

JANUARY 1
WINSTON CHURCHILL

Special Survey

Asked in Great Britain: In general, do you approve or disapprove of Mr. Churchill as Prime Minister?

Approve............................ 88%
Disapprove........................ 8
Undecided......................... 4

JANUARY 2
PAY DEDUCTIONS FOR WAR EFFORT

Interviewing Date 12/20–25/41
Survey #256–K   Question #7

Would you be willing to have your employer take a small part — say two cents out of every dollar — of your wages or salary each pay day to buy defense bonds or stamps for you?

Yes.............................. 69%
No............................... 19
Undecided......................... 12

JANUARY 3
COMMON COLD

Interviewing Date 12/20–25/41
Survey #256–K   Question #10b

Do any of the people in your home, including yourself, have a cold at the present time?

Yes.............................. 34%
No............................... 66

By Age

	With Colds
Under 10 Years...................	22%
10–19 Years......................	13
20–29 Years......................	12
30–49 Years......................	13
50 Years and over................	13

By Income

Upper............................	13%
Middle...........................	13
Lower............................	15

Interviewing Date 12/20–25/41
Survey #256–K   Question #10c

Asked of those who responded in the affirmative: Was a doctor consulted about the cold?

Yes.............................. 26%
No............................... 74

Among the 26% who had consulted a doctor, approximately two thirds went to the doctor's office, while in the remaining one-third of the cases the doctor called at the home.

JANUARY 5
DAYLIGHT SAVING TIME

Interviewing Date 12/20–25/41
Survey #256–K   Question #2

As long as the war lasts, would you favor, or oppose daylight saving time in your community for the entire year?

Favor............................ 57%
Oppose........................... 30
Undecided......................... 13

By Region
New England and Middle Atlantic

Favor............................ 69%
Oppose........................... 24
Undecided......................... 7

East Central

Favor............................ 52%
Oppose............................ 35
Undecided........................ 13

West Central

Favor............................ 48%
Oppose............................ 35
Undecided........................ 17

South

Favor............................ 45%
Oppose............................ 36
Undecided........................ 19

West

Favor............................ 54%
Oppose............................ 28
Undecided........................ 18

By Community Size
100,000 and Over

Favor............................ 72%
Oppose............................ 19
Undecided........................ 9

10,000–100,000

Favor............................ 61%
Oppose............................ 30
Undecided........................ 9

Towns Under 10,000

Favor............................ 49%
Oppose............................ 34
Undecided........................ 17

Farm Areas

Favor............................ 36%
Oppose............................ 45
Undecided........................ 19

JANUARY 7
LENGTH OF WAR

Special Survey

Asked of Britons: How much longer do you think the war will last?

6 months.......................... 5%
12 months......................... 15
18 months......................... 13
2 years........................... 29
3 years........................... 18
More than 3 years................. 16
No opinion........................ 4

JANUARY 9
DRAFTING OF WOMEN

Interviewing Date 12/21–26/41
Survey #257–K   Question #1

Would you be in favor of starting now to draft single women between the ages of 21 and 35 to train them for wartime jobs?

Yes............................... 68%
No................................ 26
Undecided......................... 6

By Sex
Men

Yes............................... 63%
No................................ 31
Undecided......................... 6

Women

Yes............................... 73%
No................................ 20
Undecided......................... 7

Women Aged 21–35 Only

Yes............................... 75%
No................................ 19
Undecided......................... 6

JANUARY 10
JOINT WAR COUNCIL

Interviewing Date 12/21–26/41
Survey #257–K   Question #4a

Do you think the United States, Britain, Russia, and their allies should form a joint war council which would plan all war operations against the Axis powers?

Yes................................ 80%
No................................. 10
No opinion......................... 10

Interviewing Date 12/21–26/41
Survey #257–K   Question #4b

If such a council is formed, should the army, navy, and air force of every country, including the United States, be controlled by the war council?

Yes................................ 68%
No................................. 15
No opinion......................... 17

JANUARY 12
WARTIME GOVERNMENT CONTROL

Interviewing Date 12/21–26/41
Survey #257–K   Question #2a

In time of war, should the Government have the right to tell factory owners and businessmen what products they can make and what prices they can charge?

Yes................................ 78%
No................................. 12
Qualified answers.................. 4
Undecided.......................... 6

Businessmen Only

Yes................................ 81%
No................................. 11
Qualified answers.................. 4
Undecided.......................... 4

Interviewing Date 12/21–26/41
Survey #257–K   Question #2b

In time of war, should the Government have the right to tell workers what job they are to work at, what they will be paid, and how many hours they shall work?

Yes................................ 67%
No................................. 22
Qualified answers.................. 4
Undecided.......................... 7

Skilled, Semiskilled, and Unskilled Workers Only

Yes................................ 64%
No................................. 25
Qualified answers.................. 4
Undecided.......................... 7

Interviewing Date 12/20–25/41
Survey #256–K   Question #3

In time of war, should the Government have the right to tell farmers what crops they must raise and what prices they are to get?

Yes................................ 61%
No................................. 26
Qualified answers.................. 4
Undecided.......................... 9

Farmers Only

Yes................................ 51%
No................................. 33
Qualified answers.................. 7
Undecided.......................... 9

JANUARY 14
NATIONAL SALES TAX

Interviewing Date 12/21–26/41
Survey #257–K   Question #5

In order to help pay the cost of the war, should the Federal Government put a national sales tax of 2% on everything you buy, in addition to taxes now in effect?

Yes................................ 47%
No................................. 46
No opinion......................... 7

By Income
Upper

Yes................................ 58%
No................................. 34
No opinion......................... 8

Middle

Yes................................ 48%
No................................. 46
No opinion......................... 6

Lower

Yes	43%
No	50
No opinion	7

By Community Size
Farms

Yes	53%
No	39
No opinion	8

10,000 and Under

Yes	49%
No	44
No opinion	7

10,000–100,000

Yes	46%
No	46
No opinion	8

100,000 and Over

Yes	44%
No	50
No opinion	6

JANUARY 16
BRITISH ADVICE

Special Survey

Asked of Britons: From your own experience, what would you say are the best preparations an American, living in the United States, can make in case this is a long war?

The following are listed in order of frequency of mention:

Get used to doing without things now. Live simply; cut out luxuries. Conserve your money, lend as much as possible in war savings.

Volunteer for war work immediately and be prepared to make all necessary sacrifices for the war effort.

Insist on efficient civilian defense. See that there are sufficient shelters and that people know where those shelters are. Also, be sure the fire fighting service is thoroughly organized.

Save everything possible. Avoid waste. Throw nothing away. Americans are too wasteful.

Keep fit; keep calm; don't worry. Don't listen to rumors. Be prepared to take the rough with the smooth. Above all, don't talk too much.

Insist on immediate rationing of goods that may become scarce. Don't wait.

Insist on price control and stabilization of wages now. Don't postpone it until inflation is upon you.

JANUARY 17
SERVICE ACADEMIES

Interviewing Date 12/21–26/41
Survey #257–K   Question #6

Should young men who want to go to West Point or Annapolis be permitted to apply directly for entrance, or should they first be required to get an appointment from their congressman, as at present?

Apply directly	68%
Apply through congressman	18
No opinion	14

JANUARY 21
LENGTH OF WAR

Interviewing Date 1/8–13/42
Survey #258–K   Question #3

About how much longer do you think the war will last?

Less than 2 years	21%
2 years	29
3 years	16
Longer than 3 years	22
Unwilling to guess	12

JANUARY 23
AUTOMOBILES

Interviewing Date 1/8–13/42
Survey #258–K   Question #8e

Asked of car owners: If it were not possible for you to use your car, would this make any great difference to you?

Yes............................... 46%
No............................... 54

JANUARY 24
TIRE RATIONING

Interviewing Date 1/8–13/42
Survey #258–K   Question #8b

Asked of car owners: Have you heard about the tire rationing program?

Yes............................... 99%
No............................... 1

Interviewing Date 1/8–13/42
Survey #258–K   Question #8c

Asked of car owners: Do you think that tire rationing is necessary at this time?

Yes............................... 81%
No............................... 19

Interviewing Date 1/8–13/42
Survey #258–K   Question #8d

Asked of car owners: How long do you think the Government regulation of tire sales will be in effect?

Until the end of the war............. 44%
From 2 to 5 years.................. 12
Less than 1 year................... 10
Other guesses, no opinion........... 36

JANUARY 26
DRIVING HABITS

Interviewing Date 1/8–13/42
Survey #258–K   Question #8g

Asked of car owners: About how many miles does your car go a month?

Median average................ 750 miles

Interviewing Date 1/8–13/42
Survey #258–K   Question #8i

Asked of car owners: Have you made any plans to cut down the number of miles you drive?

Yes............................... 53%
No............................... 46
Not using car at present............. 1

Interviewing Date 1/8–13/42
Survey #258–K   Question #8j

Asked of car owners: How much do you plan to cut down on your car mileage?

Median average.................... 45%

Interviewing Date 1/8–13/42
Survey #258–K   Question #9

It has been suggested that to save rubber and reduce automobile accidents every state should pass a law against people driving more than 35 miles an hour on any road. Would you approve, or disapprove, of such a law in every state in the country?

Approve........................... 67%
Disapprove........................ 28
No opinion........................ 5

Car Owners Only

Approve........................... 61%
Disapprove........................ 36
No opinion........................ 3

JANUARY 28
PRESIDENT ROOSEVELT'S
VOTER APPEAL

Interviewing Date 1/8–13/42
Survey #258–K   Question #10b

Do you approve or disapprove of the way Franklin Roosevelt is handling his job as President today?

Approve............................ 84%
Disapprove........................ 9
No opinion........................ 7

JANUARY 30
CONSCRIPTION IN CANADA

Special Survey

Asked of Canadians: If you were asked to vote in the next few weeks on the question of selective service for overseas duty, would you vote for it, or against it?

For it............................. 60%
Against it.......................... 30
Undecided.......................... 10

JANUARY 31
FEDERAL LOTTERIES

Interviewing Date 1/8–13/42
Survey #258–K   Question #2b

Would you favor lotteries run by the Federal Government to help pay part of the cost of carrying on the war?

Yes............................... 54%
No................................ 37
No opinion........................ 9

FEBRUARY 2
WORK WEEK

Interviewing Date 1/8–13/42
Survey #258–K   Question #7f

How many hours a week do you work?

Farmers.......................... 62 hrs.
Employers and administrators....... 61 hrs.
Skilled workers.................... 51 hrs.
Professional....................... 50 hrs.
Semiskilled and unskilled.......... 49 hrs.
White collar...................... 47 hrs.

FEBRUARY 4
IDENTIFICATION CARDS

Interviewing Date 1/8–13/42
Survey #258–K   Question #1

Do you believe everyone in the United States should be required to carry an identification card containing, among other things, his picture and his fingerprints?

Yes............................... 69%
No................................ 25
No opinion........................ 6

FEBRUARY 6
PROBLEMS OF ORGANIZED LABOR

Special Survey

Asked of union leaders and union members: What do you consider the most important problem that organized labor must solve in the next few months?

Union Leaders Only

Increased production of war materials and settlement of disputes between labor and capital in order to win the war............................. 54%
Achieving unity within labor.......... 15
Combating restrictive labor legislation.. 12
Unemployment due to industry's changing over to war basis.............. 8
Wage adjustments to fit cost of living.... 5
Organizing more workers into unions... 7
Getting radicals and racketeers out of unions........................ 1
                                   ‾‾‾‾
                                   102%

(Note: table adds to more than 100% because some persons gave more than one answer.)

Union Members Only

Increased production of war materials and settlement of disputes between

labor and capital in order to win the
war.............................. 48%
Achieving unity within labor......... 14
Combating restrictive labor legislation.. 5
Unemployment due to industry's chang-
ing over to war basis.............. 7
Wage adjustments to fit cost of living.... 6
Organizing more workers into unions... 4
Getting radicals and racketeers out of
unions........................ 3
No opinion....................... 13

*In time of war, should the Government
have the right to tell workers what jobs they
are to work at, what they will be paid, and
how many hours they shall work?*

Union Leaders Only

Yes.............................. 55%
No.............................. 30
No opinion....................... 15

Union Members Only

Yes.............................. 58%
No.............................. 29
No opinion....................... 13

FEBRUARY 7
LABOR UNION DUES

Special Survey

*Asked of labor union leaders and union
members: Should companies having a
closed or union shop take union dues out of
the workers' pay envelopes and turn the
money over to the unions (the check-off),
or should the unions collect the dues
themselves?*

Union Leaders Only

Companies should collect............. 46%
Unions should collect................ 42
Qualified answers.................... 6
No opinion....................... 6

Union Members Only

Companies should collect............. 29%
Unions should collect................ 61
Qualified answers.................... 4
No opinion....................... 6

FEBRUARY 9
WAR EFFORT

Interviewing Date 1/25–30/42
Survey #259–K   Question #6a

*Do you think the United States is doing all
it can toward winning the war?*

Yes.............................. 78%
No.............................. 17
Undecided........................ 5

By Political Affiliation
Democrats

Yes.............................. 82%
No.............................. 15
Undecided........................ 3

Republicans

Yes.............................. 69%
No.............................. 24
Undecided........................ 7

By Education
College

Yes.............................. 62%
No.............................. 33
Undecided........................ 5

High School

Yes.............................. 80%
No.............................. 15
Undecided........................ 5

Grade School

Yes.............................. 82%
No.............................. 11
Undecided........................ 7

Interviewing Date 1/25–30/42
Survey #259–K   Question #6b

Asked of those who answered no to the question: What more can we do?

The following are listed in order of frequency of mention:

Make better use of labor and production facilities, work longer hours, stop strikes.

The psychological attitude is wrong — we need all-out effort, less disagreement, more sacrifices.

Send more men and equipment to the Far East.

Cut out graft and red tape; get better administrative direction, more businessmen like Donald Nelson.

Strike at the enemy, take the offensive.

FEBRUARY 13
EQUAL PAY FOR WOMEN

Interviewing Date 1/25–30/42
Survey #259–K   Question #12

If women replace men in industry should they be paid the same wages as men?

Yes	78%
No	14
Undecided	8

By Sex
Men

Yes	71%
No	20
Undecided	9

Women

Yes	85%
No	7
Undecided	8

FEBRUARY 14
LIQUOR REGULATIONS

Interviewing Date 11/15–20/41
Survey #253–K   Question #2a

Do you think liquor regulations in your community are too strict or not strict enough?

Too strict	6%
Not strict enough	55
About right	39

Interviewing Date 11/15–20/41
Survey #253–K   Question #2b

Do you think there is more drunkenness or less drunkenness in your community than there was ten years ago?

More	43%
Less	31
About the same	26

FEBRUARY 16
PROHIBITION

Interviewing Date 1/25–30/42
Survey #259–K   Question #4

If the question of national prohibition should come up again, would you vote for prohibition or against it?

For	36%
Against	64

Ten per cent expressed no opinion.

By Sex

	For	Against
Men	29%	71%
Women	43	57

By Community Size

	For	Against
Farms	50%	50%
Under 10,000	43	57
10,000–100,000	31	69
Over 100,000	23	77

Interviewing Date 1/25–30/42
Survey #259–K   Question #5

Do you think it would be better for young people if we had national prohibition again?

Yes.............................. 45%
No............................... 55

Nine per cent expressed no opinion.

FEBRUARY 18
PENSIONS FOR CONGRESSMEN

Special Survey

Have you heard or read about the bill passed by the House of Representatives which would allow members of Congress to place themselves under the Civil Service Retirement System if they have served five years?

Yes.............................. 75%
No............................... 25

Asked of those who had heard about the plan: Do you approve or disapprove of giving a pension to congressmen when they leave office?

Approve........................... 10%
Disapprove........................ 84
No opinion........................ 6

FEBRUARY 22
EIRE

Interviewing Date 2/5–10/42
Survey #260–K   Question #5a

Do you happen to know whether the Irish Free State (Eire) has gone to war against Germany?

Yes, has (incorrect)................. 50%
No, has not (correct)................ 50

Irish-Americans Only

Yes.............................. 82%
No............................... 18

Interviewing Date 2/5–10/42
Survey #260–K   Question #5b

Asked of those who were correct about Eire's neutral status: Would you like to see Eire let the Allies use war bases along the Irish coast?

Yes.............................. 90%
No............................... 5
No opinion........................ 5

Irish-Americans Only

Yes.............................. 72%
No............................... 21
No opinion........................ 7

Interviewing Date 2/5–10/42
Survey #260–K   Question #5c

Asked of those who were correct about Eire's neutral status: Should Eire join the Allies in declaring war against Germany?

Yes.............................. 71%
No............................... 16
No opinion........................ 13

Irish-Americans Only

Yes.............................. 56%
No............................... 32
No opinion........................ 12

FEBRUARY 25
TIRE RATIONING

Interviewing Date 2/12–17/42
Survey #261–K   Question #3e

Asked of car owners: About how long do you think it will be before your tires are so worn out that you will not be able to drive your car?

Tires worn out now.................. 2%
6 months or less.................... 21
6 months to 1½ years................ 47
2 years............................ 19
More than 2 years................... 11

Interviewing Date 2/12–17/42
Survey #261–K   Question #3i

Asked of car owners: Have you cut down on the speed of your driving?

Yes............................... 63%
No............................... 37

Interviewing Date 2/12–17/42
Survey #261–K   Question #3g

Asked of car owners: Have you cut down on your car mileage from what you would normally drive at this time of year?

Yes............................... 73%
No............................... 27

FEBRUARY 27
PENSIONS FOR CONGRESSMEN

Interviewing Date 2/12–17/42
Survey #261–K   Question #10b

Do you approve or disapprove of giving a pension to congressmen when they leave office?

Approve........................... 9%
Disapprove........................ 83
Undecided......................... 8

MARCH 2
PUNISHMENT FOR SABOTAGE IN SWEDEN

Special Survey

Asked in Sweden: What punishment should be given to persons convicted of espionage or sabotage against Sweden?

Re-introduce death sentence.......... 33%
Longer prison sentences than at present. 22
Undecided......................... 45

MARCH 11
TOTAL WAR MOBILIZATION

Interviewing Date 2/25–3/2/42
Survey #262–K   Question #3b

After finding out what each person can do, should the Government have the power to tell each citizen what to do as his part in the war effort and require him or her to do it?

Yes............................... 61%
No............................... 32
No opinion....................... 7

By Sex
Men

Yes............................... 66%
No............................... 29
No opinion....................... 5

Women

Yes............................... 55%
No............................... 36
No opinion....................... 9

By Region
New England

Yes............................... 57%
No............................... 36
No opinion....................... 7

Middle Atlantic

Yes............................... 60%
No............................... 33
No opinion....................... 7

East Central

Yes............................... 56%
No............................... 35
No opinion....................... 9

West Central

Yes............................... 62%
No............................... 32
No opinion....................... 6

South

Yes................................ 66%
No................................ 25
No opinion........................ 9

Mountain

Yes................................ 69%
No................................ 24
No opinion........................ 7

Pacific

Yes................................ 63%
No................................ 33
No opinion........................ 4

By Income
Upper

Yes................................ 62%
No................................ 34
No opinion........................ 4

Middle

Yes................................ 61%
No................................ 33
No opinion........................ 6

Lower

Yes................................ 60%
No................................ 30
No opinion........................ 10

By Political Affiliation
Democrats

Yes................................ 67%
No................................ 26
No opinion........................ 7

Republicans

Yes................................ 57%
No................................ 37
No opinion........................ 6

By Age
21–29 Years

Yes................................ 56%
No................................ 38
No opinion........................ 6

30–49 Years

Yes................................ 61%
No................................ 31
No opinion........................ 8

50 Years and Over

Yes................................ 62%
No................................ 30
No opinion........................ 8

New York State Only

Yes................................ 60%
No................................ 33
No opinion........................ 7

Massachusetts Only

Yes................................ 53%
No................................ 39
No opinion........................ 8

Philadelphia Only

Yes................................ 67%
No................................ 29
No opinion........................ 4

MARCH 13
STRIKES IN WAR INDUSTRIES

Interviewing Date 2/25–3/2/42
Survey #262–K   Question #5

Should Congress pass a law forbidding strikes in war industries until the war is over, or should the workers in war industries continue to have the right to go on strike?

Congress should pass law............. 86%
Workers should have right........... 9
No opinion........................ 5

Democrats vote 86% for an anti-strike law, and the rank and file of Republicans 89%. The vote of the upper, middle, and lower income groups in favor of the law is respectively 90%, 89%, and 82%.

The workers of the country — skilled, semi-skilled and unskilled — vote for the curb by a majority of 81%.

MARCH 14
DEFENSE WORK

Interviewing Date 2/25–3/2/42
Survey #262–K   Question #2c

Is your regular job in any way connected with the war effort?

Yes...................................... 21%
No...................................... 79

Interviewing Date 2/25–3/2/42
Survey #262–K   Question #2e

Asked of employed persons who answered no: Would you be willing to change your job to one in a defense factory at whatever pay the defense job would give you?

Yes...................................... 57%
No...................................... 40
Undecided............................ 3

Interviewing Date 2/25–3/2/42
Survey #262–K   Question #2h

Asked of housewives: Would you be willing to take a job in a defense factory?

Yes...................................... 49%
No...................................... 50
Undecided............................ 1

Interviewing Date 2/25–3/2/42
Survey #262–K   Question #2g

Asked of all persons who stated they would take a defense job: Would you be willing to take a defense job in another city?

Yes...................................... 38%
No...................................... 50
Undecided............................ 12

MARCH 18
OVERSEAS SERVICE FOR
CANADIAN TROOPS

Special Survey

Asked in Canada: Are you in favor of conscription for overseas duty?

Yes...................................... 70%
No...................................... 30

Eight per cent expressed no opinion.

MARCH 20
PRESIDENT ROOSEVELT'S
VOTER APPEAL

Interviewing Date 3/12–17/42
Survey #263–K   Question #16c

In general do you approve or disapprove of the way Franklin Roosevelt is handling his job as President?

Approve.............................. 78%
Disapprove.......................... 13
No opinion........................... 9

MARCH 23
DRAFTING OF MEN
WITH DEPENDENTS

Interviewing Date 2/25–3/2/42
Survey #262–K   Question #1a

Would you favor or oppose a plan to draft men who have dependents if this would be necessary to win the war?

Favor................................. 71%
Oppose............................... 23
No opinion........................... 6

MARCH 25
SCRAP MATERIALS

Interviewing Date 3/12–17/42
Survey #263–K   Question #2a

Has anyone called at your home to pick up scrap materials for national defense?

Yes...................................... 32%
No...................................... 62
Don't know.......................... 6

Interviewing Date 3/12–17/42
Survey #263–K   Question #2b

If you made a thorough search, about how many pounds of scrap metal including old farm machinery do you think you could find that you could give to national defense?

Median average............... 175 pounds

MARCH 27
DRAFTING OF WOMEN

Interviewing Date 3/12–17/42
Survey #263–K   Question #1

Would you be in favor of starting now to draft single women between the ages of 21 and 35 to train them for war time jobs?

Yes................................ 69%
No................................. 23
No opinion......................... 8

By Region
New England and Middle Atlantic

Yes................................ 69%
No................................. 23
No opinion......................... 8

East Central

Yes................................ 70%
No................................. 22
No opinion......................... 8

West Central

Yes................................ 68%
No................................. 24
No opinion......................... 8

South

Yes................................ 72%
No................................. 18
No opinion......................... 10

West

Yes................................ 69%
No................................. 25
No opinion......................... 6

MARCH 28
SALARY OF ARMY PRIVATES

Interviewing Date 3/12–17/42
Survey #263–K   Question #4a

How much pay per month do you think a private should get when he enters the army?

Median average..................... $38

Interviewing Date 3/12–17/42
Survey #263–T   Question #4

Do you think an army private should be paid $42 a month instead of $21 when he enters the army?

Yes................................ 73%
No................................. 18
Undecided.......................... 9

MARCH 30
WORK WEEK

Interviewing Date 3/12–17/42
Survey #263–K   Question #9

How many hours do you think workers in war industries should work in a week before time and one-half pay for overtime starts?

40 hours........................... 27%
40–47 hours........................ 4
48 hours........................... 25
49–59 hours........................ 8
60 hours or more................... 9
No overtime pay at all............. 21
No opinion......................... 6

By Occupation

	Median Average
Farmers........................	60 hrs.
White collar....................	48 hrs.
Skilled and unskilled.............	48 hrs.

By Income

Upper...........................	48 hrs.
Middle..........................	48 hrs.
Lower...........................	48 hrs.

New England.................... 48 hrs.
Middle Atlantic................. 48 hrs.
East Central.................... 48 hrs.
West Central................... 48 hrs.
South.......................... 56 hrs.
West........................... 48 hrs.

APRIL 1
CONDUCT OF WAR

Special Survey

Asked in Great Britain: Are you satisfied or dissatisfied with the Government's conduct of the war?

Satisfied........................ 35%
Dissatisfied..................... 50
No opinion...................... 15

Asked in Great Britain: Would you favor an offensive operation this year — or should our Government continue defensive operations this year?

Offensive....................... 67%
Defensive....................... 10
No opinion...................... 23

APRIL 3
LABOR UNION FINANCES

Interviewing Date 3/12–17/42
Survey #263–K   Question #6

Do you think all labor unions should be required to register with the Federal Government and report the amount of money they take in and spend each year?

Yes............................. 80%
No.............................. 6
No opinion...................... 14

APRIL 4
REGULATION OF WARTIME BUSINESS PROFITS

Interviewing Date 3/20–25/42
Survey #264–K   Question #5b

It has been suggested that Congress pass laws regulating business firms and profits to a much greater extent. Would you approve or disapprove of this?

Approve......................... 69%
Disapprove...................... 20
No opinion...................... 11

APRIL 6
WAGE AND PRICE CONTROLS

Interviewing Date 3/20–25/42
Survey #264–K   Question #1

A law in Canada keeps wage and salary rates from going higher than they are now and also keeps all prices, including prices of farm products, from going higher. Would you approve or disapprove of such a law in the United States?

Approve......................... 66%
Disapprove...................... 24
No opinion...................... 10

Manual Workers Only

Approve......................... 63%
Disapprove...................... 26
No opinion...................... 11

Farmers Only

Approve......................... 64%
Disapprove...................... 27
No opinion...................... 9

APRIL 8
USE OF SUGAR

Interviewing Date 3/12–17/42
Survey #263–K   Question #13

Asked of housewives: About how many pounds of sugar a week does your family use?

Median average.......One pound per person

Interviewing Date 3/12–17/42
Survey #263–K   Question #14

Asked of housewives: What is the smallest amount of sugar your family could get along on each week?

Median average.......9½ ounces per person

APRIL 10
WAR MOBILIZATION

Interviewing Date 3/12–17/42
Survey #263–K   Question #3a

Should all men and women over 18 who are not already in military service be required to register with the Government for some kind of civilian defense or war work?

Yes................................ 80%
No................................ 14
No opinion........................ 6

Interviewing Date 3/12–17/42
Survey #263–K   Question #3b

After finding out what each person can do, should the Government have the power to tell each citizen what to do as his part in the war effort and require him or her to do it (total mobilization)?

Yes................................ 58%
No................................ 33
No opinion........................ 9

By Special States

	Yes	No	No Opinion
California...........	62%	32%	6%
Illinois..............	61	31	8
Indiana..............	60	32	8
Michigan............	55	36	9
Massachusetts........	57	35	8
New Jersey..........	60	29	11
New York...........	57	36	7
Ohio...............	53	37	10
Pennsylvania........	59	33	8

APRIL 11
LENGTH OF WAR

Inteviewing Date 3/12–17/42
Survey #263–K   Question #7

About how much longer do you think the war will last?

Less than 2 years.................... 15%
2 years........................... 22
3 years........................... 16
More than 3 years................. 28
Don't know....................... 19

Among persons with a college education, only 9% think the war will be over in two years, as compared to 18% among persons with less than a high school education.

Thirty-four per cent of the college group think the war will go on for another three years or more, as contrasted to 25% of the group with less than a high school education.

APRIL 13
POLITICAL AWARENESS

Interviewing Date 3/20–25/42
Survey #264–K   Question #10a

Do you happen to know the name of the congressman from your district?

Correct answers..................... 50%
Incorrect answers................... 50

By Region
New England and Middle Atlantic

Correct answers..................... 44%
Incorrect answers................... 56

East Central

Correct answers..................... 50%
Incorrect answers................... 50

West Central

Correct answers..................... 56%
Incorrect answers................... 44

South

Correct answers................... 64%
Incorrect answers.................. 36

West

Correct answers................... 50%
Incorrect answers.................. 50

Farmers Only

Correct answers................... 67%
Incorrect answers.................. 33

APRIL 15
PROFESSIONAL SPORTS
IN WARTIME

Interviewing Date 3/12–17/42
Survey #263–K   Question #8

Do you think that professional sports should be continued during the war, or should they be stopped until after the war?

Should be continued............... 66%
Should be stopped.................. 24
No opinion........................ 10

Seventy-eight per cent of voters between 21 and 29 years would continue sports, while only 56% of those above 50 years of age are in favor.

Poor people are less anxious to continue with professional sports than the above average-income groups. Seventy-six per cent of those in the upper-income bracket want sports continued, as compared to 62% in the lower-income groups.

APRIL 15
WAGE-PRICE CONTROL

Special Survey

A law in Canada keeps wage and salary rates from going higher than they are now and also keeps all prices, including prices of farm products, from going higher. Would you approve or disapprove of such a law in the United States?

Approve........................... 66%
Disapprove........................ 24
No opinion........................ 10

By State

	Approve	Disapprove	Undecided
California...........	67%	23%	10%
Illinois..............	63	27	10
Indiana..............	62	26	12
Iowa................	72	19	9
Massachusetts.......	67	21	12
Michigan...........	65	25	10
Minnesota..........	66	25	9
Missouri............	66	20	14
New Jersey.........	68	21	11
New York..........	57	34	9
Ohio...............	69	21	10
Pennsylvania........	66	29	5
Texas..............	68	22	10
Wisconsin..........	62	30	8

APRIL 17
WAR EFFORT

Interviewing Date 4/2–7/42
Survey #265–K   Question #1a

Do you think business and industry are going all-out to win the war?

Yes............................... 58%
No................................ 33
Undecided......................... 9

Interviewing Date 4/2–7/42
Survey #265–K   Question #1b

Do you think labor unions are going all-out to win the war?

Yes............................... 37%
No................................ 50
Undecided......................... 13

Interviewing Date 4/2–7/42
Survey #265–K   Question #1c

Do you think farmers are going all-out to win the war?

Yes............................... 69%
No............................... 12
Undecided........................ 19

APRIL 18
NEW DEAL PROGRAMS

Interviewing Date 4/2–7/42
Survey #265–K   Question #9a

Should the Civilian Conservation Corps in its present form be done away with until the end of the war?

Yes............................... 54%
No............................... 37
No opinion....................... 9

Interviewing Date 4/2–7/42
Survey #265–K   Question #9b

Should the National Youth Administration be done away with until the end of the war?

Yes............................... 38%
No............................... 43
No opinion....................... 19

Interviewing Date 4/2–7/42
Survey #265–K   Question #9c

Should farm benefits be done away with until the end of the war?

Yes............................... 43%
No............................... 40
No opinion....................... 17

Farmers Only

Yes............................... 46%
No............................... 46
No opinion....................... 8

APRIL 20
INCOME TAX

Interviewing Date 3/12–17/42
Survey #263–K   Question #5a

In order to help pay for the war, the Government will be forced to increase income taxes. If you were the one to decide, how much income tax, if any, would you ask a typical family of four with an income of $1,000 a year to pay?

If public decided tax.................. $7
Proposed Treasury Department rate...... $0

Interviewing Date 3/12–17/42
Survey #263–K   Question #5b

How much income tax, if any, would you ask a typical family of four with an income of $1,500 a year to pay?

If public decided tax.................. $24
Proposed Treasury Department rate..... $ 0

Interviewing Date 3/12–17/42
Survey #263–K   Question #5c

How much income tax, if any, would you ask a typical family of four with an income of $2,000 a year to pay?

If public decided tax.................. $54
Proposed Treasury Department rate..... $ 0

Interviewing Date 3/12–17/42
Survey #263–K   Question #5d

How much income tax, if any, would you ask a typical family of four with an income of $3,000 a year to pay?

If public decided tax................. $201
Proposed Treasury Department rate.... $118

Interviewing Date 3/12–17/42
Survey #263–K   Question #5e

How much income tax, if any, would you ask a typical family of four with an income of $5,000 a year to pay?

If public decided tax................. $470
Proposed Treasury Department rate.... $587

Interviewing Date 3/12–17/42
Survey #263–K   Question #5f

How much inocme tax, if any, would you ask a typical family of four with an income of $10,000 a year to pay?

If public decided tax............... $1,640
Proposed Treasury Department rate.. $2,143

Interviewing Date 3/12–17/42
Survey #263–K   Question #5g
   How much income tax, if any, would you
   ask a typical family of four with an income
   of $50,000 a year to pay?

If public decided tax.............. $13,700
Proposed Treasury Department rate. $26,537

Interviewing Date 3/12–17/42
Survey #263–K   Question #5h
   How much income tax, if any, would you
   ask a typical family of four with an income
   of $100,000 a year to pay?

If public decided tax.............. $33,700
Proposed Treasury Department rate. $68,261

APRIL 24
CANADIAN MILITARY SERVICE

Special Survey
   Asked in Canada: Will you vote for or
   against freeing the Government from any
   pledges it has made on restricting the
   methods of raising men for military service?

Yes.............................. 65%
No............................... 35

APRIL 25
PARTY STRENGTH

Interviewing Date 4/2–7/42
Survey #265–K   Question #10
   In politics do you consider yourself a Re-
   publican, Democrat, Independent, or So-
   cialist?

Republican....................... 37%
Democrat......................... 46
Independent...................... 16
Socialist, others................. 1

APRIL 27
WARTIME PROBLEMS

Interviewing Date 4/2–7/42
Survey #265–K   Question #12
   What do you regard as the greatest problem
   the country now faces in winning the war?

Speeding up war production......... 28%
Shipping and transportation shortage... 19
Uniting the people behind the war effort. 15
Getting labor into line, and eliminating
   fights between labor and industry..... 9
Increasing the armed forces.......... 5
Solving the problem of war material
   shortage........................ 5
Eliminating government red tape and
   political inefficiency............... 4
Getting an offensive started........... 3
Cleaning up fifth columnists.......... 3
Financing the war.................. 3
Miscellaneous and undecided......... 17
                                   ─────
                                    111%

Note: table adds to more than 100% because
some persons gave more than one answer.

APRIL 29
NAME FOR WORLD WAR

Interviewing Date 4/17–22/42
Survey #266–K   Question #3a
   President Roosevelt has asked the public to
   think up a good name to call the present
   war. What would you suggest?

By and large most of the country thinks the
war should be called "World War II" or
"Second World War."

Interviewing Date 4/17–22/42
Survey #266–K   Question #3b
   Here are a few names that have been sug-
   gested (on card): Which do you like best?

War of World Freedom.............. 26%
War of Freedom.................... 14

War of Liberty..................... 13
Anti-Dictator War.................. 11
War for Humanity.................. 9
Survival War...................... 7
The People's War.................. 6
Anti-Nazi War.................... 5
Total War........................ 5
War of Liberation................. 4

MAY 1
WAGE-PRICE CONTROLS

Interviewing Date 3 /20–25 /42
Survey #264–K   Question #1

A recent law in Canada keeps wage and salary rates from going higher than they are now, and also keeps all prices, including the prices of farm products, from going higher. Would you approve or disapprove of such a law in the United States?

Approve........................... 66%
Disapprove........................ 24
Undecided......................... 10

MAY 2
THE DRAFT

Interviewing Date 4 /17–22 /42
Survey #266–K   Question #4

Do you think the draft is being handled fairly in your community?

Yes.............................. 88%
No............................... 12

Sixteen per cent had no opinion.

By Region

	Yes	No
New England and Middle Atlantic.................	88%	12%
East Central..................	85	15
West Central.................	84	16
South.......................	90	10
West........................	91	9

MAY 4
FEDERAL SALES TAX

Interviewing Date 4 /17–22 /42
Survey #266–K   Question #6

In order to help pay the cost of the war, should the Federal Government put a national sales tax of 2% on everything that people buy?

Yes.............................. 54%
No............................... 46

Interviewing Date 4 /18–23 /42
Survey #266–T   Question #6

In order to help pay the cost of the war, should the Federal Government put a national sales tax of 3% on everything that people buy?

Yes.............................. 46%
No............................... 54

Interviewing Date 4 /2–7 /42
Survey #265–K   Question #4

In order to help pay the cost of the war, should the Federal Government put a national sales tax of 5% on everything that people buy?

Yes.............................. 43%
No............................... 57

MAY 6
FARM UNIONS

Special Survey

Asked of farmers: John L. Lewis is planning to organize the dairy farmers of the country into a branch of the C.I.O. union. Do you favor or oppose this movement to organize farmers into labor unions?

Favor............................ 11%
Oppose........................... 70
Undecided........................ 19

MAY 13
PRESIDENT ROOSEVELT'S
VOTER APPEAL

Interviewing Date 4/17–22/42
Survey #266–K   Question #12c

Do you approve or disapprove of the way Franklin Roosevelt is handling his job as President?

Approve............................ 78%
Disapprove........................ 13
No opinion........................ 9

MAY 15
WAR BONDS AND STAMPS

Interviewing Date 5/1–6/42
Survey #267–K   Question #6c

Would you be willing to have your employer take a regular part of your wages or salary each pay day to buy war savings bonds or stamps for you?

Already covered by such a plan........ 25%
Would be willing.................... 43
Would not be....................... 32

Interviewing Date 5/1–6/42
Survey #267–K   Question #6d

What is the largest amount out of each dollar of your salary or wages you would be able to put into war savings bonds or stamps?

Median average..................... 9¢

MAY 16
WINSTON CHURCHILL

Special Survey

Asked of Britons: Are you satisfied or dissatisfied with Mr. Churchill as Prime Minister?

Satisfied.......................... 82%
Dissatisfied....................... 13
No opinion........................ 5

Asked of Britons: If anything should happen to Winston Churchill, who would you like to see succeed him?

Anthony Eden...................... 37%
Sir Stafford Cripps................. 34
Ernest Bevin...................... 2
Clement Attlee.................... 2
Lord Beaverbrook................. 2
Others........................... 23

MAY 18
AUTOMOBILE TIRES

Interviewing Date 5/1–6/42
Survey #267–K   Question #5d

Asked of automobile owners: About how long do you think it will be before your tires are so worn out that you will not be able to drive your car?

Tires completely worn out now........ 2%
5 months.......................... 22
One year.......................... 35
Two years......................... 32
More than two years................ 9

MAY 22
TAXES

Special Survey

Asked of civic and community leaders: Do you favor a 2% national sales tax?

Yes............................... 69%
No................................ 28
No opinion....................... 3

Asked of civic and community leaders: In the case of income taxes would you be in favor of reducing the amount of personal exemptions — that is, broadening the base — so that more people would have to pay income taxes?

Yes............................... 57%
No................................ 41
No opinion....................... 2

Asked of civic and community leaders: At what income level do you think a typical family of four — a married man with two children — should start paying a federal income tax?

Median average.................... $1,800

Under exemptions of present law a family of four does not start paying income taxes until $2,300 is earned.

MAY 25
AUSTRALIAN BLUE LAWS

Special Survey

Asked in Australia: Are you in favor of opening places of amusement to soldiers on Sundays?

Yes............................... 8%
No............................... 71
No opinion....................... 21

MAY 25
WAGE CEILING

Special Survey

Asked of civic and community leaders: Do you favor a Government ceiling over wages?

Yes............................... 82%
No............................... 15
No opinion....................... 3

Asked of civic and community leaders: Do you think the Government will put a ceiling over wages?

Yes............................... 52%
No............................... 35
No opinion....................... 13

MAY 27
UNIFIED COMMAND FOR ARMED FORCES

Special Survey

Asked of civic and community leaders: Should the President, as commander-in-chief of the armed forces of the country, name a military leader to direct both the army and the navy?

Favor............................. 49%
Oppose........................... 40
Undecided........................ 11

MAY 29
AVIATION TRAINING

Interviewing Date 5/1–6/42
Survey #267–K   Question #10

Do you favor aviation instruction for boys in high schools?

Yes............................... 77%
No............................... 12
No opinion....................... 11

MAY 30
PEACE OFFER TO FINLAND AND ITALY

Special Survey

Asked of civic and community leaders: Should the Allies offer peace terms at this time to Finland?

Yes............................... 43%
No............................... 45
No opinion....................... 12

Asked of civic and community leaders: Should the Allies offer peace terms at this time to Italy?

Yes................................ 16%
No................................ 79
No opinion........................ 5

Depression........................ 51%
Prosperity........................ 36
Undecided......................... 13

JUNE 3
AUSTRALIAN STATE GOVERNMENTS

Special Survey

Asked in Australia: Are you in favor of abolishing state governments?

Yes................................ 57%
No................................ 19
No opinion........................ 24

JUNE 6
WINSTON CHURCHILL

Special Survey

Asked in Great Britain: In general, do you approve or disapprove of Mr. Churchill as Prime Minister?

Approve........................... 87%
Disapprove........................ 8
Undecided......................... 5

JUNE 5
ECONOMIC OUTLOOK

Interviewing Date 5/23–28/42
Survey #268–K   Question #11

Which do you think the United States will have for the first two or three years after the war — depression or prosperity?

Depression........................ 43%
Prosperity........................ 45
Undecided......................... 12

By Occupation
Business and Professional

Depression........................ 34%
Prosperity........................ 57
Undecided......................... 9

White Collar

Depression........................ 39%
Prosperity........................ 50
Undecided......................... 11

Manual Workers

Depression........................ 42%
Prosperity........................ 44
Undecided......................... 14

JUNE 7
LENGTH OF WAR

Interviewing Date 6/1–6/42
Survey #269–K   Question #6a

About how much longer do you think the war will last?

Less than two years............... 35%
Two years......................... 26
Three years....................... 14
More than three years............. 15
No opinion........................ 10

JUNE 10
FARM UNIONS AND FARM PRICES

Special Survey

Asked of dairy farmers: John L. Lewis is planning to organize the dairy farmers of the country into a branch of the C.I.O. union. Do you favor or oppose this movement to organize farmers into labor unions?

Favor............................. 16%
Oppose............................ 74
No opinion........................ 10

Among all farmers as a group the percentage favoring the union is lower — 14%.

Asked of farmers: Are you satisfied with the price you are now getting for your chief cash crop?

Yes............................ 58%
No............................. 28
Undecided...................... 14

By Farm Type
Dairy

Satisfied........................ 52%
Dissatisfied..................... 45
Undecided....................... 3

Wheat

Satisfied........................ 52%
Dissatisfied..................... 43
Undecided....................... 5

Cotton

Satisfied........................ 57%
Dissatisfied..................... 31
Undecided....................... 12

Corn

Satisfied........................ 67%
Dissatisfied..................... 25
Undecided....................... 8

Hog

Satisfied........................ 87%
Dissatisfied..................... 9
Undecided....................... 4

Others

Satisfied........................ 55%
Dissatisfied..................... 20
Undecided....................... 25

JUNE 12
THE DRAFT

Interviewing Date 6/1–6/42
Survey #269–K   Question #1

Do you think young men 18 and 19 years old should be drafted for military service?

Yes............................ 42%
No............................. 52
No opinion...................... 6

JUNE 13
GERMAN PEOPLE

Interviewing Date 5/23–28/42
Survey #268–K   Question #10

In the war with Germany, do you think that our chief enemy is the German people as a whole, or the German government?

German people.................... 6%
German government................ 79
No opinion...................... 15

JUNE 17
PAYMENTS FOR SOLDIERS' WIVES

Interviewing Date 6/1–6/42
Survey #269–K   Question #11a

How much money should an army private's wife, without children, receive to live on?

Median average................... $40 mo.

Interviewing Date 6/1–6/42
Survey #269–K   Question #11b

How much would you add to this for each child?

Median average................... $15 mo.

JUNE 19
INCOME TAXES

Interviewing Date 6/1–6/42
Survey #269–K   Question #5b

Would you like to have a regular amount deducted from each pay check to pay your federal income tax next year?

Yes............................. 50%
No............................. 43
Undecided....................... 7

JUNE 20
REPUBLICAN PRESIDENTIAL CANDIDATES

Interviewing Date 5/23–28/42
Survey #568–K   Question #6

Asked of Republicans: If it came to a choice between Wendell Willkie and Thomas Dewey for Republican candidate for President in 1944, which man would you prefer?

Willkie........................... 52%
Dewey........................... 48

Sixteen per cent expressed no opinion.

JUNE 24
PRISONERS FOR WAR SERVICE

Interviewing Date 6/11–16/42
Survey #270–K   Question #6

It has been suggested that men in American prisons who are eligible for parole in the next two or three years be paroled now to enlist in the armed forces. Do you favor or oppose this proposal?

Favor............................ 66%
Oppose........................... 21
Qualified answer.................. 6
No opinion....................... 7

JUNE 26
TRANSPORTATION TO WORK

Interviewing Date 6/1–6/42
Survey #269–K   Question #2

How do you get to work?

Walk............................ 40%
Drive........................... 36
Public conveyance.................. 23
Bicycle.......................... 1

JUNE 27
REPUBLICANS AND THE WAR EFFORT

Interviewing Date 5/23–28/42
Survey #268–K   Question #7

Which way do you think the Government's war effort would go ahead faster — if the Republicans had more power in Washington, or if the Republicans had less power in Washington?

Faster if they had more power........ 21%
Faster if they had less power......... 31
Would make no difference............ 27
No opinion....................... 21

JUNE 29
CHIEF WAR ENEMY

Interviewing Date 6/11–16/42
Survey #270–K   Question #13

Which do you think is our number one enemy in the war — Japan or Germany?

Japan........................... 25%
Germany.......................... 50
Both............................ 23
No opinion....................... 2

By Region
New England and Middle Atlantic

Japan........................... 26%
Germany.......................... 50
Both............................ 22
No opinion....................... 2

East Central

Japan	26%
Germany	49
Both	23
No opinion	2

West Central

Japan	26%
Germany	52
Both	21
No opinion	1

South

Japan	19%
Germany	51
Both	29
No opinion	1

Mountain

Japan	28%
Germany	50
Both	21
No opinion	1

Pacific

Japan	31%
Germany	45
Both	21
No opinion	3

JULY 1
PUNISHMENT FOR NAZI LEADERS

Interviewing Date 6/11–16/42
Survey #270–K   Question #14a

What do you think should be done with the Nazi leaders after the war?

Hang or shoot	35%
Imprison or put in asylum	31
Treat as Nazis have treated others	5
Won't be alive — will have committed suicide or been killed by then	2
Exile	2
Slow torture: mental and physical suffering	2

Be lenient in punishment	2
Not our affair	2
Court-martial	2
No opinion	17

Interviewing Date 6/11–16/42
Survey #270–K   Question #14b

What do you think should be done with Hitler after the war?

Hang or shoot	39%
Imprison or put in asylum	23
Exile	6
Treat as Nazis have treated others	5
Won't be alive — will have committed suicide or been killed by then	6
Slow torture: mental and physical suffering	3
Be lenient in punishment	2
Not our affair	2
Court-martial	1
No opinion	13

JULY 3
NATIONAL SALES TAX

Interviewing Date 6/11–16/42
Survey #270–K   Question #2

In order to help pay the cost of the war, should the Federal Government put a national sales tax of two per cent on everything that people buy?

Yes	58%
No	42

Eight per cent expressed no opinion.

By Region

	Yes	No
New England	54%	46%
Middle Atlantic	54	46
East Central	56	44
West Central	62	38
South	65	35
West	56	44

JULY 4
CANADIAN VIEWS ON A SECOND FRONT

Special Survey

Asked in Canada: One hears and reads a lot of arguments for and against opening a second front against the Germans. What is your opinion of this?

Should open second front now........ 46%
When ready but not before........... 18
Should leave to authorities, or no
  opinion.......................... 29
Against second front................. 6
It has already been opened........... 1

JULY 6
POSTWAR LEAGUE OF NATIONS

Interviewing Date 6/11–16/42
Survey #270–K   Question #1

Would you like to see the United States join a league of nations after this war is over?

Yes............................... 73%
No................................ 27

By Region

	Yes	No
New England and Middle Atlantic	71%	29%
East Central	72	28
West Central	76	24
South	78	22
West	74	26

JULY 8
RATIONING VIOLATIONS

Interviewing Date 6/11–16/42
Survey #270–K   Question #22a

Without giving any names, have you heard of any cases where service stations or ga-
rages sell gasoline to customers without punching the full amount on ration cards?

Yes............................... 43%
No................................ 57

Interviewing Date 6/11–16/42
Survey #270–K   Question #22b

Do you think there should be any punishment of service station or garage operators who disobey gasoline ration rules?

Yes............................... 69%
No................................ 17
No opinion........................ 14

Interviewing Date 6/11–16/42
Survey #270–K   Question #22c

Asked of those who think there should be punishment: What do you think that punishment should be?

They should lose selling privileges, have
  their licenses revoked.............. 26%
They should be fined................ 25
Should have jail sentences........... 3
Should be let off with a warning....... 1
Operators should be fired............ 1
No opinion as to what punishment
  should be........................ 13
                                    ——
                                    69%

JULY 11
THE CHURCH AND THE WAR

Special Survey

Asked of clergymen: In general, what attitude do you think the church should take toward the war?

The following are listed in order of frequency of mention:

Support the war and give full cooperation to the Government in the war effort
Give spiritual strength to the people and maintain morale

Aid in creating a lasting peace
"Keep the Christian spirit alive"
Be loyal to the Government but oppose war
   as evil

Yes	48%
No	36
No opinion	16

JULY 15
IDENTIFICATION CARDS

Interviewing Date 7/1–6/42
Survey #271–K   Question #1

Do you believe everyone in the United States should be required to carry an identification card containing, among other things, his picture and his fingerprints?

Yes	72%
No	22
Undecided	6

JULY 17
SECOND EUROPEAN FRONT

Interviewing Date 7/1–6/42
Survey #271–K   Question #2

Would you like to see England and the United States attempt a large-scale attack on Germany in Western Europe in the near future or do you think we should wait until they are stronger?

Now	48%
Wait	34
No opinion	18

JULY 18
UNIFIED COMMAND FOR ARMED FORCES

Interviewing Date 7/1–6/42
Survey #271–K   Question #3

Should the President, as Commander-in-Chief of the armed forces of the country, name a military leader to direct both the army and the navy?

JULY 19
FAMILY INCOME

Interviewing Date 3/12–17/42
Survey #263–K   Question #17d

Is the income of your family higher or lower today than it was a year ago?

Higher	39%
Same	46
Lower	15

By Occupation
Professional

Higher	40%
Same	46
Lower	14

Businessmen

Higher	31%
Same	54
Lower	15

White Collar

Higher	41%
Same	45
Lower	14

Skilled

Higher	46%
Same	40
Lower	14

Semiskilled

Higher	41%
Same	41
Lower	18

Unskilled

Higher	31%
Same	54
Lower	15

Farmers

Higher	45%
Same	45
Lower	10

Interviewing Date 5/1–6/42
Survey #267–K   Question #9

What is your weekly family income today?

Median average	$35 wk.

$100 wk. or more	7%
$60–$99 wk.	13
$49–$59 wk.	22
$30–$48 wk.	17
$20–$29 wk.	19
$15–$19 wk.	8
$10–$14 wk.	7
Under $10 wk.	7

JULY 22
WAR IN AFRICA

Interviewing Date 7/1–6/42
Survey #271–K   Question #6

What do you think was responsible for the loss of Tobruk and for other British reverses in Africa?

Shortage of men and equipment	26%
No competent leadership in battle; Germans outsmarted them and had better strategy	25
British were too slow and unprepared	10
British won't fight, not good fighters	8
British were overconfident	5
Blundering and bad planning by Government	1
Miscellaneous	3
No opinion	33
	111%

(Note: table adds to more than 100% because some persons gave more than one answer.)

JULY 24
WINSTON CHURCHILL

Special Survey

Asked of Britons: Are you satisfied or dissatisfied with Mr. Churchill as Prime Minister?

Satisfied	78%
Dissatisfied	15
No opinion	7

JULY 25
CANADIAN PRICE-WAGE LAW

Special Survey

Asked of Canadians: Do you think the law that keeps prices and wages from going higher should remain in effect after the war?

Yes	50%
No	33
No opinion	17

JULY 29
ESPIONAGE

Interviewing Date 7/16–21/42
Survey #272–K   Question #13

What punishment should be given to spies caught in this country?

Death penalty	85%
Imprisonment	8
Deportation	1
Miscellaneous	3
No opinion	3

JULY 31
WAR STRATEGY

Special Survey

Asked in Great Britain: Should the Allies try to invade Europe this year?

Yes.............................. 60%
No.............................. 12
No opinion....................... 28

AUGUST 1
AUTOMOBILE TIRES

Interviewing Date 7/16–21/42
Survey #272–K   Question #6b

If the Government needs tires, would you offer to sell some of your tires to the Government for a fair price?

Yes.............................. 73%
No.............................. 22
No opinion....................... 5

Farmers Only

Yes.............................. 62%
No.............................. 30
No opinion....................... 8

City Dwellers Only

Yes.............................. 76%
No.............................. 19
No opinion....................... 5

AUGUST 3
MOBILIZATION

Interviewing Date 7/16–21/42
Survey #272–K   Question #7b

Do you think a law should be passed giving the Government the right to require workers not employed in war industries to take jobs in war industries?

Yes.............................. 71%
No.............................. 23
Undecided....................... 6

Interviewing Date 7/16–21/42
Survey #272–K   Question #7c

Should a law be passed giving the Government the right to require workers to move to any place in the country to take jobs in war industries?

Yes.............................. 53%
No.............................. 39
Undecided....................... 8

AUGUST 5
GERMAN SUBMARINES

Interviewing Date 7/16–21/42
Survey #272–K   Question #20

How do you account for the success of German submarines in sinking our ships along the Atlantic Coast?

Greater part of navy diverted elsewhere; navy not large enough yet to handle situation; patrol ships more necessary elsewhere........................ 27%
Spies in this country, fifth-column work, loose talk........................ 18
Germans had large number of submarines already built and use them cleverly.......................... 17
Our navy caught off guard; not smart enough.......................... 13
Insufficient cooperation between army and navy........................ 2
No opinion....................... 23

AUGUST 7
ALLIED LEADERSHIP

Interviewing Date 7/1–6/42
Survey #271–K   Question #15

Do you think that Roosevelt and Churchill should have the final decision on the military and naval plans of the war, or do you think these plans should be decided by the military and naval leaders of the United Nations?

Roosevelt and Churchill.............. 21%
Military and naval leaders........... 64
Undecided....................... 15

AUGUST 8
GASOLINE RATIONING

Interviewing Date 7/16–21/42
Survey #272–K   Question #21

Do you think we will have gasoline rationing throughout the entire country within the next six months?

Yes.............................. 47%
No............................... 41
No opinion....................... 12

Rationed Areas Only

Yes.............................. 52%
No............................... 34
No opinion....................... 14

Non-Rationed Areas Only

Yes.............................. 45%
No............................... 44
No opinion....................... 11

Interviewing Date 7/16–21/42
Survey #272–K   Question #22

Do you think it necessary to ration gasoline throughout the country in order to conserve tires?

Yes.............................. 49%
No............................... 44
No opinion....................... 7

Rationed Areas Only

Yes.............................. 63%
No............................... 29
No opinion....................... 8

Non-Rationed Areas Only

Yes.............................. 41%
No............................... 52
No opinion....................... 7

AUGUST 12
LEON HENDERSON

Interviewing Date 8/1–6/42
Survey #273–K   Question #11a

In your opinion, how good a job has Leon Henderson done as head of the Office of Price Administration?

Good job or doing best he can with his
  powers........................ 54%
Poor job.......................... 16
No opinion....................... 30

AUGUST 19
BRITISH VIEWS OF AMERICANS

Special Survey

Asked in Great Britain: Do you think Americans are more democratic than Britishers?

Yes.............................. 52%
No............................... 33
Undecided........................ 15

Do you think most Americans adopt a superior attitude toward the British without any grounds?

Yes.............................. 37%
No............................... 44
Undecided........................ 19

Would we be better off if we were more like the Americans in many respects?

Yes.............................. 41%
No............................... 39
Undecided........................ 20

As a result of participating in the war, will the United States want: A. More than their share of credit for helping to win the war?

Yes.............................. 36%
No............................... 44
Undecided........................ 20

B. More than their fair share of world markets after the war?

Yes........................... 26%
No............................ 45
Undecided..................... 29

C. More than their fair say in settling the peace terms?

Yes........................... 28%
No............................ 49
Undecided..................... 23

D. More than their fair share of power and influence in the postwar world?

Yes........................... 29%
No............................ 46
Undecided..................... 25

Do you think Americans are too willing to let others do their fighting?

Yes........................... 28%
No............................ 55
Undecided..................... 17

AUGUST 21
WAR STRATEGY

Interviewing Date 8/1–6/42
Survey #273–K   Question #6a

If the Allies build a strong enough air force do you think they can win the war virtually by air attacks alone?

Yes........................... 40%
No............................ 49
No opinion.................... 11

AUGUST 24
INCOME TAXES

Interviewing Date 8/1–6/42
Survey #273–K   Question #8

Should every family not on relief pay a federal income tax?

Yes........................... 70%
No............................ 25
No opinion.................... 5

By Income
Upper and Middle

Yes........................... 73%
No............................ 23
No opinion.................... 4

Lower

Yes........................... 66%
No............................ 27
No opinion.................... 7

AUGUST 26
JAMES PETRILLO

Interviewing Date 8/15–20/42
Survey #274–K   Question #12b

Asked of those persons who said they were familiar with James Petrillo's attempts to ban phonograph records from the radio: What is your opinion of Mr. Petrillo's rulings?

Favorable comments............ 8%
Unfavorable................... 75
No opinion.................... 17

Interviewing Date 8/15–20/42
Survey #274–K   Question #12c

Asked of those same persons: Do you approve or disapprove of the Government taking legal action to stop Petrillo?

Approve....................... 73%
Disapprove.................... 12
Undecided..................... 15

AUGUST 28
NATIONAL SALES TAX

Interviewing Date 8/15–20/42
Survey #274–K   Question #9

Do you favor or oppose a national sales tax?

Favor............................ 61%
Oppose........................... 39

AUGUST 28
FUEL SHORTAGE

Special Survey

Asked in Ohio, Indiana, Illinois, and Michigan: Would you be willing to have the Government reduce everybody's driving by as much as one-third to release transportation facilities to send fuel oil to New England where there is a shortage?

Yes.............................. 67%
No............................... 21
Undecided........................ 12

Asked in Ohio, Indiana, Illinois, and Michigan: Would you be willing to have the Government cut down on the amount of fuel oil the people in Ohio, Indiana, Illinois, and Michigan can have this winter in order to send some to New England?

Yes.............................. 68%
No............................... 18
Undecided........................ 14

AUGUST 29
WAR EFFORT

Interviewing Date 8/15–20/42
Survey #274–K   Question #10

As long as the war lasts, would you favor or oppose the appointment of a committee of judges with full power to set aside any peacetime laws and regulations that they felt were slowing up the war effort?

Favor............................ 58%
Oppose........................... 23
No opinion....................... 19

AUGUST 31
WAR EFFORT

Interviewing Date 8/15–20/42
Survey #274–K   Question #6

If you were the President, what would you do to speed up the war effort?

The following are listed according to frequency of mention:

Stop strikes
Cut red tape
Control inflation
Mobilize more men
Cut politics for duration of war
Open a second front

SEPTEMBER 2
PRESIDENT ROOSEVELT'S
VOTER APPEAL

Interviewing Date 8/15–20/42
Survey #274–K   Question #23c

Do you approve or disapprove of the way Franklin Roosevelt is handling his job as President today?

Approve.......................... 70%
Disapprove....................... 16
No opinion....................... 14

By Region

	Approve	Disapprove
New England.........	70%	30%
Middle Atlantic........	70	30
East Central..........	69	31
West Central..........	70	30
South................	72	28
West.................	71	29

SEPTEMBER 5
AIR FORCE

Interviewing Date 8/15–20/42
Survey #274–K   Question #2a

Have you heard or read about the discussions over a separate air force, coequal with the army and navy?

Yes............................... 44%

No................................ 56

Interviewing Date 8/15–20/42
Survey #274–K   Question #2b

Asked of those answering yes to the above question: Do you favor or oppose the idea of a separate air force?

Favor............................. 57%

Oppose........................... 27

No opinion........................ 16

SEPTEMBER 7
THE DRAFT

Interviewing Date 8/1–6/42
Survey #273–K   Question #1

If the Government had to choose between drafting 18 and 19 year old men, or married men with children, which should it choose?

18–19 year group.................. 77%

Married men with children........... 13

Undecided......................... 10

Interviewing Date 7/16–21/42
Survey #272–K   Question #1

If the Government had to choose between drafting 18 and 19 year old men, or married men without children, which should it choose?

18–19 year group.................. 43%

Married men without children........ 47

Undecided......................... 10

SEPTEMBER 11
COMPLUSORY UNION MEMBERSHIP IN DEFENSE FACTORIES

Interviewing Date 8/27–9/1/42
Survey #275–K   Question #11b

At the present time, workers who take jobs in some war factories that have unions must join the union before they can start work.

Do you think that workers who start to work in a factory because the Government has told them to, should have to join the union, or should they be able to go to work without joining the union?

Should be made to join.............. 17%

Should not have to join............. 76

No opinion........................ 7

SEPTEMBER 12
THE MOVIES

Special Survey

It has been suggested that the Government issue an order forbidding double feature movies for the duration of the war, in order to save film. Would you favor or oppose such an order?

Favor............................. 71%

Oppose........................... 11

Undecided......................... 18

SEPTEMBER 13
NEW YORK POLITICS

Special Survey

Asked in New York State: For whom do you plan to vote for Governor?

Thomas Dewey..................... 54%

John Bennett...................... 36

Dean Alfange...................... 10

Seventeen per cent expressed no opinion.

SEPTEMBER 15
WAGE-PRICE CONTROLS

Interviewing Date 8/1–6/42
Survey #273–K   Question #13c

To keep the cost of living from going higher do you favor keeping salaries and wages, *and the prices of farm products, from going higher?*

Favor............................ 71%
Oppose........................... 11
Qualified........................ 12
No opinion....................... 6

By City
Baltimore

Favor............................ 82%
Oppose........................... 4
Qualified........................ 7
No opinion....................... 7

Chicago

Favor............................ 85%
Oppose........................... 4
Qualified........................ 4
No opinion....................... 7

St. Louis

Favor............................ 87%
Oppose........................... 9
Qualified........................ 2
No opinion....................... 2

Omaha

Favor............................ 78%
Oppose........................... 3
Qualified........................ 6
No opinion....................... 13

Los Angeles

Favor............................ 73%
Oppose........................... 4
Qualified........................ 11
No opinion....................... 12

Midwestern Farmers Only

Favor............................ 71%
Oppose........................... 7
Qualified........................ 16
No opinion....................... 6

SEPTEMBER 19
PROHIBITION

Interviewing Date 8/27–9/1/42
Survey #275–K   Question #1

If the question of national prohibition should come up again, would you vote for it or against it?

For.............................. 38%
Against.......................... 62

By Sex

	For	Against
Men	30%	70%
Women	46	54

Farmers Only

For.............................. 55%
Against.......................... 45

SEPTEMBER 21
PRESIDENT ROOSEVELT'S HANDLING OF GOVERNMENT OFFICIALS

Interviewing Date 9/5–10/42
Survey #276–K   Question #10

Some people say President Roosevelt has not been tough enough in dealing with heads of Government departments concerned with war effort. Do you agree or disagree?

Agree............................ 52%
Disagree......................... 31
Undecided........................ 17

By Political Affiliation
Democrats

Agree............................ 50%
Disagree......................... 35
Undecided........................ 15

Republicans

Agree............................ 58%
Disagree......................... 25
Undecided........................ 17

SEPTEMBER 23
NEEDED LEGISLATION

Interviewing Date 9/5–10/42
Survey #276–K   Question #9

If you were elected to Congress, what laws would you want to have passed?

The following are listed in order of frequency of mention:

A law to establish ceilings over both prices and wages

Legislation for greater control and regulation of labor unions

A law to draft 18 and 19-year-old men into the armed forces

A tax bill to bring in increased revenue for war.

An anti-liquor law

Repeal of the A.A.A

Legislation to bring about Government economy in non-war spending

Legislation to consolidate overlapping bureaus of government and increase efficiency

Nationwide gas rationing

Old-age pension legislation

SEPTEMBER 25
WAGE-PRICE CONTROL

Interviewing Date 9/17–22/42
Survey #277–K   Question #5

To keep the cost of living from going higher, do you favor or oppose wage-price controls?

Favor.......................... 71%
Qualified approval.................. 12
Oppose........................... 11
No opinion........................ 6

The group with qualified opinions consists of persons who favor price control but not wage control, and vice versa.

SEPTEMBER 27
NEW YORK POLITICS

Special Survey

Asked in New York State: For whom do you plan to vote for Governor?

Thomas Dewey..................... 53%
John Bennett...................... 37
Dean Alfange..................... 10

Fourteen per cent expressed no opinion.

Upstate Only

Dewey............................ 65%
Bennett........................... 33
Alfange.......................... 2

New York City Only

Dewey............................ 42%
Bennett........................... 41
Alfange.......................... 17

Roosevelt Supporters in 1940 Only

Dewey............................ 33%
Bennett........................... 52
Alfange.......................... 15

Willkie Supporters in 1940 Only

Dewey............................ 77%
Bennett........................... 22
Alfange.......................... 1

OCTOBER 2
GASOLINE RATIONING

Interviewing Date 9/17–22/42
Survey #277–K   Question #3

Asked of car owners: Are you in favor of nationwide gasoline rationing to conserve tires?

Yes.............................. 73%
No............................... 22
No opinion........................ 5

Rationed Areas Only

Yes.............................. 89%
No............................... 8
No opinion........................ 3

Non-Rationed Areas Only

Yes.............................. 66%
No............................... 28
No opinion........................ 6

OCTOBER 3
NATIONAL SPEED LIMIT

Interviewing Date 9/17–22/42
Survey #277–K   Question #4

In order to save rubber, do you think there should be a law limiting driving speed to 35 miles per hour in every state?

Yes.............................. 87%
No.............................. 8
No opinion........................ 5

Car Owners Only

Yes.............................. 89%
No.............................. 9
No opinion........................ 2

OCTOBER 6
COMMITTEE TO STUDY MANPOWER NEEDS

Interviewing Date 9/17–22/42
Survey #277–K   Question #11

Would you approve or disapprove a committee such as the Baruch Committee investigating and reporting on the problem of drafting manpower for war industries?

Approve........................... 74%
Disapprove........................ 14
No opinion........................ 12

OCTOBER 9
CANADIAN WAR EFFORT

Special Survey

Asked of Canadians: At present the Government's policy is to try to pay about three-quarters of the cost of the war out of its present income. Do you think this is a good policy or do you think more of this expense should be left to be paid after the war is over?

Approve pay-as-you-go.............. 67%
Postpone more till after war......... 20
Undecided......................... 13

OCTOBER 10
SCRAP METAL CAMPAIGN

Interviewing Date 10/1–6/42
Survey #278–K   Question #1g

Do you think metal statues, old guns, railings, heavy chains, and other metal in parks and cemeteries in your community should be donated to the scrap metal drive?

Yes.............................. 82%
No.............................. 10
No opinion........................ 8

OCTOBER 16
NEW YORK POLITICS

Special Survey

Asked in New York State: For whom do you plan to vote for Governor?

Thomas Dewey..................... 50%
John Bennett...................... 41
Dean Alfange...................... 8
Others........................... 1

Upstate Only

Dewey............................ 64%
Bennett.......................... 34
Alfange.......................... 2
Others........................... *

*Less than ½ of 1%.

New York City Only

Dewey............................ 36%
Bennett.......................... 48
Alfange.......................... 15
Others........................... 1

New York City — By Borough
Manhattan

Dewey............................ 39%
Bennett.......................... 48
Alfange.......................... 13

Brooklyn

Dewey............................ 33%
Bennett........................... 49
Alfange........................... 18

Bronx

Dewey............................ 29%
Bennett........................... 49
Alfange........................... 22

Queens

Dewey............................ 46%
Bennett........................... 48
Alfange........................... 6

Staten Island figures are not available.

Roosevelt Supporters in 1940 Only

Dewey............................ 28%
Bennett........................... 58
Alfange........................... 14

Willkie Supporters in 1940 Only

Dewey............................ 79%
Bennett........................... 20
Alfange........................... 1

Votes for minor party candidates (1%) have been eliminated in the above tables.

OCTOBER 17
WINSTON CHURCHILL

Special Survey

Asked in Great Britain: In general do you approve or disapprove of Mr. Churchill as Prime Minister?

Approve........................... 82%
Disapprove........................ 11
No opinion........................ 7

Asked in Great Britain: Are you satisfied or dissatisfied with the Government's conduct of the war?

Satisfied.......................... 41%
Dissatisfied....................... 37
No opinion........................ 22

OCTOBER 19
WAR PRIORITIES

Interviewing Date 10/1–6/42
Survey #278–K   Question #7

If there is a shortage of raw materials for manufacture of war goods, which branch of the service do you think should have first claim on materials — the army, the navy, or the air force?

Army............................. 9%
Navy............................. 11
Air force......................... 52
Don't know....................... 28

OCTOBER 20
NEW YORK POLITICS

Special Survey

Asked in New York State: For whom do you plan to vote for Governor?

By Age
21–29 Years

Thomas Dewey..................... 52%
John Bennett..................... 36
Dean Alfange..................... 12

30–49 Years

Dewey............................ 50%
Bennett........................... 42
Alfange........................... 8

50 Years and Over

Dewey............................ 52%
Bennett........................... 41
Alfange........................... 7

Israel Amter, Communist candidate, and other minor party candidates received about 1%. This figure has been eliminated in the above tables.

OCTOBER 21
THE DRAFT

Special Survey

*Asked of young men 17–19 years old:
Would you approve or disapprove of
drafting young men 18 and 19 years old
now?*

Approve........................... 81%
Disapprove........................ 15
No opinion........................ 4

OCTOBER 23
NEW YORK POLITICS

Special Survey

*Asked in New York State: For whom do
you plan to vote for Governor?*

Thomas Dewey..................... 50%
John Bennett...................... 41
Dean Alfange...................... 8
Others............................ 1

Upstate Only

Dewey............................ 65%
Bennett........................... 33
Alfange........................... 2
Others............................ *

*Less than ½ of 1%.

New York City Only

Dewey............................ 36%
Bennett........................... 48
Alfange........................... 15
Others............................ 1

OCTOBER 28
WORK WEEK

Interviewing Date 10/15–20/42
Survey #281   Question #8

*How many hours do you think workers in
war industries should work in a week before
time and one-half pay for overtime starts?*

40 hours.......................... 33%
41–47 hours....................... 5
48 hours.......................... 29
49–59 hours....................... 4
60 hours or more.................. 4
No overtime pay at all............ 18
No opinion........................ 7

OCTOBER 30
NEW YORK POLITICS

Special Survey

*Asked in New York State: For whom do
you plan to vote for Governor?*

Thomas Dewey..................... 53%
John Bennett...................... 38
Dean Alfange...................... 8
Others............................ 1

NOVEMBER 2
NEW YORK POLITICS — FINAL POLL

Special Survey

*Asked in New York State: For whom do
you plan to vote for Governor?*

Thomas Dewey..................... 53%
John Bennett...................... 39
Dean Alfange...................... 8

Upstate Only

Dewey............................ 65%
Bennett........................... 33
Alfange........................... 2

New York City Only

Dewey............................ 39%
Bennett........................... 45
Alfange........................... 16

NOVEMBER 6
RUBBER PROGRAM

Interviewing Date 10/16–21/42
Survey #281–S   Question #2b

About how long do you think it will be be-

fore your tires are so worn out that you will not be able to drive your car?

	Families with cars in operation
Already worn out............	400,000
6 months or less............	4,800,000
7 months through 18 months....	8,800,000
2 years...................	3,600,000
More than 2 years...........	2,400,000

NOVEMBER 7
THE DRAFT

Interviewing Date 10/16–21/42
Survey #281–S   Question #6

Would you approve or disapprove of drafting young men 18 and 19 years old for the armed forces now?

Approve........................... 67%
Disapprove........................ 26
No opinion........................ 7

By Sex
Men

Approve........................... 73%
Disapprove........................ 21
No opinion........................ 6

Women

Approve........................... 60%
Disapprove........................ 32
No opinion........................ 8

NOVEMBER 9
MANPOWER CONTROL PROGRAM

Interviewing Date 10/15–20/42
Survey #281   Question #11a

Do you approve or disapprove of the Government's registering for war work all men and women not already registered or in war service?

Approve........................... 76%
Disapprove........................ 24

Interviewing Date 10/15–20/42
Survey #281   Question #11b

After finding out what each person can do, should the Government have the power to tell each citizen what to do as his part in the war effort and require him or her to do it?

Yes.............................. 53%
No............................... 36
Undecided........................ 11

NOVEMBER 11
SCRAP METAL DRIVE

Interviewing Date 10/29–11/3/42
Survey #282   Question #19b

Is there any scrap metal left around your home or other place that you could give to the war effort?

Yes.............................. 21%
No............................... 73
Don't know....................... 6

NOVEMBER 13
VENEREAL DISEASE

Interviewing Date 10/29–11/3/42
Survey #282   Question #18

In order to control the spread of venereal disease around army camps, which of these plans (on card) do you favor: A. Require all prostitutes to take a regular weekly medical examination, and quarantine those who are diseased; B. Conduct a police drive to get rid of all prostitutes?

Require weekly medical examination... 55%
Conduct police drives to drive out all
  prostitutes..................... 45

	Weekly Exam.	Drive Out
Men	61%	39%
Women	49	51

NOVEMBER 14
WAR BONDS AND STAMPS

Interviewing Date 10/29–11/3/42
Survey #282   Question #10a

Do you happen to have bought any war bonds or stamps?

Yes	78%
No	22

By Income

	Yes	No
Upper	90%	10%
Middle	90	10
Lower	68	32

By Occupation

Professional	92%	8%
Businessmen	88	12
White collar	88	12
Skilled and semiskilled	78	22
Unskilled	65	35
Farmers	71	29

NOVEMBER 16
INCOME TAX

Interviewing Date 10/29–11/3/42
Survey #282   Question #10b

Do you know about how much your federal income tax will be next March on your earnings of this year?

Know how much	23%
Don't know how much	51
Don't think will have to pay any tax	26

Interviewing Date 10/29–11/3/42
Survey #282   Question #10c

Have you started saving any money for the special purpose of paying your income tax?

Yes	25%
No	75

By Income

	Yes	No
Upper	47%	53%
Middle	36	64
Lower	15	85

NOVEMBER 18
RUML PLAN

Special Survey

Are you familiar with the Ruml Plan, a proposal for paying taxes on current income rather than on the previous year's income?

Familiar	22%
Not familiar	78

Next March 15 the Government will collect an income tax on money that you earned throughout this year. Would you like to have that plan continue, or would you prefer to pay your taxes on the money as you earn it?

Satisfied with old plan	35%
Prefer to pay as earn	65

NOVEMBER 20
VACATIONS

Interviewing Date 10/1–6/42
Survey #278   Question #3a

Did you take a vacation last winter?

Yes	8%
No	92

Interviewing Date 10/1–6/42
Survey #278   Question #3b

Did you plan to take a vacation this winter?

Yes.............................. 4%
No.............................. 96

The Institute survey discloses that the average distance to be traveled by this year's vacationers will be only about two-thirds that of last winter.

NOVEMBER 21
THE DRAFT

Interviewing Date 10/29–11/3/42
Survey #282   Question #12a

Do you think the draft is being handled fairly in your community?

Yes.............................. 82%
No.............................. 18

NOVEMBER 27
WORK WEEK

Interviewing Date 10/15–20/42
Survey #281   Question #8a

Would you be willing to work at least 48 hours a week in your present job?

War Workers Only

Yes.............................. 79%
No.............................. 11
Qualified......................... 5
No opinion........................ 5

Non-War Workers Only

Yes.............................. 74%
No.............................. 17
Qualified......................... 5
No opinion........................ 4

Interviewing Date 10/15–20/42
Survey #281   Question #8b

How many hours do you think workers in war industries should work in a week before time and one-half pay for overtime starts?

War Workers Only

40 hours.......................... 53%
41–47 hours....................... 4
48 hours.......................... 30
49–59 hours....................... 3
60 hours or more.................. 2
Should pay no overtime............ 7
No opinion........................ 1

Non-War Workers Only

40 hours.......................... 29%
41–47 hours....................... 4
48 hours.......................... 38
49–59 hours....................... 3
60 hours or more.................. 3
Should pay no overtime............ 17
No opinion........................ 6

NOVEMBER 28
WORK WEEK

Interviewing Date 11/12–17/42
Survey #283–K   Question #4

Would you favor or oppose a law requiring workers connected with war industries to work at least 48 hours a week?

Yes.............................. 78%
No.............................. 12
No opinion........................ 10

NOVEMBER 29
REPUBLICAN PRESIDENTIAL CANDIDATES

Special Survey

Do you have a favorable or unfavorable opinion of the following Republican presidential possibilities for 1944?

	Favorable	Unfavorable	No Opinion
Willkie.........	49%	38%	13%
Dewey.........	53	21	26
Stassen.........	15	11	74
Bricker.........	12	11	77
Taft............	26	29	45

DECEMBER 2
PROHIBITION

Interviewing Date 11/12–17/42
Survey #283–K   Question #1

If the question of national prohibition should come up again, would you vote wet or dry?

Wet............................... 64%
Dry............................... 36

Eight per cent expressed no opinion.

By Sex

	Dry	Wet
Men........................	29%	71%
Women.....................	43	57

By Age

21–29 Years.................	29%	71%
30–49 Years.................	32	68
50 Years and over............	46	54

By Region

New England and Middle Atlantic.............	24%	76%
East Central.................	35	65
West Central.................	42	58
South.......................	59	41
Mountain and West...........	37	63

By Community Size

Farms.......................	49%	51%
Under 10,000................	48	52
10,000–100,000..............	32	68
100,000 and over............	22	78

DECEMBER 4
GERMAN PEOPLE

Interviewing Date 11/19–24/42
Survey #284–K   Question #2

In the war with Germany do you feel that our chief enemy is the German people as a whole, or the German Government?

German people..................... 6%
German Government................ 74
Both............................. 18
No opinion....................... 2

DECEMBER 5
WAR EFFORT

Interviewing Date 11/12–17/42
Survey #283–K   Question #6a

Is there anything that you dislike about the way the present Administration is conducting the war effort?

Yes............................. 31%
No.............................. 58
Undecided....................... 21

Interviewing Date 11/12–17/42
Survey #283–K   Question #6b

Asked of those who responded in the affirmative: What?

The following are listed in order of frequency of mention:

Too much talking, too little action
Too much politics
Coddling of labor
Extravagance
Handling of manpower
Handling of war news

DECEMBER 9
ELEANOR ROOSEVELT

Interviewing Date 11/19–24/42
Survey #284–K   Question #13a, b

Is there anything about Mrs. Roosevelt of which you especially disapprove? Is there anything about Mrs. Roosevelt of which you especially approve?

The criticism most frequently given was that "she is too much in the public eye . . . she ought to stay at home, where a wife belongs." With about equal frequency came approval of the fact that "she has a personality of her own and doesn't allow herself just to sit at home and do nothing."

An appreciable percentage of those who specifically approved something about her liked her "great interest in current affairs and the fact that she is able to take a stand on almost any current problem."

In contrast was more frequent criticism of the fact that "she is always getting her nose into the Government's business."

About as large a group as the preceding were those who said, "She talks too much." About half as great a percentage commended her "ability and courage to speak out on what she believes, in spite of criticism."

A large percentage of those approving Mrs. Roosevelt on some specific count, commended her "social consciousness . . . her efforts on behalf of mankind . . . on behalf of the poor." Criticism by a group smaller than the above centered on the fact that she "interferes in things that are none of her affair," that she "is stirring up racial prejudice."

About three in every hundred questioned approved of "everything" about the President's wife, and another three in one hundred disapproved of "everything" about her.

Those interested enough to comment on her recent trip to England were about equally divided in approving and disapproving.

Among other things mentioned less frequently were approval of her "sociability, her friendliness, her genuine interest in people, her courage."

Other targets for those who disapproved were her newspaper column and the criticism that she has "commercialized her position as the President's wife."

DECEMBER 11
BEVERIDGE PLAN

Special Survey

Asked in Great Britain: Are you in favor of the Beveridge Plan which would require weekly payments by employers and employees to provide social security benefits in case of sickness or unemployment?

Yes............................. 70%
No.............................. 16
No opinion....................... 14

DECEMBER 12
BIBLE READING

Interviewing Date 11/21–26/42
Survey #284–T   Question #15a

Do you read the Bible every day?

Yes............................. 10%
No.............................. 90

Five in every one hundred persons say they are reading the Bible more often today than they did before the war.

A small percentage say they are not reading the Bible as much as they did before the war because of the pressure of extra work since Pearl Harbor.

Many of those who are not reading the Bible any more frequently than heretofore point out that they are reading it more seriously now, either because they have come to depend upon their religion more than before the war or because they hope to get a better understanding of the war and the future of the world from their reading.

More than twice as many women than men read the Bible daily. More men than women have not looked into the Bible within the past year.

Farmers and residents of small communities are more given to daily reading of the Bible than those who live in large cities.

More than three times as many persons 50 years of age or over read the Bible daily than do men and women between the ages of 21 and 29. More than half the younger people have not looked at the Bible within the past year, while this is true of only 29% of those 50 or over.

Which of the books or parts of the Bible do you find the most interesting?

Ten per cent replied "all of it," while among those who had special preferences more persons mentioned the New Testament than the Old Testament.

In the New Testament, one or more of the Gospels came as first choice among those questioned, and *Revelations* came second. Also frequently mentioned were *Paul's Letters*, *Life of Christ*, and *Luke*.

The *Psalms* were first choice of those who mentioned the Old Testament. Next came *Genesis*, then the *Ten Commandments*. Other books and parts of the Old Testament mentioned most frequently were the *Proverbs*, *Ruth*, *Job*, and the *Prophets*.

DECEMBER 13
DEMOCRATIC PRESIDENTIAL CANDIDATES

Interviewing Date 11/19–24/42
Survey #284–K   Question #11a

Asked of Democrats: What is your opinion of the following men as Democratic presidential candidates for 1944:

Franklin Roosevelt?

Favorable........................ 73%
Unfavorable...................... 22
No opinion....................... 5

Henry Wallace?

Favorable........................ 50%
Unfavorable...................... 22
Not familiar..................... 14
No opinion....................... 14

Paul McNutt?

Favorable........................ 26%
Unfavorable...................... 31
Not familiar..................... 25
No opinion....................... 18

James Byrnes?

Favorable........................ 13%
Unfavorable...................... 14
Not familiar..................... 57
No opinion....................... 16

William Douglas?

Favorable........................ 14%
Unfavorable...................... 11
Not familiar..................... 57
No opinion....................... 18

Interviewing Date 11/19–24/42
Survey #284–K   Question #11b

Asked of Republicans: What is your opinion of the following men as Democratic presidential candidates for 1944?

Franklin Roosevelt?

Favorable........................ 21%
Unfavorable...................... 74
No opinion....................... 5

Henry Wallace?

Favorable........................ 20%
Unfavorable...................... 57
Not familiar..................... 11
No opinion....................... 12

Paul McNutt?

Favorable........................ 16%
Unfavorable...................... 52
Not familiar..................... 17
No opinion....................... 15

James Byrnes?

Favorable........................ 11%
Unfavorable...................... 23
Not familiar..................... 51
No opinion....................... 15

William Douglas?

Favorable	9%
Unfavorable	23
Not familiar	52
No opinion	16

DECEMBER 16
WAR AIMS

Interviewing Date 12/4–9/42
Survey #285–K   Question #4

Do you feel that you have a clear idea of what the war is all about — that is, what we are fighting for?

Yes	68%
No	32

By Income

	Yes	No
Upper	80%	20%
Middle	69	31
Lower	65	35

Among those who say they do have a clear idea of why we are fighting, there is some evidence of a failure to understand the underlying issues.

Many of these people, when asked to state what they thought the war was about, indulged in catch phrases such as "We're fighting for freedom and liberty," or "We're fighting to lick the Nazis," or "We're fighting to keep Democracy."

Only a negligible number of those questioned mentioned the Atlantic Charter or the "Four Freedoms" as our purpose in the war. And even fewer of those who brought up the Four Freedoms could name them.

DECEMBER 18
RUML PLAN

Interviewing Date 12/4–9/42
Survey #285–K   Question #5a

Next March 15 the Government will collect an income tax on money that you earned throughout this year. Would you like to have that plan continue, or would you prefer to pay your taxes on money as you earn it?

Satisfied with present plan	29%
Prefer to pay as earn	71

Seven per cent expressed no opinion.

Interviewing Date 12/4–9/42
Survey #285–K   Question #6a

Asked of taxpayers: Have you heard of the Ruml pay-as-you-go plan for income taxes?

Yes	44%
No	56

Interviewing Date 12/4–9/42
Survey #285–K   Question #6b

Asked of those who responded in the affirmative: Do you favor or oppose the Ruml Plan?

Favor	76%
Oppose	24

Twenty-three per cent expressed no opinion.

DECEMBER 21
GASOLINE RATIONING

Interviewing Date 12/4–9/42
Survey #285–K   Question #1a

Do you think that gasoline rationing in your area is necessary?

Yes	62%
No	31
No opinion	7

By Region
New England and Middle Atlantic

Yes	74%
No	18
No opinion	8

East Central

Yes............................... 55%
No................................ 41
No opinion........................ 4

West Central

Yes............................... 51%
No................................ 40
No opinion........................ 9

South

Yes............................... 59%
No................................ 34
No opinion........................ 7

West

Yes............................... 60%
No................................ 37
No opinion........................ 3

States Placed Under Gasoline Rationing This Month

Yes............................... 50%
No................................ 47
No opinion........................ 3

States Previously Under Gasoline Rationing

Yes............................... 76%
No................................ 19
No opinion........................ 5

Automobile Owners Only

Yes............................... 60%
No................................ 36
No opinion........................ 4

DECEMBER 23
UNION FINANCES

Interviewing Date 12/4–9/42
Survey #285–K   Question #8

Do you think all labor unions should be required to register with the Federal Government and report the amount of money they take in and spend each year?

Yes............................... 81%
No................................ 6
Undecided......................... 13

By Occupation
Business and Professional

Yes............................... 90%
No................................ 3
Undecided......................... 7

White Collar

Yes............................... 83%
No................................ 4
Undecided......................... 13

Manual Workers

Yes............................... 77%
No................................ 8
Undecided......................... 15

Farmers

Yes............................... 81%
No................................ 5
Undecided......................... 14

DECEMBER 24
NEWSBOYS

Interviewing Date 10/29–11/3/42
Survey #282   Question #7a

If you had a son who wanted to deliver newspapers, would you permit him to do so?

Yes............................... 90%
No................................ 7
Undecided......................... 3

Interviewing Date 10/29–11/3/42
Survey #282   Question #7b

Asked of those answering in the affirmative: If he had to get up at 6 o'clock in the morning to deliver his newspapers, would you permit him to do so?

Yes............................... 79%
No................................ 14
Undecided......................... 7

Interviewing Date 11/19–24/42
Survey #284–K   Question #14

If you had a boy 14 years old, who wanted to deliver papers, would you permit him to do so, or do you think this is too young?

Would permit at 14................. 90%
Would not permit.................. 7
Undecided........................ 3

DECEMBER 26
UNIVERSAL MILITARY TRAINING

Interviewing Date 12/4–9/42
Survey #285–K   Question #3

After this war is over, do you think every young man should be required to serve one year in the army or navy?

Yes.............................. 66%
No............................... 27
Undecided........................ 7

DECEMBER 28
POSTWAR WORLD ORGANIZATION

Interviewing Date 12/4–9/42
Survey #285–K   Question #2

Should the Government take steps now, before the end of the war, to set up with our allies a world organization to maintain the future peace of the world?

Yes.............................. 64%
No............................... 24
No opinion....................... 12

DECEMBER 30
WEST COAST JAPANESE

Special Survey

Asked of West Coast residents: Would you be willing to hire Japanese servants to work in your home after the war is over?

Yes.............................. 26%
No............................... 69
Undecided........................ 5

Asked of West Coast residents: Would you be willing to trade at Japanese-owned stores after the war is over?

Yes.............................. 38%
No............................... 58
Undecided........................ 4

1943

JANUARY 2
ITALY

Interviewing Date 12/4–9/42
Survey #285–K   Question #15a

Would you approve or disapprove of our offering Italy generous peace terms if she will stop fighting now?

Approve........................... 52%
Disapprove....................... 48

Sixteen per cent had no opinion on this issue.

JANUARY 3
WORLD WAR II

Interviewing Date 12/17–22/42
Survey #286–K   Question #4

In looking back over the first year of the war, what do you wish the Government had done differently?

Forty per cent of those interviewed were either satisfied or had no opinion. The remaining 60% offered the following criticisms, listed in order of frequency of mention:

Should have shown more foresight and acted sooner on rationing of scarce goods.

Should have tightened up Government efficiency, cut red tape in administering war programs.

Should have dealt more firmly with labor unions and strikes.

Should have given public more information about war problems — less "sugar coating" of bad news.

JANUARY 6
LABOR CONTROLS

Interviewing Date 12/17–22/42
Survey #286–K   Question #5b

Do you favor or oppose giving the Government the right to tell workers where to work and at what jobs?

Favor............................. 56%
Oppose........................... 35
Undecided........................ 9

JANUARY 8
IRISH FREE STATE

Interviewing Date 12/17–22/42
Survey #286–K   Question #12a

Do you happen to know whether or not the Irish Free State (Eire) has gone to war against Germany?

Yes, it has....................... 3%
No, it has not.................... 50
Don't know....................... 47

JANUARY 9
WAGES AND SALARIES

Interviewing Date 12/17–22/42
Survey #286–T   Question #18a

Do you think there should be any limit on the amount of income (including wages and salary) that each person should be allowed to keep per year in war time after paying all taxes?

Yes.............................. 47%
No............................... 38
No opinion....................... 15

Of the 47% who favor limitation, the largest number said $25,000 should be the top sum.

JANUARY 10
RATIONING

Interviewing Date 12/17–22/42
Survey #286–K   Question #1a

Do you think the rationing of various products is being handled fairly?

Yes................................. 64%
No.................................. 29
No opinion......................... 7

Interviewing Date 12/17–22/42
Survey #286–K   Question #2

If there is a shortage of a given product would you rather see the Government ration it, or would you prefer to take the chance of being able to obtain it yourself?

Government should ration............ 89%
Prefer to take chance on getting the
   product......................... 9
No opinion......................... 2

Interviewing Date 12/17–22/42
Survey #286–K   Question #3

Within the next six months do you think clothing will be rationed?

Yes................................. 42%
No.................................. 33
No opinion......................... 25

Will shoes be rationed?

Yes................................. 48%
No.................................. 26
No opinion......................... 26

Will dairy products be rationed?

Yes................................. 84%
No.................................. 7
No opinion......................... 9

Will meat be rationed?

Yes................................. 93%
No.................................. 2
No opinion......................... 5

JANUARY 13
LENGTH OF WAR

Special Survey

Britons were asked: How much longer do you think the war will last?

Six months......................... 14%
1 year............................. 35
1½ years........................... 21
2 years............................ 19
3 years............................ 5
More than 3 years.................. 3
Undecided.......................... 3

Britons were asked: Winston Churchill says that when Germany is beaten Britain will continue fighting until Japan is defeated. Do you approve or disapprove of this course?

Approve............................ 88%
Disapprove......................... 6
Undecided.......................... 6

JANUARY 15
VOTING AGE

Interviewing Date 10/29–11/3/42
Survey #282   Question #15

At the present time American citizens cannot vote until they become 21 years of age. Would you favor changing the law to allow men and women 18, 19, and 20 years old to vote?

Yes................................. 39%
No.................................. 52
Undecided.......................... 9

By Age
21–29 Years

Yes................................. 41%
No.................................. 53
Undecided.......................... 6

30–49 Years

Yes..............................38%
No..............................52
Undecided.......................10

50 Years and Over

Yes..............................37%
No..............................52
Undecided.......................11

JANUARY 16
WINSTON CHURCHILL

Special Survey

Britons were asked: In general do you approve or disapprove of Mr. Churchill as Prime Minister?

Approve..........................93%
Disapprove.......................5
Undecided.......................2

Britons were asked: If anything should happen to Mr. Churchill, whom would you like to see succeed him as Prime Minister?

Eden.............................39%
Cripps...........................24
Bevin............................4
Attlee...........................3
Beaverbrook......................2
Morrison.........................2
Miscellaneous, undecided.........26

Britons were asked: Are you satisfied or dissatisfied with the government's conduct of the war?

Satisfied........................75%
Dissatisfied.....................17
Undecided.......................8

JANUARY 20
STRIKES

Interviewing Date 12/17–22/42
Survey #286–K   Question #14

Should Congress pass a law forbidding strikes in war industries, or should the workers in war industries continue to have the right to go on strike?

Forbid strikes...................81%
Continue right to strike.........13
Undecided.......................6

By Occupation
Farmers

Forbid strikes...................89%
Continue right to strike.........6
Undecided.......................5

Businessmen

Forbid strikes...................85%
Continue right to strike.........11
Undecided.......................4

White Collar

Forbid strikes...................85%
Continue right to strike.........12
Undecided.......................3

Professional

Forbid strikes...................78%
Continue right to strike.........16
Undecided.......................6

Skilled and Unskilled Workers

Forbid strikes...................75%
Continue right to strike.........17
Undecided.......................8

JANUARY 22
OVERTIME IN WAR PLANTS

Interviewing Date 11/12–17/42
Survey #283–K   Question #5

How long do you think people in war factories should work before time and a half pay for overtime begins?

40 hours........................... 29%
41–47 hours....................... 4
48 hours.......................... 30
49–59 hours...................... 5
60 hours or more................. 5
No overtime pay at all............. 23
Undecided........................ 4

JANUARY 23
"VICTORY GARDENS"

Interviewing Date 1/9–14/43
Survey #287–K   Question #3a

Do you plan to have a "victory garden" this spring?

Yes.............................. 54%
No............................... 44
Undecided........................ 2

Interviewing Date 1/9–14/43
Survey #287–K   Question #3b

Did you have a "victory garden" last spring?

Yes.............................. 48%
No............................... 52

JANUARY 25
RUML PLAN

Interviewing Date 12/4–9/42
Survey #285–K   Question #6a

Have you heard of the Ruml pay-as-you-go income tax plan?

Yes.............................. 81%
No............................... 19

Interviewing Date 12/4–9/42
Survey #285–K   Question #6b

Those who responded in the affirmative were asked: Do you favor or oppose the Ruml Plan?

Favor............................ 90%
Oppose........................... 10

Seventeen per cent of those who heard of the Ruml Plan did not express an opinion about it.

JANUARY 27
LEND-LEASE

Interviewing Date 1/9–14/43
Survey #287–K   Question #7a

Do you know what the lend-lease program is?

Yes.............................. 77%
No............................... 23

Interviewing Date 1/9–14/43
Survey #287–K   Question #7b

Those who responded in the affirmative were asked: Do you favor or oppose the lend-lease program?

Favor............................ 82%
Oppose........................... 9
No opinion....................... 9

Interviewing Date 1/9–14/43
Survey #287–K   Question #8a

Those who responded in the affirmative also were asked: Do you think the nations now getting lend-lease materials from us will repay us for these materials either in money or in goods, or will not repay us at all?

Will repay....................... 29%
Will not......................... 58
No opinion....................... 13

JANUARY 29
CABINET MEMBERS

Special Survey

Which of these cabinet members has done the best job with his department during the past year? (on card)

Hull............................ 36%
Knox............................ 18
Morgenthau...................... 13
Wickard......................... 10
Stimson......................... 8
Ickes........................... 6
Walker.......................... 4
Biddle.......................... 4
Perkins......................... 4
Jones........................... 4
No opinion...................... 13
                               ────
                               120%

(Note: table adds to more than 100% as multiple answers were frequent.)

Do you approve or disapprove of having some Republicans in the President's cabinet?

Approve......................... 77%
Disapprove...................... 4
No opinion...................... 19

JANUARY 31
WAR EMPLOYMENT

Interviewing Date 12/17–22/42
Survey #286–K   Question #8

Men were asked: Would you be willing to take a job in a war plant at your present rate of pay?

Yes............................. 49%
No.............................. 40
Qualified answers............... 6
Don't know...................... 5

Interviewing Date 12/17–22/42
Survey #286–K   Question #10a

Women were asked: Would you be willing to take a full-time job running a machine in a war plant?

Yes............................. 40%
No.............................. 40
Qualified answers............... 17
Don't know...................... 3

Interviewing Date 12/17–22/42
Survey #286–K   Question #9

Married men were asked: Would you be willing to have your wife take a full-time job running a machine in a war plant?

Yes............................. 30%
Qualified yes................... 11
No.............................. 50
Don't know...................... 9

FEBRUARY 3
RUSSIA

Interviewing Date 1/9–14/43
Survey #287–K   Question #9a

Do you think Russia can be trusted to cooperate with us when the war is over?

Yes............................. 46%
No.............................. 29
No opinion...................... 25

FEBRUARY 6
GERMANY

Interviewing Date 1/29–2/3/43
Survey #288–K   Question #10

If Hitler offered peace now to all countries on the basis of not going farther, but of leaving matters as they are now, would you favor or oppose such a peace?

Favor........................... 4%
Oppose.......................... 92
No opinion...................... 4

FEBRUARY 7
PEARL HARBOR INVESTIGATION

Special Survey

Do you think the Navy Department was right in holding up the full report of our naval losses at Pearl Harbor for one year?

Yes.............................. 73%
No............................... 19
Undecided....................... 8

FEBRUARY 8
DIET

Interviewing Date 1/9–14/43
Survey #287–K   Question #4

We want to find out what you eat in the course of a day. Can you tell me what you, yourself, eat for breakfast, lunch, and dinner?

Fruits and raw greens............... 55%
Eggs............................ 62
Milk and/or cheese................. 66
Green or yellow vegetables........... 75
Meat or fish or poultry.............. 88
Fruit............................ 92
Cereals or bread................... 97

FEBRUARY 10
MOST IMPORTANT BRITISH PROBLEM

Special Survey

Britons were asked: What do you think is the most important problem the British Government must solve during the next few months?

Shipping losses..................... 30%
Invasion of Continent............... 15
Speedy victory..................... 6
Organization of manpower........... 6
Maintaining food supplies........... 6
Production........................ 5
North Africa...................... 5
Post war reconstruction............. 4
Miscellaneous..................... 13
Undecided........................ 10

FEBRUARY 12
CROP PRODUCTION

Special Survey

Farmers were asked: Do you expect to increase production on any of your crops or products this year?

Yes.............................. 64%
No............................... 29
Undecided....................... 7

FEBRUARY 13
FARM PRICE CEILINGS

Special Survey

Farmers were asked: Would you rather have the Government keep price ceilings on agricultural products, or leave them uncontrolled?

Favor price ceilings................. 56%
Leave prices uncontrolled............ 28
Qualified answers................... 8
Undecided....................... 8

Considering costs of production, do you think you get a fair price for all your chief crops or products?

Fair............................. 59%
Unfair........................... 41

By Region

	Fair	Un-fair
New England and Middle Atlantic.................	47%	53%
East Central................	62	38
West Central................	75	25
South......................	55	45
West.......................	56	44

FEBRUARY 15
FARM PROBLEMS

Special Survey

Farmers were asked: What is the biggest problem facing farmers in this area today?

Shortage of labor.................... 77%
Shortage of machinery and parts....... 19
Lack of money..................... 8
Other............................. 5
                                  ———
                                  109%

(Note: table adds to more than 100% as some farmers gave more than one response.)

Those farmers who cited shortage of labor were asked: What do you think should be done to meet the farm labor shortage?

Defer farm hands from draft, leave experienced men on farms, stop drafting
  farm labor....................... 39%
Obtain outside labor, especially from
  towns........................... 10
Release soldiers who have been farmers,
  especially during busy season........ 8
Raise prices so farm labor can be paid
  more; make farm pay and industrial
  pay more equal.................... 8
Freeze farm jobs so farm hands cannot
  go to war factories................ 7
Other............................. 15
                                  ———
                                  87%

(Note: table adds to more than 77% as some farmers gave more than one response.)

Farmers also were asked: It has been suggested that in order to meet the farm labor shortage problem, many women will have to take jobs on farms this summer. Would this help you?

Yes.............................. 41%
No............................... 54
Undecided........................ 5

Farmers also were asked: It has been suggested that high school students be given jobs on farms this summer. Would this help you?

Yes.............................. 56%
No............................... 38
Undecided........................ 6

FEBRUARY 17
FARM MACHINERY

Special Survey

Farmers were asked: As one way to keep production up, it has been suggested that farmers with tractors, harvesters, and other machinery loan out this machinery to neighboring farms if convenient. Would you favor or oppose such a program?

Favor............................. 45%
Oppose........................... 48
Undecided........................ 7

FEBRUARY 19
VIEWS OF FARMERS

Special Survey

Farmers were asked: Which of these groups do you think has received the best treatment from our Government — farmers, labor, or business?

Farmers........................... 10%
Labor............................. 72
Business.......................... 7
No opinion........................ 11

Farmers also were asked: Do you think there should be more Government control of labor unions, or less control?

More.............................. 76%
Less.............................. 4
Same.............................. 2
No opinion........................ 18

Farmers also were asked: How long should people working in war plants be required to work before time and a half pay for overtime begins?

Median average................. 60 hours

FEBRUARY 24
NATION'S CHIEF ENEMY

Interviewing Date 2/5–10/43
Survey #289–K   Question #1

In this war, which do you think is our chief enemy — Japan or Germany?

Japan............................ 53%
Germany......................... 34
No opinion....................... 13

By Region
New England and Middle Atlantic

Japan............................ 51%
Germany......................... 34
No opinion....................... 15

East Central

Japan............................ 56%
Germany......................... 31
No opinion....................... 13

West Central

Japan............................ 53%
Germany......................... 35
No opinion....................... 12

South

Japan............................ 47%
Germany......................... 39
No opinion....................... 14

Mountain

Japan............................ 55%
Germany......................... 34
No opinion....................... 11

Pacific

Japan............................ 65%
Germany......................... 27
No opinion....................... 8

FEBRUARY 26
LENGTH OF WAR

Interviewing Date 2/5–10/43
Survey #289–K   Question #2a

How much longer do you think the war with Germany will last?

Less than 6 months................ 5%
6 to 11 months.................... 28
1 year........................... 33
1 to 2 years...................... 9
2 years.......................... 14
2 to 3 years...................... 1
3 years.......................... 3
3 to 5 years...................... 1
5 years or more................... 1
No opinion....................... 5

Interviewing Date 2/5–10/43
Survey #289–K   Question #2b

How much longer do you think the war with Japan will last?

Less than 6 months................ 1%
6 to 11 months.................... 7
1 year........................... 16
1 to 2 years...................... 16
2 years.......................... 26
2 to 3 years...................... 5
3 years.......................... 10
3 to 5 years...................... 5
5 years or more................... 5
No opinion....................... 9

FEBRUARY 27
NATIONAL LOTTERIES

Interviewing Date 2/5–10/43
Survey #289–T   Question #3b

Would you favor lotteries run by the Federal Government to help pay the cost of the war?

Favor............................ 49%
Oppose........................... 42
No opinion....................... 9

Men are more in favor of lotteries than women — 54% of the men favor the idea while 43% of the women support it. Those in lower income brackets are more in favor than those in the middle and upper income brackets.

MARCH 1
FRANKLIN ROOSEVELT

Interviewing Date 1/29–2/3/43
Survey #288–K   Question #8a

If the war is over and President Roosevelt runs for a fourth term next year, do you think you will vote for him or against him?

For.............................. 39%
Against........................... 50
Undecided......................... 11

Interviewing Date 1/28–2/3/43
Survey #288–T   Question #8a

If the war is still going on and President Roosevelt runs for a fourth term next year, do you think you will vote for him or against him?

For.............................. 51%
Against........................... 37
Undecided......................... 12

Interviewing Date 1/28–2/3/43
Survey #288–K   Question #8b

Those who had a definite opinion were asked: Do you think President Roosevelt will run for a fourth term next year?

Yes.............................. 60%
No............................... 40

MARCH 3
INCOME TAX

Interviewing Date 2/5–10/43
Survey #289–K   Question #5b

Employed persons who will have to pay an income tax on March 15 were asked: Would you like to pay your federal income tax by having your employer deduct a regular amount from your wage or salary each time you are paid?

Yes.............................. 76%
No............................... 19
No opinion....................... 5

MARCH 5
FOOD RATIONING

Interviewing Date 2/25–3/1/43
Survey #290–K   Question #1a

Do you think food rationing is necessary?

Yes.............................. 85%
No............................... 15

Interviewing Date 2/25–3/1/43
Survey #290–K   Question #1b

Do you understand how the food point rationing system works?

By Sex

	Men	Women
Yes	53%	76%
No	47	24

MARCH 6
HOME HEATING AND FUEL OIL RATIONING

Interviewing Date 2/5–10/43
Survey #289–K   Question #11b

Those who use oil to heat their homes were asked: At what temperature do you keep your home during the day?

Under 65 degrees................... 11%
At 65 degrees...................... 33
At 68 degrees...................... 19
At 70 degrees...................... 23
Above 70 degrees.................. 14

Whereas 65 degrees is the recommended temperature in order to conserve fuel oil, 56% of all oil furnace owners keep homes heated above 65 degrees.

Interviewing Date 2/5–10/43
Survey #289–K   Question #11g

Oil furnace owners also were asked: Do you think the rationing of fuel oil has been handled fairly in your area?

Yes............................... 68%
No............................... 23
No opinion....................... 9

Among the 23% not satisfied, the chief complaint is not so much against the amount of fuel allowed as against alleged inefficiency among ration boards and inequality or favoritism in the apportionment of oil.

MARCH 8
REPUBLICAN PRESIDENTIAL CANDIDATES

Interviewing Date 2/5–10/43
Survey #289–K   Question #8

Asked of Republicans: Can you tell me your opinion of the following possible candidates for the Republican presidential nomination in 1944?

Thomas Dewey?

Favorable......................... 69%
Unfavorable....................... 13
Unfamiliar, no opinion............. 18

Wendell Willkie?

Favorable......................... 49%
Unfavorable....................... 43
Unfamiliar, no opinion............. 8

Harold Stassen?

Favorable......................... 31%
Unfavorable....................... 10
Unfamiliar, no opinion............. 59

John Bricker?

Favorable......................... 25%
Unfavorable....................... 10
Unfamiliar, no opinion............. 65

Leverett Saltonstall?

Favorable......................... 15%
Unfavorable....................... 9
Unfamiliar, no opinion............. 76

MARCH 8
WORKING WOMEN

Special Survey

Asked of women workers in war plants: After the war do you plan to go on working?

Yes............................... 56%
No............................... 31
No opinion....................... 13

Single Women Only

Yes............................... 75%
No............................... 14
No opinion....................... 11

Married Women Only

Yes............................... 35%
No............................... 49
No opinion....................... 16

MARCH 9
WAR PLANT WORKERS

Special Survey

Asked of war plant workers: For about how long could you get by if you had no work at all after the war?

3 months or less	32%
4–6 months	16
7 months–1 year	16
1 year–2 years	4
Over 2 years	8
Don't know	24

Asked of war plant workers who had to relocate: Do you find living here more enjoyable or less enjoyable than in the place where you formerly lived?

	Length of Time in New Location	
	2 yrs. or more	Less than 2 yrs.
More enjoyable	55%	36%
Less	13	42
About same	19	19
Undecided	13	3

Asked of war plant workers who had to relocate: Do you plan to stay in this area after the war?

	Yes
Detroit area	48%
Cleveland-Buffalo and Ohio area	35
Philadelphia-Baltimore area	37
New England	32
California	49

MARCH 10
INCOME TAX

Interviewing Date 2/25–3/1/43
Survey #290–K   Question #10

Single persons making more than $500 a year were asked: Do you happen to know how much money a single person had to make last year before he has to file an income tax report this March 15?

Correct ($500)	54%
Incorrect, did not know	46

Interviewing Date 2/25–3/1/43
Survey #290–K   Question #11

Married men earning more than $1,200 a year were asked: Do you happen to know how much money a married person had to make last year before he has to file an income tax report this March 15?

Correct ($1,200)	67%
Incorrect, did not know	33

MARCH 12
INCOME TAX

Interviewing Date 2/25–3/1/43
Survey #290–K   Question #8a

Do you think that you (or your husband) will have to file a federal income tax report by March 15 on the money you made last year?

Findings indicate that unless last minute efforts to acquaint people with the provisions of the new tax law and the penalty for not filing are effective, the number of persons who file a return on March 15 may fall below the 40,000,000 mark.

Interviewing Date 2/25–3/1/43
Survey #290–K   Question #8f

Those who responded in the affirmative were asked: Will you have to cash in any war bonds or stamps to meet your March 15 payment?

Yes	4%
No	96

MARCH 13
STANDARD TIME

Interviewing Date 2/25–3/1/43
Survey #290–K   Question #2

A resolution in Congress calls for a return to standard time throughout the nation. If the question were voted on in this state would you vote for returning to standard time or staying on war time?

Favor war time...................... 44%
Favor standard time................ 42
No opinion........................ 14

By Community Size
Farms

Favor war time...................... 23%
Favor standard time............... 66
No opinion........................ 11

Under 10,000

Favor war time...................... 39%
Favor standard time............... 46
No opinion........................ 15

10,000 and Over

Favor war time...................... 53%
Favor standard time................ 32
No opinion........................ 15

MARCH 14
INCOME TAX

Interviewing Date 2/25–3/1/43
Survey #290–K   Question #8g

Do you regard the income tax which you will have to pay this year as fair?

Fair............................... 85%
Unfair.......................... 15

Those who had no opinion numbered less than 10%.

MARCH 17
ARMED FORCES

Interviewing Date 2/25–3/1/43
Survey #290–K   Question #3

There is an argument in Washington as to whether this country should build up our

armed forces to 11,000,000 men this year. Do you think we should or should not increase our armed forces to 11,000,000 men this year?

Should........................... 43%
Should not......................... 33
No opinion........................ 24

By Community Size
Farms

Should........................... 29%
Should not......................... 43
No opinion........................ 28

Under 10,000

Should........................... 39%
Should not......................... 36
No opinion........................ 25

10,000–100,000

Should........................... 43%
Should not......................... 31
No opinion........................ 26

Over 100,000

Should........................... 52%
Should not......................... 27
No opinion........................ 21

Single Men Only

Should........................... 50%
Should not......................... 36
No opinion........................ 14

Married Men Only

Should........................... 36%
Should not......................... 42
No opinion........................ 22

MARCH 19
DEMOCRATIC PRESIDENTIAL CANDIDATES

Interviewing Date 2/5–10/43
Survey #289–K   Question #8a

Democrats were asked: Will you tell me what you think of Henry Wallace? Do you have a favorable or unfavorable opinion of him?

Favorable	57%
Unfavorable	20
No opinion	23

By Region
East

Favorable	61%
Unfavorable	16
No opinion	23

Midwest

Favorable	54%
Unfavorable	25
No opinion	21

South

Favorable	52%
Unfavorable	22
No opinion	26

West

Favorable	59%
Unfavorable	20
No opinion	21

Interviewing Date 2/5–10/43
Survey #289–K   Question #8b

Democrats were asked: Will you tell me what you think of William O. Douglas? Do you have a favorable or unfavorable opinion of him?

Favorable	21%
Unfavorable	10
No opinion	69

By Region
East

Favorable	25%
Unfavorable	11
No opinion	64

Midwest

Favorable	20%
Unfavorable	9
No opinion	71

South

Favorable	19%
Unfavorable	11
No opinion	70

West

Favorable	19%
Unfavorable	11
No opinion	70

Interviewing Date 2/5–10/43
Survey #289–K   Question #8c

Democrats were asked: Will you tell me what you think of Paul V. McNutt? Do you have a favorable or unfavorable opinion of him?

Favorable	28%
Unfavorable	31
No opinion	41

By Region
East

Favorable	29%
Unfavorable	29
No opinion	42

Midwest

Favorable	32%
Unfavorable	32
No opinion	36

South

Favorable	24%
Unfavorable	32
No opinion	44

West

Favorable	20%
Unfavorable	33
No opinion	47

Interviewing Date 2/5–10/43
Survey #289–K   Question #8d

Democrats were asked: Will you tell me what you think of James Byrnes? Do you have a favorable or unfavorable opinion of him?

Favorable......................... 19%
Unfavorable....................... 12
No opinion........................ 69

By Region
East

Favorable......................... 19%
Unfavorable....................... 13
No opinion........................ 68

Midwest

Favorable......................... 19%
Unfavorable....................... 11
No opinion........................ 70

South

Favorable......................... 25%
Unfavorable....................... 12
No opinion........................ 63

West

Favorable......................... 12%
Unfavorable....................... 12
No opinion........................ 76

MARCH 20
BRITISH POLITICS

Special Survey

Britons were asked: If anything should happen to Mr. Churchill, whom would you like to see succeed him as Prime Minister?

Eden............................. 39%
Cripps........................... 24
Bevin............................ 4
Attlee........................... 3
Beaverbrook...................... 2
Morrison......................... 2
Miscellaneous, undecided......... 26

MARCH 21
RUML PLAN

Interviewing Date 2/25–3/1/43
Survey #290–K   Question #15c

Have you heard of the Ruml income tax plan?

Yes.............................. 71%
No............................... 29

Interviewing Date 2/25–3/1/43
Survey #290–K   Question #15d

Those persons who had heard of the Ruml Plan were asked: Do you favor or oppose the Ruml Plan?

By Political Affiliation
Republicans

Favor............................ 87%
Oppose........................... 13

Democrats

Favor............................ 83%
Oppose........................... 17

By Income
Upper Half of Income Bracket

Favor............................ 83%
Oppose........................... 17

Lower Half of Income Bracket

Favor............................ 86%
Oppose........................... 14

By Region
New England

Favor............................ 87%
Oppose........................... 13

East Central

Favor............................ 85%
Oppose........................... 15

West Central

Favor............................ 85%
Oppose........................... 15

South

Favor............................ 85%
Oppose........................... 15

Mountain and Far West

Favor............................ 86%
Oppose........................... 14

MARCH 24
POSTWAR ROLE FOR UNITED STATES

Interviewing Date 12/4–9/42
Survey #285–K   Question #2

Should the Government take steps now, before the end of the war, to set up with our allies a world organization to maintain the future peace of the world?

Yes.............................. 64%
No............................... 24
No opinion....................... 12

By Political Affiliation
Republicans

Yes.............................. 63%
No............................... 28
No opinion....................... 9

Democrats

Yes.............................. 65%
No............................... 23
No opinion....................... 12

Interviewing Date 1/29–2/3/43
Survey #288–K   Question #5a

Do you think the United States, Britain, Russia, China, and their allies should form a joint war council which would plan all war operations against the Axis powers?

Yes.............................. 74%
No............................... 9
No opinion....................... 17

By Political Affiliation
Republicans

Yes.............................. 75%
No............................... 10
No opinion....................... 15

Democrats

Yes.............................. 74%
No............................... 8
No opinion....................... 18

Interviewing Date 1/29–2/3/43
Survey #288–T   Question #9

After this war, do you think the United States should stay out of world affairs, or take an active part in world affairs?

Active part...................... 76%
Stay out......................... 14
No opinion....................... 10

By Political Affiliation
Republicans

Active part...................... 76%
Stay out......................... 15
No opinion....................... 9

Democrats

Active part...................... 78%
Stay out......................... 12
No opinion....................... 10

MARCH 26
WAR PLANT ABSENTEES

Interviewing Date 3/12–17/43
Survey #291–K   Question #10

What do you think should be done with workers in war factories who are regularly absent from work without good excuse?

The most frequently mentioned suggestion — given by 48% of those questioned — is to draft habitual men absentees into the army.

The second most frequently mentioned penalty — suggested by about 11% — is that workers be laid off or discharged from their jobs. Institute policies of "enforced furloughs" for absenteeism without a good excuse.

The remaining 32% who mentioned penalties offered a variety of suggestions ranging from fines to jail sentences.

About one per cent of those questioned thought absenteeism without cause is non-existent and wanted no penalties, and 8% had no opinion.

MARCH 27
CLARE BOOTHE LUCE

Interviewing Date 3/12–17/43
Survey #291–K   Question #17a

Have you heard or read about Mrs. Clare Boothe Luce?

Yes............................... 50%
No............................... 50

Interviewing Date 3/12–17/43
Survey #291–K   Question #17b

Those who answered in the affirmative were asked: Can you tell me what her job is now?

Eight out of every ten correctly identified her as a member of Congress.

When the figures are analyzed they reveal that Mrs. Luce is better known among women than men, better known among the upper and middle income groups than among the lower income groups, and better known among Republicans than Democrats.

Interviewing Date 3/12–17/43
Survey #291–K   Question #17c

Those who answered in the affirmative also were asked: What is your opinion of her?

Women have a more favorable opinion of Mrs. Luce than do men. In fact, a slightly higher proportion of men express an unfavorable opinion than express a favorable opinion. The reverse is true of women.

MARCH 28
WOMEN IN WAR INDUSTRIES

Interviewing Date 3/12–17/43
Survey #291–K   Question #14e

Women were asked: If you were offered a job in a war plant today, would you take it?

On the basis of the findings, approximately 8,800,000 women would take a job in a war plant if they were asked to do so. To this total can be added 2,300,000 married women, with children under ten years of age, who would be willing to take war jobs today if, at no expense to themselves, provision were made for the care of their children.

Interviewing Date 3/12–17/43
Survey #291–K   Question #11

Should all women over 18 be required to register with the government for jobs in war industries?

Yes............................... 61%
No............................... 31
No opinion....................... 8

APRIL 2
"VICTORY GARDENS"

Interviewing Date 3/12–17/43
Survey #291–K   Question #1a

Do you plan to have a vegetable garden for home consumption this year?

Results show that an estimated 21,000,000 families plan to have a victory garden.

Interviewing Date 3/12–17/43
Survey #291–K   Question #1c

Those who plan to have a garden were asked: How large will it be?

According to the survey, the average size of garden plots planned this year in cities of

100,000 or more population will be approximately 500 square feet, or a plot 20 by 25 feet. In towns or cities of 100,000 down to and including rural non-farm areas, gardens will average 40 by 95 feet, or 3,800 square feet. Gardens on farms will run to an average of about half an acre. The greatest number of "victory gardens" will be in towns and villages under 10,000 population.

APRIL 3
WAR STRATEGY

Special Survey

Britons were asked: Do you think it will be necessary for the Allies to invade the continent before Germany can be defeated?

Yes.............................. 76%
No.............................. 10
Undecided........................ 14

Britons were asked: Should Britain, America, Russia, and China form a supreme war council to plan and direct the war on all fronts?

Yes.............................. 76%
No.............................. 9
Undecided........................ 15

APRIL 7
PROFESSIONAL SPORTS

Interviewing Date 3 /26–31 /43
Survey #292–K   Question #2b

Do you think that professional baseball should be continued during the war, or should it be stopped until after the war?

Continued........................ 59%
Stopped.......................... 28
No opinion....................... 13

Interviewing Date 3 /26–31 /43
Survey #292–T   Question #2b

Do you think that professional sports should be continued during the war, or should they be stopped until after the war?

Continued........................ 64%
Stopped.......................... 25
No opinion....................... 11

APRIL 9
VOTING AGE

Interviewing Date 3 /26–31 /43
Survey #292–K   Question #1

At present, American citizens cannot vote until they become 21 years of age. Would you favor changing the law to allow men and women 18, 19, and 20 years old to vote?

Favor............................ 42%
Oppose........................... 52
No opinion....................... 6

APRIL 10
VENEREAL DISEASE

Interviewing Date 1 /29–2 /3 /43
Survey #288–K   Question #3

In order to control the spread of venereal diseases around army camps, which of these plans (on card) do you favor? A. Require all prostitutes to take a regular weekly medical examination and quarantine those who are diseased. B. Rely upon continuous police action to get rid of all prostitutes around army camps.

Require weekly examinations......... 61%
Use police action................... 29
Undecided.......................... 10

APRIL 12
NATIONAL RESOURCES BOARD

Interviewing Date 3/26–31/43
Survey #292–K   Question #14a

Have you heard or read about the National Resources Board plan for the postwar period?

Yes................................. 34%
No.................................. 66

Interviewing Date 3/26–31/43
Survey #292–K   Question #14b

Those who had heard about the report were asked: Can you tell me briefly what it is about?

Fewer than half of those who had heard about the report could name anything that it contained. In terms of the whole population, the group familiar with any provisions of the report represented only 13% or one person in every eight.

Interviewing Date 3/26–31/43
Survey #292–K   Question #14c

Those who had heard of the plan were asked: What is your opinion of the plan?

Favorable........................... 69%
Unfavorable........................ 18
No opinion......................... 13

Interviewing Date 3/26–31/43
Survey #292–K   Question #10a

Do you think your present job will continue after the war, or do you think you will have to find a new one?

Will continue...................... 79%
Have to find new one.............. 13
Undecided......................... 8

Interviewing Date 3/26–31/43
Survey #292–K   Question #10b

Those who think they will have to find new jobs were asked: Do you think you will have any difficulty in finding a new job?

Yes................................. 5%
No.................................. 5
Don't know......................... 3
                    —
                    13%

APRIL 14
JOHN BRICKER

Interviewing Date 2/5–10/43
Survey #289–K   Question #8

Will you tell me what you think of Governor John Bricker of Ohio? Generally speaking, do you think he is presidential material?

Among Republican voters, 65% were unfamiliar with him or had no opinion. Among all voters who had an opinion, the ratio of favorable to unfavorable was better than 2 to 1.

APRIL 16
RATING OF STATE GOVERNORS

Interviewing Date 3/26–31/43
Survey #292–K   Question #15

What kind of a job would you say the governor of your state is doing — outstanding, better than average, average, or poor?

Outstanding........................ 17%
Better than average................ 14
Average............................ 42
Poor............................... 8
No opinion......................... 19

New York State Only

Outstanding........................ 26%
Better than average................ 15
Average............................ 31
Poor............................... 4
No opinion......................... 24

Ohio Only

Outstanding........................ 29%
Better than average................ 18
Average............................ 31
Poor............................... 8
No opinion......................... 14

APRIL 17
RATIONING

Interviewing Date 4/8–13/43
Survey #293–K   Question #1

Which of the things now rationed do you find it hardest to cut down on?

The following are listed according to frequency of mention:

Meat
Coffee
Gasoline
Sugar
Butter
Canned goods
Shoes
Fuel oil
Tires
Cheese

APRIL 20
INCOME TAX

Interviewing Date 4/8–13/43
Survey #293–K   Question #5

Each year the Federal Government collects income taxes on money earned the previous year. Would you like to have that plan continue or would you prefer to pay your taxes on the money as you earn it?

Pay as money is earned.............. 79%
Present system..................... 21

The 7% no opinion vote has been eliminated.

Interviewing Date 4/8–13/43
Survey #293–K   Question #8d

Do you favor or oppose the Ruml Plan which would put the nation on a pay-as-you-go basis without calling for the payment of two years taxes in one year?

Favor............................ 72%
Oppose.......................... 28

By Political Affiliation
Republicans

Favor............................ 77%
Oppose.......................... 23

Democrats

Favor............................ 66%
Oppose.......................... 34

APRIL 21
PARTY BEST FOR PEACE AND PROSPERITY

Interviewing Date 4/8–13/43
Survey #293–K   Question #9a

After the war which party do you think is more likely to bring better times to the country, the Republicans or the Democrats?

Republicans....................... 32%
Democrats......................... 27
Makes no difference................ 21
No opinion........................ 20

Interviewing Date 4/8–13/43
Survey #293–K   Question #9b

Which party do you think can handle the problems of peace better, the Republicans or the Democrats?

Republicans....................... 20%
Democrats......................... 32
Makes no difference................ 33
No opinion........................ 15

APRIL 24
TWO TERM AMENDMENT

Interviewing Date 4/8–13/43
Survey #293–K   Question #14

Would you favor adding an amendment to the Federal Constitution to prevent any president of the United States from serving a third term?

Favor............................ 46%
Oppose.......................... 54

By Region

	Favor	Oppose
New England and Middle Atlantic	41%	59%
East Central	52	48
West Central	58	42
South	42	58
Far West	42	58

By Political Affiliation

Democrats	28%	72%
Republicans	74	26

APRIL 28
SHOP FOREMEN

Interviewing Date 4/8–13/43
Survey #293–K   Question #3

At present shop foremen in factories are generally not members of a labor union. Do you think they should or should not become members of a labor union?

Should	42%
Should not	58

Twenty-four per cent had no opinion on this issue.

By Occupation

	Should	Should Not
Skilled workers	58%	42%
Semiskilled and unskilled	50	50
Business and professional	31	69
White collar	38	62
Farmers	30	70

APRIL 30
RUSSIA

Interviewing Date 4/8–13/43
Survey #293–T   Question #13a

Do you think Russia can be trusted to cooperate with us when the war is over?

Yes	44%
No	34
No opinion	22

By Income
Upper

Yes	53%
No	31
No opinion	16

Middle

Yes	45%
No	38
No opinion	17

Lower

Yes	41%
No	33
No opinion	26

By Region
New England and Middle Atlantic

Yes	45%
No	33
No opinion	22

East Central

Yes	41%
No	37
No opinion	22

West Central

Yes	48%
No	34
No opinion	18

South

Yes	39%
No	33
No opinion	28

Far West

Yes	45%
No	37
No opinion	18

MAY 1
HAROLD STASSEN

Interviewing Date 4/8–13/43
Survey #293–K   Question #15

Minnesota voters were asked: What kind of job would you say Governor Stassen is doing — outstanding, better than average, average, or poor?

Outstanding	45%
Better than average	12
Average	34
Poor	5
No opinion	4

Interviewing Date 2/5–10/43
Survey #289–K   Question #8

Asked of Minnesota voters: Will you tell me what you think of Harold Stassen as presidential material for 1944? Is your opinion of him favorable or unfavorable?

Favorable	62%
Unfavorable	29
No opinion	9

MAY 3
INTERNATIONAL POLICE FORCE

Interviewing Date 4/8–13/43
Survey #293–K   Question #10

Should the countries fighting the Axis set up an international police force after the war is over to try to keep peace throughout the world?

Yes	74%
No	14
No opinion	12

MAY 5
STRIKES

Special Survey

War plant workers were asked: Do you think there should be a law forbidding strikes in war plants?

Yes	72%
No	22
No opinion	6

Union Members Only

Yes	64%
No	30
No opinion	6

MAY 7
ABSENTEEISM IN WAR PLANTS

Special Survey

War plant workers were asked: How do you, yourself, account for absenteeism among workers?

Illness	28%
Fatigue from long hours	26
Irresponsibility, laziness	13
Too much pay	12
Drinking	10
Transportation difficulties	2
Miscellaneous	6
No opinion	12
	109%

(Note: table adds to more than 100% as some workers cited more than one cause.)

MAY 8
POSTWAR WORK FOR WOMEN

Special Survey

Women workers in war plants were asked: After the war do you plan to go on working?

Yes	54%
No	33
Undecided	13

Married Women Only

Yes	34%
No	49
Undecided	17

Single Women Only

Yes.............................. 73%
No............................... 16
Undecided....................... 11

MAY 12
VOTER INTEREST

Special Survey

War plant workers were asked: Did you vote in 1942?

Yes.............................. 42%
No............................... 58

Of those who voted in 1942, 63% said they plan to vote Democratic in 1944. Of those who did not vote in 1942, 74% said they favor the Democrats for 1944.

MAY 14
LABOR UNIONS

Interviewing Date 4/29–5/4/43
Survey #294–K   Question #10a

Has your attitude toward labor unions changed in any way during the last year?

Yes.............................. 43%
No............................... 57

Interviewing Date 4/29–5/4/43
Survey #294–K   Question #10b

Those who responded in the affirmative were asked: Are you more in favor or less in favor of labor unions than you were a year ago?

More in favor.................... 5%
Less in favor.................... 38
                                 ‾‾‾
                                 43%

MAY 15
BOMBING OF ROME

Interviewing Date 4/29–5/4/43
Survey #294–K   Question #9c

Do you think the Allied air forces should bomb Rome?

Yes.............................. 37%
No............................... 51
No opinion....................... 12

By Religion
Protestants

Yes.............................. 36%
No............................... 52
No opinion....................... 12

Catholics

Yes.............................. 24%
No............................... 67
No opinion....................... 9

Non-Church Members

Yes.............................. 47%
No............................... 40
No opinion....................... 13

MAY 16
REPUBLICAN PRESIDENTIAL CANDIDATES

Interviewing Date 4/29–5/4/43
Survey #294–K   Question #13b

Republicans were asked: Which one of these men would you prefer as the Republican candidate for President next year?

Dewey........................... 38%
Willkie......................... 28
MacArthur....................... 17
Bricker......................... 8
Stassen......................... 7
Saltonstall..................... 1
Warren.......................... 1

MAY 19
DEMOCRATIC PRESIDENTIAL CANDIDATES

Interviewing Date 4/29–5/4/43
Survey #294–K   Question #13b

Democrats were asked: Which one of these men would you prefer as the Democratic candidate for President next year?

Roosevelt............................ 79%
Wallace............................. 8
Farley.............................. 5
McNutt............................. 4
Douglas............................ 2
Byrnes............................. 1
Winant............................. 1

MAY 21
WAR PLANTS

Special Survey

War plant workers were asked: What do you think is the greatest mistake that your company makes?

Poor planning in production, lack of co-ordination between departments, failure to supply materials on time....... 13%
Poor employer-employee relations, no interest taken in employees or their problems, failure to profit by suggestions and ideas of the workers....... 8
Unfair wages, lack of proper pay-scale for different types of work, lack of incentive payments for better work.... 6
Wrong types hired for certain jobs, workers not properly trained, jobs not suitable to abilities of workers.......... 6
Bosses too lenient, too much loafing permitted, too many workers sitting around doing nothing.............. 5
Lack of competent supervisors, men in key jobs who don't know their business 4
No modern equipment, slow in improving methods or standardizing products 3
Miscellaneous...................... 9
No important mistakes made.......... 46

War plant workers also were asked: Do you find many people in your plant loaf on the job?

Yes................................ 40%
No................................. 55
Don't know........................ 5

MAY 22
POSTWAR AMERICAN BASES IN AUSTRALIA

Special Survey

Australians were asked: Would you favor or oppose letting the United States navy and air forces use bases in Australia after the war?

Favor.............................. 77%
Oppose............................. 15
Undecided.......................... 8

Those who responded in the affirmative were asked: Should this right be granted permanently or should bases be leased for a limited period, say 25 years?

Permanently........................ 23%
Limited period..................... 47
Undecided.......................... 7
                                    ——
                                    77%

Should compulsory cadet training of youths of 16 and 17 begin immediately?

Yes................................ 79%
No................................. 16
Undecided.......................... 5

MAY 23
PRESIDENTIAL TRIAL HEAT

Interviewing Date 4/29–5/4/43
Survey #294–K   Question #14

Suppose Franklin Roosevelt and Henry Wallace were the Democratic candidates for President and Vice President in the election next year and Thomas Dewey and Douglas MacArthur were the Republican candidates for President and Vice President, which ticket would you vote for?

Roosevelt-Wallace................... 54%
Dewey-MacArthur................... 46

Thirteen per cent refrained from making a choice.

By Region

	Roosevelt-Wallace	Dewey-MacArthur
East..............	55%	45%
Midwest..........	47	53
South............	75	25
West.............	50	50

By Income

	Roosevelt-Wallace	Dewey-MacArthur
Upper and middle..	46%	54%
Lower............	62	38

By Age

	Roosevelt-Wallace	Dewey-MacArthur
21–29 Years.......	66%	34%
30–49 Years.......	55	45
50 Years and over..	48	52

MAY 26
WAR BONDS

Interviewing Date 4/29–5/4/43
Survey #294–K   Question #6

Would you be willing to have your employer take 15 cents out of every dollar of your wages or salary each pay day to buy war bonds for you?

Would be........................... 52%
Would not......................... 43
Undecided........................ 5

MAY 28
STRIKES

Interviewing Date 5/14–19/43
Survey #295–K   Question #15

Would you approve or disapprove of making it a crime for anyone to urge workers to strike in companies taken over by the Government?

Approve........................... 78%
Disapprove........................ 14
Undecided........................ 8

Union Members Only

Approve........................... 67%
Disapprove........................ 22
Undecided........................ 11

MAY 29
LENGTH OF WAR

Special Survey

Britons were asked: How much longer do you think the war will last?

Six months....................... 7%
1 year........................... 27
1½ years......................... 22
2 years.......................... 26
3 years.......................... 9
More than 3 years................. 6
Undecided........................ 3

MAY 31
LABOR UNIONS

Special Survey

War workers were asked: Would you like to see labor unions change their way of handling things?

Yes.............................. 53%
No.............................. 23
Undecided........................ 24

Union Members Only

Yes.............................. 45%
No............................... 38
Undecided........................ 17

JUNE 2
LABOR UNIONS

Interviewing Date 5/14–19/43
Survey #295–K   Question #14

Do you think all labor unions should be required to register with the Federal Government and report the amount of money they take in and spend each year?

Yes.............................. 85%
No............................... 7
Undecided........................ 8

Union Members Only

Yes.............................. 80%
No............................... 12
Undecided........................ 8

JUNE 4
SEX EDUCATION

Interviewing Date 5/14–19/43
Survey #295–K   Question #19

It has been suggested that a course in sex education be given to students in high schools. Do you approve or disapprove of this plan?

Approve........................... 68%
Disapprove........................ 16
No opinion........................ 16

By Region
New England and Middle Atlantic

Approve........................... 72%
Disapprove........................ 16
No opinion........................ 12

East Central

Approve........................... 72%
Disapprove........................ 15
No opinion........................ 13

West Central

Approve........................... 65%
Disapprove........................ 17
No opinion........................ 18

South

Approve........................... 61%
Disapprove........................ 16
No opinion........................ 23

Far West

Approve........................... 71%
Disapprove........................ 14
No opinion........................ 15

By Age
21–29 Years

Approve........................... 77%
Disapprove........................ 13
No opinion........................ 10

30–49 Years

Approve........................... 69%
Disapprove........................ 15
No opinion........................ 16

50 Years and Over

Approve........................... 61%
Disapprove........................ 20
No opinion........................ 19

JUNE 5
INTERNATIONAL POLICE FORCE

Interviewing Date 5/14–19/43
Survey #295–K   Question #10

Should the countries fighting the Axis set up an international police force after the war is over to try to keep peace throughout the world?

Yes............................... 76%
No............................... 12
Undecided........................ 12

JUNE 7
FRANKLIN ROOSEVELT

Interviewing Date 5/14–19/43
Survey #295–K   Question #21

If the war is over and President Roosevelt runs for a fourth term next year, do you think you will vote for him or against him?

For............................... 31%
Against........................... 69

Interviewing Date 5/14–19/43
Survey #295–K   Question #20a

If the war is still going on and Roosevelt runs for a fourth term next year, do you think you will vote for him or against him?

For............................... 56%
Against........................... 44

Interviewing Date 5/14–19/43
Survey #295–K   Question #20b

If the war is not entirely over next year but looks as though it might be over soon, do you think you will vote for or against Roosevelt for a fourth term?

For............................... 51%
Against........................... 49

JUNE 9
POSTWAR TRADE WITH UNITED STATES

Special Survey

Canadians were asked: After the war, do you think we should have free trade with the United States, that is, that all products and merchandise crossing the border either way should be free of all tariffs and customs duties?

Yes............................... 67%
No............................... 17
Undecided........................ 16

By Occupation
Business and Professional

Yes............................... 50%
No............................... 30
Undecided........................ 20

White Collar

Yes............................... 65%
No............................... 19
Undecided........................ 16

Manual Workers

Yes............................... 71%
No............................... 15
Undecided........................ 14

Farmers

Yes............................... 72%
No............................... 13
Undecided........................ 15

JUNE 11
GERMANY AND JAPAN

Interviewing Date 4/29–5/4/43
Survey #294–K   Question #2

Which country do you think we can get along with better after the war — Germany or Japan?

Germany.......................... 67%
Japan............................. 8
No opinion....................... 25

By Race
White

Germany.......................... 70%
Japan............................. 7
No opinion....................... 23

Negro

Germany.......................... 30%
Japan............................. 22
No opinion........................ 48

By Region
East

Germany.......................... 65%
Japan............................. 7
No opinion........................ 28

Midwest

Germany.......................... 74%
Japan............................. 6
No opinion........................ 20

South

Germany.......................... 59%
Japan............................. 13
No opinion........................ 28

West

Germany.......................... 70%
Japan............................. 9
No opinion........................ 21

JUNE 12
"VICTORY GARDENS"

Interviewing Date 5/14–19/43
Survey #295–K   Question #1a

Did you plant a "victory garden" this spring?

By Region

	Number of Gardens
East......................	4,000,000
Midwest...................	6,500,000
South.....................	6,500,000
West......................	2,800,000

The average size of the garden plot, on the basis of gardeners' plans at the start of the season is approximately 500 square feet in cities of 100,000 or more population — a plot of about 20 by 25 feet. In towns or cities of less than 100,000 down to and including rural non-farm areas, gardens were expected to average 40 by 95 feet or 3,800 square feet. Gardens on farms were estimated to run to an average of about half an acre.

The total acreage under cultivation, if those who have gardens followed their estimates on the sizes of their gardens, is about 7,000,000 acres — an area equivalent to all of the land put to crops in North Carolina in 1940.

JUNE 18
JOHN L. LEWIS

Interviewing Date 6/4–9/43
Survey #296–K   Question #5

What is your opinion of John L. Lewis?

Favorable......................... 9%
Unfavorable....................... 87
No opinion........................ 4

JUNE 23
POSTWAR CANADA

Special Survey

Canadians were asked: Which of these things would you like to see Canada do after the war? A. Continue as a member of the British Commonwealth as at present. B. Leave the British Commonwealth and become a part of the United States. C. Leave the British Commonwealth and become a completely independent nation.

Continue in Commonwealth......... 49%
Become part of the U.S........... 21
Become an independent nation..... 24
Undecided........................ 6

By Region
Maritime

Continue in Commonwealth......... 58%
Become part of the U.S........... 23
Become an independent nation..... 12
Undecided........................ 7

Quebec

Continue in Commonwealth	24%
Become part of the U.S.	18
Become an independent nation	50
Undecided	8

Ontario

Continue in Commonwealth	64%
Become part of the U.S.	20
Become an independent nation	11
Undecided	5

Prairie

Continue in Commonwealth	57%
Become part of the U.S.	26
Become an independent nation	11
Undecided	6

British Columbia

Continue in Commonwealth	48%
Become part of the U.S.	33
Become an independent nation	15
Undecided	4

JUNE 25
LENGTH OF WAR

Interviewing Date 6/4–9/43
Survey #296–K Question #1a

How much longer do you think the war with Germany will last?

Median average............... one year

Interviewing Date 6/4–9/43
Survey #296–K Question #1b

How much longer do you think the war with Japan will last?

Median average............... two years

JUNE 26
DEMOBILIZATION

Interviewing Date 6/4–9/43
Survey #296–K Question #7a

Do you think the men in the armed forces will have trouble finding jobs when the war is over?

Yes	56%
No	35
Don't know	9

Families with a Member in Armed Forces

Yes	55%
No	35
Don't know	10

Interviewing Date 6/4–9/43
Survey #296–K Question #7b

Do you think men should be released from the armed forces after the war if they have no jobs, or should they be kept in service until they can show they have jobs?

Released after war	38%
Kept in service till they find jobs	50
Undecided	12

Families with a Member in Armed Forces

Released after war	41%
Kept in service till they find jobs	48
Undecided	11

JUNE 27
REPUBLICAN PRESIDENTIAL CANDIDATES

Interviewing Date 6/4–9/43
Survey #296–K Question #6b

Republicans were asked: Which one of these men would you prefer as the Republican candidate for President next year?

Dewey	37%
Willkie	28
MacArthur	15
Bricker	10
Stassen	7
Saltonstall	2
Warren	1

JULY 2

DEMOCRATIC PRESIDENTIAL CANDIDATES

Interviewing Date 6/4–9/43
Survey #296–K   Question #6b

Southern Democrats were asked: Which one of these men would you prefer as the Democratic candidate for President next year?

Roosevelt........................... 80%
Byrnes............................. 8
Wallace............................ 6
Farley............................. 3
McNutt............................ 2
William Douglas.................... 1

JULY 3

PARTY BEST FOR BUSINESSMEN AND WORKERS

Interviewing Date 6/4–9/43
Survey #296–K   Question #9b

Do you think businessmen will be better off if the Republicans or the Democrats win the presidential election next year?

Views of Businessmen Outside South

Business better off under Republicans.. 78%
Business better off under Democrats... 22

Views of Workers

Business better off under Republicans... 59%
Business better off under Democrats... 41

Interviewing Date 6/4–9/43
Survey #296–K   Question #9c

Do you think skilled and unskilled workers will be better off if the Republicans or the Democrats win the presidential election next year?

Views of Businessmen Outside South

Workers better off under Republicans... 49%
Workers better off under Democrats.... 51

Views of Workers

Workers better off under Republicans... 27%
Workers better off under Democrats.... 73

JULY 4

WAR BONDS

Interviewing Date 6/4–9/43
Survey #296–K   Question #19a

Have you purchased any war bonds or stamps since January 1, 1943?

Yes................................ 60%
No................................ 40

By Community Size

	Yes	No
Farm areas.................	50%	50%
Towns under 10,000..........	57	43
10,000–100,000..............	69	31
100,000 and over............	65	35

Union Members

Yes................................ 73%
No................................ 27

Interviewing Date 6/4–9/43
Survey #296–K   Question #19b

Do you own any war bonds or stamps now?

Yes................................ 81%
No................................ 19

JULY 7

ROOSEVELT ADMINISTRATION

Interviewing Date 6/5–10/43
Survey #296   Question #2b

Southerners were asked: What do you like least about the Roosevelt Administration?

Poor handling of labor unions........ 22%
Extravagance, waste of public funds, pay-

ing people who don't work as hard as
they should...................... 11
Inefficiency, bureaucracy, red tape..... 11
Sponsoring too much equality of Negroes 5
Unfair treatment of Southern farmers... 5
Stimulating liquor trade by repeal of
prohibition...................... 2
Failure to curb inflation.............. 1
Too high taxes..................... 1
Unpreparedness for war............. 1
No opinion, no criticism............. 41

JULY 9
FEATHERBEDDING

Interviewing Date 6/5–10/43
Survey #296–T   Question #4

Some labor unions make jobs for their
members by requiring employers to hire
more men than are actually needed to do a
particular job. The unions say this is
necessary in order to give work to all their
members. Do you think a law should be
passed prohibiting this practice?

Yes.............................. 69%
No............................... 19
Undecided........................ 12

Union Members

Yes.............................. 57%
No............................... 31
Undecided........................ 12

JULY 10
POSTWAR WORLD AFFAIRS

Interviewing Date 6/24–29/43
Survey #297–K   Question #5

Do you want your Congressman to vote for
or against this resolution (Fulbright Resolution on card): That the Congress hereby
expresses itself as favoring the creation of
appropriate international machinery with
power adequate to establish and to maintain

a just and lasting peace among the nations
of the world, and as favoring participation
by the United States therein?

For.............................. 78%
Against........................... 9
Undecided........................ 13

JULY 11
ROOSEVELT ADMINISTRATION

Interviewing Date 6/24–29/43
Survey #297–K   Question #4a

Do you approve or disapprove of the way
President Roosevelt is handling our foreign
policy — that is, our relations with other
nations?

Approve.......................... 73%
Disapprove....................... 14
Undecided........................ 13

Interviewing Date 6/24–29/43
Survey #297–K   Question #4b

Do you approve or disapprove of the way
President Roosevelt is handling our domestic policy — that is local problems here
at home?

Approve.......................... 49%
Disapprove....................... 42
Undecided........................ 9

By Region
New England and Middle Atlantic

Approve.......................... 53%
Disapprove....................... 37
Undecided........................ 10

East Central

Approve.......................... 48%
Disapprove....................... 42
Undecided........................ 10

West Central

Approve.............................. 47%
Disapprove........................... 47
Undecided........................... 6

South

Approve.............................. 48%
Disapprove........................... 42
No opinion.......................... 10

West

Approve.............................. 44%
Disapprove........................... 47
No opinion........................... 9

By Occupation
Professional and Business

Approve.............................. 34%
Disapprove........................... 59
No opinion........................... 7

Farmers

Approve.............................. 39%
Disapprove........................... 53
No opinion........................... 8

White Collar

Approve.............................. 44%
Disapprove........................... 47
No opinion........................... 9

Manual Workers

Approve.............................. 62%
Disapprove........................... 28
No opinion.......................... 10

JULY 14
REPUBLICAN PRESIDENTIAL CANDIDATES

Interviewing Date 6/24–29/43
Survey #297–K   Question #17

Which one of these men would you prefer as the Republican candidate for President next year?

New York Republicans Only

Dewey............................... 53%
Willkie.............................. 27
MacArthur.......................... 8
Bricker............................. 5
Stassen............................. 4
Saltonstall......................... 2
Warren.............................. 1

Pennsylvania Republicans Only

Dewey............................... 38%
Willkie.............................. 33
MacArthur.......................... 14
Bricker............................. 9
Stassen............................. 5
Warren.............................. 1
Saltonstall......................... *

Illinois Republicans Only

Dewey............................... 41%
Willkie.............................. 19
MacArthur.......................... 18
Bricker............................. 11
Stassen............................. 10
Saltonstall......................... 1
Warren.............................. *

*Less than 1%

JULY 16
WAR CONTRIBUTIONS

Special Survey
Interviewing Date 6/24–29/43 (U.S. only)
Survey #297–K   Question #1

Which of these countries do you think has done the most toward winning the war so far — Russia, China, Britain, or the United States?

Views of Britons

Russia.............................. 50%
Britain............................. 42
China............................... 5
United States....................... 3

Views of Americans

United States............... 55%
Russia..................... 32
Britain.................... 9
China...................... 4

JULY 17
SEX EDUCATION

Interviewing Date 6/24–29/43
Survey #297–K   Question #9

Some people say that sex problems should be scientifically and frankly discussed by medical authorities in daily newspapers. Do you approve or disapprove of this?

Approve.................... 40%
Disapprove................. 44
Undecided.................. 16

By Sex
Men

Approve.................... 43%
Disapprove................. 38
No opinion................. 19

Women

Approve.................... 38%
Disapprove................. 49
No opinion................. 13

By Age
21–29 Years

Approve.................... 49%
Disapprove................. 38
No opinion................. 13

30–49 Years

Approve.................... 41%
Disapprove................. 43
No opinion................. 16

50 Years and Over

Approve.................... 35%
Disapprove................. 48
No opinion................. 17

By Education
College

Approve.................... 51%
Disapprove................. 41
No opinion................. 8

High School

Approve.................... 45%
Disapprove................. 44
No opinion................. 11

Grade School

Approve.................... 35%
Disapprove................. 44
No opinion................. 21

JULY 21
REPUBLICAN PRESIDENTIAL CANDIDATES

Interviewing Date 6/24–29/43
Survey #297–K   Question #17

Which one of these men would you prefer as the Republican candidate for President in 1944?

Republicans

Dewey...................... 39%
Willkie.................... 28
Bricker.................... 15
MacArthur.................. 10
Stassen.................... 6
Warren..................... 1
Saltonstall................ 1

Republicans Who Say They Might Vote Democratic

Dewey...................... 35%
Willkie.................... 34
Bricker.................... 11
MacArthur.................. 9
Stassen.................... 8
Warren..................... 2
Saltonstall................ 1

Independents

Willkie............................ 39%
Dewey............................. 29
MacArthur......................... 17
Stassen........................... 6
Bricker........................... 5
Warren............................ 2
Saltonstall....................... 2

Democrats Who Say They Might Vote Republican

Willkie............................ 45%
Dewey............................. 22
MacArthur......................... 17
Stassen........................... 7
Bricker........................... 5
Warren............................ 2
Saltonstall....................... 2

JULY 23
CONNALLY-SMITH ACT

Interviewing Date 7/9–14/43
Survey #298–K   Question #11a

Have you heard or read about the Connally-Smith Act?

Yes.............................. 75%
No............................... 25

Interviewing Date 7/9–14/43
Survey #298–K   Question #11b

Those who responded in the affirmative were asked: In general, are you for or against the Connally-Smith Act?

For.............................. 67%
Against.......................... 24
Undecided........................ 9

JULY 25
FOOD SHORTAGE

Interviewing Date 7/9–14/43
Survey #298–K   Question #3

Do you think there is a need for an im-partial committee to study and report on the current food problem?

Yes.............................. 67%
No............................... 22
Undecided........................ 11

Interviewing Date 7/9–14/43
Survey #298–T   Question #3

Would you be for or against having Herbert Hoover take over the entire food problem in the United States?

For.............................. 59%
Against.......................... 41

Fifteen per cent of those interviewed had no opinion.

Interviewing Date 7/9–14/43
Survey #298–K   Question #4b

Have you lost weight or gained weight since food rationing began?

Lost weight...................... 19%
Gained weight.................... 12
Remained same.................... 69

Interviewing Date 7/9–14/43
Survey #298–T   Question #4c

In general, do you think most people you know would be healthier if they ate less?

Yes.............................. 64%
No............................... 21
Undecided........................ 15

By Income
Upper and Middle

Yes.............................. 70%
No............................... 19
Undecided........................ 11

Lower

Yes.............................. 59%
No............................... 23
Undecided........................ 18

By Sex
Men

Yes............................... 61%
No................................ 22
Undecided......................... 17

Women

Yes............................... 67%
No................................ 20
Undecided......................... 13

By Age
21–29 Years

Yes............................... 56%
No................................ 25
Undecided......................... 19

30–49 Years

Yes............................... 65%
No................................ 21
Undecided......................... 14

50 Years and Over

Yes............................... 68%
No................................ 18
Undecided......................... 14

JULY 28
RACE RIOTS

Interviewing Date 7/9–14/43
Survey #298–K   Question #6

What do you think is the real cause of race riots such as the one Detroit has had?

Views of Detroiters

A high percentage of the persons interviewed in Detroit are inclined to ascribe the recent trouble there to "floaters and drifters attracted to the city by war work." Particularly, they are inclined to blame Southerners who have recently taken jobs in Detroit, and the lack of segregation of races both in the city proper and in Detroit factories. Others in Detroit are inclined to blame "young hoodlums" of both

races and the present day "fast living" in the city, as well as bad housing conditions.

Views of Southern Whites

White persons interviewed in states south of the Mason-Dixon line blame lack of segregation, "trying to put Negroes and whites on an equal basis," labor leaders, and politics. Some white persons in the South think the trouble lies in the fact that "the Northerners don't understand the Negro." A few are inclined to blame agitators and ignorant people.

Views of Negroes Outside South

Negroes outside the South who were interviewed in the study ascribe the Detroit riot to "jealousy on the part of the whites," the fact that "white people don't ever try to like us." Others believe the cause to be Southerners who have migrated to the North since the war. A surprising number of Negroes are, however, willing to blame "hoodlums" among their own race as well as among the whites.

JULY 30
PRESIDENTIAL TRIAL HEAT

Interviewing Date 7/9–14/43
Survey #298–K   Question #14

Laborers were asked: If the presidential election were being held today, and Franklin Roosevelt were running for President on the Democratic ticket against Wendell Willkie on the Republican ticket, how do you think you would vote?

Roosevelt.......................... 65%
Willkie............................ 35

Four per cent expressed no opinion.

Union Members Only

Roosevelt.......................... 71%
Willkie............................ 29

JULY 31
PRESIDENTIAL TRIAL HEAT

Interviewing Date 7/9–14/43
Survey #298–K   Question #14a

Farmers were asked: If the presidential election were held today, and Franklin Roosevelt were running for President on the Democratic ticket against Wendell Willkie on the Republican ticket, how do you think you would vote?

Roosevelt.......................... 50%
Willkie............................ 50

Among the nation's farmers, 16% were undecided.

Farmers Outside South

Roosevelt.......................... 48%
Willkie............................ 52

AUGUST 1
PRESIDENTIAL TRIAL HEAT

Interviewing Date 7/9–14/43
Survey #298–K   Question #14c

If the presidential election were being held today and Franklin Roosevelt were running for President on the Democratic ticket against Wendell Willkie on the Republican ticket, how do you think you would vote?

Roosevelt.......................... 59%
Willke............................ 41

Eight per cent expressed no opinion.

By Income
Upper

Roosevelt.......................... 39%
Willkie............................ 61

Middle

Roosevelt.......................... 53%
Willkie............................ 47

Lower

Roosevelt.......................... 66%
Willkie............................ 34

By Age
21–29 Years

Roosevelt.......................... 67%
Willkie............................ 33

30–49 Years

Roosevelt.......................... 58%
Willkie............................ 42

50 Years and Over

Roosevelt.......................... 55%
Willkie............................ 45

By Region
East

Roosevelt.......................... 58%
Willkie............................ 42

Midwest

Roosevelt.......................... 54%
Willkie............................ 46

South

Roosevelt.......................... 71%
Willkie............................ 29

West

Roosevelt.......................... 56%
Willkie............................ 44

AUGUST 2
SOUTHERN FACTORIES AND FREIGHT RATES

Interviewing Date 6/5–10/43
Survey #296   Question #8

Southerners were asked: Would you like to see the South get more factories, that is, become industrial, or should it remain largely agricultural?

Would like more factories........... 71%
Would like to remain agricultural...... 21
Undecided........................ 8

Interviewing Date 6/5–10/43
Survey #296   Question #9

Southerners also were asked: Do you think the South gets a fair break on freight rates?

Yes.............................. 11%
No............................... 89

A large proportion of those polled — 55% — had no opinion.

AUGUST 4
REPUBLICAN PRESIDENTIAL CANDIDATES

Interviewing Date 7/9–14/43
Survey #298–K   Question #13b

Which one of these men would you prefer as the Republican candidate for President next year?

Choice of Ohio Republicans

Bricker........................... 54%
Dewey............................ 19
MacArthur........................ 12
Willkie........................... 11
Stassen........................... 4
Saltonstall........................ *
Warren........................... *

*Less than 1%.

Choice of New York Republicans

Dewey............................ 53%
Willkie........................... 27
MacArthur........................ 8
Bricker........................... 5
Stassen........................... 4
Saltonstall........................ 2
Warren........................... 1

Choice of Pennsylvania Republicans

Dewey............................ 38%
Willkie........................... 33
MacArthur........................ 14
Bricker........................... 9
Stassen........................... 5
Warren........................... 1
Saltonstall........................ *

*Less than 1%.

Choice of Illinois Republicans

Dewey............................ 41%
Willkie........................... 19
MacArthur........................ 18
Bricker........................... 11
Stassen........................... 10
Saltonstall........................ 1
Warren........................... *

*Less than 1%.

AUGUST 6
PARTY STRENGTH

Interviewing Date 6/25–30/43
Survey #297   Question #3

Southerners were asked: Do you think the South would be better off, in general, if there were two political parties of about equal strength instead of one strong party as there is at present?

Yes.............................. 59%
No............................... 41

AUGUST 8
PRESIDENTIAL TRIAL HEAT

Interviewing Date 7/9–14/43
Survey #298–K   Question #14b

If the presidential election were being held today and Franklin Roosevelt were running for President on the Democratic ticket against Thomas E. Dewey on the Republican ticket, how do you think you would vote?

Roosevelt......................... 55%
Dewey............................. 45

By Income
Upper
Roosevelt......................... 43%
Dewey............................. 57

Middle
Roosevelt......................... 50%
Dewey............................. 50

Lower
Roosevelt......................... 61%
Dewey............................. 39

By Occupation
Workers
Roosevelt......................... 59%
Dewey............................. 41

Farmers
Roosevelt......................... 45%
Dewey............................. 55

Farmers Outside South
Roosevelt......................... 39%
Dewey............................. 61

By Age
21–29 Years
Roosevelt......................... 64%
Dewey............................. 36

30–49 Years
Roosevelt......................... 54%
Dewey............................. 46

50 Years and Over
Roosevelt......................... 51%
Dewey............................. 49

By Region
East
Roosevelt......................... 55%
Dewey............................. 45

Midwest
Roosevelt......................... 51%
Dewey............................. 49

South
Roosevelt......................... 72%
Dewey............................. 28

West
Roosevelt......................... 55%
Dewey............................. 45

Union Members Only
Roosevelt......................... 67%
Dewey............................. 33

AUGUST 11
SEPARATE AIR FORCE

Interviewing Date 7/9–14/43
Survey #298–K   Question #5b

Those who were able to define what is meant by a separate air force were asked: Would you approve or disapprove of a separate air force for the United States?

Approve........................... 59%
Disapprove........................ 41

AUGUST 13
LENGTH OF WAR

Interviewing Date 7/30–8/4/43
Survey #299–K   Question #1a

How much longer do you think the war with Germany will last?

Will end this year................... 8%
First half of 1944.................. 31
Last half of 1944................... 34
First half of 1945.................. 6
Last half of 1945.................. 12
During 1946....................... 3
Later than 1946................... 2
Unwilling to guess................. 4

Interviewing Date 7 /30–8 /4 /43
Survey #299–K   Question #1b

How much longer do you think the war with Japan will last?

Will end this year................... 1%
First half of 1944................... 6
Last half of 1944................... 17
First half of 1945................... 9
Last half of 1945................... 27
During 1946........................ 19
Later than 1946.................... 16
Unwilling to guess................. 5

AUGUST 14
SOCIAL SECURITY

Interviewing Date 7 /31–8 /4 /43
Survey #299–K   Question #12

At present farmers, domestic servants, Government employees, and professional persons are not included under Social Security. Do you think the Social Security program should be changed to include these groups?

Yes............................... 64%
No................................ 19
Undecided......................... 17

Interviewing Date 7 /31–8 /4 /43
Survey #299–K   Question #13a

At present the Social Security program provides benefits for old age, death, and unemployment. Would you favor changing the program to include payment of benefits for sickness, disability, doctor, and hospital bills?

Yes............................... 59%
No................................ 29
Undecided......................... 12

Interviewing Date 7 /31–8 /4 /43
Survey #299–K   Question #13b

Those who responded in the affirmative were asked: Would you be willing to pay (or have your husband pay) 6% of your salary or wages in order to make this program possible?

Yes............................... 44%
No................................ 11
Undecided......................... 4
                                   ―――
                                   59%

AUGUST 16
DEMOCRATIC PRESIDENTIAL CANDIDATES

Interviewing Date 7 /30–8 /4 /43
Survey #299–K   Question #8a

Which one of these men would you prefer as Democratic candidate for President next year?

Choice of New York Democrats

Roosevelt.......................... 88%
Wallace............................ 5
McNutt............................. 2
Farley............................. 2
Douglas............................ 1
Winant............................. 1
Byrnes............................. 1

Choice of Pennsylvania Democrats

Roosevelt.......................... 91%
Wallace............................ 5
Farley............................. 2
McNutt............................. 1
Winant............................. 1
Douglas............................ *
Byrnes............................. *

*Less than 1%.

Choice of Illinois Democrats

Roosevelt.......................... 87%
Wallace............................ 5
Farley............................. 4
Byrnes............................. 2
McNutt............................. 1
Douglas............................ 1
Winant............................. *

*Less than 1%.

Choice of Ohio Democrats

Roosevelt	91%
Farley	3
Byrnes	3
Wallace	2
Douglas	1
Winant	*
McNutt	*

*Less than 1%.

Choice of California Democrats

Roosevelt	86%
Wallace	6
Farley	4
McNutt	1
Douglas	1
Byrnes	1
Winant	1

AUGUST 18
DRAFTING OF WOMEN

Interviewing Date 7/30–8/4/43
Survey #299–K   Question #2

Do you favor drafting single women between the ages of 21 and 35 to serve in the WACS, WAVES, or other similar branches of the armed service?

Yes	45%
No	48
Undecided	7

By Sex
Men

Yes	39%
No	54
Undecided	7

Women

Yes	51%
No	42
Undecided	7

Women 21–35 Years

Yes	58%
No	36
Undecided	6

By Region
East

Yes	45%
No	49
Undecided	6

Midwest

Yes	44%
No	48
Undecided	8

South

Yes	44%
No	46
Undecided	10

West

Yes	47%
No	46
Undecided	7

AUGUST 20
POLITICAL CONTRIBUTIONS

Interviewing Date 7/31–8/4/43
Survey #299–K   Question #3a

Do you think labor unions should or should not be allowed to give money to campaign funds of political parties?

Should	17%
Should not	65
Undecided	18

By Political Affiliation
Republicans

Should	14%
Should not	70
Undecided	16

Democrats

Should............................ 20%
Should not........................ 61
Undecided......................... 19

Union Members Only

Should............................ 24%
Should not........................ 58
Undecided......................... 18

Interviewing Date 7/31–8/4/43
Survey #299–K   Question #3b

Do you think business corporations should or should not be allowed to give money to campaign funds of political parties?

Should............................ 23%
Should not........................ 59
Undecided......................... 18

By Political Affiliation
Republicans

Should............................ 23%
Should not........................ 60
Undecided......................... 17

Democrats

Should............................ 24%
Should not........................ 57
Undecided......................... 19

AUGUST 21
CONTROL OF GOVERNMENT

Interviewing Date 7/30–8/4/43
Survey #299–K   Question #10

Most people believe the Government should not be controlled by any one group. However, if you had to choose which would you prefer to have control of the Government— big business or labor unions?

Big business...................... 45%
Labor unions...................... 26
Undecided......................... 29

By Political Affiliation
Republicans

Big business...................... 58%
Labor unions...................... 17
Undecided......................... 25

Democrats

Big business...................... 35%
Labor unions...................... 34
Undecided......................... 31

By Income
Upper

Big business...................... 72%
Labor unions...................... 9
Undecided......................... 19

Middle

Big business...................... 55%
Labor unions...................... 19
Undecided......................... 26

Lower

Big business...................... 33%
Labor unions...................... 34
Undecided......................... 33

AUGUST 22
POSTWAR REFORMS

Interviewing Date 7/30–8/4/43
Survey #299–K   Question #11a

After the war would you like to see many changes or reforms made in the United States, or would you rather have the country remain pretty much the way it was before the war?

Reforms........................... 32%
No reforms........................ 58
Undecided......................... 10

By Age
21–29 Years

Reforms........................... 35%
No reforms........................ 55
Undecided......................... 10

30-49 Years

Reforms	32%
No reforms	58
Undecided	10

50 Years and Over

Reforms	30%
No reforms	60
Undecided	10

Interviewing Date 7/30–8/4/43
Survey #299–K   Question #11b

Those who said they favored reforms were asked: What changes would you like to see after the war?

The people who want changes are rather evenly divided between those who see the need for greater social security, and those who want to return to the pre-New Deal era. The first group advocates better working conditions, prevention of unemployment, better housing conditions, greater distribution of wealth, and more tolerance toward racial and religious minorities.

The second group wants stricter control over labor unions, less government bureaucracy and "meddling" in private affairs, reduced taxes, and a free hand for business enterprise.

AUGUST 25
POLL TAX

Interviewing Date 6/25–30/43
Survey #297   Question #10

Asked of white voters living in those Southern states with a poll tax: Do you think the people in your state should have to continue paying a poll tax in order to vote?

Yes	53%
No	37
No opinion	10

AUGUST 27
PROHIBITION

Interviewing Date 7/30–8/4/43
Survey #299–K   Question #6

If the question of national prohibition should come up again, would you vote wet, or dry?

Dry	34%
Wet	66

Eight per cent expressed no opinion.

By Sex

	Dry	Wet
Men	27%	73%
Women	41	59

By Community Size

Farmers	51%	49%
Towns under 10,000	45	55
10,000–100,000	30	70
100,000 and over	19	81

AUGUST 28
NEGROES

Interviewing Date 6/25–30/43
Survey #297   Question #6

Southern whites were asked: Do you think the present Administration in Washington has done a good job, a fair job, or a poor job in dealing with the Negro problem?

Good job	13%
Fair job	27
Poor job	35
No opinion	25

AUGUST 29
MANPOWER DRAFT

Interviewing Date 7/30–8/4/43
Survey #299–K   Question #9a

If there is a shortage of men and women workers for war industries this fall, should the Government draft persons to fill these jobs?

Yes................................ 79%
No................................ 14
No opinion........................ 7

Interviewing Date 7/30–8/4/43
Survey #299–K   Question #9b, c

If such a law is passed, do you think that you might be drafted to take a war job?

Approximately three out of four said they might be drafted for such service.

Asked of those who thought they might be drafted: If there is a shortage of men and women workers for war industries this fall, should the Government draft persons to fill these jobs?

Yes................................ 91%
No................................ 6
No opinion........................ 3

SEPTEMBER 1
INCOME TAX

Interviewing Date 8/19–24/43
Survey #300–K   Question #11b

Taxpayers were asked: Do you favor the present pay-as-you-go plan for income taxes, or would you prefer to go back to the system of paying each year's income tax the following year?

Favor pay-as-you-go tax.............. 82%
Favor paying the following year....... 12
Undecided......................... 6

SEPTEMBER 3
IMPORTANT PROBLEMS

Interviewing Date 8/19–24/43
Survey #300–K   Question #2a

If you could sit down and talk with the Congressman from your district before he returns to Washington, what questions would you like to ask him about problems here in the United States?

The responses in order of frequency mentioned are:

High cost of living
Gasoline rationing
Postwar problems
The draft
Labor disputes
Government bureaucracy
Racial conflicts and discrimination
Government spending
Farm problem
Pensions and social security
Drinking

SEPTEMBER 4
GERMANY

Interviewing Date 8/19–24/43
Survey #300–K   Question #9

If Hitler offered peace now to all countries on the basis of not going any farther, but of leaving matters as they are now, would you favor or oppose such a peace?

Favor............................. 8%
Oppose............................ 89
Undecided......................... 3

Interviewing Date 8/20–25/43
Survey #300–T   Question #9

If the German military leaders removed Hitler from office and offered peace to all countries on the basis of not going farther, but of leaving matters as they are now, would you favor or oppose such a peace?

Favor............................. 10%
Oppose............................ 84
Undecided......................... 6

The present survey reveals that what little appeasement sentiment there is confines itself largely to voters of the lower educational level — those who had no opportunity to go beyond grade school. On the question of making peace with the German leaders, this group shows a favorable vote of 14%, as compared to a 5% favorable vote among those who attended high school or college.

SEPTEMBER 5
VOTING AGE

Interviewing Date 8/20–25/43
Survey #300–T   Question #1

Congress may be called upon to consider a constitutional amendment to allow persons 18, 19, and 20 years old to vote in elections. Would you like to have your Congressman vote for or against this proposal?

For............................ 52%
Against......................... 42
No opinion...................... 6

By Region
New England and Middle Atlantic

For............................ 53%
Against......................... 41
No opinion...................... 6

East Central

For............................ 50%
Against......................... 45
No opinion...................... 5

West Central

For............................ 50%
Against......................... 45
No opinion...................... 5

South

For............................ 52%
Against......................... 40
No opinion...................... 8

West

For............................ 53%
Against......................... 40
No opinion...................... 7

SEPTEMBER 8
POSTWAR ALLIANCES

Interviewing Date 8/19–24/43
Survey #300–K   Question #7a

After the war, should the United States and Great Britain make a permanent military alliance, that is, agree to come to each other's defense immediately if the other is attacked at any future time?

Yes............................ 61%
No............................. 25
Undecided...................... 14

By Political Affiliation
Republicans

Yes............................ 57%
No............................. 29
Undecided...................... 14

Democrats

Yes............................ 67%
No............................. 19
Undecided...................... 14

By Region
New England and Middle Atlantic

Yes............................ 60%
No............................. 27
Undecided...................... 13

East Central

Yes............................ 58%
No............................. 27
Undecided...................... 15

West Central

Yes............................ 60%
No............................. 26
Undecided...................... 14

South

Yes............................ 72%
No............................. 11
Undecided...................... 17

West

Yes................................ 59%
No................................ 27
Undecided......................... 14

SEPTEMBER 10
THE DRAFT

Interviewing Date 8/26–9/1/43
Survey #301–K   Question #2

The Army can either draft 300,000 single women, aged 21–35, for the WACS for non-fighting jobs, or it can draft the same number of married men with families for the same work. Which plan would you favor?

Single women should be drafted........ 81%
Married men with families should be
    drafted........................... 13
No opinion......................... 6

The vote of all women is 84% in favor of such a draft, and the vote of single women interviewed in the survey is approximately the same. As for the males, the married men with children vote 80% in favor of drafting the women, and the vote of both single and married men combined is 78%.

SEPTEMBER 11
SACRIFICES FOR THE WAR

Interviewing Date 8/26–9/1/43
Survey #301–K   Question #7a

In general, do you think the Government has gone too far or not far enough in asking people to make sacrifices for the war?

Too far............................ 8%
Not far enough..................... 44
About right........................ 40
Undecided.......................... 8

By Income
Upper

Too far............................ 7%
Not far enough..................... 55
About right........................ 30
Undecided.......................... 8

Middle

Too far............................ 7%
Not far enough..................... 48
About right........................ 40
Undecided.......................... 5

Lower

Too far............................ 8%
Not far enough..................... 39
About right........................ 44
Undecided.......................... 9

Interviewing Date 8/26–9/1/43
Survey #301–K   Question #7b

Have you had to make any real sacrifices?

Yes................................ 31%
No................................. 69

SEPTEMBER 12
POSTWAR ALLIANCES

Interviewing Date 8/19–24/43
Survey #300–K   Question #7b

After the war, should the United States and Russia make a permanent military alliance, that is, agree to come to each other's defense immediately if the other is attacked at any future time?

Yes................................ 39%
No................................. 37
Undecided.......................... 24

By Political Affiliation
Republicans

Yes................................ 36%
No................................. 48
Undecided.......................... 21

Democrats

Yes............................. 45%
No............................... 31
Undecided........................ 24

SEPTEMBER 15
THE DRAFT

Interviewing Date 8/26–9/1/43
Survey #301–K   Question #1

If the army needs more men, who do you think should be drafted first — single men who are employed in essential war industries, or fathers who are not employed in essential war industries?

Single men in war industries.......... 68%
Fathers............................ 24
Undecided......................... 8

SEPTEMBER 17
REPUBLICAN PRESIDENTIAL
CANDIDATES

Interviewing Date 8/26–31/43
Survey #301–K   Question #4b

If Harold Stassen, Leverett Saltonstall, Douglas MacArthur, John Bricker, Earl Warren, Robert Taft, Thomas Dewey, and Wendell Willkie were candidates for the Republican presidential nomination next year, which one would you prefer?

Choice of New York Republicans

Dewey............................ 51%
Willkie........................... 29
MacArthur........................ 11
Taft.............................. 3
Bricker........................... 2
Saltonstall........................ 2
Warren........................... 1
Stassen........................... 1

Choice of Pennsylvania Republicans

Dewey............................ 39%
Willkie........................... 30
MacArthur........................ 16
Taft.............................. 7
Bricker........................... 5
Stassen........................... 1
Saltonstall........................ 1
Warren........................... 1

Choice of Illinois Republicans

Dewey............................ 39%
Willkie........................... 20
MacArthur........................ 20
Taft.............................. 10
Bricker........................... 6
Stassen........................... 5
Saltonstall........................ *
Warren........................... *

*Less than 1%.

Choice of Ohio Republicans

Bricker........................... 47%
Dewey............................ 16
Willkie........................... 14
MacArthur........................ 12
Taft.............................. 9
Stassen........................... 2
Warren........................... *
Saltonstall........................ *

*Less than 1%.

Choice of California Republicans

Willkie........................... 35%
Dewey............................ 27
MacArthur........................ 14
Warren........................... 13
Taft.............................. 4
Bricker........................... 3
Stassen........................... 3
Saltonstall........................ 1

Choice of New Jersey Republicans

Dewey............................	43%
Willkie...........................	30
MacArthur........................	14
Taft...............................	8
Bricker...........................	3
Saltonstall........................	1
Stassen...........................	1
Warren...........................	*

*Less than 1%.

Choice of Michigan Republicans

Dewey............................	46%
Willkie...........................	21
MacArthur........................	16
Bricker...........................	8
Taft...............................	5
Stassen...........................	3
Saltonstall........................	1
Warren...........................	*

*Less than 1%.

Choice of Indiana Republicans

Willkie...........................	30%
Dewey............................	30
MacArthur........................	13
Bricker...........................	12
Taft...............................	11
Stassen...........................	4
Saltonstall........................	*
Warren...........................	*

*Less than 1%.

Choice of Massachusetts Republicans

Willkie...........................	45%
Dewey............................	29
Saltonstall........................	16
MacArthur........................	9
Bricker...........................	1
Taft...............................	*
Stassen...........................	*
Warren...........................	*

*Less than 1%.

Choice of Missouri Republicans

Dewey............................	32%
Willkie...........................	27
MacArthur........................	23
Taft...............................	7
Bricker...........................	5
Stassen...........................	4
Warren...........................	1
Saltonstall........................	1

SEPTEMBER 19
PRESIDENTIAL TRIAL HEAT

Interviewing Date 8/26–9/1/43
Survey #301–K   Question #5c

If the presidential election were being held today, and Franklin Roosevelt were running for President on the Democratic ticket against Douglas MacArthur on the Republican ticket, how do you think you would vote?

Roosevelt.........................	58%
MacArthur........................	42

By Region

	Roosevelt	MacArthur
New England........	60%	40%
Middle Atlantic......	60	40
East Central.........	54	46
West Central.........	49	51
South..............	69	31
Mountain...........	51	49
Pacific..............	60	40

By Income

Upper...............	50%	50%
Middle..............	55	45
Lower..............	62	38

By Age

21–29 Years.........	71%	29%
30–49 Years.........	59	41
50 Years and over.....	51	49

Farmers Only

Roosevelt........................... 44%
MacArthur......................... 56

Farmers Outside South Only

Roosevelt........................... 42%
MacArthur......................... 58

SEPTEMBER 22
VOTING AGE

Interviewing Date 8/20–25/43
Survey #300–T   Question #1

Voters in the ten states with the largest number of votes cast in 1940 were asked: Congress may be called upon to consider a constitutional amendment to allow persons 18, 19, and 20 years old to vote in elections. Would you like to have your congressman vote for or against this proposal?

	For	Against	Undecided
New York	55%	40%	5%
Pennsylvania	53	40	7
Illinois	48	47	5
Ohio	51	43	6
California	52	42	6
Michigan	52	44	4
Massachusetts	47	46	7
New Jersey	58	36	6
Missouri	48	47	5
Indiana	49	44	7

SEPTEMBER 24
PRESIDENTIAL TRIAL HEAT

Interviewing Date 8/26–9/1/43
Survey #301–K   Question #6b

If the presidential election were being held today and Henry Wallace were running for President on the Democratic ticket against Thomas Dewey on the Republican ticket, how do you think you would vote?

Dewey.............................. 60%
Wallace............................ 40

By Region

	Dewey	Wallace
New England	69%	31%
Middle Atlantic	64	36
East Central	62	38
West Central	61	39
South	36	64
Rocky Mountain	61	39
Pacific Coast	64	36

Interviewing Date 9/16–21/43
Survey #302–J   Question #5a

If the presidential election were being held today and Franklin Roosevelt were running for President on the Democratic ticket against Thomas Dewey on the Republican ticket, how do you think you would vote?

Dewey.............................. 45%
Roosevelt.......................... 55

SEPTEMBER 25
POLITICAL REFUGE IN SWEDEN

Special Survey

Swedes were asked: Should Sweden give persons holding power in belligerent or occupied countries asylum if they seek refuge, or should such persons not be admitted to the country?

Would admit anyone................. 5%
Would admit some.................. 61
Would admit none.................. 17
Undecided......................... 17

SEPTEMBER 26
INTERNATIONAL POLICE FORCE

Interviewing Date 8/26–9/1/43
Survey #301–K   Question #13d

All persons who could explain the term "international police force" were asked: Taking into account the arguments for, and those against, how do you yourself stand — are you for or against an international police force?

For	75%
Against	17
Undecided	8

Reforms	32%
Remain as was	58
Undecided	10

SEPTEMBER 29
POSTWAR EMPLOYMENT OUTLOOK

Special Survey

American soldiers stationed in England were asked: Do you have a definite job ready for you when you return after the war?

Yes	62%
No	27
Plan to continue schooling	3
Don't know	8

Those who responded in the negative were asked: Do you think it will be hard to find a job?

Yes	24%
No	56
Don't know	20

The soldiers also were asked: Which way do you think there will be more jobs after the war — if the Republicans are in power in Washington, or if the Democrats are?

Republicans in power	11%
Democrats in power	45
No difference	23
Don't know	21

OCTOBER 1
POSTWAR REFORMS

Interviewing Date 7/31–8/4/43
Survey #299–K   Question #11a

After the war would you like to see many changes or reforms made in the nation, or would you rather the country remain pretty much as it was before the war?

OCTOBER 2
VEGETARIANS

Interviewing Date 9/16–21/43
Survey #302–V   Question #7a

Some people in the United States are vegetarians, that is, people who eat no fish, fowl, or meat of any kind. Do you happen to be a vegetarian?

When the percentage claiming to be vegetarians is applied to the number of adults in the population, excluding members of the armed forces, the total comes to 2,800,000.

OCTOBER 3
MOST IMPORTANT PROBLEM

Interviewing Date 8/26–9/1/43
Survey #301–K   Question #5a

Looking ahead to the next presidential term, that is, from 1945 through 1949, what do you think will be the greatest problem facing this country?

Jobs, economic readjustment	58%
Lasting peace	13
Reducing taxes, paying off national debt	11
Food shortages	6
Labor problems	4
Growing bureaucracy in government	3
Others	15

OCTOBER 6
LENGTH OF WAR

Interviewing Date 9/16–21/43
Survey #302–V   Question #1

How much longer do you think the war with Germany will last?

Six months	12%
One year	28
Eighteen months	38
Two years	11
More than two years	4
No opinion	7

Interviewing Date 9/16–21/43
Survey #302–V   Question #2

How much longer do you think the war with Japan will last?

Six months	1%
One year	7
Eighteen months	20
Two years	40
More than two years	25
No opinion	7

OCTOBER 8
POSTWAR ALLIANCES

Interviewing Date 9/16–21/43
Survey #302–J   Question #3

After the war should the United States and China make a permanent military alliance, that is, agree to come to each other's defense immediately if the other is attacked at any future time?

Yes	56%
No	23
Undecided	21

OCTOBER 9
PROHIBITION

Special Survey

Soldiers stationed in England were asked: If the question of national prohibition in the United States should come up again would you vote wet or dry?

Wet	85%
Dry	9
No opinion	6

OCTOBER 13
TREATIES

Interviewing Date 8/26–31/43
Survey #301–K   Question #8b

Which of these would you favor as the best way to have peace treaties approved after the war: 1.) Approval only by the President; 2.) Approval by the President and a majority of the whole Congress; or 3.) Approval by the President and two-thirds of the Senate?

Approval by President	7%
Approval by President and majority of Congress	54
Approval by President and two-thirds of Senate	25
No opinion	14

OCTOBER 15
WAR BONDS

Interviewing Date 10/1–5/43
Survey #303–K   Question #11a

Have you, yourself, purchased any war bonds or stamps during the last four weeks?

Yes	34%
No	66

Interviewing Date 10/1–5/43
Survey #303–K   Question #11b

Do you or your family happen to own any war bonds or stamps?

By Region

	Yes	No
New England and Middle Atlantic	88%	12%
East Central	85	15
West Central	82	18
South	68	32
Mt. states and Pacific Coast	85	15

By Education

	Yes	No
Grade School	73%	27%
High School	91	9
College	94	6

OCTOBER 16
LABOR SHORTAGE

Interviewing Date 9/16–21/43
Survey #302–J   Question #10a

Do you think there is a shortage of workers in war plants in this country?

Yes............................... 36%
No................................ 42
Undecided......................... 22

OCTOBER 17
PARTY STRENGTH

Interviewing Date 10/1–5/43
Survey #303–K   Question #2

Leaving the question of candidates aside, if the presidential election were being held today, which party would you vote for — the Democratic or the Republican?

Democratic........................ 54%
Republican........................ 46

By Region

	Dem.	Rep.
New England	51%	49%
Middle Atlantic	52	48
East Central	49	51
West Central	46	54
South	76	24
Rocky Mountain	55	45
Pacific Coast	53	47

OCTOBER 20
REPUBLICAN PRESIDENTIAL CANDIDATES

Interviewing Date 9/16–21/43
Survey #302–J   Question #4c

Missouri Republicans were asked: Which one of these men would you prefer as the Republican candidate for President next year?

Dewey............................. 28%
MacArthur......................... 26
Willkie........................... 25
Taft.............................. 7
Bricker........................... 7
Stassen........................... 5
Warren............................ 1
Saltonstall....................... 1

OCTOBER 23
THE DRAFT

Interviewing Date 8/26–9/1/43
Survey #301–K   Question #2

The army can either draft 300,000 single women, aged 21–35, for the WACS for non-fighting jobs, or it can draft the same number of married men with families for the same work. Which plan would you favor?

Single women should be drafted....... 73%
Married men with families should be
  drafted......................... 19
No opinion........................ 8

Views of Women

Single women should be drafted....... 77%
Married men with families should be
  drafted......................... 16
No opinion........................ 7

Views of Single Women

Single women should be drafted....... 72%
Married men with families should be
  drafted......................... 23
No opinion........................ 5

Views of Married Men

Single women should be drafted....... 70%
Married men with families should be
  drafted......................... 21
No opinion........................ 9

OCTOBER 25
REPUBLICAN PRESIDENTIAL CANDIDATES

Interviewing Date 9/16–21/43
Survey #302–J   Question #4c

Republicans were asked: Which one of these men would you prefer as the Republican candidate for President next year?

Dewey............................ 32%
Willkie........................... 28
MacArthur........................ 19
Bricker........................... 8
Stassen........................... 6
Taft.............................. 5
Warren............................ 1
Saltonstall....................... 1

By Region
New England

Dewey............................ 30%
Willkie........................... 40
MacArthur........................ 15
Bricker........................... 2
Others............................ 13

Middle Atlantic

Dewey............................ 41%
Willkie........................... 29
MacArthur........................ 17
Bricker........................... 4
Others............................ 9

East Central

Dewey............................ 30%
Willkie........................... 18
MacArthur........................ 19
Bricker........................... 19
Others............................ 14

West Central

Dewey............................ 30%
Willkie........................... 26
MacArthur........................ 20
Bricker........................... 5
Others............................ 19

South

Dewey............................ 24%
Willkie........................... 35
MacArthur........................ 26
Bricker........................... 5
Others............................ 10

Mountain

Dewey............................ 26%
Willkie........................... 33
MacArthur........................ 22
Bricker........................... 6
Others............................ 13

Pacific

Dewey............................ 25%
Willkie........................... 32
MacArthur........................ 17
Bricker........................... 4
Others............................ 22

OCTOBER 27
GERMANY

Interviewing Date 10/8–13/43
Survey #304–K   Question #4

Suppose the German army gets rid of Hitler, gives up all the countries Germany has conquered, and offers to make peace. If that happens, should we make peace, or should we continue the war until the German army is completely defeated?

Make peace if German army gives up
  conquered lands.................. 24%
Continue fighting.................... 70
Undecided......................... 6

By Sex
Men

Make peace if German army gives up
  conquered lands.................. 19%
Continue fighting.................... 76
Undecided......................... 5

Women

Make peace if German army gives up
   conquered lands.................. 30%
Continue fighting.................... 64
Undecided........................ 6

OCTOBER 29
WARTIME SHORTAGES

Interviewing Date 9/16–21/43
Survey #302–J   Question #6a

   *Aside from food, what things that you
need very much right now for your home or
family would you buy if you could get them?*

The following are listed in order of frequency
of mention:

Tires and tubes
Stockings
Refrigerators
Automobiles
Washing machines
Electric irons
Shoes
Hairpins
Stoves
Kitchen utensils
Elastic articles
Radios
Safety pins

OCTOBER 30
IMPORTANT PROBLEMS

Interviewing Date 10/8–13/43
Survey #304–K   Question #2

   *If you could sit down and talk with the
Congressman from your district before he
returns to Washington, what questions
would you like to ask him about problems
here in the United States?*

The following are listed in order of frequency
of mention:

Postwar employment
High cost of living
Rationing
Taxation
The draft
Government bureaucracy
Labor disputes

OCTOBER 31
WENDELL WILLKIE

Interviewing Date 10/1–5/43
Survey #303–K   Question #10a

   *We would like to find out what things
people like and dislike about Wendell
Willkie. What do you, yourself, like most
about him?*

The following are listed in order of frequency
of mention:

Sincerity, frankness, ability
Winning personality
Fine appearance
Speaking ability
Open-mindedness
Progressiveness
Interest in world affairs

Interviewing Date 10/1–5/43
Survey #303–K   Question #10b

   *Now what would you say you like least
about him?*

The following are listed in order of frequency
of mention:

Too changeable
Talks too much
Judgments are not sound
Too much like Roosevelt
Lacks political experience
Is a Republican

Interviewing Date 10/1–5/43
Survey #303–K   Question #10d

   *Do you think Mr. Willkie could handle
big problems like unemployment better
than President Roosevelt, as well as
Roosevelt, or not so well?*

Better............................ 16%
As well........................... 30
Not so well....................... 41
No opinion........................ 13

Republicans

Better............................ 30%
As well........................... 36
Not so well....................... 23
No opinion........................ 11

Democrats

Better............................ 5%
As well........................... 24
Not so well....................... 58
No opinion........................ 13

Interviewing Date 10/1–5/43
Survey #303–K   Question #10e

Do you think Mr. Willkie would be good at handling problems which will come up after the war concerning our relations with other nations?

Yes............................... 53%
No................................ 24
No opinion........................ 23

By Political Affiliation
Republicans

Yes............................... 62%
No................................ 22
No opinion........................ 16

Democrats

Yes............................... 46%
No................................ 28
No opinion........................ 26

NOVEMBER 3
TAXES

Interviewing Date 10/8–13/43
Survey #304–K   Question #3

If the Government decided to raise taxes, which would you prefer — that the extra

amount be raised by a national sales tax on everything people buy, or that the extra amount be raised by increasing everybody's income taxes?

Prefer national sales tax.............. 53%
Prefer increasing income tax......... 34
No opinion........................ 13

By Occupation
Professional and Business

Prefer national sales tax.............. 61%
Prefer increasing income tax......... 30
No opinion........................ 9

White Collar

Prefer national sales tax.............. 57%
Prefer increasing income tax......... 31
No opinion........................ 12

Skilled Workers

Prefer national sales tax.............. 55%
Prefer increasing income tax......... 32
No opinion........................ 13

Unskilled Workers

Prefer national sales tax.............. 46%
Prefer increasing income tax......... 37
No opinion........................ 17

Farmers

Prefer national sales tax.............. 53%
Prefer increasing income tax......... 37
No opinion........................ 10

Views of Income Tax Payers

Prefer national sales tax.............. 57%
Prefer increasing income tax......... 31
No opinion........................ 12

NOVEMBER 5
WARTIME PROSPERITY

Interviewing Date 10/8–13/43
Survey #304–K   Question #1a

Are you now able to buy or do things that you could not afford a year ago?

Yes................................ 29%
No................................ 71%

By Age

	Yes	No
21–29 Years.......	43%	57%
30–49 Years.......	30	70
50 Years and over.	19	81

By Occupation

	Yes	No
Professional and business	23%	77%
White collar............	31	69
Skilled labor..........	30	70
Unskilled labor........	31	69
Farmers................	30	70

Interviewing Date 10/8–13/43
Survey #304–K   Question #1b

Those who responded in the affirmative were asked: What things can you now buy?

The following are listed in order of frequency of mention:

Finer clothing
House furnishings
Better food
Home improvements
Automobiles
Real estate
Jewelry
Gifts
Everything

NOVEMBER 6
FREE ENTERPRISE

Interviewing Date 10/8–13/43
Survey #304–K   Question #8

Will you tell me in your own words what you understand by the term "free enterprise"?

The great majority of Americans are either without any idea of the term free enterprise or hold an erroneous one.

Only one out of every four women can give a correct definition of free enterprise. Only about one out of six among unskilled laboring groups knows what the term means. Only one out of every four Democrats has a clear idea about its meaning; only three out of ten Republicans can define the term. Best able to define the term, from a percentage point of view, are professional and business people, including teachers, small shopkeepers, etc. About half among these can give a satisfactory definition.

NOVEMBER 7
PARTY STRENGTH

Interviewing Date 10/8–13/43
Survey #304–K   Question #9

Midwestern farmers were asked: Leaving the question of candidates aside, if the presidential election were being held today, which party would you vote for?

Democratic........................ 40%
Republican........................ 60

NOVEMBER 10
POSTWAR WAGES

Interviewing Date 10/8–13/43
Survey #304–K   Question #13a

Do you think the wages now being paid in industries producing war materials will continue to be as high when these same industries produce peace-time goods?

Yes................................ 9%
No................................ 85
No opinion........................ 6

Interviewing Date 10/8–13/43
Survey #304–K   Question #13c

What do you think the average weekly wage will be for these same workers after the war?

The median response was $30—$20 below the estimated $50 the average war plant worker now receives weekly.

NOVEMBER 12
LEND-LEASE

Interviewing Date 10/8–13/43
Survey #304–K   Question #5b

What is your understanding of our agreement with England on lend-lease materials sent to her — is England supposed to pay us back in some way after the war, or are we supposed to give her this material?

England supposed to pay............. 57%
U. S. supposed to give.............. 13
Don't know........................ 30

Interviewing Date 10/8–13/43
Survey #304–K   Question #5c

Does England furnish us with any war materials under the lend-lease program?

Yes............................... 30%
No................................ 23
No opinion........................ 47

Interviewing Date 10/8–13/43
Survey #304–K   Question #5a

Those who understood the workings of lend-lease were asked: Do you think England should pay us back in some way after the war for the lend-lease material we send her?

Yes............................... 50%
No................................ 50

NOVEMBER 13
WAGES

Interviewing Date 10/8–13/43
Survey #304–T   Question #12b

In some war plants, workers are paid on a piecework basis, that is, they are paid for what they actually turn out, and not on an hourly or daily basis. Would you favor or oppose putting such a plan into operation in all war plants in this country?

Favor............................. 54%
Oppose............................ 33
Undecided......................... 13

Employed Persons Only

Favor............................. 46%
Oppose............................ 42
Undecided......................... 12

NOVEMBER 14
REPUBLICAN PRESIDENTIAL
CANDIDATES

Interviewing Date 10/8–13/43
Survey #304–K   Question #10

Republicans were asked: If you had to choose between Thomas Dewey and Wendell Willkie for the Republican presidential nomination, which one would you prefer?

Dewey............................. 55%
Willkie........................... 35
Undecided......................... 10

By Region
New England and Middle Atlantic

Dewey............................. 52%
Willkie........................... 40
Undecided......................... 8

East Central

Dewey............................. 69%
Willkie........................... 23
Undecided......................... 8

West Central

Dewey............................. 57%
Willkie........................... 32
Undecided......................... 11

South

Dewey............................ 36%
Willkie........................... 45
Undecided........................ 19

West

Dewey............................ 48%
Willkie........................... 42
Undecided........................ 10

NOVEMBER 17
COMPULSORY MILITARY TRAINING

Interviewing Date 10/28–11/2/43
Survey #305–K   Question #1

After this war is over, do you think every young man should be required to serve one year in the army or navy?

Yes.............................. 63%
No............................... 29
No opinion....................... 8

By Sex
Men

Yes.............................. 67%
No............................... 28
No opinion....................... 5

Women

Yes.............................. 60%
No............................... 30
No opinion....................... 10

NOVEMBER 19
NATIONAL SALES TAX

Interviewing Date 10/28–11/2/43
Survey #305–K   Question #7

It is suggested that a nation-wide sales tax be put on everything people buy, except bare necessities. On less essential things, the tax would start at 2 cents out of every dollar, and rise to 30 or 40 cents out of every dollar on luxuries. Would you favor or oppose a sales tax of this type?

Favor............................ 45%
Oppose........................... 46
Undecided........................ 9

NOVEMBER 21
STRIKES

Interviewing Date 10/28–11/2/43
Survey #305–K   Question #2a

What do you think is the chief cause of strikes in this country?

The following are listed in order of frequency of mention:

Unjust demands of workers
Labor leaders who seek personal power
Wartime conditions
Higher prices
Government has not accepted its responsibility to prevent strikes
Foreign saboteurs

Interviewing Date 10/28–11/2/43
Survey #305–K   Question #2b

What do you think should be done about strikes?

The following are listed in order of frequency of mention:

Strong measures such as punishment of strikers and strike leaders
Forbid strikes by law
Draft strikers into army
Compulsory arbitration
Give strikers increases

Interviewing Date 10/29–11/3/43
Survey #305–T   Question #2

Should Congress pass a law forbidding strikes in war industries, or should the workers in war industries continue to have the right to strike?

Make strikes illegal................. 69%
Permit strikes...................... 23
No opinion........................ 8

NOVEMBER 24
GERMANY

Interviewing Date 11/11–16/43
Survey #306–K   Question #11

What do you think we should do with Germany, as a country, after the war?

Strict supervision.................... 49%
Destroy completely.................. 21
Rehabilitate........................ 19
Do nothing........................ 4
No opinion........................ 14
                                      107%

(Note: table adds to more than 100% as some people gave more than one reply.)

NOVEMBER 26
RUSSIA

Interviewing Date 11/12–17/43
Survey #306–T   Question #10b

Have you heard or read about the Moscow Conference between Cordell Hull, Anthony Eden, and V. M. Molotov?

Yes............................... 70%
No............................... 30

Interviewing Date 11/12–17/43
Survey #306–T   Question #10c

Those who responded in the affirmative were asked: Did the Moscow Conference produce greater or smaller results than you expected?

Greater........................... 48%
Same as expected.................. 13
Smaller........................... 8
No opinion........................ 31

Interviewing Date 11/11–16/43
Survey #306–K   Question #10b

Do you think Russia can be trusted to cooperate with us after the war is over?

Yes............................... 47%
No............................... 27
No opinion........................ 26

By Political Affiliation
Republicans

Yes............................... 43%
No............................... 34
No opinion........................ 23

Democrats

Yes............................... 50%
No............................... 21
No opinion........................ 29

Those Who Heard of Moscow Conference

Yes............................... 57%
No............................... 27
No opinion........................ 16

NOVEMBER 27
REPUBLICAN PRESIDENTIAL CANDIDATES

Interviewing Date 9/16–21/43
Survey #302–J   Question #4c

Ohio Republicans were asked: Which one of the following would you prefer as the Republican presidential candidate next year?

Bricker........................... 40%
Dewey............................ 18
Willkie........................... 16
MacArthur........................ 16
Taft.............................. 7
Stassen........................... 3

NOVEMBER 28
ROOSEVELT ADMINISTRATION

Interviewing Date 11/11–16/43
Survey #306–K   Question #3

Those voters in New York, New Jersey, and Kentucky who shifted to the Republican party at the last election were asked: What do you like least about the way the Roosevelt Administration is handling things?

The following reasons are listed in order of frequency of mention:

Incompetent and dictatorial management of home affairs
Coddling of labor
Government extravagance
Failure to keep prices down
Bad job of rationing

DECEMBER 1
LABOR UNIONS

Interviewing Date 11/11–16/43
Survey #306–K   Question #12

Do you think all labor unions should be required to register with the Federal Government and report the amount of money they take in and spend each year?

Yes............................. 75%
No............................. 10
No opinion...................... 15

Union Members Only

Yes............................. 71%
No............................. 15
No opinion...................... 14

DECEMBER 3
THE DRAFT

Interviewing Date 11/12–17/43
Survey #306–T   Question #1

The army can either draft 300,000 single women aged 21–35 for the WAC's for non-fighting jobs, or it can draft the same number of married men with families for the same work. Which plan do you favor?

Single women should be drafted....... 78%
Married men with families should be drafted.......................... 15
No opinion...................... 7

By Sex
Men

Single women should be drafted....... 75%
Married men with families should be drafted.......................... 17
No opinion...................... 8

Women

Single women should be drafted....... 81%
Married men with families should be drafted.......................... 12
No opinion...................... 7

DECEMBER 8
FARM SUBSIDIES

Interviewing Date 11/26–12/1/43
Survey #307–T   Question #13b

Will you tell me in your own words what you think is meant by a price subsidy to farmers?

Farmers

Correct............................ 35%
Incorrect......................... 65

Non-farmers

Correct............................ 29%
Incorrect......................... 71

DECEMBER 10
REPUBLICAN PRESIDENTIAL CANDIDATES

Interviewing Date 11/25–12/1/43
Survey #307–K   Question #6

Pennsylvania Republicans were asked: Which one of the following would you like to see nominated for President by the Republican party next year?

Dewey.......................... 36%
Willkie.......................... 29
MacArthur....................... 19
Taft............................. 6
Bricker.......................... 5
Stassen.......................... 5
Others.......................... *

*Less than 1%.

DECEMBER 11
REPUBLICAN PRESIDENTIAL CANDIDATES

Interviewing Date 11/25–12/1/43
Survey #307–K   Question #6a

New Jersey Republicans were asked: Which one of the following would you like to see nominated for President by the Republican party next year?

Dewey	39%
Willkie	30
MacArthur	17
Taft	7
Bricker	4
Stassen	3
Others	*

*Less than 1%.

DECEMBER 15
GEORGE PATTON

Interviewing Date 11/28–12/3/43
Survey #307   Question #1a

Have you heard or read about the incident in which General Patton slapped an enlisted man, to whom he later apologized?

Yes	85%
No	15

Interviewing Date 11/28–12/3/43
Survey #307   Question #1b

Those who responded in the affirmative were asked: Leaving aside questions of military policy, which way would you as a citizen have greater confidence in the army high command — if General Patton is brought back to the United States, or if he is left in charge of his troops in Italy?

Brought back to U.S.	22%
Left in charge of his troops in Italy	70
Undecided	8

DECEMBER 17
REPUBLICAN PRESIDENTIAL CANDIDATES

Interviewing Date 11/25–12/1/43
Survey #307–K   Question #6b

Massachusetts Republicans were asked: Which one of the following would you like to see nominated for President by the Republican party next year?

Willkie	40%
Dewey	30
Saltonstall	15
MacArthur	9
Bricker	4
Stassen	2
Others	*

*Less than 1%.

DECEMBER 18
REPUBLICAN PRESIDENTIAL CANDIDATES

Interviewing Date 11/25–12/1/43
Survey #307–K   Question #6c

Kentucky Republicans were asked: Which one of the following would you like to see nominated for President by the Republican party next year?

Willkie	31%
Dewey	26
MacArthur	20
Taft	13
Bricker	8
Warren	1
Stassen	1
Others	*

*Less than 1%.

DECEMBER 19
REPUBLICAN PRESIDENTIAL CANDIDATES

Interviewing Date 11/25–12/1/43
Survey #307–K   Question #7

Republicans were asked: Which one of the following would you like to see nominated for President by the Republican party next year?

Dewey	36%
Willkie	25
MacArthur	15
Bricker	10
Stassen	6
Taft	5
Saltonstall	1
Warren	1
Eric Johnston	1

By Region
New England

Dewey	35%
Willkie	39
MacArthur	9
Bricker	5
Others	12

Middle Atlantic

Dewey	42%
Willkie	27
MacArthur	14
Bricker	7
Others	10

East Central

Dewey	37%
Willkie	13
MacArthur	15
Bricker	21
Others	14

West Central

Dewey	34%
Willkie	22
MacArthur	16
Bricker	6
Others	22

South

Dewey	25%
Willkie	34
MacArthur	21
Bricker	9
Others	11

Mountain

Dewey	32%
Willkie	28
MacArthur	20
Bricker	5
Others	15

Pacific

Dewey	29%
Willkie	28
MacArthur	10
Bricker	6
Others	22

DECEMBER 22
EXECUTIVE BRANCH PRIVILEGE

Interviewing Date 11/26–12/1/43
Survey #307–T   Question #5a

A member of Congress has suggested that heads of Government departments and agencies appear before Congress, when requested, to answer questions about what their departments are doing. Do you approve or disapprove of this idea?

Approve	72%
Disapprove	7
No opinion	21

DECEMBER 24
DEMOCRATIC PRESIDENTIAL CANDIDATES

Interviewing Date 11/25–12/1/43
Survey #307–K   Question #6

Democrats were asked: Will you look over these possible candidates (on card) and tell me which one you would like to see as the next President of the United States?

Roosevelt.......................... 85%
Wallace........................... 6
Farley............................ 3
Byrd.............................. 2
McNutt........................... 1
Marshall.......................... 1
Byrnes............................ 1
Douglas........................... 1

By Region
New England and Middle Atlantic
Roosevelt.......................... 88%
Wallace........................... 5
Farley............................ 3
Byrd.............................. 2
Others............................ 2

East Central
Roosevelt.......................... 83%
Wallace........................... 7
Farley............................ 3
Byrd.............................. 1
Others............................ 6

West Central
Roosevelt.......................... 82%
Wallace........................... 9
Farley............................ 3
Byrd.............................. 1
Others............................ 5

South
Roosevelt.......................... 81%
Wallace........................... 4
Farley............................ 3
Byrd.............................. 5
Others............................ 7

West
Roosevelt.......................... 89%
Wallace........................... 5
Farley............................ 2
Byrd.............................. 1
Others............................ 3

DECEMBER 25
BIBLE READING

Interviewing Date 11/26–12/1/43
Survey #307–T   Question #16a

Have you, yourself, read the Bible or any part of it at home within the last month?

Yes............................... 64%
No................................ 36

By Age
21–29 Years
Yes............................... 57%
No................................ 43

30–49 Years
Yes............................... 60%
No................................ 40

50 Years and Over
Yes............................... 71%
No................................ 29

Interviewing Date 11/26–12/1/43
Survey #307–T   Question #16b

Those who responded in the affirmative were asked: What book or part of the Bible do you think is the most interesting?

New Testament or part of it.......... 29%
Old Testament or part of it.......... 26
No opinion........................ 45

DECEMBER 26
ROOSEVELT ADMINISTRATION

Interviewing Date 11/25–12/1/43
Survey #307–K   Question #2b

Farmers were asked: What do you dislike most about the way the Roosevelt Administration is handling things?

Government extravagance............ 20%
Incompetent and dictatorial management
    of home affairs, especially with farm
    problems........................ 15
Coddling of labor.................. 13
Farm programs not effective........ 11
Bad job of rationing............... 6
Failure to keep prices down........ 2
Miscellaneous...................... 13
No complaint....................... 20

DECEMBER 29
TWO TERM AMENDMENT

Interviewing Date 11/25–12/1/43
Survey #307–K   Question #3a

Would you favor adding a law to the Constitution that would prevent any President of the United States from being reelected in the future if he has already served two terms?

Yes............................... 54%
No................................ 46

Seven per cent expressed no opinion.

Interviewing Date 11/25–12/1/43
Survey #307–T   Question #3b

Would you favor changing the term of office of the President hereafter to one six-year term with no reelection?

Yes............................... 34%
No................................ 66

Ten per cent expressed no opinion.

DECEMBER 31
POSTWAR SHORTAGES

Interviewing Date 11/25–12/1/43
Survey #307–K   Question #1a

For a year or two after the war, should people in the United States continue to put up with shortages of butter, sugar, meat, and other rationed food products in order to give food to people who need it in Europe?

Yes............................... 67%
No................................ 21
Qualified......................... 4
Undecided......................... 8

By Sex
Men

Yes............................... 62%
No................................ 26
Qualified......................... 5
Undecided......................... 7

Women

Yes............................... 71%
No................................ 16
Qualified......................... 4
Undecided......................... 9

1944

Interviewing Date 11 /25–30 /43
Survey #307–T   Question #12a

Asked of Republicans: Would you approve or disapprove if both the Republican and Democratic parties agreed to name Cordell Hull Secretary of State again after the next election?

Approve............................ 52%
Disapprove........................ 22
Undecided......................... 26

JANUARY 1
PROHIBITION

Interviewing Date 7 /30–8 /4 /43
Survey #299–K   Question #6

If the question of national prohibition should come up again, would you vote wet or dry?

Wet............................... 66%
Dry............................... 34

Seven per cent expressed no opinion.

By Sex

	Wet	Dry
Men	73%	27%
Women	59	41

JANUARY 3
BIPARTISAN FOREIGN POLICY

Interviewing Date 11 /25–30 /43
Survey #307–K   Question #12a

Asked of Republicans: Do you think that both the Republicans and the Democrats should take exactly the same stand for an active part in world affairs in their party platforms in 1944?

Yes............................... 58%
No................................ 21
Undecided......................... 21

JANUARY 5
THE DRAFT

Interviewing Date 12 /17–22 /43
Survey #308–K   Question #1a

Do you think the draft is being handled fairly in your neighborhood?

Yes............................... 75%
No................................ 25

No significant differences of attitude toward the draft were found by age groups or by size of community. Nor is there much difference between the opinions of men and women.

JANUARY 6
REPUBLICAN PRESIDENTIAL CANDIDATES

Special Survey

Asked of Republicans: Whom would you like to see the Republican party nominate for President?

Midwest Only

Dewey............................ 35%
Willkie........................... 22
MacArthur........................ 13
Bricker........................... 13
Taft.............................. 11
Stassen........................... 4
Eric Johnston..................... 2

JANUARY 8
THE FLU

Interviewing Date 12/17–22/43
Survey #308–K   Question #17a

Do any of the people in your home, including yourself, have the flu at the present time?

Yes.............................. 13%
No.............................. 87

JANUARY 10
POSTWAR GERMANY

Interviewing Date 11/11–16/43
Survey #306–K   Question #11

What do you think we should do with Germany, as a country, after the war?

Supervise and control............... 44%
Destroy her as a political entity, divide
    into small states.................. 21
Rehabilitate, re-educate, encourage trade 17
Miscellaneous and no opinion........ 18

JANUARY 12
PARTY STRENGTH

Interviewing Date 12/17–22/43
Survey #308–K   Question #9a

Have you ever voted in the election district where you now live?

Yes.............................. 75%
No.............................. 25

Interviewing Date 12/17–22/43
Survey #308–K   Question #9b

Asked of those who responded in the affirmative: Which party would you like to see win the presidential election next November?

Democratic........................ 49%
Republican........................ 51

Interviewing Date 12/17–22/43
Survey #308–K   Question #9c

Asked of those who responded in the negative: Which party would you like to see win the presidential election next November?

Democratic........................ 61%
Republican........................ 39

JANUARY 14
REPUBLICAN PRESIDENTIAL CANDIDATES

Special Survey

Asked of Republicans: Whom would you like to see the Republican party nominate for President?

Maine, New Hampshire, and Vermont Only

Willkie........................... 55%
Dewey............................ 29
MacArthur........................ 10
Bricker........................... 4
Stassen........................... 2

JANUARY 15
HOME CANNING

Interviewing Date 10/29–11/3/43
Survey #305–K   Question #16a

Did you or your family put up (home can) any cans or jars of food this year?

Yes.............................. 75%
No.............................. 25

Interviewing Date 10/29–11/3/43
Survey #305–K   Question #16b

Asked of those who responded in the affirmative: How many cans or jars did you put up?

Median average.......... 165 cans or jars

JANUARY 17
PARTY STRENGTH

Interviewing Date 1 /6–11 /44
Survey #309–K   Question #7

Which party would you like to see win the presidential election in November?

By Sex

	Republican	Democratic
Men	49%	51%
Women	47	53

JANUARY 18
DEMOCRATIC PRESIDENTIAL CANDIDATES

Interviewing Date 1 /6–11 /44
Survey #309–K   Question #8a

Asked of Democrats: Whom would you like to see the Democratic party nominate for President?

By Sex
Men

Roosevelt	82%
Wallace	7
Farley	3
Byrd	2
Marshall	2
Byrnes	2
Others	2

Women

Roosevelt	88%
Wallace	4
Farley	2
Byrd	2
Others	4

JANUARY 18
REPUBLICAN PRESIDENTIAL CANDIDATES

Interviewing Date 1 /6–11 /44
Survey #309–K   Question #8b

Asked of Republicans: Whom would you like to see the Republican party nominate for President?

By Sex
Men

Dewey	38%
Willkie	27
MacArthur	13
Bricker	11
Stassen	7
Eric Johnston	2
Others	2

Women

Dewey	37%
Willkie	23
MacArthur	19
Bricker	9
Stassen	7
Others	5

JANUARY 22
DURATION OF WAR

Interviewing Date 1 /6–11 /44
Survey #309–K   Question #1a

How much longer do you think the war with Germany will last?

Will end in first half of 1944	12%
Will end in second half of 1944	46
Will end in 1945	31
Will end in 1946	5
Will end in 1947 or later	1
No opinion	5

Interviewing Date 1 /6–11 /44
Survey #309–K   Question #1b

How much longer do you think the war with Japan will last?

Will end in first half of 1944	1%
Will end in second half of 1944	5
Will end in 1945	33
Will end in 1946	33
Will end in 1947 or later	20
No opinion	8

JANUARY 24
"MUSTERING OUT" PAY
FOR VETERANS

Interviewing Date 1/6–11/44
Survey #309–K   Question #11a

A bill in Congress provides that members of the armed forces be given a certain sum of money by the Government when they leave the service. Do you approve or disapprove of this idea?

Approve............................ 88%
Disapprove......................... 8
No opinion......................... 4

Interviewing Date 1/6–11/44
Survey #309–K   Question #11b

Would you, personally, be willing to pay higher taxes in order to make these payments possible?

Yes................................ 70%
No................................. 20
Undecided.......................... 10

JANUARY 26
REPUBLICAN PRESIDENTIAL
CANDIDATES

Special Survey

Asked of Wisconsin Republicans: Whom would you like to see the Republican party nominate for President?

Dewey.............................. 40%
Willkie............................ 20
MacArthur.......................... 15
Stassen............................ 11
Bricker............................ 8
Eric Johnston...................... 6

JANUARY 28
WAR REPORTING

Interviewing Date 1/6–11/44
Survey #309–K   Question #6

Should newspapers and newsreels show war pictures with men dead or wounded on battlefields, or should such pictures not be shown?

Should be shown.................... 56%
Should not......................... 36
No opinion......................... 8

JANUARY 29
SERVICEWOMEN'S UNIFORMS

Interviewing Date 1/6–11/44
Survey #309–K   Question #3a

Which uniform worn by women in the armed services do you like best — the Wac, Wave, Spar, Marine?

Wac uniform....................... 15%
Wave or Spar uniform.............. 49
Marine uniform.................... 26
No opinion........................ 10

By Sex
Men

Wac uniform....................... 17%
Wave or Spar uniform.............. 40
Marine uniform.................... 28
No opinion........................ 15

Women

Wac uniform....................... 13%
Wave or Spar uniform.............. 57
Marine uniform.................... 24
No opinion........................ 6

JANUARY 31
REPUBLICAN PRESIDENTIAL
CANDIDATES

Interviewing Date 1/20–25/44
Survey #310–K   Question #6a

Asked of Republicans: Whom would you like to see the Republican party nominate for President?

Dewey............................ 42%
Willkie........................... 23
MacArthur........................ 18
Bricker........................... 8
Stassen........................... 6
Others............................ 3

By Region
New England
Willkie........................... 41%
Dewey............................ 38
MacArthur........................ 14
Bricker........................... 3
Others............................ 4

Middle Atlantic
Dewey............................ 54%
Willkie........................... 21
MacArthur........................ 16
Bricker........................... 4
Others............................ 5

East Central
Dewey............................ 35%
Bricker........................... 21
MacArthur........................ 17
Willkie........................... 15
Others............................ 12

West Central
Dewey............................ 40%
Willkie........................... 23
MacArthur........................ 19
Bricker........................... 3
Others............................ 15

South
Willkie........................... 36%
Dewey............................ 30
MacArthur........................ 24
Bricker........................... 6
Others............................ 4

Mountain
Dewey............................ 37%
Willkie........................... 26
MacArthur........................ 21
Bricker........................... 7
Others............................ 9

West
Dewey............................ 35%
Willkie........................... 27
MacArthur........................ 12
Bricker........................... 4
Others............................ 22

FEBRUARY 2
REPUBLICAN PRESIDENTIAL CANDIDATES

Special Survey

Asked of Missouri Republicans: Whom would you like to see the Republican party nominate for President?

Dewey............................ 41%
MacArthur........................ 27
Willkie........................... 24
Stassen........................... 3
Bricker........................... 3
Others............................ 2

FEBRUARY 4
REPUBLICAN PRESIDENTIAL CANDIDATES

Special Survey

Asked of Michigan Republicans: Whom would you like to see the Republican party nominate for President?

Dewey............................ 47%
Willkie........................... 19
MacArthur........................ 16
Bricker........................... 8
Stassen........................... 7
Others............................ 3

FEBRUARY 5
REPUBLICAN PRESIDENTIAL CANDIDATES

Special Survey

Asked of Minnesota Republicans: Whom would you like to see the Republican party nominate for President?

Stassen	31%
Willkie	28
Dewey	25
MacArthur	12
Bricker	3
Warren	1

Dewey	41%
MacArthur	29
Willkie	20
Bricker	5
Stassen	3
Others	2

FEBRUARY 6
PARTY STRENGTH

Interviewing Date 1/20–25/44
Survey #310–K   Question #5

Which party would you like to see win the presidential election this November?

Labor Union Members Only

Democratic	64%
Republican	36

C.I.O. Members Only

Democratic	66%
Republican	34

FEBRUARY 7
DEMOCRATIC PRESIDENTIAL CANDIDATES

Interviewing Date 1/20–25/44
Survey #310–K   Question #6a

Asked of Democratic labor union members: Whom would you like to see the Democratic party nominate for President?

Roosevelt	88%
Wallace	6
Farley	3
Others	3

FEBRUARY 7
REPUBLICAN PRESIDENTIAL CANDIDATES

Interviewing Date 1/20–25/44
Survey #310–K   Question #6b

Asked of Republican labor union members: Whom would you like to see the Republican party nominate for President?

FEBRUARY 9
WARTIME PROHIBITION

Interviewing Date 1/21–26/44
Survey #310–T   Question #1

There is a bill in Congress which would forbid the sale of liquor in this country until the war is over. Do you think this bill should be passed?

Yes	36%
No	64

Five per cent expressed no opinion.

By Sex

	Yes	No
Men	30%	70%
Women	42	58

FEBRUARY 11
REBUILDING OF RUSSIAN CITIES

Interviewing Date 12/17–22/43
Survey #308–T   Question #2

After the war should three or four million German men be sent to Russia to help rebuild destroyed cities there?

Yes	50%
No	30
No opinion	20

FEBRUARY 12
AID TO EUROPEAN CHILDREN

Special Survey

Should the United States send food by neutral Swedish ships to the children of

France, Belgium, Holland, and other countries now occupied by German troops?

Yes............................. 65%
No.............................. 22
No opinion...................... 13

By Sex
Men

Yes............................. 62%
No.............................. 26
No opinion...................... 12

Women

Yes............................. 67%
No.............................. 18
No opinion...................... 15

FEBRUARY 14
NATIONAL SERVICE ACT

Interviewing Date 2/3–8/44
Survey #311–K   Question #7a

If there is a shortage of men and women workers for war industries this spring, should the Government draft persons to fill these jobs?

Yes............................. 65%
No.............................. 26
No opinion...................... 9

Interviewing Date 2/3–8/44
Survey #311–K   Question #7b

Do you think there is a good chance that you might be called to take a war job?

Yes............................. 20%
No.............................. 66
Don't know...................... 14

Interviewing Date 2/3–8/44
Survey #311–K   Question #7c

Do you think there is a shortage of workers in war plants in this country as a whole now?

Yes............................. 16%
No.............................. 59
No opinion...................... 25

Interviewing Date 2/4–9/44
Survey #311–T   Question #7a

Have you heard or read about President Roosevelt's proposal for a national service law?

Yes............................. 62%
No.............................. 38

Interviewing Date 2/4–9/44
Survey #311–T   Question #7b

If so, what is your understanding of what this proposed law stands for?

Among those who had heard about the proposal, approximately one-third gave a vague or incorrect definition of what it seeks to do, or were unable to define it. The remaining two-thirds gave a reasonably accurate definition.

FEBRUARY 16
REPUBLICAN PRESIDENTIAL CANDIDATES

Special Survey

Asked of New Jersey Republicans: Whom would you like to see the Republican party nominate for President?

Dewey.......................... 55%
Willkie......................... 21
MacArthur...................... 16
Stassen......................... 4
Bricker......................... 3
Others.......................... 1

FEBRUARY 18
REPUBLICAN PRESIDENTIAL CANDIDATES

Special Survey

Asked of Pennsylvania Republicans: Whom would you like to see the Republican party nominate for President?

Dewey............................. 51%
Willkie............................ 22
MacArthur......................... 18
Stassen............................ 4
Bricker............................ 3
Warren............................ 1
Eric Johnston...................... 1

By Region

	Democratic	Republican
New England........	52%	48%
Middle Atlantic......	53	47
East Central........	45	55
West Central........	42	58
South..............	71	29
Mountain........	48	52
Pacific.	49	51

FEBRUARY 19
"FEATHERBEDDING"

Interviewing Date 2/3–8/44
Survey #311–K   Question #5

Some labor unions make jobs for more of their members by requiring employers to hire more men than are actually needed to do a particular job. The unions say this is necessary in order to give work to all their members. Do you think a law should be passed stopping this practice?

Yes............................... 62%
No................................ 17
No opinion........................ 21

Union Members Only

Yes............................... 49%
No................................ 30
No opinion........................ 21

FEBRUARY 21
PARTY STRENGTH

Interviewing Date 2/3–8/44
Survey #311–K   Question #6

Which party do you want to see win the presidential election next fall — the Republican or Democratic?

Democratic........................ 51%
Republican........................ 49

FEBRUARY 23
REPUBLICAN PRESIDENTIAL CANDIDATES

Special Survey

Asked of New York State Republicans: Whom would you like to see the Republican party nominate for President?

Dewey............................. 57%
Willkie............................ 20
MacArthur......................... 16
Bricker............................ 4
Stassen............................ 2
Eric Johnston...................... 1

FEBRUARY 25
SCRAP PAPER DRIVE

Interviewing Date 2/3–8/44
Survey #311–K   Question #1a

Have you heard or read about the present drive to collect scrap paper?

Yes............................... 75%
No................................ 25

Interviewing Date 2/3–8/44
Survey #311–K   Question #1b

Are you saving scrap paper regularly?

Yes............................... 53%
No................................ 47

Interviewing Date 2/3–8/44
Survey #311–K   Question #1c

*Has anyone called at your home in the
present scrap drive to collect your scrap
paper?*

Yes.............................. 45%
No............................... 55

Interviewing Date 2/3–8/44
Survey #311–K   Question #1d

*Is there scrap paper around your home now
that could be collected if someone came for
it?*

The survey finds that there are about 13.5
million households containing scrap paper
that could be collected.

FEBRUARY 25
ELECTION FORECAST

Interviewing Date 11/11–16/43
Survey #306–K   Question #2a

*Regardless of what party you yourself
favor, which party do you think will win the
presidential election?*

By Political Affiliation
Democrats

Democratic........................ 65%
Republican........................ 17
No opinion........................ 18

Republicans

Democratic........................ 31%
Republican........................ 49
No opinion........................ 20

FEBRUARY 28
REPUBLICAN PRESIDENTIAL
CANDIDATES

Interviewing Date 2/18–23/44
Survey #312–K   Question #4a

*Asked of Republicans: Whom would you
like to see the Republican party nominate
for President?*

Dewey............................ 45%
Willkie........................... 21
MacArthur........................ 19
Bricker........................... 7
Stassen........................... 5
Others............................ 3

FEBRUARY 29
REPUBLICAN PRESIDENTIAL
CANDIDATES

Special Survey

*Asked of Iowa Republicans: Whom would
you like to see the Republican party
nominate for President?*

Dewey............................ 40%
Willkie........................... 25
MacArthur........................ 19
Stassen........................... 13
Bricker........................... 2
Others............................ 1

MARCH 3
REPUBLICAN PRESIDENTIAL
CANDIDATES

Special Survey

*Asked of Ohio Republicans: Whom would
you like to see the Republican party
nominate for President?*

Bricker........................... 41%
Dewey............................ 25
MacArthur........................ 18
Willkie........................... 11
Stassen........................... 3
Eric Johnston..................... 2

MARCH 4
WHITE HOUSE PRESS CONFERENCE

Interviewing Date 2/3–8/44
Survey #311–K   Question #2

*Suppose you could attend a press conference
at the White House — what question would*

you like to ask the President about problems here in the United States?

The following are listed according to frequency of mention:

How will we avoid a depression after the war?
Will there be jobs for all of us?
Will the soldiers be able to find work?
Why are the tax forms so complicated?
Why is so much money being wasted by our Government?
Why doesn't the farmer get a higher price for his crops?
Why do we have to have ceilings on farm prices?
Why aren't strikes stopped?
When is the Government going to crack down on labor unions?

MARCH 6
DEMOCRATIC VICE-PRESIDENTIAL CANDIDATES

Interviewing Date 2/18–23/44
Survey #312–K   Question #4a

Asked of Democrats: Whom would you like to see the Democratic party nominate for Vice President this year?

Wallace	46%
Hull	21
Farley	13
Rayburn	12
Byrnes	5
Byrd	3

By Region
East

Wallace	47%
Hull	22
Farley	14
Rayburn	9
Byrnes	5
Byrd	3

Midwest

Wallace	46%
Hull	20
Rayburn	14
Farley	12
Byrnes	5
Byrd	3

South

Wallace	42%
Hull	20
Farley	15
Rayburn	14
Byrnes	6
Byrd	3

West

Wallace	47%
Hull	21
Farley	13
Rayburn	11
Byrnes	5
Byrd	3

MARCH 8
REPUBLICAN PRESIDENTIAL CANDIDATES

Special Survey

Asked of Republicans: Whom would you like to see the Republican party nominate for President?

Connecticut Only

Dewey	50%
Willkie	26
MacArthur	17
Bricker	4
Stassen	3

West Virginia

Dewey	48%
MacArthur	23
Willkie	15
Bricker	13
Stassen	1

MARCH 10
DRAFTING OF WOMEN

Interviewing Date 2/18–23/44
Survey #312–T   Question #1

The army can either draft 300,000 single women aged 21–35 for the Wacs for non-fighting jobs, or it can draft the same number of married men with families for the same work. Which plan would you favor?

Draft single women................. 75%
Draft married men................. 16
No opinion........................ 9

By Sex
Men

Draft single women................. 72%
Draft married men................. 19
No opinion........................ 9

Women

Draft single women................. 78%
Draft married men................. 13
No opinion........................ 9

MARCH 11
REPUBLICAN PRESIDENTIAL CANDIDATES

Special Survey

Asked of Kansas Republicans: Whom would you like to see the Republican party nominate for President?

Dewey............................ 58%
MacArthur........................ 20
Willkie.......................... 11
Bricker.......................... 6
Stassen.......................... 5

MARCH 13
REPUBLICAN PRESIDENTIAL CANDIDATES

Interviewing Date 1/20–25/44
Survey #310–K   Question #6b

Asked of Republicans: If your choice of Republican candidates for President were limited to Wendell Willkie and Thomas Dewey, which would you prefer?

Dewey............................ 64%
Willkie.......................... 27
Undecided........................ 9

By Region
New England

Dewey............................ 50%
Willkie.......................... 42
Undecided........................ 8

Middle Atlantic

Dewey............................ 69%
Willkie.......................... 25
Undecided........................ 6

East Central

Dewey............................ 74%
Willkie.......................... 16
Undecided........................ 10

West Central

Dewey............................ 63%
Willkie.......................... 27
Undecided........................ 10

South

Dewey............................ 47%
Willkie.......................... 39
Undecided........................ 14

Mountain

Dewey............................ 63%
Willkie.......................... 29
Undecided........................ 8

West

Dewey	56%
Willkie	36
Undecided	8

Bricker Supporters Only

Dewey	77%
Willkie	11
Undecided	12

MacArthur Supporters Only

Dewey	60%
Willkie	18
Undecided	22

Stassen Supporters Only

Dewey	55%
Willkie	31
Undecided	14

MARCH 15
TAXES

Interviewing Date 2/18–23/44
Survey #312–K   Question #11d

Do you regard the amount of taxes you have to pay as fair?

Yes	90%
No	10

In general a slightly larger number of complaints about tax rates comes from business and professional men, salaried workers, and persons who have had to file tax returns in previous years, than among wage earners, unskilled workers, and new taxpayers. However, the differences are not large.

MARCH 17
REPUBLICAN PRESIDENTIAL CANDIDATES

Special Survey

Asked of Illinois Republicans: Whom would you like to see the Republican party nominate for President?

Dewey	43%
MacArthur	28
Bricker	10
Willkie	7
Stassen	6
Eric Johnston	5
Warren	1

MARCH 18
REPUBLICAN PRESIDENTIAL CANDIDATES

Special Survey

Asked of Maine Republicans: Whom would you like to see the Republican party nominate for President?

Willkie	57%
Dewey	23
MacArthur	14
Bricker	3
Stassen	3

MARCH 20
TAXES

Interviewing Date 2/18–23/44
Survey #312–K   Question #9

If larger taxes are voted by Congress, which would you prefer — a national sales tax on everything people buy, or an increase in everyone's income tax?

Sales tax	55%
Income tax	34
No opinion	11

By Political Affiliation
Democrats

Sales tax	51%
Income tax	38
No opinion	11

Republicans

Sales tax	60%
Income tax	30
No opinion	10

Interviewing Date 2/18–23/44
Survey #312–K   Question #8a

Would you be willing to pay higher taxes this year so that the Government could pay a larger part of our present war costs?

Yes	48%
No	42
No opinion	10

Interviewing Date 2/18–23/44
Survey #312–K   Question #8b

Asked of those willing to pay higher taxes: How much more would you be willing to pay — one quarter, one half, three quarters, or twice as much as you pay now?

Twenty-six per cent said they would be willing to pay a quarter more. They constitute nearly two-thirds of all those who named a specific increase. Another 8% said they would be willing to pay one-half more, while the rest indicated other proportions or said that they did not know yet just how much more they could pay.

MARCH 21
REPUBLICAN PRESIDENTIAL CANDIDATES

Special Survey

Asked of Oklahoma Republicans: Whom would you like to see the Republican party nominate for President?

Dewey	36%
MacArthur	27
Willkie	22
Bricker	10
Eric Johnston	3
Stassen	2

MARCH 24
REPUBLICAN PRESIDENTIAL CANDIDATES

Special Survey

Asked of Kentucky Republicans: Whom would you like to see the Republican party nominate for President?

Dewey	37%
Willkie	30
MacArthur	25
Bricker	7
Warren	1

MARCH 25
"VICTORY GARDENS"

Interviewing Date 3/3–8/44
Survey #313–K   Question #9b

Do you plan to have a vegetable garden this year?

The survey found that approximately 19.6 million persons plan a "victory garden."

MARCH 27
PARTY BEST FOR PEACE AND PROSPERITY

Interviewing Date 2/18–23/44
Survey #312–K   Question #5

Which party do you think is more likely to bring the war to a successful end at the earliest time — the Democratic or the Republican?

Democratic	36%
Republican	22
No difference	29
Undecided	13

Interviewing Date 2/18–23/44
Survey #312–K   Question #7

After the war, which party do you think will make the best peace arrangements?

Democratic........................ 32%
Republican........................ 29
No difference..................... 25
Undecided........................ 14

Interviewing Date 2/18–23/44
Survey #312–K   Question #6

After the war, which party do you think will bring the greatest prosperity and the greatest number of jobs?

Republican........................ 34%
Democratic........................ 31
No difference..................... 22
Undecided........................ 13

Union Members Only

Democratic........................ 41%
Republican........................ 24
No difference..................... 21
No opinion........................ 14

MARCH 29
REPUBLICAN PRESIDENTIAL CANDIDATES

Special Survey

Asked of Indiana Republicans: Whom would you like to see the Republican party nominate for President?

Dewey............................ 47%
Willkie........................... 18
MacArthur........................ 16
Bricker........................... 13
Eric Johnston..................... 4
Stassen........................... 2

MARCH 31
DURATION OF WAR

Interviewing Date 3/3–8/44
Survey #313–K   Question #7a

When do you think the war with Germany will end?

First half of 1944................. 2%
Second half of 1944............... 31
First half of 1945................. 39
Second half of 1945............... 7
1946.............................. 12
1947 or later..................... 2
Undecided........................ 7

Interviewing Date 3/3–8/44
Survey #313–K   Question #7b

When do you think the war with Japan will end?

1944.............................. 6%
1945.............................. 33
1946.............................. 32
1947 or later..................... 21
Undecided........................ 8

APRIL 1
PARTY STRENGTH

Special Survey

Asked in Texas: Which party would you like to see win the presidential election in November?

Democratic........................ 74%
Republican........................ 26

APRIL 3
DRAFTING OF WOMEN

Interviewing Date 3/17–22/44
Survey #314–K   Question #2

The army can either draft 300,000 single women aged 21–35 for the Wacs for non-fighting jobs, or it can draft the same number of married men with families for the same work. Which plan would you prefer?

Draft single women................ 76%
Draft fathers..................... 16
No opinion........................ 8

Single Women 21–35 Years Only

Draft single women.................. 75%
Draft fathers....................... 18
No opinion......................... 7

APRIL 5
IRELAND

Interviewing Date 3/17–22/44
Survey #314–K   Question #8a

Have you heard or read about the United States' request to the Irish Free State to send German and Japanese representatives home?

Three out of four stated they had heard or read about the United States' request.

Interviewing Date 3/17–22/44
Survey #314–K   Question #8b

Asked of those who stated they had heard or read about the United States' request: Ireland has said that because she is neutral in this war she will not send the German and Japanese representatives home. Do you think the United States should do anything further about this?

Yes.............................. 66%
No............................... 30
No opinion........................ 4

APRIL 7
POLITICS

Special Survey

Asked in Florida: Which party would you like to see win the presidential election this year?

Democratic....................... 66%
Republican....................... 34

Asked of Florida Republicans: Whom would you like to see the Republican party nominate for President?

Willkie.......................... 12%
Dewey............................ 12
MacArthur........................ 5
Bricker.......................... 3
Stassen.......................... 2
                                 ———
                                 34%

Asked of Florida Democrats: Whom would you like to see the Democratic party nominate for President?

Roosevelt........................ 53%
Byrnes........................... 4
Byrd............................. 3
Wallace.......................... 3
McNutt........................... 2
Farley........................... 1
                                 ———
                                 66%

APRIL 8
POLITICS

Special Survey

Asked in Georgia: Which party would you like to see win the presidential election this year?

Democratic....................... 77%
Republican....................... 23

Asked of Georgia Republicans: Whom would you like to see the Republican party nominate for President?

MacArthur........................ 9%
Dewey............................ 7
Willkie.......................... 5
Bricker.......................... 1
Stassen.......................... 1
                                 ———
                                 23%

Asked of Georgia Democrats: Whom would you like to see the Democratic party nominate for President?

Roosevelt	71%
Byrd	2
Wallace	1
Farley	1
Byrnes	1
McNutt	1
	77%

	Roosevelt	Wallace	Byrnes	Others
Alabama	72%	3%	1%	3%
Florida	53	3	4	6
Georgia	71	1	1	4
Louisiana	69	3	1	7
Mississippi	62	3	3	13
South Carolina	60	1	15	12
Texas	65	3	1	5

APRIL 10
POLITICS

Special Survey

Asked in the Deep South: Which party would you like to see win the presidential election this year?

	Democratic	Republican
Alabama	79%	21%
Florida	66	34
Georgia	77	23
Louisiana	80	20
Mississippi	81	19
South Carolina	88	12
Texas	74	26

Asked of Republicans in the Deep South: Whom would you like to see the Republican party nominate for President?

	Dewey	Willkie	MacArthur	Others
Alabama	9%	2%	6%	4%
Florida	12	12	5	5
Georgia	7	5	9	2
Louisiana	7	6	2	5
Mississippi	6	3	8	2
South Carolina	4	2	5	1
Texas	10	5	6	5

Asked of Democrats in the Deep South: Whom would you like to see the Democratic party nominate for President?

APRIL 12
REPUBLICAN PRESIDENTIAL CANDIDATES

Special Survey

Asked of Michigan Republicans: Whom would you like to see the Republican party nominate for President?

Dewey	47%
Willkie	19
MacArthur	16
Bricker	8
Stassen	7
Others	3

APRIL 13
REPUBLICAN PRESIDENTIAL CANDIDATES

Special Survey

Asked of Republicans: Whom would you like to see the Republican party nominate for President?

California Only

Dewey	46%
Willkie	25
Warren	11
MacArthur	6
Bricker	6
Stassen	4
Eric Johnston	2

Oregon Only

Dewey............................ 46%
Willkie............................ 23
MacArthur........................ 18
Stassen........................... 6
Warren........................... 4
Bricker........................... 3

Washington Only

Dewey............................ 38%
Willkie............................ 27
Eric Johnston...................... 14
Stassen........................... 7
MacArthur........................ 7
Bricker........................... 4
Warren........................... 3

APRIL 17
CONSCRIPTION

Interviewing Date 3/31–4/4/44
Survey #315–T   Question #3b

Do you think that men who are turned down by the army because they are not physically fit for fighting, but who are able to work in war plants, should be taken into the army and given jobs in order to free young men in war plants for combat service?

Yes.............................. 78%
No.............................. 15
No opinion....................... 7

APRIL 19
BOMBING OF RELIGIOUS BUILDINGS

Interviewing Date 3/31–4/4/44
Survey #315–K   Question #9

If military leaders believe it will be necessary to bomb historic religious buildings and shrines in Europe, would you approve or disapprove of their bombing them?

Approve.......................... 74%
Disapprove....................... 19
No opinion....................... 7

By Religion
Protestants

Approve.......................... 75%
Disapprove....................... 19
No opinion....................... 6

Catholics

Approve.......................... 63%
Disapprove....................... 28
No opinion....................... 9

APRIL 21
COMBAT PAY

Interviewing Date 3/31–4/4/44
Survey #315–K   Question #1a

It has been suggested that American servicemen who take part in actual fighting should get a 50% increase in pay. Should Congress pass such a law?

Yes.............................. 70%
No.............................. 23
No opinion....................... 7

By Region
New England and Middle Atlantic

Yes.............................. 72%
No.............................. 21
No opinion....................... 7

East Central

Yes.............................. 71%
No.............................. 22
No opinion....................... 7

West Central

Yes.............................. 68%
No.............................. 26
No opinion....................... 6

South

Yes.............................. 67%
No.............................. 25
No opinion....................... 8

West

Yes.............................. 67%
No............................... 25
No opinion....................... 8

Interviewing Date 3/31–4/4/44
Survey #315–K   Question #1b

Would you yourself be willing to pay higher taxes to make this possible?

Yes.............................. 60%
No............................... 8
No opinion....................... 9
Disapprove of plan.............. 23

APRIL 22
IRELAND

Interviewing Date 3/31–4/4/44
Survey #315–K   Question #11a

Have you heard or read about the United States request to Ireland that it expel Axis representatives?

Yes.............................. 60%
No............................... 40

Interviewing Date 3/31–4/4/44
Survey #315–K   Question #11b

Asked of those who replied in the affirmative: Do you think we should stop all trade with the Irish Free State if it doesn't send home the German and Japanese representatives?

Yes.............................. 69%
No............................... 19
No opinion....................... 12

APRIL 24
PRESIDENTIAL TRIAL HEAT

Interviewing Date 3/31–4/4/44
Survey #315–K   Question #14a

If the war is still going on and President Roosevelt runs for the Democrats against Governor Dewey for the Republicans, how do you think you will vote?

Roosevelt........................ 55%
Dewey............................ 45

Interviewing Date 3/31–4/4/44
Survey #315–K   Question #14b

If the war is over and President Roosevelt runs for the Democrats against Governor Dewey for the Republicans, how do you think you will vote?

Roosevelt........................ 42%
Dewey............................ 58

Interviewing Date 3/31–4/4/44
Survey #315–K   Question #14c

Suppose the war is still going on in Europe, but it looks as though it might be over in a few weeks or a few months, how do you think you will vote — for President Roosevelt or Governor Dewey?

Roosevelt........................ 51%
Dewey............................ 49

APRIL 26
PRESIDENTIAL TENURE

Interviewing Date 3/17–22/44
Survey #314–K   Question #12

Would you favor adding a law to the Constitution that would prevent any President of the United States from being reelected in the future if he has already served two terms?

Favor............................ 57%
Oppose........................... 43

By Political Affiliation

	Favor	Oppose
Democrats.................	32%	68%
Republicans...............	84	16

APRIL 28
PRESIDENTIAL TRIAL HEAT

Special Survey

> Asked of farmers: If the presidential election were held today and if Franklin Roosevelt were running against Thomas Dewey, which one would you vote for?

Roosevelt........................... 42%
Dewey.............................. 58

Farmers Outside South Only

Roosevelt........................... 35%
Dewey.............................. 65

APRIL 29
PRESIDENTIAL TRIAL HEAT

Special Survey

> Asked of labor union members: If the presidential election were held today and if Franklin Roosevelt were running against Thomas Dewey, which one would you vote for?

Roosevelt........................... 65%
Dewey.............................. 35

APRIL 30
REPUBLICAN PRESIDENTIAL CANDIDATES

Interviewing Date 4/14–19/44
Survey #316–K   Question #4a

> Asked of Republicans: Whom would you like to see the Republican party nominate for President?

Dewey.............................. 55%
MacArthur.......................... 20
Bricker............................ 9
Stassen............................ 7
Willkie............................ 7
Others............................. 2

By Region
New England

Dewey.............................. 57%
MacArthur.......................... 17
Bricker............................ 4
Stassen............................ 4
Others............................. 18

Middle Atlantic

Dewey.............................. 62%
MacArthur.......................... 19
Bricker............................ 7
Stassen............................ 4
Others............................. 8

East Central

Dewey.............................. 53%
MacArthur.......................... 20
Bricker............................ 19
Stassen............................ 5
Others............................. 3

West Central

Dewey.............................. 54%
MacArthur.......................... 19
Stassen............................ 17
Bricker............................ 4
Others............................. 6

South

Dewey.............................. 48%
MacArthur.......................... 27
Bricker............................ 6
Stassen............................ 4
Others............................. 15

Mountain

Dewey.............................. 53%
MacArthur.......................... 18
Stassen............................ 8
Bricker............................ 6
Others............................. 15

Pacific

Dewey.............................. 52%
MacArthur.......................... 14
Stassen............................ 8
Bricker............................ 6
Others............................. 20

Interviewing Date 4/14–19/44
Survey # 316–K   Question #4b

Asked of Douglas MacArthur supporters: Who is your second choice?

Dewey............................. 11%
Bricker............................ 2
Stassen........................... 2
Others............................ 5
                                 20%

MAY 3
REPUBLICAN PRESIDENTIAL CANDIDATES

Special Survey

Asked of Ohio Republicans: Whom would you like to see the Republican party nominate for President?

Bricker........................... 43%
Dewey............................ 36
MacArthur........................ 14
Stassen........................... 3
Willkie............................ 3
Eric Johnston..................... 1

MAY 5
PRESIDENTIAL TRIAL HEAT

Interviewing Date 3/31–4/4/44
Survey #315–K   Question #14c

Asked of business people and professionals: Suppose the war were still going on in Europe, but it seemed as if it might end in a few weeks or a few months, how do you think you would vote for President if the candidates were Franklin Roosevelt and Thomas Dewey?

Roosevelt......................... 42%
Dewey............................ 58

MAY 6
MONTGOMERY-WARD CASE

Special Survey

Do you think the Government did the right thing in taking over the Montgomery-Ward plants, or was it a mistake?

Government did right thing........... 39%
Government made a mistake.......... 61

Twelve per cent expressed no opinion.

MAY 8
CIVILIAN ATTITUDE TOWARD WAR

Interviewing Date 4/14–19/44
Survey #316–K   Question #2a

Soldiers back from the war front say most people in this country do not take the war seriously enough. Do you think this is true?

Yes............................... 66%
No............................... 26
No opinion........................ 8

MAY 10
BIPARTISAN FOREIGN POLICY

Interviewing Date 4/14–19/44
Survey #316–T   Question #10a

Secretary Cordell Hull recently suggested that a committee made up of Republicans as well as Democrats work with him in shaping our country's foreign policy. Do you think this is a good suggestion?

Yes............................... 83%
No............................... 6
No opinion........................ 11

By Political Affiliation
Democrats

Yes............................... 81%
No............................... 7
No opinion........................ 12

Republicans

Yes............................... 86%
No................................ 6
No opinion........................ 8

MAY 12
POLITICS

Interviewing Date 4/27–5/2/44
Survey #317–K   Question #5

Do you think that President Roosevelt will run for a fourth term?

Yes............................... 79%
No................................ 8
No opinion........................ 13

Interviewing Date 4/27–5/2/44
Survey #317–K   Question #3b

Whom would you like to see as the next President of the United States?

Choice of Those Who Named a Democrat

Roosevelt......................... 89%
Hull.............................. 4
Wallace........................... 3
Barkley........................... 2
Byrnes............................ 1
McNutt............................ 1

Interviewing Date 4/27–5/2/44
Survey #317–K   Question #3a

Asked of all those who named President Roosevelt as their first choice: Who is your second choice for President?

A Republican candidate............. 50%
A Democratic candidate............. 50

MAY 13
ELEANOR ROOSEVELT

Interviewing Date 4/27–5/2/44
Survey #317–K   Question #2

What do you think about the trips that Mrs. Eleanor Roosevelt makes?

Approve........................... 36%
Disapprove........................ 45
Not our concern................... 13
No opinion........................ 6

By Sex
Men

Approve........................... 33%
Disapprove........................ 50
Not our concern, no opinion........ 17

Women

Approve........................... 40%
Disapprove........................ 39
Not our concern, no opinion........ 21

MAY 15
WAGES AND PRICES

Interviewing Date 4/14–19/44
Survey #316–T   Question #8a

Do you think prices on most products should be allowed to go up, or should prices be held where they are now?

Let prices go up................... 4%
Hold at present level.............. 91
No opinion........................ 5

Interviewing Date 4/14–19/44
Survey #316–T   Question #8b

Do you think wages for most workers should be allowed to go up, or should wages be held where they are now?

Let wages go up.................... 18%
Hold at present level.............. 72
No opinion........................ 10

MAY 17
RATIFICATION OF TREATIES

Interviewing Date 4/27–5/1/44
Survey #317–K   Question #7a

When the war is over it will be necessary for the Allies to decide on peace terms for the Axis. Which of these three ways would you, personally, favor as the best way to have peace treaties approved — have them approved solely by the President, have them approved by the President and a majority of the whole Congress, or have them approved by the President and two-thirds of the Senate?

President only...................... 7%
President and a majority of the whole Congress........................ 60
President and two-thirds of the Senate... 19
No opinion........................ 14

MAY 19
POSTWAR AFFAIRS

Interviewing Date 4/27–5/1/44
Survey #317–K   Question #8

Do you agree with those people who think that the United States should take an active part in world affairs after the war, or with those people who think we should stay out of world affairs?

Take active part.................... 73%
Stay out........................... 18
No opinion........................ 9

Interviewing Date 4/27–5/1/44
Survey #317–K   Question #9

Should the Government take steps now, before the end of the war, to try to set up with our allies a world organization to maintain the future peace of the world, or should we wait until after the war is won?

Act now........................... 58%
Wait till war ends.................. 30
No opinion........................ 12

By Region
New England and Middle Atlantic

Act now........................... 55%
Wait till war ends.................. 34
No opinion........................ 11

East Central

Act now........................... 59%
Wait till war ends.................. 26
No opinion........................ 15

West Central

Act now........................... 62%
Wait till war ends.................. 30
No opinion........................ 8

South

Act now........................... 54%
Wait till war ends.................. 33
No opinion........................ 13

West

Act now........................... 62%
Wait till war ends.................. 28
No opinion........................ 10

MAY 20
AUSTRALIAN MILITARY BASES

Special Survey

Asked of Australians: It has been suggested that we should let the American navy and air forces use bases in Australia after the war. Do you favor or oppose this suggestion?

Favor............................. 65%
Oppose........................... 20
Undecided........................ 15

All those in favor of granting bases were asked whether this arrangement should be permanent, or whether the bases should simply be leased for a period of time. The weight of sentiment was strongly in favor of leasing.

MAY 21
PRESIDENTIAL TRIAL HEAT

Interviewing Date 5/12–17/44
Survey #318–T   Question #7a

If the presidential election were held today and if Franklin Roosevelt were running against Thomas Dewey, which one would you vote for?

Roosevelt........................... 51%
Dewey............................. 49

MAY 24
PACIFIC ISLANDS

Interviewing Date 4/27–5/2/44
Survey #317–K   Question #16

After the war should the United States keep all of the Japanese islands we conquer between Hawaii and the Philippines?

Yes................................ 69%
No................................ 17
No opinion......................... 14

MAY 26
PRESIDENTIAL TRIAL HEAT

Special Survey

Asked in New York State: If the presidential election were held today and if Franklin Roosevelt were running against Thomas Dewey, which one would you vote for?

Roosevelt........................... 52%
Dewey............................. 48

MAY 27
MONTGOMERY-WARD CASE

Interviewing Date 5/11–16/44
Survey #318–K   Question #5c

Have you heard or read anything about the Montgomery-Ward affair?

Yes................................ 87%
No................................ 13

Interviewing Date 5/11–16/44
Survey #318–K   Question #5d

Asked of those familiar with the case: From what you know about this case, which side

are you more inclined to believe is in the right — Montgomery-Ward, or the Government?

Montgomery-Ward.................. 60%
Government....................... 40

MAY 29
REPUBLICAN PRESIDENTIAL CANDIDATES

Interviewing Date 5/11–16/44
Survey #318–K   Question #3a

Asked of Republicans: Whom would you like to see the Republican party nominate for President?

Dewey............................. 65%
Bricker............................ 9
Stassen............................ 5
Warren............................ 2
Others............................. 19

MAY 31
"VICTORY GARDENS"

Interviewing Date 5/11–16/44
Survey #318–K   Question #1c

Do you plan to have a "victory garden" this year?

By Region

	Yes
New England and Middle Atlantic.	3,000,000
Midwest.......................	6,000,000
South.........................	6,000,000
West..........................	2,500,000

JUNE 2
LABOR STRIKES

Interviewing Date 5/12–17/44
Survey #318–T   Question #2

Do you think there is a need for a law to prevent strikes in war industries?

Yes............................. 70%
No.............................. 15
No opinion....................... 15

Union Members Only

Yes............................. 64%
No.............................. 26
No opinion....................... 10

Among Democrats interviewed in the survey 67% say there is need for anti-strike legislation, while among Republicans the vote is 72%.

JUNE 3
THE DRAFT

Interviewing Date 5/12–17/44
Survey #318–T   Question #6

Are you in favor of drafting 4-F's for jobs in war plants in order to release able-bodied men in those plants for military service?

Yes............................. 78%
No.............................. 18
No opinion....................... 4

JUNE 3
WARTIME EMPLOYMENT

Interviewing Date 5/12–17/44
Survey #318–K   Question #6

A law has been proposed which would require every man of draft age in a war job to get permission from his draft board before he can quit his present job. If he quits without permission, he would be subject to draft into the army. Do you think this law should be passed?

Yes............................. 56%
No.............................. 32
No opinion....................... 12

JUNE 7
PRESIDENTIAL TRIAL HEAT

Special Survey

Asked in Pennsylvania: If the presidential election were held today and if Franklin Roosevelt were running against Thomas Dewey, which one would you vote for?

Roosevelt........................ 52%
Dewey........................... 48

JUNE 9
PRESIDENTIAL TRIAL HEAT

Special Survey

Asked in Illinois: If the presidential election were held today and if Franklin Roosevelt were running against Thomas Dewey, which one would you vote for?

Roosevelt........................ 47%
Dewey........................... 53

Cook County Only

Roosevelt........................ 54%
Dewey........................... 46

JUNE 10
GERMANY

Interviewing Date 4/14–19/44
Survey #316–K   Question #9a

As soon as Germany is defeated, do you think she will start making plans for another world war?

Yes............................. 60%
No.............................. 21
No opinion....................... 19

JUNE 11
PRESIDENTIAL TRIAL HEAT

Interviewing Date 5/25–30/44
Survey #319–K   Question #6a

If the presidential election were held today and if Franklin Roosevelt were running against Thomas Dewey, which one would you vote for?

Union Members Only

Roosevelt...........................66%
Dewey..............................34

Skilled, Semiskilled, and Unskilled Only

Roosevelt...........................59%
Dewey..............................41

JUNE 14
PRESIDENTIAL TRIAL HEAT

Special Survey

Asked in Michigan: If the presidential election were held today and if Franklin Roosevelt were running against Thomas Dewey, which one would you vote for?

Roosevelt...........................46%
Dewey..............................54

JUNE 16
PRESIDENTIAL TRIAL HEAT

Special Survey

Asked in New Jersey: If the presidential election were held today and if Franklin Roosevelt were running against Thomas Dewey, which one would you vote for?

Roosevelt...........................51%
Dewey..............................49

JUNE 16
PRESIDENTIAL TRIAL HEAT

Special Survey

Asked in Massachusetts: If the presidential election were held today and if Franklin Roosevelt were running against Thomas Dewey, which one would you vote for?

Roosevelt...........................53%
Dewey..............................47

JUNE 19
REPUBLICAN PLATFORM

Interviewing Date 5/25–30/44
Survey #319–K   Question #12a

Asked of Republicans: Is there any particular idea or plank that you would like your party to include in its platform for the coming presidential election?

The following are listed — in addition to the obvious pledge to support the war — according to frequency of mention:

Eliminate wasteful non-war spending
Stricter control of labor unions
Steps should be taken to prevent a postwar depression
Cut down on federal control wherever possible
Support for some sort of world union
Support for a Constitutional amendment limiting a President's tenure to two terms

JUNE 21
PRESIDENTIAL TRIAL HEAT

Special Survey

Asked in Indiana: If the presidential election were held today and if Franklin Roosevelt were running against Thomas Dewey, which one would you vote for?

Roosevelt...........................44%
Dewey..............................56

REPUBLICAN PRESIDENTIAL CANDIDATES

Special Survey

Asked of Republicans: Whom would you like to see the Republican party nominate for President?

New England States

Dewey	64%
Bricker	14
Stassen	4
Others	18

Middle Atlantic States

Dewey	66%
Bricker	7
Stassen	4
Others	23

REPUBLICAN PRESIDENTIAL CANDIDATES

Special Survey

Asked of Republicans: Whom would you like to see the Republican party nominate for President?

Pacific States Only

Dewey	63%
Bricker	6
Stassen	6
Others	25

Mountain States Only

Dewey	54%
Bricker	7
Stassen	5
Others	34

Southern States Only

Dewey	59%
Bricker	10
Stassen	6
Others	25

REPUBLICAN PRESIDENTIAL CANDIDATES

Special Survey

Asked of Republicans: Whom would you like to see the Republican party nominate for President?

East Central States Only

Dewey	45%
Bricker	21
Stassen	4
Others	30

West Central States Only

Dewey	58%
Bricker	8
Stassen	15
Others	19

REPUBLICAN PRESIDENTIAL CANDIDATES

Interviewing Date 6/9–14/44
Survey #320–K   Question #3

Asked of Republicans: Whom would you like to see the Republican party nominate for President?

Dewey	58%
Bricker	12
Stassen	6
Others	24

By Region
New England

Dewey	64%
Bricker	14
Stassen	4
Others	18

Middle Atlantic

Dewey	66%
Bricker	7
Stassen	4
Others	23

East Central

Dewey	45%
Bricker	21
Stassen	4
Others	30

West Central

Dewey	58%
Bricker	8
Stassen	15
Others	19

South

Dewey	59%
Bricker	10
Stassen	6
Others	25

Mountain

Dewey	54%
Bricker	7
Stassen	5
Others	34

Pacific

Dewey	63%
Bricker	6
Stassen	6
Others	25

JUNE 28
THE DE GAULLE GOVERNMENT

Interviewing Date 6/9–14/44
Survey #320–K   Question #8b

Have you heard or read about the de Gaulle Committee?

Yes	50%
No	50

Interviewing Date 6/9–14/44
Survey #320–K   Question #8c

Asked of those who responded in the affirmative: Should the United States recognize the de Gaulle Committee as the provisional government of France?

Yes	66%
No	34

JUNE 30
REGULATION OF EMPLOYMENT

Interviewing Date 6/9–14/44
Survey #320–T   Question #2

After July 1 no employer hiring more than eight people can hire men between 18 and 65 without getting approval of the United States Employment Service. Do you approve or disapprove of this measure?

Approve	33%
Disapprove	53
No opinion	14

JULY 2
LEAGUE OF NATIONS

Interviewing Date 6/9–14/44
Survey #320–K   Question #7

If a new council or union of nations is formed after the war to take the place of the old League of Nations, should this country join?

Yes................................. 72%
No................................. 13
No opinion......................... 15

By Political Affiliation
Democrats
Yes................................. 74%
No................................. 10
No opinion......................... 16

Republicans
Yes................................. 70%
No................................. 15
No opinion......................... 15

Midwest Only
Yes................................. 71%
No................................. 13
No opinion......................... 16

JULY 5
PRESIDENTIAL TENURE

Interviewing Date 6/9–14/44
Survey #320–T   Question #10

Would you favor adding a law to the Constitution that would prevent any President of the United States from being reelected after this year's election if he has already served two terms?

Favor.............................. 62%
Oppose............................. 32
No opinion......................... 6

Roosevelt Supporters Only
Favor.............................. 44%
Oppose............................. 56

Dewey Supporters Only
Favor.............................. 88%
Oppose............................. 12

Among the Roosevelt supporters, 8% say they have no opinion. Among the Dewey supporters, the no opinion vote is 3%.

JULY 7
DURATION OF WAR

Interviewing Date 6/22–27/44
Survey #321–K   Question #1a

When do you think the war with Germany will end?

In 1944............................ 59%
First half of 1945................. 28
Second half of 1945................ 3
1946 or later...................... 6
No opinion......................... 4

Interviewing Date 6/22–27/44
Survey #321–K   Question #1b

When do you think the war with Japan will end?

In 1944............................ 14%
First half of 1945................. 49
Second half of 1945................ 21
1946 or later...................... 11
No opinion......................... 5

JULY 8
SCRAP PAPER DRIVE

Interviewing Date 6/9–14/44
Survey #320–K   Question #11a

Are you saving scrap paper regularly?

Yes................................. 61%
No................................. 39

JULY 10
PRESIDENTIAL TRIAL HEAT

Special Survey

Asked in New York: If the presidential election were held today and if Franklin Roosevelt were running against Thomas Dewey, which one would you vote for?

Roosevelt.......................... 48%
Dewey............................ 52

Upstate Only

Roosevelt.......................... 41%
Dewey............................ 59

New York City Only

Roosevelt.......................... 56%
Dewey............................ 44

JULY 10
PRESIDENT ROOSEVELT

Interviewing Date 6/9–14/44
Survey #320–K   Question #6a

What would you say are the two main arguments for voting for Franklin Roosevelt?

He has a wider first-hand knowledge of the war situation than his opponent and is therefore better fitted by experience to handle it.

The middle of the war is no time to change administrations.

Interviewing Date 6/9–14/44
Survey #320–K   Question #6b

What would you say are the two main arguments for voting against Franklin Roosevelt?

His domestic policies have been wastefully and inefficiently carried out, with too much bureaucracy, red tape, and assertion of dictatorial power not only over the people, but over Congress.

No man should hold public office for as long as Roosevelt has. It is high time for a change.

JULY 11
C.I.O. POLITICAL ENDORSEMENT

Interviewing Date 5/25–30/44
Survey #319–K   Question #10a

If the C.I.O. union supported a candidate, would you be more likely to vote for that candidate, or against him?

For............................... 10%
Against............................ 53
No difference...................... 20
No opinion........................ 17

By Political Affiliation
Democrats

For............................... 14%
Against............................ 43
No difference...................... 22
No opinion........................ 21

Republicans

For............................... 6%
Against............................ 68
No difference...................... 14
No opinion........................ 12

Independents

For............................... 9%
Against............................ 46
No difference...................... 28
No opinion........................ 17

JULY 14
RUSSIA

Interviewing Date 6/9–14/44
Survey #320–K   Question #9

Do you think Russia can be trusted to cooperate with us when the war is over?

Yes............................... 47%
No................................ 36
No opinion........................ 17

By Education
College

Yes............................. 58%
No.............................. 32
No opinion....................... 10

High School

Yes............................. 51%
No.............................. 33
No opinion....................... 16

Grade School

Yes............................. 41%
No.............................. 39
No opinion....................... 20

JULY 15
BEER AND THE NAVY

Interviewing Date 5/25–30/44
Survey #319–K   Question #1

An officer in the navy says he thinks all navy men should be permitted to have beer on board navy ships. Do you agree or disagree?

Agree............................ 46%
Disagree......................... 46
No opinion....................... 8

JULY 15
DEMOCRATIC VICE-PRESIDENTIAL CANDIDATES

Interviewing Date 7/8–13/44
Survey #322–T   Question #6a

Asked of Democrats: Whom would you like to see the Democratic party nominate for Vice President?

Wallace.......................... 64%
Barkley.......................... 14
Byrd............................. 6
Others........................... 16

JULY 17
DEMOCRATIC PRESIDENTIAL CANDIDATES

Interviewing Date 6/22–27/44
Survey #321–K   Question #3a

Asked of Democrats: Whom would you like to see nominated by the Democratic party for President?

Roosevelt........................ 90%
Wallace.......................... 3
Hull............................. 3
Byrd............................. 2
Farley........................... 1
Rayburn.......................... .5
McNutt........................... .5

JULY 21
PARTY STRENGTH

Special Survey

Asked in the South: Do you think the South would be better off, in general, if there were two political parties of about equal strength instead of one strong party as there is at present?

Yes............................. 64%
No.............................. 36

Twenty per cent expressed no opinion.

JULY 22
WAR BONDS AND STAMPS

Interviewing Date 6/22–27/44
Survey #321–K   Question #18

Have you bought any war bonds or stamps yet?

Yes............................. 82%
No.............................. 18

By Occupation

	Yes	No
Professional and business.......	88%	12%
White collar..................	88	12
Skilled, semiskilled workers.....	83	17
Unskilled workers............	73	27
Farmers.....................	80	20

By Community Size

	Yes	No
100,000 and over.............	84%	16%
10,000–100,000...............	87	13
Towns under 10,000...........	80	20
Farm areas..................	80	20

JULY 24
REPUBLICAN PLATFORM

Interviewing Date 7/8–13/44
Survey #322–T   Question #7

Did you happen to read the Republican party platform drawn up at their convention in Chicago recently?

Yes................................	36%
No................................	64

Farmers Only

Yes.............................	8%
No.............................	92

JULY 28
POSTWAR EMPLOYMENT

Interviewing Date 7/8–13/44
Survey #322–T   Question #5f

Asked of persons in the civilian adult population who said they planned to work after the war: How certain are you that you will have a job after the war?

Very certain........................	40%
Fairly certain......................	25
Not at all certain...................	35

JULY 29
PRESIDENTIAL TRIAL HEAT

Interviewing Date 7/8–13/44
Survey #322–T   Question #11c

If the presidential election were held today, how would you vote — for Franklin Roosevelt or for Thomas Dewey?

Have Voted Before in Present Election District

Roosevelt...........................	48%
Dewey..............................	52

Have Not Voted Before in Present Election District

Roosevelt...........................	59%
Dewey..............................	41

JULY 30
PRESIDENTIAL TRIAL HEAT

Special Survey

If the presidential election were held today, how would you vote — for Franklin Roosevelt or for Thomas Dewey?

Illinois Only

Roosevelt...........................	46%
Dewey..............................	54

Ohio Only

Roosevelt...........................	46%
Dewey..............................	54

Michigan Only

Roosevelt...........................	43%
Dewey..............................	57

Indiana Only

Roosevelt...........................	43%
Dewey..............................	57

AUGUST 1
PRESIDENTIAL TRIAL HEAT

Special Survey

If the presidential election were held today, how would you vote — for Franklin Roosevelt or for Thomas Dewey?

Deep South Only

	Roosevelt	Dewey
Alabama...............	80%	20%
Arkansas...............	78	22
Florida.................	68	32
Georgia................	84	16
Louisiana...............	76	24
Mississippi..............	84	16
South Carolina..........	89	11
Texas..................	75	25

AUGUST 3
PRESIDENTIAL TRIAL HEAT

Special Survey

Asked in Massachusetts: If the presidential election were held today, how would you vote — for Franklin Roosevelt or for Thomas Dewey?

Roosevelt..........................	52%
Dewey.............................	48

AUGUST 5
ROBOT BOMBS

Interviewing Date 7/20–25/44
Survey #323–K   Question #1a

A Swedish newspaperman says the Germans are now building robot bombs which can hit cities on our East Coast. Do you believe this is true?

Yes..............................	20%
No..............................	61
No opinion........................	19

Interviewing Date 7/20–25/44
Survey #323–K   Question #1b

Do you think that in another 25 years such flying bombs will be able to cross the Atlantic Ocean?

Yes..............................	70%
No..............................	10
No opinion........................	20

AUGUST 6
PRESIDENTIAL TRIAL HEAT

Special Survey

If the presidential election were held today, how would you vote — for Franklin Roosevelt or for Thomas Dewey?

California Only

Roosevelt..........................	53%
Dewey.............................	47

Washington Only

Roosevelt..........................	53%
Dewey.............................	47

Oregon Only

Roosevelt..........................	49%
Dewey.............................	51

AUGUST 8
PRESIDENTIAL TRIAL HEAT

Special Survey

If the presidential election were held today, how would you vote — for Franklin Roosevelt or for Thomas Dewey?

Iowa Only

Roosevelt..........................	44%
Dewey.............................	56

Minnesota Only

Roosevelt..........................	47%
Dewey.............................	53

Wisconsin Only

Roosevelt	44%
Dewey	56

AUGUST 10
PRESIDENTIAL TRIAL HEAT

Special Survey

If the presidential election were held today, how would you vote — for Franklin Roosevelt or for Thomas Dewey?

North Dakota Only

Roosevelt	38%
Dewey	62

South Dakota Only

Roosevelt	37%
Dewey	63

Kansas Only

Roosevelt	34%
Dewey	66

Nebraska Only

Roosevelt	33%
Dewey	67

AUGUST 11
REBUILDING OF RUSSIAN CITIES

Interviewing Date 7/20–25/44
Survey #323–K   Question #2

After the war should three or four million German men be required to spend two or three years helping rebuild cities in Russia that they have destroyed?

Yes	61%
No	25
No opinion	14

AUGUST 12
PRESIDENTIAL TRIAL HEAT

Special Survey

If the presidential election were held today, how would you vote — for Franklin Roosevelt or for Thomas Dewey?

Rocky Mountain States Only

	Roosevelt	Dewey
Colorado	45%	55%
Idaho	47	53
Wyoming	45	55
Montana	57	43
Arizona	58	42
Utah	57	43
Nevada	56	44
New Mexico	56	44

AUGUST 15
BRITISH VIEWS ON AMERICAN POLITICS

Special Survey

Asked in Great Britain: Can you tell me the name of the man selected to run on the ticket with President Roosevelt?

Correct (Truman)	64%
Incorrect, no opinion	36

Asked in Great Britain: Can you tell me the name of Mr. Dewey's Republican running mate?

Correct	62%
Incorrect, no opinion	38

AUGUST 16
PRESIDENTIAL TRIAL HEAT

Special Survey

If the presidential election were held today, how would you vote — for Franklin Roosevelt or for Thomas Dewey?

Virginia Only

Roosevelt........................ 64%
Dewey........................... 36

North Carolina Only

Roosevelt........................ 67%
Dewey........................... 33

Tennessee Only

Roosevelt........................ 67%
Dewey........................... 33

AUGUST 19
PRESIDENTIAL ELECTION

Interviewing Date 7/20–25/44
Survey #323–K   Question #4

*Regardless of how you yourself plan to vote,
which presidential candidate do you think
will win — Franklin Roosevelt or Thomas
Dewey?*

Roosevelt........................ 71%
Dewey........................... 17
Undecided........................ 12

AUGUST 20
PRESIDENTIAL TRIAL HEAT

Special Survey

*If the presidential election were held today,
how would you vote — for Franklin Roosevelt or for Thomas Dewey?*

Missouri Only

Roosevelt........................ 49%
Dewey........................... 51

Kentucky Only

Roosevelt........................ 54%
Dewey........................... 46

Oklahoma Only

Roosevelt........................ 51%
Dewey........................... 49

West Virginia Only

Roosevelt........................ 53%
Dewey........................... 47

Maryland Only

Roosevelt........................ 52%
Dewey........................... 48

AUGUST 23
PRESIDENTIAL TRIAL HEAT

Special Survey — Summary

*If the presidential election were held today,
how would you vote — for Franklin Roosevelt or for Thomas Dewey?*

Safe for Roosevelt

	Roosevelt	Dewey
South Carolina..........	89%	11%
Georgia................	84	16
Mississippi..............	84	16
Alabama...............	80	20
Arkansas...............	78	22
Louisiana...............	76	24
Texas..................	75	25
Florida.................	68	32
Tennessee..............	67	33
North Carolina..........	67	33
Virginia................	64	36
Arizona................	58	42
Montana...............	57	43
Utah...................	57	43
Nevada.................	56	44
New Mexico.............	56	44
Kentucky...............	54	46

157 electoral votes.

Leaning Toward Roosevelt

West Virginia...........	53%	47%
Washington..............	53	47
California..............	53	47
Maryland................	52	48
Massachusetts...........	52	48

Pennsylvania................	52	48
Oklahoma..................	51	49
Rhode Island..............	51	49
New Hampshire...........	51	49
Connecticut...............	51	49
Delaware..................	51	49

129 electoral votes.

Safe for Dewey

Nebraska..................	33%	67%
Kansas....................	34	66
South Dakota.............	37	63
North Dakota.............	38	62
Michigan..................	43	57
Indiana...................	43	57
Iowa......................	44	56
Wisconsin.................	44	56
Wyoming..................	45	55
Colorado..................	45	55
Vermont..................	46	54
Illinois...................	46	54
Ohio......................	46	54

141 electoral votes.

Leaning Toward Dewey

Idaho.....................	47%	53%
Minnesota................	47	53
Maine....................	47	53
New York................	48	52
Oregon...................	49	51
Missouri..................	49	51
New Jersey...............	49	51

104 electoral votes.

The soldier vote is not included.

AUGUST 25
PRESIDENTIAL TRIAL HEAT

Special Survey

If the presidential election were held today, how would you vote — for Franklin Roosevelt or for Thomas Dewey?

Businessmen Only

Roosevelt...................	37%
Dewey......................	63

Professionals Only

Roosevelt...................	39%
Dewey......................	61

AUGUST 26
REGULATION OF EMPLOYMENT

Interviewing Date 7/8–13/44
Survey #322–T   Question #1a

Have you heard or read about the new ruling that requires men to get permission from the United States Employment Service before taking a new job in a business firm or factory?

Yes........................	70%
No.........................	30

Interviewing Date 7/8–13/44
Survey #322–T   Question #1c

Asked of those answering in the affirmative: Will you tell me whether you are for or against this ruling?

For........................	51%
Against....................	37
No opinion.................	12

AUGUST 27
PRESIDENTIAL TRIAL HEAT

Special Survey

Asked of farmers: If the presidential election were held today, how would you vote — for Franklin Roosevelt or for Thomas Dewey?

Roosevelt...................	45%
Dewey......................	55

Midwestern Farmers Only

Roosevelt...................	38%
Dewey......................	62

AUGUST 30
FRANKLIN ROOSEVELT'S HEALTH

Interviewing Date 7/20–25/44
Survey #323–K   Question #10

Do you think that President Roosevelt's health will or will not permit him to carry on the responsibility of the presidency for another four years?

Will permit him.................... 66%
Will not.......................... 34

Roosevelt Supporters Only

Will permit him.................... 84%
Will not.......................... 16

Dewey Supporters Only

Will permit him.................... 45%
Will not.......................... 55

SEPTEMBER 2
POSTWAR GERMANY

Interviewing Date 8/3–8/44
Survey #324–K   Question #1c

Do you think the Allies should supervise the education and training of German youth after this war?

Yes............................... 66%
No................................ 19
No opinion........................ 15

Interviewing Date 8/3–8/44
Survey #324–K   Question #1b

About how long do you think we should keep some of our armed forces in Germany to maintain peace and order after the war?

6 months and under................. 13%
1 year............................ 20
2 to 3 years...................... 18
4 to 10 years..................... 21
Over 10 years..................... 14
Don't know........................ 14

SEPTEMBER 4
PRESIDENTIAL TRIAL HEAT

Interviewing Date 8/18–23/44
Survey #325–K   Question #4a

If the presidential election were held today, how would you vote — for Franklin Roosevelt or for Thomas Dewey?

By Occupation

	Roosevelt	Dewey
Business..................	37%	63%
Professional..............	39	61
White collar.............	48	52
Skilled..................	54	46
Semiskilled..............	59	41
Unskilled................	63	37

SEPTEMBER 6
PRESIDENTIAL TRIAL HEAT

Special Survey

If the presidential election were held today, how would you vote — for Franklin Roosevelt or for Thomas Dewey?

Roosevelt......................... 49%
Dewey............................. 51

These figures are based on the 75% of those interviewed who say they are "absolutely certain" that they will vote in the election.

SEPTEMBER 8
UNEMPLOYED VETERANS

Interviewing Date 8/18–23/44
Survey #325–T   Question #1a

When the war is over and many soldiers return to civilian life, they may not find jobs. Do you think the Government should give soldiers money if they find themselves out of work after the war?

Yes............................... 83%
No................................ 13
No opinion........................ 4

Asked of those who answered in the affirmative: How much should the Government give per week to a married veteran with two children, while he is unemployed?

Under $20 weekly	6%
$20 weekly	9
$25	20
$30	12
$35	8
$40	5
Over $40	7
Estimate	16
	83%

Should the Government give war workers money if they find themselves out of work when the war is over or nearly over?

Yes	21%
No	71
No opinion	8

SEPTEMBER 8
UNEMPLOYMENT COMPENSATION

Should unemployment payments be handled by each state government or by the Federal Government in Washington?

States	52%
Federal Government	48

SEPTEMBER 11
PRESIDENTIAL TRIAL HEAT

Special Survey

Asked in Maine: If the presidential election were held today, how would you vote — for Franklin Roosevelt or for Thomas Dewey?

Roosevelt	46%
Dewey	54

SEPTEMBER 13
PRESIDENTIAL TRIAL HEAT

Special Survey

If the presidential election were held today, how would you vote — for Franklin Roosevelt or for Thomas Dewey?

Michigan Only

Roosevelt	45%
Dewey	55

Iowa Only

Roosevelt	45%
Dewey	55

Nebraska Only

Roosevelt	34%
Dewey	66

SEPTEMBER 15
PRESIDENTIAL TRIAL HEAT

Special Survey

If the presidential election were held today, how would you vote — for Franklin Roosevelt or for Thomas Dewey?

Washington Only

Roosevelt	55%
Dewey	45

Idaho Only

Roosevelt	48%
Dewey	52

SEPTEMBER 16
PRESIDENTIAL TRIAL HEAT

Special Survey

Asked in Oregon: If the presidential election were held today, how would you vote —

for *Franklin Roosevelt or for Thomas Dewey?*

Roosevelt........................... 51%
Dewey.............................. 49

SEPTEMBER 17
PRESIDENTIAL TRIAL HEAT

Special Survey

If the presidential election were held today, how would you vote — for Franklin Roosevelt or for Thomas Dewey?

California Only
Roosevelt........................... 55%
Dewey.............................. 45

Oklahoma Only
Roosevelt........................... 51%
Dewey.............................. 49

SEPTEMBER 20
PRESIDENTIAL TRIAL HEAT

Interviewing Date 9/14–19/44
Survey #328   Question #5a

If the presidential election were held today, how would you vote — for Franklin Roosevelt or for Thomas Dewey?

C.I.O. Members Only
Roosevelt........................... 72%
Dewey.............................. 28

A.F. of L. Members Only
Roosevelt........................... 63%
Dewey.............................. 37

SEPTEMBER 23
DURATION OF WAR

Interviewing Date 9/14–19/44
Survey #328   Question #1

How much longer do you think the war with Germany will last?

Less than 1 month.................. 5%
1 month........................... 18
2 months.......................... 25
3 months.......................... 19
4 months.......................... 9
5 months.......................... 2
6 months.......................... 9
More than 6 months................ 7
No opinion........................ 6

SEPTEMBER 27
PARTY STRENGTH

Interviewing Date 9/14–19/44
Survey #328   Question #7

In politics as of today, do you consider yourself a Republican, a Democrat, Socialist, or Independent?

Republican......................... 39%
Democrat.......................... 41
Independent....................... 20
Socialist.......................... *

*Less than 1%.

SEPTEMBER 28
PRESIDENTIAL TRIAL HEAT

Interviewing Date 9/14–19/44
Survey #328   Question #6

Asked of Independents: If the presidential election were held today, how would you vote — for Franklin Roosevelt or for Thomas Dewey?

Roosevelt........................... 55%
Dewey.............................. 45

Twenty per cent expressed no opinion.

SEPTEMBER 29
UNIVERSAL MILITARY TRAINING

Interviewing Date 8/31–9/4/44
Survey #326   Question #9

After this war is over, do you think every

able-bodied young man should be required to serve one year in the army or navy?

Yes.............................. 63%
No............................... 23
No opinion....................... 14

By Sex
Men

Yes.............................. 65%
No............................... 23
No opinion....................... 12

Women

Yes.............................. 62%
No............................... 23
No opinion....................... 15

By Age
21–29 Years

Yes.............................. 61%
No............................... 24
No opinion....................... 15

30–49 Years

Yes.............................. 69%
No............................... 19
No opinion....................... 12

50 Years and Over

Yes.............................. 58%
No............................... 27
No opinion....................... 15

SEPTEMBER 30
DURATION OF WAR

Interviewing Date 9/22–27/44
Survey #329   Question #1

How much longer do you think the war with Japan will last?

Will end in 1944.................... 4%
Will end in 1945................... 60
Will end in 1946................... 28
Will end in 1947 or later............. 8

OCTOBER 1
BRITISH VIEWS ON EUROPEAN WAR

Special Survey

The following questions were asked in Great Britain: Should Hitler, Himmler, Goering, and other Nazi leaders be punished after the war?

Yes.............................. 97%
No............................... 2
Uncertain........................ 1

If yes, how should they be punished?

Executed.......................... 53%
Exiled............................ 25
Other punishment (mainly torture)...... 22

Should Germans who have committed crimes against other Germans be punished by the United Nations, or by the German people?

United Nations..................... 67%
Germans........................... 26
Uncertain......................... 7

Should Germany be forced to make good the war damage she has done?

Yes.............................. 88%
No............................... 6
Uncertain........................ 6

If so, how?

By money payments................. 37%
By goods.......................... 16
By forced labor.................... 47

If German men are going to be sent to other countries to repair damage, should they be drafted from the German population as a whole, from among German war prisoners, or only from the ranks of Nazis guilty of war crimes?

From population as a whole......... 41%
From war prisoners................. 13
From guilty Nazis.................. 46

How long do you think it will be necessary to occupy Germany with armed forces after the war?

Always........................... 9%
30 yrs........................... 12
20 yrs........................... 16
10 yrs........................... 25
5 yrs............................ 21
Less than 5 yrs.................. 16
Uncertain........................ 1

Would you approve or disapprove of depriving Germany of all arms and armed forces?

Approve.......................... 94%
Disapprove....................... 4
Uncertain........................ 2

If so, for how long?

Always........................... 31%
30 yrs........................... 22
20 yrs........................... 19
10 yrs........................... 14
5 yrs............................ 7
Less than 5 yrs.................. 3
Uncertain........................ 4

Would you approve or disapprove of splitting Germany permanently into a number of smaller states?

Approve.......................... 56%
Disapprove....................... 23
Uncertain........................ 21

In general, do you approve or disapprove of the idea of giving portions of Germany to other countries?

Approve.......................... 48%
Disapprove....................... 35
Uncertain........................ 17

Specifically, would you approve or disapprove of the following: Giving East Prussia and parts of East Germany to Poland?

Approve.......................... 53%
Disapprove....................... 25
Uncertain........................ 22

Permanently taking over the whole Ruhr and Rhineland, making it into a zone under international administration?

Approve.......................... 66%
Disapprove....................... 17
Uncertain........................ 17

Which do you think is more likely to insure future peace in Europe — a hard peace on Germany, or a soft peace?

Hard peace....................... 80%
Soft peace....................... 8
Uncertain........................ 12

OCTOBER 2
PARTY STRENGTH

Interviewing Date 9/22–27/44
Survey #329   Question #9c

As you feel today, would you be more likely to vote for the Democratic or the Republican candidate for Congress from your district?

Republican....................... 50.5%
Democratic....................... 49.5

OCTOBER 6
PRESIDENTIAL TRIAL HEAT

Interviewing Date 9/22–27/44
Survey #329   Question #5a

If the presidential election were held today, how would you vote — for Franklin Roosevelt or for Thomas Dewey?

Roosevelt.......................... 51%
Dewey............................ 49

This does not include any soldier votes.

OCTOBER 9
PRESIDENTIAL TRIAL HEAT

Interviewing Date 9/22–27/44
Survey #329   Question #5a

If the presidential election were held today, how would you vote — for Franklin Roosevelt or for Thomas Dewey?

By Education

	Roosevelt	Dewey
College.................	35%	65%
High School............	47	53
Grade School...........	58	42

OCTOBER 11
PRESIDENTIAL TRIAL HEAT

Special Survey

If the presidential election were held today, how would you vote — for Franklin Roosevelt or for Thomas Dewey?

Ohio Only

Roosevelt.......................... 47%
Dewey............................ 53

Minnesota Only

Roosevelt.......................... 52%
Dewey............................ 48

Missouri Only

Roosevelt.......................... 50%
Dewey............................ 50

Nebraska Only

Roosevelt.......................... 36%
Dewey............................ 64

North Dakota Only

Roosevelt.......................... 45%
Dewey............................ 55

Michigan Only

Roosevelt.......................... 46%
Dewey............................ 54

OCTOBER 13
PRESIDENTIAL TRIAL HEAT

Special Survey

If the presidential election were held today, how would you vote — for Franklin Roosevelt or for Thomas Dewey?

Mountain States Only

	Roosevelt	Dewey
Montana...............	53%	47%
Arizona................	58	42
Colorado..............	45	55
Idaho.................	48	52
Wyoming..............	44	56
Utah..................	57	43
Nevada................	53	47
New Mexico...........	49	51

Pacific States Only

California..............	53	47
Oregon................	50	50
Washington............	54	46

OCTOBER 14
PRESIDENTIAL TRIAL HEAT

Special Survey

If the presidential election were held today, how would you vote — for Franklin Roosevelt or for Thomas Dewey?

Southern States Only

	Roosevelt	Dewey
South Carolina..........	91%	9%
Mississippi..............	87	13
Georgia................	83	17

	Roosevelt	Dewey
Alabama...............	78	22
Louisiana..............	77	23
Arkansas..............	74	26
Texas.................	74	26
Florida...............	74	26
North Carolina..........	71	29
Tennessee...............	67	33
Virginia................	64	36
Kentucky...............	55	45
Oklahoma..............	51	49

OCTOBER 16
PRESIDENTIAL TRIAL HEAT

Special Survey

If the presidential election were held today, how would you vote — for Franklin Roosevelt or for Thomas Dewey?

	No. of States	Electoral Vote
Roosevelt................	25	243
Dewey..................	19	228
On the line..............	4	60

266 electoral votes are needed to win the election.

OCTOBER 18
PRESIDENTIAL TRIAL HEAT

Interviewing Date 10/12–17/44
Survey #331–S   Question #8a

If the presidential election were held today, how would you vote — for Franklin Roosevelt or for Thomas Dewey?

C.I.O. Members Only

Roosevelt...........................	72%
Dewey.............................	28

A.F.L. Members Only

Roosevelt...........................	64%
Dewey.............................	36

OCTOBER 21
PRESIDENTIAL TRIAL HEAT

Interviewing Date 10/14–19/44
Survey #332   Question #8a

If the presidential election were held today, how would you vote — for Franklin Roosevelt or for Thomas Dewey?

By Age

	Roosevelt	Dewey
21–29 Years............	59%	41%
30–49 Years............	51	49
50 Years and over........	47	53

OCTOBER 24
THIRD PARTY VOTE

Special Survey

Do you plan to vote for a third-party candidate in the November presidential election?

Yes.............................	0.7%
No..............................	99.3

OCTOBER 28
PRESIDENTIAL TRIAL HEAT

Special Survey

If the presidential election were held today, how would you vote — for Franklin Roosevelt or for Thomas Dewey?

Upstate New York Only

Roosevelt...........................	40%
Dewey.............................	60

New York City Only

Roosevelt...........................	57%
Dewey.............................	43

NOVEMBER 1
PRESIDENTIAL TRIAL HEAT

Special Survey

If the presidential election were held today,

how would you vote — for Franklin Roosevelt or for Thomas Dewey?

New York Only

Roosevelt........................... 49%
Dewey............................. 51

New Jersey Only

Roosevelt........................... 49%
Dewey............................. 51

Massachusetts Only

Roosevelt........................... 50%
Dewey............................. 50

Connecticut Only

Roosevelt........................... 52%
Dewey............................. 48

Pennsylvania Only

Roosevelt........................... 50%
Dewey............................. 50

NOVEMBER 3
VOTER AWARENESS

Interviewing Date 10/14–19/44
Survey #332   Question #9a

Will you tell me who the Democratic vice-presidential candidate is?

Roosevelt Supporters Only

Correct answer (Truman)............ 55%
Incorrect answer.................... 45

Dewey Supporters Only

Correct answer..................... 69%
Incorrect answer.................... 31

Interviewing Date 10/14–19/44
Survey #332   Question #9b

Will you tell me who the Republican vice-presidential candidate is?

Roosevelt Supporters Only

Correct answer (Bricker)............ 54%
Incorrect answer.................... 46

Dewey Supporters Only

Correct answer..................... 81%
Incorrect answer.................... 19

NOVEMBER 5
PRESIDENTIAL TRIAL HEAT

Interviewing Date 10/28–11/3/44
Survey #334   Question #5

If the presidential election were held today, how would you vote — for Franklin Roosevelt or for Thomas Dewey?

By Sex

	Roosevelt	Dewey
Men...................	49%	51%
Women...............	52	48

NOVEMBER 6
PRESIDENTIAL TRIAL HEAT — FINAL POLL

Special Survey

If the presidential election were held today, how would you vote — for Franklin Roosevelt or for Thomas Dewey?

States Definitely for Roosevelt

	Roosevelt	Dewey
South Carolina..........	89%	11%
Mississippi..............	89	11
Georgia................	81	19
Texas..................	78	22
Louisiana..............	78	22
Alabama...............	78	22
Arkansas..............	72	28
Florida................	71	29
North Carolina..........	71	29
Tennessee..............	64	36
Virginia...............	64	36
Arizona...............	58	42
Rhode Island...........	56	44
Utah..................	56	44
Washington............	54	46
Kentucky..............	54	46
Nevada................	54	46
Montana...............	54	46

165 electoral votes.

States Definitely for Dewey

	Roosevelt	Dewey
Kansas...............	36%	64%
South Dakota...........	36	64
Nebraska..............	38	62
North Dakota...........	38	62
Colorado...............	44	56
Iowa..................	44	56
Wisconsin..............	44	56
Vermont................	45	55
Indiana................	45	55
Michigan...............	46	54

85 electoral votes.

Pivotal States

	Roosevelt	Dewey
California..............	53%	47%
Maryland..............	53	47
Connecticut............	52	48
Pennsylvania...........	51	49
Massachusetts...........	51	49
New Hampshire..........	51	49
Oklahoma..............	51	49
Oregon................	51	49
Idaho.................	51	49
West Virginia...........	51	49
Delaware...............	51	49
New York..............	50−	50+
Missouri...............	49	51
New Mexico............	49	51
Illinois................	49	51
Maine.................	48	52
Ohio..................	48	52
New Jersey.............	48	52
Wyoming...............	47	53
Minnesota..............	47	53

281 electoral votes.

These figures do not include any soldier votes.

NOVEMBER 11

PRESIDENTIAL ELECTION — ANALYSIS

Final comparisons must wait until complete and official election returns are made public. But on the basis of virtually complete returns to date,

Roosevelt received 53.3% of the total major-party vote cast, including both civilian and soldier votes, or an estimated 52.3% of the civilian votes only, excluding soldiers.

Since military regulations did not permit the poll-takers to question soldiers, their forecasts — and this is important to remember — excluded the soldier vote.

Following is the record of the three major poll-takers — Elmo Roper (Fortune Survey), the Crossley Poll, conducted by Archibald Crossley, and the Institute poll — as compared to the civilian popular vote of 52.3% for Roosevelt at last reports.

	Forecast for Roosevelt	Error
Roper.................	53.6%	1.3
Crossley..............	51.2	1.1
Institute..............	51.5	.8

Returns to date make it appear that the Institute's error state-by-state — it gave popular vote figures on each of the 48 states — averaged only 2.2 percentage points.

Following is the record for the 48 states, based on latest available election returns which are about 98% complete for the nation.

	Roosevelt (All Votes)	Roosevelt (Civilian Votes)	Roosevelt Gallup Poll	Deviation
Arizona.........	59%	58%	58%	0
Oregon.........	52	51	51	0
Pennsylvania.....	51	51	51	0
Montana........	55	54	54	0
New Hampshire...	52	51	51	0
Massachusetts....	52	51	51	0
Connecticut......	52.5	51.5	52	+ .5
Arkansas........	71.5	71.5	72	+ .5
Idaho...........	51.5	50.5	51	+ .5
Ohio...........	49.5	48.5	48	− .5
Kentucky........	54.5	53.5	54	+ .5
Colorado........	45	45	44	−1
Florida.........	70	70	71	+1
Indiana.........	47	46	45	−1

Wyoming........	49	48	47	−1
South Carolina....	87.5	87.5	89	−1.5
New Jersey......	50.5	49.5	48	−1.5
New York.......	52	51	49.5	−1.5
North Carolina...	69.5	69.5	71	+1.5
Maine..........	47.5	46.5	48	+1.5
Maryland........	51.5	51.5	53	+1.5
Rhode Island.....	58	58	56	−2
Missouri........	51	51	49	−2
Nevada.........	53	52	54	+2
Illinois..........	52	51	49	−2
Kansas.........	39	38	36	−2
Virginia.........	62.5	62	64	+2
Delaware........	54.5	53.5	51	−2.5
Georgia.........	83.5	83.5	81	−2.5
Nebraska........	41.5	40.5	38	−2.5
Iowa...........	47.5	46.5	44	−2.5
New Mexico......	53	52	49	−3
Louisiana........	81	81	78	−3
Michigan........	50	49	46	−3
Vermont.........	43	42	45	+3
Alabama........	81.5	81.5	78	−3.5
Oklahoma.......	55.5	54.5	51	−3.5
Texas..........	81.5	81.5	78	−3.5
Mississippi......	92.5	92.5	89	−3.5
Washington......	57.5	57.5	54	−3.5
West Virginia.....	56	55	51	−4
California.......	57	57	53	−4
Wisconsin........	49	48	44	−4
Tennessee.......	61	60	64	+4
South Dakota....	41.5	40.5	36	−4.5
Minnesota.......	52.5	51.5	47	−4.5
Utah...........	61	61	56	−5
North Dakota....	46	46	38	−8

NOVEMBER 13
POISON GAS

Interviewing Date 9/22–27/44
Survey #329   Question #2a

If it means an earlier end of the war in the Pacific, would you approve or disapprove of the Allies using poison gas against Japanese cities?

Approve........................... 23%
Disapprove........................ 71
No opinion........................ 6

Interviewing Date 9/22–27/44
Survey #329   Question #2b

If it means an earlier end of the war in Europe, would you approve or disapprove of the Allies using poison gas against German cities?

Approve........................... 20%
Disapprove........................ 76
No opinion........................ 4

NOVEMBER 15
UNITED NATIONS

Special Survey

Asked of Britons: Should the United Nations adopt the principle of using force against aggressor nations when this war has ended?

Yes............................... 77%
No................................ 10
No opinion........................ 13

NOVEMBER 17
PROHIBITION

Interviewing Date 10/28–11/2/44
Survey #334   Question #1

If the question of national prohibition should come up again, would you vote "wet" or "dry"?

Wet............................... 63%
Dry............................... 37

By Sex

	Wet	Dry
Men.........................	69%	31%
Women.....................	56	44

NOVEMBER 18
MAIN CAMPAIGN ISSUES IN RETROSPECT

Interviewing Date 8/3–8/44
Survey #324–K   Question #5

In your opinion, which man is more likely to get the war over in the shortest time — Thomas Dewey or Franklin Roosevelt?

Dewey............................ 22%
Roosevelt......................... 44
No opinion........................ 34

Interviewing Date 8/3–8/44
Survey #324–K   Question #6

In your opinion, which man is likely to do the best job of dealing with foreign nations and preventing future wars — Thomas Dewey or Franklin Roosevelt?

Dewey............................ 30%
Roosevelt......................... 51
No opinion........................ 19

Interviewing Date 8/3–8/44
Survey #324–K   Question #4

In your opinion, which man will handle affairs best in this country during the next four years — Thomas Dewey or Franklin Roosevelt?

Dewey............................ 41%
Roosevelt......................... 48
No opinion........................ 11

NOVEMBER 20
GERMANY

Interviewing Date 10/5–10/44
Survey #330   Question #2

What do you think we should do with Germany, as a country, after the war?

Supervise, control.................. 32%
Destroy as political entity............ 34
Rehabilitate...................... 12
Miscellaneous, no opinion........... 22

NOVEMBER 22
BRITISH DEMOBILIZATION

Special Survey

Asked of Britons: Should the Government demobilize men as soon as possible after the war and let them find jobs themselves, or should they be demobilized gradually as jobs are made available for them?

Demobilize immediately............. 16%
Demobilize gradually................ 76
No opinion........................ 8

NOVEMBER 24
DURATION OF WAR

Interviewing Date 10/14–19/44
Survey #332   Question #2

How much longer do you think the war with Germany will last?

Less than 1 month.................. 1%
1 month.......................... 3
2 months......................... 9
3 months......................... 15
4–5 months....................... 9
6 months......................... 26
More than 6 months................ 28
No opinion........................ 9

NOVEMBER 25
BRITISH POLITICS

Special Survey

Asked of Britons: What form of government would you like to see lead Britain in the period following the war?

All-Party Government............... 35%
Labor............................ 26
Conservative...................... 12
Liberal-Labor..................... 6
Liberal........................... 4
Conservative-Liberal................ 3
Uncertain........................ 14

Asked of Britons: What man would you like to see lead the Government after the war?

Churchill............................ 24%
Eden................................ 21
Attlee............................... 7
Cripps.............................. 6
Morrison............................ 3
Bevin............................... 2
Others.............................. 9
Uncertain........................... 28

NOVEMBER 27
UNIVERSAL MILITARY TRAINING

Interviewing Date 11/17–22/44
Survey #335   Question #5

After the war is over, do you think every able-bodied young man should be required to serve one year in the army or navy?

Yes................................ 63%
No................................. 23
No opinion......................... 14

By Region
New England

Yes................................ 65%
No................................. 21
No opinion......................... 14

Middle Atlantic

Yes................................ 67%
No................................. 21
No opinion......................... 12

East Central

Yes................................ 61%
No................................. 24
No opinion......................... 15

West Central

Yes................................ 64%
No................................. 24
No opinion......................... 12

South

Yes................................ 61%
No................................. 21
No opinion......................... 18

West

Yes................................ 61%
No................................. 27
No opinion......................... 12

By Political Affiliation
Democrats

Yes................................ 68%
No................................. 19
No opinion......................... 13

Republicans

Yes................................ 60%
No................................. 28
No opinion......................... 12

DECEMBER 1
RUSSIA

Interviewing Date 11/17–22/44
Survey #335   Question #4

When Germany is defeated, do you think Russia will join us in the war against Japan, or do you think Russia will stay neutral?

Will join.......................... 53%
Will stay neutral................... 31
No opinion......................... 16

Interviewing Date 11/17–22/44
Survey #335   Question #3

Do you think Russia can be trusted to co-operate with us when the war is over?

Yes................................ 47%
No................................. 35
No opinion......................... 18

DECEMBER 2
WAR BONDS AND STAMPS

Interviewing Date 11/17–22/44
Survey #335   Question #7

*Should all people receiving wages, salary,
or other income be required by law to put
ten cents out of every dollar of their income
in war savings bonds and stamps?*

Yes.................................. 38%
No................................... 58
No opinion........................ 4

Interviewing Date 11/17–22/44
Survey #335   Question #8a

*Do you believe that war bonds are a good
investment?*

Yes.................................. 91%
No................................... 5
Undecided........................ 4

DECEMBER 4
NAZI ATROCITIES

Interviewing Date 11/17–22/44
Survey #335   Question #1a

*Do you believe the stories that the Germans
have murdered many people in concentration camps?*

Yes.................................. 76%
No................................... 12
No opinion........................ 12

By Region
New England

Yes.................................. 80%
No................................... 9
No opinion........................ 11

Middle Atlantic

Yes.................................. 73%
No................................... 15
No opinion........................ 12

East Central

Yes.................................. 75%
No................................... 13
No opinion........................ 12

West Central

Yes.................................. 73%
No................................... 14
No opinion........................ 13

South

Yes.................................. 77%
No................................... 9
No opinion........................ 14

West

Yes.................................. 84%
No................................... 5
No opinion........................ 11

Interviewing Date 11/17–22/44
Survey #335   Question #1b

*Asked of those saying yes: Nobody knows,
of course, how many may have been murdered, but what would be your best guess?*

100,000 or less...................... 27%
100,000 to 500,000.................. 5
500,000 to 1,000,000................ 1
1,000,000........................... 6
2,000,000 to 6,000,000.............. 8
6,000,000 or more.................. 4
Unwilling to guess.................. 25
                                    ____
                                    76%

Interviewing Date 11/17–22/44
Survey #335   Question #1c

*What do you think should be done to punish
the Germans found guilty of these charges?*

The largest number of replies favored execu-
tion of the guilty — in poison gas chambers, by
hanging, electrocution, or by firing squad.
Others favored imprisonment, physical torture,
or some other unspecified form of punishment.
Virtually nobody expressed any desire for
leniency. A few simply said, "Give them to the
Poles."

DECEMBER 6
MINIMUM INCOME NEEDED
FOR FAMILY OF FOUR

Interviewing Date 11/17–22/44
Survey #335   Question #6

How much income per week do you think the average family of four needs for health and comfort?

Median average.................. $48 wk.

By Occupation
(*Median Average*)

Professional..................... $51 wk.
Business........................ 50 wk.
White collar..................... 50 wk.
Skilled workers.................. 49 wk.
Semiskilled workers.............. 48 wk.
Unskilled workers................ 42 wk.
Farmers......................... 38 wk.

By Region
(*Median Average*)

New England.................... $48 wk.
Middle Atlantic................. 49 wk.
East Central.................... 48 wk.
West Central.................... 42 wk.
South.......................... 40 wk.
Mountain....................... 48 wk.
Pacific......................... 50 wk.

DECEMBER 9
BIBLE READING

Interviewing Date 11/17–22/44
Survey #335   Question #17a

Have you, yourself, read any part of the Bible at home within the past year?

Yes............................ 62%
No............................. 38

Interviewing Date 11/17–24/44
Survey #335   Question #17b

How often do you read the Bible?

Interest in the Bible appears to increase with age. Sixty-four per cent of the people over 50 are Bible readers; 14% of them spend some part of each day reading the Bible; one-third of them turn to the Bible once or more each month.

Ten per cent of those questioned in the present survey are daily Bible readers. Thirteen per cent of American women read their Bibles daily. Among men the figure is much lower — 6%.

Ten per cent among farmers, 12% among small town dwellers, 8% among urbanites read Bibles every day.

DECEMBER 11
RELIGIOUS BELIEFS

Interviewing Date 11/17–22/44
Survey #335   Question #16a

Have you attended a religious service within the past four weeks?

Yes............................ 58%
No............................. 42

Interviewing Date 11/17–22/44
Survey #335   Question #18a

Do you, personally, believe in a God?

Yes............................ 96%
No............................. 1
No opinion...................... 3

By Region
New England

Yes............................ 94%
No............................. 1
No opinion...................... 5

Middle Atlantic

Yes............................ 95%
No............................. 2
No opinion...................... 3

East Central

Yes................................ 97%
No................................ 1
No opinion........................ 2

West Central

Yes................................ 97%
No................................ 1
No opinion........................ 2

South

Yes................................ 98%
No................................ 1
No opinion........................ 1

Mountain

Yes................................ 98%
No................................ 1
No opinion........................ 1

Pacific

Yes................................ 93%
No................................ 1
No opinion........................ 6

By Community Size
100,000 and Over

Yes................................ 94%
No................................ 2
No opinion........................ 4

10,000–100,000

Yes................................ 94%
No................................ 2
No opinion........................ 4

Towns Under 10,000

Yes................................ 98%
No................................ 1
No opinion........................ 1

Farms

Yes................................ 97%
No................................ 1
No opinion........................ 2

By Sex
Men

Yes................................ 95%
No................................ 1
No opinion........................ 4

Women

Yes................................ 97%
No................................ 1
No opinion........................ 2

By Age
20–29 Years

Yes................................ 93%
No................................ 3
No opinion........................ 4

30–49 Years

Yes................................ 97%
No................................ 1
No opinion........................ 2

50 Years and Over

Yes................................ 97%
No................................ 1
No opinion........................ 2

Interviewing Date 11/17–22/44
Survey #335   Question #18c

Do you believe there is a life after death?

Yes................................ 76%
No................................ 13
No opinion........................ 11

By Region
New England

Yes................................ 68%
No................................ 16
No opinion........................ 16

Middle Atlantic

Yes................................ 69%
No................................ 18
No opinion........................ 13

East Central

Yes................................ 77%
No................................. 14
No opinion......................... 9

West Central

Yes................................ 85%
No................................. 7
No opinion......................... 8

South

Yes................................ 91%
No................................. 2
No opinion......................... 7

Mountain

Yes................................ 87%
No................................. 9
No opinion......................... 4

Pacific

Yes................................ 63%
No................................. 14
No opinion......................... 23

By Community Size
100,000 and Over

Yes................................ 69%
No................................. 18
No opinion......................... 13

10,000–100,000

Yes................................ 72%
No................................. 15
No opinion......................... 13

Towns Under 10,000

Yes................................ 81%
No................................. 8
No opinion......................... 11

Farms

Yes................................ 85%
No................................. 6
No opinion......................... 9

By Sex
Men

Yes................................ 73%
No................................. 14
No opinion......................... 13

Women

Yes................................ 79%
No................................. 11
No opinion......................... 10

By Age
20–29 Years

Yes................................ 70%
No................................. 17
No opinion......................... 13

30–49 Years

Yes................................ 76%
No................................. 13
No opinion......................... 11

50 Years and Over

Yes................................ 79%
No................................. 10
No opinion......................... 11

DECEMBER 13
UNITED STATES ELECTION

Special Survey

Asked in Canada prior to the American presidential election: Can you name the American presidential candidates?

Correct............................ 88%
Incorrect.......................... 12

Asked of those correctly identifying the candidates: Which of these men would you like to see elected as President of the United States?

Roosevelt.......................... 79%
Dewey.............................. 4
No opinion......................... 5
                                   ——
                                   88%

DECEMBER 15
EDWARD STETTINIUS

Interviewing Date 12/1–6/44
Survey #336–K   Question #5

Have you ever heard or read about Edward Stettinius?

Yes............................... 58%
No............................... 42

Interviewing Date 12/1–6/44
Survey #336–K   Question #5a

Asked of those familiar with Edward Stettinius: In general, is your opinion of this man favorable or unfavorable?

Favorable......................... 92%
Unfavorable...................... 8

DECEMBER 16
ADULT EDUCATION

Interviewing Date 11/17–22/44
Survey #335   Question #13a

After the war would you like to attend classes and take special courses for adults in some school or college?

Yes............................... 34%
No............................... 66

Young people aged 20–29 were the most interested (57%) and farmers the least interested.

Interviewing Date 11/17–24/44
Survey #335   Question #13b

Asked of those who answered in the affirmative: What courses would you like to take?

Vocational — machine work, beauty operator, typing, stenography, photography, dress-making, refrigeration, building trades................... 13%
Professional and Scientific — law, engineering, journalism, international law, government, economics, psychology, social welfare, chemistry, physics, electricity....................... 12

Languages — principally Spanish and English........................... 5
Arts — music, art, painting.......... 2
Other............................. 3
Undecided........................ 3
                             38%

(Note: table adds to more than 34% because some persons named more than one course.)

DECEMBER 18
UNIVERSAL MILITARY TRAINING

Interviewing Date 12/1–6/44
Survey #336–K   Question #11

After this war is over, do you think every able-bodied young man should be required to serve one year in the army or navy?

Yes............................... 70%
No............................... 25
No opinion...................... 5

By Region
New England

Yes............................... 69%
No............................... 26
No opinion...................... 5

Middle Atlantic

Yes............................... 73%
No............................... 23
No opinion...................... 4

East Central

Yes............................... 72%
No............................... 25
No opinion...................... 3

West Central

Yes............................... 63%
No............................... 33
No opinion...................... 4

South

Yes..............................	71%
No...............................	21
No opinion.......................	8

Mountain

Yes..............................	64%
No...............................	33
No opinion.......................	3

Pacific

Yes..............................	71%
No...............................	25
No opinion.......................	4

The survey revealed no difference in attitude as between men and women, and only small variations as between age groups in the adult population.

Rural and farm communities throughout the country showed less enthusiasm for the plan than urban areas.

DECEMBER 20
JAPAN

Interviewing Date 11/17–22/44
Survey #335   Question #2a

What do you think we should do with Japan, as a country, after the war?

Supervise and control................	28%
Destroy as political entity.............	33
Kill all Japanese people..............	13
Rehabilitate, reeducate...............	8
Miscellaneous, no opinion...........	18

DECEMBER 22
SMOKING HABITS

Interviewing Date 12/1–6/44
Survey #336–K   Question #1a

Do you smoke cigarettes, a pipe, cigars, or don't you smoke at all?

Cigarettes...........................	41%
Pipes...............................	10
Cigars..............................	6
Don't smoke........................	48

By Sex

	Cigarette	Pipe	Cigars	Don't Smoke
Men...........	48%	22%	12%	29%
Women........	36	—	—	64

By Age

20–29 Years.....	55%	4%	2%	42%
30–49 Years.....	49	10	5	42
50 Years and over.	25	14	8	58

By Region

New England and Middle Atlantic	46%	7%	6%	44%
East Central.....	39	11	7	49
West Central.....	33	14	4	52
South..........	38	13	2	47
West...........	43	7	5	50

By Occupation

Professional and business.......	41%	9%	6%	49%
White collar.....	47	5	5	46
Manual workers..	44	9	6	45

By Community Size

100,000 and over..	48%	7%	5%	43%
10,000–100,000...	46	7	5	45
Under 10,000....	36	11	6	52

(Note: tables add to more than 100% because some persons use tobacco in more than one form.)

DECEMBER 23
PUNISHMENT OF JAPANESE LEADERS

Interviewing Date 11/17–22/44
Survey #335   Question #2b

After the war, do you think the Japanese military leaders should be punished in any way?

Yes............................... 88%
No............................... 5
No opinion....................... 7

Interviewing Date 11/17–22/44
Survey #335   Question #2c

*Asked of those answering in the affirmative:
In what way should they be punished?*

Here are some typical comments: "We should string them up and cut little pieces off them — one piece at a time."

"Torture them to a slow and awful death."

"Put them in a tank and suffocate them."

"Kill them, but be sure to torture them first, the way they have tortured our boys."

"Let them have it wholesale; get rid of every one of them."

"Take them to Pearl Harbor and sink them."

"Put them in Siberia and let them freeze to death."

"Turn them over to the Chinese."

"Put them in foxholes and fire bombs and grenades at them."

"Kill them like rats."

It is notable that only four in every one hundred questioned as to the means of punishing Japanese military leaders suggest that we "Treat them justly, handle them under International Law, (or) demote them."

DECEMBER 25
IDEAL CHRISTMAS PRESENT

Interviewing Date 12/14–19/44
Survey #337–K   Question #9

If you had your choice, what present would you most like for Christmas?

Far and away the greatest proportion of replies were similar to this: "To have the boys back home."

DECEMBER 27
POSTWAR EMPLOYMENT

Interviewing Date 12/1–6/44
Survey #336–K   Question #7

After the war, do you think that everyone who wants a job will be able to get one?

Yes............................... 25%
No............................... 68
No opinion....................... 7

By Sex
Men

Yes............................... 28%
No............................... 66
No opinion....................... 6

Women

Yes............................... 22%
No............................... 71
No opinion....................... 7

By Age
21–29 Years

Yes............................... 23%
No............................... 73
No opinion....................... 4

30–49 Years

Yes............................... 25%
No............................... 68
No opinion....................... 7

50 Years and Over

Yes............................... 26%
No............................... 66
No opinion....................... 8

By Occupation
Business and Professional

Yes............................... 22%
No............................... 74
No opinion....................... 4

White Collar

Yes............................... 25%
No............................... 67
No opinion....................... 8

Farmers

Yes............................... 25%
No............................... 69
No opinion....................... 6

Manual Workers

Yes.............................. 26%
No.............................. 66
No opinion....................... 8

By Region
New England and Middle Atlantic

Yes.............................. 26%
No.............................. 68
No opinion....................... 6

East Central

Yes.............................. 25%
No.............................. 67
No opinion....................... 8

West Central

Yes.............................. 27%
No.............................. 65
No opinion....................... 8

South

Yes.............................. 24%
No.............................. 67
No opinion....................... 9

Mountain and Pacific

Yes.............................. 23%
No.............................. 72
No opinion....................... 5

DECEMBER 31
NEW YEAR RESOLUTION

Interviewing Date 12/14–19/44
Survey #337–K   Question #11a

Are you going to make any New Year resolutions?

The survey findings reveal that approximately 15 million Americans are going to make resolutions.

Interviewing Date 12/14–19/44
Survey #337–K   Question #11b

Asked of those answering in the affirmative: What will they be?

The following are listed in order of frequency of mention.

By Sex
Men

Improve my character generally.
Stop drinking, or drink less.
Save more money, and budget more carefully.
Be more religious, go to church more often.
Stop smoking, or smoke less.
Do all I can to speed the end of the war.
Buy more bonds.
Try to do a better job, be more efficient and prompt.
Improve my disposition, not be jealous, control my temper.
Improve my health, keep more regular hours.

Women

Improve my character generally.
Improve my disposition, be more sympathetic and understanding.
Be more religious, go to church more often.
Save more money, budget more carefully.
Buy more bonds.
Try to do a better job, be more efficient and prompt.
Stop smoking, or smoke less.
Do all I can to help speed end of war.
Improve my health, keep more regular hours.
Stop drinking, or drink less.

1945

Next most frequently mentioned is the suggestion that the Government provide public-works programs to supplement private industry whenever and wherever needed.

This proposal is similar to that embodied in the Murray Committee proposal, which would have the President each year inform Congress of the prospects for employment for the forthcoming year and recommend a "fill the gap" Federal Government program to insure jobs for everyone, if it appeared that private industry could not provide all of the jobs required.

Two per cent suggest that we increase our foreign trade.

Other suggestions received in the survey do not bear specifically upon the problem but are related to it.

One of these is to take married women off jobs in order to make room for men, especially returning servicemen.

Another is to cut down on the length of the work week, in the hope that shortening the hours of labor would spread the available work among more people.

Still another group proposes a "back to the farm" movement, or some variation of it, to encourage city workers to find work, food, and places to live by starting small farms.

JANUARY 3
WAGE OUTLOOK

Interviewing Date 12/2–7/44
Survey #336–K   Question #8

After the war do you think the weekly income of workers will be about the same as it is now, or will it be more, or less?

About the same.................... 20%
More.............................. 5
Less.............................. 71
No opinion........................ 4

Women are inclined to be more pessimistic than men. Seventy-four per cent of the women think the weekly income will be less after the war. This compares with a vote of 68% among men. Farmers are slightly more pessimistic than members of other occupational groups. Seventy-seven per cent of farmers think wages will be lower. This compares with a vote of 68% among business and professional people and 65% among union members.

JANUARY 5
POSTWAR UNEMPLOYMENT

Interviewing Date 12/2–7/44
Survey #336–K   Question #10

After the war what do you think should be done to give most people jobs at good wages?

First in the list of suggestions — made by 22% in some form or other — is that the way to give people jobs is to encourage private enterprise.

JANUARY 6
40-HOUR WORK WEEK

Interviewing Date 12/2–7/44
Survey #336–K   Question #9

After the war how many hours per week do you think persons in business and industry should work?

30 hours or less..................... 4%
Between 30 and 40 hours............. 5
40 hours............................ 50
Between 40 and 48 hours............. 8
48 hours............................ 25
Over 48 hours....................... 5
No opinion.......................... 3

PEACE TREATIES

Interviewing Date 12/2–7/44
Survey #336–K   Question #6a

When the war is over it will be necessary for the Allies to decide on peace terms for the Axis. Which one of these three ways (on card) would you, personally, favor as the best way to have peace treaties approved after the war: have the treaties approved solely by the President, or have the treaties approved by the President and a majority of the Congress, or have them approved by the President and two-thirds of the Senate?

President only...................... 8%
President and a majority of Congress... 58
President and ⅔ of the Senate........ 22
No opinion........................ 12

By Education
College

President only...................... 3%
President and a majority of Congress... 65
President and ⅔ of the Senate........ 29
No opinion........................ 3

High School

President only...................... 5%
President and a majority of Congress... 64
President and ⅔ of the Senate........ 25
No opinion........................ 6

Grade School

President only...................... 12%
President and a majority of Congress... 52
President and ⅔ of the Senate........ 19
No opinion........................ 17

JANUARY 10
HENRY WALLACE

Interviewing Date 12/2–7/44
Survey #336–K   Question #5

Generally speaking, is your opinion of Henry Wallace favorable or unfavorable?

Favorable........................ 58%
Unfavorable...................... 23
Unfamiliar, no opinion.............. 19

JANUARY 12
SOCIAL SECURITY

Interviewing Date 12/14–19/44
Survey #337–K   Question #4

At present some groups are not included under social security. Do you think the Social Security Program should be changed to include the following groups: farmers, government employees, professional and self-employed persons, and domestic servants?

	Yes	No	Un-decided
Farmers..............	60%	23%	17%
Government employees	61	21	18
Prof. and self-employed	57	25	18
Domestic servants.....	69	15	16

The answers of people in these groups show a majority in favor of including themselves under the Social Security Program.

JANUARY 13
HEALTH

Interviewing Date 12/14–19/44
Survey #337–K   Question #10a

Do any of the people in your home, including yourself, have a cold at the present time?

About 16%, or about 21 million persons, are found to be suffering from a cold.

Interviewing Date 12/14–19/44
Survey #337–K   Question #4d

What have you found to be the best way to treat a cold?

In addition to the accepted medical remedies and aids for colds, the survey found that some parts of the public still cling to remedies that have been handed down through generations. Some of them are: "Take coal oil and mix it with sugar"; "All it takes is mental and spiritual effort"; "Use black pepper and lard"; "Nothing like a good old shot of you-know-what"; "Keep your head cold and your feet warm."

JANUARY 14
COMPULSORY MILITARY TRAINING

Interviewing Date 12/2–7/44
Survey #336–K   Question #11

After the war is over, do you think every able-bodied young man should be required to serve one year in the army or navy?

Yes.................................. 70%
No................................... 25
No opinion......................... 5

JANUARY 17
JAPAN AND POISON GAS

Interviewing Date 12/14–19/44
Survey #337–K   Question #1

The Japs say that they will execute any American bomber pilots forced to land in Japan. If the Japs do this, should we use poison gas against Japanese cities?

Yes.................................. 43%
No................................... 47
No opinion......................... 10

By Education
College

Yes.................................. 24%
No................................... 70
No opinion......................... 6

High School

Yes.................................. 42%
No................................... 51
No opinion......................... 7

Grade School

Yes.................................. 49%
No................................... 38
No opinion......................... 13

JANUARY 19
LENGTH OF WAR

Interviewing Date 12/31/44–1/4/45
Survey #338–K   Question #1a

How much longer do you think the war with Germany will last?

3 months or less.................... 4%
4 to 5 months...................... 4
6 months........................... 19
More than 6 months................ 64
No opinion......................... 9

Interviewing Date 12/31/44–1/4/45
Survey #338–K   Question #1b

Do you think that there is any chance that we will lose the war in Europe?

Yes.................................. 9%
No................................... 86
Uncertain.......................... 5

JANUARY 20
IDEAL PLACE TO LIVE

Interviewing Date 12/14–19/44
Survey #337–K   Question #7c

If you could live in any state in the nation, in which state would you most like to live?

The following are listed in order of preference:

California
Florida
New York
Texas
Colorado
Oregon
Arizona
Kentucky
Mississippi
Michigan

JANUARY 21
WAR JOBS

Interviewing Date 12/15–20/44
Survey #337–T   Question #5

What do you think should be done to keep war workers in their jobs as long as they are needed?

Freeze workers in jobs	24%
Draft workers into army if they won't work	19
Pass National Service Act	14
Provide additional wage incentives	5
Convince workers they can keep jobs after the war	4
Make it impossible for them to get another job	4
Make working conditions more pleasant	4
Impose penalties if workers leave	2
Miscellaneous	2
Nothing can be done about it	3
Nothing should be done about it	2
Don't know	16
	104%

(Note: table adds to more than 100% because some persons made more than one suggestion.)

JANUARY 24
POLITICS AS PROFESSION

Interviewing Date 12/31/44–1/4/45
Survey #338–K   Question #3a

If you had a son would you like to see him go into politics as a life's work when he gets out of school?

Yes	21%
No	68
No opinion	11

Interviewing Date 12/31/44–1/4/45
Survey #338–K   Question #3b

Why do you feel this way?

The reasons mentioned most often by those opposing politics as a career for their son were: (1) Politics is too crooked and unethical; (2) Temptations are too great even for a good man; (3) There is not much future in it and there are better jobs elsewhere; (4) It's too precarious a way to earn a living.

The two most frequently mentioned reasons for favoring a son going into politics were: (1) There is a great need for good and honest men in politics today; (2) Politics presents an opportunity to serve, to help mold national and world policies.

JANUARY 26
DEMOCRATIC PRESIDENTIAL CANDIDATES

Interviewing Date 12/14–19/44
Survey #337–K   Question #6b

Regardless of what political party you prefer, what is your guess as to who will be the Democratic candidate for President in 1948?

Roosevelt	30%
Wallace	11
Truman	6
Stettinius	4
Byrnes	1
Byrd	1
Others	5
No opinion	42

Republican voters are much more positive than Democratic voters that Roosevelt will be the candidate.

JANUARY 28
VOTER KNOWLEDGE

Interviewing Date 12/2–7/44
Survey #336–K   Question #3a

Will you tell me for how many years members of the House of Representatives are elected?

Correct............................ 38%
Incorrect.......................... 62

By Education

	Correct	Incorrect
College..................	64%	36%
High School.............	42	58
Grade School...........	29	71

Interviewing Date 12/2–7/44
Survey #336–K   Question #4a

Will you tell me how much salary a United States representative receives a year?

$5,000 or under.................... 9%
$6,000–$9,000...................... 9
$10,000 (correct answer)............. 24
Over $10,000....................... 6
Don't know........................ 52

JANUARY 31
GERMANY AND JAPAN

Special Survey

After the war, should Germany and Japan be kept permanently disarmed?

Yes............................... 92%
No................................ 6
No opinion........................ 2

Should the United States, England, Russia, and China make a written agreement now to keep Germany and Japan disarmed, or should we wait until the war is over to make such an agreement?

Make agreement now................ 57%
Wait.............................. 39
No opinion........................ 4

If it becomes necessary to use force to keep Germany and Japan from arming again, should the President have the right to order the use of American armed force immediately, or should approval of Congress be obtained first?

Give President the right............. 41%
Require approval of Congress........ 54
No opinion........................ 5

FEBRUARY 2
DRAFTING OF NURSES

Interviewing Date 1/19–24/45
Survey #339–K   Question #11a

Do you approve or disapprove of the proposal now before Congress to draft nurses to serve with the army and navy?

Approve........................... 73%
Disapprove........................ 19
No opinion........................ 8

Interviewing Date 1/19–24/45
Survey #339–K   Question #11c

Do you think there is a shortage of nurses in the armed forces now?

Yes............................... 78%
No................................ 2
No opinion........................ 20

FEBRUARY 3
PROFESSIONAL BASEBALL

Interviewing Date 1/19–24/45
Survey #339–K   Question #1b

Do you follow professional baseball?

Yes............................... 33%
No................................ 67

Interviewing Date 1/19–24/45
Survey #339–K   Question #1a

Do you think that professional baseball should be continued during the war, or should it be stopped until after the war?

Should be continued................ 46%
Should be stopped.................. 41
Undecided......................... 13

By Age
21–29 Years

Should be continued................ 57%
Should be stopped.................. 30
Undecided......................... 13

30–49 Years

Should be continued................ 49%
Should be stopped.................. 38
Undecided......................... 13

50 Years and Over

Should be continued................ 37%
Should be stopped.................. 49
Undecided......................... 14

By Sex
Men

Should be continued................ 51%
Should be stopped.................. 38
Undecided......................... 11

Women

Should be continued................ 42%
Should be stopped.................. 42
Undecided......................... 16

FEBRUARY 4
MILITARY STRENGTH

Interviewing Date 1/19–24/45
Survey #339–K   Question #7a

There are about 3,000,000 men in the United States navy at present. About how many men do you think we should have in our peacetime navy after the war?

Under 1 million.................... 18%
1 million......................... 29
1½ million........................ 13
2 million......................... 4
Over 2 million.................... 4
No opinion, no specific answer....... 32

Interviewing Date 1/19–24/45
Survey #339–K   Question #7b

There are about 8,000,000 men in the United States army at present. About how many men do you think we should have in our peacetime army after the war?

Under 1 million.................... 7%
1 million......................... 15
1½ million........................ 2
2 million......................... 17
2½ million........................ 4
3 million......................... 8
3½ million........................ 1
4 million......................... 12
Over 4 million.................... 3
No opinion........................ 31

FEBRUARY 7
WAR JOBS

Interviewing Date 1/19–24/45
Survey #339–K   Question #4a

Have you followed the discussion over a National Service Act which would require more people to take war jobs?

Yes............................... 62%
No................................ 38

Interviewing Date 1/19–24/45
Survey #339–K   Question #4b

What is your opinion of the proposal to draft people for war jobs?

Approve........................... 55%
Approve only if necessary........... 21
Disapprove........................ 24

FEBRUARY 9
WAR JOBS

Interviewing Date 1/19–24/45
Survey #339–T   Question #5

Most people in this country agree that 250,000 more war workers are needed right away. Which of these two ways of getting these workers do you think should be followed: 1) Continue to try to do it as at present by asking people to take war jobs; or 2) Pass a law which would permit the drafting of certain civilians for war jobs?

Favor voluntary method.............. 39%
Favor drafting people............... 53
Uncertain......................... 8

By Region
New England and Middle Atlantic

Favor voluntary method.............. 41%
Favor drafting people............... 53
Uncertain......................... 6

East Central

Favor voluntary method.............. 42%
Favor drafting people............... 51
Uncertain......................... 7

West Central

Favor voluntary method.............. 36%
Favor drafting people............... 53
Uncertain......................... 11

South

Favor voluntary method.............. 27%
Favor drafting method............... 63
Uncertain......................... 10

Mountain and West Coast

Favor voluntary method.............. 44%
Favor drafting people............... 50
Uncertain......................... 6

Interviewing Date 1/19–24/45
Survey #339–T   Question #5a

Government and army officials say it is absolutely necessary to have more men to work in munitions plants and war industries. Do you think Congress should pass a law to permit local draft boards to draft civilians between the ages of 21 and 45 who are able to work for these industries?

Favor............................ 56%
Oppose........................... 36
No opinion....................... 8

FEBRUARY 10
WOMEN AND POSTWAR EMPLOYMENT

Interviewing Date 1/19–24/45
Survey #339–K   Question #3b

Women were asked: Do you plan to work in any job after the war?

Yes.............................. 61%
No............................... 29
Uncertain........................ 10

FEBRUARY 11
FUEL SHORTAGE

Interviewing Date 1/19–24/45
Survey #339–K   Question #9a

At what temperature do you keep your home during the day? (This question was asked in all New England states as well as in New York, Pennsylvania, Ohio, West Virginia, Maryland, Virginia, and Kentucky.)

Under 65 degrees................... 9%
At 65 degrees..................... 18
At 68 degrees..................... 24
At 70 degrees..................... 34
Above 70 degrees.................. 19

Coal users are inclined to keep their temperatures at higher levels than oil users. Whereas about half of the oil users keep their home temperatures at or above 70 degrees, 63% — nearly two out of three — among coal users do so.

FEBRUARY 14
WARTIME SACRIFICE

Interviewing Date 1/19–24/45
Survey #339–K   Question #8a

Have you had to make any real sacrifice for the war?

Yes.............................. 36%
No.............................. 64

Among the 36% who say they think they have made real sacrifices, the greatest number mention the absence of a relative who is in the armed forces. Also frequently mentioned are financial and business sacrifices and rationing.

FEBRUARY 16
DIETS

Interviewing Date 12/31/44–1/4/45
Survey #338–K   Question #5

We want to find out what the average person eats in the course of a day. Would you tell me what you, yourself, had for breakfast today? For lunch today? For dinner today? And did you eat anything between meals?

Daily Diet Recommendations	Not living up to recommendations
Milk or milk products................	32%
Citrus fruits, tomatoes or raw greens...	46
Green or yellow vegetables............	23
Other vegetables or fruits.............	9
Meat, fish, or poultry...............	9
Eggs................................	40
Cereal or bread.....................	4
Butter or other fats.................	22

By Income
Not living up to recommendations

	Upper	Middle	Lower
Milk or milk products	26%	26%	36%
Citrus fruits, tomatoes, or raw greens......	24	36	57
Green or yellow vegetables..........	15	17	28
Other vegetables or fruits............	9	8	11
Meat, fish, or poultry	6	7	11
Eggs..............	34	38	44
Cereal or bread......	3	4	4
Butter or other fats...	13	17	27

FEBRUARY 17
RATIONING

Interviewing Date 1/19–24/45
Survey #339–K   Question #10

What one product that is now rationed do you find it hardest to cut down on or get along without?

Sugar............................ 20%
Butter............................ 19
Meat.............................. 19
Gasoline.......................... 10
Shoes............................. 5
Canned foods...................... 2
Fuel oil........................... 1
Others............................ 24

Women are more inclined to name sugar and butter than men, while a greater proportion of men mention meat and gasoline.

FEBRUARY 18
PEACE TERMS

Interviewing Date 2/3–8/45
Survey #340–K   Question #5b

Do you approve or disapprove of requiring unconditional surrender of our enemy?

Approve........................... 75%
Disapprove........................ 12
Undecided......................... 13

FEBRUARY 21
LINCOLN AND WASHINGTON

Interviewing Date 2 /3–8 /45
Survey #340–K   Question #2a

*Who do you think was the greater —
George Washington or Abraham Lincoln?*

Washington........................ 22%
Lincoln........................... 42
Equally great..................... 28
Uncertain.........................   8

While people as a whole in the South name General Washington over Lincoln, Southern Negroes and people in all other sections name Lincoln as the greater, among those making a choice.

A far greater proportion of younger people — those from 21 to 29 — say they think Lincoln was the greater man than is the case among those in the older age brackets.

Interviewing Date 2 /3–8 /45
Survey #340–K   Question #2b

Those who made a choice were asked: Why?

Here are the principal reasons why people say they choose Lincoln: "He was a greater humanitarian, more down to earth, more of a people's President . . . He eliminated the institution of slavery and maintained the Union . . . He was a self-made man . . . He had to deal with far more complicated problems than Washington faced."

Among an admiring but confused minority there were replies like these: "Abe Lincoln was the founder of the Declaration of Independence . . . He discovered America . . . He first said the world was round."

Those who think Washington was the greater of the two men think so, for the most part, because "He was the founder of our country . . . He was our first President . . . He was a great general . . . He faced greater responsibilities than Lincoln."

He was the greater man, declared one man, "because his picture is on the dollar."

FEBRUARY 23
HENRY WALLACE

Interviewing Date 2 /3–8 /45
Survey #340–K   Question #10a

Have you heard or read about the appointment of Henry Wallace as Secretary of Commerce?

Yes............................... 76%
No................................ 24

Interviewing Date 2 /3–8 /45
Survey #340–K   Question #10b

Would you like to see Congress vote for or against the appointment of Henry Wallace as Secretary of Commerce?

For............................... 40%
Against........................... 37
No opinion........................ 23

Roosevelt Voters Only

For............................... 61%
Against........................... 19
No opinion........................ 20

Dewey Voters Only

For............................... 17%
Against........................... 64
No opinion........................ 19

Interviewing Date 2 /3–8 /45
Survey #340–K   Question #10c

Do you think the money lending agency — the RFC (Reconstruction Finance Corporation) — should be kept under the direction of the Department of Commerce, or should it be separated?

Keep RFC under Department of Commerce.............................. 27%
Separate RFC..................... 35
Qualified........................ 6*
No opinion....................... 32

*Depending on who heads the Department of Commerce.

FEBRUARY 24
SLEEPING HABITS

Interviewing Date 2/3–8/45
Survey #340–K   Question #13

At about what time do you usually go to bed at night?

In bed by
8 o'clock........................... 8%
9 o'clock........................... 25
10 o'clock......................... 54
11 o'clock......................... 81
12 o'clock......................... 95

By Community Size

In bed by	Farms	Towns under 10,000	Towns and Cities 10,000 and Over
8 o'clock	19%	7%	4%
9 o'clock	58	22	13
10 o'clock	89	56	36
11 o'clock	98	86	69
12 o'clock	100*	97	92

*Less than half of 1% stay up after 12.

FEBRUARY 25
COMPULSORY MILITARY TRAINING

Interviewing Date 1/19–24/45
Survey #339–K   Question #2a

After this war is over, do you think every able-bodied young man should be required to take military or naval training for one year?

Yes.............................. 69%
No.............................. 22
No opinion...................... 9

Roosevelt Voters Only

Yes.............................. 73%
No.............................. 19
No opinion...................... 8

Dewey Voters Only

Yes.............................. 64%
No.............................. 30
No opinion...................... 6

Interviewing Date 1/19–24/45
Survey #339–K   Question #2b

Do you think a military training law should be passed now, or should this wait until after the war?

Pass law now...................... 37%
Wait until after war.............. 25
Undecided......................... 7
                                 ___
                                 69%

FEBRUARY 28
MILITARY TRAINING FOR WOMEN

Interviewing Date 2/3–8/45
Survey #340–K   Question #9

After the war is over, do you think young women should be required to take one year's training in the women's branches of the armed services?

Yes.............................. 22%
No.............................. 71
No opinion...................... 7

By Sex
Men

Yes.............................. 19%
No.............................. 74
No opinion...................... 7

Women

Yes............................... 25%
No................................ 68
No opinion........................ 7

MARCH 2
GERMANY AND JAPAN

Interviewing Date 2/3–8/45
Survey #340–K   Question #4a

After the war should Germany and Japan be kept permanently disarmed?

Roosevelt Voters Only

Yes............................... 89%
No................................ 6
No opinion........................ 5

Dewey Voters Only

Yes............................... 89%
No................................ 6
No opinion........................ 5

Interviewing Date 2/3–8/45
Survey #340–K   Question #4b

Should the United States, England, Russia, and China make a written agreement now to keep Germany and Japan disarmed, or should we wait until the war is over to make such an agreement?

Roosevelt Voters Only

Make agreement now............... 56%
Wait until war is over............ 27
Make no agreement................. 7
No opinion........................ 10

Dewey Voters Only

Make agreement now............... 53%
Wait until war is over............ 31
Make no agreement................. 8
No opinion........................ 8

Interviewing Date 2/3–8/45
Survey #340–K   Question #4c

If it becomes necessary to use force to keep Germany and Japan from arming again, should the President have the right to order the use of American armed force immediately, or should the approval of Congress be obtained first?

Roosevelt Voters Only

President should have the right....... 54%
Should first obtain approval......... 37
No opinion........................ 9

Dewey Voters Only

President should have the right....... 23%
Should first obtain approval.......... 69
No opinion........................ 8

MARCH 3
WASTE PAPER CAMPAIGN

Interviewing Date 2/3–8/45
Survey #340–K   Question #1a

Is any member of your household now regularly saving scrap paper?

On the basis of the present survey, about 19,500,000 households are now saving any waste paper regularly; 14,000,000 are not.

About 10,000,000 families still are not convinced of the need for saving waste paper.

Of the appreciable proportion (21%) who say they have to carry waste paper to salvage depots, slightly more than half say they think they would save more if someone came by to pick it up regularly.

MARCH 9
GERMAN MANPOWER

Interviewing Date 2/22–27/45
Survey #341–K   Question #5

After the war should three or four million German men be required to spend two or three years helping rebuild cities in Russia which they have destroyed?

Yes..............................	71%
No..............................	20
No opinion......................	9

MARCH 10
CRIMEAN CONFERENCE

Interviewing Date 2/22–27/45
Survey #341–K   Question #11a

Have you heard or read about the Crimean Conference between Stalin, Churchill, and Roosevelt?

Yes..............................	70%
No..............................	30

Interviewing Date 2/22–27/45
Survey #341–K   Question #11b

Those who had heard or read about the Crimean Conference were then asked: On the whole, is your opinion of what was accomplished at the conference favorable or unfavorable?

Favorable........................	61%
Unfavorable......................	9
No opinion......................	30

Roosevelt Voters Only

Favorable........................	70%
Unfavorable......................	6
No opinion......................	24

Dewey Voters Only

Favorable........................	52%
Unfavorable......................	12
No opinion......................	33

MARCH 11
RUSSIA

Interviewing Date 2/22–27/45
Survey #341–K   Question #8

Do you think Russia can be trusted to cooperate with us after the war?

Yes..............................	55%
No..............................	31
Undecided.......................	14

By Education
College

Yes..............................	62%
No..............................	30
Undecided.......................	8

High School

Yes..............................	60%
No..............................	29
Undecided.......................	11

Grade School

Yes..............................	51%
No..............................	31
Undecided.......................	18

Roosevelt Voters Only

Yes..............................	62%
No..............................	25
Undecided.......................	13

Dewey Voters Only

Yes..............................	51%
No..............................	38
Undecided.......................	11

MARCH 14
RUSSIA

Interviewing Date 2/22–27/45
Survey #341–K   Question #9

When Germany is defeated, do you think Russia will join us in the war against Japan, or do you think Russia will stay neutral?

Will join........................	65%
Will stay neutral.................	22
No opinion......................	13

There is not much difference by political parties. The survey finds that 65% of all people who voted for Dewey last fall, and 69% of those who voted for Roosevelt, agree in thinking that Russia will join us.

MARCH 16
PEACE OUTLOOK

Interviewing Date 2/22–27/45
Survey #341–K   Question #7a

Do you think the United States will find itself in another war within the next 25 years?

Yes................................. 38%
No.................................. 45
No opinion......................... 17

By Age
21–29 Years
Yes................................. 44%
No.................................. 40
No opinion......................... 16

30–49 Years
Yes................................. 39%
No.................................. 45
No opinion......................... 16

50 Years and Over
Yes................................. 34%
No.................................. 48
No opinion......................... 18

MARCH 17
DIVORCE LAWS

Interviewing Date 2/22–27/45
Survey #341–K   Question #13a

Do you think divorce laws should be the same in every state?

Yes................................. 83%
No.................................. 5
No opinion......................... 12

Interviewing Date 2/22–27/45
Survey #341–K   Question #13b

Do you think the divorce laws in your state are too strict or not strict enough?

Too strict.......................... 9%
Not strict enough................... 35
About right......................... 31
No opinion......................... 25

Older people, 50 years or over, are more inclined to feel that the laws in their state are not now strict enough than is the case among those who are under 50 years of age.

MARCH 18
INCOME OUTLOOK

Interviewing Date 2/22–27/45
Survey #341–K   Question #14

During the first year or two after the war do you think the total amount of money taken in by your family will be greater, about the same, or less than it is now?

Greater............................ 10%
Same.............................. 49
Less............................... 36
No opinion......................... 5

By Region
New England and Middle Atlantic
Greater............................ 10%
Same.............................. 47
Less............................... 37
No opinion......................... 6

East Central
Greater............................ 12%
Same.............................. 51
Less............................... 33
No opinion......................... 4

West Central
Greater............................ 8%
Same.............................. 52
Less............................... 36
No opinion......................... 4

South

Greater	9%
Same	50
Less	35
No opinion	6

West

Greater	13%
Same	45
Less	37
No opinion	5

By Occupation
Professional and Business

Greater	15%
Same	51
Less	31
No opinion	3

White Collar

Greater	13%
Same	53
Less	31
No opinion	3

Farmers

Greater	7%
Same	51
Less	37
No opinion	5

Skilled and Semiskilled

Greater	9%
Same	47
Less	39
No opinion	5

Unskilled

Greater	8%
Same	46
Less	40
No opinion	6

MARCH 21
WAR NEWS

Interviewing Date 2/22–27/45
Survey #341–K   Question #6a

Do you think the Government is giving the public as much information as it should about the war?

Yes	55%
No	36
No opinion	9

Interviewing Date 2/22–27/45
Survey #341–K   Question #6b

Asked of those dissatisfied with the news they received: What further information do you think should be given?

A sizeable proportion would like to get more of the bad news and more details.

There is also dissatisfaction with the amount of news about our losses, the pushbacks, casualties, and ship losses. People in this group say they would like to see the Government publish more of this news, or publish it more promptly.

MARCH 24
CURFEW

Interviewing Date 2/23–28/45
Survey #341–T   Question #13

The War Mobilization Director has recently requested that all places of entertainment be closed by midnight to conserve fuel and other war resources. Do you approve or disapprove of this?

Approve	82%
Disapprove	13
Undecided	5

By Age
21–29 Years

Approve.......................... 75%
Disapprove...................... 18
Undecided...................... 7

30–49 Years

Approve.......................... 82%
Disapprove...................... 13
Undecided...................... 5

50 Years and Over

Approve.......................... 86%
Disapprove...................... 10
Undecided...................... 4

MARCH 25
CANCER

Interviewing Date 2/3–8/45
Survey #340–K   Question #8a

Do you think cancer is curable

If caught in time.................. 62%
Incurable........................ 26
Don't know...................... 12

Interviewing Date 2/3–8/45
Survey #340–K   Question #8b

Do you think cancer is contagious?

Yes.............................. 21%
No............................... 59
Don't know...................... 20

Interviewing Date 2/3–8/45
Survey #340–K   Question #8d

Do you happen to know any of the symptoms of cancer?

Yes.............................. 43%
No............................... 57

Interviewing Date 2/3–8/45
Survey #340–K   Question #8a

If someone in your family had cancer that could not be cured, do you think they should be told this?

Yes.............................. 46%
No............................... 38
Don't know...................... 16

MARCH 28
INCOME TAXES

Interviewing Date 3/9–14/45
Survey #342–K   Question #6e

Do you regard the amount of tax you had to pay on your 1944 income as fair?

Yes.............................. 85%
No............................... 15

About as large a percentage in the business and professional classifications consider their taxes fair, as in the case with white-collar workers or factory workers.

MARCH 30
COMPULSORY MILITARY TRAINING

Interviewing Date 3/10–15/45
Survey #342–T   Question #2a

Do you think young men 18 years of age in the armed forces should be trained for one year in this country before being sent overseas to fight, or is it all right to send them sooner if the army thinks they have had enough training?

One year......................... 68%
Sooner........................... 26
No opinion....................... 6

By Sex
Men

One year......................... 62%
Sooner........................... 31
No opinion....................... 7

Women

One year......................... 73%
Sooner........................... 22
No opinion....................... 5

MARCH 31
STANDARD TIME

Interviewing Date 3/9–14/45
Survey #342–K   Question #1

Do you think the entire country should go back to Standard Time or should we stay on War Time the year around until the war is over?

Return to Standard Time............ 38%
Stay on War Time.................. 49
Undecided........................ 13

By Region
New England and Middle Atlantic

Return to Standard Time............ 30%
Stay on War Time.................. 59
Undecided........................ 11

East Central

Return to Standard Time............ 36%
Stay on War Time.................. 49
Undecided........................ 15

West Central

Return to Standard Time............ 56%
Stay on War Time.................. 29
Undecided........................ 15

South

Return to Standard Time............ 39%
Stay on War Time.................. 48
Undecided........................ 13

West

Return to Standard Time............ 37%
Stay on War Time.................. 49
Undecided........................ 14

APRIL 1
MOST IMPORTANT PROBLEM

Interviewing Date 3/9–14/45
Survey #342–K   Question #3

Aside from winning the war, what do you think is the most important problem facing this country today?

Jobs for everyone after the war, prevent future unemployment, make sure soldiers all get jobs.................... 20%

Solving economic problems, preventing inflation, preventing depression, getting war paid for without devaluing currency, paying off national debt, reconversion of industry, and other economic problems................ 16

A permanent world peace, making a lasting peace, world policing, handling of Axis powers.................... 15

Labor union troubles, labor vs. capital, strikes, curbing and controlling unions. 10

Rehabilitating returning veterans, wounded and maimed.................... 6

How to reduce government control and stimulate free enterprise........... 5

Racial and religious tolerance........ 5

Food shortages here and abroad, rationing, clothing shortages.............. 5

Juvenile delinquency................ 3

Return to religion, "get closer to the Lord"........................... 2

Miscellaneous problems.............. 8

No problems named................ 10
_____
105%

(Note: total adds to more than 100% because some persons named more than one problem.)

APRIL 4
"FEATHER-BEDDING"

Interviewing Date 3/10–15/45
Survey #342–T   Question #10

To make more jobs, some unions require employers to hire more persons than are actually needed to do the work. Would you favor or oppose having a law passed which would stop this practice?

Favor............................ 66%
Oppose........................... 20
Undecided........................ 14

The survey also discovered that only 4% of the public knew what the term "feather-bedding" meant.

APRIL 6
PRISONERS OF WAR

Interviewing Date 3/22–27/45
Survey #343–K   Question #13a

Have you heard or read anything about our treatment of prisoners of war now in camps in this country?

Yes................................ 84%
No................................ 16

Interviewing Date 3/22–27/45
Survey #343–K   Question #13b

Those who said yes were then asked: Do you think the treatment of prisoners of war here is too strict or not strict enough?

Too strict.......................... 1%
Not strict enough.................. 71
About right........................ 24
No opinion........................ 4

APRIL 7
THREAT OF COAL STRIKE

Interviewing Date 3/9–14/45
Survey #342–K   Question #4

What do you think the Government should do if the coal miners go on strike this spring?

Take over the mines................ 74%
Give in to miners.................. 7
Punish strikers.................... 6
Settle by arbitration.............. 4
Do nothing........................ 1
No opinion........................ 8

APRIL 8
WORLD GOVERNMENT

Interviewing Date 3/22–27/45
Survey #343–K   Question #6a

Do you think the United States should join a world organization with police power to maintain world peace?

Yes................................ 81%
No................................ 11
No opinion........................ 8

Interviewing Date 3/22–27/45
Survey #343–K   Question #6b

How important do you think it is that we join such a world organization — very important, fairly important, or not too important?

Very important..................... 83%
Fairly important................... 11
Not too important.................. 3
No opinion........................ 3

APRIL 11
WORLD GOVERNMENT

Interviewing Date 3/22–27/45
Survey #343–K   Question #6a

Do you think the United States should join a world organization with police power to maintain world peace?

By Region

	Yes
New England.......................	84%
East Central......................	81
West Central......................	83
South............................	81
West.............................	85

APRIL 13
SAVINGS

Interviewing Date 3/22–27/45
Survey #343–K   Question #3b

If you lose your present job after the war, will you have enough money saved so that you can get along till you find other work?

Yes.............................. 60%
No............................... 30
Don't know....................... 10

By Occupation
White Collar

Yes.............................. 68%
No............................... 25
Don't know....................... 7

Laborers

Yes.............................. 54%
No............................... 35
Don't know....................... 11

Interviewing Date 3/22–27/45
Survey #343–K   Question #3c

All those who said yes were then asked: For about how long could you get by if you had no work at all?

3 months or less.................... 10%
4–6 months......................... 12
7–12 months........................ 14
13 months–2 years.................. 6
Over 2 years....................... 10
Don't know......................... 8
                                   ―――
                                   60%

APRIL 14
IDEAL PLACE TO VISIT

Interviewing Date 3/22–27/45
Survey #343–K   Question #1

When this war is over, many Americans will want to travel to various parts of the world. If you could take a trip outside the United States, to which one country would you most like to go?

Great Britain tops the list of choices. France runs second. These two each receive more

than twice as many votes as the next most popular country.

Germany ranks third in choice. Russia is next. Then come Italy, Switzerland, Ireland, and Norway, in that order.

APRIL 15
LITTLE STEEL FORMULA

Interviewing Date 3/22–27/45
Survey #343–K   Question #5a

Have you heard or read anything about the Little Steel Formula?

Yes.............................. 52%
No............................... 48

Interviewing Date 3/22–27/45
Survey #343–K   Question #5b

Those who answered in the affirmative were asked: Will you tell me briefly what it is intended to do?

The number who were able to give a reasonably accurate answer constituted 30% of the population. In the case of labor union members the proportion indicating correct knowledge was 38%.

Interviewing Date 3/22–27/45
Survey #343–K   Question #5d

Do you think the Government's present policy in regard to wage and salary increases should be continued, or should it be changed to permit general increases in wages and salaries?

Continued.......................... 42%
Changed............................ 29
Qualified answers.................. 13
No opinion......................... 16

Informed Persons Only

Continued.......................... 45%
Changed............................ 30
Qualified answers.................. 16
No opinion......................... 9

Among labor union members in the informed group, the weight of opinion was found slightly in favor of change rather than the continuation of the present policy.

APRIL 18
RUSSIA

Interviewing Date 3/22–27/45
Survey #343–K   Question #7

After the war should the United States and Russia make a permanent alliance, that is, agree to come to each other's defense immediately if the other is attacked at any future time?

Yes............................... 49%
No................................ 36
Undecided......................... 15

APRIL 20
GERMANY

Interviewing Date 3/22–27/45
Survey #343–K   Question #9

What do you think should be done with German industry after the war?

Close supervision and control........ 56%
Destroy it, make the country mainly
    agricultural..................... 13
Take it over ourselves............... 10
Promote it, encourage Germany....... 4
Do nothing.......................... 4
No opinion.......................... 13

By Education
College

Close supervision and control........ 71%
Destroy it, make the country mainly
    agricultural..................... 6
Take it over ourselves............... 9
Promote it, encourage Germany....... 6
Do nothing.......................... 3
No opinion.......................... 7
                                    ‾‾‾‾
                                    102%

High School

Close supervision and control........ 60%
Destroy it, make the country mainly
    agricultural..................... 12
Take it over ourselves............... 10
Promote it, encourage Germany....... 5
Do nothing.......................... 5
No opinion.......................... 8

Grade School

Close supervision and control........ 50%
Destroy it, make the country mainly
    agricultural..................... 15
Take it over ourselves............... 10
Promote it, encourage Germany....... 4
Do nothing.......................... 4
No opinion.......................... 18
                                    ‾‾‾‾
                                    101%

(Note: some of the above tables add to more than 100% because some persons named more than one alternative.)

APRIL 21
DOMESTIC REFORM

Interviewing Date 3/22–27/45
Survey #343–K   Question #8a

After the war, would you like to see many changes or reforms made in the United States, or would you rather have the country remain pretty much the way it was before the war?

Many changes....................... 39%
Stay the same...................... 52
No opinion......................... 9

By Education
College

Many changes....................... 58%
Stay the same...................... 37
No opinion......................... 5

High School

Many changes...................... 43%
Stay the same...................... 50
No opinion........................ 7

Grade School

Many changes...................... 32%
Stay the same...................... 57
No opinion........................ 11

Interviewing Date 3/22–27/45
Survey #343–K   Question #8b

Asked of those who want changes: What changes would you like to see made after the war?

Social Reforms

Want to see jobs for all, improvement in wages, working conditions......... 9%
Want to end racial and religious discrimination.......................... 3
Want to liberalize social security provisions, increase pensions, provide national health insurance.............. 3
Want better educational opportunities.. 3
Want better housing and slum clearance 2

Pre-New Deal Changes

Want to get back to Constitution, do away with Government controls..... 7

Other Changes

Want better administration of labor unions, settlement of labor disputes without strikes................... 3
Want prices kept high............... 1
Want lower taxes.................... 1
Miscellaneous suggestions............ 9
Did not say........................ 3
         44%

(Note: table adds to more than the 39% who say they want to see changes or reforms after the war because some persons made more than one suggestion.)

APRIL 22
SAN FRANCISCO CONFERENCE

Interviewing Date 4/6–11/45
Survey #344–K   Question #9a

Have you heard or read about the San Francisco Conference to be held this month?

Yes............................... 67%
No................................ 33

Interviewing Date 4/6–11/45
Survey #344–K   Question #9b

Each person aware of the conference was asked: Will you tell me what the purpose of the conference is?

Work out peace terms, dispose of the Axis........................... 41%
Create machinery for world league, establish basis for permanent peace........ 34
Discuss postwar plans, settle economic questions, trade problems, etc....... 11
Make plans for finishing the war....... 2
Settle boundary disputes............. 1
Miscellaneous...................... 3
Don't know........................ 17
        109%

(Note: table adds to more than 100% because some people gave more than one suggestion.)

APRIL 25
ASSISTANCE FOR EUROPE

Interviewing Date 4/6–11/45
Survey #344–K   Question #1

For a year after the war in Europe is over, should people in the United States continue to put up with present shortages of butter, sugar, meat, and other rationed food products in order to give food to people who need it in Europe?

Yes............................... 65%
No................................ 27
Undecided......................... 8

By Sex
Men

Yes............................... 61%
No............................... 32
Undecided........................ 7

Women

Yes............................... 60%
No............................... 32
Undecided........................ 8

APRIL 27
NAZI WAR CRIMES

Interviewing Date 4/7–12/45
Survey #344–T   Question #7

After the war, what do you think should be done with members of the Nazi party who defend themselves by claiming that they committed crimes under orders of higher-ups in the party?

Imprison them..................... 42%
Kill them......................... 19
Try them, and punish only if found guilty 19
Try to reeducate them............. 3
Do nothing about them............. 2
No opinion........................ 15

APRIL 28
GERMANY

Interviewing Date 4/6–11/45
Survey #344–K   Question #11

Do you approve or disapprove of splitting Germany permanently into a number of smaller countries?

Approve........................... 40%
Disapprove........................ 32
Undecided......................... 28

By Education
College

Approve........................... 42%
Disapprove........................ 44
Undecided......................... 14

High School

Approve........................... 46%
Disapprove........................ 34
Undecided......................... 20

Grade School

Approve........................... 37%
Disapprove........................ 28
Undecided......................... 35

MAY 2
COMPULSORY MILITARY TRAINING

Interviewing Date 4/6–11/45
Survey #344–K   Question #3a

After the war is over, do you think every able-bodied young man should be required to take military or naval training for one year?

Yes............................... 70%
No............................... 24
No opinion........................ 6

By Sex
Men

Yes............................... 70%
No............................... 25
No opinion........................ 5

Women

Yes............................... 70%
No............................... 23
No opinion........................ 7

By Political Preference
Roosevelt Voters

Yes............................... 77%
No............................... 18
No opinion........................ 5

Dewey Voters

Yes............................... 61%
No............................... 34
No opinion........................ 5

By Region
New England–Middle Atlantic

Yes............................... 69%
No................................ 25
No opinion........................ 6

East Central–West Central

Yes............................... 66%
No................................ 29
No opinion........................ 5

South

Yes............................... 74%
No................................ 17
No opinion........................ 9

Mountain–West

Yes............................... 72%
No................................ 25
No opinion........................ 3

Interviewing Date 4/6–11/45
Survey #344–K   Question #3b

Those answering yes were then asked: Do you think a military training law should be passed now, or should this wait until after the war?

Now.............................. 33%
Later............................. 30
No opinion........................ 7
                  70%

MAY 4
TROOP DEPLOYMENT

Interviewing Date 4/6–11/45
Survey #344–K   Question #8

After Germany is defeated, do you think American soldiers in Europe who are no longer needed there will be sent home to stay, or do you think most of them will be sent to fight against Japan?

Sent home........................ 15%
Sent to Japan..................... 74
No opinion........................ 11

MAY 5
LABOR FOREMEN

Interviewing Date 4/20–25/45
Survey #345–K   Question #14a

Have you ever heard or read anything about the question of foremen in factories organizing into a union?

Yes............................... 28%
No................................ 72

Interviewing Date 4/20–25/45
Survey #345–K   Question #14b

At the present most shop foremen in factories are not members of a labor union. Do you think they should or should not become members of a labor union?

Should............................ 29%
Should not........................ 41
No opinion........................ 30

Labor Union Members Only

Should............................ 56%
Should not........................ 27
No opinion........................ 17

MAY 6
GERMAN MANPOWER

Interviewing Date 4/20–25/45
Survey #345–K   Question #2

After the war should three or four million German men be required to spend two or three years in Russia helping rebuild cities which they have destroyed?

Yes............................... 82%
No................................ 11
No opinion........................ 7

By Education
College

Yes............................... 80%
No................................ 17
No opinion........................ 3

High School

Yes	83%
No	12
No opinion	5

Grade School

Yes	82%
No	9
No opinion	9

MAY 9
OCCUPATION OF GERMANY

Special British Survey

Britons were asked this question: About how long do you think the occupation of Germany will have to last?

Up to 5 years	18%
Up to 10 years	27
Up to 15 years	10
Up to 20 years	16
Up to 25 years	8
More than 25 years	10
No opinion	11

MAY 12
PRESIDENT TRUMAN'S POLITICAL PHILOSOPHY

Interviewing Date 4/20–25/45
Survey #345–K   Question #11b

Do you think Harry Truman will be more favorable or less favorable toward business than Franklin Roosevelt?

More favorable	40%
Less favorable	7
About the same	25
No opinion	28

Interviewing Date 4/20–25/45
Survey #345–K   Question #11c

Do you think Harry Truman will be more favorable or less favorable toward labor unions than Franklin Roosevelt?

More favorable	6%
Less favorable	38
About the same	25
No opinion	31

MAY 13
PRESIDENT TRUMAN AND CONGRESS

Interviewing Date 4/20–25/45
Survey #345–K   Question #13

Some writers believe that with Harry Truman as President, Congress will have more importance and power than it had under Franklin Roosevelt. Do you think this would be a good thing or a bad thing for the country?

Good thing	65%
Bad thing	16
No opinion	19

By Education
College

Good thing	84%
Bad thing	9
No opinion	7

High School

Good thing	70%
Bad thing	16
No opinion	14

Grade School

Good thing	51%
Bad thing	24
No opinion	25

MAY 16
PRESIDENTIAL CANDIDATES

Interviewing Date 4/20–25/45
Survey #345–K   Question #7

What man would you like to see elected President of the country in 1948?

Choice of Democrats

Truman	63%
Wallace	20
Stettinius	9
Byrnes	1
Byrd	1
Others	6

Choice of Republicans

Dewey	59%
Stassen	15
Bricker	8
MacArthur	7
Vandenberg	4
Taft	2
Hoover	1
Saltonstall	1
Warren	1
Others	2

MAY 18
PARTY STRENGTH

Interviewing Date 4/20–25/45
Survey #345–K   Question #6

Which party do you want to see win the presidential election in 1948 — the Democratic or the Republican?

Democratic	54%
Republican	46

Interviewing Date 4/20–25/45
Survey #345–K   Question #8

Regardless of how you yourself feel, which party do you think will win the presidential election in 1948?

Democratic	45%
Republican	55

MAY 19
PRESIDENTIAL TENURE

Interviewing Date 4/20–25/45
Survey #345–K   Question #15

Would you favor or oppose a law which would keep all Presidents of the United States from being elected for a third term?

Favor	60%
Oppose	40

Interviewing Date 4/20–25/45
Survey #345–T   Question #15

Would you favor changing the term of office of the President of the United States in the future to one six-year term with no reelection?

Yes	27%
No	73

MAY 20
NAZI WAR CRIMES

Interviewing Date 5/4–9/45
Survey #346–K   Question #3a

What do you think of the reports that the Germans have killed many people in concentration camps or let them starve to death — are they true or not true?

True	84%
True, but exaggerated	9
Doubtful, hard to believe	1
Not true	3
Can't decide	3

Interviewing Date 5/4–9/45
Survey #346–K   Question #3b

Nobody knows how many have been killed or starved to death but what would be your best guess?

Median average	1 million

Do you think it would be a good idea or a bad idea to have movie theaters throughout the country show pictures of all the horrible things that have happened in prison camps run by Germans?

Good idea............................ 60%
Bad idea............................ 35
No opinion........................ 5

Would you like to see them?

Yes............................... 83%
No............................... 17

Do you think such pictures should be shown to all German prisoners of war in camps in the United States?

Yes............................... 87%
No............................... 9
No opinion........................ 4

Do you think such pictures should be shown to all German people in Germany?

Yes............................... 89%
No............................... 8
No opinion........................ 3

MAY 23
TRADE AGREEMENTS

Congress has to decide whether or not to continue the trade agreements program. What do you think — should the program be continued or not?

Should be continued................. 75%
Should not be..................... 7
Undecided........................ 18

Would you approve or disapprove using this program to get further reductions of tariffs in both the United States and other countries?

Approve............................ 57%
Disapprove........................ 20
No opinion........................ 23

Democrats who are familiar with the principle of reciprocal trade agreements are overwhelmingly in favor of a further reduction in tariffs. Republicans who are familiar with the agreements are more evenly divided. A slight majority of those interviewed in this survey favor further reductions.

MAY 25
TENNESSEE VALLEY AUTHORITY

Have you ever heard of the Tennessee Valley Authority?

Yes............................... 60%
No............................... 40

Will you tell me briefly what it is?

Correct answer..................... 41%
Incorrect answer................... 59

Those who gave a correct answer were then asked: From what you know, is your opinion of TVA in general favorable or unfavorable?

Favorable......................... 32%
Unfavorable....................... 5
No opinion........................ 4
                                   ——
                                   41%

Interviewing Date 4/20–25/45
Survey #345–K   Question #17d

*Those informed about the TVA were next
asked: Would you like to see something
similar organized for the Missouri Valley?*

Yes.............................. 27%
No............................... 5
No opinion....................... 9
                                  ——
                                  41%

MAY 26
BLACK MARKET

Interviewing Date 5/4–9/45
Survey #346–K   Question #11b

*Do you think that buying at black market
prices is sometimes justified?*

Sometimes justified................. 21%
Not justified....................... 74
No opinion.......................... 5

By Sex
Men

Sometimes justified................. 23%
Not justified....................... 71
No opinion.......................... 6

Women

Sometimes justified................. 18%
Not justified....................... 77
No opinion.......................... 5

By Community Size
Over 100,000

Sometimes justified................. 23%
Not justified....................... 73
No opinion.......................... 4

10,000–100,000

Sometimes justified................. 19%
Not justified....................... 78
No opinion.......................... 3

Under 10,000

Sometimes justified................. 21%
Not justified....................... 73
No opinion.......................... 6

Farm Areas

Sometimes justified................. 18%
Not justified....................... 73
No opinion.......................... 9

Interviewing Date 5/4–9/45
Survey #346–K   Question #11c

*Under what conditions do you think it is
justified?*

When questioned as to conditions under which
black market buying might be justified, the
largest number mentioned emergencies such
as illness. Others said they felt black market
buying was justified when the rationing board
was unfair after an appeal.

MAY 27
GERMANY

Interviewing Date 5/4–9/45
Survey #346–K   Question #1

*What do you think we should do with
Germany as a country?*

Be lenient, rehabilitate reeducate, en-
courage trade, start afresh.......... 8%
Supervise and control, disarm, eliminate
Nazis, control industries............ 46
Treat very severely, destroy as political
entity, cripple her.................. 34
Miscellaneous, undecided............. 12

MAY 30
GENERAL KNOWLEDGE

Interviewing Date 5/4–9/45
Survey #346–K   Question #10

Can you locate the following places?

	Correct
Guam	28%
Okinawa	33
Java	26
Singapore	14
Osaka	43
Kyushu	41
Chungking	79
Manila	74

By Education

	College	High School	Grade School
Guam	46%	35%	20%
Okinawa	54	36	26
Java	57	32	15
Singapore	37	17	6
Osaka	72	55	28
Kyushu	72	54	26
Chungking	98	91	67
Manila	95	85	63

JUNE 1
HERMANN GOERING

Interviewing Date 5/17–22/45
Survey #347–K   Question #2b

What punishment if any do you think we should give Goering?

Kill him	67%
Imprison for life	6
Give him a trial	4
Other punishment	5
Do nothing	1
No opinion	17

The 67% advocating death for Goering includes many who say that the manner of death should be made as unpleasant as possible.

JUNE 2
POSTWAR PUNISHMENT

Interviewing Date 5/18–23/45
Survey #347–T   Question #2

What do you think should be done with Gestapo agents and storm troopers after the war?

Nearly half (45%) would like to see Gestapo agents and Nazi Storm Troopers quickly destroyed.

"Kill them . . . hang them . . . wipe them off the face of the Earth " are typical replies.

About a fifth of the people would "punish them" without designating just what form the punishment should take. Half of these people would, however, take time out to try the Gestapo and storm troop prisoners, make certain of their guilt before punishing.

One in ten think in terms of more than death. They want SS troopers and Gestapo men to die, but they want them to die slowly; they want to torture them, some suggesting "hard work and starvation" as the means.

"Imprison them . . . jail them . . . cage them (at least some part of the public always wants to put enemies on public display) . . . exile them . . . isolate them . . . treat them as they treated others. . . . No punishment is bad enough." These are just a few of the other suggestions.

JUNE 3
ADOLF HITLER

Interviewing Date 5/17–22/45
Survey #347–K   Question #1

Do you personally think that Hitler is dead?

Yes	17%
No	68
No opinion	15

By Education
College

Yes.................................. 23%
No................................... 65
No opinion........................... 12

High School

Yes.................................. 15%
No................................... 72
No opinion........................... 13

Grade School

Yes.................................. 16%
No................................... 66
No opinion........................... 18

JUNE 6
RUSSIA

Interviewing Date 5/17–22/45
Survey #347–K   Question #12

Do you think Russia can be trusted to cooperate with us after the war?

Yes.................................. 45%
No................................... 38
Undecided............................ 17

The decrease in confidence in Russia's intentions is found to be the same among both Republican and Democratic voters, and among both men and women. While there are some differences on the basis of education, there has been a marked drop-off in trust of Russia in all educational levels.

JUNE 8
TAXES

Interviewing Date 5/17–22/45
Survey #347–K   Question #10a

Do you think Congress should reduce income taxes this year, or should this wait until after Japan is defeated?

Cut income taxes..................... 18%
Wait................................. 77
No opinion........................... 5

Interviewing Date 5/17–22/45
Survey #347–K   Question #10b

Do you think Congress should reduce taxes on business this year, or should this wait until after Japan is defeated?

Cut business taxes................... 16%
Wait................................. 74
No opinion........................... 10

JUNE 9
CANADIAN POLITICS

Special Survey

Asked of Canadian voters: If the election were being held today what party would you vote for?

Liberal party........................ 40%
Progressive-Conservative............. 27
Co-operative Commonwealth Federation 19
Bloc Populaire....................... 5
Others............................... 9

JUNE 10
GERMANY AND JAPAN

Interviewing Date 5/17–22/45
Survey #347–K   Question #5a

To what extent do you think the German people have approved of the killing and starving of prisoners in Germany — entirely, partly, or not at all?

Entirely............................. 31%
Partly............................... 51
Not at all........................... 4
German people didn't know............ 8
No opinion........................... 6

Interviewing Date 5/17–22/45
Survey #347–K   Question #5b

To what extent do you think the Japanese people approve of the killing and starving of prisoners — entirely, partly, or not at all?

Entirely............................ 63%
Partly.............................. 25
Not at all.......................... 2
Japanese people don't know........... 4
No opinion......................... 6

Interviewing Date 5/17–22/45
Survey #347–K   Question #5c

Which people do you think are more cruel at heart — the Germans or the Japanese?

Japanese........................... 82%
Germans........................... 18

Attitudes toward the German and Japanese people do not vary to any important extent by education levels in this country. Today's poll finds that the typical college-trained person feels about the same way as the person who has had only a high school education or a grade school education, the majority in all groups thinking that the Japanese people show instincts considerably less civilized than the German people.

JUNE 13
COMPULSORY MILITARY TRAINING

Interviewing Date 6/1–5/45
Survey #348–K   Question #14

After the war is over do you think every able-bodied young man should be required to take military or naval training for one year?

Yes................................ 70%
No................................. 24
No opinion......................... 6

JUNE 15
RATION POINTS

Interviewing Date 6/1–5/45
Survey #348–K   Question #1

Do you think restaurants should collect ration points from people who eat meals which include meat?

Yes................................ 33%
No................................. 56
No opinion......................... 11

Persons Who Eat in Restaurants

	Often	Occasionally	Rarely, Never
Yes...........	26%	33%	40%
No...........	70	59	34
No opinion.....	4	8	26

JUNE 16
TREATIES

Interviewing Date 5/17–22/45
Survey #347–K   Question #13a

Which one of these three ways would you, personally, favor as the best way to have peace treaties approved? (1) Approval by the President only, (2) Approval by the President and a majority of the whole Congress, (3) Approval by the President and two-thirds of the Senate — the present method.

President only..................... 7%
President and majority whole Congress 58
President and two-thirds Senate....... 21
Don't know......................... 14

JUNE 17
AID TO EUROPE

Interviewing Date 5/17–22/45
Survey #347–K   Question #4a

Do you think many people in Europe will starve this year unless we send them food?

Yes................................ 70%
No................................ 23
No opinion........................ 7

Interviewing Date 5/17–22/45
Survey #347–K   Question #4d

Do you think there is enough food in this country to keep Europeans from starving and still not reduce the amount people eat here?

Yes................................ 35%
No................................ 56
No opinion........................ 9

Interviewing Date 5/18–23/45
Survey #347–T   Question #4c

Would you be willing to continue to put up with present shortages of butter, sugar, meat, and other rationed food products in order to give food to people who need it in Europe?

Yes................................ 85%
No................................ 12
No opinion........................ 3

Interviewing Date 5/17–22/45
Survey #347–K   Question #4c

If necessary, would you and your family be willing to eat about one-fifth less than you are now eating in order to send more food to Europe?

Yes................................ 70%
No................................ 23
No opinion........................ 7

JUNE 22
PROPAGANDA AGENCY

Interviewing Date 6/1–5/45
Survey #348–T   Question #13a

Do you think we should have a permanent governmental agency that would explain the views and policies of this country to the people of other nations of the world?

Yes................................ 49%
No................................ 23
No opinion........................ 28

By Political Affiliation
Democrats

Yes................................ 56%
No................................ 19
No opinion........................ 25

Republicans

Yes................................ 47%
No................................ 34
No opinion........................ 19

Interviewing Date 6/1–5/45
Survey #348–T   Question #13b

Can you tell me what the OWI is?

Correct answer..................... 31%
Incorrect answer................... 69

Interviewing Date 6/1–5/45
Survey #348–T   Question #13c

Those answering correctly were asked: As far as you know, do you think the OWI has done its job well or poorly?

Well............................... 14%
Fair job........................... 9
Poorly............................. 4
No opinion......................... 4
                                  ‾‾‾‾
                                  31%

JUNE 23
DISCHARGE FROM ARMY

Interviewing Date 6/1–5/45
Survey #348–K   Question #3a

Do you think the point system for releasing men from the Army is fair?

Yes................................ 72%
No................................ 15
No opinion........................ 13

Interviewing Date 6/1–5/45
Survey #348–K　　　　　　　Question #3b

What changes, if any, would you like to see made in the point system?

Only 30% suggested changes. These, in order of frequency, are as follows:

Credit for children should be higher. Men who have served the longest should be released first. Men in combat longest should be released first. Years of overseas service should be given more points. Age should be given more consideration. Point requirements should be lowered generally. The point system should be extended to include the Marines, the Navy, the Medical Corps. Men who have enough points should not be kept in, no matter how essential they are considered to be. More points should be given for wounds. Officers should be included in the system. Dependents other than children should be counted. Married men should be released first; men should be given points for wives.

Interviewing Date 6/1–5/45
Survey #348–K　　　　　　　Question #4

Do you think the draft is being handled fairly in your community?

Yes................................ 79%
No................................ 21

JUNE 24
WINSTON CHURCHILL

Interviewing Date 6/1–5/45
Survey #348–K　　　　　　　Question #5b

Persons who indicated an awareness of the upcoming British elections were asked: Would you like to see Winston Churchill reelected as Prime Minister?

Yes................................ 71%
No................................ 15
No opinion........................ 14

JUNE 27
WAGES

Interviewing Date 6/1–5/45
Survey #348–K　　　　　　　Question #11

After the war, are you expecting the general level of wages to be higher, lower, or about the same as it is now?

Higher............................ 5%
Lower............................. 63
About same........................ 27
No opinion........................ 5

By Occupation
Professional and Business

Higher............................ 8%
Lower............................. 60
About same........................ 29
No opinion........................ 3

White Collar

Higher............................ 4%
Lower............................. 68
About same........................ 27
No opinion........................ 1

Farmers

Higher............................ 2%
Lower............................. 73
About same........................ 20
No opinion........................ 5

Skilled and Unskilled

Higher............................ 4%
Lower............................. 60
About same........................ 29
No opinion........................ 7

JUNE 29
EMPEROR HIROHITO

Interviewing Date 6/1–5/45
Survey #348–K　　　　　　　Question #18a

Can you tell me the name of the Emperor of Japan?

Correct answer...................... 54%
Incorrect answer.................... 46

Five per cent said Tojo is the Emperor. Others said the Emperor is named Hari-Kari, Yoko-hoama, or Fujiyama.

Interviewing Date 6/1–5/45
Survey #348–K   Question #18b

What do you think we should do with the Japanese emperor after the war?

Execute him....................... 33%
Let court decide his fate............. 17
Keep him in prison the rest of his life.. 11
Exile him.......................... 9
Do nothing — he's only a figurehead for
    war lords....................... 4
Use him as a puppet to run Japan....... 3
Miscellaneous, no opinion........... 23

JUNE 30
ECONOMIC CONDITIONS

Interviewing Date 6/1–5/45
Survey #348–K   Question #10a

What class or group of people in this country has done best financially during the war compared to before the war?

Labor, war workers, other workers..... 60%
Business executives, upper class people.. 15
Farmers........................... 5
White collar workers................ 3
Miscellaneous...................... 5
No particular group................. 12

Interviewing Date 6/1–5/45
Survey #348–K   Question #10b

Do you think any class or group of people in this country is not making as much money as it should?

Yes............................... 59%
No................................ 26
No opinion........................ 15

Interviewing Date 6/1–5/45
Survey #348–K   Question #10c

Those answering yes were asked: Which group?

White collar....................... 25%
Labor, skilled, semiskilled, and unskilled
    workers....................... 13
Farmers........................... 10
Business and professional............ 9
Miscellaneous...................... 5
                        62%

(Note: total is more than 59% because some persons named more than one group.)

JULY 1
PRESIDENT TRUMAN'S POPULARITY

Interviewing Date 6/1–5/45
Survey #348–K   Question #19

Do you approve or disapprove of the way Harry Truman is handling his job as President?

Approve........................... 87%
Disapprove........................ 3
No opinion........................ 10

By Political Affiliation
Democrats

Approve........................... 88%
Disapprove........................ 2
No opinion........................ 10

Republicans

Approve........................... 89%
Disapprove........................ 3
No opinion........................ 8

The favorable opinion on Mr. Truman was found in all sections of the country, with comparatively little difference between areas. The highest percentage of approval — 92% — came from the West Central section.

JULY 4
"VICTORY GARDENS"

Interviewing Date 6/1–5/45
Survey #384–K   Question #8b

Have you started a vegetable garden this year?

Based on the findings, approximately 17,000,-000 families have started gardens.

Interviewing Date 6/1–5/45
Survey #384–K   Question #8c

Do you plan to have one?

Approximately 1,400,000 families say that they will be starting a vegetable garden.

JULY 6
CONGRESSIONAL PAY

Interviewing Date 6/15–20/45
Survey #349–T   Question #4

President Truman says that he favors raising the salaries of congressmen from $10,000 to at least $15,000 a year after general wage ceilings are removed. Would you approve or disapprove of this?

Approve.............................. 31%
Disapprove.......................... 50
No opinion........................... 19

By Occupation
Business and Professional

Approve.............................. 55%
Disapprove.......................... 32
No opinion........................... 13

White Collar

Approve.............................. 41%
Disapprove.......................... 46
No opinion........................... 13

Farmers

Approve.............................. 24%
Disapprove.......................... 55
No opinion........................... 21

Manual Workers

Approve.............................. 22%
Disapprove.......................... 56
No opinion........................... 22

JULY 7
MERCHANT MARINE

Interviewing Date 6/1–5/45
Survey #348–K   Question #2a

Are all men in the merchant marine members of the armed forces?

Yes................................. 25%
No.................................. 75

Interviewing Date 6/1–5/45
Survey #348–K   Question #2b

Does the GI Bill of Rights apply to all men in the merchant marine?

Yes................................. 19%
No.................................. 81

Interviewing Date 6/1–5/45
Survey #348–K   Question #2c

Informed persons (those answering no to the above two questions) were then asked: Should the GI bill of rights be extended to include all men in the merchant marine?

Yes................................. 60%
No.................................. 33
No opinion........................... 7

JULY 8
FRATERNIZATION

Interviewing Date 6/14–19/45
Survey #349–K   Question #1b

Do you think American soldiers in Germany should be allowed to have dates with German girls?

Yes................................ 30%
No................................. 59
No opinion......................... 11

By Sex
Men

Yes................................ 41%
No................................. 48
No opinion......................... 11

Women

Yes................................ 22%
No................................. 67
No opinion......................... 11

Families with a member in the armed forces in Germany are more opposed to fraternization than those with no member of the family in the occupying forces.

JULY 11
POSTWAR PRESTIGE

Special Survey

Persons in the United States and several European countries were asked: After the war, which country do you think will actually have the most influence in world affairs?

France Says

United States..................... 43%
Russia............................ 41
England........................... 4
No one in particular.............. 4
Undecided......................... 8

Canada Says

United States..................... 36%
Russia............................ 24
England........................... 19
Miscellaneous..................... 2
Undecided......................... 19

Sweden Says

United States..................... 50%
Russia............................ 21
England........................... 8
No one in particular.............. 5
Undecided......................... 16

Denmark Says

United States..................... 21%
Russia............................ 19
England........................... 9
United States and England......... 12
United States and Russia.......... 7
Others............................ 4
Undecided......................... 28

United States Says

United States..................... 63%
Russia............................ 24
England........................... 5
United States and Russia.......... 2
United States and England......... 1
Undecided......................... 5

JULY 13
UNEMPLOYMENT COMPENSATION

Interviewing Date 6/15–20/45
Survey #349–T   Question #5a

Do you think the Government should give money to workers who are unemployed for a limited length of time until they can find another job?

Yes................................ 63%
No................................. 32
No opinion......................... 5

By Occupation
Business and Professional

Yes................................ 58%
No................................. 38
No opinion......................... 4

White Collar

Yes.................................. 56%
No................................... 40
No opinion........................... 4

Farmers

Yes.................................. 50%
No................................... 42
No opinion........................... 8

Skilled and Unskilled

Yes.................................. 72%
No................................... 23
No opinion........................... 5

When the public was asked how much per week should be given in the way of unemployment compensation for a man with a wife and two children, the median average figure, including those opposed to the principle of giving anything, was $20 per week. The median average sum named by farmers was $15, and by business and professional people, white collar workers, and manual workers, $25.

JULY 14
OVERSEAS TRIPS FOR SOLDIERS' WIVES

Interviewing Date 4/20–25/45
Survey #345–K   Question #1a

It has been suggested that wives of servicemen be permitted to visit their husbands who have to stay abroad to police conquered countries. Do you approve or disapprove of this plan?

Approve.............................. 64%
Disapprove........................... 29
No opinion........................... 7

Interviewing Date 4/20–25/45
Survey #345–K   Question #1b

How do you think these trips should be paid for — by the Government or by the people themselves?

Government........................... 42%
People themselves.................... 30
Share the cost....................... 5
No opinion........................... 23

JULY 15
RUSSIA

Interviewing Date 6/15–20/45
Survey #349–T   Question #2b

Do you want to see Russia join us in the war against Japan, or would you rather not see her join us?

Want Russia to join.................. 77%
Do not want.......................... 14
No opinion........................... 9

By Education
College

Want Russia to join.................. 75%
Do not want.......................... 21
No opinion........................... 4

High School

Want Russia to join.................. 80%
Do not want.......................... 12
No opinion........................... 8

Grade School

Want Russia to join.................. 73%
Do not want.......................... 13
No opinion........................... 14

Interviewing Date 6/15–20/45
Survey #349–T   Question #2a

Do you think Russia will join us in the war against Japan?

Yes.................................. 39%
No................................... 31
No opinion........................... 30

JULY 18
COMPULSORY MILITARY TRAINING

Interviewing Date 6/29–7/4/45
Survey #350–K   Question #1

After this war is over, do you think every able-bodied young man should be required to take military or naval training for one year?

Yes............................... 69%
No................................ 24
No opinion........................ 7

By Sex
Men

Yes............................... 68%
No................................ 25
No opinion........................ 7

Women

Yes............................... 70%
No................................ 23
No opinion........................ 7

By Age
21–29 Years

Yes............................... 72%
No................................ 22
No opinion........................ 6

30–49 Years

Yes............................... 69%
No................................ 24
No opinion........................ 7

50 Years and Over

Yes............................... 68%
No................................ 25
No opinion........................ 7

JULY 20
LENGTH OF WAR

Interviewing Date 6/29–7/4/45
Survey #350–T   Question #8a

How much longer do you think the war with Japan will last?

Until end of 1945.................. 20%
First half of 1946................. 42
Second half of 1946................ 12
1947 or later...................... 20
Unwilling to guess................. 6

JULY 21
CANCER FUND

Interviewing Date 6/14–19/45
Survey #349–K   Question #11a

Should Congress pass a law that would provide $200 million for the study and treatment of cancer in this country?

Yes............................... 81%
No................................ 10
No opinion........................ 9

Interviewing Date 6/14–19/45
Survey #349–K   Question #11b

Would you be willing to pay more taxes to provide this money?

Yes............................... 75%
No................................ 20
No opinion........................ 5

JULY 22
UNITED NATIONS CHARTER

Interviewing Date 6/29–7/4/45
Survey #350–K   Question #3a

Should the United States Senate approve the United Nations Charter for a world organization as adopted at the San Francisco Conference?

Yes............................... 66%
No................................ 3
No opinion........................ 31

By Region
New England and Middle Atlantic

Yes............................... 64%
No................................ 3
No opinion........................ 33

East Central and West Central

Yes	68%
No	3
No opinion	29

South

Yes	62%
No	2
No opinion	36

West

Yes	65%
No	4
No opinion	31

JULY 25
UNITED NATIONS CHARTER

Interviewing Date 6/29–7/4/45
Survey #350–K   Question #3c

Do you think the Charter worked out at San Francisco will prevent future wars?

Yes	15%
Qualified yes	27
No	36
No opinion	22

The group answering with a qualified "yes," or a "yes if —," stipulated many different things that would have to be done to insure permanent peace. The chief qualifications:

"If all nations obey the Charter rules . . . if we work in accord . . . if political leaders aren't cynical but really put their minds and souls into maintaining a world peace organization . . . if the Big Five stick together . . . if the big nations are willing to fight to stop aggressive countries . . . if the United States takes the lead in keeping peace . . . if we don't go back to isolationism."

The study reveals that Republican voters are less optimistic than Democratic voters about the efficacy of the Charter as a peace measure. Forty-three per cent of the Republicans questioned said they did not think the Charter would prevent future wars, as compared to 29% among Democrats.

JULY 27
VETERANS AND POLITICS

Interviewing Date 6/29–7/4/45
Survey #350–T   Question #13

If war veterans get organized after this war into a strong political group, do you think that would be a good thing or a bad thing for the country?

Good	43%
Bad	28
No opinion	29

By Occupation
Business and Professional

Good	40%
Bad	40
No opinion	20

White Collar

Good	42%
Bad	37
No opinion	21

Farmers

Good	40%
Bad	32
No opinion	28

Manual Workers

Good	49%
Bad	18
No opinion	33

JULY 28
PRESIDENTIAL PENSION

Interviewing Date 7/14–19/45
Survey #351–K   Question #1

Would you approve or disapprove of the Government giving $25,000 a year to a United States President for the rest of his life after he leaves office?

Approve............................ 26%
Disapprove......................... 64
No opinion......................... 10

Opinion does not divide along party lines, for about the same proportion of Republican voters as Democratic voters oppose the plan. There is some difference of sentiment according to occupation, however, with business and professional people most in favor of the idea and farmers most opposed.

JULY 29
PRESIDENTIAL TENURE

Interviewing Date 7/14–19/45
Survey #351–T   Question #5

Would you favor or oppose a law that would keep all Presidents of the United States from being elected for a third term?

Favor............................. 58%
Oppose............................ 42

By Political Affiliation

	Favor	*Oppose*
Republicans................	74%	26%
Democrats.................	47	53

AUGUST 1
RETIRED PRESIDENTS

Interviewing Date 7/14–19/45
Survey #351–K   Question #1

It has been suggested that after a United States President has finished his term he automatically be given a seat and a vote in the United States Senate for as long as he wishes. Do you approve or disapprove of this?

Approve............................ 34%
Disapprove......................... 53
No opinion......................... 13

Interviewing Date 7/14–19/45
Survey #351–K   Question #1

It has been suggested that after a United States President has finished his term he automatically be given a seat in the House of Representatives for as long as he wishes. Do you approve or disapprove of this?

Approve............................ 38%
Disapprove......................... 48
No opinion......................... 14

AUGUST 4
WARTIME DATING

Interviewing Date 7/14–19/45
Survey #351–K   Question #3

Do you think a woman whose husband is overseas should accept dates with other men?

Yes............................... 6%
Yes, qualified..................... 5
No................................ 85
No opinion........................ 4

By Sex
Men

Yes............................... 7%
Yes, qualified..................... 4
No................................ 83
No opinion........................ 6

Women

Yes............................... 5%
Yes, qualified..................... 6
No................................ 87
No opinion........................ 2

People who wanted to qualify their approval of the idea said, among other things, "Yes — if the dates are in groups . . . if the husband approves . . . if the man is a personal friend of the husband, or a relative."

AUGUST 5
PARTY STRENGTH

Interviewing Date 7/14–19/45
Survey #351–K   Question #6

If the presidential election were being held today, which party would you vote for — the Democratic or Republican?

Democratic........................ 58%
Republican........................ 42

AUGUST 10
CLOSED SHOP

Interviewing Date 7/14–19/45
Survey #351–K   Question #12a

Are you in favor of the closed shop — that is, requiring every worker in a company to belong to a union before he can be hired?

Favor............................. 13%
Oppose............................ 75
No opinion........................ 13

Union Members Only

Favor............................. 39%
Oppose............................ 54
No opinion........................ 7

Non-Union Members Only

Favor............................. 11%
Oppose............................ 77
No opinion........................ 12

AUGUST 11
DIVORCE

Interviewing Date 7/14–19/45
Survey #351–K   Question #4

Do you think the courts of this state should recognize divorces granted by Reno courts?

Yes............................... 34%
No................................ 51
No opinion........................ 15

By Age
21–29 Years

Yes............................... 43%
No................................ 44
No opinion........................ 13

30–49 Years

Yes............................... 36%
No................................ 50
No opinion........................ 14

50 Years and Over

Yes............................... 26%
No................................ 56
No opinion........................ 18

AUGUST 12
LABOR UNIONS

Interviewing Date 7/14–19/45
Survey #351–K   Question #9

There has been some discussion about changing the laws concerning labor unions. What changes, if any, would you like to see made?

Eliminate unions................... 8%
Increase union restrictions........ 50
Increase employers' powers......... 2
Improve mediation system........... 2
Miscellaneous (anti-union)......... 15
Effect changes favoring unions..... 4
No changes......................... 31
                                   ‾‾‾‾
                                   112%

(Note: table adds to more than 100% because some persons suggested more than one change.)

AUGUST 15
SPAIN

Interviewing Date 7/27–8/1/45
Survey #352–T   Question #8c

Should Spain, under its present government, become a member of the United Nations?

Yes............................. 12%
No............................. 76
No opinion...................... 12

Interviewing Date 7/27–8/1/45
Survey #352–T   Question #8a

Can you tell me who General Franco is?

Correct answer.................... 53%
Incorrect answer.................. 47

AUGUST 17
RATIONING

Interviewing Date 7/27–8/1/45
Survey #352–K   Question #1

If you could have any one of these four things, which would you prefer: 15 gallons of gasoline, 25 pounds of sugar, 5 pounds of butter, or 5 pounds of beefsteak?

Sugar........................... 47%
Beefsteak....................... 29
Gasoline........................ 14
Butter.......................... 10

By Community Size
Cities 100,000 and Over

Sugar........................... 27%
Beefsteak....................... 40
Gasoline........................ 22
Butter.......................... 11

Towns, Cities up to 100,000

Sugar........................... 48%
Beefsteak....................... 28
Gasoline........................ 12
Butter.......................... 12

Farm Areas

Sugar........................... 71%
Beefsteak....................... 14
Gasoline........................ 10
Butter.......................... 5

AUGUST 18
NAVY UNIFORMS

Interviewing Date 7/27–8/1/45
Survey #352–K   Question #5

It has been suggested that the uniforms of sailors in the navy be changed. Do you think they should be changed?

Yes............................. 34%
No............................. 45
No opinion...................... 21

By Age
21–29 Years

Yes............................. 44%
No............................. 40
No opinion...................... 16

30–49 Years

Yes............................. 34%
No............................. 47
No opinion...................... 19

50 Years and Over

Yes............................. 31%
No............................. 45
No opinion...................... 24

AUGUST 19
MINIMUM WAGE

Interviewing Date 7/27–8/1/45
Survey #352–K   Question #2a

What does the term "minimum wage" mean to you?

Correct answer.................... 48%
Incorrect answer.................. 22
Don't know....................... 30

Among people who attended college, 75% gave a correct answer; among those with no more than a grade school education, 32% gave correct replies.

Interviewing Date 7/27–8/1/45
Survey #352–K   Question #2b

Those who knew what the term "minimum wage" meant were asked: Do you happen to know what the minimum wage rate per hour throughout the country is now?

Median average of replies......... $.45 hr.

Interviewing Date 7/27–8/1/45
Survey #352–K   Question #c

Asked of those familiar with the meaning of "minimum wage": Would you favor or oppose making the minimum wage 65 cents an hour for all workers in business and industry?

Favor.............................. 56%
Oppose............................ 32
No opinion........................ 12

AUGUST 22
JAPAN

Interviewing Date 7/27–8/1/45
Survey #352–K   Question #6

How should we treat the Japanese people after the war?

Control strictly, punish war criminals.. 53%
Treat fairly, start reeducating them.... 33
Treat with extreme harshness......... 14
Miscellaneous..................... 3
No opinion........................ 7
                                   ─────
                                   110%

(Note: table adds to more than 100% because some persons suggested more than one treatment.)

AUGUST 24
STRIKES

Interviewing Date 7/14–19/45
Survey #351–T   Question #11a

Would you favor a law requiring employers and unions to take their differences to a Federal Labor Board before a strike could be called in any industry?

Yes............................... 70%
No................................ 10
No opinion........................ 20

Labor Union Members Only

Yes............................... 71%
No................................ 18
No opinion........................ 11

AUGUST 25
POSTWAR PROBLEMS

Special Survey

Britons were asked: What do you think will be the chief postwar problem?

Housing........................... 54%
Employment....................... 13
Preparing for return of troops........ 4
Other............................. 29

French citizens were asked: What do you think will be the chief postwar problem?

Food.............................. 38%
Internal politics................... 14
Collaborationists.................. 11
Cost of living..................... 8
Other............................. 29

Americans were asked: What do you think will be the chief postwar problem?

Jobs.............................. 20%
Avoiding a depression.............. 16
Permanent peace.................. 15
Strikes........................... 10
Other............................. 39

AUGUST 26
WEAPONS AND JAPAN

Interviewing Date 8/10–15/45
Survey #353–K   Question #8c

Do you approve or disapprove of using the new atomic bomb on Japanese cities?

Approve........................... 85%
Disapprove........................ 10
No opinion........................ 5

When this vote is broken down there is hardly any difference of opinion by sex, age, or education.

Interviewing Date 6/14–19/45
Survey #349–K   Question #3a

Would you favor or oppose using poison gas against the Japanese if doing so would reduce the number of American soldiers who are killed and wounded?

Favor............................. 40%
Oppose............................ 49
No opinion........................ 11

A majority of young people favor the use of poison gas, while persons 50 years and older are substantially opposed to the idea. Men oppose the idea of using gas to a greater extent than women, and college-trained people are more opposed than people with no more than an elementary school education.

AUGUST 29
SUPREME COURT

Interviewing Date 8/10–15/45
Survey #353–T   Question #12c

The President fills all vacancies on the Supreme Court. Do you think he should appoint about the same number of Democrats and Republicans, or should he appoint only members of his own political party?

Same number from each party........ 56%
Only from own party................ 9
Should be nonpartisan and appoint best
  qualified........................ 19
No opinion........................ 16

By Political Affiliation
Democrats

Same number from each party........ 52%
Only from own party................ 12
Should be nonpartisan and appoint best
  qualified........................ 19
No opinion........................ 17

Republicans

Same number from each party........ 64%
Only from own party................ 5
Should be nonpartisan and appoint best
  qualified........................ 20
No opinion........................ 11

AUGUST 31
WAGE-PRICE CONTROLS

Interviewing Date 8/10–15/45
Survey #353–K   Question #9a

Do you approve or disapprove of removing all wage ceilings now?

Approve........................... 25%
Disapprove........................ 62
No opinion........................ 13

Interviewing Date 8/10–15/45
Survey #353–K   Question #9b

Do you approve or disapprove of removing all price ceilings now?

Approve........................... 16%
Disapprove........................ 74
No opinion........................ 10

Interviewing Date 8/10–15/45
Survey #353–K   Question #9c

Some people believe that wage ceilings cannot be removed without also removing price ceilings. If you had to vote for or against keeping both wage and price control, would you vote to keep both or do away with both?

Keep both........................ 77%
Do away with both................ 18
No opinion....................... 5

Analysis of the vote of the various occupational groups on these questions finds every group — businessmen, professional men, white collar workers, farmers, manual workers — all with high majorities favoring retention of wage and price controls for the time being.

SEPTEMBER 1
HOUSE CONSTRUCTION

Interviewing Date 8/10–15/45
Survey #353–K   Question #15a

Do you plan to build a new home of your own after the war?

Yes.............................. 23%
No.............................. 77

Interviewing Date 8/10–15/45
Survey #353–K   Question #15b

Asked of those answering in the affirmative: About how much do you think you will spend building the house?

Median average................... $5,000

SEPTEMBER 2
TRUMAN ADMINISTRATION

Interviewing Date 8/10–15/45
Survey #353–T   Question #11a

Which of these three policies would you like to have President Truman follow: (1) Go more to the left by following more of the views of labor and other liberal groups, (2) Go more to the right by following more of the views of business and conservative groups, or (3) Follow a middle-of-the-road policy?

Go to the left.................... 16%
Go to the right................... 18
Stay middle-of-the-road.......... 55
No opinion....................... 11

By Age
21–29 Years

Go to the left.................... 19%
Go to the right................... 9
Stay middle-of-the-road.......... 60
No opinion....................... 12

30–49 Years

Go to the left.................... 17%
Go to the right................... 17
Stay middle of the road.......... 56
No opinion....................... 10

50 Years and Over

Go to the left.................... 14%
Go to the right................... 25
Stay middle-of-the-road.......... 49
No opinion....................... 12

Interviewing Date 8/10–15/45
Survey #353–T   Question #11b

Which of these three policies do you think President Truman has been following?

Left............................. 10%
Right............................ 17
Middle-of-the-road............... 54
No opinion....................... 19

SEPTEMBER 5
RUSSIA

Interviewing Date 8/10–15/45
Survey #353–K   Question #7

Do you think Russia can be trusted to cooperate with us after the war?

Yes.............................. 54%
No.............................. 30
No opinion....................... 16

By Occupation
Professional and Business

Yes.............................. 64%
No.............................. 25
No opinion....................... 11

White Collar

Yes.................................. 62%
No.................................. 30
No opinion.......................... 8

Farmers

Yes.................................. 48%
No.................................. 32
No opinion.......................... 20

Manual Workers

Yes.................................. 48%
No.................................. 33
No opinion.......................... 19

By Education
College

Yes.................................. 71%
No.................................. 23
No opinion.......................... 6

High School

Yes.................................. 58%
No.................................. 31
No opinion.......................... 11

Grade School

Yes.................................. 47%
No.................................. 32
No opinion.......................... 21

SEPTEMBER 7
IDEAL FAMILY SIZE

Interviewing Date 8/10–15/45
Survey #353–K   Question #16

What do you consider to be the ideal size of a family — a husband and wife and how many children?

1 child............................. 1%
2 children.......................... 22
3 children.......................... 28
4 children.......................... 31
5 children.......................... 9
6 or more children.................. 9

Views of Women

1 child............................. 1%
2 children.......................... 21
3 children.......................... 27
4 children.......................... 36
5 children.......................... 8
6 or more children.................. 7

Views of Women Aged 21–34 Years

1 child............................. 1%
2 children.......................... 25
3 children.......................... 33
4 children.......................... 31
5 children.......................... 7
6 or more children.................. 3

In general, women living on farms and in small towns favor larger families than women living in metropolitan areas. For example, 42% of those questioned on farms named four children ideal, as compared to only 30% in cities of more than half a million population.

SEPTEMBER 8
MONEY

Interviewing Date 8/10–15/45
Survey #353–K   Question #1

It has been suggested that the paper money bills of different value be printed in different colors. Do you think this is a good or poor idea?

Good idea........................... 42%
Poor idea........................... 42
No opinion.......................... 16

By Education
College

Good idea........................... 49%
Poor idea........................... 46
No opinion.......................... 5

High School

Good idea........................... 45%
Poor idea........................... 41
No opinion.......................... 14

Grade School

Good idea......................... 38%
Poor idea......................... 42
No opinion........................ 20

SEPTEMBER 9
INCOME TAXES

Interviewing Date 8/10–15/45
Survey #353–K   Question #4a

After the war how much do you think a married man with two children who earns $60 a week, that is $3,000 a year, should pay in federal income taxes?

Median average.................... $150

Interviewing Date 8/10–15/45
Survey #353–K   Question #4b

How about a married man with two children who earns $200 a week, that is $10,000 a year?

Median average................... $1,000

Interviewing Date 8/10–15/45
Survey #353–K   Question #4c

How about a married man with two children who earns $1,000 a week, that is $50,000 a year?

Median average.................. $12,500

Interviewing Date 8/10–15/45
Survey #353–T   Question #4a

What do you think the tax is now for a married man with two children who earns $60 a week, that is $3,000 a year?

Median average.................... $250

Interviewing Date 8/10–15/45
Survey #353–T   Question #4b

What do you think the tax is now for a married man with two children who earns $200 a week, that is $10,000 a year?

Median average................... $1,000

Interviewing Date 8/10–15/45
Survey #353–T   Question #4c

What do you think the tax is now for a married man with two children who earns $1,000 a week, that is $50,000 a year?

Median average.................. $10,000

The actual taxes now being paid on income by these three groups is, respectively, $200, $1,900, and $21,500.

SEPTEMBER 12
ATOMIC BOMB

Interviewing Date 8/24–29/45
Survey #354–K   Question #4

It has been suggested that the new United Nations Security Council use the atomic bomb to help keep peace by putting it under control of a special international air force. Would you favor such a plan, or should the United States try to keep control of this weapon?

Put under UN control............... 14%
U.S. should keep control............ 73
No opinion........................ 12

The greatest inclination to put the atomic bomb under Security Council control was found among people who have attended college and also among young people. The least inclined are people who did not go beyond grammar school and among people who are over 50 years of age.

SEPTEMBER 14
STANDARD TIME

Interviewing Date 8/24–29/45
Survey #354–K   Question #13

Which of the following would you prefer: A. Stay on war time the year 'round as at present; B. Have daylight saving time in the summer and standard time the rest of the year. C. Stay on standard time the year 'round?

Stay on war time the year 'round...... 17%
Daylight time in summer, standard time
    rest of year....................... 25
Stay on standard time the year 'round.. 46
No opinion........................ 12

By Area

	Now Favoring:			
	War Time	Summer Daylight Time	Stand. Time	Un-dec.
Cities and towns which had summer daylight time before war.....	21%	37%	31%	11%
Areas which had standard time year 'round before war.......	14	14	60	12

SEPTEMBER 15
EMPLOYMENT OUTLOOK

Interviewing Date 8/24–29/45
Survey #354–K   Question #10a

*Do you think that business firms in this
country will be able to provide enough jobs
for nearly everyone during the next five
years, or will the Government have to step
in and provide work like the W.P.A. or
P.W.A.?*

Business will be able to provide enough
    jobs............................. 42%
Government will have to provide work.. 42
No opinion........................ 16

Interviewing Date 8/24–29/45
Survey #354–K   Question #10b

*Do you think the Government will have to
provide work steadily during the next five
years, or only part of the time?*

Steadily........................... 13%
Part of the time................... 25
Don't know........................ 4
                                   ――――
                                   42%

SEPTEMBER 16
PUBLIC WELFARE DEPARTMENT

Interviewing Date 8/24–29/45
Survey #354–T   Question #12

*Do you think another Cabinet office, called
the Department of Public Welfare and
headed by a Secretary, should be set up in
Washington to include such things as
Social Security, public health, and education?*

Should be......................... 47%
Should not........................ 22
No opinion........................ 31

By Education
College

Should be......................... 53%
Should not........................ 32
No opinion........................ 15

High School

Should be......................... 50%
Should not........................ 25
No opinion........................ 25

Grade School

Should be......................... 45%
Should not........................ 17
No opinion........................ 38

By Occupation
Professional and Business

Should be......................... 53%
Should not........................ 27
No opinion........................ 20

White Collar

Should be......................... 54%
Should not........................ 22
No opinion........................ 24

Farmers

Should be......................... 35%
Should not........................ 31
No opinion........................ 34

Manual Workers

Should be........................... 47%
Should not.......................... 15
No opinion......................... 38

SEPTEMBER 19
ATOMIC BOMB

Interviewing Date 8/24–29/45
Survey #354–K   Question #3a

Do you think it was a good thing or a bad thing that the atomic bomb was developed?

Good thing......................... 69%
Bad thing........................... 17
No opinion......................... 14

Interviewing Date 8/24–29/45
Survey #354–K   Question #3c

Do you think that atomic energy will be developed in the next ten years to supply power for industry and other things?

Yes................................ 47%
No................................. 19
No opinion......................... 34

Interviewing Date 8/24–29/45
Survey #354–K   Question #3b

Some people say that some day experiments in smashing atoms will cause an explosion which will destroy the entire world. Do you think this is ever likely to happen?

Yes................................ 27%
No................................. 53
No opinion......................... 20

Interviewing Date 8/24–29/45
Survey #354–T   Question #3a

Some people say that the atomic bomb makes a large army and navy unneccessary. Do you agree or disagree with this?

Agree.............................. 35%
Disagree........................... 47
No opinion......................... 18

SEPTEMBER 21
DEMOBILIZATION

Interviewing Date 8/24–29/45
Survey #354–K   Question #7

Do you think that men in the army should be released faster than they are, or do you think they are being released fast enough?

Army should release men faster....... 23%
Release rate fast enough............. 56
No opinion......................... 21

Views of People with Relative in Army

Army should release men faster....... 29%
Release rate fast enough............. 55
No opinion......................... 16

Interviewing Date 8/24–29/45
Survey #354–T   Question #7

Do you think that men in the navy should be released faster than they are, or do you think they are being released fast enough?

Navy should release men faster....... 24%
Release rate fast enough............. 45
No opinion......................... 31

Views of People with Relative in Navy

Navy should release men faster....... 38%
Release rate fast enough............. 38
No opinion......................... 24

SEPTEMBER 22
ADOLF HITLER

Interviewing Date 9/8–13/45
Survey #355–K   Question #1

Do you personally believe that Hitler is dead?

Yes................................ 16%
No................................. 69
No opinion......................... 15

SEPTEMBER 23
CIVIL RIGHTS LEGISLATION

Interviewing Date 6/14–19/45
Survey #349–K   Question #7

Do you favor or oppose a law in your state that would require employers to hire a person if he is qualified for the job regardless of his race or color?

Favor............................. 43%
Oppose........................... 44
No opinion....................... 13

By Region
New England and Middle Atlantic

Favor............................. 58%
Oppose........................... 31
No opinion....................... 11

East Central and West Central

Favor............................. 41%
Oppose........................... 43
No opinion....................... 16

South

Favor............................. 30%
Oppose........................... 60
No opinion....................... 10

West

Favor............................. 41%
Oppose........................... 46
No opinion....................... 13

By Age
21–29 Years

Favor............................. 55%
Oppose........................... 34
No opinion....................... 11

30–49 Years

Favor............................. 42%
Oppose........................... 45
No opinion....................... 13

50 Years and Over

Favor............................. 38%
Oppose........................... 48
No opinion....................... 14

By Occupation
Business and Professional

Favor............................. 43%
Oppose........................... 48
No opinion....................... 9

White Collar

Favor............................. 41%
Oppose........................... 51
No opinion....................... 8

Farmers

Favor............................. 25%
Oppose........................... 57
No opinion....................... 18

Manual Workers

Favor............................. 52%
Oppose........................... 35
No opinion....................... 13

Interviewing Date 6/14–19/45
Survey #349–T   Question #7

Would you favor or oppose a state law that would require employees to work alongside persons of any race or color?

Favor............................. 34%
Oppose........................... 56
No opinion....................... 10

SEPTEMBER 26
PEARL HARBOR

Interviewing Date 9/8–13/45
Survey #355–K   Question #14a

Have you heard or read about the report on the Pearl Harbor disaster?

Yes............................... 72%
No................................ 28

Those answering yes were asked: Who do you think was chiefly to blame for the Pearl Habor disaster?

The Government	17%
The "whole country"	15
President Roosevelt	11
Admiral Kimmel, General Short, the army or navy at Pearl Harbor	10
Army and navy	8
Secretary Hull	1
General Marshall	1
Secretary Stimson	1
Secretary Knox	1
Miscellaneous	35

Are you satisfied with the report that has been made on Pearl Harbor, or do you think Congress should investigate this further?

Satisfied	29%
Should investigate further	55
No opinion	16

SEPTEMBER 28
LEND-LEASE

Was it your understanding that the lend-lease goods we sent to England during the war were to be paid for in full either in goods or money or not to be paid at all?

In full	44%
In part	21
Not at all	13
No opinion	22

Do you think England should pay us back in some way for the lend-lease material we sent her?

Yes	83%
No	12
No opinion	5

SEPTEMBER 29
THE DRAFT

If the Government decides to continue the draft to obtain men for occupation forces, should we draft young men eighteen years old or should the age be set higher?

Continue to draft young men 18 years old	39%
Set the draft age higher	53
No opinion	8

By Age
20–29 Years

Continue to draft young men 18 years old	46%
Set the draft age higher	45
No opinion	9

30–49 Years

Continue to draft young men 18 years old	41%
Set the draft age higher	52
No opinion	7

50 Years and Over

Continue to draft young men 18 years old	32%
Set the draft age higher	60
No opinion	8

By Sex
Men

Continue to draft young men 18 years old	41%
Set the draft age higher	51
No opinion	8

Women

Continue to draft young men 18 years old	35%
Set the draft age higher	56
No opinion	9

By Education
College
Continue to draft young men 18 years old 47%
Set the draft age higher.............. 49
No opinion....................... 4

High School
Continue to draft young men 18 years old 46%
Set the draft age higher.............. 47
No opinion....................... 7

Grade School
Continue to draft young men 18 years old 33%
Set the draft age higher.............. 57
No opinion....................... 10

SEPTEMBER 30
LOAN TO ENGLAND

Interviewing Date 9/8–13/45
Survey #355–K   Question #5a

England plans to ask this country for a loan of three to five billion dollars to help England get back on its feet. Would you approve or disapprove of the United States making such a loan?

Approve........................... 27%
Disapprove....................... 60
No opinion....................... 13

By Occupation
Business and Professional
Approve........................... 37%
Disapprove....................... 55
No opinion....................... 8

White Collar
Approve........................... 35%
Disapprove....................... 54
No opinion....................... 11

Farmers
Approve........................... 26%
Disapprove....................... 62
No opinion....................... 12

Manual Workers
Approve........................... 20%
Disapprove....................... 65
No opinion....................... 15

By Education
College
Approve........................... 45%
Disapprove....................... 50
No opinion....................... 5

High School
Approve........................... 32%
Disapprove....................... 58
No opinion....................... 10

Grade School
Approve........................... 22%
Disapprove....................... 63
No opinion....................... 15

OCTOBER 3
VETERANS' INCOME TAXES

Interviewing Date 9/8–13/45
Survey #355–T   Question #16a

Do you think that all income taxes owed by members of the armed forces on their service pay should be cancelled, or should these taxes be paid?

Should be cancelled................. 75%
Should be paid.................... 16
No opinion....................... 9

Interviewing Date 9/8–13/45
Survey #355-T   Question #16b

When persons went into the armed forces, income tax payments on that year's earnings as civilians were postponed until after they were discharged. Do you think these income taxes should be cancelled, or should they be paid?

Should be cancelled................. 56%
Should be paid.................... 34
No opinion....................... 10

OCTOBER 5
UNEMPLOYMENT COMPENSATION

Interviewing Date 9/8–13/45
Survey #355–T   Question #9a

Congress is now considering a law which would give more unemployment compensation to persons without jobs so that some would get as much as $25 a week for 26 weeks. Would you like to have your congressman vote for or against this bill?

For................................ 46%
Against............................ 40
No opinion......................... 14

By Occupation
Farmers

For................................ 28%
Against............................ 55
No opinion......................... 17

Business and Professional

For................................ 34%
Against............................ 57
No opinion......................... 9

White Collar

For................................ 42%
Against............................ 45
No opinion......................... 13

Manual Workers

For................................ 61%
Against............................ 25
No opinion......................... 14

OCTOBER 6
WORK WEEK

Interviewing Date 9/8–13/45
Survey #355–K   Question #11

How many hours a week do you think persons should work in a regular work week now that the war is over?

Under 40 hours..................... 10%
40 hours........................... 66
41–47 hours........................ 5
48 hours........................... 12
Over 48 hours...................... 1
No opinion......................... 6

OCTOBER 7
PARTY BEST ABLE TO SOLVE PROBLEMS

Interviewing Date 9/8–13/45
Survey #355–K, T   Question #12

It's another year until the congressional elections, but as you feel today, which political party, the Democratic or Republican, do you think can handle each of these different problems?

	Dem.	Rep.	No Diff.	No Opin.
Encouraging new business to start up	35%	30%	20%	15%
Reducing strikes and labor troubles	34	26	33	17
Seeing that taxes don't get too heavy	37	26	23	14
Running Gov't. efficiently	41	23	23	13
Getting business and industry back to peacetime production	41	23	20	16
Improving the health of the people	36	15	32	17
Improving the education level of the people	36	15	33	16
Keeping farmers' income high	46	19	20	15
Taking care of veterans properly	42	12	33	13
Working out a lasting peace with other countries	45	14	28	13
Keeping wages high	49	15	23	13

OCTOBER 10
STRIKES

Interviewing Date 9/21–26/45
Survey #356–K   Question #7a

Should the Government take a strong stand on labor strikes during the present reconversion period?

Yes............................... 74%
No................................ 14
No opinion........................ 12

Interviewing Date 9/21–26/45
Survey #356–K   Question #7b

Those answering in the affirmative were asked: What do you think it should do?

Crack down on labor — prohibit strikes, punish strikers, control union leaders, abolish unions, force strikers back to work............................ 24%
Get production going again — step in with mediation or enforced arbitration, seize strike-bound plants and put men back to work................. 28
Help labor — support strikers, compel employers to be fair, raise wages...... 6
Miscellaneous...................... 4
No procedure named................ 12
                                 ―――
                                 74%

OCTOBER 12
WAGES

Interviewing Date 9/21–26/45
Survey #356–T   Question #9a

Should workers in a plant who work 40 hours a week be willing to take less pay than they did for a 48-hour week during wartime?

Yes............................... 56%
No................................ 37
No opinion........................ 7

Interviewing Date 9/21–26/45
Survey #356–K   Question #9

Do you think that automobile workers should get as much pay for 40 hours in peacetime as they got for 48 hours during the war?

Yes............................... 33%
No................................ 54
No opinion........................ 13

By Occupation
Business and Professional

Yes............................... 22%
No................................ 71
No opinion........................ 7

Farmers

Yes............................... 21%
No................................ 68
No opinion........................ 11

White Collar

Yes............................... 29%
No................................ 58
No opinion........................ 13

Manual Workers

Yes............................... 44%
No................................ 40
No opinion........................ 16

Union Members Only

Yes............................... 55%
No................................ 32
No opinion........................ 13

OCTOBER 13
GOVERNMENT OWNERSHIP OF KEY INDUSTRIES

Interviewing Date 9/8–13/45
Survey #355–K   Question #13

Do you think the Government should own the following things in this country: Banks? Railroads? Coal Mines? Electric Power Companies?

Banks
Government should own............. 34%
Government should not own......... 55
No opinion....................... 11

Railroads
Government should own............. 26%
Government should not own......... 56
No opinion....................... 18

Coal Mines
Government should own............. 38%
Government should not own......... 49
No opinion....................... 13

Electric Power Companies
Government should own............. 38%
Government should not own......... 39
No opinion....................... 23

OCTOBER 14
PARTY STRENGTH

Interviewing Date 9/21–26/45
Survey #356–K　　　　　　Question #4

If you were voting for congressman today, would you be most likely to vote for the Democratic or Republican candidate?

Democratic....................... 53%
Republican....................... 47

OCTOBER 17
WAGES

Interviewing Date 9/21–26/45
Survey #356–K　　　　　　Question #10

The automobile workers' union says that workers' pay can be increased by 30% without making it necessary to increase the price of automobiles. Do you agree or disagree with this?

Agree............................ 26%
Disagree......................... 42
No opinion....................... 32

By Occupation
Business and Professional
Agree............................ 19%
Disagree......................... 56
No opinion....................... 25

Farmers
Agree............................ 16%
Disagree......................... 54
No opinion....................... 30

White Collar
Agree............................ 25%
Disagree......................... 41
No opinion....................... 34

Manual Workers
Agree............................ 34%
Disagree......................... 32
No opinion....................... 34

Union Members Only
Agree............................ 40%
Disagree......................... 30
No opinion....................... 30

Interviewing Date 9/21–26/45
Survey #356–T　　　　　　Question #10

Do you think that if wages to auto workers are increased by 30%, the price of new automobiles will be increased?

Yes.............................. 78%
No............................... 11
No opinion....................... 11

OCTOBER 19
OCCUPATION OF JAPAN

Interviewing Date 9/21–26/45
Survey #356–K　　　　　　Question #14

What is your opinion of the way we are treating the Japanese — are we being too tough or not tough enough?

Not tough enough.................. 61%
Too tough........................ 1
Treatment is about right............. 32
No opinion....................... 6

By Education
College

Not tough enough.................. 46%
Too tough........................ 2
Treatment is about right............. 44
No opinion....................... 8

High School

Not tough enough.................. 63%
Too tough........................ —
Treatment is about right............. 32
No opinion....................... 5

Grade School

Not tough enough.................. 68%
Too tough........................ —
Treatment is about right............. 27
No opinion....................... 5

By Age
21–29 Years

Not tough enough.................. 68%
Too tough........................ —
Treatment is about right............. 25
No opinion....................... 7

30–49 Years

Not tough enough.................. 60%
Too tough........................ 1
Treatment is about right............. 34
No opinion....................... 5

50 Years and Over

Not tough enough.................. 59%
Too tough........................ —
Treatment is about right............. 35
No opinion....................... 6

OCTOBER 21
FOREIGN AFFAIRS

Interviewing Date 10/5–10/45
Survey #357–K   Question #4

Do you think it would be best for the future of this country if we take an active part in world affairs, or if we stayed out of world affairs?

Take active part.................... 71%
Stay out.......................... 19
No opinion....................... 10

By Region
New England and Middle Atlantic

Take active part.................... 68%
Stay out.......................... 20
No opinion....................... 12

East Central

Take active part.................... 71%
Stay out.......................... 19
No opinion....................... 10

West Central

Take active part.................... 70%
Stay out.......................... 21
No opinion....................... 9

South

Take active part.................... 68%
Stay out.......................... 17
No opinion....................... 15

West

Take active part.................... 80%
Stay out.......................... 15
No opinion....................... 5

OCTOBER 22
MOST IMPORTANT PROBLEM

Interviewing Date 10/5–10/45
Survey #357–K   Question #2

What do you think is the most important problem facing the country during the next year?

Jobs	42%
Strikes	32
Reconversion	19
Making Peace	7
Demobilization	5
Wages	3
Food shortages	2
Atomic bomb	2
Other	9
	121%

(Note: total is more than 100% because some persons named more than one problem.)

OCTOBER 24
WAGE-PRICE CONTROLS

Interviewing Date 10/5–10/45
Survey #357–T   Question #6a

Do you approve or disapprove of removing all wage ceilings now?

Approve	30%
Disapprove	58
No opinion	12

Interviewing Date 10/5–10/45
Survey #357–K   Question #6b

Do you approve or disapprove of removing all price ceilings now?

Approve	21%
Disapprove	72
No opinion	7

Interviewing Date 10/5–10/45
Survey #357–T   Question #6c

Some people believe that wage ceilings cannot be removed without also removing price ceilings. If you had to vote for or against keeping both wage and price control, would you vote to keep both or do away with both?

Keep both	67%
Do away with both	21
No opinion	12

OCTOBER 26
LOAN TO RUSSIA

Interviewing Date 10/5–10/45
Survey #357–K   Question #11a

Russia has asked this country for a loan of six billion dollars to help Russia get back on its feet. Would you approve or disapprove of the United States making such a loan?

Approve	27%
Disapprove	60
No opinion	13

By Occupation
Professional and Business

Approve	36%
Disapprove	55
No opinion	9

White Collar

Approve	32%
Disapprove	56
No opinion	12

Farmers

Approve	22%
Disapprove	65
No opinion	13

Manual Workers

Approve	23%
Disapprove	61
No opinion	16

By Education
College

Approve	45%
Disapprove	48
No opinion	7

High School

Approve	29%
Disapprove	59
No opinion	12

Approve.......................... 22%
Disapprove....................... 62
No opinion....................... 16

Interviewing Date 10/5–10/45
Survey #357–K   Question #11d

If we lend Russia this money, do you think we will be repaid in part, in full, or not at all?

In part.......................... 26%
In full.......................... 23
Not at all....................... 35
No opinion....................... 16

OCTOBER 27
WAR BONDS

Interviewing Date 10/5–10/45
Survey #357–T   Question #15b

Some people say that since the war is over it is no longer important nor is there any need to buy war bonds. Do you agree or disagree?

Agree............................ 22%
Disagree......................... 67
No opinion....................... 11

OCTOBER 28
ATOMIC BOMB

Interviewing Date 10/5–10/45
Survey #357–K   Question #5a

Do you think the secret of making atomic bombs should be put under the control of the new United Nations Security Council, or should the United States keep this secret to itself?

Put under United Nations control...... 17%
U.S. should keep control............. 71
No opinion....................... 12

Interviewing Date 10/5–10/45
Survey #357–K   Question #5d

Do you think the United States can keep this secret to itself, or do you think other nations will develop atomic bombs?

Can keep the secret.................. 22%
Others will develop bombs............ 65
No opinion....................... 13

OCTOBER 31
INFANTILE PARALYSIS

Interviewing Date 10/5–10/45
Survey #357–K   Question #10a

Can you tell me another name for poliomyelitis or polio?

Correct answer...................... 57%
Don't know, incorrect............... 43

Interviewing Date 10/5–10/45
Survey #357–K   Question #10b

Do you think infantile paralysis is contagious (catching)?

Yes.............................. 49%
No............................... 29
No opinion....................... 22

Interviewing Date 10/5–10/45
Survey #357–K   Question #10c

What do you think causes infantile paralysis?

Germs............................ 25%
Insects.......................... 8
Unsanitary conditions............... 6
Malnutrition..................... 3
Over-exertion, weak system.......... 4
Nerve defect..................... 2
Inherited........................ 1
Poor blood circulation.............. 1
Miscellaneous.................... 7
Cause not yet discovered............ 2
Don't know....................... 48
                                 ———
                                 107%

(Note: table adds to more than 100% because some persons gave more than one cause.)

Interviewing Date 10/5–10/45
Survey #357–T Question #10b

Can you tell me any of the signs or symp-toms that tell whether people are coming down with infantile paralysis?

Fever	21%
Aches, pains	21
Headache	9
Vomiting	8
Cold, sore throat	8
Stiff neck	7
Others	8
Don't know	56
	138%

(Note: table adds to more than 100% because some persons named more than one symptom.)

Interviewing Date 10/5–10/45
Survey #357–T Question #10d

Have you heard or read about Sister Kenny or the Kenny method of treating infantile paralysis?

Yes	52%
No	48

Interviewing Date 10/5–10/45
Survey #357–T Question #10e

Those who had heard of the Kenny method were asked: From what you have heard do you think it is a good way or a bad way to treat the disease?

Good way	38%
Fair	4
Uncertain	10
	52%

Interviewing Date 10/5–10/45
Survey #357–K Question #10d

Does infantile paralysis leave all people who have had it crippled or paralyzed?

Yes	30%
No	56
No opinion	14

NOVEMBER 2
PRESIDENT TRUMAN'S POPULARITY

Interviewing Date 10/5–10/45
Survey #357–K Question #18

Do you approve or disapprove of the way Harry Truman is handling his job as President?

Approve	82%
Disapprove	9
No opinion	9

NOVEMBER 2
CLEMENT ATTLEE

Special Survey

Britons were asked: Do you approve or dis-approve of Mr. Attlee as Prime Minister?

Approve	66%
Disapprove	19
No opinion	15

NOVEMBER 3
OCCUPATION OF JAPAN

Interviewing Date 10/5–10/45
Survey #357–K Question #9a

Do you think we will have to police the Japanese many years, or do you think we can withdraw our troops in a few years?

Many years	64%
Few years	23
Undecided	13

Interviewing Date 10/5–10/45
Survey #357–K Question #9b

How many years?

1 through 5 years	24%
6 through 10 years	19
11 through 20 years	20
21 through 50 years	13
51 through 100 years	2
Forever	4
Miscellaneous	1
Undecided	17

NOVEMBER 4
WAGES

Interviewing Date 10/5–10/45
Survey #357–K   Question #13a

Because there is no overtime now, the total weekly pay of many factory workers is less than it was during the war. So that their total weekly pay will be the same as it was during the war, these workers want a 30% increase in their hourly rate. Do you think they should or should not receive this increase?

Should............................ 55%
Should not........................ 33
No opinion........................ 12

By Occupation
Professional and Business

Should............................ 60%
Should not........................ 33
No opinion........................ 7

White Collar

Should............................ 66%
Should not........................ 27
No opinion........................ 7

Farmers

Should............................ 49%
Should not........................ 38
No opinion........................ 13

Manual Workers

Should............................ 71%
Should not........................ 19
No opinion........................ 10

Union Members Only

Should............................ 83%
Should not........................ 14
No opinion........................ 3

Interviewing Date 10/5–10/45
Survey #357–K   Question #13b

Those not in favor of a 30% wage boost were asked: Would you favor increasing factory workers' hourly rates by 15%?

Those favoring this step and those already in favor of a 30% raise form nearly two-thirds of all persons interviewed in the survey.

NOVEMBER 7
TAXES

Interviewing Date 10/19–24/45
Survey #358–T   Question #15

Congress is considering cutting income taxes next year. Under one plan many families now paying a small tax would no longer have to pay any tax, and the rest would have their taxes cut by about 10%. Do you think these cuts would be enough for the present, or should they be cut some more?

Would be enough................... 52%
Taxes should be cut more.......... 31
Undecided......................... 17

By Occupation
Professional and Business

Would be enough................... 64%
Taxes should be cut more.......... 26
No opinion........................ 10

White Collar

Would be enough................... 57%
Taxes should be cut more.......... 32
Undecided......................... 11

Farmers

Would be enough................... 53%
Taxes should be cut more.......... 28
Undecided......................... 19

Manual Workers

Would be enough................... 45%
Taxes should be cut more.......... 33
Undecided......................... 22

NOVEMBER 9
ARMY-NAVY MERGER

Interviewing Date 10/19–24/45
Survey #358–T   Question #8a

Will you tell me what your understanding is of the term "unified command" for the armed forces of the United States?

Reasonably correct answer........... 52%
Incorrect answer.................... 48

Interviewing Date 10/19–24/45
Survey #358–T   Question #8b

The group indicating some knowledge of the matter was asked: Do you approve or disapprove of a unified command for the armed forces of this country?

Approve........................... 64%
Disapprove........................ 23
No opinion........................ 13

By Education
College

Approve........................... 73%
Disapprove........................ 17
No opinion........................ 10

High School

Approve........................... 64%
Disapprove........................ 24
No opinion........................ 12

Grade School

Approve........................... 57%
Disapprove........................ 27
No opinion........................ 16

NOVEMBER 11
LABOR-MANAGEMENT STRIFE

Interviewing Date 10/5–10/45
Survey #357–T   Question #14

Would you favor a law requiring employers and unions to take their differences to a Government arbitrator before a strike could be called in any industry?

Yes............................... 79%
No................................ 11
No opinion........................ 10

Interviewing Date 10/5–10/45
Survey #358–K   Question #4

It has been suggested that the Government create special courts to handle labor disputes. When a strike is threatened, unions and employers would go before a special labor court to state their case and the decision of the court would be final. Would you favor or oppose setting up a special labor court?

Favor............................. 70%
Oppose............................ 16
No opinion........................ 14

Interviewing Date 10/5–10/45
Survey #358–T   Question #4

It has been suggested that to settle some labor disputes, communities set up their own boards of persons from civic groups, industry, and labor, to help the Government settle these differences. Do you think this would be a good idea or a poor one?

Good idea......................... 60%
Poor idea......................... 20
No opinion........................ 20

NOVEMBER 11
COMPULSORY MILITARY TRAINING

Interviewing Date 10/19–24/45
Survey #358–T   Question #2

In the future, do you think every able-bodied young man should be required to take military and naval training for one year?

Yes............................... 70%
No................................ 24
No opinion........................ 6

NOVEMBER 14
GERMAN PRISONERS

Interviewing Date 10/19–24/45
Survey #358–T   Question #13

What is your opinion of the way we are treating the Germans — are we being too tough or not tough enough?

Too tough........................ 2%
About right....................... 37
Not tough enough.................. 50
No opinion........................ 11

By Sex
Men

Too tough........................ 1%
About right....................... 42
Not tough enough.................. 47
No opinion........................ 10

Women

Too tough........................ 2%
About right....................... 32
Not tough enough.................. 53
No opinion........................ 13

By Political Affiliation
Democrats

Yes.............................. 59%
No............................... 12
No opinion....................... 29

Republicans

Yes.............................. 56%
No............................... 20
No opinion....................... 24

By Education
College

Yes.............................. 70%
No............................... 20
No opinion....................... 10

High School

Yes.............................. 65%
No............................... 17
No opinion....................... 18

Grade School

Yes.............................. 49%
No............................... 12
No opinion....................... 39

NOVEMBER 14
VETO POWERS

Interviewing Date 9/21–26/45
Survey #356–K   Question #11

At the present time when Congress passes a bill to spend money, the President cannot veto parts of that bill but must accept it in full or veto it. Do you think this should be changed so that the President can veto some items in a bill to spend money without vetoing the entire bill?

Yes.............................. 57%
No............................... 14
No opinion....................... 29

NOVEMBER 17
GEORGE PATTON

Interviewing Date 10/19–24/45
Survey #358–K   Question #13

What is your opinion of General George Patton?

Unqualified approval of Patton........ 50%
Qualified approval.................. 22
Disapproval........................ 7
Miscellaneous...................... 3
No opinion, never heard of him....... 18

NOVEMBER 18
COMPULSORY MILITARY TRAINING

Interviewing Date 11/2–7/45
Survey #359–K   Question #1a

In the future, do you think every able-bodied young man should be required to take military and naval training for one year?

Yes............................... 75%
No............................... 21
No opinion....................... 4

Interviewing Date 11/2–7/45
Survey #359–K   Question #1b

Do you think that giving military training in this country will result in a group being formed of military men who will try to have too much power?

Yes............................... 21%
No............................... 62
No opinion....................... 17

Interviewing Date 11/2–7/45
Survey #359–K   Question #1c

If the young men of this country receive this training, do you think the chances of our getting into another war are increased, or decreased?

Increased......................... 12%
Decreased......................... 59
No difference..................... 23
No opinion....................... 6

NOVEMBER 21
COMPULSORY MILITARY TRAINING

Interviewing Date 11/2–7/45
Survey #359–K   Question #1a

In the future do you think every able-bodied young man should be required to take military or naval training for one year?

Yes............................... 75%
No............................... 21
No opinion....................... 4

World War II Veterans Only

Yes............................... 80%
No............................... 18
No opinion....................... 2

Union Members Only

Yes............................... 76%
No............................... 19
No opinion....................... 5

By Political Affiliation
Democrats

Yes............................... 79%
No............................... 18
No opinion....................... 3

Republicans

Yes............................... 70%
No............................... 27
No opinion....................... 3

By Sex
Men

Yes............................... 76%
No............................... 21
No opinion....................... 3

Women

Yes............................... 74%
No............................... 21
No opinion....................... 5

By Age
21–29 Years

Yes............................... 78%
No............................... 19
No opinion....................... 3

30–49 Years

Yes............................... 75%
No............................... 21
No opinion....................... 4

50 Years and Over

Yes.................................. 73%
No................................... 23
No opinion........................... 4

By Occupation
Business and Professional

Yes.................................. 74%
No................................... 23
No opinion........................... 3

White Collar

Yes.................................. 76%
No................................... 22
No opinion........................... 2

Farmers

Yes.................................. 68%
No................................... 28
No opinion........................... 4

Manual Workers

Yes.................................. 78%
No................................... 17
No opinion........................... 5

NOVEMBER 23
DISCHARGES FROM ARMED FORCES

Interviewing Date 11/2–7/45
Survey #359–K   Question #13a

Do you think the army system of releasing men is fair, or do you think it needs some changes?

Army release system is fair........... 50%
Changes needed..................... 40
No opinion........................ 10

Interviewing Date 11/2–7/45
Survey #359–K   Question #13b

Do you think the navy system of releasing men is fair, or do you think it needs some changes?

Navy release system is fair........... 35%
Changes needed..................... 38
No opinion........................ 27

NOVEMBER 24
BRITISH ATTITUDES TOWARD UNITED STATES AND RUSSIA

Special Survey

Britons were asked: Are your feelings toward the United States more friendly, or less friendly, than they were a year ago?

More friendly...................... 9%
Same............................... 46
Less friendly...................... 35
Don't know......................... 10

Are your feelings toward Russia more friendly, or less friendly, than they were a year ago?

More friendly...................... 16%
Same............................... 54
Less friendly...................... 19
Don't know......................... 11

NOVEMBER 25
PRESIDENT TRUMAN AND CONGRESS

Interviewing Date 11/2–7/45
Survey #359–T   Question #6

Do you think President Truman should take a stronger stand in trying to get Congress to carry out his recommendations for things that need to be done in this country?

Yes.................................. 52%
No................................... 21
No opinion........................... 27

By Political Affiliation
Democrats

Yes.................................. 55%
No................................... 16
No opinion........................... 29

Yes.............................. 49%
No.............................. 29
No opinion....................... 22

NOVEMBER 28
OCCUPATION OF JAPAN

Interviewing Date 10/19–24/45
Survey #358–T   Question #14

Do you think we should continue ruling Japan as we are, or should an Allied council with representatives from England, Russia, China, and the United States rule Japan?

Continue as we are................. 60%
Use Allied council................. 27
No opinion....................... 13

NOVEMBER 30
WAGES

Interviewing Date 11/2–7/45
Survey #359–T   Question #12a

Because of loss of overtime, the total weekly pay of many factory workers is less than it was during the war. So that their total weekly pay will be the same as it was during the war, these workers want a 30% increase in their hourly rates. Do you think they should or should not receive this increase?

Should........................... 52%
Should not....................... 38
No opinion....................... 10

Interviewing Date 11/2–7/45
Survey #359–T   Question #12b

All voters not in favor of a 30% wage boost were asked: Would you favor increasing factory workers' hourly rates by 15%?

Favor............................ 69%
Oppose........................... 22
No opinion....................... 9

DECEMBER 1
INTERNATIONAL LANGUAGE

Interviewing Date 11/2–7/45
Survey #359–K   Question #4a

Should the school children in all countries be required to learn, in addition to their own language, some one language which would be understood in all countries so that people of every nation could understand each other better?

Yes.............................. 71%
No.............................. 17
No opinion....................... 12

Interviewing Date 11/2–7/45
Survey #359–K   Question #4c

Those in favor of the idea were asked: Do you think the United Nations should appoint a group to study various languages and select one to use?

Yes.............................. 57%
No.............................. 8
No opinion....................... 6
                                 ——
                                 71%

Interviewing Date 11/2–7/45
Survey #359–T   Question #4b

If some language other than ours were selected, which one would you choose?

French........................... 19%
Spanish.......................... 19
German........................... 5
Russian.......................... 3
Latin............................ 2
Esperanto........................ 2
Miscellaneous.................... 6
No choice, no opinion............. 19
                                 ——
                                 75%

(Note: table adds to more than 71% because some named more than one language.)

Interviewing Date 11/2–7/45
Survey #359–K   Question #4b

If the people of all nations could speak the same language do you think this would increase the chances of maintaining world peace?

Yes.................................. 60%
No................................... 23
No opinion........................ 17

DECEMBER 2
MILITARY STRENGTH

Interviewing Date 11/2–7/45
Survey #359–K   Question #11

Some people say that with the discovery of the atomic bomb, armed forces, except those to handle the bombs, are no longer useful. Do you agree or disagree with this?

Agree............................... 13%
Disagree........................... 67
No opinion........................ 20

Interviewing Date 10/19–24/45
Survey #358–K   Question #9

Before the war the regular army of the United States had about 190,000 men. During the war it had about 8,000,000 men. Just making your best guess, about how many men should we have in our peacetime army about five years from now?

Median average................ 1,000,000

Interviewing Date 10/19–24/45
Survey #359–T   Question #9

Before the war the regular navy of the United States had about 140,000 men. During the war it had over 3,000,000 men. Just making your best guess, about how many men should we have in our peacetime navy about five years from now?

Median average................. 500,000

Interviewing Date 11/2–7/45
Survey #359–K   Question #9

Some people say that if there is another war, a nation can be defeated in one blow by atomic bombs and the war will be over in a few days. Do you agree or disagree with this?

Agree............................... 36%
Disagree........................... 49
No opinion........................ 15

By Education
College

Agree............................... 30%
Disagree........................... 62
No opinion........................ 8

High School

Agree............................... 38%
Disagree........................... 50
No opinion........................ 12

Grade School

Agree............................... 35%
Disagree........................... 46
No opinion........................ 19

DECEMBER 5
COMPULSORY MILITARY TRAINING

Interviewing Date 11/2–7/45
Survey #359–K   Question #1a

In the future, do you think every able-bodied young man should be required to take military and naval training for one year?

By State
New York

Yes.................................. 78%
No................................... 18
No opinion........................ 4

Massachusetts

Yes.................................. 75%
No................................... 21
No opinion........................ 4

New Jersey

Yes............................... 79%
No............................... 20
No opinion........................ 1

Pennsylvania

Yes............................... 74%
No............................... 22
No opinion........................ 4

DECEMBER 7
COMPULSORY MILITARY TRAINING

Interviewing Date 11/2–7/45
Survey #359–K   Question #1

In the future, do you think every able-bodied young man should be required to take military or naval training for one year?

By State
Illinois

Yes............................... 74%
No............................... 24
No opinion........................ 2

Ohio

Yes............................... 75%
No............................... 22
No opinion........................ 3

Indiana

Yes............................... 69%
No............................... 27
No opinion........................ 4

Michigan

Yes............................... 76%
No............................... 21
No opinion........................ 3

DECEMBER 8
COMPULSORY MILITARY TRAINING

Interviewing Date 11/2–7/45
Survey #359–K   Question #1a

In the future, do you think every able-bodied young man should be required to take military or naval training for one year?

By State
Wisconsin

Yes............................... 70%
No............................... 26
No opinion........................ 4

Missouri

Yes............................... 70%
No............................... 25
No opinion........................ 5

Kansas

Yes............................... 70%
No............................... 26
No opinion........................ 4

Kentucky

Yes............................... 75%
No............................... 18
No opinion........................ 7

Oklahoma

Yes............................... 74%
No............................... 22
No opinion........................ 4

Texas

Yes............................... 78%
No............................... 16
No opinion........................ 6

California

Yes............................... 77%
No............................... 20
No opinion........................ 3

DECEMBER 9
COMPULSORY MILITARY TRAINING

Interviewing Date 11/23–28/45
Survey #360–K   Question #1

In the future, do you think every able-bodied young man should be required to take military or naval training for one year?

Yes............................... 70%
No................................ 25
No opinion........................ 5

By Political Affiliation
Democrats

Yes............................... 76%
No................................ 20
No opinion........................ 4

Republicans

Yes............................... 63%
No................................ 32
No opinion........................ 5

By Age
21–29 Years

Yes............................... 72%
No................................ 24
No opinion........................ 4

30–49 Years

Yes............................... 70%
No................................ 25
No opinion........................ 5

50 Years and Over

Yes............................... 69%
No................................ 25
No opinion........................ 6

By Education
College

Yes............................... 68%
No................................ 29
No opinion........................ 3

High School

Yes............................... 72%
No................................ 23
No opinion........................ 5

Grade School

Yes............................... 69%
No................................ 25
No opinion........................ 6

By Occupation
Professional and Business

Yes............................... 71%
No................................ 25
No opinion........................ 4

White Collar

Yes............................... 72%
No................................ 24
No opinion........................ 4

Farmers

Yes............................... 58%
No................................ 35
No opinion........................ 7

Manual Workers

Yes............................... 73%
No................................ 22
No opinion........................ 5

By Region
New England and Middle Atlantic

Yes............................... 70%
No................................ 25
No opinion........................ 5

East Central and West Central

Yes............................... 69%
No................................ 27
No opinion........................ 4

South

Yes............................... 76%
No................................ 17
No opinion........................ 7

West

Yes.............................. 69%
No.............................. 26
No opinion....................... 5

DECEMBER 12
WAGES

Interviewing Date 11/23–28/45
Survey #360–K   Question #5a

President Truman thinks the wages and salaries of civil service workers in the Federal Government should be raised 20% Do you favor or oppose such a raise?

Favor............................ 53%
Oppose.......................... 33
No opinion....................... 14

By Occupation
Professional and Business

Favor............................ 56%
Oppose.......................... 33
No opinion....................... 11

Manual Workers

Favor............................ 57%
Oppose.......................... 26
No opinion....................... 17

White Collar

Favor............................ 58%
Oppose.......................... 31
No opinion....................... 11

Farmers

Favor............................ 32%
Oppose.......................... 53
No opinion....................... 15

Union Members Only

Favor............................ 65%
Oppose.......................... 22
No opinion....................... 13

Interviewing Date 6/1–5/45
Survey #348–K   Question #10a

What class or group of people in this country has done best financially during the war compared to what they made before the war?

Labor, war workers, other workers..... 60%
Business executives, upper class people.. 15
Farmers........................... 5
White collar workers................ 3
Miscellaneous, no particular group.... 17

Interviewing Date 6/1–5/45
Survey #348–K   Question #10b

Do you think any class or group of people in this country is not making as much money as it should?

Yes.............................. 59%
No, no opinion................... 41

Those who replied in the affirmative were then asked: What group do you have in mind?

White collar workers................ 25%
Skilled and manual labor............ 13
Farmers........................... 10
Business and professional............ 9
Miscellaneous..................... 5
                                    62%

(Note: table adds to more than 59% because some voters named more than one group.)

DECEMBER 14
PARTY STRENGTH

Interviewing Date 11/23–28/45
Survey #360–K   Question #11

If the presidential election were being held today, which party would you vote for — the Democratic or Republican?

World War II Veterans Only

Democratic........................ 63%
Republican........................ 37

The survey also found that a preference for the Democratic party is as high among voters in their twenties who have not had military service as it is among veterans.

DECEMBER 15
WOMEN IN POLITICS

Interviewing Date 11/23–28/45
Survey #360–K   Question #6a

A woman leader says not enough of the capable women are holding important jobs in the United States Government. Do you agree or disagree with this?

Agree........................... 32%
Disagree........................ 48
No opinion...................... 20

By Sex
Men

Agree........................... 26%
Disagree........................ 53
No opinion...................... 21

Women

Agree........................... 38%
Disagree........................ 43
No opinion...................... 19

Interviewing Date 11/23–28/45
Survey #360–K   Question #6d

If the party whose candidate you most often support nominated a woman for President of the United States, would you vote for her if she seemed best qualified for the job?

Yes............................. 33%
No.............................. 55
No opinion...................... 12

By Sex
Men

Yes............................. 29%
No.............................. 58
No opinion...................... 13

Women

Yes............................. 37%
No.............................. 51
No opinion...................... 12

Interviewing Date 11/23–28/45
Survey #360–K   Question #6c

Would you approve or disapprove of having a capable woman in the President's cabinet?

Approve......................... 38%
Disapprove...................... 48
No opinion...................... 14

By Sex
Men

Approve......................... 33%
Disapprove...................... 52
No opinion...................... 15

Women

Approve......................... 43%
Disapprove...................... 43
No opinion...................... 14

Interviewing Date 11/23–28/45
Survey #360–T   Question #6c

Would you approve or disapprove of having a capable woman on the Supreme Court?

Approve......................... 47%
Disapprove...................... 40
No opinion...................... 13

By Sex
Men

Approve......................... 42%
Disapprove...................... 46
No opinion...................... 12

Women

Approve......................... 52%
Disapprove...................... 35
No opinion...................... 13

Interviewing Date 11/23–28/45
Survey #360–T   Question #6d

If the party you most often support nominated a woman for governor of this state, would you vote for her if she seemed qualified for the job?

Yes............................. 56%
No.............................. 35
No opinion...................... 9

By Sex
Men

Yes............................. 52%
No.............................. 40
No opinion...................... 8

Women

Yes............................. 60%
No.............................. 30
No opinion...................... 10

DECEMBER 16
PROHIBITION AND DRINKING HABITS

Interviewing Date 11/23–28/45
Survey #360–K   Question #7b

If the question of national prohibition should come up again, would you vote wet or dry?

Wet............................. 67%
Dry............................. 33

Interviewing Date 11/23–28/45
Survey #360–K   Question #7a

Do you ever have occasion to use any alcoholic beverages such as liquor, wine, or beer, or are you a total abstainer?

Drink any alcoholic beverage on occasion 52%
Total abstainers.................... 33
Drink only beer, wine.............. 15

Drinking falls off sharply among men 50 years of age and older the survey finds. Only two of ten are nondrinkers among men up to 50. After that about one out of three is a total abstainer.

More women than men are nondrinkers, the survey finds, with 25% among men reporting themselves as nondrinkers, compared to 41% among women. Fifty-seven per cent among the women over 50 years of age are nondrinkers.

In farm areas, total abstainers number better than five out of ten; whereas in cities barely two out of ten say they do not drink.

DECEMBER 19
COMPULSORY MILITARY TRAINING

Interviewing Date 11/23–28/45
Survey #360–K   Question #1

This question was asked of young men, aged 15 to 18, and parents of young men between the ages of 12 and 18: In the future, do you think every able-bodied young man should be required to take military or naval training for one year?

Young Men Only

Yes............................. 76%
No.............................. 22
No opinion...................... 2

Parents Only

Yes............................. 60%
No.............................. 36
No opinion...................... 4

DECEMBER 21
LOAN TO ENGLAND

Interviewing Date 11/23–28/45
Survey #360–K   Question #2c

Do you think England needs the proposed $4 billion loan to get back on its feet?

Yes............................. 26%
No.............................. 52
No opinion...................... 22

Interviewing Date 11/23–28/45
Survey #360–K   Question #2b

If we make this loan, do you think that the United States as well as England will benefit from this in addition to the interest paid us on the loan?

Yes................................. 31%
No................................. 49
No opinion......................... 20

DECEMBER 22
PARENTHOOD

Interviewing Date 11/23–28/45
Survey #360–S   Question #3

Asked of young men, aged 15 to 18: If you were a parent, what one thing would you do differently than most parents do?

The two largest single groups of replies deal with parental strictness. One group would act a little more leniently toward their children. The other group, of identical size, would act a little more strictly.

Another sizeable group declare they would work more with the children, try to understand their viewpoints, help them to make up their minds.

Many of these replies carry a serious note: "I'd treat my children as adults; let them decide things for themselves . . . I'd try not to tell my son what he ought to be when he grows up . . . I'd be more of a companion to my children . . . I'd give my children proper sexual education instead of letting them find out about sex the wrong way."

Other replies:

"I'd bring more religion into the home . . . I'd let my son have the car more than some people I know . . . I'd increase my son's allowance . . . I'd stop opening up other people's mail . . . I'd let my son take a part-time job if he wanted to earn some money . . . I'd see that my son stayed in school and got a proper education . . . I'd give the children more responsibility."

Only about two out of every ten with whom reporters talked said they have no complaint, that they would do things just about the way their parents are now doing them.

DECEMBER 23
PRESIDENTIAL CANDIDATES

Interviewing Date 8/10–15/45
Survey #353–K   Question #13

It is often said that many people who have not held public office would make good Presidents. Can you think of anyone in this state or nation who you think might make a good President?

MacArthur......................... 26%
Eisenhower........................ 24
Kaiser............................. 8
Ford.............................. 2
Baruch............................ 2
Eleanor Roosevelt.................. 2
Others............................ 36

DECEMBER 26
UNIFICATION OF ARMED FORCES

Interviewing Date 12/7–12/45
Survey #361–K   Question #7a

Will you tell me what your understanding is of the term "unified command" for the armed forces of the United States?

Correct answer..................... 62%
Incorrect.......................... 38

Interviewing Date 12/7–12/45
Survey #361–K   Question #7b

Those giving correct answers were then asked: Do you approve or disapprove of a unified command for the armed forces of this country?

Approve........................... 52%
Disapprove........................ 34
No opinion........................ 14

The better educated and better informed throughout the country tend to be the most in favor of the idea of merger.

Among World War II veterans included in the poll, the vote runs 53% approval, 40% disapproval, 7% no opinion.

DECEMBER 28
PEARL HARBOR

Interviewing Date 12/7–12/45
Survey #361–K   Question #5a

Have you heard or read about the congressional investigation of the Pearl Harbor attack?

Yes.................................. 83%
No.................................. 17

Interviewing Date 12/7–12/45
Survey #361–K   Question #5b

Asked of those who replied in the affirmative: Who or what do you think was most to blame for the Pearl Harbor disaster?

The American people — all of us.......	12%
The Government, Washington.........	11
The army and the navy (including particular people)....................	10
President Roosevelt..................	9
The army and navy at Pearl Harbor....	8
The Japanese.......................	5
The army (including particular people).	4
Negligence and unpreparedness........	3
The navy (including particular people)..	2
State Department (including Secretary Hull)............................	2
Congress...........................	2
Isolationists........................	1
Army and navy intelligence...........	1
Others.............................	7
No opinion.........................	23

DECEMBER 29
TELEVISION

Interviewing Date 12/7–12/45
Survey #361–K   Question #6a

Do you know what television is?

Yes.................................. 85%
No.................................. 15

Interviewing Date 12/7–12/45
Survey #361–K   Question #6b

Have you ever seen a television set in operation?

Yes.................................. 19%
No.................................. 81

DECEMBER 30
GENERAL MOTORS STRIKE

Interviewing Date 12/7–12/45
Survey #361–K   Question #3d

Do you think workers at General Motors should get more pay?

Yes.................................. 60%
No.................................. 22
No opinion......................... 18

By Occupation
Business and Professional

Yes.................................. 56%
No.................................. 26
No opinion......................... 18

Farmers

Yes.................................. 45%
No.................................. 35
No opinion......................... 20

White Collar

Yes.................................. 62%
No.................................. 20
No opinion......................... 18

Manual Workers

Yes.................................. 67%
No.................................. 16
No opinion......................... 17

Interviewing Date 12/7–12/45
Survey #361–K   Question #3c

Asked of those who answered in the affirmative: How much more should they get?

Median average.................... 15%

1946

JANUARY 6
LABOR DISPUTES

Interviewing Date 12/7–12/45
Survey #361–T   Question #2a

President Truman has proposed a law requiring a 30-day cooling off period before a major strike could start. During this time a committee would look into the facts and causes of the dispute and make public its report. Would you favor or oppose such a law?

Favor.............................. 78%
Oppose............................ 10
No opinion........................ 12

By Region
New England and Middle Atlantic

Favor.............................. 77%
Oppose............................ 10
No opinion........................ 13

East Central and West Central

Favor.............................. 78%
Oppose............................ 12
No opinion........................ 10

South

Favor.............................. 79%
Oppose............................ 5
No opinion........................ 16

West

Favor.............................. 77%
Oppose............................ 12
No opinion........................ 11

By Occupation
Business and Professional

Favor.............................. 80%
Oppose............................ 12
No opinion........................ 8

White Collar

Favor.............................. 80%
Oppose............................ 11
No opinion........................ 9

JANUARY 2
FOOD FOR GERMANY

Interviewing Date 12/7–12/45
Survey #361–K   Question #4a

Do you think the German people in the part of Germany that the United States occupies and controls will all get enough to eat to live on this winter?

Yes............................... 49%
No................................ 34
No opinion........................ 17

World War II Veterans Only

Yes............................... 49%
No................................ 36
No opinion........................ 15

Interviewing Date 12/7–12/45
Survey #361–K   Question #4b

Should we ship more food into this area which we occupy?

Yes............................... 48%
No................................ 35
No opinion........................ 17

World War II Veterans Only

Yes............................... 38%
No................................ 46
No opinion........................ 16

Farmers

Favor.............................. 83%
Oppose............................ 5
No opinion........................ 12

Manual Workers

Favor.............................. 73%
Oppose............................ 12
No opinion........................ 15

Union Members Only

Favor.............................. 70%
Oppose............................ 16
No opinion........................ 14

Interviewing Date 12/7–12/45
Survey #361–T   Question #2b

*Do you think this law would operate to re-
duce the number of strikes?*

Yes............................... 72%
No................................ 14
No opinion........................ 14

Union Members Only

Yes............................... 68%
No................................ 21
No opinion........................ 11

JANUARY 9
PALESTINE

Interviewing Date 12/7–12/45
Survey #361–K   Question #11a

*Have you followed the discussion about
permitting Jews to settle in Palestine?*

Yes............................... 55%
No................................ 45

Interviewing Date 12/7–12/45
Survey #361–K   Question #11b

*Asked of those who replied in the affirma-
tive: What is your opinion of the issue?*

Favor the idea..................... 76%
Favor if Jews do................... 4
Against the idea................... 7
Favor leaving question up to British..... 1
Favor leaving question up to Arabs..... 1
Miscellaneous...................... 3
Don't know........................ 8

Jews Only

Favor the idea..................... 90%
Oppose the idea.................... 10

JANUARY 9
UNITED NATIONS

Special Survey

*Asked of newspaper publishers: On the
basis of the United Nations Organization
decision to locate its permanent headquarters in the eastern part of the United
States, in your opinion which of the following areas would seem to be most suitable —
Boston, Hyde Park, Philadelphia, or New
York?*

Philadelphia....................... 34.1%
Hyde Park......................... 30.9
Boston............................ 20.4
New York......................... 14.6

JANUARY 12
TRAVEL

Interviewing Date 10/19–24/45
Survey #358–T   Question #1

*If you had the money and wanted to take a
thousand mile trip across the country, and
the cost was the same, would you prefer to
go by railroad or airplane?*

Railroad.......................... 54%
Airplane.......................... 46

By Sex

	Railroad	Airplane
Men.................	50%	50%
Women..............	57	43

By Age

21–29 Years...........	32%	68%
30–49 Years...........	51	49
50 Years and over.......	68	32

JANUARY 14
IMMIGRATION

Interviewing Date 12/7–12/45
Survey #361–K   Question #12a

Should we permit more persons from Europe to come to this country each year than we did before the war, should we keep the number about the same, or should we reduce the number?

More............................	5%
Same............................	32
Fewer............................	37
None at all.........................	14
No opinion........................	12

By Education
College

More, same.......................	49%
Fewer, none at all..................	41
No opinion........................	10

High School

More, same.......................	40%
Fewer, none at all..................	52
No opinion........................	8

Grade School

More, same.......................	34%
Fewer, none at all..................	52
No opinion........................	14

World War II Veterans Only

More, same.......................	34%
Fewer, none at all..................	56
No opinion........................	10

Labor Union Members Only

More, same.......................	38%
Fewer, none at all..................	53
No opinion........................	9

Interviewing Date 12/7–12/45
Survey #361–K   Question #12b

Asked of those who favored more, the same number, or fewer immigrants or who had no opinion: From which countries would you like to see the people come?

The following are listed according to frequency of mention:

Scandinavian countries
Holland
Belgium
England
France
Czechoslovakia
Poland
Greece
Russia
Germany
Spain
Italy

JANUARY 16
MOST IMPORTANT PROBLEM

Interviewing Date 12/21–26/45
Survey #362–K   Question #1

What is the most important problem that you and your family face today?

High cost of living...................	28%
Housing...........................	15
Difficulty buying food, clothing, fuel, equipment......................	10
Finding a job......................	9
Others............................	38

JANUARY 18
COLDS AND FLU

Interviewing Date 12/21–26/45
Survey #362–K   Question #6a

Do any of the people in your home, including yourself, have a cold — not the flu — at the present time?

Yes................................ 19%
No................................ 81

Interviewing Date 12/21–26/45
Survey #362–K   Question #7a

Do any of the people in your home, including yourself, have the flu at the present time?

Yes................................ 4%
No................................ 96

JANUARY 19
LABOR DISPUTES

Interviewing Date 12/21–26/45
Survey #362–T   Question #4a

President Truman has proposed a law requiring a 30-day cooling off period before a major strike could start. During this time a committee would look into the facts and causes of the dispute and make public its report. Would you favor or oppose such a law?

By Political Affiliation
Democrats

Favor.............................. 74%
Oppose............................ 14
No opinion........................ 12

Republicans

Favor.............................. 83%
Oppose............................ 7
No opinion........................ 10

JANUARY 21
PARTY STRENGTH

Interviewing Date 12/21–26/45
Survey #362–K   Question #15

If a presidential election were being held today, which party would you vote for — the Democratic or Republican?

Union Members Only

Democratic........................ 70%
Republican........................ 30

C.I.O. Members Only

Democratic........................ 74%
Republican........................ 26

A.F.L. Members Only

Democratic........................ 69%
Republican........................ 31

JANUARY 23
PARTY STRENGTH

Interviewing Date 12/21–26/45
Survey #362–K   Question #10

If a presidential election were being held today, which party would you vote for — the Democratic or Republican?

Farmers Only

Democratic........................ 51%
Republican........................ 49

Midwestern Farmers Only

Democratic........................ 42%
Republican........................ 58

JANUARY 25
PARTY STRENGTH

Interviewing Date 12/21–26/45
Survey #362–K   Question #10

If a presidential election were being held today, which party would you vote for — the the Democratic or Republican?

By Age

	Democratic	Republican
15–18 Years.........	65%	35%
21–29 Years.........	62	38
30–49 Years.........	55	45
50 Years and over....	49	51

JANUARY 26
PARTY STRENGTH

Interviewing Date 12/21–26/45
Survey #362–K   Question #10

If a presidential election were being held today, which party would you vote for — the Democratic or Republican?

World War II Veterans Only

Democratic........................ 65%
Republican........................ 35

21–29 Years Only

Democratic........................ 62%
Republican........................ 38

JANUARY 28
PARTY STRENGTH

Interviewing Date 12/21–26/45
Survey #362–K   Question #10

If a presidential election were being held today, which party would you vote for — the Democratic or Republican?

Cities 100,000–500,000 Only

Democratic........................ 60%
Republican........................ 40

Nation's 13 Largest Cities Only

Democratic........................ 62%
Republican........................ 38

JANUARY 30
CONGRESSIONAL ELECTIONS

Interviewing Date 12/21–26/45
Survey #362–K   Question #3a

In the coming congressional election which will be held next November, what do you think will be the main issue?

The following are listed according to frequency of mention:

Labor legislation and strikes
Full (or high) employment
Inflation
Reconversion
Veterans affairs
Housing
Military training
Taxes

FEBRUARY 1
PRESIDENT TRUMAN'S POPULARITY

Interviewing Date 1/5–10/46
Survey #363–K   Question #10a

Do you approve or disapprove of the way Harry Truman is handling his job as President?

Approve........................... 63%
Disapprove........................ 22
No opinion........................ 15

By Political Affiliation
Democrats

Approve........................... 75%
Disapprove........................ 13
No opinion........................ 12

Republicans

Approve........................... 46%
Disapprove........................ 37
No opinion........................ 17

FEBRUARY 2
HARRY TRUMAN

Interviewing Date 1/5–10/46
Survey #363–K   Question #10c

What one thing do you like best about the way Harry Truman is handling his job?

The following are listed according to frequency of mention:

His honesty, sincerity, and friendliness.
The fact that he is doing the best he can under present conditions.
His carrying on of Roosevelt policies.
His handling of foreign affairs.
His interest in the general welfare and in the common man.
His handling of strikes and labor difficulties.
The rapidity of demobilization.
His continued attempts to get congressional cooperation.
His willingness to take sound advice.
His essential independence of attitude.

Interviewing Date 1/5–10/45
Survey #363–K   Question #10d

Which one thing do you like least about the way Harry Truman is handling his job?

The following are listed according to frequency of mention:

The way he is handling the labor problem.
His lack of leadership.
The fact that he is too easily influenced, too easily led.
His playing of politics and taking care of his friends in his appointments.
His inability to get along with Congress.
His foreign policy — loans to Britain and Russia.
His failure to take his job seriously enough.
His handling of demobilization.
His poor advisers.
His lack of experience and stature for the job.

FEBRUARY 4
TRUMAN ADMINISTRATION

Interviewing Date 12/21–26/45
Survey #362–K   Question #14a

Which of these three policies (on card) would you like to see the Government follow— (1) go more to the left by following more of the views of labor and other liberal groups, (2) go more to the right by following more of the views of business and conservative groups, or (3) follow a policy halfway between the two?

Go to the left...................... 18%
Go to the right..................... 21
Follow middle road.................. 52
No opinion......................... 9

By Political Affiliation
Democrats

Go to the left...................... 27%
Go to the right..................... 10
Follow middle road.................. 52
No opinion......................... 11

Republicans

Go to the left...................... 6%
Go to the right..................... 36
Follow middle road.................. 51
No opinion......................... 7

Interviewing Date 12/21–26/45
Survey #362–K   Question #14b

Which of these three policies do you think the Truman administration has been following?

Going left.......................... 44%
Going right......................... 13
Middle road........................ 27
No opinion......................... 16

By Political Affiliation
Democrats

Going left.......................... 30%
Going right......................... 15
Middle road........................ 35
No opinion......................... 20

Republicans

Going left..........................	63%
Going right.........................	9
Middle road........................	16
No opinion.........................	12

FEBRUARY 6
REPUBLICAN PRESIDENTIAL CANDIDATES

Interviewing Date 1/5–10/46
Survey #363–K   Question #4a

Asked of Republicans: What man would you like to see elected President in 1948?

Dewey.............................	38%
Stassen............................	27
Bricker............................	8
MacArthur.........................	6
Vandenberg........................	4
Taft...............................	4
Eisenhower........................	3
Saltonstall.........................	2
Warren............................	1
Johnston...........................	1
Others.............................	6

FEBRUARY 8
DEMOCRATIC PRESIDENTIAL CANDIDATES

Interviewing Date 1/5–10/46
Survey #363–K   Question #4b

Asked of Democrats: What man would you like to see elected President in 1948?

Truman............................	67%
Wallace............................	15
Eisenhower........................	6
Byrnes.............................	3
Stettinius..........................	2
La Guardia........................	1
Farley.............................	1
Barkley............................	1
Others.............................	4

FEBRUARY 9
REPUBLICAN PRESIDENTIAL CANDIDATES

Interviewing Date 1/25–30/46
Survey #364–K   Question #11

Asked of Republicans in the Midwest: Whom would you like to see the Republican party nominate for President in 1948?

Stassen............................	33%
Dewey.............................	30
Bricker............................	11
Taft...............................	6
Vandenberg........................	6
MacArthur.........................	5
Eisenhower........................	3
Others.............................	6

FEBRUARY 10
PARTY BEST FOR VARIOUS INCOME GROUPS

Interviewing Date 1/5–10/46
Survey #363–K   Question #11a

Which political party — the Democratic or the Republican — do you think is most interested in persons of above average income?

Democratic........................	14%
Republican........................	57
No difference......................	17
No opinion........................	12

Interviewing Date 1/5–10/46
Survey #363–K   Question #11b

Which political party is most interested in persons of average income?

Democratic........................	46%
Republican........................	21
No difference......................	21
No opinion........................	12

Interviewing Date 1/5–10/46
Survey #363–K
Question #11c

Which political party is most interested in persons of below average income?

Democratic........................ 61%
Republican........................ 10
No difference..................... 18
No opinion........................ 11

FEBRUARY 13
DEMOCRATIC PRESIDENTIAL CANDIDATES

Interviewing Date 1/25–30/46
Survey #364–K
Question #11

Asked of Democrats: What man would you like to see elected President of the country in 1948?

Truman........................... 67%
Wallace.......................... 15
Eisenhower....................... 6
Byrnes........................... 3
Stettinius....................... 2
La Guardia....................... 1
Farley........................... 1
Others........................... 5

Democratic Union Members Only

Truman........................... 65%
Wallace.......................... 19
Eisenhower....................... 4
Byrnes........................... 3
Stettinius....................... 2
La Guardia....................... 1
Farley........................... 1
Others........................... 5

MARCH 1
ARMY ENLISTMENTS

Interviewing Date 1/25–30/46
Survey #364–K
Question #6

What more do you think the army should do to get hundreds of thousands of men to enlist?

The following are listed in order of frequency of mention:

Raise army pay.

Make army life more attractive. This includes suggestions for longer furloughs, with provisions for visits home once a year, etc., and better allowances and housing facilities for families of men in the army.

Make the officers treat the enlisted men better, and provide for getting a better type of officer material.

Offer more educational programs, more recreation, and more job training to help men when they return to civilian life.

World War II Veterans Only

Raise army pay.

Inject greater degree of democracy into the army. Less difference between the officers and enlisted personnel.

Offer more educational programs and training of a kind which will be useful in civilian life.

Provide more opportunity for advancement.

Increase family allowances.

MARCH 2
FAMILY LIFE

Interviewing Date 1/25–30/46
Survey #364–T
Question #18

Asked of married women: What is the chief fault of your husband?

The following are listed in order of frequency of mention:

Thoughtlessness
Bossiness
Other women
Stinginess
Lack of interest in domestic problems
Nagging
Gambling and smoking

Four per cent declared that their husbands are faultless and 8% expressed no opinion.

MARCH 4
PRICE CONTROLS

Interviewing Date 1/25–30/46
Survey #364–K   Question #9a

The present price ceiling law ends in June. Do you think the price ceiling should be continued or should it end in June?

Should be continued.................. 73%
Should end......................... 21
No opinion......................... 6

Interviewing Date 1/25–30/46
Survey #364–K   Question #9b

What kind of a job do you think the OPA has done?

Excellent, very good................ 40%
Fair, fairly good................... 40
Poor............................... 13
No opinion......................... 7

MARCH 6
LOANS TO ENGLAND

Interviewing Date 2/15–20/46
Survey #365–T   Question #5a

Have you followed the discussion about the United States lending money to England?

Yes................................ 57%
No................................. 43

Interviewing Date 2/15–20/46
Survey #365–T   Question #5b

Asked of those who responded in the affirmative: What do you think is the best argument in favor of granting the loan?

It will promote world trade and stimulate business within the United States. 16%
England is still suffering from the war and is badly in need of the loan....... 7
We should make the loan in the interests of a good neighbor policy.......... 4

England is our ally, and important to us as a first line of defense in Europe..... 4
Miscellaneous...................... 5
No answers......................... 28
                                  ⎯⎯
                                  64%

(Note: total is greater than 57% as some people gave more than one response.)

Interviewing Date 2/15–20/46
Survey #365–T   Question #5c

Asked also of those who responded in the affirmative: What do you think is the best argument against granting the loan?

Britain won't pay the loan back...... 28%
U.S. needs the money itself.......... 6
We've already given Britain too much... 4
England doesn't need or want the loan.. 2
England will use the loan to further her own interests and against the U.S..... 2
The loan will increase our already heavy tax burden...................... 1
Miscellaneous...................... 4
No answer.......................... 17
                                  ⎯⎯
                                  64%

(Note: total is greater than 57% as some people gave more than one response.)

Interviewing Date 2/15–20/46
Survey #365–T   Question #5d

Asked of those who responded in the affirmative: Do you think Congress should or should not approve the loan?

Should............................. 22%
Should not......................... 29
Undecided.......................... 6
                                  ⎯⎯
                                  57%

MARCH 9
MINIMUM AMOUNT NEEDED FOR FOOD

Interviewing Date 2/15–20/46
Survey #365–K   Question #3

On the average, how much does your family spend on food, including milk, each week?

Median average...................... $17

$5 or less........................... 4%
$6–$10.............................. 19
$11–$15............................. 25
$16–$20............................. 24
$21–$25............................. 14
Over $25............................ 14

By Community Size
(*Median Average*)

100,000 and over.................... $20
10,000–99,999...................... 15
Under 9,999........................ 15
Farms.............................. 10

By Occupation
(*Median Average*)

Professional and business............ $20
White collar........................ 18
Manual workers..................... 15

MARCH 9
FAMILY LIFE

Interviewing Date 1/25–30/46
Survey #364–K   Question #17

Asked of married men: What is the chief fault of your wife?

The following are listed in order of frequency of mention:

Nagging
Extravagance
Poor homemaker
Drinking
Gossiping
Selfishness
Too many outside interests
Too bossy
Untidy

Eight per cent declared that their wives are faultless and 14% expressed no opinion.

MARCH 10
FOOD SHIPMENTS TO EUROPE

Interviewing Date 2/15–20/46
Survey #365–K   Question #2

Would you eat less meat and use less flour in order to send more food to the people of Europe?

Yes................................ 67%
No................................. 22
No opinion......................... 11

Women showed a higher vote of approval than men. The vote of women was 72%, that of men 61%.

MARCH 13
ATOMIC TESTING

Interviewing Date 2/15–20/46
Survey #365–K   Question #11a

This summer our navy plans to make tests at sea to find out how effective the atom bombs would be in naval warfare. Do you think that representatives of other nations should or should not be allowed to watch these tests?

Should............................. 26%
Should not......................... 66
No opinion......................... 8

By Education
College

Should............................. 45%
Should not......................... 49
No opinion......................... 6

High School

Should............................. 31%
Should not......................... 63
No opinion......................... 6

Grade School

Should............................. 19%
Should not......................... 72
No opinion......................... 9

MARCH 15
STATEHOOD FOR HAWAII

Interviewing Date 2/15–20/46
Survey #365–T   Question #7a

Would you favor or oppose having Hawaii admitted as the 49th state in the Union?

Favor........................... 60%
Oppose.......................... 19
No opinion...................... 21

By Region
New England and Middle Atlantic

Favor........................... 62%
Oppose.......................... 20
No opinion...................... 18

East Central and West Central

Favor........................... 59%
Oppose.......................... 20
No opinion...................... 21

South

Favor........................... 55%
Oppose.......................... 16
No opinion...................... 29

Mountain

Favor........................... 66%
Oppose.......................... 15
No opinion...................... 19

West

Favor........................... 68%
Oppose.......................... 18
No opinion...................... 14

By Political Affiliation
Democrats

Favor........................... 61%
Oppose.......................... 17
No opinion...................... 22

Republicans

Favor........................... 61%
Oppose.......................... 21
No opinion...................... 18

MARCH 16
INCOME TAX

Interviewing Date 2/28–3/5/46
Survey #366–K   Question #14b

Do you think that the income tax you now pay is fair or unfair?

Fair............................ 62%
Unfair.......................... 38

By Income

	Fair	Unfair
Upper	64%	36%
Middle	64	36
Lower	59	41

MARCH 19
FEATHERBEDDING PRACTICES

Interviewing Date 12/21–26/45
Survey #362–K   Question #16

To make more jobs, some unions require employers to hire more persons than are actually needed to do the work. Would you favor or oppose having a law which would stop this practice?

Favor........................... 60%
Oppose.......................... 23
No opinion...................... 17

By Region
New England and Middle Atlantic

Favor........................... 57%
Oppose.......................... 24
No opinion...................... 19

East and West Central

Favor........................... 62%
Oppose.......................... 24
No opinion...................... 14

South

Favor........................... 66%
Oppose.......................... 17
No opinion...................... 17

Mountain and West

Favor	60%
Oppose	24
No opinion	16

By Political Affiliation
Democrats

Favor	55%
Oppose	26
No opinion	19

Republicans

Favor	69%
Oppose	20
No opinion	11

Union Members Only

Favor	52%
Oppose	31
No opinion	17

World War II Veterans Only

Favor	58%
Oppose	26
No opinion	16

MARCH 18
WORLD POLITICS

Interviewing Date 1/25–30/46
Survey #364–K   Question #15a

Do you believe any nation would like to dominate or run the rest of the world?

Yes	59%
No	27
No opinion	14

Interviewing Date 1/25–30/46
Survey #364–K   Question #15b

Asked of those who said yes to the above question: Which nation?

Russia	26%
Britain	12
Germany	10
Japan	6
United States	2
Others	1
All big nations	1
No opinion	1
	59%

MARCH 22
SECRET SERVICE

Interviewing Date 2/28–3/5/46
Survey #366–K   Question #13

Do you think Congress should provide money to maintain a large force of secret service agents who would operate throughout the world to keep us informed of what other nations are doing?

Yes	77%
No	17
No opinion	6

MARCH 23
OVERSEAS MARRIAGES

Interviewing Date 2/28–3/5/46
Survey #366–K   Question #1

Do you think the army should or should not let soldiers serving overseas marry girls who live in occupied countries in Europe?

Should	44%
Should not	48
No opinion	8

By Sex
Men

Should	53%
Should not	39
No opinion	8

Women

Should.............................. 36%
Should not.......................... 56
No opinion.......................... 8

By Age
21–29 Years

Should.............................. 53%
Should not.......................... 40
No opinion.......................... 7

30–49 Years

Should.............................. 46%
Should not.......................... 46
No opinion.......................... 8

50 Years and Over

Should.............................. 37%
Should not.......................... 54
No opinion.......................... 9

World War II Veterans Only

Should.............................. 61%
Should not.......................... 33
No opinion.......................... 6

MARCH 24
RUSSIA

Interviewing Date 2/28–3/5/46
Survey #366–K   Question #9

Do you think Russia will cooperate with us in world affairs?

Yes................................ 35%
No................................. 52
No opinion.......................... 13

By Political Affiliation
Democrats

Yes................................ 37%
No................................. 49
No opinion.......................... 14

Republicans

Yes................................ 33%
No................................. 57
No opinion.......................... 10

By Education
College

Yes................................ 54%
No................................. 38
No opinion.......................... 8

High School

Yes................................ 37%
No................................. 51
No opinion.......................... 12

Grade School

Yes................................ 29%
No................................. 56
No opinion.......................... 16

By Age
21–29 Years

Yes................................ 38%
No................................. 49
No opinion.......................... 13

30–49 Years

Yes................................ 35%
No................................. 52
No opinion.......................... 13

50 Years and Over

Yes................................ 33%
No................................. 54
No opinion.......................... 13

World War II Veterans Only

Yes................................ 45%
No................................. 43
No opinion.......................... 12

MARCH 27
FOREIGN AFFAIRS

Interviewing Date 2/28–3/5/46
Survey #366-K   Question #3

Do you think it would be best for the future of this country if we take an active part in world affairs, or if we stay out of world affairs?

Take active part.................... 72%
Stay out.......................... 22
No opinion........................ 6

By Region
New England and Middle Atlantic

Take active part.................... 71%
Stay out.......................... 25
No opinion........................ 4

East Central

Take active part.................... 74%
Stay out.......................... 20
No opinion........................ 6

West Central

Take active part.................... 71%
Stay out.......................... 23
No opinion........................ 6

South

Take active part.................... 69%
Stay out.......................... 23
No opinion........................ 8

Mountain and Pacific

Take active part.................... 77%
Stay out.......................... 18
No opinion........................ 5

By Political Affiliation
Democrats

Take active part.................... 72%
Stay out.......................... 22
No opinion........................ 6

Republicans

Take active part.................... 72%
Stay out.......................... 23
No opinion........................ 5

World War II Veterans Only

Take active part.................... 80%
Stay out.......................... 17
No opinion........................ 3

MARCH 29
DISARMAMENT

Interviewing Date 3/15–20/46
Survey #367-K   Question #4

It has been suggested that Russia, Britain, and the United States get together and do away with armaments and military training. Do you think we should agree to this?

Yes............................... 30%
No............................... 62
No opinion........................ 8

MARCH 29
THE DRAFT

Interviewing Date 3/15–20/46
Survey #367-K   Question #1a

The Selective Service Draft Law expires in May. Do you think Congress should or should not vote to continue the Draft Law for another year?

Should............................ 65%
Should not........................ 27
No opinion........................ 8

MARCH 30
FUTURE WARS

Interviewing Date 3/15–20/46
Survey #367-K   Question #2

Do you think the United States will find itself in another war within say the next 25 years?

Yes................................ 69%
No................................. 19
No opinion......................... 12

By Age
21–29 Years

Yes................................ 70%
No................................. 17
No opinion......................... 13

30–49 Years

Yes................................ 70%
No................................. 18
No opinion......................... 12

50 Years and Over

Yes................................ 65%
No................................. 22
No opinion......................... 13

MARCH 31
RUSSIA

Interviewing Date 3/15–20/46
Survey #367–K   Question #5

In general, do you approve or disapprove of the policy Russia is following in world affairs?

Approve............................ 7%
Disapprove......................... 71
No opinion......................... 22

Interviewing Date 3/15–20/46
Survey #367–K   Question #7

If Russia continues her present course what should we do, if anything?

Be firm, no appeasement............. 44%
Cut off lend-lease.................. 5
Sever relations.................... 1

Go before UN....................... 8%
Work things out.................... 7
Try to appease Russia.............. 1

Do nothing......................... 12%
Others, no opinion................. 22

Interviewing Date 3/15–20/46
Survey #367–T   Question #9a

Have you heard or read about Winston Churchill's speech in which he suggested a continuation of the present military co-operation between the United States and Great Britain as a check on Russia's present moves?

Yes................................ 68%
No................................. 32

Interviewing Date 3/15–20/46
Survey #367–T   Question #9b

Asked of those who responded in the affirmative: What is your opinion of this suggestion?

Approve............................ 22%
Disapprove......................... 40
No opinion......................... 6
                                    ——
                                    68%

APRIL 3
HOUSING SHORTAGE

Interviewing Date 2/28–3/5/46
Survey #366–T   Question #11a

Are you or your immediate family now being directly affected by the housing shortage?

Yes................................ 27%
No................................. 73

APRIL 5
LABOR STRIKES

Interviewing Date 3/15–20/46
Survey #367–T   Question #11a

Do you think that Congress should or should not do anything about the strike situation?

Should............................ 70%
Should not........................ 18
No opinion........................ 12

Union Members Only

Should............................ 52%
Should not........................ 36
No opinion........................ 12

Interviewing Date 3/15–20/46
Survey #367–T   Question #11b

Asked of those saying Congress should do something about the strike situation: What should Congress do?

Discipline labor unions.............. 31%
Pass provisions making a cooling-off
  period mandatory.................. 15
Adopt general policy of giving in to labor
  demands.......................... 4
Miscellaneous...................... 20
                                   ───
                                   70%

APRIL 6
FLYING

Interviewing Date 2/28–3/5/46
Survey #366–K   Question #11a

Would you like to learn to fly an airplane?

Yes............................... 27%
No................................ 69
No opinion........................ 4

By Sex
Men

Yes............................... 30%
No................................ 67
No opinion........................ 3

Women

Yes............................... 22%
No................................ 74
No opinion........................ 4

By Age
21–29 Years

Yes............................... 50%
No................................ 47
No opinion........................ 3

30–49 Years

Yes............................... 28%
No................................ 68
No opinion........................ 4

50 Years and Over

Yes............................... 9%
No................................ 89
No opinion........................ 2

APRIL 7
MINIMUM WAGE

Interviewing Date 2/28–3/5/46
Survey #366–T   Question #8b

At the present time the minimum wage that can be paid to workers in every state in most businesses and industries is 40 cents an hour. This means that all persons, including young people who have never worked before, cannot be paid less than 40 cents an hour. Would you approve or disapprove of raising this minimum to 65 cents an hour?

Approve........................... 65%
Disapprove........................ 29
No opinion........................ 6

By Political Affiliation
Democrats

Approve........................... 70%
Disapprove........................ 25
No opinion........................ 5

Republicans

Approve........................... 59%
Disapprove........................ 36
No opinion........................ 5

Union Members Only

Approve............................. 80%
Disapprove......................... 14
No opinion......................... 6

Farmers Only

Approve............................. 50%
Disapprove......................... 42
No opinion......................... 8

APRIL 10
FOOD

Interviewing Date 3/15–20/46
Survey #367–K   Question #3b

Have you heard or read about the plan to send food to other nations during the next four months?

Yes............................... 92%
No................................ 8

Interviewing Date 3/15–20/46
Survey #367–K   Question #3d

Is your family doing anything now to save on food?

Yes............................... 56%
No................................ 40
Don't know........................ 4

Interviewing Date 3/15–20/46
Survey #367–K   Question #3e

Asked of those stating they are doing something to save food: What are you doing?

The following are listed in order of frequency of mention:

Cutting down on food; eating less; doing without things.
Making it a point to use leftovers at the next (or another) meal.
Saving fats and drippings.
Eating more of foods that are not especially needed.

Growing own vegetables.
Eating rye and/or whole wheat bread instead of white.

Interviewing Date 3/15–20/46
Survey #367–K   Question #3a

Do you think your health would be better or worse if you ate less?

Better............................. 44%
Worse............................. 27
Same.............................. 25
Undecided......................... 4

Professional and business people are particularly prone to consider themselves overeaters. More than half of them think they should do less eating. More women than men think they should eat less. This is particularly true of women over 30 years of age. The same trend of thinking is found among the men. Those over 30 are more inclined to think they eat too much than those between 21 and 29 years of age.

APRIL 12
REPUBLICAN PRESIDENTIAL CANDIDATES

Interviewing Date 2/28–3/5/46
Survey #366–K   Question #16

Asked of Republicans: What man would you like to see elected President in 1948?

Dewey............................. 37%
Stassen........................... 33
Bricker........................... 11
Vandenberg........................ 6
MacArthur......................... 3
Taft.............................. 3
Eisenhower........................ 2
Saltonstall....................... 1
Warren............................ 1
Hoover............................ 1
Others............................ 2

APRIL 13
VEGETABLE GARDENS

Interviewing Date 3/15–20/46
Survey #367–K   Question #10b

Do you plan to have a vegetable garden this year?

The survey finds that eighteen and a half million families are planning to have gardens.

APRIL 15
AUTOMOBILE DRIVERS

Interviewing Date 3/29–4/3/46
Survey #368–T   Question #27

Would you rather ride in a car driven by a man or a woman?

Rather ride with man driver.......... 66%
Rather ride with woman driver....... 12
No opinion........................ 22

By Sex
Men

Rather ride with man driver.......... 74%
Rather ride with woman driver....... 6
No opinion........................ 20

Women

Rather ride with man driver.......... 58%
Rather ride with woman driver....... 18
No opinion........................ 24

APRIL 17
STRIKES IN PUBLIC SERVICE INDUSTRIES

Interviewing Date 2/28–3/5/46
Survey #366–K   Question #7

Should laws be passed to forbid all strikes in public service industries such as electric, gas, telephone, and local transportation companies?

Yes.............................. 60%
No.............................. 32
No opinion...................... 8

By Political Affiliation
Democrats

Yes.............................. 57%
No.............................. 35
No opinion...................... 8

Republicans

Yes.............................. 71%
No.............................. 24
No opinion...................... 5

Union Members Only

Yes.............................. 40%
No.............................. 52
No opinion...................... 8

APRIL 19
FOOD TO FOREIGN NATIONS

Interviewing Date 3/29–4/3/46
Survey #368–K   Question #6

Would you be willing to go back to food rationing in order to send food to people in other nations?

Yes.............................. 59%
No.............................. 36
No opinion...................... 5

By Sex
Men

Yes.............................. 53%
No.............................. 41
No opinion...................... 6

Women

Yes.............................. 64%
No.............................. 31
No opinion...................... 5

By Age
21–29 Years

Yes.............................. 56%
No............................... 38
No opinion....................... 6

30–49 Years

Yes.............................. 60%
No............................... 35
No opinion....................... 5

50 Years and Over

Yes.............................. 57%
No............................... 37
No opinion....................... 6

By Political Affiliation
Democrats

Yes.............................. 65%
No............................... 31
No opinion....................... 4

Republicans

Yes.............................. 55%
No............................... 39
No opinion....................... 6

APRIL 20
JUVENILE DELINQUENCY

Interviewing Date 3/29–4/3/46
Survey #368–K   Question #17

Police records show that a large number of crimes are being committed by teen-age boys and girls. What do you think is the main reason for this juvenile delinquency?

Seven out of every ten questioned blame the parents for the rise in crime among youth throughout the nation.

Those blaming the parents put the fault under two main headings: lack of supervision and control, and lack of proper training.

Another sizable group thinks the problem has risen because of a lack of recreational facilities for the young. The consequence is, they turn to bad movies, bad books, bad company, and liquor.

APRIL 22
ATOMIC BOMB TESTS

Interviewing Date 3/29–4/3/46
Survey #368–K   Question #10

Do you think the United States should carry out the atom bomb tests on Bikini Island, or should this be given up?

Hold the tests..................... 43%
Call off the tests................. 37
No opinion......................... 20

By Education
College

Hold the tests..................... 53%
Call off the tests................. 36
No opinion......................... 11

High School

Hold the tests..................... 52%
Call off the tests................. 36
No opinion......................... 12

Grade School

Hold the tests..................... 35%
Call off the tests................. 40
No opinion......................... 25

World War II Veterans Only

Hold the tests..................... 65%
Call off the tests................. 25
No opinion......................... 10

Interviewing Date 3/29–4/3/46
Survey #368–K   Question #11

Some persons say that animals should not be used in making atom bomb tests at Bikini Island. Do you agree or disagree?

Agree.............................. 42%
Disagree........................... 42
No opinion......................... 16

By Education
College

Agree............................ 53%
Disagree.......................... 34
No opinion........................ 13

High School

Agree............................ 46%
Disagree.......................... 42
No opinion........................ 12

Grade School

Agree............................ 36%
Disagree.......................... 44
No opinion........................ 20

By Sex
Men

Agree............................ 37%
Disagree.......................... 43
No opinion........................ 20

Women

Agree............................ 47%
Disagree.......................... 40
No opinion........................ 13

World War II Veterans Only

Agree............................ 36%
Disagree.......................... 53
No opinion........................ 11

APRIL 24
DAYLIGHT SAVING TIME

Interviewing Date 3/29–4/3/46
Survey #368–K   Question #3

Which of the following would you prefer: 1. Have daylight saving time the year round? 2. Have daylight saving time in summer and standard time the rest of the year? 3. Have standard time the whole year, including summer?

Year round........................ 19%
Just in summer.................... 31
Stay on standard time............. 45
No opinion........................ 5

Farmers Only

Year round........................ 12%
Just in summer.................... 16
Stay on standard time............. 68
No opinion........................ 4

Persons in Cities Over 100,000

Year round........................ 23%
Just in summer.................... 39
Stay on standard time............. 32
No opinion........................ 6

APRIL 26
PARTY FIDELITY

Interviewing Date 3/29–4/3/46
Survey #368–K   Question #19

If a congressman is elected on the Democratic ticket and does not vote with his party on all major issues, should he be prevented from running for office again as a Democrat?

Yes............................... 21%
No................................ 69
No opinion........................ 10

Democrats Only

Yes............................... 25%
No................................ 64
No opinion........................ 11

APRIL 27
FAULTS OF FARMERS AND CITY DWELLERS

Interviewing Date 3/29–4/3/46
Survey #368–T   Question #4

Asked of city dwellers: What do you think are the chief faults of farmers?

The following are listed in order of frequency of mention:

Provincialism, narrowness
Constant complaining
Poor managing
Stubbornness
Make too much money

Interviewing Date 3/29–4/3/46
Survey #368–K   Question #4

Asked of farmers: What do you think are the chief faults of city people?

The following are listed in order of frequency of mention:

Feel too superior
Selfishness
Laziness
Live too hurried a life
Ignorance of farm problems

APRIL 29
STRIKES AND LOCKOUTS

Interviewing Date 3/29–4/3/46
Survey #368–K   Question #8a

Bernard Baruch has suggested that all strikes and lockouts be called off for a year. Do you agree or disagree with this?

Agree	70%
Disagree	21
No opinion	9

Interviewing Date 3/29–4/3/46
Survey #368–K   Question #8b

Do you think a law should be passed forbidding all strikes and lockouts for a year?

Yes	54%
No	36
No opinion	10

MAY 1
HOLIDAYS

Interviewing Date 3/29–4/3/46
Survey #368–K   Question #1

Would you approve or disapprove of having all holidays like Decoration Day or Washington's Birthday, but not Christmas, celebrated on Mondays, in order to have a longer weekend?

Approve	52%
Disapprove	37
No opinion	11

By Age
21–29 Years

Approve	56%
Disapprove	35
No opinion	9

30–49 Years

Approve	55%
Disapprove	34
No opinion	11

50 Years and Over

Approve	45%
Disapprove	41
No opinion	14

By Occupation
Professional and Business

Approve	55%
Disapprove	39
No opinion	6

White Collar

Approve	59%
Disapprove	32
No opinion	9

Manual Workers

Approve	56%
Disapprove	33
No opinion	11

Farmers

Approve............................ 33%
Disapprove........................ 47
No opinion........................ 20

MAY 3
VETERANS' BONUSES

Interviewing Date 3/29–4/3/46
Survey #368–K   Question #5a

Would you be willing to pay higher taxes to have your state government pay a bonus to war veterans at this time?

Yes............................... 52%
No................................ 39
No opinion........................ 9

World War II Veterans Only

Yes............................... 63%
No................................ 33
No opinion........................ 4

Interviewing Date 3/29–4/3/46
Survey #368–K   Question #5b

How much do you think the bonus should be?

Median average.................... $200

MAY 4
ARMY PROTOCOL

Interviewing Date 4/12–17/46
Survey #369–K   Question #18

Do you think it would be a good idea or a poor idea if army officers and enlisted men had the same food, clubs, and social privileges?

Good idea......................... 72%
Poor idea......................... 20
No opinion........................ 8

World War II Veterans Only

Good idea......................... 78%
Poor idea......................... 19
No opinion........................ 3

MAY 5
FOOD SHORTAGE

Interviewing Date 4/12–17/46
Survey #369–K   Question #6a

Have you heard or read about the program to send food to other nations during the next three months?

Yes............................... 94%
No................................ 6

Interviewing Date 4/12–17/46
Survey #369–K   Question #6c

Is your family doing anything now to save on food?

Yes............................... 60%
No................................ 36
Don't know........................ 4

Interviewing Date 4/12–17/46
Survey #369–T   Question #6b

Have you heard or read anything that told you exactly how much less bread and how much less fat you are to use?

Only 12% were able to give an estimate of what they thought the Government expects people to save. The average of their estimates was 25%, or fairly close to the 20% reduction recommended by the Government.

MAY 8
ARMED FORCES MERGER

Interviewing Date 4/12–17/46
Survey #369–K   Question #9a

Will you tell me what your understanding is of the term "unified command" for the armed forces of the United States?

Correct............................ 60%
Incorrect.......................... 40

Interviewing Date 4/12–17/46
Survey #369–K   Question #9b

Asked of those giving correct answers: Do you approve or disapprove of a unified command for the armed forces of this country?

Approve........................... 59%
Disapprove........................ 28
No opinion........................ 13

By Education
College

Approve........................... 68%
Disapprove........................ 25
No opinion........................ 7

High School

Approve........................... 62%
Disapprove........................ 27
No opinion........................ 11

Grade School

Approve........................... 51%
Disapprove........................ 30
No opinion........................ 19

Veterans Only

Approve........................... 65%
Disapprove........................ 29
No opinion........................ 6

MAY 10
THE DRAFT

Interviewing Date 4/26–5/1/46
Survey #370–T   Question #1

The Selective Service Law ends in May. Do you think Congress should or should not vote to continue the Draft Law for another year?

Should............................ 63%
Should not........................ 29
No opinion........................ 8

Interviewing Date 4/26–5/1/46
Survey #370–K   Question #2

The House of Representatives has passed a bill postponing the drafting of any men from May to October to see if enough volunteers will join the army and make the draft unnecessary. Do you think enough people will volunteer?

Yes............................... 37%
No................................ 52
No opinion........................ 11

Interviewing Date 4/26–5/1/46
Survey #370–K   Question #1

The House of Representatives has passed a bill that forbids the drafting of anyone under 20 years of age. Do you think the Senate also should pass this bill?

Should............................ 60%
Should not........................ 33
No opinion........................ 7

Interviewing Date 4/26–5/1/46
Survey #370–T   Question #1b

If the Draft Law is continued, would you approve or disapprove of keeping young men 18 and 19 years old in this country, and sending older men overseas to serve in occupied countries?

Approve........................... 57%
Disapprove........................ 35
No opinion........................ 8

MAY 11
VETERAN REENLISTMENT

Interviewing Date 4/26–5/1/46
Survey #370–K   Question #26b

Asked of World War II veterans: Would you be interested in going back into some branch of the service if the pay were increased 50 per cent?

Yes.................................. 23%
No.................................... 74
No opinion............................ 3

MAY 12
BRITISH RATIONING

Special Survey

Asked in Great Britain: Would you approve or disapprove if rationing of bread were introduced in this country, having regard to the world shortage of wheat?

Approve.............................. 41%
Disapprove........................... 50
No opinion............................ 9

MAY 12
FOOD SHORTAGES

Interviewing Date 4/26–5/1/46
Survey #370–T   Question #16a

Did you hear or read about President Truman's speech concerning the food shortage in other nations?

Yes.................................. 72%
No.................................... 28

Interviewing Date 4/26–5/1/46
Survey #370–K   Question #17

Would you be willing to go back to food rationing in order to send food to people in other nations?

Yes.................................. 70%
No.................................... 26
No opinion............................ 4

Interviewing Date 4/26–5/1/46
Survey #370–T   Question #16b

Do you think the Government has gone too far or not far enough in taking steps to take food from here to send abroad?

Too far.............................. 21%
About right.......................... 44
Not far enough....................... 26
No opinion............................ 9

MAY 12
A WOMAN'S LIFE

Interviewing Date 4/26–5/1/46
Survey #370–K   Question #15b

Generally speaking, whose life is more difficult — a man's or a woman's?

A man's life......................... 24%
A woman's life....................... 54
No opinion........................... 22

By Sex
Men

A man's life......................... 30%
A woman's life....................... 47
No opinion........................... 23

Women

A man's life......................... 18%
A woman's life....................... 61
No opinion........................... 21

MAY 15
UNITED NATIONS

Interviewing Date 4/26–5/1/46
Survey #370–K   Question #3a

Are you satisfied or dissatisfied with the progress the UN has made to date?

Satisfied............................ 37%
Dissatisfied......................... 37
No opinion........................... 26

World War II Veterans Only

Satisfied............................ 37%
Dissatisfied......................... 45
No opinion........................... 18

By Political Affiliation
Democrats

Satisfied............................ 41%
Dissatisfied........................ 32
No opinion......................... 27

Republicans

Satisfied............................ 36%
Dissatisfied........................ 43
No opinion......................... 21

By Education
College

Satisfied............................ 39%
Dissatisfied........................ 51
No opinion......................... 10

High School

Satisfied............................ 35%
Dissatisfied........................ 43
No opinion......................... 22

Grade School

Satisfied............................ 39%
Dissatisfied........................ 29
No opinion......................... 32

Interviewing Date 4/26–5/1/46
Survey #370–K   Question #3b

Asked of those expressing dissatisfaction with the United Nations: Why are you dissatisfied?

The principal reasons are as follows:

The UN is not accomplishing anything. It is not making any progress at all.

There is too much distrust in the UN and too little attempt at cooperation.

The whole thing is on a selfish plane, each country trying to get everything for itself.

The whole thing is power politics and a system of appeasing such countries as Russia, Britain, etc.

The UN has spent all of its time dealing with petty issues and has sidestepped every important issue that has faced it.

The UN has been far too slow in getting started.

The UN needs more power if it is to operate effectively.

MAY 17
REPUBLICAN PRESIDENTIAL CANDIDATES

Interviewing Date 4/12–17/46
Survey #369–K   Question #10

Asked of Republicans: What man would you like to see elected President of the country in 1948?

Dewey.............................. 35%
Stassen............................. 34
Bricker............................. 10
Vandenberg........................ 5
MacArthur......................... 5
Taft................................. 3
Eisenhower........................ 2
Hoover............................. 2
Saltonstall......................... 1
Others.............................. 3

MAY 18
DEMOCRATIC PRESIDENTIAL CANDIDATES

Interviewing Date 4/12–17/46
Survey #369–T   Question #10

Asked of Democrats: What man would you like to see elected President of the country in 1948?

Truman............................. 61%
Wallace............................ 24
Eisenhower........................ 4
Byrnes............................. 3
Stettinius.......................... 1
Others.............................. 7

MAY 20

HEALTH INSURANCE

Interviewing Date 4/12–17/46
Survey #369–T   Question #14

What do you think should be done, if anything, to provide for the payment of doctor, dental, and hospital bills for people in this country?

Voluntary health insurance............ 17%
Insurance under Social Security........ 12
Special grants to care for needy........ 11
Private charity...................... 6
Miscellaneous....................... 12
Don't know......................... 16
Nothing............................ 26

Interviewing Date 4/12–17/46
Survey #369–T   Question #15a

Have you heard or read about the Wagner-Murray-Dingell health insurance bill which would require weekly pay deductions from every worker and employer for medical, dental, and hospital insurance?

Yes................................ 37%
No................................. 63

Interviewing Date 4/12–17/46
Survey #369–K   Question #16a

Just making a guess, about how much did you pay for doctor, hospital, and dental bills during the past year?

Nothing............................ 16%
Under $25.......................... 21
$25 to $50......................... 16
$50–$100........................... 16
Over $100.......................... 28
Don't know......................... 3

Interviewing Date 4/12–17/46
Survey #369–K   Question #15d

How much would you be willing to pay a year for you and your dependents to join a health insurance plan that would pay all doctor, hospital, and dental bills?

Nothing............................ 9%
Under $25.......................... 30
$25 to $50......................... 23
$50–$100........................... 15
Over $100.......................... 4
Don't know......................... 19

Interviewing Date 4/12–17/46
Survey #369–K   Question #15c

If the Government handled a health insurance program do you think you would get better medical care or not as good medical care as you are now getting?

Better............................. 32%
Same............................... 23
Not as good........................ 35
No opinion......................... 10

MAY 22

ATOM BOMB

Interviewing Date 4/12–17/46
Survey #369–K   Question #4

Should the United States continue to manufacture the atom bomb?

Yes................................ 61%
No................................. 30
No opinion......................... 9

Interviewing Date 4/12–17/46
Survey #369–K   Question #5a

Do you think any other country is already making atom bombs?

Yes................................ 42%
No................................. 40
No opinion......................... 18

Interviewing Date 4/12–17/46
Survey #369–K   Question #5b

Asked of those who answered yes to the above question: What country?

The largest number said they thought Russia was making atom bombs. England was mentioned next. A few expressed the belief that experiments in bomb making were going on in Spain or in Argentina.

MAY 24
PRICE CONTROLS

Interviewing Date 4/26–5/1/46
Survey #370–T   Question #5

For the next year would you like to have O.P.A. price ceilings kept on or taken off the following: Food? Rent? Clothing? Automobiles, radios, and other manufactured goods?

	Keep Price Ceilings	Remove Price Ceilings	No Opinion
Food............	75%	21%	4%
Rent............	78	17	5
Clothing.........	70	26	4
Automobiles, radios, and other manufactured goods...	66	27	7

Interviewing Date 4/26–5/1/46
Survey #370–T   Question #6

A year from now, which way do you think prices would be lower — if O.P.A. is done away with now, or if it is kept on?

Done away with.................... 21%
Is kept on........................ 68
No opinion....................... 11

Interviewing Date 4/26–5/1/46
Survey #370–K   Question #6

Do you think O.P.A. price ceilings make it impossible for some manufacturers to make a profit?

Yes.............................. 51%
No.............................. 35
No opinion....................... 14

Interviewing Date 4/26–5/1/46
Survey #370–K   Question #7

Should O.P.A. put high enough ceilings on products to allow manufacturers to make a profit?

Yes.............................. 84%
No.............................. 9
No opinion....................... 7

MAY 25
SPAIN

Interviewing Date 4/26–5/1/46
Survey #370–T   Question #14a

Will you tell me what the arguments are in favor of breaking our diplomatic relations with Spain?

The following are listed according to frequency of mention:

Spain is harboring Nazis and German scientists.
The Franco government is a Fascist government.
Spain aided the Axis during the war.
Spain is a menace to world peace.

Interviewing Date 4/26–5/1/46
Survey #370–T   Question #14b

Will you tell me what the arguments are against breaking our diplomatic relations with Spain?

The following are listed according to frequency of mention:

We have to have a united world, with everyone friendly toward everyone else.
Breaking off relations with Spain might mean another war.
We should not interfere with Spain's internal affairs.
Spain is not endangering world peace or giving any provocation for a diplomatic break.
It would hurt trade with Spain.
Russia would have her way again.
It might cause civil war in Spain.
We would not know what is going on in Spain.

Interviewing Date 4/26–5/1/46
Survey #370–T   Question #14c

Asked of those responding citing any argument for or against breaking of diplomatic relations: Do you think we should or should not break off diplomatic relations with Spain?

Should............................ 43%
Should not........................ 43
Undecided......................... 14

By Political Affiliation
Democrats

Should............................ 49%
Should not........................ 35
Undecided......................... 16

Republicans

Should............................ 36%
Should not........................ 52
Undecided......................... 12

MAY 29
PARTY STRENGTH

Interviewing Date 4/26–5/1/46
Survey #370–T   Question #10

If a presidential election were being held today, which party would you vote for — the Democratic or Republican?

Democratic....................... 52.5%
Republican....................... 47.5

By Occupation

	Democratic	Republican
Professional and business..........	42%	58%
White collar.........	45	55
Manual workers......	64	36
Farmers.............	45	55

MAY 29
LABOR STRIKES

Special Survey

President Truman has proposed that employers and employees be compelled to run strike-bound essential industries which Government has taken over. In general do you approve or disapprove of this?

Approve........................... 65%
Disapprove........................ 26
No opinion........................ 9

President Truman has proposed that employers and employees who refuse to run strike-bound essential industries taken over by Government be drafted into armed forces and sent back to their jobs. Do you approve or disapprove of this?

Approve........................... 53%
Disapprove........................ 38
No opinion........................ 9

MAY 31
LABOR STRIKES

Interviewing Date 5/17–22/46
Survey #371–K   Question #8

Should laws be passed to forbid all strikes in public service industries such as electric, gas, telephone, and local transportation companies?

Yes.............................. 64%
No.............................. 29
No opinion........................ 7

By Political Affiliation
Democrats

Yes.............................. 61%
No.............................. 32
No opinion........................ 7

Republicans

Yes............................... 70%
No............................... 24
No opinion....................... 6

Union Members Only

Yes............................... 49%
No............................... 44
No opinion....................... 7

JUNE 1
JOHN L. LEWIS

Interviewing Date 5/17–22/46
Survey #371–K   Question #9

What is your opinion of John L. Lewis?

Favorable opinion................... 13%
Unfavorable opinion................ 69
No opinion....................... 18

JUNE 3
FRENCH RECOVERY

Special Survey

Asked in France: Which nation in your opinion has helped most toward the recovery of France?

United States..................... 58%
Russia........................... 17
Great Britain..................... 8
Canada........................... 2
Others........................... 1
No opinion....................... 14

JUNE 5
EMPLOYMENT OUTLOOK

Interviewing Date 5/17–22/46
Survey #371–K   Question #13

During the next year do you think there is any chance that you (your husband) will be unemployed?

A great chance..................... 9%
A slight chance.................... 21
No chance........................ 55
Don't know....................... 15

By Occupation
Professional and Business

A great chance..................... 5%
A slight chance.................... 14
No chance........................ 69
Don't know....................... 12

White Collar

A great chance..................... 9%
A slight chance.................... 21
No chance........................ 58
Don't know....................... 12

Manual Workers

A great chance..................... 14%
A slight chance.................... 29
No chance........................ 38
Don't know....................... 19

Farmers

A great chance..................... 4%
A slight chance.................... 11
No chance........................ 76
Don't know....................... 9

Union Members Only

A great chance..................... 14%
A slight chance.................... 29
No chance........................ 41
Don't know....................... 16

JUNE 7
RUSSIA

Interviewing Date 5/17–22/46
Survey #371–K   Question #17

As you hear and read about Russia these days, do you believe Russia is trying to build herself up to be the ruling power of the world, or is Russia just building up protection against being attacked in another war?

Wants to rule world.................. 58%
Builds for protection................ 29
No opinion......................... 13

By Occupation
Professional and Business

Wants to rule world.................. 52%
Builds for protection................ 36
No opinion......................... 12

White Collar

Wants to rule world.................. 55%
Builds for protection................ 33
No opinion......................... 12

Farmers

Wants to rule world.................. 59%
Builds for protection................ 29
No opinion......................... 12

Manual Workers

Wants to rule world.................. 60%
Builds for protection................ 26
No opinion......................... 14

JUNE 8
FOOD SHORTAGE

Interviewing Date 5/17–22/46
Survey #371–T   Question #2c

> Is your family doing anything now to save on food?

Yes.............................. 74%
No.............................. 21
Don't know....................... 5

Interviewing Date 5/17–22/46
Survey #371–K   Question #2

> Would you be willing to go back to rationing in order to send food to people in other nations?

Yes.............................. 65%
No.............................. 31
Undecided........................ 4

By Sex
Men

Yes.............................. 58%
No.............................. 37
Undecided........................ 5

Women

Yes.............................. 72%
No.............................. 25
Undecided........................ 3

JUNE 9
OCCUPATION OF GERMANY AND JAPAN

Interviewing Date 5/17–22/46
Survey #371–K   Question #11a

> Do you think we have done a good job or a poor job in handling our occupation of Japan?

Good job......................... 60%
Fair job......................... 15
Poor job......................... 4
No opinion....................... 21

Interviewing Date 5/17–22/46
Survey #371–K   Question #11b

> Do you think we have done a good job or a poor job in handling our occupation of Germany?

Good job......................... 31%
Fair job......................... 24
Poor job......................... 21
No opinion....................... 24

World War II Veterans Only

Good job......................... 23%
Fair job......................... 27
Poor job......................... 40
No opinion....................... 10

JUNE 12
CANCER RESEARCH

Interviewing Date 5/17–22/46
Survey #371–K   Question #1a

Do you approve or disapprove of having the Government spend $100 million to find possible ways of preventing or curing cancer in this country?

Approve........................... 87%
Disapprove........................ 9
No opinion........................ 4

Interviewing Date 5/17–22/46
Survey #371–K   Question #1b

Asked of those approving the plan: Would you be willing to pay more taxes to provide this money?

Yes............................... 72%
No................................ 27
No opinion........................ 1

Interviewing Date 5/17–22/46
Survey #371–T   Question #1a

Should Congress pass a law that would provide $200 million for the study and treatment of cancer in this country?

Yes............................... 82%
No................................ 11
No opinion........................ 7

Interviewing Date 5/17–22/46
Survey #371–T   Question #1b

Asked of those answering that Congress should pass a law: Would you be willing to pay more taxes to provide this money?

Yes............................... 69%
No................................ 27
No opinion........................ 4

JUNE 14
LABOR STRIKES

Interviewing Date 6/1–6/46
Survey #372–K   Question #12

President Truman has proposed that employers and employees who refuse to run strike-bound essential industries taken over by the Government be drafted into the armed forces and sent back to their jobs. Do you approve or disapprove of this?

Approve........................... 47%
Disapprove........................ 43
No opinion........................ 10

Union Members Only

Approve........................... 30%
Disapprove........................ 60
No opinion........................ 10

Interviewing Date 6/1–6/46
Survey #372–K   Question #11

President Truman has proposed that employers and employees be compelled to run strike-bound essential industries which the Government has taken over. In general, do you approve or disapprove of this?

Approve........................... 61%
Disapprove........................ 28
No opinion........................ 11

JUNE 15
MIDDLE AGE

Interviewing Date 4/26–5/1/46
Survey #370–K   Question #8

At what age does middle age begin?

Under 40 years.................... 23%
At 40 years....................... 30
Between 41 and 49 years........... 24
At 50 years....................... 17
Over 50 years..................... 4

By Age

	Median Averages
21–29 Years..............	40 years
31–49 Years..............	40 years
50 Years and over........	40 years

By Sex

Men...................	40 years
Women.................	45 years

By Occupation

Professional and business....	45 years
White collar..............	41 years
Farmers................	40 years
Manual workers..........	40 years

By Education

College.................	42 years
High School..............	40 years
Grade School............	40 years

JUNE 17
MOST ADMIRED PERSON

Interviewing Date 4/26–5/1/46
Survey #370–K   Question #13

What person living today in any part of the world do you admire the most?

The following are listed according to frequency of mention:

Douglas MacArthur
Dwight D. Eisenhower
Harry S. Truman
Mrs. Franklin D. Roosevelt
Winston Churchill
Herbert Hoover
Henry A. Wallace
Thomas E. Dewey
Harold Stassen
James Byrnes

JUNE 19
JEWS AND PALESTINE

Interviewing Date 5/17–22/46
Survey #371–K   Question #19a

Have you heard or read about the Jewish migration into Palestine?

Yes.............................	50%
No..............................	50

Interviewing Date 5/17–22/46
Survey #371–K   Question #19b

Asked of those answering yes to the above question: Do you think it is a good idea or a poor idea to admit 100,000 Jews to settle in Palestine?

Good idea........................	78%
Poor idea........................	14
No opinion.......................	8

Interviewing Date 5/17–22/46
Survey #371–K   Question #20

England has suggested that we send troops to Palestine to help keep order there if the Arabs oppose letting 100,000 Jews enter Palestine. Do you approve or disapprove of our sending troops to Palestine to help England keep order there?

Approve..........................	21%
Disapprove.......................	74
No opinion.......................	5

Interviewing Date 5/17–22/46
Survey #371–K   Question #21

It has been suggested that the United Nations handle the problem of letting Jews settle in Palestine. Do you think this is a good idea or a poor idea?

Good idea........................	72%
Poor idea........................	19
No opinion.......................	9

JUNE 21
BRITISH ATTITUDES REGARDING SPAIN

Special Survey

Asked in Great Britain: The United States, France, and Britain have expressed disapproval of Franco. Would you agree if they took stronger steps such as cutting off all trade with Spain?

Agree............................ 48%
Disagree.......................... 22
No opinion........................ 30

JUNE 21
FRENCH ATTITUDES REGARDING SPAIN

Special Survey

Asked in France: Do you approve of the measures that have just been taken by the French Government in regard to Franco (closing of French-Spanish border)?

Approve........................... 47%
Disapprove........................ 33
No opinion........................ 20

Asked in France: Should France immediately recognize the Spanish Republican (anti-Franco) Government?

Should............................ 40%
Should not........................ 35
No opinion........................ 25

JUNE 23
PARTY BEST FOR HANDLING LABOR PROBLEMS

Interviewing Date 6/1–6/46
Survey #372–T   Question #6

As you feel today, which political party — the Democratic or Republican — can better handle the problem of reducing strikes and labor trouble?

Democratic........................ 33%
Republican........................ 41
Makes no difference............... 26

Manual Workers Only

Democratic........................ 39%
Republican........................ 33
Makes no difference............... 28

JUNE 26
SOUTHERN POLITICS

Special Survey

Asked of Southerners: Do you think the South would be better off, in general, if there were two political parties of about equal strength instead of one strong party as there is at present?

Two parties....................... 62%
One party......................... 38

In the less solidly Democratic Southern states — North Carolina, Virginia, Florida, Kentucky, Oklahoma, and Tennessee, taken as a group — the vote favoring a strong two-party system is 69%. In the other states, South Carolina, Alabama, Arkansas, Georgia, Louisiana, Mississippi, and Texas the aggregate vote is 51% in favor.

JUNE 28
SUPREME COURT

Interviewing Date 6/14–19/46
Survey #373–K   Question #19a

Has your attitude toward the Supreme Court changed in recent years?

Yes............................... 30%
No................................ 45
No opinion........................ 25

Interviewing Date 6/14–19/46
Survey #373–K   Question #19b

Asked of those who answered yes: Do you have a higher regard or a lower regard for the Supreme Court now?

Higher............................ 3%
Lower............................. 27
                                   ⎯⎯
                                   30%

Interviewing Date 6/14–19/46
Survey #373–T   Question #19

Some people say that the Supreme Court decides many questions largely on the basis of politics. Do you agree or disagree with this?

Agree............................. 43%
Disagree.......................... 36
No opinion........................ 21

JUNE 29
PARTY BEST ABLE TO MAINTAIN HIGH WAGES

Interviewing Date 6/1–6/46
Survey #372–K   Question #6b

As you feel today, which political party — the Democratic or Republican — can better handle the problem of keeping wages high?

Democratic........................ 53%
Republican........................ 26
Makes no difference............... 21

Twelve per cent were without an opinion.

By Political Affiliation
Democrats

Democratic........................ 73%
Republican........................ 10
Makes no difference............... 17

Republicans

Democratic........................ 30%
Republican........................ 48
Makes no difference............... 22

Union Members Only

Democratic........................ 62%
Republican........................ 18
Makes no difference............... 20

Manual Workers Only

Democratic........................ 56%
Republican........................ 26
Makes no difference............... 18

JUNE 30
POLITICAL PARTICIPATION

Interviewing Date 6/1–6/46
Survey #372–K   Question #2a

Have you ever written or wired your congressman or senator in Washington?

Yes............................... 14%
No................................ 86

By Occupation

	Yes	No
Professional and business	32%	68%
White collar	17	83
Farmers	12	88
Manual workers	7	93

By Education

	Yes	No
College	35%	65%
High School	15	85
Grade School	9	91

Interviewing Date 6/1–6/46
Survey #372–K   Question #2c

Asked of those answering yes to the above question: Did you do it on your own or did some organization suggest you do it?

On own............................ 9%
Someone suggested it.............. 5
                                   ⎯⎯
                                   14%

JULY 3
ARMAMENTS CONTROL

Interviewing Date 6/14–19/46
Survey #373–K   Question #4

Would you be willing to have the United States turn over control of all her armed forces and war weapons, including atomic bombs, to a world parliament or congress, provided that other countries did the same?

Education is the most important determining factor in separating those who favor and those who oppose the principle of world government. Voters with college training show the greatest acceptance, with a majority of those with opinions voting "yes".

Veterans of World War II included in the poll show themselves substantially opposed to this country's turning over all military and atomic controls to a world parliament.

Among both Democratic and Republican voters the weight of opinion is against the proposal, the Republicans more markedly than the Democrats.

People who call themselves "Independent" voters, are somewhat more inclined than are Democrats or Republicans to having the United States relinquish military and atomic controls to an international group; opinion in this group is fairly evenly divided on the issue.

By Occupation
Professional and Business

Kill or imprison them	36%
Curb them, make them inactive	18
Watch them carefully	10
Do nothing	20
No opinion	16

White Collar

Kill or imprison them	34%
Curb them, make them inactive	15
Watch them carefully	8
Do nothing	21
No opinion	22

Manual Workers

Kill or imprison them	37%
Curb them, make them inactive	14
Watch them carefully	5
Do nothing	14
No opinion	30

Farmers

Kill or imprison them	40%
Curb them, make them inactive	21
Watch them carefully	9
Do nothing	4
No opinion	26

JULY 6
AMERICAN COMMUNISTS

Interviewing Date 6/14–19/46
Survey #373–K   Question #13

What do you think should be done about the Communists in this country?

Kill or imprison them	36%
Curb them, make them inactive	16
Watch them carefully	7
Do nothing	16
No opinion	25

JULY 7
PRESIDENT TRUMAN'S POPULARITY

Interviewing Date 6/14–19/46
Survey #373–K   Question #21c

Do you approve or disapprove of the way Harry Truman is handling his job as President?

Approve	43%
Disapprove	45
No opinion	12

JULY 10

PRESIDENT TRUMAN AND STRIKES

Interviewing Date 6/14–19/46
Survey #373–K   Question #1

Do you approve or disapprove of the way President Truman is handling the strike problem?

Approve........................... 36%
Disapprove........................ 49
No opinion........................ 15

By Occupation

Business and Professional

Approve........................... 37%
Disapprove........................ 56
No opinion........................ 7

White Collar

Approve........................... 34%
Disapprove........................ 52
No opinion........................ 14

Manual Workers

Approve........................... 34%
Disapprove........................ 48
No opinion........................ 18

Farmers

Approve........................... 42%
Disapprove........................ 43
No opinion........................ 15

Union Members Only

Approve........................... 30%
Disapprove........................ 56
No opinion........................ 14

JULY 12

REPUBLICAN PRESIDENTIAL CANDIDATES

Interviewing Date 6/28–7/3/46
Survey #374–K   Question #15

Asked of Republicans: What man would you like to see elected President of the country in 1948?

West Central States Only

Stassen........................... 49%
Dewey............................. 29
Bricker........................... 6
Vandenberg........................ 5
MacArthur......................... 5
Taft.............................. 3
Eisenhower........................ 2
Others............................ 1

East Central States Only

Dewey............................. 31%
Stassen........................... 21
Bricker........................... 19
Vandenberg........................ 11
MacArthur......................... 7
Taft.............................. 6
Eisenhower........................ 2
Others............................ 3

JULY 13

REPUBLICAN PRESIDENTIAL CANDIDATES

Interviewing Date 6/28–7/3/46
Survey #374–K   Question #15

Asked of Republicans: What man would you like to see elected President of the country in 1948?

Dewey............................. 38%
Stassen........................... 28
Bricker........................... 9
Vandenberg........................ 7
MacArthur......................... 6
Taft.............................. 4
Eisenhower........................ 2
Others............................ 6

JULY 22

PARTY STRENGTH

Interviewing Date 6/28–7/3/46
Survey #374–K   Question #6

If a presidential election were being held today, which party would you vote for, the Democratic or Republican?

Democratic........................ 49%
Republican........................ 51

By Region

	Democratic	Republican
New England........	44%	56%
Middle Atlantic......	45	55
East Central.........	44	56
West Central........	44	56
South..............	72	28
Mountain...........	48	52
Pacific..............	52	48

JULY 24
UNITED NATIONS

Interviewing Date 6/14–19/46
Survey #373–K   Question #9a

Are you satisfied or dissatisfied with the progress that the United Nations has made to date?

Satisfied........................... 26%
Dissatisfied....................... 49
No opinion........................ 25

By Education
College

Satisfied........................... 23%
Dissatisfied....................... 69
No opinion........................ 8

High School

Satisfied........................... 26%
Dissatisfied....................... 53
No opinion........................ 21

Grade School

Satisfied........................... 27%
Dissatisfied....................... 42
No opinion........................ 31

World War II Veterans Only

Satisfied........................... 27%
Dissatisfied....................... 60
No opinion........................ 13

Interviewing Date 6/14–19/46
Survey #373–K   Question #9b

Asked of those expressing dissatisfaction: Why are you dissatisfied?

People over and over made such comments as, "Too much arguing and disagreeing"..."They talk their heads off and get nowhere" ... "Too much dissension among the delegates" ... "Just a bunch of international politicians each playing his own little game" ... "We'll never have peace until they quit wrangling and get down to business."

The second main objection raised is that the UN is "letting Russia get away with too much."

JULY 29
PARTY STRENGTH

Interviewing Date 6/28–7/3/46
Survey #374–K   Question #6

If a presidential election were being held today, which party would you vote for — the Democratic or Republican?

Democratic........................ 49%
Republican........................ 51

By Occupation

	Democratic	Republican
Professional and business..........	39%	61%
White collar.........	45	55
Manual workers......	58	42
Farmers............	44	56

By Age

	Democratic	Republican
21–29 Years........	53%	47%
30–49 Years........	50	50
50 Years and over....	46	54

Union Members Only

Democratic........................ 62%
Republican........................ 38

World War II Veterans Only

Democratic........................ 51%
Republican........................ 49

JULY 31
PARTY AFFILIATION

Interviewing Date 6/28–7/3/46
Survey #374–K   Question #16

In politics, as of today, do you consider yourself a Republican, a Democrat, a Socialist, or Independent?

Republican........................ 40%
Democrat......................... 39
Independent...................... 21
Socialist......................... *

*Less than 1%.

AUGUST 3
MOST IMPORTANT PROBLEM

Interviewing Date 6/28–7/3/46
Survey #374–T   Question #2a

What do you think will be the most important problem facing this country during the next year?

Control of inflation (high prices, O.P.A.) 46%
Food and other shortages............ 20
Maintenance of peace and conducting
  foreign affairs................... 10
Strikes and labor troubles........... 9
Housing.......................... 5
Jobs............................. 4
Reconversion..................... 3
Atom bomb....................... 3
Miscellaneous.................... 7
No opinion....................... 4
                                 ‾‾‾‾
                                 111%

(Note: total is more than 100% because some people gave more than one answer.)

Interviewing Date 6/28–7/3/46
Survey #374–T   Question #2b

Which political party do you think can deal best with this particular problem?

Democratic........................ 34%
Republican........................ 35
Undecided........................ 31

AUGUST 4
REPUBLICAN PRESIDENTIAL CANDIDATES

Special Survey

Asked of a cross section of Republicans listed in Who's Who in America: *If you had to decide today, who would be your choice for President in 1948?*

Stassen.......................... 48%
Dewey............................ 15
Vandenberg....................... 9
Warren........................... 7
Taft............................. 6
Bricker........................... 4
Saltonstall........................ 3
MacArthur........................ 2
Eisenhower....................... 2
Others........................... 4

AUGUST 9
UNIONIZATION OF BASEBALL PLAYERS

Interviewing Date 6/28–7/3/46
Survey #374–K   Question #12

Would you like to see baseball players join labor unions?

Yes.............................. 21%
No............................... 79

Union Members Only

Yes.............................. 34%
No............................... 66

AUGUST 11
PRICE OUTLOOK

Interviewing Date 6/28–7/3/46
Survey #374–K   Question #7a

Do you think prices will go up in the next six months?

Yes................................ 92%
No................................. 5
No opinion......................... 3

Interviewing Date 6/28–7/3/46
Survey #374–K   Question #7b

If prices do go up in the next six months, whose fault do you think this will be?

Congress........................... 20%
The people, everybody.............. 17
Big business....................... 12
Government officials................ 9
Laxness of O.P.A................... 7
Truman administration.............. 7
Labor unions, strikers............. 5
Others............................. 8
No one, rises are to be expected....... 7
Don't know......................... 14
            106%

(Note: table totals more than 100% because some people gave more than one answer.)

AUGUST 14
FUTURE WARS

Special Survey

Asked of people listed in Who's Who in America: *Do you think the United States will find itself in another war within, say, the next 25 years?*

Yes................................ 39%
No................................. 34
No opinion......................... 27

AUGUST 16
RUSSIA

Interviewing Date 7/27–8/1/46
Survey #375–T   Question #12a

In general do you approve or disapprove of the policy Russia is following in world affairs?

Approve............................ 7%
Disapprove......................... 71
No opinion......................... 22

Interviewing Date 7/26–31/46
Survey #375–K   Question #12

As you hear and read about Russia these days, do you believe Russia is trying to build herself up to be the ruling power of the world, or is Russia just building up protection against being attacked in another war?

Wants to rule world................. 60%
Seeks protection................... 26
No opinion......................... 14

Interviewing Date 7/26–31/46
Survey #375–K   Question #13

If Russia continues to follow her present course, what should we do, if anything?

Be firm, make her stick to agreements,
 no appeasement.................. 28%
Keep militarily prepared............. 28
Economic blockade................. 4
Sever relations..................... 1
Go before the UN.................. 4
Get together and talk............... 6
Try to appease Russia............... 1
Do nothing........................ 10
Miscellaneous, no opinion........... 22
            104%

(Note: table adds to more than 100% because some persons suggested more than one course of action.)

AUGUST 17
CONGRESS

Interviewing Date 7/26–31/46
Survey #375–K   Question #9a

In general, do you think the present Congress has done a good job or a poor job?

Good............................ 23%
Fair............................ 40
Poor............................ 37

Eighteen per cent offered no opinion.

By Political Affiliation
Democrats

Good............................ 27%
Fair............................ 39
Poor............................ 34

Republicans

Good............................ 20%
Fair............................ 40
Poor............................ 40

By Education
College

Good............................ 15%
Fair............................ 38
Poor............................ 47

High School

Good............................ 21%
Fair............................ 42
Poor............................ 37

Grade School

Good............................ 27%
Fair............................ 39
Poor............................ 34

By Occupation
Professional and Business

Good............................ 14%
Fair............................ 40
Poor............................ 46

Farmers

Good............................ 23%
Fair............................ 48
Poor............................ 29

White Collar

Good............................ 24%
Fair............................ 38
Poor............................ 38

Manual Workers

Good............................ 27%
Fair............................ 38
Poor............................ 35

AUGUST 18
UNITED NATIONS

Interviewing Date 7/26–31/46
Survey #375–K   Question #2

Do you think the United Nations organization should be strengthened to make it a world government with power to control the armed forces of all nations, including the United States?

Yes............................. 54%
No.............................. 24
No opinion...................... 22

By Region
New England and Middle Atlantic

Yes............................. 51%
No.............................. 21
No opinion...................... 28

East Central and West Central

Yes............................. 56%
No.............................. 26
No opinion...................... 18

South

Yes............................. 56%
No.............................. 22
No opinion...................... 22

West

Yes	57%
No	25
No opinion	18

Persons Listed in *Who's Who in America*

Yes	59%
No	32
No opinion	9

AUGUST 21
YOUTH VOTE

Interviewing Date 7/26–31/46
Survey #375–K   Question #11

Asked of those young persons who will be eligible to vote for the first time in 1948: What man would you like to see elected President of the country in 1948?

All those who named a Republican divided as follows:

Dewey	42%
Stassen	25
MacArthur	12
Eisenhower*	6
Warren	4
Bricker	3
Taft	3
Others	5

All those who named a Democrat voted as follows:

Truman	59%
Wallace	19
Stettinius	6
Eisenhower*	5
Byrnes	4
Others	7

*Eisenhower had no announced political affiliation.

AUGUST 23
REPUBLICAN PRESIDENTIAL CANDIDATES

Interviewing Date 7/26–31/46
Survey #375–K   Question #11a

Asked of Republicans: What man would you like to see elected President of the country in 1948?

Dewey	37%
Stassen	25
Bricker	9
Vandenberg	8
Warren	6
Taft	5
MacArthur	4
Eisenhower	2
Saltonstall	1
Others	3

AUGUST 24
DEMOCRATIC PRESIDENTIAL CANDIDATES

Interviewing Date 7/26–31/46
Survey #375–K   Question #11

Asked of Democrats: What man would you like to see elected President of the country in 1948?

Truman	62%
Wallace	19
Eisenhower	5
Byrnes	4
Stettinius	1
Vinson	1
Pepper	1
McNutt	1
Others	6

AUGUST 26
COMMUNIST PARTY

Interviewing Date 7/26–31/46
Survey #375–K   Question #7a

In general, do you think most Americans who belong to the Communist party in this country are loyal to America or to Russia?

Loyal to United States.............. 23%
Loyal to Russia.................... 48
No opinion........................ 29

Interviewing Date 7/26–31/46
Survey #375–K   Question #7b

*Should United States Communists be per-
mitted to hold civil service (regular Government) jobs in this country?*

Yes................................ 17%
No................................. 69
No opinion........................ 14

Interviewing Date 7/26–31/46
Survey #375–K   Question #7c

*Do you think Russia has spies at work in the
United States?*

Yes................................ 78%
No................................. 5
No opinion........................ 17

AUGUST 28
PROMOTING DEMOCRACY

Interviewing Date 7/26–31/46
Survey #375–K   Question #6a

*Should the United States do everything it
can to tell other nations the advantages of
our type of democracy for the common
people of the world?*

Yes................................ 68%
No................................. 19
No opinion........................ 13

Interviewing Date 7/26–31/46
Survey #375–K   Question #6b

*What would you say is the greatest ad-
vantage of our type of government?*

Freedom in general................. 24%
Freedom of speech and of press....... 19
People have a voice in government...... 17
Freedom of opportunity............. 7

Freedom of worship................ 5
Equal rights...................... 5
The four freedoms................. 4
Free enterprise, competition in business. 3
Miscellaneous..................... 6
No advantages..................... 1
No opinion........................ 21
                                 ―――
                                 112%

(Note: table adds to more than 100% because
some persons named more than one advantage.)

AUGUST 30
THREAT OF DEPRESSION

Interviewing Date 7/26–31/46
Survey #375–K   Question #14a

*Do you think there will be a serious business
depression in the United States within the
next 10 years?*

Yes................................ 60%
No................................. 20
No opinion........................ 20

By Age
21–29 Years

Yes................................ 64%
No................................. 17
No opinion........................ 19

30–49 Years

Yes................................ 59%
No................................. 21
No opinion........................ 20

50 Years and Over

Yes................................ 57%
No................................. 22
No opinion........................ 21

By Occupation
Professional and Business

Yes................................ 63%
No................................. 22
No opinion........................ 15

White Collar

Yes	59%
No	23
No opinion	18

Manual Workers

Yes	56%
No	20
No opinion	24

Farmers

Yes	65%
No	17
No opinion	18

By Education
College

Yes	70%
No	20
No opinion	10

High School

Yes	64%
No	20
No opinion	16

Grade School

Yes	55%
No	20
No opinion	25

Interviewing Date 7/26–31/46
Survey #375–K   Question #14b

Asked of those who said yes: When do you think it will come?

Median average . . . . 5 years

AUGUST 30
ATOMIC TESTS

Interviewing Date 7/26–8/1/46
Survey #375–K   Question #1

Did the atom bombs in the recent tests do more damage or less than you thought they would?

More damage	18%
Less damage	53
Did damage about as expected	11
No opinion	18

AUGUST 31
FAMILY FINANCES

Interviewing Date 6/28–7/3/46
Survey #374–K   Question #10a

In some families the wife manages most of the money, while in others the husband does. Who manages most of the money in your household?

Husband	29%
Wife	32
Both	39

By Occupation
Professional and Business

Husband	30%
Wife	26
Both	44

White Collar

Husband	29%
Wife	32
Both	39

Farmers

Husband	37%
Wife	16
Both	47

Manual Workers

Husband	24%
Wife	42
Both	34

Interviewing Date 6/28–7/3/46
Survey #374–K   Question #10b

Do you think that this is the best arrangement in your case?

Yes	93%
No	4
No opinion	3

SEPTEMBER 2
DRINKING HABITS

Interviewing Date 7/26–31/46
Survey #375–K   Question #15b

If the question of national prohibition should come up again, would you vote wet or dry?

Wet............................... 69%
Dry............................... 31

Interviewing Date 7/26–31/46
Survey #375–K   Question #15a

Do you ever have occasion to use any alcoholic beverages such as liquor, wine, or beer, or are you a total abstainer?

Drinker........................... 67%
Abstainer......................... 33

The highest proportion of nondrinkers is on the farms of the country. More men than women take at least an occasional drink. Only one man in four is a teetotaler, whereas two-fifths of the women of the country shun beer, wine, and liquor.

The lowest proportion of abstainers among adults is found in the age group 20–29, the highest in the age bracket 50 and over.

SEPTEMBER 4
BALANCED BUDGET

Interviewing Date 8/16–21/46
Survey #376–K   Question #7a

Will you tell me what is meant by "balancing the federal budget"?

Generally correct answers........... 49%
Incorrect answers.................. 51

By Education

	Correct	*Incorrect*
College...............	77%	23%
High School..........	55	45
Grammar or no School..	37	63

Interviewing Date 8/16–21/46
Survey #376–K   Question #7b

Asked of those giving a correct answer: Some people say that if we're going to balance the federal budget we've got to keep income taxes at the present rates. Others say it's more important to cut income taxes than it is to balance the budget. Which do you think is the more important to do in the coming year — balance the budget or cut income taxes?

Balance budget.................... 71%
Cut income taxes.................. 20
No opinion....................... 9

By Occupation
Business and Professional

Balance budget.................... 78%
Cut income taxes.................. 15
No opinion....................... 7

White Collar

Balance budget.................... 72%
Cut income taxes.................. 21
No opinion....................... 7

Farmers

Balance budget.................... 75%
Cut income taxes.................. 17
No opinion....................... 8

Manual Workers

Balance budget.................... 64%
Cut income taxes.................. 25
No opinion....................... 11

SEPTEMBER 6
VETERANS' BATTLE IN TENNESSEE

Interviewing Date 8/16–21/46
Survey #376–K   Question #8a

Have you heard or read anything about the disturbances in Athens, Tennessee involving the war veterans?

Yes............................. 52%
No.............................. 48

World War II Veterans Only

Yes............................. 74%
No.............................. 26

Interviewing Date 8/16–21/46
Survey #376–K   Question #8b

Asked of those answering yes to the above question: What do you think about what the veterans did in the recent local election in Athens, Tennessee?

All right, or all right under the circum-
stances......................... 25%
Good idea but wrong method, they went
too far, shouldn't have used violence.. 20
No opinion....................... 7
                                  ——
                                  52%

World War II Veterans Only

All right, or all right under the circum-
stances......................... 46%
Good idea but wrong method, they went
too far, shouldn't have used violence.. 26
No opinion....................... 2
                                  ——
                                  74%

SEPTEMBER 7
JUVENILE DELINQUENCY

Interviewing Date 7/26–31/46
Survey #375–K   Question #4

In San Francisco judges require the parents of delinquent children to attend classes to learn to handle their children better. Do you think such classes should be started in this community?

Yes............................. 78%
No.............................. 12
No opinion....................... 10

By Sex
Men

Yes............................. 75%
No.............................. 14
No opinion....................... 11

Women

Yes............................. 81%
No.............................. 10
No opinion....................... 9

SEPTEMBER 9
EDUCATION

Interviewing Date 8/16–21/46
Survey #376–K   Question #2c

Are you satisfied with the school your child (or children) goes to?

Satisfied........................ 87%
Not satisfied.................... 13

Interviewing Date 8/16–21/46
Survey #376–K   Question #2d

If you were asked to criticize the school where your child goes, what would your main criticism be?

Four out of every 10 had no criticism to offer; the others offered scattered complaints with no one item standing out very much above the others. The criticisms included such things as: lack of facilities and crowded buildings, wrong subjects stressed, not enough teachers, teachers not well trained, and faulty discipline.

Interviewing Date 8/16–21/46
Survey #376–T   Question #2e

Do you think the school teachers' pay in your community is too high, too low, or about right?

Too high......................... 2%
Too low.......................... 44
About right...................... 33
No opinion....................... 21

Interviewing Date 8/16–21/46
Survey #376–K   Question #2e

In general, from what you have seen or heard, do you think the teachers in the school where your child goes do their job well or poorly?

Well............................. 60%
Fair............................. 29
Poorly........................... 8
No opinion....................... 3

SEPTEMBER 11
ELECTION FORECAST

Interviewing Date 7/26–31/46
Survey #375–K   Question #17

Regardless of how you yourself plan to vote, which party do you think will win control of the House in the congressional elections this fall — the Democratic or the Republican?

Democratic....................... 42%
Republican....................... 58

By Political Affiliation

	Republicans Will Win	Democrats Will Win
Republicans.........	79%	21%
Democrats..........	36	64

SEPTEMBER 13
JAMES F. BYRNES

Interviewing Date 8/30–9/4/46
Survey #377–K   Question #4a

James F. Byrnes has been Secretary of State a little over a year. In dealing with foreign nations would you say he has been doing an excellent, good, fair, or poor job?

Excellent........................ 16 ⎫ 57%
Good............................. 41 ⎭
Fair............................. 17
Poor............................. 10
No opinion....................... 16

By Political Affiliation
Democrats

Excellent or good................. 61%
Fair............................. 15
Poor............................. 8
No opinion....................... 16

Republicans

Excellent or good................. 54%
Fair............................. 20
Poor............................. 11
No opinion....................... 15

SEPTEMBER 14
"BABY BONUSES"

Interviewing Date 8/16–21/46
Survey #376–K   Question #1a

To encourage having children, England now pays $1 per week for each child under 16 years of age. Do you think we should have a baby bonus plan of that type in this country?

Yes............................. 30%
No.............................. 61
No opinion....................... 9

Those With Children Under 16 Only

Yes............................. 34%
No.............................. 56
No opinion....................... 10

Those Without Children Under 16 Only

Yes............................. 29%
No.............................. 63
No opinion....................... 8

Interviewing Date 8/16–21/46
Survey #376–K   Question #1b

Asked of those answering yes to the bonus plan: How much should be paid each week per child?

Median average.................. $2 wk.

Interviewing Date 8/16–21/46
Survey #376–T   Question #1a

To help parents support their children, England now pays $1 per week for each child under 16 years of age. Do you think we should have a baby bonus plan of that type in this country?

Yes.............................. 38%
No............................... 49
No opinion........................ 13

Those With Children Under 16 Only

Yes.............................. 46%
No............................... 42
No opinion........................ 12

Those Without Children Under 16 Only

Yes.............................. 34%
No............................... 55
No opinion........................ 11

SEPTEMBER 16
TROOPS OVERSEAS

Interviewing Date 8/30–9/4/46
Survey #377–K   Question #6

Do you think we are doing the best thing to keep troops in Germany and other defeated nations in Europe, or would it be better to bring all our troops home now?

Keep troops in Europe.............. 80%
Bring troops home.................. 16
No opinion........................ 4

Interviewing Date 8/30–9/4/46
Survey #377–K   Question #7

Do you think we are doing the best thing to keep troops in Japan, or would it be better to bring all our troops home now?

Keep troops in Japan............... 81%
Bring troops home.................. 15
No opinion........................ 4

Veterans of World War II are more in favor of maintaining occupation troops than the rest of the public. The vote of veterans questioned in the poll was 93% in favor of keeping troops in Germany and Europe, 94% in favor of keeping them in Japan.

SEPTEMBER 18
ATTITUDES TOWARD RUSSIA

Interviewing Date 8/30–9/4/46
Survey #377–K   Question #12a

Are your feelings toward Russia more friendly or less friendly than they were a year ago?

More friendly...................... 2%
Less friendly...................... 62
About the same..................... 28
No opinion........................ 8

SEPTEMBER 20
VETERANS

Interviewing Date 7/26–31/46
Survey #375–K   Question #26d

Asked of ex-servicemen: Has the Government given you, as a veteran, all the help you think it should?

Yes.............................. 71%
No............................... 26
No opinion........................ 3

Interviewing Date 7/26–31/46
Survey #375–K   Question #26e

Asked of those who said no: What more should it do?

The principal replies were: pay a bonus, get more living quarters for veterans, and cut out red tape in obtaining G.I. loans.

Interviewing Date 7/26–31/46
Survey #375–K   Question #26a

Generally speaking do you feel that your time in the armed forces was a waste from your point of view, or did you benefit from it?

Waste............................... 32%
Benefit............................. 62
No opinion......................... 6

Interviewing Date 7/26–31/46
Survey #375–K   Question #26b

What did you like best about being in the service?

Experience, education, training, and
   discipline........................ 47%
Travel.............................. 15
Understanding of other peoples........ 15
Independence, how to take care of myself 6
Money.............................. 2
Contacts with men................... 2
Benefits under G.I. bill.............. 2
Miscellaneous...................... 13
No benefits......................... 6
No opinion......................... 6
                           114%

Interviewing Date 7/26–31/46
Survey #375–K   Question #26c

What did you like least about being in the service?

Regimentation and discipline......... 21%
Caste system, social inequality........ 15
Officers............................ 15
Distance from home and family....... 12
Red tape, time wasting.............. 9
Not enough free time............... 4
Boring routine duties............... 4
Fighting and killing................ 3
Poor food.......................... 3
Miscellaneous...................... 11
No drawbacks...................... 5
No opinion......................... 2
                           104%

(Note: the preceding two tables add to more than 100% because some persons gave more than one answer.)

SEPTEMBER 21
ALASKAN STATEHOOD

Interviewing Date 8/30–9/4/46
Survey #377–K   Question #1

Would you favor or oppose having Alaska admitted as a 49th state in the Union?

Favor.............................. 64%
Oppose............................ 12
Undecided......................... 24

SEPTEMBER 23
PARTY STRENGTH

Interviewing Date 8/30–9/4/46
Survey #377–K   Question #11

If a presidential election were being held today, which party would you vote for — the Democratic or the Republican?

Democratic......................... 50%
Republican......................... 50

By Occupation

	Democratic	Republican
Professional and business..........	39%	61%
Farmers.............	44	56
White collar.........	47	53
Manual workers......	60	40

SEPTEMBER 25
A.F.L. AND C.I.O.

Interviewing Date 8/16–21/46
Survey #376–K   Question #16e

Asked of A.F.L. members: What is your main criticism of the C.I.O.?

The following are listed in order of frequency of mention:

The C.I.O. is run by communists and radicals
It calls too many strikes
It has poor leadership
It doesn't look after the welfare of its members enough
It holds too much power and abuses that power
The C.I.O. is never satisfied; always complaining and trying to get more
It dictates too much to its members

Interviewing Date 8 /16–21 /46
Survey #376–K   Question #16d

Asked of C.I.O. members: What is your main criticism of the A.F.L.?

The following are listed in order of frequency of mention:

The A.F.L. doesn't do enough for its members; not energetic and ambitious enough
It isn't run democratically — the rank and file don't get enough to say
A.F.L. leaders are inefficient, old, and tired
It calls too many strikes
Too many crooks and gangsters in the A.F.L.
A.F.L. plays ball too much with management

SEPTEMBER 27
ARMED FORCES

Interviewing Date 8 /30–9 /4 /46
Survey #377–T   Question #2a

Before the war, the regular army of the United States had about 190,000 men. During the war it had about 8,000,000 men. Just making your best guess, about how many men should we have in our peacetime army about five years from now?

Median average................. 1,000,000

Fewer than one voter in 14 wanted to go back to the old peacetime strength of 190,000, or less.

Interviewing Date 8 /3–90 /4 /46
Survey #377–K   Question #2b

Before the war, the regular navy of the United States had about 140,000 men. During the war it had over 3,000,000 men. Just making your best guess, about how many should we have in our peacetime navy about five years from now?

Median average................. 1,000,000

Interviewing Date 8 /30–9 /4 /46
Survey #377–K   Question #2a

Would you be willing to have a son of yours go into the service for a year and a half to make up an army of this size?

Yes............................. 80%
No.............................. 11
No opinion...................... 9

People with sons who are now of draft age or who will come of draft age in the next few years expressed the same willingness to have them go into the armed forces as did the rest of the country.

SEPTEMBER 28
GREAT BRITAIN

Interviewing Date 8 /30–9 /4 /46
Survey #377–K   Question # 12a

Are your feelings toward Britain more friendly or less friendly than they were a year ago?

More friendly................... 8%
About the same.................. 53
Less friendly................... 30
No opinion...................... 9

SEPTEMBER 30
CAMPAIGN ISSUES

Interviewing Date 9 /13–18 /46
Survey #378–K   Question #2b

What do you personally regard as the most important issue that should be discussed in the coming November election campaigns?

The following are listed in order of frequency of mention:

Foreign policy, relations with Russia
Lowering the cost of living
Curbing strikes and regulating labor troubles
Working out world peace, making the United Nations succeed
Housing
Shortages of food, clothing, and other necessities
Veteran's welfare

"Independent" voters (numbering about 13,-000,000 out of the voting population of 65,-000,000), the group holding the balance of power in elections, look upon the issues in the same order as the general voting public — foreign policy first, high cost of living second, strikes third, etc.

Voters who call themselves Democrats show more concern over the cost of living than Republicans. Republicans point to strikes and labor troubles as the top issue.

OCTOBER 2
NEW YORK ELECTION

Special Survey

For Governor of New York do you favor the Republican candidate Thomas Dewey, or the Democratic candidate James Mead?

Dewey	52%
Mead	34
Undecided	14

OCTOBER 4
VOTER INTEREST

Interviewing Date 9/13–18/46
Survey #378–K   Question #6a

Have you paid much attention to the coming elections this fall?

Yes	46%
No	54

By Political Affiliation

	Yes	No
Republicans	52%	48%
Democrats	41	59

By Education

College	69%	31%
High School	48	52
Grade School	38	62

Interviewing Date 9/13–18/46
Survey #378–K   Question #6c

Do you think it makes much difference or only a little difference which party wins the elections for Congress this fall?

Much difference	49%
Little difference	31
No difference at all	11
No opinion	9

The people most inclined to say that it will make little or no difference who wins the elections are Democrats and people whose schooling did not go beyond grade school.

OCTOBER 5
PRICE CONTROLS

Interviewing Date 9/13–18/46
Survey #378–K   Question #9

Do you think the present price ceilings should be kept on or taken off the following items?

	Kept On	Taken Off	No Opin.
Meats	42%	53%	5%
Other foods	42	51	7
Clothing	49	44	7
Autos, radios, and other mfd. goods	45	46	9
Rents	67	27	6

OCTOBER 6
OHIO ELECTION

Special Survey

In the election for United States Senator from Ohio which do you favor — James Huffman or John Bricker?

Bricker............................ 56%
Huffman........................... 28
Undecided......................... 16

OCTOBER 9
HOUSE OF REPRESENTATIVES

Interviewing Date 9/13–18/46
Survey #378–K   Question #4a

When a man is elected to the United States House of Representatives, how many years does he serve in one term of office?

Correct answers (two years).......... 47%
Incorrect answers................... 53

By Education

	Correct	Don't know, Incorrect
College..................	75%	25%
High School.............	55	45
Grade School............	36	64

Interviewing Date 9/13–18/46
Survey #378–K   Question #4b

It has been suggested that the Constitution be changed to make the term of office of Congressmen in Washington four years instead of two. Would you approve or disapprove of this change?

Approve............................ 40%
Disapprove......................... 51
No opinion......................... 9

By Education
College

Approve............................ 52%
Disapprove......................... 41
No opinion......................... 7

High School

Approve............................ 36%
Disapprove......................... 53
No opinion......................... 11

Grade School

Approve............................ 39%
Disapprove......................... 53
No opinion......................... 8

OCTOBER 11
ELECTION FORECAST

Interviewing Date 9/27–10/2/46
Survey #379–K   Question #9

Regardless of how you yourself plan to vote, which party do you think will win control of the House in the Congressional elections this fall — the Democratic or the Republican?

Republican......................... 63%
Democratic......................... 37

By Political Affiliation

	Republican	Democratic
Republicans..........	84%	16%
Democrats..........	36	64

OCTOBER 12
AIR AND NAVAL BASES OVERSEAS

Interviewing Date 9/27–10/2/46
Survey #379–K   Question #1

Do you think we should keep the air and naval bases that we have in the Pacific, or should we turn them over to the UN?

Keep them......................... 76%
Turn them over.................... 12
No opinion........................ 12

OCTOBER 13
WALLACE-BYRNES DEBATE

Interviewing Date 9/27–10/2/46
Survey #379–K   Question #7a

Have you followed the arguments about Byrnes's ideas and Wallace's ideas for dealing with Russia?

Yes............................... 42%
No................................ 58

Interviewing Date 9/27–10/2/46
Survey #379–K   Question #7d

Asked of those who answered yes: Whose policy do you think we should follow — Byrnes's or Wallace's?

Byrnes's........................... 78%
Wallace's.......................... 16
No opinion......................... 6

Interviewing Date 9/27–10/2/46
Survey #379–K   Question #7b

Asked of those who answered yes to the first question: In general, what do you understand Byrnes's ideas to be regarding Russia?

Byrnes wants to be firm with Russia; fair
  but firm; tell them just where we stand 76%
Wants to cooperate with Russia....... 7
Miscellaneous and don't know........ 17

Interviewing Date 9/27–10/2/46
Survey #379–K   Question #7c

Asked of those who answered yes to the first question: In general, what do you understand Wallace's ideas to be regarding Russia?

Wallace wants to be easy with Russia,
  lenient; wants to appease her....... 50%
Try to see Russia's viewpoint, side with
  her a little more.................. 16
Pro-Russian, a communist............ 17
Miscellaneous and don't know........ 17

OCTOBER 16
PARTY STRENGTH

Interviewing Date 9/13–18/46
Survey #378–K   Question #6b

If you were voting for a congressman today, would you be most likely to vote for the Democrat, the Republican, or the candidate of some other party?

Democrat........................... 43%
Republican......................... 57

Interviewing Date 9/27–10/2/46
Survey #379–K   Question #11

If a presidential election were being held today which party would you vote for — the Democratic or Republican?

Democratic......................... 47%
Republican......................... 53

OCTOBER 16
PRESIDENT TRUMAN'S POPULARITY

Interviewing Date 9/13–18/46
Survey #378–K   Question #19

Do you approve or disapprove of the way Harry Truman is handling his job as President?

Only 32% of voters polled said they were satisfied with the way Harry Truman has handled the Presidency.

OCTOBER 19
MEAT SHORTAGE

Interviewing Date 10/5–10/46
Survey #379–S   Question #14a

Whom or what do you blame for the present meat shortage?

Blame the Democrats................ 30%
Blame the Republicans.............. 4
Blame something or someone other than
  political party.................. 66

The voters who say the fault lies with no political party, who place the blame on something or someone other than the political parties, assign the blame as follows, with the items listed in descending order of importance.

The OPA
The Government, Washington, Congress
Meat packers
Profiteers
Farmers
Big business
All people
Extent of meat exports

OCTOBER 20
PARTY BEST ABLE TO HANDLE LABOR PROBLEMS

Interviewing Date 9/27–10/2/46
Survey #379–K   Question #4a

As you feel today which political party — the Democratic or the Republican — can best handle the problem of reducing strikes and labor troubles?

Democratic......................... 23%
Republican......................... 46
No difference...................... 31

OCTOBER 23
NEW YORK AND OHIO ELECTIONS

Special Survey

Asked in New York: In the election for Governor of New York, which do you favor — James Mead or Thomas Dewey?

Mead.............................. 38%
Dewey............................. 62

Seventeen per cent expressed no opinion.

Asked in Ohio: In the election for United States Senator, which do you favor — James Huffman or John Bricker?

Huffman........................... 35%
Bricker........................... 65

OCTOBER 25
PARTY STRENGTH

Interviewing Date 9/27–10/2/46
Survey #379–K   Question #8b

If you were voting for a congressman today, would you be more likely to vote for a Democrat, a Republican, or for the candidate of another party?

By Region

	Democrat	Republican
New England........	40%	60%
Middle Atlantic......	45	55
East Central........	38	62
West Central........	37	63
South..............	73	27
West...............	48	52

NOVEMBER 1
REPUBLICAN PRESIDENTIAL CANDIDATES

Interviewing Date 10/12–17/46
Survey #380   Question #14

Asked of Republicans: If you had to decide today, who would be your choice for President in 1948?

Dewey............................. 40%
Stassen........................... 22
Bricker........................... 8
Vandenberg........................ 7
Taft.............................. 6
Warren............................ 6
MacArthur......................... 5
Eisenhower........................ 2
Saltonstall....................... 1
Hoover............................ 1
Others............................ 2

NOVEMBER 3
CONGRESSIONAL ELECTIONS —
FINAL POLL

Special Survey
Interviewing Date 10/18–23/46

If you were voting for a congressman today, would you be most likely to vote for the Democrat, the Republican, or the candidate of some other party?

Democrat.......................... 42%
Republican......................... 58

NOVEMBER 8
ECONOMIC CONDITIONS IN BRITAIN

Special Survey

Asked in Great Britain: In general, do you approve or disapprove of the Government's record to date?

Approve............................ 46%
Disapprove......................... 41
Don't know......................... 13

Do you think that we shall or shall not have a Conservative Government in Britain within five years?

Yes, we shall...................... 29%
No, we shall not................... 48
Undecided.......................... 23

NOVEMBER 8
ECONOMIC CONDITIONS

Interviewing Date 10/18–23/46
Survey #381   Question #3

Compared with last year, are you finding it harder, easier, or about the same to make both ends meet?

Harder............................. 71%
About the same..................... 21
Easier............................. 6
Undecided.......................... 2

NOVEMBER 10
VITAL ISSUES

Interviewing Date 10/12–17/46
Survey #380   Question #16

Should the Congress elected in November pass new laws to control labor unions?

Yes............................... 66%
No................................ 22
Undecided......................... 12

By Political Affiliation
Republicans

Yes............................... 77%
No................................ 12
Undecided......................... 11

Democrats

Yes............................... 60%
No................................ 28
Undecided......................... 12

Independents

Yes............................... 57%
No................................ 30
Undecided......................... 13

Interviewing Date 10/12–17/46
Survey #380   Question #17

Should the Congress elected in November pass a law to require every physically fit young man who has not served in the armed forces to take military or naval training for one year?

Yes............................... 67%
No................................ 25
Undecided......................... 8

By Political Affiliation
Republicans

Yes............................... 67%
No................................ 26
Undecided......................... 7

Democrats

Yes................................ 68%
No................................ 25
Undecided........................ 7

Independents

Yes................................ 66%
No................................ 26
Undecided........................ 8

Interviewing Date 10/12–17/46
Survey #380   Question #19

Should the Congress elected in November reduce income taxes in 1947, or should this wait until some of the national debt has been paid off?

Reduce............................ 41%
Wait.............................. 49
Undecided........................ 10

By Political Affiliation
Republicans

Reduce............................ 45%
Wait.............................. 48
Undecided........................ 7

Democrats

Reduce............................ 38%
Wait.............................. 50
Undecided........................ 12

Independents

Reduce............................ 41%
Wait.............................. 50
Undecided........................ 9

Interviewing Date 10/12–17/46
Survey #380   Question #18

Should the Congress elected in November pass a law raising minimum wages throughout the country from 40 to 65 cents an hour — that is, no worker could receive less than 65 cents an hour?

Yes................................ 66%
No................................ 26
Undecided........................ 8

By Political Affiliation
Republicans

Yes................................ 61%
No................................ 31
Undecided........................ 8

Democrats

Yes................................ 70%
No................................ 24
Undecided........................ 6

Independents

Yes................................ 70%
No................................ 23
Undecided........................ 7

NOVEMBER 13
STRIKES

Interviewing Date 9/27–10/2/46
Survey #379–K   Question #13

In Toledo, Ohio, strikes have been settled by a local committee of citizens. Do you think that this method would work in your community?

Yes................................ 52%
No................................ 23
No opinion........................ 25

By Occupation
Professional and Business

Yes................................ 60%
No................................ 25
No opinion........................ 15

Farmers

Yes................................ 52%
No................................ 13
No opinion........................ 35

White Collar

Yes................................. 53%
No.................................. 27
No opinion.......................... 20

Manual Workers

Yes................................. 49%
No.................................. 24
No opinion.......................... 27

Union Members Only

Yes................................. 50%
No.................................. 30
No opinion.......................... 20

NOVEMBER 15
FRANCE AND THE UNITED STATES

Special Survey

Asked in France: If Russia and the United States went to war against one another, which side would you favor?

United States....................... 40%
Russia.............................. 21
Neither............................. 33
No opinion.......................... 6

NOVEMBER 16
PARTY STRENGTH

Interviewing Date 10/23–28/46
Survey #382   Question #8

If you were voting for congressmen today, would you be most likely to vote for the Democrat, the Republican or the candidate of some other party?

By Occupation

	Republican	Democratic
Professional and business	70%	30%
White collar	65	35
Farmers	67	33
Manual workers	53	47

Union Members Only

Republican.......................... 49%
Democratic.......................... 51

NOVEMBER 22
STRIKES AND LOCKOUTS

Interviewing Date 10/18–23/46
Survey #381   Question #12b

Do you think a law should be passed forbidding all strikes and lockouts for a year?

Yes................................. 50%
No.................................. 41
Undecided........................... 9

NOVEMBER 23
SMOKING BY WOMEN TEACHERS

Interviewing Date 10/12–17/46
Survey #380   Question #3

The school boards in many communities do not allow women teachers to smoke. Do you think this rule should be changed to allow women teachers to smoke while outside the classroom?

Yes................................. 62%
No.................................. 32
No opinion.......................... 6

Analysis of voting by groups and geographical areas brings out this interesting fact: Among no group and in no part of the country, except the thirteen states comprising the South, do more people vote to keep teachers from smoking than vote in favor of allowing them to smoke.

People 50 years of age or more and farmers are the groups in the population least inclined to give women teachers the right to smoke. But even here, the weight of opinion is on the side of permitting the women to smoke.

The most liberal attitude on the subject is to be found among college trained people, young people (21 to 29), people in the medium sized towns (10,000 to 100,000 population), white collar workers, and people generally in the New England and Middle Atlantic states.

NOVEMBER 27
SUPERSTITIONS

Interviewing Date 8/16–21/46
Survey #376–K   Question #14a

Do you have any superstitions?

Yes................................ 48%
No................................. 52

Interviewing Date 8/16–21/46
Survey #376–K   Question #14b

Asked of those who responded in the affirmative: What are they?

Knocking on wood.................. 33%
Black cats........................ 20
Spilling salt..................... 10
Others............................ 37

NOVEMBER 29
INCOME TAX

Interviewing Date 11/15–20/46
Survey #384–K   Question #3a

Do you think the new Congress should reduce income taxes in 1947, or should this wait until some of the national debt has been paid off?

Cut taxes......................... 48%
Wait.............................. 44
No opinion........................ 8

Income Taxpayers Only

Cut taxes......................... 51%
Wait.............................. 44
No opinion........................ 5

Interviewing Date 11/15–20/46
Survey #384–K   Question #3c

Do you regard the income tax you pay this year as fair?

Yes................................ 60%
No................................. 34
No opinion......................... 6

NOVEMBER 30
UNITED NATIONS

Interviewing Date 11/15–20/46
Survey #384–K   Question #8

The United States has as much national income as all of the other nations in the UN put together. In view of this, do you think the United States should pay one half of all costs of the United Nations Organization?

Yes................................ 16%
No................................. 69
Undecided.......................... 15

By Political Affiliation
Democrats

Yes................................ 19%
No................................. 67
Undecided.......................... 14

Republicans

Yes................................ 13%
No................................. 74
Undecided.......................... 13

By Education
College

Yes................................ 23%
No................................. 71
Undecided.......................... 6

High School

Yes................................ 17%
No................................. 71
Undecided.......................... 12

Grade School

Yes	14%
No	67
Undecided	19

World War II Veterans Only

Yes	18%
No	75
Undecided	7

DECEMBER 2
CONGRESS

Interviewing Date 11/15–20/46
Survey #384–K   Question #2a

In the recent election, the Republicans won control of Congress. What is the first problem you would like to see the new Congress take up?

The following are listed according to frequency of mention:

Control of strikes
Prices and high cost of living
Tax reforms
Housing shortage

DECEMBER 4
UNITED NATIONS

Interviewing Date 11/15–20/46
Survey #384–K   Question #7a

Should the permanent United Nations headquarters stay in the United States, or should it move to some other nation?

Should stay	70%
Should move	8
Undecided	22

By Region
New England and Middle Atlantic

Should stay	70%
Should move	11
Undecided	19

East Central and West Central

Should stay	67%
Should move	8
Undecided	25

South

Should stay	74%
Should move	3
Undecided	23

West

Should stay	72%
Should move	7
Undecided	21

Interviewing Date 11/15–20/46
Survey #384–K   Question #7b

If the United Nations headquarters stays in this country, in what state do you think it should be located?

New York	28%
California	9
Washington, D.C.	7
Pennsylvania	3
Massachusetts	2
Illinois	2
Washington State	1
South Dakota	1
Anywhere	9
Others	10
Undecided	28

DECEMBER 6
PRICE OUTLOOK

Interviewing Date 11/15–20/46
Survey #384–K   Question #5

Do you think prices in general will be higher, lower, or about the same six months from now?

Higher	31%
Lower	38
Same	26
No opinion	5

By Sex
Men

Higher	32%
Lower	40
Same	24
No opinion	4

Women

Higher	30%
Lower	35
Same	27
No opinion	8

By Education
College

Higher	36%
Lower	39
Same	21
No opinion	4

High School

Higher	31%
Lower	40
Same	26
No opinion	3

Grade School

Higher	30%
Lower	37
Same	26
No opinion	7

By Occupation
Professional and Business

Higher	33%
Lower	41
Same	22
No opinion	4

White Collar

Higher	32%
Lower	42
Same	22
No opinion	4

Manual Workers

Higher	31%
Lower	35
Same	27
No opinion	7

Farmers

Higher	27%
Lower	38
Same	30
No opinion	5

DECEMBER 7
THIRD PARTY MOVEMENT

Interviewing Date 9/27–10/2/46
Survey #379–K   Question #17

If a third party is formed in this country by Henry Wallace, Claude Pepper, the C.I.O., and other labor groups, do you think you would vote for that party?

Yes	10%
No	78
No opinion	12

By Political Affiliation
Democrats

Yes	13%
No	73
No opinion	14

Republicans

Yes	3%
No	91
No opinion	6

Independents

Yes	18%
No	65
No opinion	17

By Occupation
Professional and Business

Yes	11%
No	80
No opinion	9

White Collar

Yes..................................... 10%
No..................................... 80
No opinion........................... 10

Manual Workers

Yes..................................... 11%
No..................................... 74
No opinion........................... 15

Farmers

Yes..................................... 5%
No..................................... 88
No opinion........................... 7

Union Members Only

Yes..................................... 17%
No..................................... 69
No opinion........................... 14

Non-Union Members Only

Yes..................................... 9%
No..................................... 76
No opinion........................... 15

DECEMBER 8
REPUBLICAN PRESIDENTIAL CANDIDATES

Interviewing Date 11/15–20/46
Survey #384–K   Question #15

Asked of Republicans: If you had to decide today, who would be your choice for President in 1948?

Dewey.................................. 52%
Stassen................................ 17
Vandenberg........................... 9
Bricker................................. 8
Warren................................. 5
Taft..................................... 2
MacArthur............................ 2
Eisenhower............................ 2
Saltonstall............................ 1
Others.................................. 2

Twenty-three per cent expressed no opinion.

DECEMBER 11
DEMOCRATIC PRESIDENTIAL CANDIDATES

Interviewing Date 11/15–20/46
Survey #384–K   Question #15a

Asked of Democrats: If you had to decide today, who would be your choice for President in 1948?

Truman................................ 48%
Wallace................................ 24
Byrnes................................. 10
Eisenhower............................ 8
Byrd.................................... 1
Pepper................................. 1
Vinson................................. 1
Douglas................................ 1
Barkley................................ 1
Farley.................................. 1
Eleanor Roosevelt.................... 1
Others.................................. 3

Fifty-three per cent expressed no opinion.

DECEMBER 13
SPAIN

Interviewing Date 11/16–21/46
Survey #384–T   Question #9

Do you think the member countries of the United Nations should or should not break off trade and political relations with Spain?

Should.................................. 24%
Should not............................ 37
No opinion........................... 39

By Political Affiliation
Democrats

Should.................................. 27%
Should not............................ 36
No opinion........................... 37

Republicans

Should 22%
Should not............................ 36
No opinion........................... 37

Do you think the Franco Government of Spain is a threat to world peace?

Yes, it is............................ 34%
No, it is not........................ 29
No opinion.......................... 37

Do you think that a citizen of Spain has more freedom or less freedom than a citizen of Russia?

More.............................. 31%
Less............................... 13
Same.............................. 17
No opinion........................ 39

DECEMBER 14
PARTY STRENGTH

Regardless of how you yourself feel, which party do you think will win the presidential election in 1948?

Democratic......................... 9%
Republican......................... 79
No opinion......................... 12

By Political Affiliation
Democrats

Democratic......................... 16%
Republican......................... 69
No opinion......................... 15

Republicans

Democratic......................... 1%
Republican......................... 93
No opinion......................... 6

DECEMBER 15
ATOM BOMB

Do you think the United States should stop making atom bombs and destroy all those we now have?

Yes.............................. 21%
No............................... 72
No opinion........................ 7

Do you think that the United States should stop making atom bombs and destroy those already made to prove our good intentions in asking for international control of atomic bombs?

Yes.............................. 19%
No............................... 65
Qualified......................... 5
No opinion........................ 11

Suppose the United States stopped making atom bombs and destroyed those already made. Do you think Russia would then agree to let a United Nations committee check to see that Russia does not make atom bombs?

Yes.............................. 13%
No............................... 72
No opinion........................ 15

Do you believe that this (ceasing to make bombs and destroying those already made) would help in bringing about an agreement with Russia regarding international control of atomic bombs?

Yes.............................. 28%
No............................... 52
No opinion........................ 20

DECEMBER 18
LABOR UNION FINANCES

Interviewing Date 11/29–12/4/46
Survey #385–K   Question #8

Do you think labor unions should be required by law to make yearly public reports of the money they collect and spend?

Yes	84%
No	10
Undecided	6

Union Members Only

Yes	80%
No	14
Undecided	6

DECEMBER 20
RENTS

Interviewing Date 11/29–12/4/46
Survey #385–K   Question #3c

Asked of tenants: Do you think that the rent you now have to pay is high, low, or about right?

High	24%
Low	11
About right	64
No opinion	1

When the responses were divided into two groups — those paying a rent of less than $45 a month for living quarters and those paying $45 and over — the vote by each group was as follows:

	Those Paying: Rent Under $45	Rent $45 and Over
High	22%	28%
Low	10	12
Right	66	59
No opinion	2	1

Interviewing Date 11/29–12/4/46
Survey #385–K   Question #3d

Asked of tenants: Considering the increase in costs of operation, do you think it would be fair to let your landlord increase the rent?

Yes	24%
No	71
No opinion	5

	Those Paying: Rent Under $45	Rent $45 and Over
Yes	22%	27%
No	73	67
No opinion	5	6

DECEMBER 21
IDEAL CHRISTMAS GIFT

Interviewing Date 11/29–12/4/46
Survey #385–K   Question #11

If you had your choice, what present would you most like to have for Christmas?

The following are listed in order of frequency of mention:

Automobile
House
Clothes
Household equipment
Permanent peace
Personal health
Money
Job security

DECEMBER 23
WAGES AND PRICES

Interviewing Date 11/29–12/4/46
Survey #385–T   Question #9

Would you be willing to keep wages where they are now provided that prices remain where they are now?

Yes.............................. 49%
No............................... 43
No opinion....................... 8

Manual Workers Only

Yes.............................. 46%
No............................... 47
No opinion....................... 7

Labor Union Members Only

Yes.............................. 46%
No............................... 49
No opinion....................... 5

Interviewing Date 11/29–12/4/46
Survey #385–K   Question #9

Labor leaders say that because of the increased cost of living since the raise in wages of last spring, workers should be given another wage increase of about 20%. Do you agree or disagree with this?

Agree............................ 42%
Disagree......................... 46
No opinion....................... 12

Manual Workers Only

Agree............................ 54%
Disagree......................... 36
No opinion....................... 10

Labor Union Members Only

Agree............................ 62%
Disagree......................... 31
No opinion....................... 7

DECEMBER 27
DEFENSE SPENDING

Interviewing Date 11/29–12/4/46
Survey #385–K   Question #10

About half the cost of our Government today goes to support the army and navy. Which of these do you think should be done: A. Reduce taxes by cutting down our army

and navy. B. Keep our army and navy as they are for another two or three years?

Reduce taxes..................... 20%
Keep army and navy same.......... 70
No opinion....................... 10

By Political Affiliation
Democrats

Reduce taxes..................... 19%
Keep army and navy same.......... 71
No opinion....................... 10

Republicans

Reduce taxes..................... 20%
Keep army and navy same.......... 71
No opinion....................... 9

By Education
College

Reduce taxes..................... 19%
Keep army and navy same.......... 76
No opinion....................... 5

High School

Reduce taxes..................... 20%
Keep army and navy same.......... 74
No opinion....................... 6

Grade School

Reduce taxes..................... 21%
Keep army and navy same.......... 66
No opinion....................... 13

DECEMBER 28
NEW YEAR RESOLUTIONS

Interviewing Date 12/13–18/46
Survey #386–K   Question #1a

Are you going to make any New Year resolutions?

Yes.............................. 27%
No............................... 73

Interviewing Date 12/13–18/46
Survey #386–K
Question #1b

Asked of those who responded in the affirmative: What resolutions are you going to make?

The following are listed in order of frequency of mention:

Save more money, budget more carefully.
Improve my character, live a better life.
Improve my disposition, be more understanding.
Be more religious, go to church more often.
Stop smoking, smoke less.
Help family and friends more than last year.
Be more efficient and prompt.
Earn more money.
Stop drinking, drink less.
Get more sleep, take better care of my health.

DECEMBER 30
HAROLD STASSEN

Interviewing Date 12/13–18/46
Survey #386–T
Question #4i

Can you tell me who Harold Stassen is or what he does?

Correct answers.................... 33%
Incorrect or don't know............. 67

1947

United States in the future from serving more than two terms in a row?

Yes.............................. 52%
No............................... 40
No opinion........................ 8

Among Republican voters, 69% indicated approval of prohibiting more than two terms in a row. Among Democrats, the vote of approval is only 35%.

JANUARY 3
RUSSIA

Interviewing Date 12/13–18/46
Survey #386–K   Question #13a

Do you think Russia will cooperate with us in world affairs?

Yes.............................. 43%
No............................... 40
No opinion........................ 17

By Education
College

Yes.............................. 60%
No............................... 33
No opinion........................ 7

High School

Yes.............................. 49%
No............................... 40
No opinion........................ 11

Grade School

Yes.............................. 35%
No............................... 42
No opinion........................ 23

JANUARY 4
PRESIDENTIAL TENURE

Interviewing Date 11/29–12/4/46
Survey #385–K   Question #12

Would you favor adding a law to the Constitution to prevent any President of the

JANUARY 5
UNITED NATIONS

Interviewing Date 12/13–18/46
Survey #386–K   Question #7a

Are you satisfied or dissatisfied with the progress that the United Nations has made to date?

Satisfied......................... 39%
Dissatisfied...................... 33
No opinion........................ 28

World War II Veterans Only

Satisfied......................... 41%
Dissatisfied...................... 38
No opinion........................ 21

JANUARY 8
PRESIDENT TRUMAN'S POPULARITY

Interviewing Date 12/13–18/46
Survey #386–K   Question #3

Do you approve or disapprove of the way Harry Truman is handling his job as President?

Approve........................... 35%
Disapprove........................ 47
No opinion........................ 18

JANUARY 10
WAGNER ACT

Interviewing Date 11/29–12/4/46
Survey #385–K   Question #6a

What is your understanding of what the Wagner Labor Act provides — or is supposed to do?

Generally correct answers............ 19%
Incorrect.......................... 12
Don't know........................ 69

Interviewing Date 11/29–12/4/46
Survey #385–K   Question #6c

Asked of those generally familiar with the Wagner Labor Act: Do you think the Wagner Labor Act should be left as it is, changed, or done away with?

Left as is.......................... 36%
Changed........................... 53
Done away with.................... 11

Interviewing Date 11/29–12/4/46
Survey #385–K   Question #6d

Asked of those who wanted the Act changed: How would you change the Act?

Management and labor should be on a more equal basis; the Act should be strengthened to protect employers more; it should have more restrictions on strikes; and it should limit the power of labor leaders.

JANUARY 11
GERMAN SCIENTISTS

Interviewing Date 12/13–18/46
Survey #386–K   Question #5a

It has been suggested that we bring over to America 1,000 German scientists who used to work for the Nazis and have them work with our own scientists on scientific problems. Do you think this is a good or bad idea?

Good idea......................... 35%
Bad idea.......................... 52
No opinion........................ 13

By Education
College

Good idea......................... 60%
Bad idea.......................... 33
No opinion........................ 7

High School

Good idea......................... 43%
Bad idea.......................... 48
No opinion........................ 9

Grade School

Good idea......................... 24%
Bad idea.......................... 59
No opinion........................ 17

Interviewing Date 12/13–18/46
Survey #386–K   Question #5c

Asked of those answering in the affirmative: Do you think these German scientists should be permitted to become citizens if they want to, or should they be sent back to Germany when we are through with them?

Let them become citizens............ 73%
Send them back.................... 19
No opinion........................ 8

JANUARY 13
FACTORY WORKERS' WAGES

Interviewing Date 12/13–18/46
Survey #386–K   Question #9a

Many unions of factory workers are going to ask for a pay increase within the next month or two. Do you think these factory workers should get more pay?

Yes............................... 38%
No................................ 49
No opinion........................ 13

By Occupation

Professional and Business

Yes............................... 31%
No............................... 56
No opinion........................ 13

White Collar

Yes............................... 37%
No............................... 48
No opinion........................ 15

Manual Workers

Yes............................... 50%
No............................... 37
No opinion........................ 13

Farmers

Yes............................... 19%
No............................... 71
No opinion........................ 10

Union Members Only

Yes............................... 59%
No............................... 30
No opinion........................ 11

Interviewing Date 12/13–18/46
Survey #386–K   Question #9c

Do you think pay increases could be given by most factories without increasing the prices of the goods they make?

Yes............................... 47%
No............................... 40
No opinion........................ 13

Manual Workers Only

Yes............................... 50%
No............................... 35
No opinion........................ 15

JANUARY 15
BRITISH WORKERS

Special Survey

Asked in Great Britain: What do you think is the main reason why many people are not prepared to work harder than they are doing at the present time?

High level of taxation............... 18%
War weariness..................... 12
Insufficient food.................. 9
Wages are too low.................. 6
People are lazy..................... 6
Not enough goods to buy with money
  earned......................... 5
Lack of security................... 4
Poor working conditions............. 3
Too much coddling of workers........ 3
Not enough incentive............... 2
Others, no opinion................. 32

JANUARY 17
PORTAL-TO-PORTAL PAY

Interviewing Date 1/2–7/47
Survey #387–K   Question #8a

Will you tell me what is meant by the term "portal-to-portal" pay?

Correct........................... 41%
Incorrect......................... 8
Don't know....................... 51

Interviewing Date 1/2–7/47
Survey #387–K   Question #8b

Asked of those who correctly identified the term: What is your opinion of the union's effort to collect this portal-to-portal pay for the last several years?

Fair.............................. 17%
Fair in some cases................. 3
Unfair............................ 72
No reply.......................... 8

Interviewing Date 1/2–7/47
Survey #387–K   Question #8c

Why do you feel this way?

Those disapproving portal-to-portal pay for the last several years responded:

Companies cannot afford to pay without going bankrupt.

Workers should be paid for the time they spend working.

This time was not included in contracts.

Workers already earn enough money.

The consumer will end up paying for the time.

Those approving portal-to-portal pay for the last several years responded:

The workers deserve it.

Workers don't get enough pay now.

It is a good way to put more money into circulation.

It is especially justified in the case of miners who go over dangerous routes to their actual work.

Interviewing Date 1/2–7/47
Survey #387–K Question #8d

The unions have been trying to collect pay for the last several years for workers to cover the time they needed to get from the factory gates to where they actually began to work on the job. Should workers be paid for this time for the last several years?

Yes............................... 20%
No............................... 72
No opinion........................ 8

Skilled, Semiskilled, and Unskilled Workers Only

Yes............................... 30%
No............................... 59
No opinion........................ 11

Interviewing Date 1/2–7/47
Survey #387–K Question #8e

How strongly do you feel about this — very strongly, fairly strongly, or not at all strongly?

	Those Who Favor	Those Who Oppose
Very strongly......	48%	58%
Fairly strongly.....	38	29
Not strongly.......	12	12
No opinion........	2	1

Interviewing Date 1/2–7/47
Survey #387–K Question #8f

How about in the future — should workers be paid for this time?

Yes............................... 45%
No............................... 43
No opinion........................ 12

Skilled, Semiskilled, and Unskilled Workers Only

Yes............................... 55%
No............................... 32
No opinion........................ 13

JANUARY 18
BUSINESS OUTLOOK

Interviewing Date 1/2–7/47
Survey #387–K Question #1a

Do you think there will be a business depression in 1947?

Yes............................... 31%
No............................... 60
No opinion........................ 9

Interviewing Date 1/2–7/47
Survey #387–K Question #1b

Asked of those who predicted a depression: Well, how serious a depression — very serious, fairly serious, or not too serious?

Very serious....................... 5%
Fairly serious..................... 9
Not too serious................... 17
                                   ——
                                   31%

JANUARY 19
LABOR UNIONS

Interviewing Date 11/29–12/4/46
Survey #385–K   Question #7d

Which one of the three types of shop do you prefer — the closed shop, the union shop, the open shop?: (on card) (1) The closed shop requires every worker in a company to belong to a union before he can be hired. (2) The union shop requires every worker in a company where there is a union to join that union after he is hired. (3) The open shop does not require a worker to join a union but lets him decide for himself whether to join or not?

Closed shop...................... 8%
Union shop...................... 18
Open shop...................... 66
No opinion...................... 8

By Occupation
Business and Professional

Closed shop...................... 7%
Union shop...................... 14
Open shop...................... 73
No opinion...................... 6

White Collar

Closed shop...................... 6%
Union shop...................... 17
Open shop...................... 69
No opinion...................... 8

Manual Workers

Closed shop...................... 11%
Union shop...................... 23
Open shop...................... 56
No opinion...................... 10

Farmers

Closed shop...................... 3%
Union shop...................... 11
Open shop...................... 78
No opinion...................... 8

Union Members Only

Closed shop...................... 19%
Union shop...................... 33
Open shop...................... 41
No opinion...................... 7

JANUARY 22
PRICE OUTLOOK

Interviewing Date 12/13–18/46
Survey #386–K, #386–T   Question #8

Do you think that prices on the following items will be higher, lower, or about the same six months from now?

	Higher or Same	Lower	No Opinion
Food...........	46%	48%	6%
Rent...........	83	13	4
Clothing........	55	38	7
Automobiles.....	70	19	11
Manufactured goods.........	65	30	5
Real estate.......	56	37	7

JANUARY 24
INCOME TAXES

Interviewing Date 1/2–7/47
Survey #387–K   Question #4a

About how much do you think a married man with two children who earns $60 a week, that is $3,000 a year, should pay in federal income taxes?

Median average..................... $50

Interviewing Date 1/2–7/47
Survey #387–K   Question #4b

About how much do you think a married man with two children who earns $200 a week, that is $10,000 a year, should pay in federal income taxes?

Median average..................... $900

About how much do you think a married man with two children who earns $1,000 a week, that is $50,000 a year, should pay in federal income taxes?

Median average.................... $7,500

JANUARY 25
CONSCIENTIOUS OBJECTORS

During the war, some conscientious objectors were sent to prison for refusing to serve in any way in the armed forces. Do you think these men should now be let out of prison?

Yes............................... 69%
No................................ 23
No opinion........................ 8

By Sex
Men

Yes............................... 65%
No................................ 27
No opinion........................ 8

Women

Yes............................... 73%
No................................ 19
No opinion........................ 8

By Education
College

Yes............................... 77%
No................................ 18
No opinion........................ 5

High School

Yes............................... 70%
No................................ 23
No opinion........................ 7

Grade School

Yes............................... 66%
No................................ 25
No opinion........................ 9

World War II Veterans Only

Yes............................... 61%
No................................ 33
No opinion........................ 6

JANUARY 26
MILITARY SERVICE

If you had a son or brother 18, 19, or 20 years of age, would you advise him to volunteer for service in the army or navy for a year?

Yes............................... 53%
No................................ 40
No opinion........................ 7

Asked of persons with a brother or son 18, 19, or 20 years old: If the army and navy changed their training program to include regular high school or college courses, would you then advise him to volunteer?

Yes............................... 64%
No................................ 28
No opinion........................ 8

Would you be in favor of giving these volunteers enough regular school work in the army or navy so that they could earn one year of high school or college credit for each year in the service?

Yes............................... 79%
No................................ 12
No opinion........................ 9

JANUARY 29
GOVERNMENT OWNERSHIP
OF INDUSTRY

Interviewing Date 1/2–7/47
Survey #387–K   Question #9

Do you think the United States Government should own the following things in this country: banks, railroads, coal mines, electric power companies?

	Yes	No	No Opinion
Banks	26%	66%	8%
Railroads	26	67	7
Coal mines	33	61	6
Electric power companies	28	64	8

In every case, Government ownership is opposed by substantial majorities throughout all occupation groups, education levels, and political parties.

JANUARY 31
MOST IMPORTANT PROBLEM

Interviewing Date 1/2–7/47
Survey #387–K   Question #2

In your opinion, what is the most important problem the United States Government must solve in the next year?

Strikes and labor problems	40%
International relations, including atomic energy control	26
Inflation, high prices	13
Housing	10
Taxation	4
Employment	2
Shortages	1
Miscellaneous	10
No opinion	4
	110%

(Note: replies total more than 100% because some persons named more than one problem.)

FEBRUARY 1
MOST IMPORTANT PERSONAL
PROBLEM

Interviewing Date 1/2–7/47
Survey #387–T   Question #2

What is the most important problem that you and your family face today?

The following are listed in order of frequency of mention:

The high cost of living
Housing
Shortages: household equipment, food, automobiles
Personal family problems, health

FEBRUARY 2
PRESIDENT TRUMAN'S POPULARITY

Interviewing Date 1/17–22/47
Survey #388–K   Question #5

Do you approve or disapprove of the way Harry Truman is handling his job as President?

Approve	48%
Disapprove	39
No opinion	13

By Sex
Men

Approve	49%
Disapprove	40
No opinion	11

Women

Approve	48%
Disapprove	37
No opinion	15

By Political Affiliation
Democrats

Approve	59%
Disapprove	30
No opinion	11

Republicans

Approve.......................... 41%
Disapprove........................ 46
No opinion........................ 13

By Age
21–29 Years

Approve.......................... 48%
Disapprove........................ 41
No opinion........................ 11

30–49 Years

Approve.......................... 48%
Disapprove........................ 38
No opinion........................ 14

50 Years and Over

Approve.......................... 50%
Disapprove........................ 37
No opinion........................ 13

By Occupation
Professional and Business

Approve.......................... 41%
Disapprove........................ 50
No opinion........................ 9

White Collar

Approve.......................... 44%
Disapprove........................ 43
No opinion........................ 13

Manual Workers

Approve.......................... 51%
Disapprove........................ 35
No opinion........................ 14

Farmers

Approve.......................... 59%
Disapprove........................ 28
No opinion........................ 13

Union Members Only

Approve.......................... 43%
Disapprove........................ 42
No opinion........................ 15

FEBRUARY 5
PRESIDENT TRUMAN'S POLICIES

Interviewing Date 1/17–22/47
Survey #388–K   Question #6a

*Which of these three policies would you like
to have President Truman follow (on card):
(1) Go more to the left by following more
of the views of labor and other liberal
groups. (2) Go more to the right by following more of the views of business and
conservative groups. (3) Follow a policy
halfway between the two?*

Go more to left.................... 14%
Go more to right................... 20
Keep middle-of-the-road............. 56
No opinion........................ 10

Interviewing Date 1/17–22/47
Survey #388–K   Question #6b

*Which of these three policies do you think
President Truman has been following?*

Think policies have been to left....... 19%
Think policies have been to right..... 22
Think policies have been middle-of-the-
road........................... 37
No opinion........................ 22

By Political Affiliation
Democrats

Think policies have been to left....... 15%
Think policies have been to right..... 25
Think policies have been middle-of-the-
road........................... 37
No opinion........................ 23

Republicans

Think policies have been to left....... 23%
Think policies have been to right..... 21
Think policies have been middle-of-the-
road........................... 36
No opinion........................ 20

FEBRUARY 7
GERMANY

Interviewing Date 1/2–7/47
Survey #387–K   Question #5a

At the present time, do you feel friendly or unfriendly toward the people of Germany as a whole?

Friendly............................ 45%
Unfriendly......................... 28
No opinion......................... 27

Interviewing Date 1/2–7/47
Survey #387–K   Question #5b

Do you think Germany will become a peace-loving democratic nation, or do you think she will again some day become an aggressor nation and want to start a war?

Will become peaceful................ 22%
Will become aggressive.............. 58
No opinion......................... 20

FEBRUARY 8
BRITISH POLITICS

Special Survey

Asked of Britons: Are you satisfied or dissatisfied with Mr. Attlee as Prime Minister?

Satisfied........................... 52%
Dissatisfied........................ 30
No opinion......................... 18

Asked of Britons: Do you think that Ernest Bevin is or is not doing a good job as Foreign Secretary?

Yes, he is.......................... 54%
No, he is not....................... 20
No opinion......................... 26

FEBRUARY 9
GREAT INVENTIONS

Interviewing Date 1/17–22/47
Survey #388–K   Question #13a

What do you think is the greatest invention that has ever been made?

Electric light, electrical appliances..... 29%
Atom bomb......................... 17
Radio.............................. 12
The wheel.......................... 6
Airplane........................... 6
Telephone.......................... 4
Automobile......................... 4
Steam engine....................... 2
Radar.............................. 2
Printing press...................... 2
Washing machine................... 1
Television.......................... 1
Others............................. 9
No opinion......................... 5

Interviewing Date 1/17–22/47
Survey #388–K   Question #13b

Asked of all those who named an invention: Do you happen to know who invented it?

In connection with the airplane, the Wright Brothers, Leonardo da Vinci, and Lindbergh were the names most often mentioned. The inventors of the telephone were listed as Alexander Graham Bell, Don Ameche, and Samuel F.B. Morse, who invented the telegraph.

The names of Edison and Benjamin Franklin were given most frequently in connection with electricity. As for the inventor of the wheel, those who attempted any guess at all said mostly, "some Egyptian."

Henry Ford got more credit than any one else for the automobile, while the invention of radio was ascribed to Marconi, Farraday, the Radio Corporation of America, and many others.

FEBRUARY 12
JURISDICTIONAL STRIKES

Interviewing Date 1/17–22/47
Survey #388–K   Question #10a

What does the term "jurisdictional strike" mean to you?

Correct answers.................... 12%
Incorrect answers.................. 17
Don't know........................ 71

Interviewing Date 1/17–22/47
Survey #388–K   Question #10b

Asked of those able to define jurisdictional strikes: Do you think Congress should or should not forbid jurisdictional strikes?

Should forbid...................... 68%
Should not........................ 25
No opinion........................ 7

FEBRUARY 14
DWIGHT EISENHOWER AND DOUGLAS MACARTHUR

Interviewing Date 1/2–7/47
Survey #387–K   Question #11a

Do you think General Dwight Eisenhower will become a candidate for President in 1948?

Yes............................... 21%
No................................ 61
No opinion........................ 18

Interviewing Date 1/2–7/47
Survey #387–T   Question #11a

Do you think General Douglas MacArthur will become a candidate for President in 1948?

Yes............................... 12%
No................................ 71
No opinion........................ 17

Interviewing Date 1/2–7/47
Survey #387–K   Question #11b

If General Eisenhower does become a candidate which ticket do you think he will run on — the Democratic or Republican?

Democratic........................ 29%
Republican........................ 29
Undecided......................... 42

Interviewing Date 1/2–7/47
Survey #387–T   Question #11b

If General MacArthur does become a candidate which ticket do you think he will run on — the Democratic or Republican?

Democratic........................ 18%
Republican........................ 46
Undecided......................... 36

FEBRUARY 16
UNIVERSAL MILITARY TRAINING

Interviewing Date 1/17–22/47
Survey #388–K   Question #1

In the future, do you think every able-bodied young man should be required to take military or naval training for one year?

Yes............................... 72%
No................................ 23
No opinion........................ 5

By Political Affiliation
Democrats

Yes............................... 73%
No................................ 22
No opinion........................ 5

Republicans

Yes............................... 72%
No................................ 23
No opinion........................ 5

By Region
New England
Yes............................ 73%
No............................. 22
No opinion...................... 5

Middle Atlantic
Yes............................ 70%
No............................. 25
No opinion...................... 5

East Central
Yes............................ 71%
No............................. 23
No opinion...................... 6

West Central
Yes............................ 73%
No............................. 22
No opinion...................... 5

South
Yes............................ 69%
No............................. 26
No opinion...................... 5

West
Yes............................ 75%
No............................. 20
No opinion...................... 5

By Age
21–29 Years
Yes............................ 73%
No............................. 22
No opinion...................... 5

30–49 Years
Yes............................ 71%
No............................. 24
No opinion...................... 5

50 Years and Over
Yes............................ 71%
No............................. 24
No opinion...................... 5

By Education
College
Yes............................ 66%
No............................. 30
No opinion...................... 4

High School
Yes............................ 69%
No............................. 26
No opinion...................... 5

Grade School
Yes............................ 73%
No............................. 21
No opinion...................... 6

FEBRUARY 19
GEORGIA POLITICS

Interviewing Date 2/1–5/47
Survey #389–T   Question #2a

Have you heard or read about the fight in Georgia over who is to be governor?

Yes............................ 84%
No............................. 16

Interviewing Date 2/1–5/47
Survey #389–T   Question #2b

Asked of those responding in the affirmative: What is your opinion about this fight?

Bad, shameful, disgraceful, etc......... 38%
Talmadge is wrong.................. 11
Calls for another election............ 4
Laws should be passed to take care of
   succession...................... 4
Undemocratic...................... 3
Talmadge should wait for court decision. 2
Talmadge is right.................. 2
Miscellaneous replies................ 8
No opinion, paid no attention........ 28

Interviewing Date 2/1–5/47
Survey #389–T   Question #2c

Asked of those responding in the affirmative: Who do you think should be governor of Georgia — Herman Talmadge or M.E. Thompson?

Talmadge......................... 11%
Thompson......................... 49
No opinion....................... 40

By Education
College

Talmadge......................... 8%
Thompson......................... 61
No opinion....................... 31

High School

Talmadge......................... 10%
Thompson......................... 52
No opinion....................... 38

Grade School

Talmadge......................... 13%
Thompson......................... 43
No opinion....................... 44

FEBRUARY 21
JAMES BYRNES AND GEORGE MARSHALL

Interviewing Date 2/1–5/47
Survey #389–K   Question #5a

James Byrnes was Secretary of State for about a year. In dealing with foreign nations do you think that he did an excellent, good, fair, or poor job?

Excellent........................ 21%
Good............................. 36
Fair............................. 17
Poor............................. 6
No opinion....................... 20

By Political Affiliation
Democrats

Excellent........................ 25%
Good............................. 34
Fair............................. 15
Poor............................. 6
No opinion....................... 20

Republicans

Excellent........................ 20%
Good............................. 40
Fair............................. 19
Poor............................. 5
No opinion....................... 16

Interviewing Date 2/1–5/47
Survey #389–K   Question #5b

Do you approve or disapprove of President Truman's appointment of General George Marshall as the new Secretary of State?

Approve.......................... 64%
Disapprove....................... 8
No opinion....................... 28

By Political Affiliation
Democrats

Approve.......................... 63%
Disapprove....................... 8
No opinion....................... 29

Republicans

Approve.......................... 67%
Disapprove....................... 9
No opinion....................... 24

Interviewing Date 2/1–5/47
Survey #389–K   Question #5d

In dealing with Russia do you think that Mr. Marshall should follow Mr. Byrnes' policy, be firmer with Russia than Mr. Byrnes was, or easier?

Follow Byrnes' policy............ 19%
Be firmer........................ 51
Follow easier policy............. 5
No opinion....................... 25

By Political Affiliation
Democrats

Follow Byrnes' policy............ 20%
Be firmer........................ 44
Follow easier policy............. 8
No opinion....................... 28

Republicans

Follow Byrnes' policy............... 20%
Be firmer......................... 59
Follow easier policy.............. 1
No opinion........................ 20

FEBRUARY 22
SENATORIAL TENURE

Interviewing Date 1/17–22/47
Survey #388–K   Question #11a

A United States senator now serves six years in one term of office. Do you think there should be a limit on the number of terms a senator could serve?

Yes.............................. 54%
No............................... 39
No opinion....................... 7

By Political Affiliation
Democrats

Yes.............................. 50%
No............................... 42
No opinion....................... 8

Republicans

Yes.............................. 58%
No............................... 38
No opinion....................... 4

By Age
21–29 Years

Yes.............................. 49%
No............................... 45
No opinion....................... 6

30–49 Years

Yes.............................. 52%
No............................... 41
No opinion....................... 7

50 Years and Over

Yes.............................. 61%
No............................... 33
No opinion....................... 6

By Education
College

Yes.............................. 40%
No............................... 58
No opinion....................... 2

High School

Yes.............................. 55%
No............................... 41
No opinion....................... 4

Grade School

Yes.............................. 58%
No............................... 33
No opinion....................... 9

Interviewing Date 1/17–22/47
Survey #388–K   Question #11b

Asked of those who responded in the affirmative: What do you think the limit should be?

Median average................... 2 terms

FEBRUARY 23
PRESIDENTIAL TENURE

Interviewing Date 2/1–5/47
Survey #389–K   Question #18

Would you favor adding a law to the Constitution to prevent any President of the United States from serving more than two terms?

Favor............................ 57%
Oppose........................... 43

Eight per cent expressed no opinion.

By Political Affiliation

	Favor	Oppose
Democrats	41%	59%
Republicans	74	26

By Region

	Favor	Oppose
New England	54%	46%
Middle Atlantic	54	46
East Central	58	42
West Central	69	31
South	54	46
West	55	45

FEBRUARY 26
VOTING AGE

Interviewing Date 2/1–5/47
Survey #389–K   Question #12

At the present time, American citizens cannot vote until they become 21 years of age. Would you favor changing the law to allow persons 18, 19, and 20 years old to vote?

Yes	35%
No	60
No opinion	5

By Political Affiliation
Democrats

Yes	37%
No	58
No opinion	5

Republicans

Yes	33%
No	63
No opinion	4

By Region
New England and Middle Atlantic

Yes	32%
No	63
No opinion	5

East Central

Yes	38%
No	58
No opinion	4

West Central

Yes	35%
No	61
No opinion	4

South

Yes	37%
No	53
No opinion	10

West

Yes	36%
No	61
No opinion	3

By Age
21–29 Years

Yes	34%
No	62
No opinion	4

30–49 Years

Yes	39%
No	57
No opinion	4

50 Years and Over

Yes	31%
No	63
No opinion	6

By Education
College

Yes	31%
No	66
No opinion	3

High School

Yes	34%
No	62
No opinion	4

Grade School

Yes	37%
No	57
No opinion	6

FEBRUARY 28
TEACHERS' SALARIES

Interviewing Date 2/1–5/47
Survey #389–K   Question #3a

Do you think that school teachers' pay in your community is too high, too low, or about right?

Too high..........................	2%
Too low...........................	64
About right.......................	22
No opinion.......................	12

Interviewing Date 2/1–5/47
Survey #389–K   Question #3b

Asked of those who replied "too low": Would you be willing to pay higher taxes in order to raise teachers' salaries?

Yes..............................	51%
No...............................	11
No opinion.......................	2
	64%

By Education
College

Yes..............................	76%
No...............................	7
No opinion.......................	*
Do not think it too low.............	17

*Less than 1%.

High School

Yes..............................	57%
No...............................	10
No opinion.......................	2
Do not think it too low.............	31

Grade School

Yes..............................	41%
No...............................	13
No opinion.......................	3
Do not think it too low.............	43

MARCH 1
BIRTH CONTROL

Interviewing Date 2/1–5/47
Survey #389–K   Question #4

Would you approve or disapprove of having Government health clinics furnish birth control information to married people who want it in this country?

Approve...........................	64%
Disapprove........................	23
No opinion.......................	13

By Education
College

Approve...........................	76%
Disapprove........................	18
No opinion.......................	6

High School

Approve...........................	70%
Disapprove........................	19
No opinion.......................	11

Grade School

Approve...........................	57%
Disapprove........................	26
No opinion.......................	17

By Age
Under 50 Years

Approve...........................	73%
Disapprove........................	17
No opinion.......................	10

Over 50 Years

Approve...........................	49%
Disapprove........................	32
No opinion.......................	19

MARCH 2
REPUBLICAN PRESIDENTIAL CANDIDATES

Interviewing Date 2/1–5/47
Survey #389–K   Question #9

Asked of Republicans: If you had to decide

today, who would be your choice for President in 1948?

Dewey	45%
Stassen	18
Taft	8
Vandenberg	8
Bricker	6
Eisenhower	6
MacArthur	3
Warren	3
Others	3

Twenty percent expressed no opinion.

MARCH 5
PARTY STRENGTH

Interviewing Date 2/1–5/47
Survey #389–K   Question #10

If the presidential election were being held today, which party would you vote for — the Democratic or the Republican?

Democratic	51%
Republican	49

MARCH 7
GOVERNMENT SPENDING

Interviewing Date 2/14–19/47
Survey #390–K   Question #12a

Do you think the United States Government can cut its spending without doing away with activities that you think are necessary?

Yes	62%
No	21
No opinion	17

By Political Affiliation
Democrats

Yes	52%
No	29
No opinion	19

Republicans

Yes	72%
No	19
No opinion	9

By Education
College

Yes	76%
No	19
No opinion	5

High School

Yes	65%
No	23
No opinion	12

Grade School

Yes	56%
No	20
No opinion	24

MARCH 8
SPANKING OF CHILDREN

Interviewing Date 8/30–9/4/46
Survey #377–K   Question #20a

Asked of parents: Do you approve or disapprove of spanking children?

Approve	74%
Disapprove	24
No opinion	2

Fathers Only

Approve	73%
Disapprove	24
No opinion	3

Mothers Only

Approve	76%
Disapprove	22
No opinion	2

Parents Who Were Spanked as Children

Approve	81%
Disapprove	17
No opinion	2

Parents Who Were Not Spanked as Children

Approve........................... 38%
Disapprove........................ 58
No opinion........................ 4

Interviewing Date 8/30–9/4/46
Survey #377–K   Question #20c

Asked of parents: Were you spanked as a child?

Yes.............................. 84%
No............................... 15
No answer........................ 1

Interviewing Date 8/30–9/4/46
Survey #377–K   Question #20d

Asked of parents: Do you think teachers in grade schools should have the right to spank children at school?

Yes.............................. 38%
No............................... 59
No opinion....................... 3

Fathers Only

Yes.............................. 43%
No............................... 54
No opinion....................... 3

Mothers Only

Yes.............................. 34%
No............................... 63
No opinion....................... 3

Parents Who Were Spanked as Children

Yes.............................. 41%
No............................... 56
No opinion....................... 3

Parents Who Were Not Spanked as Children

Yes.............................. 20%
No............................... 77
No opinion....................... 3

MARCH 9
MOST ADMIRED PERSON

Interviewing Date 2/14–19/47
Survey #390–K   Question #5

What person living today in any part of the world do you admire most?

The following are listed according to frequency of mention:

Douglas MacArthur
Dwight Eisenhower
Winston Churchill
Harry Truman
George Marshall
Mrs. Franklin Roosevelt
James Byrnes
Pope Pius XII
Sister Kenny
Thomas Dewey

MARCH 14
INCOME TAXES

Interviewing Date 2/14–19/47
Survey #390–T   Question #7a

For purposes of income taxes, in eight states a man and wife can divide their income equally between themselves to reduce their income tax. Should married couples in the other 40 states be allowed to do the same thing?

Yes.............................. 74%
No............................... 10
No opinion....................... 16

By Political Affiliation
Democrats

Yes.............................. 72%
No............................... 10
No opinion....................... 18

Republicans

Yes.............................. 77%
No............................... 9
No opinion....................... 14

MARCH 15
GRACE BEFORE MEALS

Interviewing Date 2/14–19/47
Survey #390–K   Question #6b

At your family meals at home, does anyone say grace or give thanks to God aloud before meals?

Yes................................ 43%
No................................. 57

Interviewing Date 2/14–19/47
Survey #390–K   Question #6c

When you were a child, did your family say grace or pray at the table?

Yes................................ 59%
No................................. 41

MARCH 16
PRESIDENTIAL SUCCESSION

Interviewing Date 2/14–19/47
Survey #390–K   Question #11a

If anything should happen to President Truman, do you know who would become President?

Correct............................ 46%
Don't know or incorrect............. 54

Interviewing Date 2/14–19/47
Survey #390–K   Question #11b

Asked of those who gave a correct reply: President Truman has suggested that the Speaker of the House of Representatives instead of the Secretary of State should become President if the President and Vice President both die. Would you favor or oppose this change?

Favor............................. 41%
Oppose............................ 44
No opinion........................ 15

By Political Affiliation
Democrats

Favor............................. 38%
Oppose............................ 46
No opinion........................ 16

Republicans

Favor............................. 44%
Oppose............................ 43
No opinion........................ 13

By Age
21–29 Years

Favor............................. 30%
Oppose............................ 55
No opinion........................ 15

30–49 Years

Favor............................. 40%
Oppose............................ 45
No opinion........................ 15

50 Years and Over

Favor............................. 50%
Oppose............................ 36
No opinion........................ 14

MARCH 19
DAVID LILIENTHAL

Interviewing Date 2/28–3/4/47
Survey #391–K   Question #2a

Have you heard or read about the appointment of David Lilienthal to head the Atomic Energy Commission?

Yes................................ 73%
No................................. 27

Interviewing Date 2/28–3/4/47
Survey #391–K   Question #2c

Asked of those who responded in the affirmative: Do you think the United States Senate should or should not approve Mr. Lilienthal's appointment?

Should.............................. 47%
Should not........................... 18
No opinion........................... 35

By Political Affiliation
Democrats

Should.............................. 59%
Should not........................... 9
No opinion........................... 32

Republicans

Should.............................. 37%
Should not........................... 27
No opinion........................... 36

By Education
College

Should.............................. 57%
Should not........................... 20
No opinion........................... 23

High School

Should.............................. 45%
Should not........................... 18
No opinion........................... 37

Grade School

Should.............................. 44%
Should not........................... 16
No opinion........................... 40

MARCH 21
VIEWS OF OTHER NATIONS

Interviewing Date 2/1–5/47
Survey #389–K   Question #1a

Do you believe any nation or nations would like to dominate or run the world?

Yes................................ 65%
No................................. 24
No opinion......................... 11

Interviewing Date 2/1–5/47
Survey #389–K   Question #1b

Asked of those who responded in the affirmative: Which nation do you think would like to dominate the world?

Russia............................. 52%
Germany............................ 10
Great Britain...................... 9
United States...................... 5
Japan.............................. 3
Others............................. 2
All big nations.................... 1
No opinion......................... 3
                                  ‾‾‾‾
                                  85%

(Note: table adds to more than 65% as some people named more than one nation.)

MARCH 22
FOOD CONDITIONS IN GERMANY

Interviewing Date 2/28–3/4/47
Survey #391–K   Question #15a

Have you heard or read about Herbert Hoover's report to President Truman on food conditions in Germany?

Yes, have heard.................... 67%
No, have not....................... 33

Interviewing Date 2/28–3/4/47
Survey #391–K   Question #15b

Asked of those who responded in the affirmative: What is your opinion of Mr. Hoover's report?

Favor recommendations.............. 60%
Oppose recommendations............. 30
No opinion......................... 10

MARCH 23
ARMY-NAVY BUDGET

Interviewing Date 2/28–3/4/47
Survey #391–K   Question #10a

Have you heard or read about the arguments in Congress for and against reducing the army-navy budget?

Yes............................... 43%
No............................... 57

Interviewing Date 2/28–3/4/47
Survey #391–K   Question #10b

Asked of those who replied in the affirmative: Do you think Congress should reduce the amount of money that the army and navy have asked for?

Should............................ 34%
Should not........................ 60
No opinion........................ 6

MARCH 26
THE PERFECT MEAL

Interviewing Date 1/2–7/47
Survey #387–K   Question #13a

If cost were no factor and you could have absolutely anything that you wanted to eat, what would you choose for a perfect meal?

Approximately one person in every four polled would start with a drink of some kind. The chief preferences are for some variety of gin cocktail or a plain Manhattan.

Here's the complete menu for the perfect meal:

Fruit or shrimp cocktail
Vegetable soup or chicken broth
Steak
Mashed or French fried potatoes
Peas
Vegetable salad
Rolls and butter
Apple pie a la mode
Coffee

Second choice in meat is roast beef, third choice roast chicken.

MARCH 29
INCOME TAX

Interviewing Date 3/14–19/47
Survey #392–K   Question #1b

Asked of those who filed an income tax return: Do you consider the amount of income tax that you had to pay as too high, too low, or about right?

Too high.......................... 54%
Too low........................... *
About right....................... 40
No opinion........................ 6

By Political Affiliation
Democrats

Too high.......................... 51%
Too low........................... *
About right....................... 43
No opinion........................ 6

Republicans

Too high.......................... 57%
Too low........................... 1
About right....................... 37
No opinion........................ 5

*Less than 1%.

MARCH 30
PRESIDENT TRUMAN'S POPULARITY

Interviewing Date 3/14–19/47
Survey #392–K   Question #6

Do you approve or disapprove of the way Harry Truman is handling his job as President?

Approve........................... 60%
Disapprove........................ 23
No opinion........................ 17

APRIL 4
AID TO GREECE

Interviewing Date 3/14–19/47
Survey #392–K   Question #14c

Have you heard or read about President Truman's program to aid Greece?

Yes............................... 75%
No................................ 25

Interviewing Date 3/14–19/47
Survey #392–K   Question #14d

Asked of those who responded in the affirmative: Do you approve or disapprove of the bill asking for $250 million to aid Greece?

Approve........................... 56%
Disapprove........................ 32
No opinion........................ 12

By Political Affiliation
Democrats

Approve........................... 56%
Disapprove........................ 32
No opinion........................ 12

Republicans

Approve........................... 56%
Disapprove........................ 31
No opinion........................ 13

By Education
College

Approve........................... 65%
Disapprove........................ 26
No opinion........................ 9

High School

Approve........................... 57%
Disapprove........................ 30
No opinion........................ 13

Grade School

Approve........................... 48%
Disapprove........................ 36
No opinion........................ 16

World War II Veterans Only

Approve........................... 57%
Disapprove........................ 36
No opinion........................ 7

APRIL 5
FILIBUSTERS

Interviewing Date 2/14–19/47
Survey #390–K   Question #2a

Can you tell me what the term "filibuster" in Congress means to you?

Correct........................... 48%
Don't know, incorrect.............. 52

Interviewing Date 2/14–19/47
Survey #390–K   Question #2b

Asked of those who gave a correct reply: Do you think Congress should do something about filibusters?

Yes............................... 78%
No................................ 13
No opinion........................ 9

Interviewing Date 2/14–19/47
Survey #390–K   Question #2c

Asked of those who gave a correct reply to the first question: It has been suggested that the Senate change its rules so that a simple majority can call for an end to discussion instead of a two-thirds majority as is now the case. Do you approve or disapprove of this?

Approve........................... 57%
Disapprove........................ 30
No opinion........................ 13

By Political Affiliation
Democrats

Approve........................... 58%
Disapprove........................ 29
No opinion........................ 13

Republicans

Approve........................... 57%
Disapprove........................ 31
No opinion........................ 12

APRIL 7
LABOR STRIKES

Interviewing Date 3/14–19/47
Survey #392–K   Question #13a

Should the people who work for the Government be allowed to go on strike?

Yes............................... 22%
No................................ 69
No opinion........................ 9

Interviewing Date 3/14–19/47
Survey #392–K   Question #13b

Should laws be passed to forbid all strikes in public service industries such as electric, gas, telephone, and local transportation companies?

Yes............................... 58%
No................................ 30
No opinion........................ 12

By Occupation
Professional and Business

Yes............................... 61%
No................................ 32
No opinion........................ 7

White Collar

Yes............................... 59%
No................................ 32
No opinion........................ 9

Manual Workers

Yes............................... 52%
No................................ 33
No opinion........................ 15

Farmers

Yes............................... 67%
No................................ 22
No opinion........................ 11

APRIL 9
PARTY BEST ABLE TO HANDLE ECONOMIC PROBLEMS

Interviewing Date 3/14–19/47
Survey #392–K   Question #8

If hard times come again, would you rather have the Republicans or Democrats in office?

Republicans....................... 30%
Democrats......................... 51
Makes no difference............... 19

Interviewing Date 3/14–19/47
Survey #392–K   Question #7b

As you feel today, which political party — the Democratic or Republican — can better handle the problem of keeping wages high?

Republican........................ 22%
Democratic........................ 54
Makes no difference............... 24

APRIL 11
FAULTS OF EMPLOYERS

Interviewing Date 1/17–22/47
Survey #388–K   Question #3

What do you think are the chief faults of employers in this country?

The following are listed according to frequency of mention:

They lack human understanding of the workers' problems.

They don't pay enough wages but are greedy for profits.

They make work hours too long and production requirements too stiff.

They don't give enough recognition and reward for ability and hard work.

APRIL 12
TIPPING

Interviewing Date 3/14–19/47
Survey #392–K   Question #5a

Do you believe in the practice of tipping?

Yes............................... 49%
No................................ 51

By Sex

	Yes	No
Men....................	48%	52%
Women.................	51	49

By Age

21–29 Years................	66%	34%
30–49 Years................	53	47
50 Years and over..........	34	66

By Occupation

Professional and business.......	45%	55%
White collar.................	59	41
Manual workers..............	52	48
Farmers....................	32	68

Interviewing Date 3/14–19/47
Survey #392–K   Question #5b

As a rule do you tip a waiter or a waitress?

Yes............................... 66%
No................................ 34

APRIL 13
AID TO GREECE AND TURKEY

Interviewing Date 3/28–4/2/47
Survey #393–K   Question #3a

Do you think the problem of aid to Greece and Turkey should be turned over to the United Nations organization?

Yes............................... 63%
No................................ 23
No opinion........................ 14

APRIL 16
DAYLIGHT SAVING TIME

Interviewing Date 2/28–3/4/47
Survey #391–K   Question #7

Which of the following would you prefer: (a) have daylight saving time the year round, (b) have daylight saving time in summer and standard time the rest of the year, (c) have standard time the whole year, including summer?

Year round........................ 15%
In summer only.................... 33
Never............................. 47
No opinion........................ 5

By Community Size
Cities Over 100,000

Year round........................ 22%
In summer only.................... 42
Never............................. 29
No opinion........................ 7

Farm Areas

Year round........................ 7%
In summer only.................... 16
Never............................. 74
No opinion........................ 3

APRIL 18
AMERICAN COMMUNISTS

Interviewing Date 3/28–4/2/47
Survey #393–K   Question #8a

In general do you think most American citizens who belong to the Communist party in this country are loyal to America or to Russia?

Loyal to America.................. 18%
Loyal to Russia................... 61
No opinion........................ 21

Interviewing Date 3/28–4/2/47
Survey #393–K   Question #8c

Should Americans who are members of the Communist party be forbidden to hold civil service jobs or should they have the same rights as others to hold government jobs?

Should be forbidden................. 67%
Should have same rights............. 19
No opinion......................... 14

By Political Affiliation
Democrats

Should be forbidden................. 62%
Should have same rights............. 23
No opinion......................... 15

Republicans

Should be forbidden................. 78%
Should have same rights............. 12
No opinion......................... 10

APRIL 19
COMMUNIST PARTY

Interviewing Date 3/28–4/2/47
Survey #393–K   Question #8b

Do you think membership in the Communist party in this country should be forbidden by law?

Yes................................ 61%
No................................. 26
No opinion......................... 13

Only one segment of the population — those with college educations — think it unwise to ban membership in the Communist party.

APRIL 20
REPUBLICAN PRESIDENTIAL CANDIDATES

Interviewing Date 3/28–4/2/47
Survey #393–K   Question #9

Asked of Republicans: If you had to decide today, who would be your choice for President in 1948?

Dewey............................. 51%
Stassen............................ 15
Vandenberg......................... 10
Taft............................... 7
Bricker............................ 6
Eisenhower......................... 4
Warren............................. 3
MacArthur.......................... 2
Others............................. 2

APRIL 23
DEMOCRATIC PRESIDENTIAL CANDIDATES

Interviewing Date 3/28–4/2/47
Survey #393–K   Question #9a

Asked of Democrats: If you had to decide today, who would be your choice for President in 1948?

Truman............................ 79%
Wallace............................ 9
Eisenhower......................... 5
Byrnes............................. 1
Marshall........................... 1
Others............................. 5

APRIL 25
UNITED NATIONS

Interviewing Date 4/11–16/47
Survey #394–K   Question #1a

Are you satisfied or dissatisfied with the progress that the United Nations organization has made to date?

Satisfied.......................... 26%
Dissatisfied....................... 50
No opinion......................... 24

APRIL 26
PRICES

Interviewing Date 4/11–16/47
Survey #394–K   Question #11a

Do you think that prices, in general, will be higher, lower, or about the same six months from now?

Higher............................ 22%
Lower............................. 46
About same........................ 24
No opinion........................ 8

By Sex
Men

Higher............................ 20%
Lower............................. 51
About same........................ 22
No opinion........................ 7

Women

Higher............................ 24%
Lower............................. 42
About same........................ 25
No opinion........................ 9

By Political Affiliation
Democrats

Higher............................ 24%
Lower............................. 43
About same........................ 24
No opinion........................ 9

Republicans

Higher............................ 18%
Lower............................. 53
About same........................ 24
No opinion........................ 5

By Education
College

Higher............................ 13%
Lower............................. 57
About same........................ 26
No opinion........................ 4

High School

Higher............................ 20%
Lower............................. 48
About same........................ 25
No opinion........................ 7

Grade School

Higher............................ 25%
Lower............................. 43
About same........................ 22
No opinion........................ 10

Interviewing Date 4/11–16/47
Survey #394–K   Question #11b

Why do you think so?

The following are listed in order of frequency of mention:

Reasons for Higher Prices

More strikes will cause prices to go higher.
Manufacturers, enjoying high profits, will oppose any drop.
The tremendous demand will send prices even higher than now.

Reasons for Lower Prices

People will simply stop buying; they can't pay present prices.
Production will ease shortages and bring prices down.

APRIL 27
FUTURE WARS

Interviewing Date 3/28–4/2/47
Survey #393–T   Question #1

Do you think the United States will find itself in another war within, say, the next 25 years?

Yes............................... 73%
No................................ 18
No opinion........................ 9

APRIL 29
TELEPHONE STRIKE

Interviewing Date 4/11–16/47
Survey #394–K   Question #16b

In the current telephone strike are your sympathies on the side of the telephone company or on the side of the workers?

Telephone company.................. 24%
Workers.......................... 48
No opinion....................... 28

Telephone Owners Only

Telephone company.................. 30%
Workers.......................... 41
No opinion....................... 29

Non-Owners Only

Telephone company.................. 17%
Workers.......................... 56
No opinion....................... 27

Interviewing Date 4/11–16/47
Survey #394–K   Question #16d

Should the United States Government require the telephone workers to go back to work while the strike is being settled?

Yes.............................. 57%
No............................... 28
No opinion....................... 15

Telephone Owners Only

Yes.............................. 61%
No............................... 27
No opinion....................... 12

Non-Owners Only

Yes.............................. 51%
No............................... 29
No opinion....................... 20

Interviewing Date 4/11–16/47
Survey #394–K   Question #16e

Asked of telephone owners: If telephone workers receive an increase in wages, do you think your telephone bill will go up?

Yes.............................. 71%
No............................... 17
No opinion....................... 12

MAY 2
ECONOMIC OUTLOOK

Interviewing Date 3/28–4/2/47
Survey #393–K   Question #10a

When you read about a business recession, what does that mean to you?

Correct answer.................... 52%
Incorrect answer.................. 48

Interviewing Date 3/28–4/2/47
Survey #393–K   Question #10b

Asked of those giving a correct answer: Do you think there will be a business recession this year?

Yes.............................. 18%
No............................... 28
No opinion....................... 6
                                 ——
                                 52%

MAY 3
MOST IMPORTANT PERSONAL PROBLEM

Interviewing Date 3/14–19/47
Survey #392–K   Question #4

What is the most important problem that you and your family face today?

The following are listed in order of frequency of mention:

High cost of living
Housing
Personal problems
Jobs
Shortages: food, automobiles, household equipment

MAY 5
DEMOCRACY

Interviewing Date 2/14–19/47
Survey #390–K, #390–T   Question #13a

Do you think there is democracy in the following countries (on card)?

	Yes	No	*No Opin.*
United States	88%	8%	4%
England	48	35	17
France	32	40	28
Holland	28	30	42
Argentina	12	59	29
Poland	9	63	28
Russia	5	83	12
Yugoslavia	4	59	37
Spain	4	72	24

MAY 7
PRESIDENTIAL TENURE

Interviewing Date 3/28–4/2/47
Survey #393–K   Question #4

Would you favor adding a law to the Constitution to prevent any President of the United States from serving more than two terms?

Favor.............................. 59%
Oppose............................ 41

By Political Affiliation

	Favor	*Oppose*
Democrats	43%	57%
Republicans	79	21

MAY 9
PIECEWORK PAYMENT

Special Survey
Interviewing Date 3/28–4/2/47 (U.S. only)
Survey #393–K   Question #12a

Do you agree or disagree that production per man must go up before wages can be increased by factories or industry?

Agree.............................. 53%
Disagree.......................... 33
No opinion........................ 14

Great Britain Only

Agree.............................. 69%
Disagree.......................... 20
No opinion........................ 11

Special Survey
Interviewing Date 3/28–4/2/47 (U.S. only)
Survey #393–K   Question #12b

Do you approve or disapprove of paying for work on a piecework basis?

Approve........................... 59%
Disapprove........................ 28
No opinion........................ 13

Great Britain Only

Approve........................... 50%
Disapprove........................ 30
Qualified approval................ 7
No opinion........................ 13

Special Survey
Interviewing Date 3/28–4/2/47 (U.S. only)
Survey #393–K   Question #12c

Do you agree or disagree that payment on a piecework basis is likely to increase production in most factories?

Agree.............................. 75%
Disagree.......................... 12
No opinion........................ 13

Great Britain Only

Agree.............................. 66%
Disagree.......................... 20
No opinion........................ 14

MAY 10
CHURCH ATTENDANCE

Interviewing Date 3/14–19/47
Survey #392–K   Question #10d

Asked of those who said they belong to a church: Did you, yourself, happen to go to church this last Sunday?

Yes............................ 45%
No............................. 55

By Education

	Yes	No
College.....................	49%	51%
High School.................	45	55
Grade School...............	43	57

By Sex

Men........................	42%	58%
Women.....................	47	53

By Age

21–29 Years................	42%	58%
30–49 Years................	46	54
50 Years and over..........	44	56

By Community Size

Farm areas..................	49%	51%
Under 10,000...............	42	58
10,000–100,000.............	42	58
Over 100,000...............	46	54

Interviewing Date 3/14–19/47
Survey #392–K   Question #10c

Asked of those who said they belong to a church: Have you attended church since last Easter?

Yes............................ 86%
No............................. 14

By Education

	Yes	No
College.....................	91%	9%
High School.................	88	12
Grade School...............	84	16

By Sex

Men........................	84%	16%
Women.....................	88	12

By Age

21–29 Years................	89%	11%
30–49 Years................	88	12
50 Years and over..........	82	18

By Community Size

Farms......................	87%	13%
Under 10,000...............	85	15
10,000–100,000.............	86	14
Over 100,000...............	88	12

MAY 11
REPUBLICAN PRESIDENTIAL CANDIDATES

Interviewing Date 3/28–4/2/47
Survey #393–K   Question #11

Asked of Republicans: Will you tell me frankly what you think of each of these men as Republican presidential material for 1948? Generally speaking is your opinion of them favorable or unfavorable?

Thomas Dewey?

Favorable........................ 74%
Unfavorable...................... 19
Not familiar with................. 3
No opinion....................... 4

Harold Stassen?

Favorable........................ 44%
Unfavorable...................... 21
Not familiar with................. 25
No opinion....................... 10

Arthur Vandenberg?

Favorable........................ 49%
Unfavorable...................... 18
Not familiar with................. 21
No opinion....................... 12

Robert Taft?

Favorable........................ 37%
Unfavorable...................... 37
Not familiar with................. 16
No opinion....................... 10

John Bricker?

Favorable......................... 39%
Unfavorable....................... 27
Not familiar with................. 22
No opinion........................ 12

Earl Warren?

Favorable......................... 31%
Unfavorable....................... 17
Not familiar with................. 38
No opinion........................ 14

Leverett Saltonstall?

Favorable......................... 17%
Unfavorable....................... 16
Not familiar with................. 54
No opinion........................ 13

MAY 14
ROLE OF GOVERNMENT

Interviewing Date 3/28–4/2/47
Survey #393–K   Question #15

Which one of these statements do you most agree with (on card): 1. The most important job for the Government is to make certain that there are good opportunities for each person to get ahead on his own; 2. The most important job for the Government is to guarantee every person a decent and steady job and standard of living?

Make sure opportunities are there..... 50%
Government should guarantee jobs..... 43
No opinion........................ 7

By Political Affiliation
Democrats

Make sure opportunities are there..... 44%
Government should guarantee jobs..... 50
No opinion........................ 6

Republicans

Make sure opportunities are there..... 60%
Government should guarantee jobs..... 35
No opinion........................ 5

By Occupation
Business and Professional

Make sure opportunities are there...... 67%
Government should guarantee jobs..... 28
No opinion........................ 5

White Collar

Make sure opportunities are there..... 57%
Government should guarantee jobs..... 38
No opinion........................ 5

Manual Workers

Make sure opportunities are there..... 37%
Government should guarantee jobs..... 56
No opinion........................ 7

By Sex
Men

Make sure opportunities are there..... 54%
Government should guarantee jobs..... 41
No opinion........................ 5

Women

Make sure opportunities are there..... 46%
Government should guarantee jobs..... 46
No opinion........................ 8

By Education
College

Make sure opportunities are there..... 73%
Government should guarantee jobs..... 24
No opinion........................ 3

High School

Make sure opportunities are there..... 57%
Government should guarantee jobs..... 39
No opinion........................ 4

Grade School

Make sure opportunities are there..... 40%
Government should guarantee jobs..... 51
No opinion........................ 9

By Age
21–29 Years

Make sure opportunities are there..... 48%
Government should guarantee jobs..... 46
No opinion........................ 6

30–49 Years

Make sure opportunities are there..... 51%
Government should guarantee jobs..... 43
No opinion........................ 6

50 Years and Over

Make sure opportunities are there..... 48%
Government should guarantee jobs..... 43
No opinion........................ 9

MAY 16
POLITICAL QUIZ

Interviewing Date 3/14–19/47
Survey #392–K   Question #2a

*Do you happen to know which party — the
Democratic or Republican — has the most
members in the United States House of
Representatives?*

Democratic....................... 10%
Republican (correct)................ 64
Don't know....................... 26

By Education
College

Democratic....................... 6%
Republican (correct)................ 88
Don't know....................... 6

High School

Democratic....................... 9%
Republican (correct)................ 72
Don't know....................... 19

Grade School

Democratic....................... 11%
Republican (correct)................ 53
Don't know....................... 36

By Age
21–29 Years

Democratic....................... 11%
Republican (correct)................ 66
Don't know....................... 23

30–49 Years

Democratic....................... 10%
Republican (correct)................ 64
Don't know....................... 26

50 Years and Over

Democratic....................... 9%
Republican (correct)................ 63
Don't know....................... 28

By Sex
Men

Democratic....................... 9%
Republican (correct)................ 71
Don't know....................... 20

Women

Democratic....................... 11%
Republican (correct)................ 72
Don't know....................... 17

Interviewing Date 3/14–19/47
Survey #392–K   Question #2b

*And do you happen to know which political
party has the most members in the Senate?*

Democratic....................... 9%
Republican (correct)................ 58
No opinion....................... 33

By Education
College

Democratic....................... 9%
Republican (correct)................ 82
No opinion....................... 9

High School

Democratic....................... 9%
Republican (correct)................ 64
No opinion....................... 27

Grade School

Democratic	9%
Republican (correct)	48
No opinion	43

By Age
21–29 Years

Democratic	9%
Republican (correct)	60
No opinion	31

30–49 Years

Democratic	10%
Republican (correct)	57
No opinion	33

50 Years and Over

Democratic	8%
Republican (correct)	58
No opinion	34

By Sex
Men

Democratic	8%
Republican (correct)	66
No opinion	26

Women

Democratic	10%
Republican (correct)	60
No opinion	30

By Sex
Men

Yes	55%
No	41
No opinion	4

Women

Yes	47%
No	49
No opinion	4

By Education
College

Yes	70%
No	26
No opinion	4

High School

Yes	57%
No	39
No opinion	4

Grade School

Yes	42%
No	53
No opinion	5

World War II Veterans Only

Yes	61%
No	36
No opinion	3

MAY 17
ADOLF HITLER

Interviewing Date 4/11–16/47
Survey #394–K   Question #5a

Do you think Adolf Hitler is dead?

Yes	51%
No	45
No opinion	4

MAY 18
ELECTION FORECAST

Interviewing Date 4/11–16/47
Survey #394–K   Question #3

Regardless of how you, yourself, feel, which party do you think will win the presidential election in 1948?

Republican	53%
Democratic	30
No opinion	17

By Political Affiliation
Democrats

Republican.......................... 49%
Democratic......................... 33
No opinion........................ 18

Republicans

Republican.......................... 77%
Democratic......................... 11
No opinion........................ 12

MAY 20
BRITISH POLITICS

Special Survey

Asked in Great Britain: If an election were held today how would you vote?

Labor............................. 44%
Conservative....................... 44
Liberal............................ 10
Other............................. 2

MAY 23
LABOR

Interviewing Date 4/25–30/47
Survey #395–K   Question #3e

If a bill that cuts down labor's power a great deal is passed by Congress, would you like to have President Truman give it his okay or veto it?

President should okay bill........... 46%
President should veto bill............ 38
No opinion........................ 16

By Political Affiliation
Democrats

President should okay bill............ 35%
President should veto bill............ 49
No opinion........................ 16

Republicans

President should okay bill........... 63%
President should veto bill............ 23
No opinion........................ 14

By Occupation
Professional and Business

President should okay bill........... 53%
President should veto bill............ 33
No opinion........................ 14

White Collar

President should okay bill........... 52%
President should veto bill............ 33
No opinion........................ 15

Farmers

President should okay bill........... 53%
President should veto bill............ 33
No opinion........................ 14

Manual Workers

President should okay bill........... 37%
President should veto bill............ 45
No opinion........................ 18

Interviewing Date 4/25–30/47
Survey #395–K   Question #3f

Asked of those who thought the President should approve the bill: Why do you feel this way?

The following are listed according to frequency of mention:

Labor is too powerful today.
Too many strikes are occurring.
Labor has run prices up.

Interviewing Date 4/25–30/47
Survey #395–K   Question #3g

Asked of those who thought the President should veto the bill: Why do you feel this way?

The following are listed according to frequency of mention:

The laboring class needs some power. It has never had a fair chance.

The working class of people need all the help they can get now in order to get along. Management should not have all the power.

MAY 24
IDEAL FAMILY SIZE

Interviewing Date 2/1–5/47
Survey #389–T   Question #11

What do you consider is the ideal size of a family — a husband, and wife, and how many children?

One	1%
Two	26
Three	26
Four	29
More than four	12
No opinion	6

MAY 26
COOPERATION WITH RUSSIA

Interviewing Date 4/25–30/47
Survey #395–K   Question #7

Should the United States continue to try to get Russia to cooperate with us in setting up a world organization or should we go ahead with other nations, such as England and France, and leave out Russia and other nations friendly to her?

Continue cooperate	62%
Leave Russia out	31
No opinion	7

By Political Affiliation
Democrats

Continue cooperate	64%
Leave Russia out	30
No opinion	6

Republicans

Continue cooperate	60%
Leave Russia out	33
No opinion	7

By Education
College

Continue cooperate	74%
Leave Russia out	22
No opinion	4

High School

Continue cooperate	66%
Leave Russia out	28
No opinion	6

Grade School

Continue cooperate	56%
Leave Russia out	35
No opinion	9

World War II Veterans Only

Continue cooperate	67%
Leave Russia out	28
No opinion	5

MAY 28
PERSONAL FINANCES

Interviewing Date 4/25–30/47
Survey #395–K   Question #11a

Are you better off or worse off, financially, than you were a year ago?

Better off	31%
Worse off	31
About same	38

By Sex
Men

Better off	34%
Worse off	30
About same	36

Women

Better off	28%
Worse off	32
About same	40

By Age
21–29 Years

Better off	38%
Worse off	32
About same	30

30–49 Years

Better off	31%
Worse off	33
About same	36

50 Years and Over

Better off	22%
Worse off	30
About same	48

By Occupation
Business and Professional

Better off	36%
Worse off	30
About same	34

White Collar

Better off	35%
Worse off	31
About same	34

Farmers

Better off	36%
Worse off	21
About same	43

Manual Workers

Better off	27%
Worse off	34
About same	39

Union Members Only

Better off	30%
Worse off	35
About same	35

World War II Veterans Only

Better off	44%
Worse off	29
About same	27

MAY 30
SURPLUS REVENUE

Interviewing Date 4/25–30/47
Survey #395–K   Question #12

The United States today has a billion dollars surplus in its running expenses. Should this money be used to reduce income taxes, or should it be used to reduce the national debt?

Cut taxes	38%
Reduce debt	53
No opinion	9

JUNE 2
PRESIDENT TRUMAN'S POPULARITY

Interviewing Date 4/25–30/47
Survey #395–K   Question #6a

Do you approve or disapprove of the way Harry Truman is handling his job as President?

Approve	57%
Disapprove	25
No opinion	18

By Region
New England and Middle Atlantic

Approve	55%
Disapprove	26
No opinion	19

East Central

Approve	50%
Disapprove	30
No opinion	20

West Central

Approve........................... 61%
Disapprove........................ 20
No opinion........................ 19

South

Approve........................... 68%
Disapprove........................ 17
No opinion........................ 15

Mountain and Pacific

Approve........................... 61%
Disapprove........................ 24
No opinion........................ 15

JUNE 4
PERSONAL WEALTH

Interviewing Date 4/25–30/47
Survey #395–K   Question #2a

Do you think it will ever be possible for another American to build up a fortune like Henry Ford?

Yes............................... 49%
No................................ 45
No opinion........................ 6

By Education
College

Yes............................... 47%
No................................ 51
No opinion........................ 2

High School

Yes............................... 55%
No................................ 40
No opinion........................ 5

Grade School

Yes............................... 45%
No................................ 46
No opinion........................ 9

By Age
21–29 Years

Yes............................... 59%
No................................ 36
No opinion........................ 5

30–49 Years

Yes............................... 47%
No................................ 47
No opinion........................ 6

50 Years and Over

Yes............................... 45%
No................................ 48
No opinion........................ 7

By Occupation
Professional and Business

Yes............................... 44%
No................................ 53
No opinion........................ 3

White Collar

Yes............................... 53%
No................................ 41
No opinion........................ 6

Manual Workers

Yes............................... 50%
No................................ 44
No opinion........................ 6

Farmers

Yes............................... 49%
No................................ 44
No opinion........................ 7

Interviewing Date 4/25–30/47
Survey #395–K   Question #2b

If a man makes $1 million a year, how much of it do you think he has to pay in income taxes?

The median average of all guesses is 50%. The actual amount that a man making that much would have to pay is 84%.

JUNE 6
PRICES

Interviewing Date 5/9–14/47
Survey #396–K   Question #12a

Do you blame anyone for present high prices?

Yes............................... 49%
No................................ 41
No opinion........................ 10

Interviewing Date 5/9–14/47
Survey #396–K   Question #12b

Asked of those who said yes: Whom do you blame?

Business and industry................. 16%
Government......................... 15
Labor unions or leaders.............. 10
War................................ 1
Farmers............................ 1
Everyone........................... 7
Miscellaneous...................... 5
                                   ——
                                   55%

(Note: table adds to more than 49% because some persons named more than one factor.)

JUNE 7
TUBERCULOSIS

Interviewing Date 2/28–3/4/47
Survey #391–K   Question #9a

What do you think is the cause of tuberculosis?

Germs............................. 22%
Undernourishment.................. 19
Neglect of health.................. 16
Low vitality....................... 16
Unhealthy living................... 12
Heredity........................... 7
Other causes....................... 13
Don't know......................... 16
                                   ——
                                   121%

(Note: table adds to more than 100% because some persons named more than one cause.)

Interviewing Date 2/28–3/4/47
Survey #391–K   Question #9b

Do you think tuberculosis is catching?

Yes............................... 70%
No................................ 24
No opinion........................ 6

Interviewing Date 2/28–3/4/47
Survey #391–K   Question #9c

Asked of those who thought tuberculosis was catching: How do you think tuberculosis is catching?

Principal answers: contact with people infected, and through germs.

Interviewing Date 2/28–3/4/47
Survey #391–T   Question #9b

Do you think a baby can be born with tuberculosis?

Yes............................... 47%
No................................ 35
No opinion........................ 18

Interviewing Date 2/28–3/4/47
Survey #391–K   Question #9f

Do you think a person who has tuberculosis can get well?

Yes............................... 83%
No................................ 13
No opinion........................ 4

Interviewing Date 2/28–3/4/47
Survey #391–K   Question #9g

What do you think a person who has tuberculosis should do to get well?

Principal answers: rest in bed, good food, proper medical care, go to sanitorium, fresh air, dry climate.

Interviewing Date 2/28–3/4/47
Survey #391–T   Question #9d

Have you ever had an X-ray taken of your chest?

Yes................................. 42%
No.................................. 58

JUNE 8
PRESIDENTIAL VETO

Interviewing Date 5/9–14/47
Survey #396–K   Question #2a

Will you tell me what the term "veto" means to you? For example, what does it mean when the President vetoes a bill sent him by Congress?

Correct answers.................... 80%
Incorrect, don't know............... 20

Interviewing Date 5/9–14/47
Survey #396–K   Question #2d

Asked of those who gave a correct answer: At the present time, when Congress passes a bill, the President cannot veto parts of that bill, but must accept it in full or veto it. Do you think this should be changed so that the President can veto some items in a bill without vetoing the entire bill?

Yes................................. 49%
No.................................. 21
Don't know.......................... 10
                                    ————
                                    80%

Interviewing Date 5/9–14/47
Survey #396–K   Question #2c

Asked of those who gave a correct answer to the first question: If the President vetoes a bill, can Congress override his veto?

Yes................................. 70%
No.................................. 4
Don't know.......................... 6
                                    ————
                                    80%

Interviewing Date 5/9–14/47
Survey #396–K   Question #2b

Asked of those who gave a correct answer to the first question: How much of a majority is required for the Senate and House to override a presidential veto?

Correct answer (⅔ majority)......... 44%
Incorrect, don't know............... 56

JUNE 11
INFORMATION PROGRAM
FOR RUSSIA

Interviewing Date 5/23–28/47
Survey #397–K   Question #15a

Do you think our Government should spend money for radio broadcasts to the Russian people — giving them an honest picture of America and of our Government's policies?

Yes................................. 43%
No.................................. 46
No opinion.......................... 11

By Education
College

Yes................................. 62%
No.................................. 34
No opinion.......................... 4

High School

Yes................................. 48%
No.................................. 43
No opinion.......................... 9

Grade School

Yes................................. 35%
No.................................. 51
No opinion.......................... 14

JUNE 13
UNIVERSAL MILITARY TRAINING

Interviewing Date 5/23–28/47
Survey #397–K   Question #16

In the future, do you think every physically fit young man (who has not already been in the armed forces) should be required to take military or naval training for one year?

Yes.............................. 74%
No.............................. 21
No opinion....................... 5

By Political Affiliation
Democrats

Yes.............................. 77%
No.............................. 18
No opinion....................... 5

Republicans

Yes.............................. 71%
No.............................. 24
No opinion....................... 5

By Age
21–29 Years

Yes.............................. 74%
No.............................. 23
No opinion....................... 3

30–49 Years

Yes.............................. 75%
No.............................. 21
No opinion....................... 4

50 Years and Over

Yes.............................. 73%
No.............................. 20
No opinion....................... 7

By Education
College

Yes.............................. 70%
No.............................. 26
No opinion....................... 4

High School

Yes.............................. 73%
No.............................. 24
No opinion....................... 3

Grade School

Yes.............................. 76%
No.............................. 18
No opinion....................... 6

By Sex
Men

Yes.............................. 73%
No.............................. 22
No opinion....................... 5

Women

Yes.............................. 75%
No.............................. 20
No opinion....................... 5

World War II Veterans Only

Yes.............................. 76%
No.............................. 21
No opinion....................... 3

JUNE 14
MINIMUM WAGE

Interviewing Date 5/23–28/47
Survey #397–K   Question #12b

At the present time, the minimum wage that can be paid to workers in every state in most businesses and industries is 40 cents an hour. This means that all persons working in such businesses, in every state, including young people who have never worked before, cannot be paid less than 40 cents an hour. Would you approve or disapprove of raising this minimum to 65 cents an hour?

Approve.......................... 71%
Disapprove....................... 24
No opinion....................... 5

By Occupation
Professional and Business

Approve.......................... 60%
Disapprove....................... 35
No opinion....................... 5

White Collar

Approve............................ 71%
Disapprove........................ 25
No opinion........................ 4

Manual Workers

Approve............................ 85%
Disapprove........................ 12
No opinion........................ 3

Farmers

Approve............................ 50%
Disapprove........................ 40
No opinion........................ 10

JUNE 15
DEMOCRATIC PRESIDENTIAL CANDIDATES

Interviewing Date 5/23–28/47
Survey #397–K   Question #10

Asked of Democrats: Will you tell me frankly what you think of each of these men as Democratic presidential material for 1948? Generally speaking, is your opinion favorable or unfavorable?

Harry Truman?

Favorable......................... 71%
Unfavorable....................... 24
No opinion........................ 5

George Marshall?

Favorable......................... 46%
Unfavorable....................... 31
Not familiar with................. 13
No opinion........................ 10

James Byrnes?

Favorable......................... 43%
Unfavorable....................... 25
Not familiar with................. 20
No opinion........................ 12

James Farley?

Favorable......................... 23%
Unfavorable....................... 49
Not familiar with................. 15
No opinion........................ 13

Henry Wallace?

Favorable......................... 22%
Unfavorable....................... 63
Not familiar with................. 6
No opinion........................ 9

Alben Barkley?

Favorable......................... 16%
Unfavorable....................... 37
Not familiar with................. 32
No opinion........................ 15

Claude Pepper?

Favorable......................... 16%
Unfavorable....................... 39
Not familiar with................. 29
No opinion........................ 16

Harry Byrd?

Favorable......................... 13%
Unfavorable....................... 26
Not familiar with................. 49
No opinion........................ 12

Lewis Douglas?

Favorable......................... 10%
Unfavorable....................... 17
Not familiar with................. 59
No opinion........................ 14

JUNE 18
PRE-PRESIDENTIAL TRAINING

Interviewing Date 5/23–28/47
Survey #397–K   Question #5

In your opinion, which qualifies a man better for President — serving as governor of a state or serving as a United States senator?

Senator.............................. 41%
Governor............................ 38
Neither.............................. 3
No opinion.......................... 18

By Political Affiliation
Democrats

Senator.............................. 43%
Governor............................ 36
Neither.............................. 3
No opinion.......................... 18

Republicans

Senator.............................. 41%
Governor............................ 40
Neither.............................. 2
No opinion.......................... 17

JUNE 21
EUTHANASIA

Interviewing Date 6/6–11/47
Survey #398–K   Question #12a

When a person has a disease that cannot be cured, do you think doctors should be allowed by law to end the patient's life by some painless means if the patient and his family request it?

Yes.................................. 37%
No................................... 54
No opinion.......................... 9

By Age
21–29 Years

Yes.................................. 46%
No................................... 47
No opinion.......................... 7

30–49 Years

Yes.................................. 36%
No................................... 54
No opinion.......................... 10

50 Years and Over

Yes.................................. 33%
No................................... 58
No opinion.......................... 9

JUNE 22
EMPLOYMENT OUTLOOK

Interviewing Date 5/9–14/47
Survey #396–K   Question #8a

During the next year, do you think there is any chance that you (your husband) will be unemployed?

Yes.................................. 21%
No................................... 63
No opinion.......................... 16

By Occupation
Professional and Business

Yes.................................. 11%
No................................... 83
No opinion.......................... 6

White Collar

Yes.................................. 17%
No................................... 70
No opinion.......................... 13

Manual Workers

Yes.................................. 28%
No................................... 51
No opinion.......................... 21

By Education
College

Yes.................................. 15%
No................................... 82
No opinion.......................... 3

High School

Yes.................................. 18%
No................................... 68
No opinion.......................... 14

Grade School

Yes.............................. 25%
No.............................. 54
No opinion....................... 21

Interviewing Date 5/9–14/47
Survey #396–K   Question #8b

Asked of those who responded in the affirmative: How great a chance is there — very great, fairly great, or only a slight chance?

Very great chance................... 6%
Fairly great chance................. 6
Slight chance....................... 8
No opinion.......................... 1
                                   ―――
                                   21%

JUNE 27
NEWFOUNDLAND

Special Survey

Asked of Canadians: Do you think Canada should invite Newfoundland to become the tenth province, or not?

Should........................... 49%
Should not....................... 16
No opinion....................... 35

JUNE 27
OWNING A BUSINESS

Interviewing Date 6/6–11/47
Survey #398–K   Question #11

If you could have your choice, would you prefer to own your own business (or have your husband own his) and assume all the risks — or would you prefer to work for someone else and let that person assume all the risks?

Own business..................... 68%
Work for someone else............. 24
No opinion....................... 8

By Occupation
Professional and Business

Own business..................... 81%
Work for someone else............. 14
No opinion....................... 5

Farmers

Own business..................... 80%
Work for someone else............. 13
No opinion....................... 7

White Collar

Own business..................... 63%
Work for someone else............. 30
No opinion....................... 7

Manual Workers

Own business..................... 61%
Work for someone else............. 31
No opinion....................... 8

JUNE 28
MENTAL RECALL

Interviewing Date 6/6–11/47
Survey #398–K   Question #6b

Offhand, can you tell me the exact license number of your car?

Yes.............................. 32%
Not sure......................... 20
No.............................. 48

Among men, 37% say they know the number, while the rest don't know or aren't sure. Among women, only 24% know.

JUNE 29
THIRD PARTY STRENGTH

Interviewing Date 6/6–11/47
Survey #398–K   Question #7a

If Henry Wallace starts a new liberal political party, do you think you would vote for the presidential candidate of that party in the next election?

Yes............................... 13%
No................................ 68
No opinion........................ 19

A Wallace party would draw its strength more from labor union members than from any other major group. Among union members polled, 22% say they would be for such a party.

JULY 2
ANTI-LYNCHING LEGISLATION

Interviewing Date 6/6–11/47
Survey #398–K   Question #5c

At present, state governments deal with most crimes committed in their own state. In the case of a lynching, do you think the United States Government should have the right to step in and deal with the crime if the state government doesn't deal with it justly?

Yes.............................. 69%
No.............................. 20
No opinion........................ 11

South Only

Yes.............................. 56%
No................................ 35
No opinion........................ 9

Interviewing Date 6/6–11/47
Survey #398–K   Question #5d

Do you think this would reduce the number of lynchings in the United States or would it make little difference?

Would reduce...................... 60%
Little difference.................. 24
No opinion........................ 16

South Only

Would reduce...................... 48%
Little difference.................. 37
No opinion........................ 15

Interviewing Date 6/6–11/47
Survey #398–K   Question #5a

Have you heard or read about the recent trial for the lynching of a Negro in Greenville, South Carolina, where 31 taxi drivers were accused of the crime?

Yes.............................. 75%
No.............................. 25

Interviewing Date 6/6–11/47
Survey #398–K   Question #5b

Asked of those answering yes to the above question: Do you approve or disapprove of the verdict (aquitted)?

Approve........................... 12%
Disapprove........................ 70
Don't care........................ 3
No opinion........................ 15

South Only

Approve........................... 21%
Disapprove........................ 62
Don't care........................ 2
No opinion........................ 15

JULY 3
CLEMENT ATTLEE

Special Survey

Asked in Great Britain: On the whole, do you approve or disapprove of Mr. Attlee as Prime Minister?

Approve........................... 51%
Disapprove........................ 36
No opinion........................ 13

Asked in Great Britain: If an election were held today how would you vote?

Labor............................. 44%
Conservative...................... 44
Liberal, other.................... 12

JULY 5
WOMEN IN PROFESSIONS

Interviewing Date 5/9–14/47
Survey #396–K   Question #14a

*Some churches now permit women to be
ministers. Do you think a woman would
make as good a minister as a man?*

Yes................................. 43%
No................................. 47
Qualified........................... 2
No opinion......................... 8

By Religion
Catholics

Yes................................. 30%
No................................. 58
Qualified........................... 1
No opinion......................... 11

Protestants

Yes................................. 44%
No................................. 48
Qualified........................... 2
No opinion......................... 6

Non-Church Goers

Yes................................. 52%
No................................. 37
Qualified........................... 1
No opinion......................... 10

Interviewing Date 5/9–14/47
Survey #396–K   Question #14b

*What is your feeling about having more
women serve as governors, senators, doctors, lawyers, and in other professions?*

Approve............................ 46%
Qualified........................... 7
Disapprove......................... 41
No opinion......................... 6

More women than men would like to see wom-
en move out of the kitchen to become lawyers, doctors, and politicians. Those who gave
qualified approval think more use should be
made of feminine talents in the professions but
that women shouldn't meddle in politics. The
amount of education a voter has received
evidently affects his opinion on this question:
61% of college graduates approve, compared
with only 38% of those with grammar school
education.

JULY 6
ADULT EDUCATION

Interviewing Date 6/6–11/47
Survey #398–T   Question #8a

*Would you like to attend classes and take
special courses for adults in some school
or college?*

Yes................................. 41%
No................................. 59

Interviewing Date 6/6–11/47
Survey #398–T   Question #8b

*Asked of those who said they would like to
attend: What courses would you like to
take?*

Social science — government, economics,
   psychology, history, etc............. 22%
Professional — nursing, law, research,
   journalism, engineering............. 16
Languages — chiefly Spanish, French,
   English, Russian.................. 16
Commercial — typing, shorthand, book-
   keeping.......................... 14
Homemaking — dressmaking, house-
   keeping, home economics.......... 11
Vocational — trade school, beauticians,
   mechanics, etc.................... 8
Fine arts — music, art, painting....... 8
Technical — radio, navigation, radar,
   designing........................ 5
Physical sciences — physics, chemistry,
   astronomy....................... 2
Religion — theology, religious education 2
Miscellaneous..................... 6
                                 ‾‾‾‾‾
                                 110%

(Note: table adds to more than 100% because some persons named more than one course.)

JULY 12

DEMOCRATIC PRESIDENTIAL CANDIDATES

Interviewing Date 6/20–25/47
Survey #399–K   Question #5

Asked of Democrats: What man would you like see elected President of the country in 1948?

Truman	71%
Wallace	12
Eisenhower	6
Marshall	3
Byrnes	2
Others	6

Twenty-seven per cent expressed no opinion.

JULY 13

PARTY STRENGTH

Interviewing Date 6/20–25/47
Survey #399–K   Question #14

If a presidential election were being held to-day, which party would you vote for, the Democratic or Republican?

Democratic	55%
Republican	45

By Occupation

	Democratic	Republican
Business and professional	43%	57%
White collar	52	48
Farmers	58	42
Manual workers	61	39

By Community Size

Under 10,000	53%	47%
10,000–500,000	52	48
Over 500,000	63	37

JULY 16

REPUBLICAN PRESIDENTIAL CANDIDATES

Interviewing Date 6/20–25/47
Survey #399–K   Question #5

Asked of Republicans: What man would you like to see elected President of the country in 1948?

Dewey	50%
Stassen	15
Taft	9
Vandenberg	9
Warren	4
Eisenhower	4
Bricker	3
MacArthur	3
Others	3

Twenty-three per cent expressed no opinion.

JULY 18

PARTY STRENGTH

Interviewing Date 6/20–25/47
Survey #399–K   Question #14

Asked of Independent voters: If a presidential election were being held today, which party would you vote for — the Democratic or Republican?

Democratic	61%
Republican	39

JULY 19

NATIONAL ANTHEM

Interviewing Date 6/20–25/47
Survey #399–K   Question #13a

Will you tell me the name of the song that is our national anthem?

"Star Spangled Banner"	31%
"God Bless America"	31
"My Country 'tis of Thee"	18
"America the Beautiful"	13
"Columbia"	5
Don't know	2

GEOGRAPHY QUIZ

Interviewing Date 6/20–25/47
Survey #399–K   Question #12

Can you locate the following countries? (Copies of an outline map of Europe were handed to each voter.)

	Correct	Incorrect	Don't Know
England	72%	10%	18%
Italy	72	9	19
France	65	18	17
Spain	53	21	26
Poland	41	34	25
Holland	38	34	28
Greece	33	40	27
Czechoslovakia	25	46	29
Yugoslavia	22	50	28
Hungary	18	51	31
Romania	17	51	32
Bulgaria	13	56	31

JULY 23
MARSHALL PLAN

Interviewing Date 7/4–9/47
Survey #400–K   Question #10a

Have you heard or read about the Marshall Plan for helping Europe?

Yes............................... 49%
No................................ 51

Interviewing Date 7/4–9/47
Survey #400–K   Question #10c

Asked of those who replied in the affirmative: What is your opinion of the plan?

Approve........................... 57%
Disapprove........................ 21
No opinion........................ 22

By Education
College

Approve........................... 67%
Disapprove........................ 17
No opinion........................ 16

High School

Approve........................... 55%
Disapprove........................ 22
No opinion........................ 23

Grade School

Approve........................... 49%
Disapprove........................ 27
No opinion........................ 24

Interviewing Date 7/4–9/47
Survey #400–K   Question #10e

Would you favor or oppose giving European countries credit of about five billion dollars a year so that they could buy the things they need in this country?

Favor............................. 55%
Oppose............................ 35
No opinion........................ 10

Interviewing Date 7/4–9/47
Survey #400–K   Question #10g

Would you be willing to pay more taxes, if necessary, to raise this money?

Yes............................... 41%
No................................ 50
No opinion........................ 9

JULY 25
UNIVERSAL MILITARY TRAINING

Interviewing Date 6/20–25/47
Survey #399–K   Question #2a

In the future, do you think every physically fit young man (who has not already been in the armed forces) should be required to take military or naval training for one year?

Yes............................... 75%
No................................ 18
No opinion........................ 7

By Age
21–29 Years

Yes............................... 75%
No................................ 19
No opinion........................ 6

30–49 Years

Yes............................... 75%
No............................... 18
No opinion....................... 7

50 Years and Over

Yes............................... 74%
No............................... 18
No opinion....................... 8

By Sex
Men

Yes............................... 74%
No............................... 20
No opinion....................... 6

Women

Yes............................... 76%
No............................... 16
No opinion....................... 8

By Education
College

Yes............................... 72%
No............................... 23
No opinion....................... 5

High School

Yes............................... 78%
No............................... 17
No opinion....................... 5

Grade School

Yes............................... 71%
No............................... 17
No opinion....................... 12

By Political Affiliation
Democrats

Yes............................... 76%
No............................... 16
No opinion....................... 8

Republicans

Yes............................... 75%
No............................... 20
No opinion....................... 5

By Region
New England and Middle Atlantic

Yes............................... 74%
No............................... 18
No opinion....................... 8

East Central

Yes............................... 73%
No............................... 20
No opinion....................... 7

West Central

Yes............................... 72%
No............................... 20
No opinion....................... 8

South

Yes............................... 80%
No............................... 14
No opinion....................... 6

West

Yes............................... 73%
No............................... 20
No opinion....................... 7

JULY 28
PRESIDENTIAL TRIAL HEAT

Interviewing Date 7/4–9/47
Survey #400–K   Question #8

If the presidential election were being held today and Thomas Dewey were running for President on the Republican ticket, against Harry Truman on the Democratic ticket, how do you think you would vote?

Truman........................... 51%
Dewey............................ 49

Ten per cent expressed no opinion.

JULY 30
PEACE TERMS FOR GERMANY AND JAPAN

Interviewing Date 6/6–11/47
Survey #398–T   Question #9a

Some people say that if Russia and the United States cannot agree on peace terms for Germany and Japan, the United States should go ahead without Russia and make a separate peace with these two countries. Do you approve or disapprove of this idea?

Yes............................. 56%
No.............................. 25
No opinion...................... 19

By Education
College

Yes............................. 53%
No.............................. 35
No opinion...................... 12

High School

Yes............................. 55%
No.............................. 30
No opinion...................... 15

Grade School

Yes............................. 58%
No.............................. 19
No opinion...................... 23

By Political Affiliation
Democrats

Yes............................. 54%
No.............................. 27
No opinion...................... 19

Republicans

Yes............................. 61%
No.............................. 21
No opinion...................... 18

JULY 31
MARSHALL PLAN

Interviewing Date 7/4–9/47
Survey #400–K   Question #10d

If Russia will not agree to the Marshall Plan, do you think the other European nations should go ahead on the plan without Russia?

Yes............................. 82%
No.............................. 7
No opinion...................... 11

AUGUST 1
TEACHERS' SALARIES

Interviewing Date 6/6–11/47
Survey #398–K   Question #4a

It has been suggested that the lowest yearly wage that could be paid to any teacher in a public grade or high school anywhere in the United States should be $2400 a year — that is, $200 a month. Do you agree or disagree with this idea?

Agree........................... 74%
Disagree........................ 20
No opinion...................... 6

AUGUST 2
THOUSAND-DOLLAR GIFT

Interviewing Date 5/23–28/47
Survey #397–K   Question #1

If someone made you a gift of $1,000 tomorrow, what would you do with it?

Save it, put in the bank, invest it...... 31%
Buy home, pay on mortgage, repair house................... 24
Buy car, furniture, home appliances, clothes......................... 14
Pay bills........................... 8
Travel.............................. 6
Go into business, add it to my business.. 6

Buy presents, give to charities 5
Spend it, have a good time 3
Save it for education, use it for education 2
Use it for every day expenses 2
Miscellaneous 2
Don't know 4
                                              ——
                                             107%

(Note: table adds to more than 100% as some people gave more than one reply.)

AUGUST 3
OUTLOOK FOR WAR

Interviewing Date 7/4–9/47
Survey #400–K   Question #3

Do you think the United States will find itself in another war within, say, the next ten years?

Yes 53%
No 36
No opinion 11

By Age
21–29 Years

Yes 56%
No 36
No opinion 8

30–49 Years

Yes 55%
No 34
No opinion 11

50 Years and Over

Yes 49%
No 39
No opinion 12

Interviewing Date 7/4–9/47
Survey #400–K   Question #3

Do you think the United States will find itself in another war within, say, the next 25 years?

Yes 73%
No 18
No opinion 9

AUGUST 6
WORLD DOMINATION

Interviewing Date 7/4–9/47
Survey #400–K   Question #1a

Do you believe any nation or nations would like to dominate or run the world?

Yes 71%
No 19
No opinion 10

Interviewing Date 7/4–9/47
Survey #400–K   Question #1b

Asked of those who replied in the affirmative: Which country do you think would like to dominate the world?

Russia 78%
Others 22

AUGUST 10
TAFT-HARTLEY LAW

Interviewing Date 7/4–9/47
Survey #400–K   Question #6a

Have you heard or read about the Taft-Hartley Law which deals with labor unions?

Yes 61%
No 39

Interviewing Date 7/4–9/47
Survey #400–K   Question #6b

Those who had heard or read about the Taft-Hartley Law were asked: What is your opinion of this law?

Approve 33%
Disapprove 39
Qualified, no opinion 28

By Political Affiliation

Democrats

Approve............................ 17%
Disapprove........................ 52
Qualified, no opinion............... 31

Republicans

Approve............................ 53%
Disapprove........................ 22
Qualified, no opinion............... 25

Interviewing Date 7/4–9/47
Survey #400–K   Question #6c

Those who had heard or read about the Taft-Hartley Law were asked: Can you recall specific provisions or points in the law that you think are particularly good?

No................................. 75%
Eliminates closed shop.............. 9
Mediation before strikes............ 8
Outlaws jurisdictional strikes.......... 4
Accounting of union funds........... 3
Other.............................. 5
                                                  104%

Interviewing Date 7/4–9/47
Survey #400–K   Question #6d

Those who had heard or read about the Taft-Hartley Law were asked: Can you recall specific provisions or points in the law that you think are particularly poor?

No................................. 85%
Eliminates closed shop.............. 6
Curbs right to strike................. 6
Curbs union political rights.......... 3
Other.............................. 2
                                                  102%

(Note: the above two tables add to more than 100% as some people gave more than one answer.)

Interviewing Date 7/4–9/47
Survey #400–K   Question #6h

Those who had heard or read about the Taft-Hartley Law were asked: Do you think the Taft-Hartley Law should be revised, repealed, or left unchanged?

Revised............................ 32%
Repealed........................... 21
Left unchanged..................... 22
No opinion......................... 25

Interviewing Date 7/4–9/47
Survey #400–K   Question #6n

Those who had heard or read about the Taft-Hartley Law were asked: As a result of this law, do you think there will be more strikes during the next three years, or fewer?

More strikes........................ 24%
Same number....................... 8
Fewer strikes....................... 26
No opinion......................... 42

AUGUST 13
CONGRESS

Interviewing Date 7/25–30/47
Survey #401–K   Question #10a

In general, do you think the present Congress has done a good job or a poor job?

Good.............................. 17%
Fair............................... 37
Poor............................... 27
No opinion......................... 19

By Political Affiliation

Democrats

Good.............................. 12%
Fair............................... 35
Poor............................... 34
No opinion......................... 19

Republicans

Good.............................. 24%
Fair............................... 41
Poor............................... 18
No opinion......................... 17

Interviewing Date 7/25–30/47
Survey #401–K
Question #10c

Generally speaking, do you think the present Congress which has been in session since January 5, has done a better job, poorer job, or about the same kind of job as sessions of Congress in recent years?

Better.............................. 18%
Poorer............................ 21
Same.............................. 39
Qualified, no opinion............... 22

Interviewing Date 7/25–30/47
Survey #401–K
Question #11a

Can you remember offhand the name of the United States congressman from your district?

Correct............................ 38%
Incorrect.......................... 9
No answer......................... 53

AUGUST 15
"FLYING SAUCERS"

Interviewing Date 7/25–30/47
Survey #401–K
Question #1a

Have you heard or read about "flying saucers"?

Yes............................... 90%
No............................... 10

Interviewing Date 7/25–30/47
Survey #401–K
Question #1b

Asked of those who answered yes to the first question: What do you think these saucers are?

Optical illusion, imagination......... 29%
A hoax............................ 10
U.S. secret weapon................. 15
Weather forecasting devices.......... 3
Russian secret weapon.............. 1
Airplane searchlights................ 2
Other answers, don't know.......... 42
                                    ——
                                   102%

(Note: table adds to more than 100% because some persons gave more than one explanation.)

AUGUST 16
LABOR UNION MERGER

Interviewing Date 7/25–30/47
Survey #401–K
Question #15a

Asked of union members: Would you like to see the A.F. of L. and the C.I.O. join in one organization?

Yes............................... 55%
No............................... 25
No opinion........................ 20

AUGUST 17
MOST IMPORTANT PROBLEM

Interviewing Date 7/25–30/47
Survey #401–K
Question #2

What do you think is the most important problem facing this country today?

High prices, high cost of living, inflation. 24%
Foreign policy, getting along with other
   nations, helping Europe............. 22
Preventing war, working out a peace.... 21
Strikes and labor problems........... 8
Housing........................... 6
Controlling atom bomb, military pre-
   paredness........................ 3
Communism........................ 1
Future of the UN................... 1
Taxes............................. 1
Miscellaneous...................... 14
                                    ——
                                   101%

(Note: the table adds to more than 100% because some persons named more than one problem.)

AUGUST 20
DISEASES

Interviewing Date 7/25–30/47
Survey #401–K   Question #7b

What disease or illness would you dread having most?

Cancer............................. 57%
Tuberculosis........................ 15
Heart trouble....................... 5
Infantile paralysis.................. 5
Venereal diseases................... 2
Other.............................. 15
No answer, don't know.............. 4
None............................... 2
                                         105%

(Note: the table adds to more than 100% because some persons named more than one disease.)

AUGUST 22
WOMEN IN THE ARMED FORCES

Interviewing Date 7/25–30/47
Survey #401–K   Question #16a

During the last war, women served in the armed forces as members of the Wacs, Waves, Spars, and Marine Woman's Reserve. In peacetime, do you think there should be units in the armed forces in which young women could enlist?

Yes............................... 53%
No................................ 35
No opinion........................ 12

By Sex
Men

Yes............................... 52%
No................................ 36
No opinion........................ 12

Women

Yes............................... 54%
No................................ 34
No opinion........................ 12

There is considerable difference of attitude by age groups. The young women of the country — those under 30 — approve the plan by a larger vote than older women.

AUGUST 23
FOREIGN POLICY INFORMATION

Interviewing Date 7/25–30/47
Survey #401–K   Question #13a

Do you think our Government is giving the people all the important facts about world conditions today, or do you think the Government is holding back on a lot of important information which the people ought to have?

Is giving enough..................... 18%
Is holding back..................... 59
No opinion......................... 23

Interviewing Date 7/25–30/47
Survey #401–K   Question #13c

Asked of those saying the Government is holding back information: Is there anything in particular on which you would like to have more information?

Russia............................. 8%
World conditions................... 4
Marshall Plan...................... 2
Atomic bomb....................... 1
Big three talks.................... 1
Relief shipments................... 1
Miscellaneous..................... 9
Nothing in particular.............. 33
                                         59%

AUGUST 27
DWIGHT EISENHOWER

Interviewing Date 7/25–30/47
Survey #401–K   Question #14b

Do you regard General Eisenhower as a Republican or a Democrat?

Republican......................... 22%
Democrat.......................... 20
Don't know........................ 58

Interviewing Date 7/25–30/47
Survey #401–K   Question #14a

Would you like to see General Eisenhower become a candidate for President in 1948?

Yes............................... 35%
No................................ 48
No opinion........................ 17

By Occupation
Professional and Business
Yes............................... 25%
No................................ 64
No opinion........................ 11

White Collar
Yes............................... 31%
No................................ 54
No opinion........................ 15

Manual Workers
Yes............................... 44%
No................................ 37
No opinion........................ 19

Farmers
Yes............................... 24%
No................................ 54
No opinion........................ 22

AUGUST 29
PRESIDENTIAL SUCCESSION

Interviewing Date 8/8–13/47
Survey #402–K   Question #14

If anything should happen to President Truman, do you know who would be President?

Speaker of the House (correct)....... 22%
Secretary of State.................. 19
Other incorrect replies.............. 8
Don't know........................ 51

By Education
College
Speaker of the House (correct)....... 48%
Secretary of State.................. 28
Other incorrect replies.............. 8
Don't know........................ 16

High School
Speaker of the House (correct)....... 29%
Secretary of State.................. 24
Other incorrect replies.............. 8
Don't know........................ 39

Grade School
Speaker of the House (correct)....... 12%
Secretary of State.................. 13
Other incorrect replies.............. 8
Don't know........................ 67

AUGUST 30
EMPLOYMENT PREFERENCE

Interviewing Date 8/8–13/47
Survey #402–K   Question #12a

Assuming that the pay is the same, would you prefer to work for the United States Government or for a private firm?

Government........................ 41%
Private firm....................... 40
No opinion........................ 19

By Occupation
Professional and Business
Government........................ 33%
Private firm....................... 53
No opinion........................ 14

Farmers
Government........................ 39%
Private firm....................... 47
No opinion........................ 14

White Collar
Government........................ 36%
Private firm....................... 39
No opinion........................ 25

Manual Workers

Government...................... 49%
Private firm...................... 31
No opinion...................... 20

Interviewing Date 8/8–13/47
Survey #402–K   Question #12b

Asked of those who expressed an opinion: Why do you feel this way?

The chief reasons for favoring Government employment are, listed in order of frequency of mention:

The Federal Government is a permanent thing; not so many ups and downs in employment. You don't get laid off every six months while they re-tool.

Government pension plan is good.

Better working conditions; not so much pressure.

The chief reasons for favoring private employment are, listed in order of frequency of mention:

Better opportunity for advancement; in Government work you get in a rut.

Less red tape; too much politics connected with Government jobs.

In a private firm you can use your own initiative and ability; you can be more on your own.

AUGUST 31
LABOR UNIONS

Interviewing Date 7/4–9/47
Survey #400–K   Question #4

In general, do you approve or disapprove of labor unions?

Approve.......................... 64%
Disapprove...................... 25
No opinion...................... 11

Interviewing Date 7/4–9/47
Survey #400–K   Question #5

Should Congress pass a law forbidding strikes in all industries, or should workers have the right to go on strike?

Congress should pass law........... 28%
Workers should have right to strike.... 62
No opinion...................... 10

By Occupation
Business and Professional

Congress should pass law........... 26%
Workers should have right to strike.... 67
No opinion...................... 7

White Collar

Congress should pass law........... 26%
Workers should have right to strike.... 65
No opinion...................... 9

Manual Workers

Congress should pass law........... 26%
Workers should have right to strike.... 65
No opinion...................... 9

Farmers

Congress should pass law........... 40%
Workers should have right to strike.... 47
No opinion...................... 13

SEPTEMBER 2
MARSHALL PLAN

Special Survey

Asked in France: Sixteen European nations are meeting in Paris to discuss the Marshall Plan. The following nations have refused to participate in the discussion — Albania, Bulgaria, Finland, Hungary, Poland, Romania, Czechoslovakia, Russia, and Yugoslavia. Do you think that the Marshall Plan can succeed in spite of this?

Can succeed...................... 46%
Cannot.......................... 22
No opinion...................... 32

Do you believe that France was right or wrong to participate in discussions of the Marshall Plan?

Right........................... 64%
Wrong.......................... 8
No opinion...................... 28

In your opinion is the Marshall Plan any threat to the independence of France?

Yes............................. 23%
No.............................. 38
No opinion...................... 39

In your opinion, by which of the following was the proposal of Mr. Marshall dictated?

The desire of America to intervene in internal affairs of Europe............. 17%
A sincere desire to aid Europe's recovery 18
The need to find external markets to avoid an economic crisis in the U.S.... 47
No opinion...................... 18

Do you believe it is a good thing or a bad thing that Russia refused to participate in discussions of the Marshall Plan?

Good thing...................... 27%
Bad thing....................... 43
No opinion...................... 30

Do you believe Russia was right or wrong in refusing to participate?

Right........................... 18%
Wrong.......................... 47
No opinion...................... 35

SEPTEMBER 3
PARTY STRENGTH

Interviewing Date 7/25–30/47
Survey #401–K   Question #5

Regardless of how you yourself feel, which party do you think will win the presidential election in 1948?

Republican...................... 46%
Democratic...................... 30
No opinion...................... 24

By Political Affiliation
Democrats

Republican...................... 30%
Democratic...................... 46
No opinion...................... 24

Republicans

Republican...................... 70%
Democratic...................... 12
No opinion...................... 18

SEPTEMBER 5
PRICE OUTLOOK

Interviewing Date 8/8–13/47
Survey #402–K   Question #1a

Do you think that prices in general will be higher, lower, or about the same six months from now?

Higher.......................... 41%
Lower........................... 21
About the same.................. 30
No opinion...................... 8

SEPTEMBER 6
FOOD EXPENSES

Interviewing Date 8/8–13/47
Survey #402–K   Question #2a

On the average about how much does your family spend on food, including milk, each week?

$5 or less...................... 3%
$6–$10.......................... 11
$11–$15......................... 21
$16–$20......................... 23
$21–$25......................... 17
Over $25........................ 25

Interviewing Date 8/8–13/47
Survey #402–K   Question #2b

What is the smallest amount of money a family of four (husband, wife, and two children) needs each week to get along on in this community?

By Region

(*Median Average*)

New England and Middle Atlantic...	$45 wk.
East and West Central...........	38 wk.
South.........................	33 wk.
Mountain and Pacific.............	42 wk.

SEPTEMBER 7
WAGE OUTLOOK

Interviewing Date 8/8–13/47
Survey #402–K   Question #3

Do you think wage rates, in general will be higher, lower, or about the same a year from now?

Higher............................	18%
Lower.............................	27
About the same....................	44
No opinion........................	11

Interviewing Date 8/8–13/47
Survey #402–T   Question #3

Do you think wage rates for the business you (your husband) are in will be higher, lower, or about the same a year from now?

Higher...........................	15%
Lower.............................	15
About the same....................	60
No opinion........................	10

Union Members Only

Higher...........................	19%
Lower.............................	10
About the same....................	65
No opinion........................	6

SEPTEMBER 10
PRESIDENTIAL TRIAL HEAT

Interviewing Date 8/29–9/3/47
Survey #403–K–1   Question #14

Asked of union members: What man would you like to see elected President of the United States in 1948?

Harry Truman.....................	28%
Thomas Dewey....................	14
Henry Wallace....................	7
Harold Stassen...................	6
General Dwight Eisenhower..........	4
General Douglas MacArthur.........	2
Arthur Vandenberg.................	2
Earl Warren......................	2
Robert Taft......................	1
Others...........................	8
No choice........................	26

SEPTEMBER 12
LABOR UNION AND
CORPORATION FUNDS

Interviewing Date 8/8–13/47
Survey #402–K   Question #13a

Do you think labor unions should be permitted to spend labor funds to help elect or defeat candidates for political offices?

Yes..............................	17%
No...............................	71
No opinion.......................	12

Union Members Only

Yes..............................	26%
No...............................	64
No opinion.......................	10

Interviewing Date 8/8–13/47
Survey #402–K   Question #13b

Do you think business corporations should be permitted to spend corporation funds to help elect or defeat candidates for political offices?

Yes................................ 16%
No................................ 72
No opinion........................ 12

Union Members Only

Yes................................ 21%
No................................ 68
No opinion........................ 11

SEPTEMBER 13
LOYALTY PURGES

Interviewing Date 8/8–13/47
Survey #402–K   Question #8

If questions of national security are involved, should our Government have the right to fire any employee at any time if his dependability or his loyalty to the United States is questioned — or should every United States Government employee have the right to present his side of the case?

Should have right to fire............. 24%
Should have right to present case...... 68
No opinion........................ 8

By Age
21–29 Years

Should have right to fire............. 19%
Should have right to present case...... 75
No opinion........................ 6

30–49 Years

Should have right to fire............. 23%
Should have right to present case...... 69
No opinion........................ 8

50 Years and Over

Should have right to fire............. 29%
Should have right to present case...... 62
No opinion........................ 9

SEPTEMBER 14
UNITED NATIONS

Interviewing Date 8/8–13/47
Survey #402–K   Question #6a

Are you in favor of the United Nations organization?

Yes................................ 85%
No................................ 6
No opinion........................ 9

Are you satisfied or dissatisfied with the progress made to date by the United Nations organization?

Satisfied........................... 33%
Dissatisfied........................ 51
No opinion........................ 16

Do you think there are any weak points in the United Nations organization?

Yes................................ 56%
No................................ 12
No opinion........................ 32

Asked of those who replied in the affirmative: What are the weak points?

The following are listed in order of frequency of mention:

Veto power
Lack of cooperation and unity
Lack of power to carry out decisions
Difficulty with Russia

What do you think has been the main value of the United Nations up to now?

The following are listed in order of frequency of mention:

Effort to get together and talk things over
Efforts to maintain peace
Laying groundwork for future
Stopping the Dutch-Indonesian war

What do you think should have been achieved by the United Nations to date?

The following are listed in order of frequency of mention:

Settlement of Palestine, Balkan, Greece, and Chinese issues
More harmony among members
Settlement of atomic bomb control
Settlement of differences between Russia and the West

It has been suggested that a world conference be called to work out plans for making the United Nations stronger. Do you approve or disapprove of this idea?

Approve........................... 83%
Disapprove....................... 9
No opinion....................... 8

How important do you think it is that the United States try to make the United Nations a success — very important, fairly important, or not at all important?

Very important.................... 82%
Fairly important.................. 9
Not so important................. 5
No opinion....................... 4

Will you tell me who the chief delegate to the United Nations organization is from each of these countries:

United States?

Warren Austin.................... 11%
Incorrect......................... 24
Don't know....................... 65

Great Britain?

Sir Alexander Cadogan.............. 2%
Incorrect......................... 21
Don't know....................... 77

France?

Alexander Parodi.................. 1%
Others............................ 8
Don't know....................... 91

Russia?

Andrei Gromyko................... 34%
Others............................ 24
Don't know....................... 42

These questions on the United Nations were contained in a single poll.

SEPTEMBER 19
WOMEN'S FASHIONS

Interviewing Date 8/29–9/3/47
Survey #403–K–1   Question #5c

Do you think women should adopt the new longer skirt length — or should they refuse to adopt it and stick to the present shorter length?

Adopt longer skirts................ 31%
Stick to present skirts............ 53
No opinion....................... 16

By Sex
Men

Adopt longer skirts................ 23%
Stick to present skirts............ 55
No opinion....................... 22

Women

Adopt longer skirts................ 39%
Stick to present skirts............ 50
No opinion....................... 11

By Age
21–29 Years

Adopt longer skirts................ 34%
Stick to present skirts............ 55
No opinion....................... 11

30–49 Years

Adopt longer skirts................ 36%
Stick to present skirts............ 53
No opinion....................... 11

50 Years and Over

Adopt longer skirts.................. 48%
Stick to present skirts............... 40
No opinion......................... 12

SEPTEMBER 20
WAR CONTRACTS

Interviewing Date 8/29–9/3/47
Survey #403–K–1   Question #2

Do you think there were any companies who made too much profit on their contracts with the Government during the war?

Yes................................ 73%
No................................. 7
No opinion......................... 20

Interviewing Date 8/29–9/3/47
Survey #403–K–1   Question #3a

Do you think the problem of graft in war contracts was serious enough for Congress to carry on investigations?

Yes................................ 68%
No................................. 15
No opinion......................... 17

Interviewing Date 8/29–9/3/47
Survey #403–K–1   Question #4a

Have you heard or read about the United States Senate Committee which is investigating Howard Hughes?

Yes................................ 76%
No................................. 24

Interviewing Date 8/29–9/3/47
Survey #403–K–1   Question #4b

Asked of those who responded in the affirmative: What is your opinion of the Hughes investigation?

Favorable......................... 25%
Unfavorable....................... 56
No opinion......................... 19

SEPTEMBER 21
PRICES

Interviewing Date 8/29–9/3/47
Survey #403–T–1   Question #1a

Do you blame anyone for present high prices?

Yes................................ 50%
No................................. 36
No opinion......................... 14

Interviewing Date 8/29–9/3/47
Survey #403–T–1   Question #1b

Asked of those responding in the affirmative: Whom do you blame?

Government........................ 17%
Business and industry.............. 14
Labor............................. 9
Everyone.......................... 7
Republicans....................... 2
Farmers........................... 1
Miscellaneous..................... 4
                                 ——
                                 54%

(Note: table adds to more than 50% because some persons named more than one factor.)

Interviewing Date 8/29–9/3/47
Survey #403–K–1   Question #1b

What do you think could be done to bring about lower prices?

Buyers' strike, stop unnecessary buying.. 20%
Return to Government regulation...... 13
Eliminate strikes, reduce wages........ 12
Increase production................. 12
Lower business profits.............. 5
Stop exporting so much............. 3
Business should voluntarily lower prices 2
Change the Administration.......... 2
Everybody should cooperate......... 1
Miscellaneous..................... 7
No way to bring prices down......... 4
Don't know........................ 24
                                 ——
                                 105%

(Note: table adds to more than 100% because persons made more than one suggestion.)

SEPTEMBER 24
GREECE

Interviewing Date 8 /29–9 /3 /47
Survey #403–K–1   Question #9a

As you know the United States is now sending military supplies and other aid to Greece to keep her and neighboring countries from coming under Russia's control. If we find within the next few weeks that this help is not enough, which one of these steps (on card) do you think we should take:

Step 1 — Let Russia control Greece and any other countries she wants to; Step 2 — Let Russia control Greece but plan to stop Russia from getting control of any other countries later on; Step 3 — In cooperation with the United Nations organization, send United States troops to patrol the Greek border to stop armed men from coming into the country to make trouble; or Step 4 — In cooperation with the United Nations, tell Russia that any further move into Greece will be considered a declaration of war against the rest of the world?

Step 1............................. 4%
Step 2............................. 6
Step 3............................. 28
Step 4............................. 40
Other answers..................... 5
No opinion........................ 17

Interviewing Date 8 /29–9 /3 /47
Survey #403–K–1   Question #9b

Some experts say that Russia will have atomic bombs in about a year. If she does, our advantage of being the only country that makes atomic bombs would end one year from now. In view of this, which of the four steps (on card used for first question) do you think we should take now concerning the present situation in Greece?

Step 1............................. 3%
Step 2............................. 4
Step 3............................. 24
Step 4............................. 46
Other answers..................... 4
No opinion........................ 19

SEPTEMBER 26
FUTURE WARS

Interviewing Date 8 /8–13 /47
Survey #402–K   Question #3

Do you think there will or will not be another war within the next 10 years?

Will be............................ 58%
Will not........................... 31
No opinion........................ 11

Interviewing Date 8 /8–13 /47
Survey #402–K   Question #3a

Do you think there will or will not be another war within the next 25 years?

Will be............................ 75%
Will not........................... 16
No opinion........................ 9

SEPTEMBER 27
FRENCH POLITICS

Special Survey

Asked in France: Is the Government in your opinion too far to the right or too far to the left?

Too far right...................... 26%
Too far left....................... 15
Fine as it is...................... 33
No opinion........................ 26

SEPTEMBER 27
THE MEDIA IN GREAT BRITAIN

Special Survey

Asked in Great Britain: What do you rely on most in forming your opinions — maga-

zines, newspapers, books, radio broadcasts, or some other source?

Newspapers............................ 58%
Radio................................. 41
Books................................. 13
Magazines............................. 8
Other................................. 24
                                      ‾‾‾‾
                                      144%

(Note: table adds to more than 100% as some persons gave more than one answer.)

SEPTEMBER 28
PRESIDENTIAL TRIAL HEAT

Interviewing Date 8/29–9/3/47
Survey #403–K–1   Question #16

If the presidential election were being held today, and General Dwight Eisenhower were running for President on the Republican ticket against Harry Truman on the Democratic ticket, how do you think you would vote?

Eisenhower............................ 48%
Truman................................ 39
No opinion............................ 13

OCTOBER 1
TAFT-HARTLEY LAW

Interviewing Date 8/29–9/3/47
Survey #403–K–1   Question #12a

Have you heard or read about the Taft-Hartley Law which deals with labor unions?

Yes................................... 72%
No.................................... 28

Interviewing Date 8/29–9/3/47
Survey #403–K–1   Question #12b

Asked of those who replied in the affirmative: Do you think the Taft-Hartley Law

should be revised, repealed, or left unchanged?

Revised............................... 27%
Repealed.............................. 18
Left unchanged........................ 28
No opinion............................ 27

By Political Affiliation
Democrats

Revised............................... 29%
Repealed.............................. 26
Left unchanged........................ 17
No opinion............................ 28

Republicans

Revised............................... 24%
Repealed.............................. 9
Left unchanged........................ 42
No opinion............................ 25

Interviewing Date 8/29–9/3/47
Survey #403–K–1   Question #12c

Asked of those who replied in the affirmative: The Taft-Hartley Law requires officers of labor unions to swear that they are not Communists before they can take a case before the National Labor Relations Board. Do you think Congress should or should not change this provision?

Should................................ 18%
Should not............................ 64
No opinion............................ 18

OCTOBER 3
WORLD OUTLOOK

Interviewing Date 9/12–17/47
Survey #404–K, T   Question #9

Do you think conditions in general will be better or worse in the coming year than they have been during the last year in the following countries?

	Better	Worse	Same	No Opin.
China............	20%	30%	17%	33%
Italy.............	25	25	14	36
England.........	29	33	13	25
France..........	31	20	16	33
Germany........	37	22	17	24
Japan...........	51	9	12	28

OCTOBER 4
RAISING CHILDREN

Interviewing Date 9/12–17/47
Survey #404–K   Question #5e

Which do you, yourself, think is easier to raise — a boy or a girl?

A boy.............................	42%
A girl..............................	23
Makes no difference..................	24
No opinion.........................	11

Views of Parents Having Boys and Girls

A boy.............................	40%
A girl..............................	22
Makes no difference................	35
No opinion.........................	3

Interviewing Date 9/12–17/47
Survey #404–K   Question #5c

If you had a (another) child, would you rather have a boy or girl?

A boy.............................	40%
A girl.............................	25
Would make no difference............	27
No opinion.........................	8

By Sex
Men

A boy.............................	45%
A girl.............................	19
Would make no difference............	27
No opinion.........................	9

Women

A boy.............................	34%
A girl.............................	32
Would make no difference...........	27
No opinion.......................	7

OCTOBER 5
PRESIDENTIAL TRIAL HEAT

Interviewing Date 9/12–17/47
Survey #404–K   Question #16b

If the presidential election were being held today, and General Douglas MacArthur were running for President on the Republican ticket, against Harry Truman on the Democratic ticket, how do you think you would vote?

Truman..........................	49%
MacArthur........................	37
No opinion.......................	14

By Political Affiliation
Democrats

Truman..........................	73%
MacArthur........................	17
No opinion.......................	10

Republicans

Truman..........................	24%
MacArthur........................	65
No opinion.......................	11

OCTOBER 8
MARSHALL PLAN

Interviewing Date 9/12–17/47
Survey #404–K   Question #10a

Have you heard or read about the Marshall Plan?

Yes...............................	49%
No...............................	51

Interviewing Date 9 /12–17 /47
Survey #404–K   Question #10b

Asked of those who responded in the affirmative: What is your understanding of the purpose of the plan?

About one in five gave an essentially correct definition — that is, a plan for European recovery which supplements self-help on the part of European countries with needed assistance from us.

The rest have a less complete idea, varying from those with a very general notion down to those with only a vague idea or no idea at all what the plan means.

Interviewing Date 9 /12–17 /47
Survey #404–K   Question #10d

Would you favor or oppose lending Western European countries like England, France, Holland, and Norway about 5 billion dollars a year for 3 or 4 years to improve conditions and help get business going in their countries?

Those Best Informed About the Marshall Plan

Favor.............................. 49%
Oppose............................ 34
Qualified.......................... 10
No opinion........................ 7

Those Less Well-Informed About the Marshall Plan

Favor.............................. 40%
Oppose............................ 41
Qualified.......................... 14
No opinion........................ 5

Those with Vague Ideas About the Marshall Plan

Favor.............................. 34%
Oppose............................ 46
Qualified.......................... 13
No opinion........................ 7

Those Who Do Not Know About the Marshall Plan

Favor.............................. 25%
Oppose............................ 54
Qualified.......................... 10
No opinion........................ 11

OCTOBER 10
SCIENCE RESEARCH

Interviewing Date 9 /12–17 /47
Survey #404–K   Question #13a

It has been suggested that the United States spend 2 billion dollars a year for various kinds of scientific and military research. Do you think this is a good idea or a poor idea?

Good idea......................... 76%
Poor.............................. 13
No opinion........................ 11

Interviewing Date 9 /12–17 /47
Survey #404–K   Question #13c

Would you be willing to pay more taxes to make this possible?

Yes............................... 50%
No................................ 38
No opinion........................ 12

By Occupation
Business and Professional

Yes............................... 60%
No................................ 32
No opinion........................ 8

White Collar

Yes............................... 55%
No................................ 36
No opinion........................ 9

Farmers

Yes............................... 54%
No................................ 32
No opinion........................ 14

Manual Workers

Yes................................ 43%
No................................ 42
No opinion........................ 15

OCTOBER 11
WORLD WAR II

Interviewing Date 9/12–17/47
Survey #404–K   Question #8a

Do you think it was a mistake for the United States to enter World War II?

Yes................................ 24%
No................................ 66
No opinion........................ 10

Interviewing Date 9/12–17/47
Survey #404–K   Question #8b

Why do you think it was a mistake (not a mistake)?

The main reasons given by voters approving American intervention are: we had no other choice since we were attacked; we had to defend our country; and we would probably have been dragged in ultimately anyhow.

Those who claim it was a mistake feel: America got nothing out of the war and is no better off; we should stay out of other countries' affairs; and war is too expensive for our economy.

OCTOBER 12
VOTER PHILOSOPHY

Interviewing Date 9/12–17/47
Survey #404–K   Question #4a

Which of these three policies would you like to have President Truman follow: go more to the right, by following more of the views of business and conservative groups; go more to the left, by following more of views of labor and other liberal groups; follow a policy half-way between the two? (on card)

Go more to the right................ 19%
Go more to the left................. 18
Stay middle-of-the-road............. 50
No opinion.......................... 13

OCTOBER 15
GEORGE MARSHALL

Special Survey

Do you think Secretary of State George Marshall has been doing a good or a poor job in handling our relations with Russia?

Good job........................... 63%
Fair job........................... 20
Poor job........................... 2
No opinion......................... 15

OCTOBER 17
FRENCH VIEWS

Special Survey

Asked in France: In your opinion, does the United States or Russia have the advantage in the struggle for influence on an international scale?

United States...................... 50%
Russia............................. 14
No opinion......................... 36

Asked in France: Do you think things are going well or badly in France today?

Well............................... *
Rather well........................ 4%
Rather badly....................... 50
Badly.............................. 43
No opinion......................... 3

*Less than 1%.

Asked in France: In a general way, do you think France is moving toward a more serious and troubled political scene or toward a more peaceful one?

More serious........................ 77%
More peaceful..................... 7
No opinion........................ 16

Asked in France: Do you think that the position of the Communist party has grown stronger or weaker in the past two months?

Weaker........................... 34%
Stronger.......................... 21
No change........................ 24
No opinion........................ 21

OCTOBER 17
DISEASES

Special Survey

Asked in Great Britain: What disease or illness would you dread having most?

Cancer........................... 29%
Tuberculosis...................... 13
Poliomyelitis..................... 11
Rheumatism, arthritis.............. 4
Insanity.......................... 2
Blindness......................... 2
Heart trouble..................... 2
Others........................... 12
None............................. 16
No opinion........................ 9

OCTOBER 18
ATOMIC BOMB

Special Survey

Do you think it was a good thing or a bad thing that the atomic bomb was developed?

Good thing........................ 55%
Bad thing......................... 38
No opinion........................ 7

Should the United States continue to manufacture the atomic bomb?

Should............................ 70%
Should not........................ 26
No opinion........................ 4

OCTOBER 19
POLITICS

Interviewing Date 9/12–17/47
Survey #404–K   Question #16

If a presidential election were being held today, which party would you vote for — the Democratic or Republican?

Democratic........................ 56%
Republican........................ 44

Interviewing Date 9/12–17/47
Survey #404–K   Question #6a

Do you approve or disapprove of the way Harry Truman is handling his job as President?

Approve........................... 55%
Disapprove........................ 29
No opinion........................ 16

Interviewing Date 9/12–17/47
Survey #404–K   Question #2a

What do you consider the most important issue before the country today?

High prices, inflation, high cost of living. 37%
Foreign policy, Russia, danger of war... 30
The food problem.................. 12
Strikes and labor troubles............ 5
Housing........................... 5
Other............................. 14
No opinion........................ 4
                                   ____
                                   107%

(Note: table adds to more than 100% as some people named more than one issue.)

Interviewing Date 8/8–13/47
Survey #402–K   Question #18a

As you feel today, which political party — the Democratic or Republican — do you think serves the interest of the following groups best: white-collar workers (office workers); unskilled workers, such as manual laborers; skilled workers, such as electricians, plumbers, carpenters, etc., business owners and professional people; farmers?

	Dem.	Rep.	No Diff.	No Opin.
Unskilled	63%	10%	11%	16%
Skilled	61	16	14	9
Farmers	52	20	16	12
White collar	28	37	23	12
Business and professional	16	66	9	9

OCTOBER 22
UNITED NATIONS

Interviewing Date 8/29–9/3/47
Survey #403–K   Question #6a

Do you think it would be best for the future of this country if we take an active part in world affairs, or if we stay out of world affairs?

Active part 65%
Stay out 26
No opinion 9

Interviewing Date 8/29–9/3/47
Survey #403–K   Question #6b

Some people say that the United States should pull out of the UN organization if Russia continues to block the will of the majority of member nations. Other people say that the United States should stay in the UN even though Russia continues to block the majority. Which of these ideas do you agree with?

Stay in 73%
Pull out 13
No opinion 14

By Education
College
Stay in 91%
Pull out 7
No opinion 2

High School
Stay in 81%
Pull out 10
No opinion 9

Grade School
Stay in 63%
Pull out 17
No opinion 20

By Occupation
Professional and Business
Stay in 82%
Pull out 10
No opinion 8

White Collar
Stay in 76%
Pull out 13
No opinion 11

Manual Workers
Stay in 67%
Pull out 16
No opinion 17

Farmers
Stay in 75%
Pull out 11
No opinion 14

OCTOBER 25
RATIONING

Interviewing Date 10/3–8/47
Survey #405–T   Question #3c

It has been suggested that in order to get enough food to feed people in Western European countries this winter, this country should go back to food rationing. Do you approve or disapprove of having rationing again to feed people in other nations?

Approve.......................... 22%
Disapprove....................... 68
No opinion....................... 10

OCTOBER 29
RUSSIA

Special Survey

Do you think that in dealing with Russia and other countries the United States is insisting too much on having its own way?

Yes.............................. 12%
No............................... 78
No opinion....................... 10

Do you think the United States is being too soft or too tough in its policy toward Russia?

Too soft.......................... 62%
Too tough........................ 6
About right....................... 24
No opinion....................... 8

OCTOBER 31
RUSSIA

Special Survey

As you hear and read about Russia these days, do you believe Russia is trying to build herself up as the ruling power of the world, or is Russia just building up protection against being attacked in another war?

Ruling power..................... 76%
Protection....................... 18
No opinion....................... 6

Do you think Communists would destroy the Christian religion if they could?

Yes.............................. 72%
No............................... 15
No opinion....................... 13

As you know, very few people are allowed to enter or visit Russia. Why do you think Russia is so secretive?

The following are listed in order of frequency of mention:

She is hiding something, preparing for war, keeping secrets for military and security reasons
She doesn't want the world to know anything about what she's doing; Russians are secretive by nature and always will be
She's afraid to show her poverty and weakness
She doesn't want her people to know about the outside world because they might become discontented.

Which of the following nations, if any, does Russia control today — that is, which of these countries is a satellite of Russia:

Poland?

Yes.............................. 78%
No............................... 5
No opinion....................... 15
                                  98%

Yugoslavia?

Yes.............................. 74%
No............................... 5
No opinion....................... 19
                                  98%

Czechoslovakia?

Yes.............................. 69%
No............................... 8
No opinion....................... 21
                                  98%

Hungary?

Yes.............................. 67%
No............................... 9
No opinion....................... 22
                                  98%

Albania?

Yes................................ 55%
No................................ 12
No opinion........................ 31
                                   ‾‾‾‾
                                   98%

Finland?

Yes................................ 51%
No................................ 27
No opinion........................ 20
                                   ‾‾‾‾
                                   98%

Norway?

Yes................................ 14%
No................................ 53
No opinion........................ 31
                                   ‾‾‾‾
                                   98%

Sweden?

Yes................................ 8%
No................................ 64
No opinion........................ 26
                                   ‾‾‾‾
                                   98%

(Note: the above tables add to 98% because 2% said no country is a satellite of Russia.)

Do you think the split between Russia and the United States will affect the United Nations — that is, will it help it, hurt it, or will it make no difference?

Help.............................. 6%
Hurt.............................. 72
No difference..................... 16
No opinion........................ 6

Do you think that Russia will leave the United Nations?

Yes................................ 42%
No................................ 34
Qualified......................... 5
No opinion........................ 19

NOVEMBER 1
ELECTION DAY AS HOLIDAY

Interviewing Date 9/12–17/47
Survey #404–K   Question #1a

Would you like to see the day on which presidential elections are held (once every four years) declared a national holiday?

Yes................................ 52%
No................................ 33
No opinion........................ 15

Union Members Only

Yes................................ 57%
No................................ 29
No opinion........................ 14

NOVEMBER 2
MARSHALL PLAN

Interviewing Date 10/24–29/47
Survey #406–K   Question #5a

Have you heard or read about the Marshall Plan?

Yes................................ 61%
No................................ 39

By Education

	Yes	No
College...	91%	9%
High School	71	29
Grade School	47	53

Interviewing Date 10/24–29/47
Survey #406–K   Question #5b

Asked of those who had heard or read about the Marshall Plan: What is your opinion of the Plan?

Favorable opinion................. 47%
Unfavorable opinion............... 15
No opinion........................ 38

Those Best-Informed About Marshall Plan

Favor.............................. 75%
Oppose............................. 15
No opinion......................... 10

Those Less Well-Informed About Marshall Plan

Favor.............................. 65%
Oppose............................. 20
No opinion......................... 15

Those with Vague Ideas About Marshall Plan

Favor.............................. 61%
Oppose............................. 20
No opinion......................... 19

Interviewing Date 10/24–29/47
Survey #406–K   Question #5d

   Asked of those who had not heard of the Marshall Plan: Would you favor or oppose lending Western European countries like England, France, Holland, and Norway about 20 billion dollars over the next four years to be spent for goods to be bought in this country?

Yes............................... 26%
No................................ 48
Qualified.......................... 4
No opinion......................... 22

Interviewing Date 10/24–29/47
Survey #406–T   Question #5d

   Asked of those who had not heard of the Marshall Plan: Would you favor or oppose sending Western European countries like England, France, Holland, and Norway about 20 billion dollars worth of goods from this country in order to improve conditions there and keep these countries from going communistic?

Yes............................... 47%
No................................ 33
Qualified.......................... 4
No opinion......................... 16

NOVEMBER 5
BRITISH POLITICS

Special Survey

   Asked of Britons: If there were a general election tomorrow, how would you vote?

Labor............................. 40%
Conservative...................... 44
Liberal........................... 11
Others............................. 5

NOVEMBER 7
"UNITED STATES OF EUROPE"

Interviewing Date 10/3–8/47
Survey #405–K   Question #5a

   Every now and then you hear or read about a "United States of Europe." Will you tell me what the term "United States of Europe" means to you?

Familiar with term................. 49%
Unfamiliar........................ 51

Interviewing Date 10/3–8/47
Survey #405–K   Question #5b

   Asked of those familiar with the term: What do you think of this idea?

Good idea......................... 55%
Qualified......................... 13
Bad idea.......................... 24
No opinion......................... 8

NOVEMBER 8
POLITICAL IDENTIFICATION TEST

Interviewing Date 10/3–8/47
Survey #405–K   Question #6a

   Will you please look over this list of names and tell me which of these people you have heard of? Will you tell me who each one is or what he does?

	Correctly Identifying
Harry Truman	98%
Douglas MacArthur	97
Dwight Eisenhower	95
Thomas Dewey	91
Robert Taft	82
George Marshall	79
Henry Wallace	75
Arthur Vandenberg	65
James Byrnes	58
Claude Pepper	58
James Forrestal	53
Alben Barkley	51
Harold Stassen	50
Earl Warren	41
Joseph Martin	33
Harry Byrd	32

NOVEMBER 9
MAP TEST

Interviewing Date 10/3–8/47
Survey #405–K   Question #10

Will you please identify for me the location of each of the following countries? (on card: an outline map of South America)

	Correct	Incorrect	Don't Know
Brazil	60%	15%	25%
Argentina	49	23	28
Chile	44	25	31
Peru	21	43	36
Bolivia	17	44	39
Paraguay	16	45	39
Ecuador	16	44	40
Colombia	16	44	40

NOVEMBER 12
ARMISTICE HOLIDAYS

Interviewing Date 10/24–29/47
Survey #406–K   Question #2

Do you think the ending of both World Wars, I and II, should be celebrated on November 11 (ending of World War I); should they be celebrated on August 14 (ending of World War II); or should the ending of each war be celebrated on its own date?

Both on Nov. 11	22%
Both on Aug. 14	7
Each on own date	46
Immaterial	13
No opinion	12

NOVEMBER 14
RUSSIA

Interviewing Date 8/29–9/3/47
Survey #403–K   Question #9a

Which one of these four statements do you agree with most? (on card)

It is very important that we make every effort to keep on friendly terms with Russia even if we have to make many concessions to her 6%

It is important that we be on friendly terms with Russia, but we should not make too many concessions to her 50

If Russia wants to be on friendly terms with us, that's all right, but we should not make any special effort to be friendly 18

We will be better off if we have just as little as possible to do with Russia 21

No opinion 5

Interviewing Date 8/29–9/3/47
Survey #403–K   Question #9b

Our scientists think that Russia will be making atomic bombs in a few years. When Russia does have atomic bombs, which one of these four statements do you think you would agree with most? (on card)

It is very important that we make every effort to keep on friendly terms with Russia even if we have to make many concessions to her 7%

It is important that we be on friendly
terms with Russia, but we should not
make too many concessions to her.... 46
If Russia wants to be on friendly terms
with us, that's all right, but we should
not make any special effort to be
friendly........................... 17
We will be better off if we have just as
little as possible to do with Russia.... 25
No opinion......................... 5

NOVEMBER 15
VOLUNTARY FOOD SAVING

Interviewing Date 10/24–29/47
Survey #406–K   Question #3e

*Do you plan to follow the suggestion of
meatless Tuesdays or will this be too difficult for you to follow?*

Plan to follow...................... 38%
Already doing it.................... 22
Too difficult....................... 29
Don't know........................ 11

NOVEMBER 16
INCOME TAXES

Interviewing Date 10/24–29/47
Survey #406–K   Question #4a

*For purposes of income taxes, in 13
states a man and wife can divide their income equally between themselves to reduce
their income tax. Should married couples in
the other states be allowed to do the same?*

Yes............................... 77%
No................................ 6
No opinion......................... 17

By Occupation
Professional and Business

Yes............................... 84%
No................................ 7
No opinion......................... 9

White Collar

Yes............................... 81%
No................................ 7
No opinion......................... 12

Manual Workers

Yes............................... 74%
No................................ 5
No opinion......................... 21

Farmers

Yes............................... 76%
No................................ 6
No opinion......................... 18

NOVEMBER 19
PALESTINE

Interviewing Date 10/24–29/47
Survey #406–K   Question #12c

*The UN has recommended that Palestine
be divided into two states — one for the
Arabs and one for the Jews — and that
150,000 Jews be permitted now to enter the
Jewish state. Do you favor or oppose this
idea?*

Favor............................. 65%
Oppose............................ 10
No opinion......................... 25

Interviewing Date 10/24–29/47
Survey #406–K   Question #13a

*If England pulls her troops out of Palestine
and war breaks out between the Arabs and
the Jews do you think the United States
should send troops to keep the peace or
should this be done by a United Nations
volunteer army?*

United States troops................ 3%
UN army.......................... 65
Neither........................... 18
No opinion......................... 14

Interviewing Date 10/24–29/47
Survey #406–K   Question #13b

If war breaks out between the Arabs and the Jews in Palestine, which side would you sympathize with?

Jews............................... 24%
Arabs.............................. 12
Neither............................ 38
No opinion......................... 26

NOVEMBER 21
FOREIGN INVOLVEMENT

Interviewing Date 10/24–29/47
Survey #406–K   Question #7a

If we lend England and other nations food or money, do you think we should insist on having something to say about the way they run their own affairs, or should we stay out of England's and other countries' affairs?

Have a say......................... 41%
Stay out........................... 48
No opinion......................... 11

NOVEMBER 22
BRITISH PROBLEMS

Special Survey

Asked of Britons: What do you think is the most urgent problem the Government must solve in the next few months?

Food.............................. 38%
Housing........................... 14
Fuel.............................. 10
Overall postwar crisis............. 8
Production........................ 6
Export............................ 4
Prices............................ 3
Foreign policy.................... 3
Miscellaneous..................... 14

Asked of Britons: Which do you think could best tackle this problem, a Labor, a Conservative, or a Liberal Government?

Labor............................. 34%
Conservative...................... 39
Liberal........................... 9
No opinion........................ 18

Asked of Britons: Do you think the power of the House of Lords should be increased, decreased, or left as it is?

Increase power of Lords............ 5%
Decrease power of Lords............ 32
Leave "as is"...................... 45
No opinion......................... 18

NOVEMBER 23
PARTY BEST ABLE TO HANDLE DOMESTIC AND FOREIGN AFFAIRS

Interviewing Date 10/24–29/47
Survey #406–K   Question #10a

As you feel today, which political party — the Democratic or the Republican — do you think can best handle foreign affairs — that is, dealing with Russia and other countries?

Democratic........................ 33%
Republican........................ 28
Makes no difference............... 22
No opinion........................ 17

By Occupation
Professional and Business

Democratic........................ 23%
Republican........................ 42
Makes no difference............... 19
No opinion........................ 16

White Collar

Democratic........................ 36%
Republican........................ 26
Makes no difference............... 22
No opinion........................ 16

Manual Workers

Democratic........................ 36%
Republican........................ 23
Makes no difference............... 24
No opinion........................ 17

Farmers

Democratic........................ 35%
Republican........................ 25
Makes no difference................. 21
No opinion........................ 19

Interviewing Date 10/24–29/47
Survey #406–K   Question #10b

*As you feel today, which political party —
the Democratic or the Republican — do
you think can best handle domestic affairs?*

Democratic........................ 35%
Republican........................ 29
Makes no difference................. 21
No opinion........................ 15

By Occupation
Professional and Business

Democratic........................ 25%
Republican........................ 45
Makes no difference................. 17
No opinion........................ 13

White Collar

Democratic........................ 36%
Republican........................ 30
Makes no difference................. 19
No opinion........................ 15

Manual Workers

Democratic........................ 39%
Republican........................ 23
Makes no difference................. 23
No opinion........................ 15

Farmers

Democratic........................ 36%
Republican........................ 27
Makes no difference................. 21
No opinion........................ 16

NOVEMBER 26
THANKSGIVING

Interviewing Date 11/7–12/47
Survey #407–K   Question #1

*What do you feel most thankful for this
year?*

Good health, and being alive......... 52%
War is over, family is out of the service.. 18
Having family and friends, happy home. 9
Good job......................... 6
A place to live.................... 4
Living in America.................. 4
"Everything"...................... 2
Miscellaneous..................... 16
Nothing.......................... 1
No answer........................ 2
                                 ———
                                 114%

(Note: table adds to more than 100% because
some persons named more than one thing.)

NOVEMBER 28
EUROPE

Interviewing Date 11/7–12/47
Survey #407–K   Question #8a

*Which European country do you regard as
worst off today?*

Germany.......................... 25%
Greece........................... 12
Poland........................... 8
Italy............................ 8
England.......................... 8
France........................... 7
Russia........................... 4
Czechoslovakia.................... 1
Norway........................... 1
Bulgaria......................... 1
Holland.......................... 1
Others........................... 1
"All Europe"...................... 8
No opinion....................... 17
                                 ———
                                 102%

(Note: table adds to more than 100% because some people named more than one
country.)

NOVEMBER 29
HISTORIC EVENTS

Interviewing Date 11/7–12/47
Survey #407–K   Question #15

If you could have been present and seen any one event in the whole history of the United States — which event would you like to have seen?

Signing of the Declaration of Independence........................... 13%
Lincoln delivering his address at Gettysburg............................ 4
Japanese surrender aboard the *Missouri*. 4
Explosion of the atom bomb — Hiroshima........................... 3
End of World War II in Europe........ 2
Landing of the Pilgrims.............. 2
Signing of the Emancipation Proclamation............................ 2
The Constitutional Convention....... 2
Civil War......................... 1
Any of F.D.R's inaugurals........... 1
Miscellaneous..................... 25
Don't know....................... 18
"Couldn't select just one"............ 23

NOVEMBER 30
HOLLYWOOD INVESTIGATIONS

Interviewing Date 11/7–12/47
Survey #407–K   Question #11a

Have you heard or read about the Congressional Committee's investigation of Hollywood?

Yes............................... 80%
No............................... 20

Interviewing Date 11/7–12/47
Survey #407–K   Question #11b

Asked of those who had heard of the investigation: What is your opinion of this investigation — do you approve or disapprove of the way it was handled?

Approve.......................... 37%
Disapprove....................... 36
No opinion....................... 27

Interviewing Date 11/7–12/47
Survey #407–K   Question #11d

Asked of those who had heard of the investigation: Do you think the Hollywood writers who refused to say whether they were members of the Communist party should be punished or not?

Should be......................... 47%
Should not........................ 39
No opinion....................... 14

By Education
College

Should be......................... 34%
Should not........................ 54
No opinion....................... 12

High School

Should be......................... 44%
Should not........................ 43
No opinion....................... 13

Grade School

Should be......................... 53%
Should not........................ 31
No opinion....................... 16

By Occupation
Professional and Business

Should be......................... 41%
Should not........................ 47
No opinion....................... 12

White Collar

Should be......................... 36%
Should not........................ 51
No opinion....................... 13

Manual Workers

Should be......................... 49%
Should not........................ 35
No opinion....................... 16

Farmers

Should be	62%
Should not	23
No opinion	15

DECEMBER 3
PARTY BEST ABLE TO KEEP PRICES DOWN

Interviewing Date 11/7–12/47
Survey #407–K   Question #6a

Which political party — the Democratic or Republican — do you think can best handle the problem of high prices during the next few years?

Democratic	35%
Republican	30
Makes no difference	19
No opinion	16

By Occupation
Professional and Business

Democratic	28%
Republican	39
Makes no difference	23
No opinion	10

White Collar

Democratic	35%
Republican	33
Makes no difference	19
No opinion	13

Manual Workers

Democratic	38%
Republican	26
Makes no difference	18
No opinion	18

Farmers

Democratic	36%
Republican	27
Makes no difference	21
No opinion	16

DECEMBER 5
AMERICAN COMMUNISTS

Interviewing Date 10/24–29/47
Survey #406–K   Question #14c

In general, do you think most American citizens who belong to the Communist party in this country are loyal to America or to Russia?

Loyal to United States	19%
Loyal to Russia	59
No opinion	22

Interviewing Date 10/24–29/47
Survey #406–K   Question #14b

Do you think membership in the Communist party in this country should be forbidden by law?

Yes	62%
No	23
No opinion	15

By Education
College

Yes	46%
No	48
No opinion	6

High School

Yes	63%
No	25
No opinion	12

Grade School

Yes	66%
No	15
No opinion	19

Interviewing Date 10/24–29/47
Survey #406–T   Question #15a

Do you think the communists in this country actually take orders from Moscow?

Yes	62%
No	13
No opinion	25

DECEMBER 6
AMERICAN INDIANS

Interviewing Date 11/7–12/47
Survey #407–K   Question #7b

From what you have heard or read, do you think the United States Government has treated the Indians fairly?

Yes.................................. 44%
No................................... 38
No opinion.......................... 18

Interviewing Date 11/7–12/47
Survey #407–K   Question #7c

Asked of those who thought the Indians have been treated unfairly: How do you think they have been treated unfairly?

Indians don't have full citizenship rights 10%
Segregation on reservations unfair..... 7
Indians given poor land for their reserva-
tions............................. 6
Economic opportunities poor.......... 4
Educational opportunities poor........ 3
Miscellaneous....................... 11
Don't know.......................... 8
                                 ——
                                 49%

(Note: table adds to more than 44% because some people gave more than one answer.)

Interviewing Date 11/7–12/47
Survey #407–K   Question #7d

Do you think Indians should or should not have the right to vote in New Mexico and Arizona?

Should have......................... 80%
Should not.......................... 4
No opinion.......................... 16

DECEMBER 7
MARSHALL PLAN

Interviewing Date 11/7–12/47
Survey #407–K   Question #9a

Have you heard or read about the Marshall Plan?

Yes.................................. 64%
No................................... 36

By Education

	Yes	No
College.....................	90%	10%
High School.................	73	27
Grade School................	52	48

Interviewing Date 11/7–12/47
Survey #407–K   Question #9c

Asked of those who had heard of the Marshall Plan: What is your opinion of the plan?

Favorable opinion................... 56%
Unfavorable opinion................. 17
No opinion.......................... 27

Interviewing Date 11/7–12/47
Survey #407–K   Question #9d

Would you favor or oppose lending Western European countries like England, France, Holland, and Norway about $20 billion over the next four years to be spent for goods to be bought in this country?

Best-Informed Group Only

Favor............................... 50%
Oppose.............................. 28
Qualified........................... 12
No opinion.......................... 10

Less Well-Informed Group Only

Favor............................... 51%
Oppose.............................. 31
Qualified........................... 10
No opinion.......................... 8

Vaguely Informed Group Only

Favor............................... 49%
Oppose.............................. 32
Qualified........................... 10
No opinion.......................... 9

Uninformed Group Only

Favor................................ 44%
Oppose.............................. 38
Qualified........................... 5
No opinion......................... 13

Interviewing Date 11/7–12/47
Survey #407–T   Question #9d

Would you favor or oppose sending Western European countries like England, France, Holland, and Norway about $20 billion worth of goods from this country in order to improve conditions there and to keep these countries from going communistic?

Best-Informed Group Only

Favor................................ 61%
Oppose.............................. 18
Qualified........................... 14
No opinion......................... 7

Less Well-Informed Group Only

Favor................................ 56%
Oppose.............................. 24
Qualified........................... 12
No opinion......................... 8

Vaguely Informed Group Only

Favor................................ 51%
Oppose.............................. 30
Qualified........................... 15
No opinion......................... 4

Uninformed Group Only

Favor................................ 47%
Oppose.............................. 28
Qualified........................... 17
No opinion......................... 8

The above two questions contained a brief description of the Marshall Plan including estimated dollar costs of the plan. One question explained the plan in terms of spending dollars for goods in the United States. The other, put to a separate but comparable cross section of voters, explained it in terms of improving conditions in Europe and keeping European nations from going communist.

DECEMBER 10
PARTY STRENGTH

Special Survey

If a presidential election were held today, which party would you vote for — the Republican or Democratic?

Pennsylvania Only

Democratic......................... 51%
Republican......................... 49

Ohio Only

Democratic......................... 51%
Republican......................... 49

DECEMBER 12
TRADE WITH RUSSIA

Special Survey

Do you happen to know whether the United States Government is now shipping oil, machinery and industrial products to Russia?

Yes, it is.......................... 52%
No, it isn't....................... 48

Would you like to see the United States Government stop shipments of oil, machinery, and industrial products to Russia or should we continue to send these things to Russia?

Stop................................ 71%
Continue........................... 16
Qualified.......................... 6
No opinion......................... 7

DECEMBER 13
CARD PLAYING

Interviewing Date 10/3–8/47
Survey #405–K   Question #4a

Do you play cards regularly, only occasionally, or not at all?

Regularly.......................... 9%
Occasionally...................... 47
Never............................. 44

Interviewing Date 10/3–8/47
Survey #405–K   Question #4b

Asked of those who play regularly or occasionally: What card game do you yourself like best?

By Sex
Men

Bridge............................ 14%
Poker............................. 27
Pinochle.......................... 21
Other games....................... 38

Women

Bridge............................ 30%
Poker.............................. 9
Pinochle.......................... 16
Other games....................... 45

By Education
College

Bridge............................ 45%
Poker............................. 17
Pinochle.......................... 12
Other games....................... 26

High School

Bridge............................ 22%
Poker............................. 18
Pinochle.......................... 20
Other games....................... 40

Grade School

Bridge............................. 9%
Poker............................. 19
Pinochle.......................... 22
Other games....................... 50

By Age
21–29 Years

Bridge............................ 14%
Poker............................. 22
Pinochle.......................... 21
Other games....................... 43

30–49 Years

Bridge............................ 22%
Poker............................. 19
Pinochle.......................... 18
Other games....................... 41

50 Years and Over

Bridge............................ 26%
Poker............................. 13
Pinochle.......................... 18
Other games....................... 43

DECEMBER 17
PARTY STRENGTH

Special Survey

Asked in New York State: If a presidential election were held today, which party would you vote for — the Democratic or the Republican?

Democratic........................ 53%
Republican........................ 47

DECEMBER 19
DRINKING

Interviewing Date 10/3–8/47
Survey #405–K   Question #1b

Do you, yourself, use any alcoholic beverages such as liquor, wine, or beer, or are you a total abstainer?

Drinkers.......................... 63%
Abstainers........................ 37

By Sex

	Drinkers	Abstainers
Men	72%	28%
Women	54	46

By Age

	Drinkers	Abstainers
21–29 Years	72%	28%
30–49 Years	68	32
50 Years and over	51	49

By Region

	Drinkers	Abstainers
New England and Middle Atlantic	73%	27%
East Central	61	39
West Central	56	44
South	45	55
West	67	33

By Community Size

	Drinkers	Abstainers
500,000 and over	76%	24%
100,000–500,000	67	33
10,000–100,000	64	36
Towns under 10,000	59	41
Farm areas	49	51

Interviewing Date 10/3–8/47
Survey #405–K   Question #1c

Do you object to women drinking in public places, such as bars or restaurants?

	Don't Object	Object
Abstainers	84%	16%
Drinkers	38	62

By Age

	Don't Object	Object
21–29 Years	42%	58%
30–49 Years	51	49
50 Years and over	76	24

Interviewing Date 10/3–8/47
Survey #405–K   Question #1d

Has liquor ever been a cause of trouble, in your home?

Yes	15%
No	85

DECEMBER 20
FAMILY BUDGETS

Interviewing Date 11/28–12/3/47
Survey #408–K   Question #9

Compared with last year, are you finding it harder, easier, or about the same to make both ends meet?

Harder	72%
Easier	3
About the same	25

By Occupation
Professional and Business

Harder	70%
Easier	3
About the same	27

White Collar

Harder	76%
Easier	3
About the same	21

Manual Workers

Harder	76%
Easier	2
About the same	22

Farmers

Harder	58%
Easier	4
About the same	38

DECEMBER 21
THE INDEPENDENT VOTE

Interviewing Date 11/7–12/47
Survey #407–K   Question #4a

Asked of Independent voters (22% of the voting population): If a presidential election were being held today, which party would you vote for — the Democratic or the Republican?

Democratic	57%
Republican	43

Interviewing Date 11/7–12/47
Survey #407–K   Question #16

Also asked of Independents: Suppose you had a chance to vote for your favorite candidate for President in 1948. If such an election were being held today, which one of these men would you vote for?

Dwight Eisenhower.................. 18%
Harry Truman...................... 17
Thomas Dewey..................... 13
Harold Stassen.................... 10
George Marshall................... 10
Henry Wallace.................... 10
Douglas MacArthur................ 8
Arthur Vandenberg................ 4
Earl Warren....................... 4
Robert Taft....................... 3
Leverett Saltonstall............... 1
Joseph Martin.................... 1
Others........................... 1

DECEMBER 24
UNITED NATIONS

Special Survey
Interviewing Date 12/12–17/47 (U.S. only)
Survey #409–T   Question #1

Do you think the United Nations should be strengthened to make it a world government with power to control the armed forces of all nations, including the United States?

United States Only

Yes............................... 56%
No............................... 30
No opinion....................... 14

Holland Only

Yes............................... 44%
No............................... 20
No opinion....................... 36

Sweden Only

Yes............................... 47%
No............................... 15
No opinion....................... 38

DECEMBER 24
CHRISTMAS CAROLS

Special Survey

What is your favorite Christmas carol?

The following are listed in order of frequency of mention:

Silent Night, Holy Night
White Christmas
Little Town of Bethlehem
The First Noel
Jingle Bells
O, Come All Ye Faithful
Hark, the Herald Angels Sing
Joy to the World

DECEMBER 26
TARIFF CUTS

Interviewing Date 11/28–12/3/47
Survey #408–K   Question #12a

Have you heard or read about the recent international trade agreement, signed by the United States and 22 nations at Geneva, Switzerland, which lowers tariffs next year on many products?

Yes............................... 34%
No............................... 66

Interviewing Date 11/28–12/3/47
Survey #408–K   Question #12b

Asked of those who replied in the affirmative: Do you favor or oppose this agreement?

Favor............................ 63%
Oppose........................... 12
No opinion....................... 25

By Political Affiliation
Democrats

Favor............................ 64%
Oppose........................... 10
No opinion....................... 26

Republicans

Favor............................ 63%
Oppose........................... 14
No opinion....................... 23

DECEMBER 27
PARTY STRENGTH

Special Survey

Asked in Michigan: If a presidential election were held today, which party would you vote for — the Democratic or the Republican?

Democratic........................ 47%
Republican........................ 53

DECEMBER 29
NEWS AND SPORTS EVENTS

Interviewing Date 12/12–17/47
Survey #409–K   Question #4

Which of the following news events interested you the most (on a card listing 24 top news stories)?

The following are listed in order of frequency of mention:

High cost of living
Russian-American conflict
Marshall Plan
Taft-Hartley Labor Law passage and litigation
Palestine Partition Plan
Investigation of Hollywood communism
John L. Lewis' difficulties with the Government
Princess Elizabeth's wedding
School teachers' strikes
Texas City, Texas, disaster
Hughes-Meyers investigation
Truman food-saving program
Telephone strike
Long skirts
Battle of Georgia governors

Interviewing Date 12/12–17/47
Survey #409–T   Question #4b

Which one of these sports events of 1947 interested you the most (on a card listing 20 top athletic events)?

The following are listed in order of frequency of mention:

"Jersey Joe" Walcott's fight against Joe Louis.
World Series.
Illinois' one-sided victory over U.C.L.A. in Rose Bowl.
Jackie Robinson, first major league Negro baseball player.
New York Giants' new home run record for a season.
Leo Durocher's suspension from baseball.
The Rocky Graziano scandal and his championship victory.
Columbia's defeat of Army eleven.
Babe Didrikson (Mrs. Zaharia) becomes first American to win British women's golf title.
Jet Pilot wins Kentucky Derby in upset.

DECEMBER 31
NEW YEAR RESOLUTIONS

Interviewing Date 12/12–17/47
Survey #409–K   Question #1a

Are you going to make any New Year resolutions?

Yes.............................. 25%
No.............................. 75

Interviewing Date 12/12–17/47
Survey #409–K   Question #1b

Asked of those who plan to make resolutions: What will they be?

The following are listed in order of frequency of mention:

Improve my disposition, be more understanding, control temper.
Improve my character, live better life.
Stop smoking, smoke less.
Save more money.
Stop drinking, drink less.
Be more religious, go to church oftener.
Be more efficient, do a better job.
Take better care of my health.
Take greater part in home life.
Lose (or gain) weight.

1948

JANUARY 2
PARTY STRENGTH

Special Survey

Asked of Illinois voters: If a presidential election were held today, which party would you vote for, the Democratic or Republican?

Democratic........................ 51%
Republican........................ 49

JANUARY 3
PARTY STRENGTH

Special Survey

Asked of California voters: If a presidential election were held today, which party would you vote for — the Democratic or the Republican?

Democratic........................ 53.5%
Republican........................ 46.5

JANUARY 4
PRESIDENTIAL TRIAL HEAT

Interviewing Date 11/28–12/2/47
Survey #408–K   Question #17a

If a presidential election were being held today, and Harry Truman were running for President on the Democratic ticket against Robert Taft on the Republican ticket, how would you vote?

Truman........................... 55%
Taft.............................. 33
No opinion....................... 12

By Region
New England and Middle Atlantic

Truman........................... 52%
Taft.............................. 35
No opinion....................... 13

East Central

Truman........................... 50%
Taft.............................. 40
No opinion....................... 10

West Central

Truman........................... 55%
Taft.............................. 34
No opinion....................... 11

South

Truman........................... 74%
Taft.............................. 16
No opinion....................... 10

West

Truman........................... 60%
Taft.............................. 28
No opinion....................... 12

By Education
College

Truman........................... 55%
Taft.............................. 36
No opinion....................... 9

High School

Truman........................... 57%
Taft.............................. 32
No opinion....................... 11

Grade School

Truman........................... 57%
Taft.............................. 28
No opinion....................... 15

By Occupation
Business and Professional

Truman............................ 48%
Taft............................... 42
No opinion......................... 10

White Collar

Truman............................ 58%
Taft............................... 32
No opinion......................... 10

Farmers

Truman............................ 58%
Taft............................... 31
No opinion......................... 11

Manual Workers

Truman............................ 60%
Taft............................... 27
No opinion......................... 13

Union Members Only

Truman............................ 65%
Taft............................... 22
No opinion......................... 13

JANUARY 7
INCOME TAXES

Interviewing Date 11/28–12/2/47
Survey #408–K   Question #6

At present, some people with large incomes have to pay more than half of their income in income taxes. Do you think an income tax limit should be placed on large incomes so that no one would pay more than half of his income in federal income tax?

Favor............................. 50%
Oppose............................ 38
No opinion......................... 12

JANUARY 9
INCOME TAXES

Interviewing Date 11/28–12/2/47
Survey #408–T   Question #5c

Asked of those households paying federal income tax: Do you consider the amount of income tax which you have to pay as too high, or about right?

Tax Paid	Too High	About Right	No Opin.
Under $50 a year........	48%	42%	10%
$50–149................	56	39	5
$150–249...............	67	28	5
$250–499...............	70	26	4
$500 and over..........	71	25	4

JANUARY 10
RELIGIOUS BELIEFS

Special Survey
Interviewing Date 11/7–12/47 (U.S. Only)
Survey #407–K   Question #2a

Do you, personally, believe in God?

	Yes	No	Don't Know
Brazil.................	96%	3%	1%
Australia..............	95	5	—
Canada.................	95	2	3
United States..........	94	3	3
Norway.................	84	7	9
Finland................	83	5	12
Holland................	80	14	6
Sweden.................	80	8	12
Denmark................	80	9	11
France.................	66	20	14

By Political Affiliation in France

	Yes	No	Don't Know
Communists............	17%	64%	19%
Socialists.............	50	29	21
Union of Left..........	62	18	20
R.P.F. (Gaullists)........	88	5	7
M.R.P.................	92	5	3
P.R.I.................	93	7	—

Interviewing Date 11/7–12/47 (U.S. Only)
Survey #407–K   Question #2c

Do you believe in life after death?

	Yes	No	No Opin.
Canada	78%	9%	13%
Brazil	78	18	4
Norway	71	15	14
Finland	69	11	20
United States	68	13	19
Holland	68	26	6
Australia	63	20	17
France	58	22	20
Denmark	55	27	18
Sweden	49	17	34
Britain	49	27	24

Interviewing Date 11/7–12/47 (U.S. Only)
Survey #407–K   Question #2d

Asked of Americans: How do you imagine life after death?

The principal replies were:

Complete happiness, joy, peace, quiet
Reward for virtue, punishment for sin; heaven or hell
Dreamlike, disembodied, inanimate, spiritual
As described in the Bible

JANUARY 11
PRESIDENTIAL TRIAL HEAT

Interviewing Date 1/2–7/48
Survey #410–K   Question #13a

Asked of New York voters: If a presidential election were being held today, and Harry Truman were running for President on the Democratic ticket against Thomas Dewey on the Republican ticket and against Henry Wallace on a third party ticket, how would you vote?

Truman	39%
Dewey	41
Wallace	14
No opinion	6

Interviewing Date 1/2–7/48
Survey #410–K   Question #13b

Asked of New York voters: If a presidential election were being held today, and Harry Truman were running for President on the Democratic ticket against Dwight Eisenhower on the Republican ticket and against Henry Wallace on a third party ticket, how would you vote?

Truman	29%
Eisenhower	53
Wallace	11
No opinion	7

Interviewing Date 1/2–7/48
Survey #410–K   Question #13c

Asked of New York voters: If a presidential election were being held today, and Harry Truman were running for President on the Democratic ticket against Robert Taft on the Republican ticket and against Henry Wallace on a third party ticket, how would you vote?

Truman	43%
Taft	31
Wallace	16
No opinion	10

JANUARY 14
INCOME TAXES

Interviewing Date 12/12–17/47
Survey #409–K   Question #2a

Some people say we should reduce income taxes now because of the high cost of living. Others say we should not reduce taxes now because we must give food and other aid to Europe and reduce our national debt first. What is your opinion on this — do you think income taxes should or should not be reduced now?

Should	51%
Should not	36
No opinion	13

JANUARY 16
WAGES

Interviewing Date 12/12–17/47
Survey #409–K   Question #5

Some people say workers' wages should be increased again because of today's high prices. Other people say that if wages are raised, prices will go still higher. How do you stand on this — are you for or against increasing the wages of workers?

For.. 31%
Against...................................... 53
Qualified.................................... 7
No opinion.................................. 9

By Education
College

For.. 19%
Against...................................... 70
Qualified, no opinion.................. 11

High School

For.. 27%
Against...................................... 57
Qualified, no opinion.................. 16

Grade School

For.. 38%
Against...................................... 45
Qualified, no opinion.................. 17

By Occupation
Professional and Business

For.. 23%
Against...................................... 65
Qualified, no opinion.................. 12

White Collar

For.. 31%
Against...................................... 50
Qualified, no opinion.................. 19

Farmers

For.. 18%
Against...................................... 66
Qualified, no opinion.................. 16

Manual Workers

For.. 41%
Against...................................... 43
Qualified, no opinion.................. 16

Union Members Only

For.. 45%
Against...................................... 39
Qualified, no opinion.................. 16

JANUARY 17
DOMESTIC ARGUMENTS

Interviewing Date 12/12–17/47
Survey #409–K   Question #16

What do you argue about most with your husband (wife)?

The following are listed according to frequency of mention:

Money
Personal habits
Bringing up children
Lateness
"Where to go, what to do"
Politics
Household chores
Husband's job
In-laws
Everything

JANUARY 19
UNIVERSAL MILITARY TRAINING

Interviewing Date 12/12–17/47
Survey #409–K   Question #3g

Do you think Congress should or should not pass a law to require every able-bodied young man (who has not already been in the armed forces) to take military or naval training for one year?

Should.. 65%
Should not.................................. 24
No opinion.................................. 11

New England and Middle Atlantic

Should............................ 64%
Should not........................ 26
No opinion........................ 10

East Central

Should............................ 65%
Should not........................ 25
No opinion........................ 10

West Central

Should............................ 67%
Should not........................ 24
No opinion........................ 9

South

Should............................ 68%
Should not........................ 16
No opinion........................ 16

West

Should............................ 66%
Should not........................ 22
No opinion........................ 12

By Occupation

Professional and Business

Should............................ 65%
Should not........................ 26
No opinion........................ 9

White Collar

Should............................ 70%
Should not........................ 21
No opinion........................ 9

Farmers

Should............................ 56%
Should not........................ 30
No opinion........................ 14

Manual Workers

Should............................ 69%
Should not........................ 21
No opinion........................ 10

By Education

College

Should............................ 67%
Should not........................ 25
No opinion........................ 8

High School

Should............................ 68%
Should not........................ 23
No opinion........................ 9

Grade School

Should............................ 64%
Should not........................ 24
No opinion........................ 12

Union Members Only

Should............................ 68%
Should not........................ 24
No opinion........................ 8

Veterans Only

Should............................ 73%
Should not........................ 21
No opinion........................ 6

Those with Relative of Draft Age

Should............................ 63%
Should not........................ 26
No opinion........................ 11

Those with No Relative of Draft Age

Should............................ 66%
Should not........................ 23
No opinion........................ 11

Interviewing Date 12/12–17/47
Survey #409–K   Question #3c

What would you say is the strongest (best) reason for universal military training?

Preparedness, protection............. 72%
Good training, good discipline for men.. 17
Show Russia we can't be pushed around. 6
No good arguments in favor.......... 4
Don't know......................... 5
                                   ————
                                   104%

(Note: above table adds to more than 100% as some people gave more than one answer.)

Interviewing Date 12/12–17/47
Survey #409–K   Question #3d

What would you say is the strongest (best) reason against universal military training?

Unfair to interrupt careers and education of young men	18%
Will encourage war, make men warlike.	13
Undemocratic, breeds regimentation, nationalism	7
Hard on parents, young people needed at home	6
Cost too great	4
Not needed, atomic age makes obsolete	3
Miscellaneous	4
No good arguments against	30
Don't know	17
	102%

(Note: table adds to more than 100% as some people gave more than one answer.)

JANUARY 21
PRESIDENTIAL TRIAL HEAT

Interviewing Date 1/2–7/48
Survey #410–K   Question #13a

Asked of labor union members: If a presidential election were being held today, and Harry Truman were running for President on the Democratic ticket against Thomas Dewey on the Republican ticket and against Henry Wallace on a third party ticket, how would you vote?

Truman	45%
Dewey	35
Wallace	10
No opinion	10

Interviewing Date 1/2–7/48
Survey #410–K   Question #13b

Asked of labor union members: If a presidential election were being held today,
and Harry Truman were running for President on the Democratic ticket against Dwight Eisenhower on the Republican ticket and against Henry Wallace on a third party ticket, how would you vote?

Truman	37%
Eisenhower	46
Wallace	8
No opinion	9

Interviewing Date 1/2–7/48
Survey #410–K   Question #13c

Asked of labor union members: If a presidential election were being held today, and Harry Truman were running for President on the Democratic ticket against Robert Taft on the Republican ticket and against Henry Wallace on a third party ticket, how would you vote?

Truman	53%
Taft	23
Wallace	11
No opinion	13

JANUARY 23
PRESIDENTIAL TRIAL HEAT

Interviewing Date 1/2–7/48
Survey #410–K   Question #13a

If a presidential election were being held today, and Harry Truman were running for President on the Democratic ticket against Thomas Dewey on the Republican ticket and against Henry Wallace on a third party ticket, how would you vote?

Truman	46%
Dewey	41
Wallace	7
No opinion	6

Outside South Only

Truman	41%
Dewey	44
Wallace	8
No opinion	7

Interviewing Date 1/2–7/48
Survey #410–K   Question #13b

If a presidential election were being held today, and Harry Truman were running for President on the Democratic ticket against Dwight Eisenhower on the Republican ticket and against Henry Wallace on a third party ticket, how would you vote?

Truman.............................. 40%
Eisenhower......................... 47
Wallace............................. 6
No opinion......................... 7

Outside South Only

Truman.............................. 36%
Eisenhower......................... 50
Wallace............................. 6
No opinion......................... 8

Interviewing Date 1/2–7/48
Survey #410–K   Question #13c

If a presidential election were being held today, and Harry Truman were running for President on the Democratic ticket against Robert Taft on the Republican ticket and against Henry Wallace on a third party ticket, how would you vote?

Truman.............................. 51%
Taft................................. 31
Wallace............................. 8
No opinion......................... 10

Outside South Only

Truman.............................. 48%
Taft................................. 33
Wallace............................. 9
No opinion......................... 10

JANUARY 24
PRESIDENTIAL TRIAL HEAT

Interviewing Date 1/2–7/48
Survey #410–K   Question #13a

Asked of farmers: If a presidential election were being held today, and Harry Truman

were running for President on the Democratic ticket against Thomas Dewey on the Republican ticket and against Henry Wallace on a third party ticket, how would you vote?

Truman.............................. 38%
Dewey.............................. 48
Wallace............................. 5
No opinion......................... 9

Interviewing Date 1/2–7/48
Survey #410–K   Question #13b

Asked of farmers: If a presidential election were being held today, and Harry Truman were running for President on the Democratic ticket against Dwight Eisenhower on the Republican ticket and against Henry Wallace on a third party ticket, how would you vote?

Truman.............................. 36%
Eisenhower......................... 46
Wallace............................. 6
No opinion......................... 12

Interviewing Date 1/2–7/48
Survey #410–K   Question #13c

Asked of farmers: If a presidential election were being held today, and Harry Truman were running for President on the Democratic ticket against Robert Taft on the Republican ticket and against Henry Wallace on a third party ticket, how would you vote?

Truman.............................. 48%
Taft................................. 36
Wallace............................. 6
No opinion......................... 10

JANUARY 26
PRESIDENTIAL TRIAL HEAT

Interviewing Date 1/2–7/48
Survey #410–K   Question #13a

If a presidential election were being held today, and Harry Truman were running for

President on the Democratic ticket against Thomas Dewey on the Republican ticket and against Henry Wallace on a third party ticket, how would you vote?

By Region
New England and Middle Atlantic
Truman............................ 41%
Dewey............................. 45
Wallace........................... 9
No opinion........................ 5

East Central
Truman............................ 36%
Dewey............................. 49
Wallace........................... 6
No opinion........................ 9

West Central
Truman............................ 45%
Dewey............................. 44
Wallace........................... 5
No opinion........................ 6

South
Truman............................ 75%
Dewey............................. 19
Wallace........................... 1
No opinion........................ 5

West
Truman............................ 46%
Dewey............................. 38
Wallace........................... 8
No opinion........................ 8

Veterans Only
Truman............................ 45%
Dewey............................. 42
Wallace........................... 9
No opinion........................ 4

Interviewing Date 1/2–7/48
Survey #410–K   Question 13b

If a presidential election were being held today, and Harry Truman were running for

President on the Democratic ticket against Dwight Eisenhower on the Republican ticket and against Henry Wallace on a third ticket, how would you vote?

By Region
New England and Middle Atlantic
Truman............................ 35%
Eisenhower........................ 52
Wallace........................... 8
No opinion........................ 5

East Central
Truman............................ 35%
Eisenhower........................ 49
Wallace........................... 6
No opinion........................ 10

West Central
Truman............................ 37%
Eisenhower........................ 50
Wallace........................... 4
No opinion........................ 9

South
Truman............................ 69%
Eisenhower........................ 27
Wallace........................... 1
No opinion........................ 3

West
Truman............................ 39%
Eisenhower........................ 44
Wallace........................... 7
No opinion........................ 10

Veterans Only
Truman............................ 39%
Eisenhower........................ 47
Wallace........................... 9
No opinion........................ 5

Interviewing Date 1/2–7/48
Survey #410–K   Question #13c

If a presidential election were being held today, and Harry Truman were running for

President on the Democratic ticket against Robert Taft on the Republican ticket and against Henry Wallace on a third party ticket, how would you vote?

By Region
New England and Middle Atlantic

Truman........................... 45%
Taft............................... 33
Wallace........................... 11
No opinion........................ 11

East Central

Truman........................... 42%
Taft............................... 35
Wallace........................... 8
No opinion........................ 15

West Central

Truman........................... 45%
Taft............................... 38
Wallace........................... 5
No opinion........................ 12

South

Truman........................... 76%
Taft............................... 16
Wallace........................... 2
No opinion........................ 6

West

Truman........................... 49%
Taft............................... 28
Wallace........................... 10
No opinion........................ 13

Veterans Only

Truman........................... 54%
Taft............................... 29
Wallace........................... 10
No opinion........................ 7

JANUARY 28
RATIONING AND PRICE CONTROLS

Interviewing Date 1/2–7/48
Survey #410–K   Question #1a

Do you think the Government should or should not put rationing and price controls on some products?

Should............................ 51%
Should not........................ 41
No opinion........................ 8

By Occupation
Professional and Business

Should............................ 49%
Should not........................ 47
No opinion........................ 4

White Collar

Should............................ 52%
Should not........................ 41
No opinion........................ 7

Farmers

Should............................ 32%
Should not........................ 56
No opinion........................ 12

Manual Workers

Should............................ 56%
Should not........................ 34
No opinion........................ 10

By Community Size
100,000 and Over

Should............................ 58%
Should not........................ 35
No opinion........................ 7

10,000–100,000

Should............................ 55%
Should not........................ 37
No opinion........................ 8

Under 10,000

Should........................ 48%
Should not.................... 43
No opinion.................... 9

Farm Areas

Should........................ 32%
Should not.................... 56
No opinion.................... 12

By Political Affiliation
Republicans

Should........................ 40%
Should not.................... 54
No opinion.................... 6

Democrats

Should........................ 59%
Should not.................... 32
No opinion.................... 9

Interviewing Date 1/2–7/48
Survey #410–K   Question #1b

> Those who responded in the affirmative
> were asked: Which specific product would
> you like to see rationed?

The following are listed according to frequency
of mention:

Meat
Butter
All foods, groceries
Bread, wheat, flour
Clothing, shoes
Eggs
Housing, rents
Milk
Gasoline, fuel oil
Lard, fats

JANUARY 31
BRITISH POLITICS

Special Survey

> Asked of Britons: On the whole, do you
> approve or disapprove of Mr. Attlee as
> Prime Minister?

Approve....................... 44%
Disapprove.................... 46
No opinion.................... 10

> On the whole are you satisfied or dis-
> satisfied with the Government's record to
> date?

Satisfied...................... 41%
Dissatisfied................... 49
No opinion.................... 10

FEBRUARY 1
REPUBLICAN PRESIDENTIAL CANDIDATES

Interviewing Date 1/2–7/48
Survey #410–T   Question #8a

> Asked of Republicans: Will you look over
> this list of possible Republican presidential
> candidates — which one would you like to
> see elected President in 1948?

Dewey........................ 33%
Eisenhower................... 19
Taft.......................... 13
Stassen....................... 12
MacArthur.................... 10
Vandenberg................... 5
Warren....................... 5
Martin........................ 1
Name of a Democrat.......... —
No choice..................... 2

Interviewing Date 1/2–7/48
Survey #410–T   Question #8b

> Asked of Republicans: Will you look over
> this list of possible presidential candidates
> (list excluded General Eisenhower) — which
> one would you like to see elected President
> in 1948?

Dewey........................ 38%
Taft.......................... 15
Stassen....................... 15
MacArthur.................... 14
Vandenberg................... 6

Warren............................ 5
Martin............................ 1
Name of a Democrat................ 2
No choice......................... 4

FEBRUARY 2
MILITARY ALLIANCES

Interviewing Date 11/28–12/2/47
Survey #408–K   Question #15

Do you think the United States, England, and France should join together in a permanent military alliance, that is, agree to come to each other's defense immediately if the other is attacked?

Yes.............................. 51%
No............................... 36
No opinion....................... 13

Interviewing Date 11/28–12/2/47
Survey #408–T   Question #15a

Do you think the United States and England should join together in a permanent military alliance — that is, agree to come to each other's defense immediately if the other is attacked?

Yes.............................. 45%
No............................... 45
No opinion....................... 10

Interviewing Date 11/28–12/2/47
Survey #408–T   Question #15b

Do you think the United States and France should join together in a permanent military alliance — that is, agree to come to each other's defense immediately if the other is attacked?

Yes.............................. 32%
No............................... 53
No opinion....................... 15

FEBRUARY 6
TRADE WITH RUSSIA

Interviewing Date 1/2–7/48
Survey #410–T   Question #9a

The United States Government has been sending oil, machinery, and industrial products to Russia under our lend-lease program. Do you think the Government should stop sending these things to Russia — or should it continue to send these things to her?

Stop............................. 83%
Continue sending................. 8
No opinion....................... 6
Qualified........................ 3

Interviewing Date 1/2–7/48
Survey #410–T   Question #9b

American business firms are now selling oil, machinery, and industrial products to Russia. Do you think business firms should stop selling these things to Russia — or should they continue to sell these things to her?

Stop............................. 72%
Continue selling................. 15
No opinion....................... 10
Qualified........................ 3

By Occupation
Professional and Business

Stop............................. 69%
Continue selling................. 21
No opinion....................... 5
Qualified........................ 5

Farmers

Stop............................. 76%
Continue selling................. 9
No opinion....................... 13
Qualified........................ 2

White Collar

Stop.............................. 71%
Continue selling................... 20
No opinion........................ 6
Qualified......................... 3

Manual Workers

Stop.............................. 73%
Continue selling................... 12
No opinion........................ 12
Qualified......................... 3

FEBRUARY 7
WOMEN WEARING SLACKS

Interviewing Date 1/2–7/48
Survey #410–K   Question #5a

Do you approve or disapprove of women of any age wearing slacks in public, that is, for example, while shopping?

By Sex
Men

Approve........................... 34%
Disapprove........................ 39
Indifferent....................... 22
No opinion........................ 3
Qualified......................... 2

Women

Approve........................... 30%
Disapprove........................ 49
Indifferent....................... 15
No opinion........................ 1
Qualified......................... 5

FEBRUARY 9
MARSHALL PLAN

Special Survey
Interviewing Date 1/23–28/48 (U.S. Only)
Survey #411–T   Question #3a

Asked of citizens of four nations: Have you heard or read about the Marshall Plan?

	Yes	No
England.......................	89%	11%
France........................	91	9
Italy.........................	78	22
United States.................	71	29

Those who responded in the affirmative were asked: Do you favor or oppose the Marshall Plan?

England

Favor............................. 60%
Oppose............................ 20
No opinion........................ 20

France

Favor............................. 60%
Oppose............................ 13
No opinion........................ 27

Italy

Favor............................. 65%
Oppose............................ 14
No opinion........................ 21

Interviewing Date 1/23–28/48 (U.S. only)
Survey #411–T   Question #3b

For what reasons in your opinion did the United States propose the Marshall Plan?

	England	France	Italy
To help Europe, humanitarian.............	24%	23%	31%
Wants markets, profits, bolstering Europe to stave off depression..........	22	26	17
To stop communism.......	14	14	20
To get more power, imperialism...............	8	9	11
For own safety, to promote peace...............	3	1	1
Other reasons...........	3	6	3
No opinion.............	26	21	17

United States Only

To help Europe	56%
To curb communism	8
To foster better understanding with Europe	2
Other	8
No opinion	26

For what reasons in your opinion does Russia oppose the Marshall Plan?

France

To oppose U.S.A.	25%
Because it goes against Russian plans to control Europe	22
Because it threatens communism	10
Because Russia is interested in keeping Europe weak	7
For economic reasons	5
Other	4
No opinion	27

England

Fears America	18%
Russia dislikes anti-communist aim of the plan	17
Fears weakening her European position	11
Wants to dominate other countries	10
Fears a western bloc	5
Wants her own way	7
Others	7
No opinion	25

Italy

Because it menaces communism, threatens Russia's expansion	29%
Interferes with Russia's imperialistic plans	26
Russia fears improved living	8
Threatens her own safety	7
No opinion	37
	107%

(Note: table adds to more than 100% as some people gave more than one reason.)

FEBRUARY 11
WAR WITH RUSSIA

Special Survey
Interviewing Date 1/23–28/48 (U.S. Only)
Survey #411–T   Question #2a

Asked of eight nations: Do you think Russia would start a war to get something she wanted (such as more territory or more resources) — or would she fight only if attacked?

	Would Start War	Defense Only	No Opin.
United States	73%	19%	8%
Canada	60	26	14
Holland	57	27	16
France	51	22	27
Italy	50	17	33
Brazil	43	16	41
Sweden	42	21	37
Norway	37	37	26

Interviewing Date 1/23–28/48 (U.S. only)
Survey #411–T   Question #2b

Do you think the United States would start a war to get something she wanted (such as more territory or more resources) — or would she fight only if attacked?

	Would Start War	Defense Only	No Opin.
Norway	23%	55%	22%
France	20	56	24
Holland	16	60	24
Italy	16	48	36
Canada	13	77	10
Sweden	13	54	33
Brazil	9	53	38
United States	5	92	3

FEBRUARY 13
MOST IMPORTANT PROBLEM

Interviewing Date 1/2–7/48
Survey #410–K   Question #3

Suppose you could attend a press conference at the White House where news-

paper reporters put any questions they want to the President. What questions would you like to ask the President about problems here and abroad?

Inflation, danger of depression........ 25%
Marshall Plan, relations with western
    European countries................ 19
U.S. relations with Russia........... 7
High taxes, large public debt......... 7
How to keep peace, United Nations.... 6
Shortages, rationing................. 3
Housing........................... 3
Palestine.......................... 1
Labor problems.................... 1
Miscellaneous..................... 8
Don't know....................... 27
                           107%

(Note: the table adds to more than 100% because some persons named more than one problem.)

FEBRUARY 14
MINIMUM WAGE

Interviewing Date 1/23–28/48
Survey #411–K   Question #5b

At present the minimum wage that can be paid to workers in every state, in most businesses and industries is 40 cents an hour. This means that all persons working in such businesses, in every state, including young people who have never worked before cannot be paid less than 40 cents an hour. Would you approve or disapprove of raising this minimum to 75 cents an hour?

Approve........................... 66%
Disapprove........................ 29
No opinion........................ 5

Interviewing Date 1/23–28/48
Survey #411–T   Question #5b

What would you say the minimum wage per hour should be today for a single per-son, just graduated from high school, and starting out at a beginner's job in a factory in this area?

Less than 10 cents.................. 1%
40 cents to 75 cents................ 39
75 cents to $1..................... 35
$1 or over........................ 18
No answer........................ 7

FEBRUARY 16
PRESIDENTIAL TRIAL HEAT

Interviewing Date 1/23–28/48
Survey #411–K   Question #13b

If a presidential election were being held today, and Harry Truman were running for President on the Democratic ticket against Harold Stassen on the Republican ticket and against Henry Wallace on a third party ticket, how would you vote?

Truman........................... 45%
Stassen........................... 41
Wallace........................... 6
No opinion........................ 8

Outside South Only

Truman........................... 44%
Stassen........................... 42
Wallace........................... 7
No opinion........................ 7

By Region
New England and Middle Atlantic

Truman........................... 40%
Stassen........................... 44
Wallace........................... 7
No opinion........................ 9

East Central

Truman........................... 43%
Stassen........................... 43
Wallace........................... 5
No opinion........................ 9

West Central

Truman........................	41%
Stassen........................	50
Wallace........................	5
No opinion.....................	4

South

Truman........................	74%
Stassen........................	19
Wallace........................	2
No opinion.....................	5

West

Truman........................	44%
Stassen........................	40
Wallace........................	11
No opinion.....................	5

Independents Only

Truman........................	33%
Stassen........................	39
Wallace........................	15
No opinion.....................	13

FEBRUARY 18
TAFT-HARTLEY ACT

Interviewing Date 1/23–28/48
Survey #411–K   Question #1b

Have you read or heard about the Taft-Hartley Labor Law, which deals with labor unions?

Yes............................	72%
No.............................	28

Interviewing Date 1/23–28/48
Survey #411–K   Question #1c

Asked of those who responded in the affirmative: Do you think the Taft-Hartley Law should be revised, repealed, or left unchanged?

Revised........................	25%
Repealed.......................	13
Left unchanged.................	36
No opinion.....................	26

By Political Affiliation
Democrats

Revised........................	22%
Repealed.......................	12
Left unchanged.................	41
No opinion.....................	25

Republicans

Revised........................	23%
Repealed.......................	10
Left unchanged.................	38
No opinion.....................	29

Independents

Revised........................	31%
Repealed.......................	18
Left unchanged.................	26
No opinion.....................	25

Interviewing Date 1/23–28/48
Survey #411–K   Question #1d

Those who said the law should be revised were asked: How should it be revised?

Make it less hard on labor, return rights to labor........................	27%
Restore closed shops................	4
Restore political campaign privileges of unions........................	2
Remove non-Communist certification...	1
Labor should have right to refuse work, right to strike (which the Act does not prohibit)........................	3
Make act stricter, put teeth in it........	34
Miscellaneous.....................	9
Don't know.......................	22
	102%

(Note: table adds to more than 100% because some persons had more than one suggestion.)

Interviewing Date 1/23–28/48
Survey #411–K   Question #1a

Persons who said they had not heard of the Taft-Hartley Act were asked: As things stand today, do you think the laws governing labor unions are too strict, or not strict enough?

Too strict............................ 14%
About right.......................... 26
Not strict enough.................... 31
No opinion.......................... 29

FEBRUARY 20
PRESIDENTIAL TRIAL HEAT

Special Survey

Asked of Southern voters: If a presidential election were being held today, and Harry Truman were running for President on the Democratic ticket against Thomas Dewey on the Republican ticket and against Henry Wallace on a third party ticket, how would you vote?

Truman.............................. 75%
Dewey............................... 19
Wallace............................. 1
Undecided........................... 5

Asked of Southern voters: If a presidential election were being held today, and Harry Truman were running for President on the Democratic ticket against Harold Stassen on the Republican ticket and against Henry Wallace on a third party ticket, how would you vote?

Truman.............................. 74%
Stassen............................. 19
Wallace............................. 2
Undecided........................... 5

Asked of Southern voters: If a presidential election were being held today, and Harry Truman were running for President on the Democratic ticket against Robert Taft on the Republican ticket and against Henry Wallace on a third party ticket, how would you vote?

Truman.............................. 76%
Taft................................ 16
Wallace............................. 2
Undecided........................... 6

FEBRUARY 21
KINSEY REPORT

Interviewing Date 1/23–28/48
Survey #411–K   Question #11a

Dr. A. C. Kinsey has completed a nine-year study on the sex behavior of males in this country. Have you read or heard of his book?

Yes................................. 20%
No.................................. 80

Interviewing Date 1/23–28/48
Survey #411–K   Question #11b

Do you think it is a good thing or a bad thing to have this information on sex available?

Good................................ 57%
Bad................................. 11
Qualified........................... 4
No opinion.......................... 28

By Age
21–29 Years

Good................................ 70%
Bad................................. 6
Qualified........................... 2
No opinion.......................... 22

30–49 Years

Good................................ 58%
Bad................................. 11
Qualified........................... 5
No opinion.......................... 26

50 Years and Over

Good................................ 46%
Bad................................. 14
Qualified........................... 4
No opinion.......................... 36

By Religion
Protestants

Good............................ 57%
Bad.............................. 10
Qualified........................ 4
No opinion....................... 29

Catholics

Good............................ 49%
Bad.............................. 19
Qualified........................ 5
No opinion....................... 27

Others and Non-Churchgoers

Good............................ 61%
Bad.............................. 8
Qualified........................ 3
No opinion....................... 28

Under 10,000

Truman.......................... 44%
Dewey........................... 45
Wallace......................... 4
No opinion...................... 7

Farm Areas

Truman.......................... 48%
Dewey........................... 40
Wallace......................... 4
No opinion...................... 8

Profile of Wallace Supporters

Voted for Roosevelt in 1944.......... 62%
Voted for Dewey in 1944............ 6
Voted for third party in 1944......... 2
Did not vote, too young to vote in 1944 30

According to the Institute's findings, Wallace's support in New York City is 23%.

FEBRUARY 23
PRESIDENTIAL TRIAL HEAT

Interviewing Date 1/23–28/48
Survey #411–T   Question #13c

If a presidential election were being held today, and Harry Truman were running for President on the Democratic ticket against Thomas Dewey on the Republican ticket and against Henry Wallace on a third party ticket, how would you vote?

By Community Size
500,000 and Over

Truman.......................... 44%
Dewey........................... 37
Wallace......................... 15
No opinion...................... 4

10,000–500,000

Truman.......................... 48%
Dewey........................... 41
Wallace......................... 5
No opinion...................... 6

FEBRUARY 25
PRESIDENTIAL TRIAL HEAT

Special Survey

Asked of Illinois voters: If a presidential election were being held today, and Harry Truman were running for President on the Democratic ticket against Thomas Dewey on the Republican ticket and against Henry Wallace on a third party ticket, how would you vote?

Truman.......................... 37%
Dewey........................... 48
Wallace......................... 7
No opinion...................... 8

Chicago Only

Truman.......................... 42%
Dewey........................... 41
Wallace......................... 12
No opinion...................... 5

FEBRUARY 27
PRESIDENTIAL TRIAL HEAT

Special Survey

Asked of Pennsylvania voters: If a presidential election were being held today, and Harry Truman were running for President on the Democratic ticket against Thomas Dewey on the Republican ticket and against Henry Wallace on a third party ticket, how would you vote?

Truman............................ 41%
Dewey............................. 46
Wallace........................... 7
No opinion........................ 6

FEBRUARY 28
THE WEATHER BUREAU

Special Survey

Do you think the official local weather bureau man is doing a good, fair, or poor job of forecasting weather conditions for this area?

Good.............................. 51%
Fair.............................. 28
Poor.............................. 15
No opinion........................ 6

By Region
New England and Middle Atlantic

Good.............................. 46%
Fair.............................. 28
Poor.............................. 22
No opinion........................ 4

East Central

Good.............................. 57%
Fair.............................. 27
Poor.............................. 10
No opinion........................ 6

West Central

Good.............................. 53%
Fair.............................. 30
Poor.............................. 13
No opinion........................ 4

South

Good.............................. 54%
Fair.............................. 28
Poor.............................. 12
No opinion........................ 6

West

Good.............................. 51%
Fair.............................. 28
Poor.............................. 11
No opinion........................ 10

FEBRUARY 28
OUTLOOK FOR PEACE

Interviewing Date 2/6–11/48
Survey #412–T   Question #2a

Do you think the United States will find itself in another war within, say, the next ten years?

Yes............................... 54%
No................................ 32
No opinion........................ 14

By Education
College

Yes............................... 47%
No................................ 47
No opinion........................ 6

High School

Yes............................... 53%
No................................ 34
No opinion........................ 13

Grade School

Yes............................... 58%
No................................ 25
No opinion........................ 17

Interviewing Date 2/6–11/48
Survey #412–T   Question #2b

Asked of those who responded in the affirmative: Who do you think will be responsible for starting the war?

Russia	70%
United States	7
England	2
Capitalists, politicians, etc.	6
Miscellaneous	7
No opinion	13
	105%

(Note: table adds to more than 100% as some persons gave more than one answer.)

Interviewing Date 2/6–11/48
Survey #412–K   Question #2a

Do you think the United States will find itself in another war within, say, the next 25 years?

Yes	76%
No	15
No opinion	9

FEBRUARY 29
PRESIDENTIAL TRIAL HEAT

Special Survey

Asked of California voters: If the presidential election were being held today and Harry Truman were running on the Democratic ticket against Thomas Dewey on the Republican ticket and against Henry Wallace on a third party ticket, which one would you prefer?

Truman	42%
Dewey	42
Wallace	10
No opinion	6

MARCH 3
ROBERT SCHUMAN

Special Survey

Asked in France: Do you approve or disapprove of Robert Schuman as President of the Council?

Approve	46%
Disapprove	26
No opinion	28

MARCH 3
MARSHALL PLAN

Interviewing Date 2/6–11/48
Survey #412–T   Question #7a

Have you heard of the Marshall Plan?

Yes	79%
No	21

Interviewing Date 2/6–11/48
Survey #412–T   Question #7c

Those who responded in the affirmative were asked: What is your opinion of the Plan?

Favorable	57%
Unfavorable	18
No opinion	25

By Region
New England and Middle Atlantic

Favorable	61%
Unfavorable	16
No opinion	23

East Central

Favorable	50%
Unfavorable	25
No opinion	25

West Central

Favorable	56%
Unfavorable	18
No opinion	26

South

Favorable........................ 57%
Unfavorable...................... 14
No opinion....................... 29

West

Favorable........................ 58%
Unfavorable...................... 16
No opinion....................... 26

Interviewing Date 2/6–11/48
Survey #412–T   Question #7g

Do you think a separate agency, headed by a man with cabinet rank should be set up in Washington to have full control and supervision of the Marshall Plan — or do you think this problem should be handled by the State Department?

Separate agency.................. 32%
State Department................. 39
No opinion....................... 29

MARCH 5
PHOTO IDENTIFICATION QUIZ

Interviewing Date 2/6–11/48
Survey #412–K   Question #6

Here are some photographs of important men. Will you please look at the photographs and tell me their names?

	Cor-rect	Incor-rect	Don't Know
Harry Truman............	93%	—	7%
Thomas Dewey...........	84	—	16
Dwight Eisenhower.......	83	1	16
Douglas MacArthur......	76	3	21
Henry Wallace...........	62	1	37
Robert Taft..............	40	1	59
James Farley.............	31	1	68
Arthur Vandenberg.......	27	4	69
Harold Stassen..........	26	16	58
Earl Warren.............	12	2	86
Joseph Martin...........	11	1	88
Claude Pepper...........	5	2	93

MARCH 6
QUALITIES OF A GOOD HUSBAND AND A GOOD WIFE

Interviewing Date 1/23–28/48
Survey #411–K   Question #6b

What would you say is the most important quality in a good husband (wife)?

By Sex

	Married Men	Single Men
Good homemaker, good housekeeper, etc..........	47%	28%
Agreeable, good company, pleasant disposition.......	18	21
Faithfulness, loyalty.........	15	16
Cooperative, a partner......	13	8
Patience, understanding.....	11	9
Good mother.............	5	1
Loving, devoted...........	3	4
Intelligence, common sense..	2	6
Neither smoke, nor drink....	1	—
Miscellaneous.............	3	4
Don't know...............	2	19
	120%	116%

	Married Women	Single Women
Good provider...........	42%	28%
Faithfulness, steadiness.....	22	24
Kindness, consideration....	20	13
Agreeable, good company...	14	16
Cooperative, a partner.....	5	1
Neither smoke nor drink...	5	2
Loving, devoted...........	3	4
Intelligence, common sense..	1	2
Good father..............	1	—
Miscellaneous.............	3	5
Don't know...............	2	19
	118%	114%

(Note: above tables add to more than 100% as some people gave more than one answer.)

MARCH 10
FRENCH POLITICS

Special Survey

Asked in France: In your opinion which is the greatest political danger to France at the present time — the Communists, Gaullists, or the third force?

Communists	56%
Gaullists	19
Both	2
Third force	3
No opinion	20

MARCH 12
UNITED NATIONS

Interviewing Date 2/6–11/48
Survey #412–K   Question #11a

It has been suggested that a world convention of the United Nations be called in 1950 to amend and rewrite the United Nations Charter to make it a stronger organization. Do you approve or disapprove of this idea?

Approve	63%
Disapprove	13
No opinion	24

By Education
College

Approve	78%
Disapprove	13
No opinion	9

High School

Approve	64%
Disapprove	14
No opinion	22

Grade School

Approve	57%
Disapprove	13
No opinion	30

MARCH 13
MARGARINE

Interviewing Date 2/20–25/48
Survey #413–K   Question #4b

There are now certain taxes and fees which dealers who handle margarine have to pay which they do not have to pay on butter. A bill has been introduced in Congress to do away with these taxes and fees on margarine. Do you favor or oppose this bill?

Favor	69%
Oppose	15
No opinion	16

By Occupation
Professional and Business

Favor	78%
Oppose	9
No opinion	13

White Collar

Favor	72%
Oppose	13
No opinion	15

Farmers

Favor	39%
Oppose	37
No opinion	24

Manual Workers

Favor	75%
Oppose	10
No opinion	15

By Education
College

Favor	75%
Oppose	15
No opinion	10

High School

Favor	72%
Oppose	13
No opinion	15

Grade School

Favor............................ 66%
Oppose........................... 16
No opinion....................... 18

By Sex
Men

Favor............................ 67%
Oppose........................... 18
No opinion....................... 15

Women

Favor............................ 72%
Oppose........................... 11
No opinion....................... 17

By Region
New England and Middle Atlantic

Favor............................ 74%
Oppose........................... 11
No opinion....................... 15

East and West Central

Favor............................ 64%
Oppose........................... 20
No opinion....................... 16

South

Favor............................ 68%
Oppose........................... 10
No opinion....................... 22

West

Favor............................ 75%
Oppose........................... 18
No opinion....................... 7

Butter Users Only

Favor............................ 58%
Oppose........................... 22
No opinion....................... 20

Margarine Users Only

Favor............................ 84%
Oppose........................... 7
No opinion....................... 9

Butter and Margarine Users Only

Favor............................ 71%
Oppose........................... 13
No opinion....................... 16

MARCH 15
REPUBLICAN PRESIDENTIAL CANDIDATES

Interviewing Date 3/5–10/48
Survey #414–T   Question #8a

Asked of Republicans: Will you look over this list of possible Republican presidential candidates. Which one would you like to see elected President in 1948?

Dewey............................ 37%
Stassen.......................... 15
Taft............................. 14
Vandenberg....................... 13
MacArthur........................ 12
Warren........................... 6
Martin........................... 1
Saltonstall...................... 1
No choice........................ 1

MARCH 17
PRICES AND WAGES

Interviewing Date 2/20–25/48
Survey #413–K   Question #1a

Do you think that prices, in general, will be higher, lower, or about the same six months from now?

Higher........................... 14%
Lower............................ 39
Same............................. 36
No opinion....................... 11

Interviewing Date 2/20–25/48
Survey #413–K   Question #2a

Do you think wage rates, in general, will be higher, lower, or about the same six months from now?

Higher.......................... 15%
Lower........................... 13
Same............................ 62
No opinion...................... 10

Interviewing Date 2/20–25/48
Survey #413–K   Question #2b

Many unions of factory workers are going to ask for a pay increase within the next month or two. Do you think these factory workers should get more pay?

Should get increase.................. 34%
Should not get increase.............. 45
Qualified........................... 5
Don't know.......................... 16

Interviewing Date 2/20–25/48
Survey #413–K   Question #3b

Do you think there will be a serious business depression in the United States this year?

Yes.............................. 9
No.............................. 72%
No opinion...................... 19

Interviewing Date 2/20–25/48
Survey #413–T   Question #3b

Do you think there will be a serious business depression in the United States in two years?

Yes............................. 25%
No.............................. 52
No opinion...................... 23

MARCH 19
ARMED FORCES

Interviewing Date 2/6–11/48
Survey #412–K   Question #10a

Do you think the United States should increase the size of its army?

Yes............................. 61%
No.............................. 29
No opinion...................... 10

World War II Veterans Only

Yes............................. 64%
No.............................. 31
No opinion...................... 5

Of its navy?

Yes............................. 63%
No.............................. 26
No opinion...................... 11

World War II Veterans Only

Yes............................. 65%
No.............................. 29
No opinion...................... 6

Of its air force?

Yes............................. 74%
No.............................. 17
No opinion...................... 9

World War II Veterans Only

Yes............................. 78%
No.............................. 18
No opinion...................... 4

Interviewing Date 2/6–11/48
Survey #412–K   Question #10b

Would you be willing to pay more money in taxes to support a larger army?

Yes............................. 55%
No.............................. 36
No opinion...................... 9

A larger navy?

Yes............................. 55%
No.............................. 35
No opinion...................... 10

A larger air force?

Yes............................. 63%
No.............................. 28
No opinion...................... 9

MARCH 22
FRENCH AND ITALIAN POLITICS

Special Survey

Asked in France: Do you approve or disapprove of Robert Schuman as President of the Council?

Approve........................... 40%
Disapprove........................ 25
No opinion........................ 35

Asked in France: If the Schuman government were to be overthrown whom would you like to see as new President of the Council?

General de Gaulle.................. 17%
Leon Blum......................... 11
Maurice Thorez.................... 7
Edouard Herriot................... 6
Georges Bidault................... 5
Jacques Duclos.................... 4
Paul Reynaud...................... 4
Paul Ramadier.................... 1
Guy Mollet....................... 1
Others........................... 10
No opinion....................... 34

Asked in France: Which nation, in your opinion, will aid France most in her recovery?

United States..................... 70%
Russia............................ 7
Great Britain..................... 2
None.............................. 6
France alone...................... 6
Other............................. 3
No opinion........................ 6

Asked in France: Do you favor or oppose an economic union of the Western European countries (France, England, Belgium, Holland, Luxembourg, Italy, and Western Germany)?

Favor............................. 68%
Oppose............................ 14
No opinion........................ 18

Asked in Italy: In Italy's interest, which party or group should become stronger?

Christian Democrats............... 36%
Communists........................ 20
Rightist parties.................. 14
Moderate Socialists............... 13
No opinion........................ 17

By Sex
Men

Communists........................ 27%
Christian Democrats............... 26
Moderate Socialists............... 17
Rightist parties.................. 16
No opinion........................ 14

Women

Christian Democrats............... 48%
Communists........................ 12
Rightist parties.................. 11
Moderate Socialists............... 8
No opinion........................ 21

Employers Only

Christian Democrats............... 33%
Rightist parties.................. 31
Moderate Socialists............... 20
Communists........................ 7
No opinion........................ 9

Workers Only

Communists........................ 42%
Christian Democrats............... 21
Moderate Socialists............... 15
Rightist parties.................. 8
No opinion........................ 14

Farmers Only

Christian Democrats............... 39%
Communists........................ 15
Rightist parties.................. 15
Moderate Socialists............... 12
No opinion........................ 19

MARCH 24
RUSSIA

Interviewing Date 3/5–10/48
Survey #414–K   Question #1a

As you hear and read about Russia these days do you believe Russia is trying to build herself up to be the ruling power of the world, or is Russia just building up protection against being attacked in another war?

Ruling power........................ 77%
Protection........................... 12
No opinion.......................... 11

Interviewing Date 3/5–10/48
Survey #414–K   Question #1b

What policy do you think we should follow toward Russia?

Be firm, no appeasement.............. 22%
Prepare to fight, build up armed forces.. 27
Go to war........................... 17
Don't send money or supplies, try economic blockade.................... 3
Form an alliance against her.......... 3
Get together, work things out........ 2
Go before UN, let UN work things out 1
Try to appease Russia................ 1
Do nothing, get out of Europe........ 5
Miscellaneous....................... 2
No opinion.......................... 17

Interviewing Date 3/5–10/48
Survey #414–T   Question #1b

Do you think the United States is being too soft or too tough (firm) in its policy toward Russia?

Too soft............................ 73%
Too tough.......................... 3
About right......................... 11
No opinion.......................... 13

MARCH 26
STEEL PRICES AND FACTORY WAGES

Interviewing Date 3/5–10/48
Survey #414–K   Question #5b

From what you've read in the newspapers or heard on the radio, would you say the steel companies should or should not have raised the price of steel?

Should............................. 16%
Should not......................... 65
No opinion......................... 19

MARCH 27
INCOME TAXES

Interviewing Date 3/5–10/48
Survey #414–K   Question #2b

Do you consider the amount of income tax that you have had to pay as too high, too low, or about right?

Too high........................... 57%
Too low............................ 1
About right......................... 38
No opinion......................... 4

MARCH 29
REPUBLICAN PRESIDENTIAL CANDIDATES

Interviewing Date 3/19–24/48
Survey #415–K   Question #7a

Asked of Republicans: Will you look over this list of possible Republican presidential candidates (on card)—which one would you like to see elected President in 1948?

Dewey.............................. 34%
MacArthur.......................... 19
Stassen............................ 15
Vandenberg......................... 13
Taft............................... 12
Warren............................. 3
Martin............................. 1
Saltonstall......................... 1
No choice.......................... 2

MARCH 31

DUTCH VIEWS OF THE MARSHALL PLAN

Special Survey

Asked in Holland: Do you think our country should cooperate with the Marshall Plan or not?

Cooperate......................... 59%
Do not cooperate.................. 9
No opinion........................ 32

Asked in Holland: Why do you think the United States wants to give us the Marshall Plan help?

U.S. wants markets, needs to stave off
   depression....................... 38%
To stop communism................ 15
To help Europe.................... 10
To get more power, imperialism....... 7
Miscellaneous, no opinion........... 30

APRIL 2

MARSHALL PLAN

Interviewing Date 1/23–28/48
Survey #411–K   Question #3c

What is your opinion of the Marshall Plan?

Truman Supporters

Approve........................... 62%
Disapprove........................ 12
No opinion........................ 26

Dewey Supporters

Approve........................... 55%
Disapprove........................ 22
No opinion........................ 23

Wallace Supporters

Approve........................... 47%
Disapprove........................ 28
No opinion........................ 25

APRIL 3

LOUIS VS. WALCOTT

Interviewing Date 1/2–7/48
Survey #410–K   Question #16

Do you think Joe Louis can beat Jersey Joe Walcott when and if they fight again next summer?

Yes.............................. 49%
No............................... 36
No opinion....................... 15

By Sex
Men

Yes.............................. 52%
No............................... 35
No opinion....................... 13

Women

Yes.............................. 43%
No............................... 38
No opinion....................... 19

APRIL 5

CIVIL RIGHTS

Interviewing Date 3/5–10/48
Survey #414–K   Question #10c

How do you feel about Truman's civil rights program? Do you think Congress should or should not pass the program as a whole?

Should............................ 6%
Should not........................ 56
No opinion........................ 6
                                68%

Had not heard of program........... 32%

Whites Outside South

Should............................ 21%
Should not........................ 15
No opinion........................ 19
                                55%

Had not heard of program........... 45%

Negroes Outside South

Should........................... 58%
Should not........................ 2
No opinion....................... 11
                                 ————
                                 71%

Had not heard of program........... 29%

Special Survey

White Southerners were asked: Do you think the present administration in Washington has dealt fairly, in general, with the South?

Yes.............................. 34%
No............................... 51
No opinion....................... 15

APRIL 6
BRITISH COST OF LIVING

Special Survey

Asked in Great Britain: Compared with six months ago, are you finding making ends meet harder, easier, or about the same?

Harder........................... 65%
Easier........................... 4
About same....................... 30
Don't know....................... 1

APRIL 9
UNIVERSAL MILITARY TRAINING

Interviewing Date 3/19–24/48
Survey #415–T   Question #4a

Do you think Congress should or should not pass a law to require every able-bodied young man (who has not already been in the armed forces) to take military or naval training for one year?

Should........................... 77%
Should not....................... 16
No opinion....................... 7

By Education
College

Should........................... 76%
Should not....................... 20
No opinion....................... 4

High School

Should........................... 82%
Should not....................... 13
No opinion....................... 5

Grade School

Should........................... 78%
Should not....................... 13
No opinion....................... 9

By Age
21–29 Years

Should........................... 80%
Should not....................... 16
No opinion....................... 4

30–49 Years

Should........................... 78%
Should not....................... 16
No opinion....................... 6

50 Years and Over

Should........................... 74%
Should not....................... 18
No opinion....................... 8

By Occupation
Professional and Business

Should........................... 74%
Should not....................... 20
No opinion....................... 6

White Collar

Should........................... 81%
Should not....................... 14
No opinion....................... 5

Farmers

Should.............................. 69%
Should not.......................... 21
No opinion......................... 10

Manual Workers

Should.............................. 80%
Should not.......................... 14
No opinion......................... 6

By Region
New England and Middle Atlantic

Should.............................. 79%
Should not.......................... 16
No opinion......................... 5

East Central

Should.............................. 78%
Should not.......................... 16
No opinion......................... 6

West Central

Should.............................. 70%
Should not.......................... 23
No opinion......................... 7

South

Should.............................. 80%
Should not.......................... 12
No opinion......................... 8

West

Should.............................. 77%
Should not.......................... 15
No opinion......................... 8

By Sex
Men

Should.............................. 79%
Should not.......................... 17
No opinion......................... 4

Women

Should.............................. 75%
Should not.......................... 16
No opinion......................... 9

Veterans Only

Should.............................. 83%
Should not.......................... 14
No opinion......................... 3

Interviewing Date 3/19–24/48
Survey #415–T   Question #10b

Do you think Congress should pass a law that would permit the Government to draft young men to serve in the armed forces?

Should.............................. 63%
Qualified........................... 7
Should not.......................... 23
No opinion......................... 7

APRIL 10
PRESIDENT TRUMAN'S POPULARITY

Special Survey

Asked in Southern states: Do you approve or disapprove of the way Harry Truman is handling his job as President?

Approve............................. 35%
Disapprove......................... 57
No opinion......................... 8

APRIL 11
PRESIDENTIAL TRIAL HEAT

Interviewing Date 3/19–24/48
Survey #415–K   Question #14a

If a presidential election were being held today, and Harry Truman were running for President on the Democratic ticket against Thomas Dewey on the Republican ticket and against Henry Wallace on a third party ticket, how would you vote?

Truman............................. 39%
Dewey.............................. 47
Wallace............................ 7
No opinion......................... 7

Interviewing Date 3/19–24/48
Survey #415–K   Question #14b

If a presidential election were being held today, and Harry Truman were running for President on the Democratic ticket against Harold Stassen on the Republican ticket and against Henry Wallace on a third party ticket, how would you vote?

Truman.......................... 39%
Stassen........................... 44
Wallace........................... 7
No opinion....................... 10

Interviewing Date 3/19–24/48
Survey #415–K   Question #14c

If a presidential election were being held today, and Harry Truman were running for President on the Democratic ticket against Arthur Vandenberg on the Republican ticket and against Henry Wallace on a third party ticket, how would you vote?

Truman.......................... 39%
Vandenberg....................... 44
Wallace........................... 7
No opinion....................... 10

Interviewing Date 3/19–24/48
Survey #415–K   Question #14d

If a presidential election were being held today, and Harry Truman were running for President on the Democratic ticket against Douglas MacArthur on the Republican ticket and against Henry Wallace on a third party ticket, how would you vote?

Truman.......................... 41%
MacArthur........................ 44
Wallace........................... 7
No opinion....................... 8

Interviewing Date 3/5–10/48
Survey #414–K   Question #13d

If a presidential election were being held today, and Harry Truman were running for President on the Democratic ticket

against Robert Taft on the Republican ticket and against Henry Wallace on a third party ticket, how would you vote?

Truman.......................... 43%
Taft.............................. 36
Wallace........................... 9
No opinion....................... 12

APRIL 14
LIBERAL VS. CONSERVATIVE

Interviewing Date 3/19–24/48
Survey #415–T   Question #8c

Can you describe for me, in your own words, a political liberal and a political conservative?

Forty per cent of the voters were unable to give a description of what is meant by the terms. Among the other 60% the principal definition given for conservative is "cautious, goes slow, careful," while liberal is defined mainly as "in favor of change."

Interviewing Date 3/19–24/48
Survey #415–T   Question #8d

Do you consider the following men to be liberal or conservative in their political views?

	Lib.	Cons.	No Opin.
Wallace..................	41%	5%	54%
Truman..................	36	25	39
Marshall.................	30	22	48
Stassen..................	21	19	60
Vandenberg..............	20	26	54
MacArthur..............	16	38	46
Dewey..................	15	37	48
Warren.................	13	14	73
Taft....................	9	40	51
Martin..................	8	22	70
Saltonstall...............	6	12	82
Byrd...................	5	18	77

Interviewing Date 3/19–24/48
Survey #415–K   Question #8c

Do you consider yourself to be a conservative or a liberal in your political views?

Conservative........................ 38%
Liberal............................. 29
Undecided.......................... 33

Interviewing Date 3/19–24/48
Survey #415–K   Question #8d

The 67% who expressed an opinion were asked: Do you consider the following men to be liberal or conservative in their political views?

Voters Who Consider Themselves Conservatives

	Lib.	Cons.	No Opin.
Wallace	55%	5%	40%
Truman	45	33	22
Marshall	29	35	36
Stassen	21	32	47
Vandenberg	18	40	42
MacArthur	16	51	33
Dewey	17	53	30
Warren	10	20	70
Taft	14	49	37
Martin	8	27	65
Saltonstall	5	16	79
Byrd	6	22	72

Voters Who Consider Themselves Liberals

	Lib.	Cons.	No Opin.
Wallace	55%	6%	39%
Truman	49	33	18
Marshall	51	22	27
Stassen	36	18	46
Vandenberg	37	27	36
MacArthur	26	46	28
Dewey	24	44	32
Warren	27	15	58
Taft	10	59	31
Martin	13	32	55
Saltonstall	10	16	74
Byrd	8	24	68

APRIL 16
STATEHOOD FOR HAWAII

Interviewing Date 3/5–10/48
Survey #414–K   Question #14

Would you favor or oppose having Hawaii admitted as the 49th state in the union?

Favor.............................. 66%
Oppose............................. 15
No opinion......................... 19

APRIL 17
GENERAL KNOWLEDGE

Interviewing Date 3/5–10/48
Survey #414–K   Question #4a

Can you locate the following ten states on this outline map of the United States — California, Texas, Pennsylvania, New York, Illinois, Ohio, Michigan, New Jersey, Massachusetts, and Missouri?

Correct answers.................... 5.5%

By Education

	Correct Answers
College	8.0%
High School	6.3
Grade School	4.1

APRIL 19
MOST IMPORTANT PROBLEM

Interviewing Date 3/19–24/48
Survey #415–K   Question #2a

What do you think is the most important problem facing this country today?

Preventing war, peace, danger of war,
   working out peace................. 38%
Foreign policy, getting along with Russia
   and other nations, helping Europe.... 27
Domestic politics, presidential election.. 9
High prices, high cost of living, inflation. 8
Communism......................... 7

Strikes, labor problems.............. 2
Housing........................... 2
Military preparedness, U.M.T., army
  and navy....................... 1
Future of United Nations........... 1
Miscellaneous..................... 2
Don't know....................... <u>4</u>
                                101%

(Note: table adds to more than 100% because some persons named more than one problem.)

Interviewing Date 3/19–24/48
Survey #415–K   Question #2b

Which party do you think can do a better job of handling the problem you have just mentioned — the Democratic, the Republican, or the Wallace third party?

Democratic party................... 28%
Republican party................... 32
Wallace's third party.............. 3
No difference..................... 19
No opinion....................... 18

APRIL 23
PRESIDENT TRUMAN'S POPULARITY

Interviewing Date 4/9–14/48
Survey #416–K   Question #2a

Do you approve or disapprove of the way Harry Truman is handling his job as President?

Approve........................... 36%
Disapprove....................... 50
No opinion....................... 14

By Occupation
Professional and Business

Approve........................... 30%
Disapprove....................... 62
No opinion....................... 8

White Collar

Approve........................... 31%
Disapprove....................... 58
No opinion....................... 11

Farmers

Approve........................... 39%
Disapprove....................... 45
No opinion....................... 16

Manual Workers

Approve........................... 40%
Disapprove....................... 42
No opinion....................... 18

By Region
New England and Middle Atlantic

Approve........................... 35%
Disapprove....................... 50
No opinion....................... 15

East Central

Approve........................... 33%
Disapprove....................... 53
No opinion....................... 14

West Central

Approve........................... 42%
Disapprove....................... 44
No opinion....................... 14

South

Approve........................... 30%
Disapprove....................... 58
No opinion....................... 12

West

Approve........................... 39%
Disapprove....................... 48
No opinion....................... 13

By Political Affiliation
Democrats

Approve........................... 50%
Disapprove....................... 37
No opinion....................... 13

Republicans

Approve.......................... 24%
Disapprove........................ 63
No opinion........................ 13

Independents

Approve.......................... 32%
Disapprove........................ 54
No opinion........................ 14

Union Members Only

Approve.......................... 41%
Disapprove........................ 43
No opinion........................ 16

APRIL 24
DAYLIGHT SAVING TIME

Interviewing Date 4/9–14/48
Survey #416–K   Question #1

*Which of the following would you prefer:
(a) have standard time the whole year,
including summer, (b) have daylight saving
time in summer and standard time the
rest of the year, or (c) have daylight saving
time the year round?*

Standard time..................... 42%
Daylight saving time.............. 52
No opinion........................ 6

By Community Size
500,000 and Over

Standard time..................... 24%
Daylight saving time.............. 69
No opinion........................ 7

100,000–500,000

Standard time..................... 39%
Daylight saving time.............. 56
No opinion........................ 5

10,000–100,000

Standard time..................... 38%
Daylight saving time.............. 57
No opinion........................ 5

Towns Under 10,000

Standard time..................... 49%
Daylight saving time.............. 46
No opinion........................ 5

Farms

Standard time..................... 71%
Daylight saving time.............. 24
No opinion........................ 5

APRIL 25
REPUBLICAN PRESIDENTIAL CANDIDATES

Interviewing Date 4/9–14/48
Survey #416–T   Question #8a

*Asked of Republicans: Will you look over
this list of possible candidates (on card)
and tell me which one you would like to see
as the Republican candidate for President in
1948?*

Stassen.......................... 31%
Dewey............................ 29
MacArthur........................ 16
Vandenberg....................... 10
Taft............................. 9
Warren........................... 2
Martin........................... 1
No choice........................ 2

APRIL 28
AID TO NATIONALIST CHINA

Interviewing Date 4/9–14/48
Survey #416–T   Question #9b

*Do you approve or disapprove of the United
States giving the Chiang Kai-shek (Nationalist) government more military supplies, goods, and money?*

Approve.......................... 55%
Disapprove........................ 32
No opinion........................ 13

By Region

New England and Middle Atlantic

Approve.............................. 57%
Disapprove......................... 31
No opinion......................... 12

East Central

Approve.............................. 51%
Disapprove......................... 35
No opinion......................... 14

West Central

Approve.............................. 55%
Disapprove......................... 32
No opinion......................... 13

South

Approve.............................. 57%
Disapprove......................... 26
No opinion......................... 17

West

Approve.............................. 52%
Disapprove......................... 33
No opinion......................... 15

World War II Veterans Only

Approve.............................. 64%
Disapprove......................... 27
No opinion......................... 9

APRIL 28
CLEMENT ATTLEE

Special Survey

Asked in Great Britain: On the whole do you approve or disapprove of Mr. Attlee as Prime Minister?

Approve.............................. 39%
Disapprove......................... 48
No opinion......................... 13

APRIL 30
BUSINESS DEPRESSION

Special Survey

Asked in four European nations: Do you think that a serious business depression is likely in the United States within the next two years?

	Likely	Un-likely	No Opin.
Italy..................	14%	35%	51%
Holland...............	15	30	55
Britain................	33	28	39
France................	33	33	34

MAY 1
FAVORITE FIRST NAMES

Interviewing Date 4/9–14/48
Survey #416–K   Question #6a

What is your favorite first name for a boy?

The following are listed according to frequency of mention:

John
William
Robert
James
David
Charles
Michael
Richard
George
Joseph
Thomas
Frank
Paul
Donald
Henry

Interviewing Date 4/9–14/48
Survey #416–K   Question #6b

What is your favorite first name for a girl?

The following are listed in order of frequency of mention:

Mary
Elizabeth
Helen
Susan
Margaret
Ruth
Anne
Carol
Barbara
Linda
Patricia
Catherine
Jean
Nancy
Alice

MAY 3
SUMMIT CONFERENCE

Interviewing Date 4/9–14/48
Survey #416–K   Question #4a

Should President Truman call an international meeting with Premier Stalin and heads of other nations to work out more effective plans for peace?

Yes................................ 63%
No................................ 28
No opinion........................ 9

Interviewing Date 4/9–14/48
Survey #416–K   Question #4c

Those who responded in the affirmative were asked: Do you think we would be successful in coming to an agreement with Premier Stalin?

Yes................................ 39%
No................................ 35
No opinion........................ 26

MAY 5
REPUBLICAN PRESIDENTIAL CANDIDATES

Interviewing Date 4/23–28/48
Survey #417–K   Question #8a

Asked of Republicans: Whom would you like to see the Republican party nominate for President?

By Sex

	Men	Women
Stassen...................	31%	31%
Dewey....................	30	28
MacArthur................	13	18
Vandenberg...............	11	9
Taft......................	9	9
Warren...................	2	2
Martin...................	2	1
No choice................	2	2

By Age

	Age 21–35	Age 36 and over
Stassen...................	30%	31%
Dewey....................	29	29
MacArthur................	20	14
Vandenberg..............	9	10
Taft.....................	7	10
Warren...................	3	2
Martin...................	1	2
No choice................	1	2

MAY 7
FUNCTION OF GOVERNMENT

Special Survey
Interviewing Date 4/9–14/48 (U.S. only)
Survey #416–T   Question #10

If you had to choose between these two types of government, which one would you choose: (A) A government whose main purpose is to provide the people with economic security — that is, the possibility of a steady income. (B) A government whose main purpose is to insure free elections, freedom of speech, press, and religion?

United States Only

Economic security	12%
Freedom	83
Qualified	2
No opinion	3

American Zone of Germany

Economic security	60%
Freedom	31
No opinion	9

MAY 8
CITIES' WORST PROBLEMS

Special Survey

What would you say is this city's worst problem today?

By Community Size
500,000 and Over

Poor housing, slums	37%
Traffic, transportation	31
Dirt, unsightliness	12
High tax rates	8
Corrupt politics	7
Crime control	4
Race problems	3
Delinquency	3
Lack of playgrounds, parks	3
Drinking, liquor problem	1
Miscellaneous	2
No opinion	6
	117%

100,000–500,000

Traffic, transportation	31%
Poor housing, slums	18
Corrupt politics	11
Dirt, unsightliness	10
Drinking, liquor problem	7
Not enough jobs	7
Lack of playgrounds, parks	5
High tax rates	4
Crime control	4
Delinquency	4
Poor schools	4
Race problems	2
Miscellaneous	5
No opinion	7
	119%

10,000–100,000

Traffic, transportation	19%
Poor housing, slums	19
High tax rates	9
Dirt, unsightliness	7
Not enough jobs	8
Lack of playgrounds, parks	7
Corrupt politics	6
Delinquency	4
Drinking, liquor problem	4
Poor schools	4
Crime control	3
Race problems	2
Miscellaneous	9
No opinion	9
	110%

10,000 and Under

Traffic, transportation	18%
Lack of playgrounds, parks	13
Drinking, liquor problem	9
Dirt, unsightliness	9
Not enough jobs	9
High tax rates	7
Poor housing, slums	6
Corrupt politics	6
Delinquency	5
Poor schools	3
Miscellaneous	8
No opinion	13
	106%

(Note: tables add to more than 100% as some people gave more than one answer.)

MAY 10
PRESIDENTIAL TRIAL HEAT

Interviewing Date 4/23–28/48
Survey #417–K   Question #13c

If a presidential election were being held today, and Harry Truman were running for President on the Democratic ticket against Harold Stassen on the Republican ticket and against Henry Wallace on a third party ticket, how would you vote?

Truman........................... 33%
Stassen........................... 56
Wallace........................... 5
No opinion........................ 6

By Region
New England and Middle Atlantic

Truman........................... 32%
Stassen........................... 56
Wallace........................... 7
No opinion........................ 5

East Central

Truman........................... 32%
Stassen........................... 59
Wallace........................... 4
No opinion........................ 5

West Central

Truman........................... 32%
Stassen........................... 63
Wallace........................... 2
No opinion........................ 3

South

Truman........................... 41%
Stassen........................... 42
Wallace........................... 4
No opinion........................ 13

Mountain and Pacific

Truman........................... 32%
Stassen........................... 57
Wallace........................... 5
No opinion........................ 6

By Occupation
Professional and Business

Truman........................... 22%
Stassen........................... 69
Wallace........................... 5
No opinion........................ 4

White Collar

Truman........................... 26%
Stassen........................... 65
Wallace........................... 6
No opinion........................ 3

Farmers

Truman........................... 38%
Stassen........................... 53
Wallace........................... 2
No opinion........................ 7

Manual Workers

Truman........................... 41%
Stassen........................... 46
Wallace........................... 6
No opinion........................ 7

MAY 12
TRADE TREATIES

Interviewing Date 4/23–28/48
Survey #417–K   Question #9d

Some people say that because the United States is planning to spend $6 billion in the next year on the Marshall Plan it is no longer necessary to continue reciprocal trade agreements. Other people say that the Marshall Plan makes the need for trade agreements more necessary than ever. Do you think the trade agreements should or should not be continued?

Should be continued................ 80%
Should not be...................... 8
No opinion........................ 12

No major differences between Republican and Democratic voters arise in regard to continuation of the treaties. Eight out of ten in each party support the treaties, and the same proportion exists among those who call themselves independent of any party allegiance.

MAY 14
REPUBLICAN PRESIDENTIAL CANDIDATES

Interviewing Date 4/23–28/48
Survey #417–K   Question #8a

Asked of Republicans: Will you look over this list of possible Republican presidential candidates. Which one would you like to see elected President in 1948?

Stassen	37%
Dewey	24
Vandenberg	13
MacArthur	12
Taft	8
Warren	2
Martin	1
No choice	3

MAY 15
BASEBALL

Special Survey

Do you follow professional baseball?

Yes	40%
No	60

Those who responded in the affirmative were asked: Which teams do you think will win the American League and the National League championships?

American League

New York	43%
Boston	13
Cleveland	7
Others	7
No opinion	30

National League

St. Louis	24%
Brooklyn	22
New York	10
Others	13
No opinion	31

MAY 15
SPORTS

Interviewing Date 4/9–14/48
Survey #416–T   Question #11a

What sport do you, yourself, enjoy watching most?

	National	Men	Women
Baseball	39%	45%	31%
Football	17	20	15
Basketball	10	8	12
Horse racing	4	3	5
Boxing	3	4	2
Ice skating, hockey	2	2	4
Swimming, diving	2	1	3
Tennis	2	1	2
Bowling	1	1	1
Auto racing	1	1	*
Others	7	7	9
None	12	7	16

*Less than 1%.

By Education
College

Baseball	24%
Football	34
Basketball	15
Others, none	27

High School

Baseball	38%
Football	24
Basketball	11
Others, none	27

Grade School

Baseball	44%
Football	8
Basketball	7
Others, none	41

Interviewing Date 4/9–14/48
Survey #416–T   Question #11b

Do you, yourself, take part in any sport?

Yes	34%
No	66

Those who answered in the affirmative were asked: Which sport do you take part in?

Baseball	9%
Hunting, fishing	7
Swimming, diving	6
Golf	5
Bowling	5
Basketball	3
Tennis	3
Horseback riding	1
Skating	1
Football	1
Others	4
	45%

(Note: table adds to more than 34% because some respondents gave more than one answer.)

MAY 16
VICE PRESIDENCY

Interviewing Date 4/23–28/48
Survey #417–T   Question #10d

It has been suggested that the Vice President should help the President with administrative problems so that the President would have more time to deal with matters of policy. Do you agree or disagree with this idea?

Agree	80%
Disagree	8
No opinion	12

Interviewing Date 4/23–28/48
Survey #417–K   Question #10e

Do you think the Government should provide him with an official residence in Washington?

Yes	46%
No	41
No opinion	13

MAY 19
PRESIDENTIAL TRIAL HEAT

Interviewing Date 4/23–28/48
Survey #417–K   Question #13d

If the presidential election were being held today, and Truman were running for President on the Democratic ticket against Vandenberg on the Republican ticket and against Wallace on the third party ticket, how do you think you would vote?

Vandenberg	45%
Truman	39
Wallace	5
No opinion	11

By Region
New England and Middle Atlantic

Vandenberg	47%
Truman	36
Wallace	7
No opinion	10

East Central

Vandenberg	51%
Truman	34
Wallace	5
No opinion	10

West Central

Vandenberg	50%
Truman	39
Wallace	3
No opinion	8

South

Vandenberg	29%
Truman	53
Wallace	3
No opinion	15

Mountain and Pacific

Vandenberg	42%
Truman	42
Wallace	5
No opinion	11

MAY 21
EUROPEAN MILITARY ALLIANCE

Interviewing Date 4/23–28/48
Survey #417–K   Question #5

Do you think the United States and all the Western European countries participating in the Marshall Plan should join together in a permanent military alliance — that is, agree to come to each other's defense immediately if any one of them is attacked?

Yes	65%
No	21
No opinion	14

By Political Affiliation
Republicans

Yes	66%
No	22
No opinion	12

Democrats

Yes	68%
No	16
No opinion	16

Independents

Yes	57%
No	29
No opinion	14

MAY 22
FEDERAL AID TO EDUCATION

Interviewing Date 5/7–12/48
Survey #418–K   Question #3d

There is a bill now before Congress which asks that the Federal Government distribute about $300,000,000 a year to the states for school aid. Do you think Congress should provide the money for this purpose or should school aid be left up to each state?

Approve federal aid	51%
Qualified approval	5
Left up to state aid	31
No opinion	13

Interviewing Date 5/7–12/48
Survey #418–K   Question #3a

Do you think there are any states in this country which do not provide a good enough (satisfactory) education for children?

Yes	51%
No	20
No opinion	29

Interviewing Date 5/7–12/48
Survey #418–K   Question #3b

Those who responded in the affirmative were asked: Do you approve of federal aid to education?

Approve	61%
Qualified	5
Disapprove	25
No opinion	9

Interviewing Date 5/7–12/48
Survey #418–K   Question #3c

Those who responded in the negative were asked: Do you approve of federal aid to education?

Approve	37%
Qualified	3
Disapprove	46
No opinion	14

MAY 24
COMMUNIST PARTY

Interviewing Date 5/8–13/48
Survey #418–T   Question #9b

Would you favor or oppose a law requiring all members of the Communist party in this country to register with the Justice Department in Washington?

Favor............................. 77%
Oppose........................... 12
No opinion........................ 11

Interviewing Date 4/9–14/48
Survey #416–K   Question #12b

In general, do you think most American citizens who belong to the Communist party in this country are loyal to America or to Russia?

Loyal to U.S....................... 16%
Loyal to Russia.................... 65
No opinion........................ 19

MAY 26
UNITED NATIONS

Interviewing Date 4/23–28/48
Survey #417–K   Question #4a

Are you satisfied or dissatisfied with the progress that the United Nations has made to date?

Satisfied.......................... 21%
Dissatisfied....................... 54
No opinion........................ 25

Interviewing Date 4/23–28/48
Survey #417–K   Question #4d

Do you think the veto power should or should not be done away with?

Should be eliminated............... 41%
Should not be..................... 24
No opinion........................ 35

Persons Satisfied with UN

Should be eliminated............... 33%
Should not be..................... 36
No opinion........................ 31

Persons Dissatisfied with UN

Should be eliminated............... 53%
Should not be..................... 24
No opinion........................ 23

MAY 28
UN CONTROL OF ATOMIC ENERGY

Interviewing Date 4/23–28/48
Survey #417–K   Question #4e

Would you favor or oppose having the UN adopt a plan for the control of atomic energy which would permit the UN to inspect atomic plants in the United States and any other country at any time?

Favor............................. 43%
Oppose........................... 39
No opinion........................ 18

By Education
College

Favor............................. 54%
Oppose........................... 40
No opinion........................ 6

High School

Favor............................. 46%
Oppose........................... 41
No opinion........................ 13

Grade School

Favor............................. 38%
Oppose........................... 37
No opinion........................ 25

Persons Satisfied with UN

Favor............................. 49%
Oppose........................... 38
No opinion........................ 13

Persons Dissatisfied with UN

Favor.............................. 47%
Oppose............................. 44
No opinion......................... 9

MAY 30
THE DRAFT

Interviewing Date 5/8–13/48
Survey #418–T   Question #5a

If you had to choose between these two plans for building up United States military strength, which one would you choose? (on card)

Requiring every able-bodied 18-year-old
young man to take military or naval
training for one year.............. 55%
Drafting young men between the ages of
19 and 25 for two years' service in the
armed services.................... 22
Neither........................... 11
Both.............................. 5
No opinion........................ 7

Interviewing Date 5/7–12/48
Survey #418–K   Question #1c

Do you think young men (19 to 25) in college should or should not be drafted for military service before they have finished their schooling?

Should............................ 26%
Should not........................ 62
Qualified......................... 6
No opinion........................ 6

Interviewing Date 5/8–13/48
Survey #418–T   Question #5b

The armed services estimate that they need between 600,000 and 700,000 men. Do you think if the Government paid a bonus of $1,000 for two years service — or about $40 a month more pay — that enough men would volunteer?

Yes............................... 59%
No................................ 29
No opinion........................ 12

Interviewing Date 5/8–13/48
Survey #418–T   Question #5c

Do you think this is a good way or a poor way to get the men needed for the armed services?

Good way.......................... 42%
Only fair......................... 11
Poor way.......................... 38
No opinion........................ 9

JUNE 2
ADOPTION PROGRAM

Interviewing Date 4/23–28/48
Survey #417–T   Question #6a

It has been suggested that towns and cities in the United States adopt — that is, try to help — towns and cities of a similar size in friendly Western European nations. Do you think this is a good idea or a poor idea?

Good idea......................... 42%
Fair idea......................... 16
Poor idea......................... 36
No opinion........................ 6

Interviewing Date 4/23–28/48
Survey #417–T   Question #6b

If such a plan were worked out, would you, yourself, be willing to write letters and send food and clothing to a family in Europe from time to time?

Yes............................... 63%
No................................ 25
No opinion........................ 12

JUNE 4
DEMOCRATIC PRESIDENTIAL CANDIDATES

Interviewing Date 5/7–12/48
Survey #418–K   Question #7a

Democrats were asked: Will you look over all these possible candidates and tell me which one you would like to see elected President of the United States in 1948?

Truman.......................... 76%
Marshall........................ 10
Byrnes.......................... 3
Byrd............................ 2
Forrestal....................... 1
Farley.......................... 1
Douglas......................... 1
No opinion...................... 6

JUNE 5
FOREIGN LANGUAGES

Interviewing Date 4/23–28/48
Survey #417–K   Question #6a

What other languages, if any, can you speak well enough to make others understand you?

None............................ 71%
German.......................... 9
French.......................... 6
Spanish......................... 5
Italian......................... 4
Yiddish......................... 2
Polish.......................... 2
Finnish......................... 1
Swedish......................... 1
Russian......................... 1
Others.......................... 5
                               ———
                               107%

(Note: the table adds to more than 100% because some persons named more than one language.)

By Education

Speak Other Language

College......................... 41%
High School..................... 25
Grade School.................... 29

Interviewing Date 4/23–28/48
Survey #417–K   Question #6c

Would you like to be able to speak another language, and which one?

No.............................. 47%
French.......................... 21
Spanish......................... 21
German.......................... 11
Italian......................... 5
Russian......................... 2
Others.......................... 9
                               ———
                               116%

(Note: table adds to more than 100% because some persons named more than one language.)

JUNE 7
TAFT-HARTLEY LAW

Interviewing Date 5/7–12/48
Survey #418–K   Question #2

Have you ever heard or read about the Taft-Hartley Law?

Yes............................. 72%
No.............................. 28

Interviewing Date 5/7–12/48
Survey #418–K   Question #2a

Asked of all persons who answered yes: Do you think the Taft-Hartley Law should be revised, repealed, or left unchanged?

Revised......................... 34%
Repealed........................ 15
Unchanged....................... 24
No opinion...................... 27

Interviewing Date 5/7–12/48
Survey #418–K   Question #2b

*Asked of all persons answering yes to
the first question: As things stand today, do
you think the laws governing labor unions
are too strict or not strict enough?*

Too strict............................ 18%
About right.......................... 22
Not strict enough.................... 42
No opinion.......................... 18

Union Members Only

Too strict............................ 32%
About right.......................... 26
Not strict enough.................... 27
No opinion.......................... 15

JUNE 9
POLITICAL INTEREST

Interviewing Date 3/19–24/48
Survey #415–K   Question #3

*Have you given much thought or only a
little thought to the presidential election?*

Much.............................. 41%
Little............................... 50
None.............................. 9

By Sex

	"Much" thought
Men..............................	48%
Women...........................	34

By Occupation

Professional and business............. 59%
White collar........................ 41
Farmers............................ 39
Manual workers..................... 33

By Age

21–29 Years......................... 39%
30–49 Years......................... 41
50 Years and over................... 42

By Political Affiliation

Republicans......................... 50%
Democrats.......................... 43

By Education

College............................. 68%
High School......................... 42
Grade School....................... 33

JUNE 11
PRESIDENT TRUMAN'S POPULARITY

Interviewing Date 5/28–6/2/48
Survey #419–K   Question #1a

*Do you approve or disapprove of the way
Harry Truman is handling his job as President?*

Approve............................ 39%
Disapprove......................... 47
No opinion......................... 14

By Region

	Approve
New England and Middle Atlantic.....	37%
East Central........................	38
West Central.......................	44
South..............................	39
West..............................	38

JUNE 14
REPUBLICAN PRESIDENTIAL
CANDIDATES

Interviewing Date 5/28–6/2/48
Survey #419–K   Question #7a

*Asked of Republican voters: Would you
look over this list of possible Republican
candidates and tell me which one you would
like to see elected President in 1948?*

Dewey............................ 33%
Stassen........................... 26
Vandenberg....................... 13
MacArthur........................ 11
Taft.............................. 10
Warren........................... 2
Martin........................... 1
Others, no choice.................. 4

Interviewing Date 5/28–6/2/48
Survey #419–K   Question #7b

Asked of those favoring Dewey, Stassen, or Taft: If neither Dewey, Stassen, nor Taft can get a majority of votes at Philadelphia and have to drop out of the race, who would then be your choice for the Republican nomination for President?

Vandenberg....................... 31%
MacArthur........................ 13
Warren........................... 10
Martin........................... 4
Others........................... 1
Would prefer a Democrat........... 1
No choice........................ 9
                                 ――
                                 69%

JUNE 18
REPUBLICAN PRESIDENTIAL CANDIDATES

Interviewing Date 5/28–6/2/48
Survey #419–K   Question #7a

Asked of Republican voters: Would you look over this list of possible Republican candidates and tell me which one you would like to see elected President in 1948?

By Sex

	Men	Women
Dewey	33%	33%
Stassen	25	27
Vandenberg	15	11
MacArthur	11	12
Taft	10	10
Warren	2	3
Martin	1	1
Others, no choice	3	3

By Age

	21–35 Years	36 Years and over
Dewey	36%	32%
Stassen	32	24
Vandenberg	10	15
MacArthur	11	11
Taft	7	11
Warren	2	2
Martin	1	1
Others, no choice	1	4

JUNE 18
INDEPENDENT VOTERS

Interviewing Date 5/28–6/2/48
Survey #419–K   Question #12b

In politics today, do you consider yourself a Republican, Democrat, or Independent?

Persons saying Independent.......... 29%

By Education

	Independent
College	39%
High School	31
Grade or no school	23

By Occupation

Business and Professional............ 34
White collar....................... 34
Manual workers.................... 27
Farmers........................... 17

By Age

21–29 Years........................ 39%
30–49 Years........................ 29
50 Years and over.................. 21

By Region

New England and Middle Atlantic..... 30%
East Central....................... 35
West Central....................... 22
South.............................. 19
Mountain and Pacific............... 29

JUNE 19
THE PRESIDENCY

Special Survey

If you were President of the United States what would you do?

The typical American says that if he were President he would devote his energies to "helping people and trying to make them happy."

JUNE 21
PARTY PLATFORMS

Interviewing Date 5/28–6/2/48
Survey #419–K   Question #12c

Is there any particular idea or plank that you would like your party to include in its party platform for the coming presidential election?

Yes............................... 34%
No................................ 66

By Political Affiliation

	Yes	No
Republicans...................	34%	66%
Democrats....................	31	69
Independents.................	40	60

Interviewing Date 5/28–6/2/48
Survey #419–K   Question #12d

Those who responded in the affirmative were asked: What idea or plank would you like to see included?

The item most frequently mentioned by one-sixth of the total sample was "lower the cost of living."

Various suggestions having to do with labor problems came next, followed by housing. Last came a long list of ideas each of which received only a low per cent including stronger foreign policy, improved education, insuring peace, preparedness, veteran's bonus, health insurance, more old-age assistance, Government economy, etc.

JUNE 23
PARTY STRENGTH

Interviewing Date 5/28–6/2/48
Survey #419–K   Question #12a

Asked of persons living in cities with populations of over 500,000: Which party do you want to see win the presidential election this fall — the Republican, Democratic, or Wallace's third party?

Republican......................... 46%
Democratic......................... 36
Wallace's party.................... 7
No opinion......................... 11

JUNE 26
HEALTH

Interviewing Date 5/28–6/2/48
Survey #419–K   Question #2a

Would you approve or disapprove of having the Government spend $100 million for research to find the causes and cure of diseases of the heart?

Approve............................ 79%
Disapprove......................... 11
Qualified answers.................. 3
No opinion......................... 7

Interviewing Date 5/28–6/2/48
Survey #419–K   Question #2c

Asked of all those who indicated approval: Would you be willing to pay more taxes to provide this money?

Yes............................... 80%
No................................ 14
No opinion......................... 6

Interviewing Date 5/28–6/2/48
Survey #419–K   Question #2d

Will you tell me what disease causes the greatest number of deaths in this country today?

Heart disease	47%
Cancer	38
Tuberculosis	8
Infantile paralysis	1
Miscellaneous	3
Don't know	3

JUNE 27
POLITICAL CONTRIBUTIONS

Interviewing Date 12/12–17/47
Survey #409–K   Question #10

If you were asked, would you contribute five dollars to the campaign fund of the political party you prefer?

Yes	27%
No	73

JULY 3
RELIGION

Interviewing Date 5/28–6/2/48
Survey #419–K   Question #8a

Asked of Protestant churchgoers: Do you think it would or would not be a good thing for all Protestant churches in the United States to combine into one church?

Favor idea	42%
Do not favor	47
No opinion	11

Interviewing Date 5/28–6/2/48
Survey #419–K   Question #8b

What do you, yourself, think churches could do to increase their attendance?

Make services better	17%
More programs to arouse interest of youth	9
More social functions	8
Better leaders, men of higher caliber	7
Make religion more practical, more down to earth	6

More evangelism, drive for members	6
Make churches less secular, more democratic	4
Less hypocrisy	3
Miscellaneous	5
Nothing needed	4
Don't know	32
	101%

(Note: table adds to more than 100% as some persons gave more than one reason.)

JULY 5
RUSSIA

Interviewing Date 5/28–6/2/48
Survey #419–K   Question #3

Do you think the United States is too soft or too tough (firm) in its policy toward Russia?

Too soft	69%
Too tough	6
About right	14
No opinion	11

By Occupation
Business and Professional

Too soft	67%
Too tough	9
About right	16
No opinion	8

White Collar

Too soft	67%
Too tough	6
About right	16
No opinion	11

Farmers

Too soft	71%
Too tough	5
About right	12
No opinion	12

Manual Workers

Too soft	71%
Too tough	4
About right	12
No opinion	13

Interviewing Date 5/28–6/2/48
Survey #419–T   Question #3

As you hear and read about Russia these days do you believe Russia is trying to build herself up to be the ruling power of the world, or do you think Russia is just building up protection against being attacked in another war?

Ruling power	69%
Protection	17
No opinion	14

JULY 7
DEMOCRATIC PRESIDENTIAL CANDIDATES

Interviewing Date 6/18–23/48
Survey #420–K   Question #8a

Asked of Democrats: Will you look over this list of possible candidates (on card) and tell me which one you would like to see as the Democratic candidate for President?

Truman	67%
Marshall	12
Byrnes	4
Byrd	4
Farley	3
Douglas	2
Pepper	2
Forrestal	1
No choice	5

JULY 9
REPUBLICAN PARTY PLATFORM

Special Survey

Did you happen to read the Republican Party platform drawn up at their convention in Philadelphia?

Yes, all of it	7%
Yes, only part of it	21
No, not any of it	72

Republicans Only

Yes, all of it	12%
Yes, only part of it	23
No, not any of it	65

Those who had read any part of the Republican platform were asked: Will you tell me what the platform says about the part the United States should play in world affairs?

Don't know	12%
Take part, no more isolationism	6
Favor aid to Europe	5
Peace, unity, understanding	2
Be firm, keep Russia in place	2
Miscellaneous	1
	28%

Will you tell me what it says about housing?

Don't know	15%
Build more houses	7
Encourage better homes at less cost	1
Private financing best	1
Federal aid for slum clearance	1
Miscellaneous	3
	28%

Will you tell me what it says about prices?

Don't know	14%
Doesn't say anything about prices	2
Says prices are too high	9
Miscellaneous	3
	28%

JULY 10
REPUBLICAN CONVENTION

Special Survey

Did you happen to read about the Republican Convention?

Yes, most of it..................... 20%
Yes, only part of it................ 44
No, not any of it................... 36

Did you happen to listen on the radio to the Republican Convention in Philadelphia?

Yes, most of it..................... 24%
Yes, only part of it................ 50
No, not any of it................... 26

Did you happen to see any part of it on television?

Yes.................................. 4%
No................................... 96

JULY 12
CONGRESS

Interviewing Date 6/19–24/48
Survey #420–T   Question #4a

Congress has been in session since January a year ago. In your opinion, has this Congress done a good job or a poor job in dealing with problems facing the country?

Good job........................... 19%
Fair............................... 34
Poor job........................... 31
No opinion......................... 16

By Political Affiliation
Democrats

Good job........................... 13%
Fair............................... 32
Poor job........................... 35
No opinion......................... 20

Republicans

Good job........................... 27%
Fair............................... 38
Poor job........................... 21
No opinion......................... 14

JULY 14
MOST IMPORTANT PROBLEM

Interviewing Date 6/18–23/48
Survey #420–K   Question #3a

What do you think is the most important problem facing the nation today?

Foreign policy...................... 44%
High cost of living................. 23
Domestic policies; presidential election; education, racial problems.......... 9
Strikes, labor problems............. 5
Housing............................. 4
Communism at home and abroad...... 4
Preparedness, army and navy......... 3
Miscellaneous....................... 5
Don't know.......................... 4
                                    ___
                                    101%

(Note: table adds to more than 100% because some persons named more than one problem.)

Interviewing Date 6/18–23/48
Survey #420–K   Question #3b

Which political party do you think can do a better job of handling the problem you have just mentioned — the Democratic, the Republican, or Wallace's third party?

Democratic party.................... 52%
Republican party.................... 48

Based on major parties only.

JULY 16
MINIMUM NEEDS FOR FAMILY OF FOUR

Interviewing Date 6/18–23/48
Survey #420–K   Question #5c

What is the smallest amount of money a family of four (husband, wife, and two children) needs each week to get along in this community?

Median average.................... $50 wk.

Interviewing Date 6/18–23/48
Survey #420–K   Question #5d

Is your total weekly family income larger or smaller than the sum that you named?

Larger............................ 44%
Same.............................. 15
Smaller........................... 32
Don't know........................ 9

JULY 16
PARTY STRENGTH

Interviewing Date 6/18–23/48
Survey #420–K   Question #7a

Leaving aside the question of candidates which party would you like to see win the next presidential election — the Republican, the Democratic, or Wallace's third party?

Democratic........................ 41%
Republican........................ 37
Wallace's third party............. 4
No opinion........................ 18

JULY 17
ECONOMIC OUTLOOK

Interviewing Date 6/18–23/48
Survey #420–K   Question #10b

If we should have another serious business depression in four years — which political party do you think could deal with it best?

Democratic........................ 38%
Republican........................ 28
Wallace's third party............. 2
No difference..................... 19
No opinion........................ 13

Interviewing Date 6/18–23/48
Survey #420–K   Question #10c

Do you think there will be another serious business depression in the United States during the next four years?

Yes............................... 36%
No................................ 41
No opinion........................ 23

JULY 18
PRESIDENTIAL TRIAL HEAT

Interviewing Date 5/28–6/2/48
Survey #419–K   Question #10a

If the presidential election were being held today, would you vote for Thomas Dewey, Harry Truman, or Henry Wallace?

Dewey............................. 49%
Truman............................ 38
Wallace........................... 6
No opinion........................ 7

JULY 21
LEADERSHIP OF POLITICAL PARTIES

Interviewing Date 6/18–23/48
Survey #420–K   Question #16a

Do you think that the Henry Wallace third party is run by communists?

Yes............................... 51%
No................................ 21
No opinion........................ 28

By Occupation
Professional and Business

Yes............................... 54%
No................................ 28
No opinion........................ 18

White Collar

Yes............................... 51%
No................................ 25
No opinion........................ 24

Farmers

Yes............................... 54%
No................................ 16
No opinion........................ 30

Manual Workers

Yes.................................. 49%
No................................... 18
No opinion........................... 33

By Age
21–29 Years

Yes.................................. 47%
No................................... 27
No opinion........................... 26

30–49 Years

Yes.................................. 50%
No................................... 22
No opinion........................... 28

50 Years and Over

Yes.................................. 53%
No................................... 17
No opinion........................... 30

By Political Affiliation
Republicans

Yes.................................. 59%
No................................... 16
No opinion........................... 25

Democrats

Yes.................................. 50%
No................................... 19
No opinion........................... 31

Independents

Yes.................................. 42
No................................... 32
No opinion........................... 26

Union Members Only

Yes.................................. 48%
No................................... 22
No opinion........................... 30

Interviewing Date 6/18–23/48
Survey #420–K   Question #16b

Do you think the Republican party is run by a few big businessmen of the country?

Yes.................................. 47%
No................................... 37
No opinion........................... 16

Interviewing Date 6/18–23/48
Survey #420–K   Question #16c

Do you think the Democratic party is run by the labor leaders of the country?

Yes.................................. 40%
No................................... 43
No opinion........................... 17

JULY 23
HENRY WALLACE

Interviewing Date 5/28–6/2/48
Survey #419–K   Question #10a

Do you plan to vote for Henry Wallace in the forthcoming presidential election?

Yes.................................. 6%
No................................... 94

By Age

	Yes
21–29 Years	8%
30–49 Years	7
50 Years and over	4

By Region

New England	4%
Middle Atlantic	9
Central	5
South	3
West	14

By Community Size

Under 10,000	4%
10,000–100,000	6
100,000–500,000	6
Over 500,000	12

Interviewing Date 6/18–23/48
Survey #420–K   Question #14a

Have you, yourself, talked to anyone who is going to support Henry Wallace for President?

Yes............................... 14%
No............................... 86

Interviewing Date 6/18–23/48
Survey #420–K   Question #14b

What is the main reason they give for supporting Henry Wallace?

The following are listed according to frequency of mention:

Is for the "common man"
Is for peace and the prevention of war
The nation today needs another party to oppose the major parties
Is fair and not a politician
Will follow Franklin D. Roosevelt's doctrines
Has a good foreign policy program

JULY 24
EDUCATION

Special Survey
Interviewing Date 6/18–23/48 (U.S. Only)
Survey #420–K   Question #1a

Do you think children today are being educated better or worse than you were?

	Better	Worse	Same	No Opin.
Canada.....	74%	12%	10%	4%
Australia...	78	9	9	4
Britain.....	64	19	11	6
U.S.A......	59	26	10	5
Finland....	54	21	17	8
Norway....	44	30	16	10
Sweden.....	26	37	29	8
Denmark...	21	45	21	13
Italy.......	20	40	23	17
France.....	12	50	27	11
Holland....	10	46	27	17

Interviewing Date 6/18–23/48
Survey #420–K   Question #1b

Asked in the United States: What is your main criticism about the way children are being taught today?

In order of frequency of mention, these are the complaints registered:

Lack of discipline, lack of fundamental character training
Subjects taught and their presentation
Parents' lack of interest and control
Too many extracurricular activities
Schools inadequate and overcrowded, old textbooks, etc.
Teacher qualifications, shortages, competency, etc.
Underpaid teachers

JULY 25
CIVIL RIGHTS PROPOSALS

Interviewing Date 3/5–10/48
Survey #414–K   Question #10

At present state governments deal with most crimes committed in their own states. In the case of a lynching do you think the Federal Government should have the right to step in and deal with the crime — or do you think this should be left entirely to the state government?

Federal Government................ 48%
State government.................... 41
No opinion........................ 11

South Only

Federal Government................ 23%
State government.................... 65
No opinion........................ 12

Outside South Only

Federal Government................ 51%
State government.................... 38
No opinion........................ 11

Interviewing Date 3/5–10/48
Survey #414–K   Question #10f

Some Southern states require every voter to pay a poll tax amounting to about a dollar a year before they can vote. Do you think these poll taxes should be abolished?

Yes............................... 65%
No................................ 24
No opinion........................ 11

South Only

Yes............................... 48%
No................................ 43
No opinion........................ 9

Outside South Only

Yes............................... 67%
No................................ 21
No opinion........................ 12

States with Poll Taxes

Yes............................... 56%
No................................ 36
No opinion........................ 8

Interviewing Date 3/5–10/48
Survey #414–K   Question #10h

Do you think Negroes should or should not be required to occupy a separate part of a train or bus when travelling from one state to another?

Yes............................... 42%
No................................ 49
No opinion........................ 9

South Only

Yes............................... 84%
No................................ 12
No opinion........................ 4

Outside South Only

Yes............................... 36%
No................................ 54
No opinion........................ 10

Interviewing Date 3/5–10/48
Survey #414–K   Question #10i

How far do you yourself think the Federal Government should go in requiring employers to hire people without regard to race, religion, color, or nationality?

All the way....................... 32%
Should do nothing................. 45
Depends on type of work........... 7
Should leave matters to the states...... 2
Don't know........................ 14

South Only

All the way....................... 9%
Should do nothing................. 68
Depends on type of work........... 3
Should leave matters to the states...... 2
Don't know........................ 18

Outside South Only

All the way....................... 36%
Should do nothing................. 42
Depends on type of work........... 7
Should leave matters to the states...... 2
Don't know........................ 13

JULY 28
FOOD EXPENSES

Interviewing Date 6/18–23/48
Survey #420–K   Question #5e

On the average, how much does your family spend on food, including milk, each week?

Median average.................... $25

JULY 30
BERLIN

Interviewing Date 7/16–21/48
Survey #421–K   Question #5a

Do you think the United States and her Western European allies should stay in Berlin, even if it means war with Russia — or should the United States give up Berlin to the Russians?

Stay in Berlin.................... 80%
Give up Berlin.................... 11
No opinion........................ 9

By Occupation
Professional and Business

Stay in Berlin...................... 85%
Give up Berlin..................... 8
No opinion........................ 7

White Collar

Stay in Berlin...................... 80%
Give up Berlin..................... 11
No opinion........................ 9

Farmers

Stay in Berlin...................... 80%
Give up Berlin..................... 11
No opinion........................ 9

Manual Workers

Stay in Berlin...................... 78%
Give up Berlin..................... 12
No opinion........................ 10

Truman Supporters

Stay in Berlin...................... 82%
Give up Berlin..................... 9
No opinion........................ 9

Dewey Supporters

Stay in Berlin...................... 83%
Give up Berlin..................... 11
No opinion........................ 6

JULY 31
DEMOCRATIC PARTY PLATFORM

Interviewing Date 7/16–21/48
Survey #421–K   Question #7a

Did you happen to read the Democratic platform drawn up at their convention in Philadelphia?

Yes, all of it...................... 7%
Yes, only part of it................ 32
No, not any of it.................. 61

AUGUST 2
PRESIDENTIAL TRIAL HEAT

Interviewing Date 7/16–21/48
Survey #421–K   Question #3a

If the presidential election were being held today, how would you vote — for Thomas Dewey, for Harry Truman, or for Henry Wallace?

Dewey........................... 48%
Truman.......................... 37
Wallace.......................... 5
No opinion........................ 10

AUGUST 4
UNITED NATIONS

Interviewing Date 7/16–21/48
Survey #421–K   Question #2a

Do you think the United States should or should not lend money to the United Nations to go ahead with their headquarters building in New York City?

Should........................... 46%
Should not........................ 34
Qualified......................... 4
No opinion........................ 16

By Education
College

Should........................... 64%
Should not........................ 24
Qualified, no opinion............... 12

High School

Should........................... 51%
Should not........................ 31
Qualified, no opinion............... 18

Grade School

Should........................... 35%
Should not........................ 41
Qualified, no opinion............... 24

Because the United States has not yet offered to lend $65 million to the United Nations to build its headquarters, some United Nations' officials want to move the headquarters to Europe. Do you think it would be a good thing or a bad thing for the UN to move its headquarters to Europe?

Good thing	11%
Bad thing	61
No difference	15
No opinion	13

By Education
College

Good thing	11%
Bad thing	60
No difference	20
No opinion	9

High School

Good thing	12%
Bad thing	60
No difference	18
No opinion	10

Grade School

Good thing	10%
Bad thing	62
No difference	12
No opinion	16

AUGUST 6
PRESIDENTIAL TRIAL HEAT

Interviewing Date 7/16–21/48
Survey #421–K   Question #3a

Asked of farmers: If a presidential election were being held today, how would you vote — for Thomas Dewey, for Harry Truman, or for Henry Wallace?

Dewey	48%
Truman	38
Wallace	2
No opinion	12

AUGUST 7
EUROPEAN MILITARY ALLIANCE

Interviewing Date 7/16–21/48
Survey #421–K   Question #4a

Do you think the United States and all the Western European countries participating in the Marshall Plan should join together in a permanent military alliance — that is, agree to come to each other's defense immediately if any one of them is attacked?

Favor alliance	73%
Opposed	16
No opinion	11

AUGUST 8
PARTY STRENGTH

Interviewing Date 7/16–21/48
Survey #421–K   Question #9

As you feel today, would you be more likely to vote for the Democratic or for the Republican candidate for Congress from your district?

Democratic	41%
Republican	41
Other party	1
No opinion	17

AUGUST 11
PRESIDENTIAL TRIAL HEAT

Interviewing Date 7/16–21/48
Survey #421–K   Question #3a

If the presidential election were being held today, how would you vote — for Harry Truman, for Thomas Dewey, or for Henry Wallace?

Truman........................ 41%
Dewey......................... 53
Wallace....................... 6

(Note: the no opinion percentage, which is 10% nationally, has been eliminated.)

Manual Workers Only

Truman........................ 45%
Dewey......................... 38
Wallace....................... 6
No opinion.................... 11

Union Members Only

Truman........................ 46%
Dewey......................... 38
Wallace....................... 7
No opinion.................... 9

Farmers Only

Truman........................ 43%
Dewey......................... 55
Wallace....................... 2

AUGUST 13
DEFENSE WORK

Interviewing Date 6/18–23/48
Survey #420–K   Question #9

Should a law be passed now which would give the Government the right to require all citizens under 65 to register with draft boards so that citizens could take part in defense work if they are needed?

Yes........................... 60%
No............................ 33
No opinion.................... 7

Interviewing Date 3/19–24/48
Survey #415–K   Question #4a

Should the United States Government require young men of draft age who are not taken into the armed forces to spend time in training for local defense or war work?

Yes........................... 70%
No............................ 21
No opinion.................... 9

AUGUST 14
OLYMPIC GAMES

Interviewing Date 7/16–21/48
Survey #421–K   Question #6c

Will you tell me what the Olympic Games are?

Two persons in three knew what the Olympic Games are.

Interviewing Date 7/16–21/48
Survey #421–T   Question #6d

Asked of those who knew what the Olympic Games are: Do you think the Olympic Games do more good than harm to international goodwill — or more harm than good?

More good than harm............ 77%
More harm than good............ 7
No effect either way........... 8
Undecided...................... 8

AUGUST 15
AMERICAN COMMUNISTS

Interviewing Date 7/30–8/4/48
Survey #422–KNS   Question #13d

The Mundt-Nixon bill now before Congress would not stop anyone from belonging to the Communist party, but it would require every individual who belongs to the Communist party or Communist organizations to register with the Justice Department in Washington. Do you think Congress should or should not pass this bill?

Should........................ 63%
Should not.................... 22
No opinion.................... 15

Interviewing Date 7/30–8/4/48
Survey #422–T   Question #18

In general do you think most American citizens who belong to the Communist party in this country are loyal to the United States or to Russia?

Loyal to U.S. 23%
Loyal to Russia 56
No opinion 21

Interviewing Date 7/30–8/4/48
Survey #422–KNS   Question #18

If we should get into a war with Russia, do you think the Communists in the United States would help this country or would they try to work against the United States?

Would help U.S. 8%
Would work against 73
Qualified 4
No opinion 15

AUGUST 16
SWEDEN VS. RUSSIA

Special Survey

Asked in Sweden: If Sweden should come into conflict with Russia, do you believe the Swedish Communists would be for Sweden or for Russia?

For Sweden 17%
For Russia 55
No opinion 28

AUGUST 18
RATIONING AND PRICE CONTROLS

Interviewing Date 7/30–8/4/48
Survey #422–KNS   Question #1a

Do you think the Government should or should not put back rationing and price controls on some products?

Should 56%
Should not 35
Qualified, no opinion 9

By Community Size
500,000 and Over

Should 63%
Should not 29
Qualified, no opinion 8

100,000–500,000

Should 62%
Should not 30
Qualified, no opinion 8

10,000–100,000

Should 57%
Should not 33
Qualified, no opinion 10

Under 10,000

Should 55%
Should not 35
Qualified, no opinion 10

Farms

Should 41%
Should not 49
Qualified, no opinion 10

Interviewing Date 7/30–8/4/48
Survey #422–KNS   Question #2

Some people say that one of the reasons prices are high today is because the Government guarantees the price of wheat, potatoes, and other crops to farmers. Would you approve or disapprove of cutting down the amount of these guarantees to farmers to reduce food prices?

Approve 46%
Disapprove 39
No opinion 15

500,000 and Over

Approve.......................... 48%
Disapprove....................... 33
No opinion....................... 19

100,000–500,000

Approve.......................... 50%
Disapprove....................... 36
No opinion....................... 14

10,000–100,000

Approve.......................... 53%
Disapprove....................... 33
No opinion....................... 14

Towns Under 10,000

Approve.......................... 48%
Disapprove....................... 37
No opinion....................... 15

Farms

Approve.......................... 26%
Disapprove....................... 62
No opinion....................... 12

AUGUST 20
PRESIDENTIAL TRIAL HEAT

Special Survey

Asked of Southern voters: If the presidential election were being held today, how would you vote — for Harry Truman, for Thomas Dewey, for Henry Wallace, or for J. Strom Thurmond?

Truman........................... 41%
Dewey............................ 34
Wallace.......................... 2
Thurmond......................... 14
No opinion....................... 9

AUGUST 21
PRESIDENTIAL CANDIDATES AS SPEAKERS

Interviewing Date 7/30–8/4/48
Survey #422–KNS   Question #12

Leaving aside any feelings you may have about the three men, which do you think is the best radio speaker — Thomas Dewey, Harry Truman, or Henry Wallace?

Dewey............................ 41%
Truman........................... 17
Wallace.......................... 11
No difference.................... 7
No opinion....................... 24

AUGUST 22
PRESIDENTIAL TRIAL HEAT

Interviewing Date 8/13–18/48
Survey #423–K   Question #1

If the presidential election were being held today how would you vote — for Harry Truman, for Thomas Dewey, for Henry Wallace, or for J. Strom Thurmond?

Dewey............................ 48%
Truman........................... 37
Wallace.......................... 4
Thurmond......................... 2
No opinion....................... 9

Interviewing Date 8/13–18/48
Survey #423–K   Question #3b

How certain are you that you will vote in the election — absolutely certain, fairly certain, or not certain?

	Absolutely Certain	Uncertain	Don't Plan To Vote
Favor Dewey........	50%	40%	25%
Favor Truman........	36	41	38
Favor Wallace........	4	5	4
Favor Thurmond......	2	1	2
No choice at present...	8	13	31

AUGUST 25
GENERAL KNOWLEDGE

Interviewing Date 7/30–8/4/48
Survey #422–K   Question #5a

Will you tell me the names of the presidential and vice-presidential candidates for the Republican party?

	Correct
Thomas Dewey, Pres.	88%
Earl Warren, V.P.	58

Interviewing Date 7/30–8/4/48
Survey #422–K   Question #5b

Will you tell me the names of the presidential and vice-presidential candidates for the Democratic party?

	Correct
Harry Truman, Pres.	91%
Alben Barkley, V.P.	49

Interviewing Date 7/30–8/4/48
Survey #422–K   Question #5c

Will you tell me the names of the presidential and vice-presidential candidates for the Progressive party?

	Correct
Henry Wallace, Pres.	67%
Glen Taylor, V.P.	30

Interviewing Date 7/30–8/4/48
Survey #422–K   Question #5d

Will you tell me the names of the presidential and vice-presidential candidates for the States' Rights party?

	Correct
J. Strom Thurmond, Pres.	11%
Fielding Wright, V.P.	3

Interviewing Date 7/30–8/4/48
Survey #422–K   Question #5e

Will you tell me the names of the presidential and vice-presidential candidates for the Socialist party?

	Correct
Norman Thomas, Pres.	21%
Tucker Smith, V.P.	*

*Less than 1%.

AUGUST 27
PRESIDENTIAL TRIAL HEAT

Special Survey

Asked of New York voters: If the presidential election were being held today, how would you vote — for Harry Truman, for Thomas Dewey, or for Henry Wallace?

Dewey	42%
Truman	32
Wallace	14
No opinion	12

AUGUST 28
ELECTORAL COLLEGE REFORM

Interviewing Date 8/13–18/48
Survey #423–K   Question #12c

Today, the presidential candidate who gets the most popular votes in a state takes all the electoral votes of that state. Do you think this should or should not be changed so that each of the candidates would receive the same proportion of electoral votes that he gets in the popular vote? This would mean, for example, that if a candidate gets two-thirds of the popular vote in a state, he would get two-thirds of the electoral votes of that state.

Should be changed	58%
Should not be changed	15
No opinion	27

By Education
College

Should be changed	81%
Should not be changed	9
No opinion	10

High School

Should be changed	64%
Should not be changed	19
No opinion	17

Grade School

Should be changed	47%
Should not be changed	12
No opinion	41

AUGUST 30
PRESIDENTIAL TRIAL HEAT

Interviewing Date 8/13–18/48
Survey #423–K   Question #4a

Asked of voters in the West Central states: If the presidential election were being held today, how would you vote — for Harry Truman, for Thomas Dewey, or for Henry Wallace?

Dewey	48%
Truman	42
Wallace	3
No opinion	7

SEPTEMBER 1
TAFT-HARTLEY ACT

Interviewing Date 7/30–8/4/48
Survey #422–K   Question #14a

Have you heard or read about the Taft-Hartley Act?

Yes	75%
No	25

Interviewing Date 7/30–8/4/48
Survey #422–K   Question #14b

Asked of those who answered yes: Do you think the Taft-Hartley law should be revised, repealed, or left unchanged?

Revised	26%
Repealed	16
Left unchanged	31
No opinion	27

Interviewing Date 7/30–8/4/48
Survey #422–K   Question #14c

Asked of those who thought the Taft-Hartley law should be revised: If revised, should the law be more strict with labor or less strict?

More strict	12%
Less strict	14
	26%

By Political Affiliation
Democrats

More strict	9%
Less strict	16
Repealed	25
Left unchanged	22
No opinion	28

Republicans

More strict	16%
Less strict	9
Repealed	5
Left unchanged	42
No opinion	28

Independents

More strict	11%
Less strict	19
Repealed	16
Left unchanged	28
No opinion	26

By Occupation
Business and Professional

More strict	21%
Less strict	14
Repealed	10
Left unchanged	32
No opinion	23

White Collar

More strict	13%
Less strict	18
Repealed	14
Left unchanged	33
No opinion	22

Manual Workers

More strict......................... 6%
Less strict......................... 13
Repealed........................... 24
Left unchanged..................... 29
No opinion......................... 28

Farmers

More strict......................... 15%
Less strict......................... 6
Repealed........................... 7
Left unchanged..................... 31
No opinion......................... 41

Union Members Only

More strict......................... 2%
Less strict......................... 21
Repealed........................... 38
Left unchanged..................... 21
No opinion......................... 18

SEPTEMBER 3
PRESIDENTIAL TRIAL HEAT

Special Survey

Asked of Pennsylvania voters: If the presidential election were being held today, how would you vote — for Harry Truman, for Thomas Dewey, or for Henry Wallace?

Dewey............................. 53%
Truman............................ 37
Wallace........................... 3
No opinion......................... 7

SEPTEMBER 4
BUSINESS OUTLOOK

Interviewing Date 8/13–18/48
Survey #423–T   Question #8b

Do you think there will be a serious business depression in the United States during the next year?

Yes............................... 16%
No................................ 66
No opinion........................ 18

Interviewing Date 8/13–18/48
Survey #423–K   Question #8b

Do you think there will be a serious business depression in the United States during the next four years — that is, between now and 1952?

Yes............................... 37%
No................................ 40
No opinion........................ 23

Interviewing Date 8/13–18/48
Survey #423–T   Question #8c

If we should have a serious business depression in the next year, which candidate, Dewey, Truman, or Wallace, do you think could deal with it best?

Dewey............................. 39%
Truman............................ 28
Wallace........................... 4
No difference..................... 12
No opinion........................ 17

SEPTEMBER 6
SPY HEARINGS

Interviewing Date 8/13–18/48
Survey #423–K   Question #10a

Have you heard or read about the congressional spy hearings?

Yes............................... 79%
No................................ 21

Interviewing Date 8/13–18/48
Survey #423–K   Question #10c

Asked of those who had heard or read about the hearings: Do you think Congress should continue with its spy investigations — or do you think Congress should call them off?

Should continue investigations......... 79%
Should call off investigations.......... 15
No opinion....................... 6

Interviewing Date 8/13–18/48
Survey #423–K   Question #10d

Asked of those who had heard or read about the hearings: Do you think there is something to these spy investigations, or do you think it is a case of playing politics?

Something to investigations.......... 74%
Just politics...................... 17
No opinion....................... 9

By Political Affiliation
Democrats

Something to investigations.......... 71%
Just politics...................... 19
No opinion....................... 10

Republicans

Something to investigations.......... 84%
Just politics...................... 8
No opinion....................... 8

Independents

Something to investigations.......... 65%
Just politics...................... 24
No opinion....................... 11

SEPTEMBER 8
PRESIDENTIAL TRIAL HEAT

Interviewing Date 8/20–25/48
Survey #424–K   Question #5a

If the presidential election were being held today how would you vote — for Harry Truman, for Thomas Dewey, or for Henry Wallace?

Dewey........................... 48.5%
Truman.......................... 36.5
Wallace.......................... 5.0
Undecided........................ 10.0

With the undecideds eliminated the vote becomes:

Dewey........................... 54.0%
Truman.......................... 40.5
Wallace.......................... 5.5

SEPTEMBER 10
PRESIDENTIAL TRIAL HEAT

Special Survey

Asked of Missouri voters: If the presidential election were being held today, how would you vote — for Harry Truman or for Thomas Dewey.

Truman.......................... 53%
Dewey........................... 36
No opinion....................... 11

SEPTEMBER 11
PRESIDENTIAL TRIAL HEAT

Interviewing Date 8/20–25/48
Survey #424–K   Question #5a

If the presidential election were being held today, for whom would you vote — Harry Truman, Thomas Dewey, or Henry Wallace?

By Sex
Men

Dewey........................... 49.0%
Truman.......................... 36.5
Wallace.......................... 5.0
Undecided........................ 9.5

Women

Dewey........................... 48.0%
Truman.......................... 36.5
Wallace.......................... 5.0
Undecided........................ 10.5

By Age
21–29 Years

Dewey.......................... 46.5%
Truman......................... 35.5
Wallace........................ 7.0
Undecided...................... 11.0

30–49 Years

Dewey.......................... 49.5%
Truman......................... 36.0
Wallace........................ 5.0
Undecided...................... 9.5

50 Years and Over

Dewey.......................... 48.0%
Truman......................... 37.5
Wallace........................ 4.0
Undecided...................... 10.5

SEPTEMBER 13
PRESIDENTIAL TRIAL HEAT

Special Survey

Asked of South Carolina voters: If the presidential election were being held today, how would you vote — for Harry Truman, for Thomas Dewey, for J. Strom Thurmond, or for Henry Wallace?

Thurmond....................... 52%
Truman......................... 26
Dewey.......................... 10
Wallace........................ *
Undecided...................... 12

*Less than 1%.

SEPTEMBER 15
PRESIDENTIAL TRIAL HEAT

Special Survey

Asked of California voters: If the presidential election were being held today, how would you vote — for Harry Truman, for Thomas Dewey, or for Henry Wallace?

Dewey.......................... 49%
Truman......................... 35
Wallace........................ 7
Undecided...................... 9

SEPTEMBER 17
PRESIDENTIAL TRIAL HEAT

Special Survey

Asked of New Jersey voters: If the presidential election were being held today, how would you vote — for Harry Truman, for Thomas Dewey, or for Henry Wallace?

Dewey.......................... 50%
Truman......................... 38
Wallace........................ 3
No opinion..................... 9

SEPTEMBER 18
THE DRAFT

Interviewing Date 8/13–18/48
Survey #423–K   Question #9a

On August 30, all men between 18 and 25 years of age will start registering under the federal draft law. In general, do you approve or disapprove of the draft?

Approve........................ 73%
Disapprove..................... 21
No opinion..................... 6

SEPTEMBER 19
PRESIDENTIAL TRIAL HEAT

Special Survey

Asked of Ohio voters: If the presidential election were being held today, how would you vote — for Harry Truman, for Thomas Dewey, or for Henry Wallace?

Dewey.......................... 50%
Truman......................... 38
Wallace........................ 3
Undecided...................... 9

Interviewing Date 8/13–18/48
Survey #423–K   Question #6a

Do you think there will be another big war within the next ten years?

Yes.................................. 57%
No................................... 26
No opinion......................... 17

Interviewing Date 8/13–18/48
Survey #422–T   Question #3a

Do you think the United States will find itself in another war within, say, the next year?

Yes.................................. 32%
No................................... 54
No opinion......................... 14

Interviewing Date 8/13–18/48
Survey #423–K   Question #6b

Asked of those who answered "yes, within the next year": Who do you think will be responsible for starting the war?

Russia............................. 24%
United States...................... 3
Others............................. 4
Don't know........................ 3
                                   ——
                                   34%

(Note: table adds to more than 32% because some persons gave more than one answer.)

SEPTEMBER 23
PRESIDENTIAL TRIAL HEAT

Special Survey

Asked of California voters: If the presidential election were being held today, how would you vote — for Harry Truman, for Thomas Dewey, or for Henry Wallace?

Dewey.............................. 46%
Truman............................. 41
Wallace............................ 5
No opinion......................... 8

SEPTEMBER 24
PRESIDENTIAL TRIAL HEAT

Interviewing Date 9/2–7/48
Survey #425–K   Question #5

If the presidential election were being held today, how would you vote — for Harry Truman, Thomas Dewey, Henry Wallace, or some other candidate?

Dewey.............................. 46.5%
Truman............................. 39.0
Wallace............................ 3.5
Thurmond.......................... 2.0
Others............................. *
No opinion......................... 9.0

*Less than 1%.

Interviewing Date 9/2–7/48
Survey #425–K   Question #4b

How certain are you that you will vote in the election — absolutely certain, fairly certain, or not certain?

	Absolutely Certain	Fairly Certain	Not Certain
Favor Dewey.........	52%	41%	27%
Favor Truman........	37	46	37
Favor Wallace........	4	2	5
Favor Thurmond......	2	2	1
No choice at present...	5	9	30

SEPTEMBER 25
PRESIDENTIAL TRIAL HEAT

Special Survey

Asked of Wisconsin voters: If the presidential election were being held today, how would you vote — for Harry Truman, for Thomas Dewey, or for Henry Wallace?

Truman	38%
Dewey	51
Wallace	3
No opinion	8

SEPTEMBER 26
PRESIDENTIAL TRIAL HEAT

Special Survey

Asked of Minnesota voters: If the presidential election were being held today, how would you vote — for Harry Truman, for Thomas Dewey, or for Henry Wallace?

Dewey	42%
Truman	47
Wallace	4
No opinion	7

SEPTEMBER 27
PRESIDENTIAL TRIAL HEAT

Special Survey

Asked of Massachusetts voters: If the presidential election were being held today, how would you vote — for Harry Truman, for Thomas Dewey, or for Henry Wallace?

Dewey	49%
Truman	42
Wallace	3
No opinion	6

SEPTEMBER 27
PRESIDENTIAL TRIAL HEAT

Special Survey

Asked of Indiana voters: If the presidential election were being held today, how would you vote — for Harry Truman, for Thomas Dewey, or for Henry Wallace?

Dewey	49%
Truman	40
Wallace	3
No opinion	8

SEPTEMBER 28
PRESIDENTIAL TRIAL HEAT

Special Survey

Asked of California voters: If the presidential election were being held today, how would you vote — for Harry Truman, for Thomas Dewey, or for Henry Wallace?

Dewey	49%
Truman	35
Wallace	7
No opinion	9

SEPTEMBER 29
PRESIDENTIAL TRIAL HEAT

Special Survey

Asked of Illinois voters: If the presidential election were being held today, how would you vote — for Harry Truman or for Thomas Dewey?

Truman	40%
Dewey	49
No opinion	11

OCTOBER 1
PRESIDENTIAL TRIAL HEAT

Special Survey

Asked of Texas voters: If the presidential election were being held today, how would you vote — for Harry Truman, for Thomas Dewey, for Henry Wallace, or for J. Strom Thurmond?

Truman.......................... 63%
Dewey.......................... 23
Wallace.......................... 3
Thurmond........................ 6
No opinion....................... 5

OCTOBER 2
PRESIDENTIAL TRIAL HEAT

Interviewing Date 9/10–15/48
Survey #426   Question #5a

If the presidential election were being held today, how would you vote — for Harry Truman, Thomas Dewey, Henry Wallace, or for J. Strom Thurmond?

Dewey.......................... 46.5%
Truman.......................... 39.0
Wallace.......................... 3.5
Thurmond........................ 2.0
Undecided....................... 9.0

By Community Size
500,000 and Over

Dewey.......................... 47%
Truman.......................... 41
Wallace.......................... 12
Thurmond........................ *

*Less than 1%.

10,000–500,000

Dewey.......................... 51%
Truman.......................... 43
Wallace.......................... 4
Thurmond........................ 2

Towns Under 10,000

Dewey.......................... 52%
Truman.......................... 43
Wallace.......................... 3
Thurmond........................ 2

Farm Areas

Dewey.......................... 50%
Truman.......................... 44
Wallace.......................... 2
Thurmond........................ 4

OCTOBER 4
PRESIDENTIAL TRIAL HEAT

Special Survey

Asked of Kentucky and North Carolina voters: If the presidential election were being held today, how would you vote — for Harry Truman, for Thomas Dewey, for Henry Wallace, or for J. Strom Thurmond?

Kentucky

Truman.......................... 45%
Dewey.......................... 42
Wallace.......................... 2
Thurmond........................ 5
No opinion....................... 6

North Carolina

Truman.......................... 44%
Dewey.......................... 33
Wallace.......................... 1
Thurmond........................ 13
No opinion....................... 9

OCTOBER 6
PRESIDENTIAL TRIAL HEAT

Special Survey

Asked of voters in the New England and Middle Atlantic states: If the presidential election were being held today, how would you vote — for Harry Truman, for Thomas Dewey, or for Henry Wallace?

New England
Maine

Dewey.......................... 56%
Truman.......................... 34
Wallace.......................... 3
No opinion....................... 7

New Hampshire

Dewey.......................... 54%
Truman.......................... 36
Wallace.......................... 3
No opinion....................... 7

Vermont

Dewey	60%
Truman	33
Wallace	1
No opinion	6

Massachusetts

Dewey	50%
Truman	43
Wallace	2
No opinion	5

Connecticut

Dewey	43%
Truman	39
Wallace	4
No opinion	14

Rhode Island

Dewey	37%
Truman	48
Wallace	3
No opinion	12

Middle Atlantic
New York

Dewey	47%
Truman	34
Wallace	11
No opinion	8

New Jersey

Dewey	50%
Truman	38
Wallace	3
No opinion	9

Pennsylvania

Dewey	50%
Truman	41
Wallace	3
No opinion	6

Delaware

Dewey	49%
Truman	36
Wallace	1
No opinion	14

Maryland

Dewey	47%
Truman	44
Wallace	4
No opinion	5

West Virginia

Dewey	49%
Truman	43
Wallace	2
No opinion	6

OCTOBER 8
PRESIDENTIAL TRIAL HEAT

Special Survey

Asked of voters in Illinois, Michigan, Indiana, and Ohio: If the presidential election were being held today, how would you vote — for Harry Truman, for Thomas Dewey, or for Henry Wallace?

Illinois

Dewey	49%
Truman	40
Wallace	*
No opinion	11

*Interviewers did not ask respondents whether they would vote for Henry Wallace.

Michigan

Dewey	52%
Truman	41
Wallace	4
No opinion	3

Indiana

Dewey	52%
Truman	40
Wallace	2
No opinion	6

Ohio

Dewey	51%
Truman	42
Wallace	3
No opinion	4

OCTOBER 9
PRESIDENTIAL TRIAL HEAT

Special Survey

Asked of labor union members: If the presidential election were being held today, how would you vote — for Harry Truman, for Thomas Dewey, for Henry Wallace, or for J. Strom Thurmond?

Truman............................ 55%
Dewey............................. 38
Wallace........................... 7
Thurmond.......................... *

*Less than 1%.

C.I.O. Members Only

Truman............................ 58%
Dewey............................. 32
Wallace........................... 10
Thurmond.......................... *

*Less than 1%.

A.F.L. Members Only

Truman............................ 54%
Dewey............................. 40
Wallace........................... 6
Thurmond.......................... *

*Less than 1%.

In the above tables, the undecided vote has been eliminated.

OCTOBER 10
PRESIDENTIAL TRIAL HEAT

Special Survey

Asked of voters in the West Central states: If the presidential election were being held today, how would you vote — for Harry Truman, for Thomas Dewey, or for Henry Wallace?

Iowa

Truman............................ 38%
Dewey............................. 53
Wallace........................... 2
Undecided......................... 7

Kansas

Truman............................ 34%
Dewey............................. 59
Wallace........................... 2
Undecided......................... 5

Minnesota

Truman............................ 45%
Dewey............................. 45
Wallace........................... 4
Undecided......................... 6

Missouri

Truman............................ 51%
Dewey............................. 40
Wallace........................... 3
Undecided......................... 6

Nebraska

Truman............................ 39%
Dewey............................. 53
Wallace........................... *
Undecided......................... 8

*Not on ballot.

North Dakota

Truman............................ 34%
Dewey............................. 50
Wallace........................... 6
Undecided......................... 10

South Dakota

Truman............................ 38%
Dewey............................. 54
Wallace........................... 1
Undecided......................... 7

Wisconsin

Truman............................ 40%
Dewey............................. 51
Wallace........................... 3
Undecided......................... 6

OCTOBER 16
PRESIDENTIAL TRIAL HEAT

Interviewing Date 9/23–28/48
Survey #428   Question #6a

If the presidential election were being held today, for whom would you vote — Thomas Dewey, Harry Truman, Henry Wallace, or J. Strom Thurmond?

Independent Voters Only

Dewey	47%
Truman	30
Wallace	7
Thurmond	1
Undecided	15

OCTOBER 18
PRESIDENTIAL TRIAL HEAT

Interviewing Date 9/23–28/48
Survey #428   Question #6a

If the presidential election were being held today, for whom would you vote — Harry Truman, Thomas Dewey, Henry Wallace, or J. Strom Thurmond?

Dewey	46%
Truman	40
Wallace	4
Thurmond	2
Undecided	8

By Region
Dewey States

	Dewey	Truman	Wallace	Thurmond	Undec.
Maine	56%	34%	3%	*%	7%
N. Hamp	54	36	3	*	7
Vermont	60	33	1	*	6
Delaware	49	36	1	*	14
New Jersey	50	38	3	*	9
New York	47	34	11	*	8
Pennsylvania	50	41	3	*	6
Illinois	49	40	*	*	11
Michigan	52	41	4	*	3
Indiana	52	40	2	*	6
Ohio	51	42	3	*	4
Iowa	53	38	2	*	7
Kansas	59	34	2	*	5
Nebraska	53	39	*	*	8
N. Dakota	50	34	6	*	10
S. Dakota	54	38	1	*	7
Wisconsin	51	40	3	*	6
Colorado	51	41	1	*	7
Wyoming	50	41	3	*	6
Oregon	47	38	5	*	10

Truman States

	Dewey	Truman	Wallace	Thurmond	Undec.
Rhode Is.	37%	48%	3%	*%	12%
Missouri	40	51	3	*	6
New Mex.	40	49	2	*	9
Arkansas	23	55	1	12	9
Georgia	16	55	2	16	11
Kentucky	40	49	1	4	6
N. Carolina	34	44	1	13	8
Oklahoma	39	52	*	*	9
Tennessee	32	48	1	8	11
Texas	23	61	3	8	5

Thurmond States

	Dewey	Truman	Wallace	Thurmond	Undec.
Alabama	16%	32%	1%	43%	8%
Louisiana	20	28	2	34	16
Miss.	5	12	1	66	16
S. Carolina	10	26	**	54	10

On the Line

	Dewey	Truman	Wallace	Thurmond	Undec.
Connecticut	43%	39%	4%	*%	14%
Mass.	50	43	2	*	5
West Va.	49	43	2	*	6
Maryland	47	44	4	*	5
Minnesota	45	45	4	*	6
Florida	32	33	2	19	14
Virginia	43	40	1	8	8
Arizona	43	47	5	*	5
Idaho	46	42	5	*	7
Montana	40	47	7	*	6
Nevada	47	44	3	*	6
Utah	45	42	3	*	10
California	48	41	6	*	5
Washington	45	43	3	*	9

*Not on ballot.
**Less than 1%.

OCTOBER 20
POLITICAL AFFILIATION

Interviewing Date 9/30–10/5/48
Survey #429   Question #9

Asked of those who said they intended to vote on Election Day: In politics, as of today, do you consider yourself a Democrat, a Republican, a Progressive, or an Independent?

Democrat.......................... 44%
Republican........................ 35
Progressive....................... 2
Independent....................... 19

OCTOBER 23
PRESIDENTIAL TRIAL HEAT

Interviewing Date 9/30–10/5/48
Survey #429   Question #7b

Regardless of how you, yourself, plan to vote — which presidential candidate do you think will carry this state, Thomas Dewey, Harry Truman, Henry Wallace, or J. Strom Thurmond?

The public by a ratio of two to one predicts that Governor Dewey will go to the White House.

College-trained voters, of whom a majority today are Republicans, by a five-to-one ratio, say Dewey will win.

People with only a grammar school education also pick Dewey but by a four to three margin.

More than eight out of ten Dewey supporters think he will be elected, while Truman voters pick the President by a ratio of two to one.

One out of eight Wallace followers with opinions believe the Progressive candidate will win the presidency, although most Wallace voters select Dewey. One out of eight Dixiecrat voters are betting that their candidate, J. Strom Thurmond will be the next president.

OCTOBER 24
FRENCH POLITICS

Special Survey

Asked in France: Do you think that the National Assembly should or should not be dissolved and new elections held?

Hold elections....................... 51%
Do not hold elections............... 27
No opinion......................... 22

OCTOBER 29
SEMIFINAL ELECTION SURVEY

Special Survey

States Where Dewey Leads by Eight or More Percentage Points

	Dewey	Tru- man	Wal- lace
Maine..................	60%	38%	2%
New Hampshire..........	58	39	3
Vermont................	63	36	1
Connecticut............	52	43	5
New York..............	52	36	12
New Jersey.............	56	40	4
Pennsylvania...........	54	43	3
Maryland..............	54	43	3
Illinois................	55	45	*
Michigan..............	53	44	3
Indiana...............	55	43	2
Ohio..................	54	43	3
Iowa..................	56	41	3
Kansas................	62	36	2
Nebraska..............	60	40	*
North Dakota..........	57	37	6
South Dakota..........	59	40	1
Wisconsin.............	56	41	3
Oregon................	52	43	5

*Not on ballot.

States Where Truman Leads by Eight or More Percentage Points

	Dewey	Truman	Wallace	Thurmond
Rhode Island	42%	55%	3%	*%
Arkansas	30	56	1	13
Florida	35	45	2	18
Georgia	22	58	2	18
Kentucky	43	52	1	4
Louisiana	24	41	3	32
North Carolina	37	50	1	12
Oklahoma	46	54	*	*
Tennessee	39	53	1	7
Texas	22	68	3	7

States Where Thurmond Leads by Eight or More Percentage Points

	Dewey	Truman	Wallace	Thurmond
Alabama	22%	*%	1%	77%
Mississippi	10	16	1	73
South Carolina	11	32	**	57

States Where Margin Between Candidates Is Less Than Eight Percentage Points

	Dewey	Truman	Wallace	Thurmond
Massachusetts	52%	45%	3%	*%
Delaware	53	46	1	*
West Virginia	51	47	2	*
Virginia	45	44	2	9
Minnesota	50	46	4	*
Missouri	47	52	1	*
Arizona	46	50	4	*
Colorado	52	47	1	*
Idaho	49	47	4	*
Montana	45	50	5	*
Nevada	51	46	3	*
New Mexico	46	52	2	*
Utah	50	47	3	*
Wyoming	52	45	3	*
California	51	44	5	*
Washington	49	47	4	*

*Not on ballot.
**Less than 1%.

Special Survey
Interviewing Date 10/15–25/48

If the presidential election were being held today, how would you vote — for Harry Truman, for Thomas Dewey, for Henry Wallace, or for J. Strom Thurmond?

Dewey	49.5%
Truman	44.5
Wallace	4
Thurmond	2

States Where Dewey Has Substantial Lead

	Dewey	Truman	Wallace
California	52%	43%	5%
Connecticut	52	44	4
Illinois	54	46	*
Indiana	54	44	2
Iowa	54	43	3
Kansas	60	39	1
Maine	56	42	2
Maryland	53	44	3
Michigan	53	44	3
Nebraska	62	38	*
New Hampshire	54	44	2
New Jersey	54	42	4
New York	51	39	10
North Dakota	57	38	5
Ohio	55	42	3
Oregon	54	42	4
Pennsylvania	52	44	4
South Dakota	58	41	1
Vermont	64	35	1
Wisconsin	56	41	3

States Where Truman Has Substantial Lead

	Dewey	Truman	Wallace	Thurmond
Arizona	44%	53%	3%	*%
Arkansas	32	53	1	14
Florida	35	45	1	19
Georgia	22	58	1	19

*Less than 1%.

	Dewey	Tru-man	Wal-lace	Thur-mond
N. Carolina.........	36	51	1	12
Oklahoma..........	45	55	*	*
Rhode Island.......	44	54	2	*
Tennessee..........	39	51	1	9
Texas.............	24	66	2	8

States Where Lead Is Not Substantial

	Dewey	Tru-man	Wal-lace	Thur-mond
Massachusetts.......	52%	45%	3%	*%
Missouri...........	47	52	1	*
Minnesota.........	51	46	3	*
W. Virginia........	51	46	3	*
Delaware..........	51	47	2	*
Wyoming..........	51	47	2	*
N. Mexico.........	47	51	2	*
Nevada............	50	47	3	*
Montana..........	48	50	2	*
Utah..............	49	50	1	*
Colorado..........	50	49	1	*
Kentucky..........	46	49	1	4
Idaho.............	49	47	4	*
Washington........	48	47	5	*
Virginia...........	45	44	1	10

States Where Ballot Is Confusing

For the following four states, these figures should not be regarded as forecasts of the vote because of confusing ballot situations confronting the voters.

	Dewey	Tru-man	Wal-lace	Thur-mond
Alabama..........	28%	*%	2%	70%
Louisiana..........	27	39	2	32
Mississippi.........	9	15	1	75
South Carolina......	9	38	**	53

*Not on the ballot.
**Less than 1%.

NOVEMBER 5
RUSSIA

Interviewing Date 7/30–8/4/48
Survey #422–KNS   Question #17

Do you think the United States is too soft or too tough (firm) in its policy toward Russia?

By Political Affiliation
Republicans

Too soft...........................	73%
Too tough........................	3
About right.......................	14
No opinion.......................	10

Democrats

Too soft...........................	70%
Too tough........................	4
About right.......................	14
No opinion.......................	12

NOVEMBER 7
CLEMENT ATTLEE

Special Survey

Asked in Great Britain: On the whole do you approve or disapprove of Mr. Attlee as Prime Minister?

Approve...........................	37%
Disapprove........................	46
No opinion.......................	17

NOVEMBER 10
ATOMIC ENERGY

Special Survey
Interviewing Date 10/7–12/48 (U.S. Only)
Survey #430–K   Question #8a

Asked in several nations: Do you think that, in the long run, atomic energy will do more good than harm?

	More Good	More Harm	No Opin.
Holland................	25%	52%	23%
Sweden................	26	48	26
England................	33	41	26
Australia...............	36	46	18
United States..........	42	23	35

By Education
College

	United States
More good	61%
More harm	18
No opinion	21

High School

More good	47%
More harm	25
No opinion	28

Grade School

More good	31%
More harm	23
No opinion	46

NOVEMBER 13
NEIGHBORS

Special Survey

Asked in Great Britain: On the whole, would you say that you have pleasant neighbors or don't you like them much?

Mainly pleasant	68%
Like a few	15
Don't like any	5
No contact with them	12

NOVEMBER 21
THE VICE PRESIDENCY

Interviewing Date 11/3–8/48
Survey #432–K   Question #8c

It has been suggested that the Vice President should help the President with administrative problems so that the President would have more time to deal with matters of policy. Do you agree or disagree with this idea?

Agree	81%
Disagree	7
No opinion	12

NOVEMBER 23
GALLUP ANALYSIS OF POLL ERROR

Statisticians of the Gallup Poll have discovered in the first check into the reasons why Truman's popular vote was underestimated, that one of the chief reasons why polls went wrong this year was their failure to continue questioning voters right up to election eve.

For this reason, Gallup Poll findings did not reflect the views of voters who made up their minds to vote for President Truman in the closing days of the campaign.

A special report by George Gallup to publishers and editors of the newspapers carrying the poll points out that the bulk of interviewing for the final survey was completed 10 to 12 days before the election. This early termination of interviewing is believed to have contributed substantially to the error of the Gallup forecast, which showed President Truman in second place and underestimated his vote by 5.5 percentage points.

However, the report emphasizes that only the first stage of the investigation has been completed and that further checks are in progress. All data will be analyzed not only by the Gallup Poll organization but will be turned over to a group of leading social scientists for their own analysis and interpretation.

Results of the first study point to a substantial shift of votes from Governor Thomas E. Dewey to President Truman during the closing days and hours of the campaign. There was also a continuation in the last days, of the shift from Henry A. Wallace to Mr. Truman.

The number of voters who were still undecided about their choice of candidates ten days before the election was unusually large this year, the poll points out, totaling 8.7%, or some four million people. Analysis of the past voting history of this group indicates that a high proportion had voted the Democratic ticket in the 1944 election. Mr. Truman won back to the Democratic fold a substantial part of this group.

The above analysis is based on a special study initiated by the Gallup organization before the election to shed light on the actual election day voting of persons they had interviewed prior to the election.

During the period October 15–25 each person interviewed in the final Gallup election poll was handed a postcard with the following instructions:

"After voting ends on November 2, please detach this postcard and mark (X) in the appropriate box below. Mail it at your first opportunity. Thank you.

"In the Presidential election Nov. 2:

( ) I was unable to vote

I voted for: ( ) Dewey ( ) Truman ( ) Wallace ( ) Thurmond ( ) Other . . . ."

Each card had a serial number. The numbers matched those on the pre-election ballot of each individual. By comparing the postcards with the pre-election interviews, the pollsters were able to see what each person said he would do beforehand and what he actually did do on election day.

This study was patterned after an experiment conducted in an Australian election by Roy Morgan, Director of the Australian Gallup Poll, and reported by him in an article in the current issue of *The Public Opinion Quarterly*.

The postcard study sheds light on what happened to the undecided vote, the Gallup report continues. Because of apathy shown in the campaign, it had been assumed that most of the undecided would not vote. This assumption proved erroneous. Not only did many of them vote but they voted overwhelmingly for Mr. Truman.

Also shown by the returned postcards was a pronounced shift toward Mr. Truman in the closing days of the campaign. He gained votes from people who had voted Democratic in 1944 and who thought ten days before the election that they were going to vote for Mr. Dewey this year, but who changed their minds and once again voted Democratic. There was some shifting in the other direction, but analysis of the cards shows the net effect was decidedly in favor of Mr. Truman.

Mr. Truman also gained, to a lesser extent, from 1944 Democrats who had been for Mr. Wallace earlier this year but who changed their minds and voted Democratic. Our postcard experiment shows that one-third of the people who told us in late October that they were going to vote for Mr. Wallace shifted to Mr. Truman. Poll reports showed a decline in Mr. Wallace's support during the last weeks of the campaign. But we didn't catch the full impact of the shift which continued after we had stopped polling.

Commenting on lessons learned from the election, Dr. Gallup said today:

"If later analysis of other facts bears out the results of the first study, it would appear that the chief failure in election forecasts this year was due to decisions made by the poll directors rather than by any failure in the sampling system itself. Certainly, one lesson learned is that polling hereafter must continue right up to the eve of election in order to catch any last minute shifts.

"Undoubtedly, other improvements can and will be made. Sampling and interviewing procedures can undoubtedly be improved as they have been in recent years. We are wedded to no single one. We constantly seek improvement by experimenting with new techniques. We hope to see full and adequate tests made in election forecasting of the method known as area sampling. Out of such testing, I am sure, progress will come and a new type of sample design best fitted for election forecasting."

NOVEMBER 24
GALLUP ANALYSIS OF POLL ERROR

A proposal for a radically new method of reporting election polls has been submitted to member newspapers sponsoring the Gallup Poll.

The suggestion, which came from some of the sponsoring newspapers, calls for publication of a greater wealth of statistical data than has been made public in the past and a new method of presenting election poll findings.

Together with the new techniques developed as a result of lessons learned in the 1948 elections, the proposed changes in reporting will produce an entirely new kind of political journalism, George Gallup, director of the American Institute of Public Opinion, declared.

In announcing the new method, Dr. Gallup stated:

In future elections the poll will, under the plan now being considered, continue to gather its facts by nation-wide interviewing, and will report in detail the comparative strength of rival candidates among the registered voters with definite opinions who also are certain they will vote.

As in previous elections this comparative strength will be analyzed for all important voting groups: farmers, union members, new voters, independents, and so forth.

The new policy of reporting wider facts will be sought regarding two important voter groups which in the past have been perennial problems to all pollsters, namely: (1) those voters who are not sure whether or not they will vote; and (2) those voters who are undecided as to which candidate they favor.

The importance of these two groups in the last campaign can be estimated roughly from the following figures: of the 94 million people of voting age, only 67 million were registered and otherwise eligible to vote; of this 67 million approximately 48 million finally got to the polls and voted. Even in the closing days of the campaign there were probably seven or eight million voters who were not certain whether they would vote, or who had not made up their minds on their presidential choice.

In future election reports the Gallup Poll will inaugurate an exhaustive study of these undecided voters to seek evidence concerning their probable voting behavior if they turn out on Election Day.

These new techniques will be designed to ascertain how these same undecided and doubtful voters voted in previous elections, as well as to learn their attitudes on controversial issues of the campaign. The new methods will also reveal the relative number of new voters, farmers, union members, men and women, and veterans in the undecided group.

Such information has never been reported in detail by any poll in previous elections. It should prove valuable to political observers who can appraise more accurately the effect of the rival campaigns on this independent group of voters.

NOVEMBER 28
MARSHALL PLAN

Interviewing Date 11/3–8/48
Survey #432–K   Question #9a

Have you heard or read about the Marshall Plan?

Yes............................... 82%
No............................... 18

Interviewing Date 11/3–8/48
Survey #432–K   Question #9b

Asked of those familiar with the Marshall Plan: How satisfied are you with the results of the Marshall Plan to date — very satisfied, fairly satisfied, or not at all satisfied?

Very satisfied..................... 14%
Fairly satisfied..................... 48
Not at all satisfied.................. 14
No opinion........................ 24

Interviewing Date 11/3–8/48
Survey #432–K   Question #9c

Asked of those familiar with the Marshall Plan: Do you think Congress should or should not continue the Marshall Plan for next year?

Should............................ 65%
Should not........................ 13
No opinion........................ 22

Interviewing Date 11 /3–8 /48
Survey #432–K   Question #9d

Asked of those familiar with the Marshall Plan: Do you think Congress should or should not vote the money required to continue the Marshall Plan for next year?

Should............................ 62%
Should not........................ 16
No opinion........................ 22

DECEMBER 1
WESTERN ALLIANCE

Interviewing Date 11 /3–8 /48
Survey #432–K   Question #10a

Do you think the United States and all the Western European countries participating in the Marshall Plan should join together in a permanent military alliance — that is, agree to come to each other's defense immediately if any one of them is attacked?

Favor alliance.................... 68%
Oppose............................ 19
No opinion........................ 13

Interviewing Date 11 /3–8 /48
Survey #432–K   Question #10b

Would you favor or oppose the United States spending about $2 billion in the next year to help Western European countries re-arm?

Favor............................. 32%
Oppose............................ 54
No opinion........................ 14

DECEMBER 3
THE "COLD WAR"

Interviewing Date 11 /3–8 /48
Survey #432–K   Question #3a

Will you tell me what the term "cold war" means?

Generally correct answer............ 47%
Incorrect answer.................... 7
Don't know.......................... 46

Interviewing Date 11 /3–8 /48
Survey #432–K   Question #3b

Asked of those giving an answer (54%): In general, who do you think is winning the cold war — the United States or Russia?

U.S. winning....................... 17%
Russia winning..................... 15
Neither winning.................... 16
No opinion......................... 6
                                   ——
                                   54%

DECEMBER 4
SLEEPING

Interviewing Date 5 /7–12 /48
Survey #418–K   Question #4a

Do you have any difficulty getting to sleep at night — frequently, occasionally, or almost never?

Yes, frequently.................... 14%
Yes, occasionally.................. 38
No, never.......................... 48

By Sex

	No, never
Men	51%
Women	44

DECEMBER 5
1948 ELECTION

Interviewing Date 11 /3–8 /48
Survey #432–K   Question #16a

When did you definitely make up your

mind to vote for the presidential candidate of your choice?

Before campaign started............. 54%
Early in campaign.................. 12
First half of October............... 3
Second half of October............. 9
Election Day...................... 4
Indefinite........................ 18

Truman Voters

Before campaign started............. 46%
Early in campaign.................. 11
First half of October............... 4
Second half of October............. 13
Election Day...................... 5
Indefinite........................ 21

Dewey Voters

Before campaign started............. 64%
Early in campaign.................. 12
First half of October............... 2
Second half of October............. 5
Election Day...................... 3
Indefinite........................ 14

DECEMBER 8
PROPAGANDA

Interviewing Date 11/3–8/48
Survey #432–K   Question #4c

It has been suggested that the United States should spend as much money in telling our side of the story to Europe and the world as Russia spends in telling her side. Do you agree or disagree with this?

Agree............................ 58%
Disagree.......................... 27
No opinion........................ 15

Interviewing Date 11/3–8/48
Survey #432–K   Question #4d

Some people say it would cost at least one billion dollars to do the job right. Would you favor or oppose spending one billion dollars to tell our side of the story to Europe and the world?

Favor............................ 45%
Oppose........................... 41
No opinion........................ 14

DECEMBER 11
PRICE OUTLOOK

Interviewing Date 11/3–8/48
Survey #432–K   Question #1a

Do you think that prices, in general, will be higher, lower, or about the same six months from now?

Higher........................... 18%
Lower............................ 33
Same............................. 39
No opinion........................ 10

DECEMBER 12
PROHIBITION

Interviewing Date 10/16–21/48
Survey #431   Question #1

If the question of national prohibition should come up again, would you vote wet or dry?

Wet.............................. 57%
Dry.............................. 35
No opinion........................ 8

By Sex
Men

Wet.............................. 67%
Dry.............................. 27
No opinion........................ 6

Women

Wet.............................. 47%
Dry.............................. 42
No opinion........................ 11

By Age
21–29 Years

Wet............................. 63%
Dry............................. 27
No opinion...................... 10

30–49 Years

Wet............................. 61%
Dry............................. 31
No opinion...................... 8

50 Years and Over

Wet............................. 49%
Dry............................. 43
No opinion...................... 8

By Community Size
10,000 and Under

Wet............................. 52%
Dry............................. 39
No opinion...................... 9

10,000–100,000

Wet............................. 61%
Dry............................. 30
No opinion...................... 9

100,000–500,000

Wet............................. 63%
Dry............................. 27
No opinion...................... 10

Farmers Only

Wet............................. 39%
Dry............................. 53
No opinion...................... 8

DECEMBER 15
CHINA

Interviewing Date 11/26–12/1/48
Survey #433–K   Question #13a

Have you heard or read about the civil war in China?

Yes............................. 79%
No.............................. 21

By Education

	Yes	No
College	97%	3%
High School	86	14
Grade School	66	34

Interviewing Date 11/26–12/1/48
Survey #433–K   Question #13b

Asked of those who had heard of the war: Will you tell me what the status of the war is in China today?

Communists gaining ground; Nationalists losing; desperate situation for Chinese Government.............. 32%
Chinese people suffering, no food, no clothing........................ 16
General answers: there's lots of bloodshed, people are fighting........... 6
Situation confused, don't know what to believe......................... 2
Miscellaneous..................... 3
Don't know....................... 20
                                  ——
                                  79%

Interviewing Date 11/26–12/1/48
Survey #433–K   Question #13c

Asked of those who had heard of the war: Do you think the fighting in China is a real threat to world peace, or not?

It is............................. 45%
It is not......................... 22
No opinion....................... 12
                                  ——
                                  79%

Interviewing Date 11/26–12/1/48
Survey #433–K   Question #13d

Asked of those who had heard of the war: Do you think the Chinese Communists take their orders from Moscow, or not?

They do........................... 51%
They do not...................... 10
No opinion....................... 18
                                  ——
                                  79%

Interviewing Date 11/26–12/1/48
Survey #433–K   Question #13e

Asked of those who had heard of the war: Would you favor or oppose sending Chiang Kai-shek's Nationalist Government about $5 billion worth of goods and military supplies in the next year to try to keep China from going communistic?

Favor.............................. 32%
Oppose............................. 34
No opinion......................... 13
                                  ────
                                  79%

DECEMBER 17
MOST IMPORTANT PROBLEM FOR CONGRESS

Interviewing Date 11/26–12/1/48
Survey #433–K   Question #2

What is the first problem you would like to see President Truman and the new Congress take up?

High cost of living.................. 31%
Housing, rent control............... 13
Handling Russia, preventing war...... 10
Labor problems, Taft-Hartley Act...... 9
Helping Europe, German problem, Palestine, other foreign policy problems.. 4
Civil Rights, end race discrimination... 2
China............................... 2
Miscellaneous....................... 2
Don't know.......................... 27

DECEMBER 18
BRITISH VIEWS OF THE LABOR GOVERNMENT

Special Survey

Asked in Great Britain: What would you say is the best thing this Government has done since it came to office in 1945?

National health scheme............... 35%
Increased pensions, looked after old people........................... 12
Nationalization of industry........... 7
Kept rationing, kept food prices down... 4
Wage increases, holidays with pay...... 4
School meals, raising school leaving age. 2
Improved housing.................... 2
Prevented unemployment............. 2
Stood firm against Russia............ 1
Miscellaneous, no answer............. 21
Done nothing good.................. 10

DECEMBER 19
MOST ADMIRED MAN

Interviewing Date 11/26–12/1/48
Survey #433–K   Question #9

What man, living today in any part of the world, that you have heard or read about do you admire the most?

The following are listed in order of frequency of mention:

Harry Truman
Dwight Eisenhower
Douglas MacArthur
Winston Churchill
Herbert Hoover
Thomas Dewey
Pope Pius XII
Harold Stassen
Albert Einstein

DECEMBER 22
RATIONING AND PRICE CONTROLS

Interviewing Date 11/26–12/1/48
Survey #433–K   Question #3a

Do you think the Government should or should not put back rationing and price controls on some products?

For controls........................ 45%
Against controls..................... 42
Price control but not rationing........ 7
No opinion.......................... 6

Truman Voters

For controls	54%
Against controls	32
Price control but not rationing	8
No opinion	6

Dewey Voters

For controls	31%
Against controls	58
Price control but not rationing	6
No opinion	5

DECEMBER 24
NEIGHBORS

Interviewing Date 11/28–12/3/48
Survey #433–K   Question #5a

On the whole, would you say that you have pleasant neighbors — or don't you like them much?

Mainly pleasant	80%
Like a few	10
Don't like any	2
Have no contact	8

Interviewing Date 11/28–12/3/48
Survey #433–K   Question #5b

Asked of all persons except those having no contact with neighbors: Do you do any of these things with your neighbors — Lend or borrow things? Have them over to your house? Look after their children? Take in messages, parcels, etc.? Do shopping for them?

	Yes	No
Lend or borrow things	62%	38%
Have them in house	72	28
Look after children	40	60
Take in messages	72	28
Do shopping for them	46	54

DECEMBER 26
MOST ADMIRED WOMAN

Interviewing Date 11/28–12/3/48
Survey #433–T   Question #9

What woman, living today in any part of the world, that you have heard or read about do you admire the most?

The following are listed according to frequency of mention:

Mrs. Franklin Roosevelt
Madame Chiang Kai-shek
Sister Kenny
Mrs. Clare Boothe Luce
Mrs. Harry Truman
Kate Smith
Princess Elizabeth
Queen Elizabeth
Margaret Chase Smith
Former Queen Wilhelmina

DECEMBER 29
ECONOMIC OUTLOOK

Interviewing Date 11/28–12/3/48
Survey #433–K   Question #6b

Do you think there will be another serious business depression in the United States during the next four years — that is, between now and 1952?

Yes	30%
No	50
No opinion	20

By Political Affiliation
Republicans

Yes	37%
No	45
No opinion	18

Democrats

Yes	26%
No	55
No opinion	19

By Occupation
Business and Professional
Yes...............................27%
No................................56
No opinion........................17

White Collar
Yes...............................29%
No................................55
No opinion........................16

Farmers
Yes...............................35%
No................................47
No opinion........................18

Manual Workers
Yes...............................29%
No................................47
No opinion........................24

DECEMBER 31
SCANDINAVIAN VIEWS ON EAST-WEST CONFLICT

Special Survey

In case of war between Russia and Eastern Europe on one side, and the United States and Western Europe on the other, do you think that our country has a possibility of staying out of such a war?

Denmark Only
Yes............................... 1%
No................................77
No opinion........................22

Norway Only
Yes............................... 5%
No................................78
No opinion........................17

Sweden Only
Yes...............................14%
No................................64
No opinion........................22

Do you think that Denmark, Norway and Sweden ought to agree on defensive cooperation?

Denmark Only
Yes...............................59%
No................................15
No opinion........................26

Norway Only
Yes...............................60%
No................................13
No opinion........................27

Sweden Only
Yes...............................42%
No................................23
No opinion........................35

If no military agreement with the Western powers were going to be a condition, do you then think that Scandinavian defensive cooperation ought to be established?

Denmark Only
Yes...............................29%
No................................33
No opinion........................38

Norway Only
Yes...............................28%
No................................32
No opinion........................40

Sweden Only
Yes...............................18%
No................................28
No opinion........................54

If a military agreement with the Western powers were a condition, do you then think that Scandinavian defensive cooperation should be established?

Denmark Only
Yes...............................45%
No................................20
No opinion........................35

Norway Only

Yes............................... 38%
No............................... 20
No opinion........................ 42

Sweden Only

Yes............................... 26%
No............................... 22
No opinion........................ 52

Asked in Denmark: Which foreign policy do you think Denmark should follow during the present state of affairs between East and West — do you think Denmark ought not to take sides, or should the country actively join one of the sides?

Take sides........................ 46%
Stay neutral...................... 32
No opinion........................ 22

Asked of those who thought Denmark should take sides: Which side?

Join Western powers................ 44%
Join Russia....................... 1
No opinion........................ 1
                                    ‾‾‾‾
                                    46%